THE OXFORD ENGLISH LITERARY HISTORY

General Editors: Jonathan Bate and Colin Burrow

1. 1000–1350: *Conquest and Transformation*
   Laura Ashe*

2. 1350–1547: *Reform and Cultural Revolution*
   James Simpson*

3. 1533–1603: *The Elizabethans*
   Colin Burrow

4. 1603–1660: *Literary Cultures of the Early Seventeenth Century*
   Katharine Eisaman Maus*

5. 1645–1714: *The Later Seventeenth Century*
   Margaret J. M. Ezell*

6. 1709–1784: *The Eighteenth Century*
   John Mullan

7. 1785–1832: *The Romantic Period*
   Fiona Robertson

8. 1830–1880: *The Victorians*
   Philip Davis*

9. 1875–1914: *From 'Victorian' to 'Edwardian'*
   Joseph Bristow

10. 1910–1940: *The Modern Movement*
    Chris Baldick*

11. 1930–1970: *Literature among the Wars*
    Rick Rylance

12. 1960–2000: *The Last of England?*
    Randall Stevenson*

13. 1948–2000: *The Internationalization of English Literature*
    Bruce King*

* already published

This series was conceived and commissioned by Kim Walwyn (1956–2002), to whose memory it is dedicated.

The Oxford English Literary History

Volume 4
1603–1660

*Literary Cultures of the Early
Seventeenth Century*

KATHARINE EISAMAN MAUS

UNIVERSITY PRESS

Great Clarendon Street, Oxford, OX2 6DP,
United Kingdom

Oxford University Press is a department of the University of Oxford.
It furthers the University's objective of excellence in research, scholarship,
and education by publishing worldwide. Oxford is a registered trade mark of
Oxford University Press in the UK and in certain other countries

© Katharine Eisaman Maus 2025

The moral rights of the author have been asserted.

All rights reserved. No part of this publication may be reproduced, stored in a retrieval system,
transmitted, used for text and data mining, or used for training artificial intelligence, in any form or
by any means, without the prior permission in writing of Oxford University Press, or as expressly
permitted by law, by licence or under terms agreed with the appropriate reprographics rights
organization. Enquiries concerning reproduction outside the scope of the above should be sent
to the Rights Department, Oxford University Press, at the address above.

You must not circulate this work in any other form
and you must impose this same condition on any acquirer.

Published in the United States of America by Oxford University Press
198 Madison Avenue, New York, NY 10016, United States of America

British Library Cataloguing in Publication Data

Data available

Library of Congress Control Number: 2024944950

ISBN 9780198943327

DOI: 10.1093/9780198943327.001.0001

Printed and bound by
CPI Group (UK) Ltd, Croydon, CR0 4YY

Links to third party websites are provided by Oxford in good faith and
for information only. Oxford disclaims any responsibility for the materials
contained in any third party website referenced in this work.

The manufacturer's authorised representative in the EU for product safety is
Oxford University Press España S.A. of El Parque Empresarial San Fernando de Henares, Avenida
de Castilla, 2 – 28830 Madrid (www.oup.es/en or
product.safety@oup.com). OUP España S.A. also acts as importer into Spain
of products made by the manufacturer.

For Everett and Sophie

Preface

During the many years I have spent writing this book, I have been lucky to have the support of many people and institutions. In its inception my work benefited from the fellowship support from the John Simon Guggenheim Foundation, the American Council of Learned Societies, and the Leverhulme Trust. The James Branch Cabell Professorship at the University of Virginia allowed me sabbatical time for several periods of intensive research and writing. Jonathan Bate, the series editor for the Oxford English Literary History when I began this project, negotiated the Leverhulme support for me via the University of Liverpool, and gave me very helpful feedback on the first chapters I drafted. In later years Colin Burrow gave me similarly indispensable commentary on each of the later chapters as I submitted them to him. Tom Cain's invitation to me to address a conference on Robert Herrick encouraged my attention to that author; Francisco Borge's invitation to give the plenary address at the Spanish and Portuguese Society for English Renaissance Studies allowed me to present my ideas on Jacobean city comedy; an invitation to give the Dan Collins lecture at the University of Massachusetts spurred me to develop my thoughts about Francis Bacon. I have also presented lectures and seminars drawn from this book project at the University of Michigan, the University of Chicago, the University of Liverpool, Michigan State University, John Hopkins University, and the University of Virginia, at multiple Modern Language Association of America conferences, and over many years of Shakespeare Association of America Annual Meetings. Discerning and helpful audience members at all these events stimulated and refined my thinking. I am grateful for the insight and energy of Abbe Watson, my research assistant in an early phase of this project, and Jack Crouse at its conclusion. I also thank the many, many individual friends with whom I fruitfully discussed aspects of this project over the years, including Sharon Achinstein, Lucia Alden, Amanda Bailey, Mary Bly, Gordon Braden, Karen Britland, Martin Butler, Dympna Callaghan, Paul Cantor, Phil Davis, Heather Dubrow, Lars Engle, Lukas Erne, Margaret Ferguson, Elizabeth Harvey, Jonathan Goldberg, John Gillies, Suzanne Gossett, Stephen Greenblatt, Achsah Guibbory, Kim Hall, Jean Howard,

Lisa Jardine, John Kerrigan, Emelye Keyser, Arthur Kinney, Clare Kinney, Dan Kinney, Arthur Kirsch, Barbara Lewalski, Naomi Liebler, Gordon MacMullan, Leah Marcus, Arthur Marotti, Fred Maus, Jeffrey Masten, Paul Menzer, Subha Mukherji, Steven Mullaney, Carol Neely, Stephen Orgel, John Parker, Patricia Parker, Gail Paster, Ted-Larry Pebworth, Curtis Perry, Lois Potter, Diane Purkiss, Amy Rodgers, Rebecca Rush, David Schalkwyk, Michael Schoenfeldt, Laurie Shannon, Debora Shuger, Nigel Smith, Eric Song, Richard Strier, James Simpson, Tiffany Stern, Cynthia Wall, Wendy Wall, Valerie Wayne, Lee Wenzler, Michael Witmore, Jessica Wolfe, and Perez Zagorin.

This book is dedicated to my children, Everett Maus and Sophie Maus Marschner, who were elementary school students when I began it, and married homeowners by the time I finished.

Contents

Introduction	1
Giants and Ghosts	1
Jacobean and Caroline England	9
Civil Wars and Commonwealth	28
History, Literature, Literary History	33

PART I LITERATURE AND SOCIAL SYSTEMS

1. Who Were the Writers?	43
2. Literary Careers	69
Amateurs	70
Remunerated Writing	87
Writing for the Commercial Theatre	88
Patronage	103
After the Fall	141

PART II IMPORTANT LITERARY GENRES 1603–1660

3. Thinking About Genre in Seventeenth-Century England	149
4. A Sense of Place	153
Satiric City Comedy	157
The Country House Poem	179
Chorography and Landscape	192
Outlandish Spaces	200
5. Authority, Obedience, and Defiance	202
Court Masque	212
Tragedy	230
Tragicomedy	258

6. Forms of Devotion	283
Religious Poetry	283
Devotional Lyric	289
Religious Narrative Poetry	318
Intimacies: Lyrics of Love and Friendship	335
'Jacobean' Love Poetry	340
Caroline and Interregnum Poetry of Love and Friendship	366
7. Intellect and Expression: Prose in the Early Seventeenth Century	389
Intellectual Prose	395
A Tale of Three Romances	414
The Prose of Everyday Life	425
Memoir and Biography	430
Bibliography	447
Index	466

Introduction

Giants and Ghosts

At the Jewish Passover Seder the youngest child at the table traditionally poses a question: 'Why is this night different from all other nights?' *Mutatis mutandis*, the same question forces itself upon the literary historian. Why is this period different from all other periods? What are its distinctive features? What is the rationale for conceiving of it as a period or an age, separating it from the years and decades immediately prior and immediately following?

The period 1603–1660 is a time of dazzlingly various and prolific literary accomplishment. About half of William Shakespeare's plays were written during this period, as were many of John Donne's major poems and most of his surviving prose compositions, Ben Jonson's and Thomas Middleton's best-known plays and Jonson's poems and masques, many of Francis Bacon's essays and most of his scientific writing, John Milton's early poems and prose works, and beautiful lyrics by George Herbert, Aemelia Lanyer, Robert Herrick, Richard Lovelace, Andrew Marvell, Katherine Phillips, and a host of others. Yet the question of periodization seems especially pertinent to this volume because political, not literary events most obviously determine its beginning and its endpoint. It commences in 1603 with the death of Queen Elizabeth, the last Tudor monarch, and the accession to the English throne of James Stuart of Scotland. Its purview extends to 1660, with the crowning of James's grandson as King Charles II. In between lies a great deal of political controversy and, eventually, violence: an increasingly autocratic monarchy culminating in the 'Personal Rule' in which King James's son, King Charles I, attempted to rule without Parliament; a civil war between the forces of King and Parliament; the trial and execution of King Charles I; and an unprecedented attempt to govern the nation without a monarch between 1649 and 1660.

In what sense do these events help demarcate a literary epoch? Of course all 'periods', historical or literary, are merely helpful conceptual structures, the demarcations of which are always open to interrogation and revision.

Nonetheless, some period boundaries have proven more durable and convincing than others. In 1668, John Dryden, in *An Essay of Dramatic Poesy*, already finds it natural to class William Shakespeare, Ben Jonson, and John Fletcher together as playwrights 'of the last age' and to distinguish them from himself and his contemporaries, whom he characterizes as less vigorous but more polished and urbane. Almost four decades later, in 1694, Dryden provides a similar analysis in 'To My Dear Friend Mr Congreve, on his Comedy Called *The Double Dealer*. Widely acknowledged as the greatest living poet but dismissed as poet laureate on the grounds of his Catholicism, the now-elderly Dryden hails the young William Congreve as the greatest playwright since Shakespeare. Dryden fondly imagines Congreve as his own literary son and heir, though he admits that the relationship will not do Congreve much practical good given that the laureateship is now occupied by painfully inferior writers.

> Oh that your brows my laurel had sustained!
> Well had I been deposed, if you had reigned;
> The father had descended for the son,
> For only you are lineal to the throne.
> (41–44)[1]

It is not surprising that Dryden should connect his own calamity with a breach of inheritance rights, and specifically with a rupture in the royal title. Dryden's own fall followed upon the 1688 deposition of the Catholic James II, brother and heir of Charles II, in favour of the more remotely related, but Protestant, William and Mary. Congreve is thus lineal heir to a throne that, alas, is no longer Dryden's to bestow.

Yet despite its denial by a debased contemporary world, Dryden's literary affinity to Congreve is analogous to that of father and son, and that 'lineal' bond between the generations is vital for Dryden's sense of literary continuity. Dryden's relationship to his own poetic forbears is rather more complicated:

> Strong were our sires, and as they fought they writ,
> Conqu'ring with force of arms, and dint of wit,
> Theirs was the giant race, before the Flood.
> (3–5)

---

[1] *The Works of John Dryden* volume 4: Poems 1693-1696 ed. A, B. Chambers, William Frost, and Vinton Dearing pp. 432–434. For full citations of all book references, including place and date of publication, please see the Bibliography at the end of the volume.

These 'sires' are not in the same direct relation to Dryden that Dryden is to Congreve: the word can mean remote as well as immediate progenitors, and Dryden's Biblical reference suggests not intimacy but distance. According to the Book of Genesis, in the days before the Flood annihilated all human beings except for Noah and his family, a race of gigantic beings had walked the earth, the offspring of illicit unions between mortal women and angelic beings. For Dryden the earlier writers are 'the giant race before the Flood': a different, and extinct, species. As befits giants, their works and wit are overpowering (Dryden's phrase 'dint of wit' is itself slyly witty, since it can mean both 'by means of wit' and 'by blows of wit'). Closer to divinity than ordinary mortals, these literary giants are nevertheless linked by both their origins in angelic lust and their own surplus 'force' to the sin that would eventually bring on God's wrath and their own obliteration.

In 'To My Dear Friend, Mr Congreve', therefore, literary pedigree, political history, and Biblical exegesis neatly coincide. A firm believer in Stuart rule, Dryden suggests that the Civil War, and the Commonwealth that followed it, was an equivalent in his own time to the Biblical Deluge. God visited calamity upon England, Dryden implies, just as He had of old upon Noah's sinful contemporaries. The Biblical analogy explains, for Dryden, why he feels estranged from his literary 'sires'. The 'giant race' has not begotten literary sons like themselves, because the old order has been washed away. In England life goes on, as it had for Noah and his family, but now it operates, like the postdiluvian world, under a new covenant and on a reduced scale. For, as many Biblical scholars point out, not only did the Flood obliterate the giants, it diminished the human lifespan; Abraham, Isaac, and Jacob lived only a fraction of the years attributed to Methusaleh or Adam.

Dryden's simple equation between the creative energies of great writers and the aggressions of the battlefield may seem highly tenuous. Arguably, too, the gap Dryden perceives between his own age and the preceding one is less a characterization of his predecessors than a way of making room for his own gifts. He can claim that the great works of the past, however venerated, seem a bit monstrous nowadays, so hopelessly antique that they no longer pertain to the present. Revising Shakespeare's *Tempest* to suit contemporary tastes in 1667, he had patronizingly connected its improbabilities with the naiveté of Shakespeare's audience: 'he then writ, as people then believed' (Prologue to *The Tempest, or the Enchanted Island*, 26).[2] Yet Dryden cannot lay to rest the spectres of the dead. In the prologue to his revision of

---

[2] *The Works of John Dryden*, vol. 10 ed. Maximiilian Novak and George Guffey, p. 6.

Troilus and Cressida (1679), the 'ghost of Shakespeare' stalks onstage and irascibly reproaches the playwrights of the modern age, ranting like the ghost of old Hamlet imposing a horrible obligation on his reluctant son. By implication Dryden, like young Hamlet, loves and admires his impressively inordinate father but declares himself unable to match him, not only because the younger man is a different, and possibly inferior, being but also because the world has irrevocably changed. There is no going back.

Whatever may be the flaws and partialities in Dryden's retrospective account of seventeenth-century literature, the demarcation he makes has certainly proven a durable one. Textbooks, literary histories like this one, English department curricula, and the schema for training doctoral students in their historical specializations: all have tended to see the English Civil War as a watershed event in the history of literature as well as of politics, and to have implicitly endorsed Dryden's stark distinction between his own poetic generation and the writers earlier in the seventeenth century. Rightly or wrongly, we are inclined to see Dryden's relationship to Congreve—or, for that matter, to Alexander Pope or Samuel Johnson—as closer than his relationship to Shakespeare, to Jonson, or to Donne.

The year 1603—the date at which King James came to the throne and this volume commences—is a considerably dimmer line of demarcation. An unprecedented flowering of literary activity that began in the 1580s with Philip Sidney and Edmund Spenser, Thomas Kyd and Christopher Marlowe, and flourished in the 1590s, was still burgeoning unabated. In 1603 many major writers were in mid-career. William Shakespeare, age thirty-nine, had written most of his comedies and English history plays, *Romeo and Juliet*, *Julius Caesar*, and *Hamlet*, but the 'problem comedy' *Measure for Measure* (1604) was still in the future. So were most of the great tragedies, including *Othello* (1604), *King Lear* (1606), *Macbeth* (1606), *Antony and Cleopatra* (1607), and *Coriolanus* (1609–1610), and the romances, including *Cymbeline* (1610), *The Winter's Tale* (1611), and *The Tempest* (1611). Ben Jonson, about eight years Shakespeare's junior, was already notorious as a participant in an acrimoniously entertaining 'War of the Theatres' in which he and other playwrights composed satiric plays on the topic of one another's failings. John Donne, Jonson's age-mate, was very well-known for the poetry he had written as a young law student; now married and a father, he was desperately seeking patronage and employment. In James's reign he would write the *Anniversaries* (1611–1612), most of his devotional poetry, and a number of polemical treatises on religion. After he took orders in 1615, he became a famous preacher: 160 of his sermons survive. The writing careers of Thomas Dekker, George Chapman, Samuel Daniel, Michael Drayton,

Thomas Heywood, Walter Ralegh, and Francis Bacon likewise straddle the reigns of Elizabeth and James.

Thus 1603, dividing 'English Renaissance' literature into Tudor and Stuart portions, seems to mark a midpoint rather than a decisive juncture. In an era apparently swarming with great writers and overflowing with their masterpieces, subdivisions help readers manage the profusion, and a change of regime provides as good an excuse for separation as any. (The other method of categorization literary historians have favoured for this period is generic, dividing the drama of the period from its 'non-dramatic' writing—a rubric with its own advantages and disadvantages, as we shall see). Yet the choice of boundaries matters, for once one makes a division, however optional or apparently arbitrary, one inevitably begins to notice differences on either side of the line.

What are these differences? Writers active at the outset of the seventeenth century do not need to invent a literary tradition from scratch, as writers had sometimes felt themselves to be doing both in the late fourteenth century, the age of Chaucer, Langland, and the Gawain-poet, and again in the mid-sixteenth century, when an onslaught of humanist ideas and the belated influence of the Continental Renaissance produced a new wave of writing in the vernacular, very different from what had preceded it. In 1603 not a paucity of appropriate models but continuity itself presented a challenge. Writers in the early seventeenth century needed some reason to keep writing when the world already seemed surfeited with books. If they were not to reproduce, endlessly, simply more of the same, they had to differentiate themselves from the brilliant writers of the immediate past, who had brought to English letters a previously unheard-of copiousness, brilliance, and range. Moreover, if, like Shakespeare, they were already mature upon James's accession, they would eventually feel compelled to differentiate themselves not only from their predecessors but from their own former selves. Premature death fortuitously prevented many of the Elizabethans from having to confront this difficulty: Philip Sidney and Robert Greene died at thirty-two, Christopher Marlowe at twenty-nine, Thomas Nashe at thirty-four, and Thomas Kyd at thirty-eight, after careers spanning, in each case, less than a decade. Edmund Spenser lived longer, into his forties, but died in 1599 with his epic *The Faerie Queene* still unfinished. John Lyly, who survived until 1606, was not able to sustain his early brilliance after the 1591 closing of the boys' theatre companies for which he had written; his later years were ones of personal setbacks and poetic silence. By contrast, the major writers of the early seventeenth century typically managed careers that spanned twenty or thirty years, or even more. Again and again, after finishing one ambitious project, they had to decide what to do next. After writing, between 1599 and around 1608, a series of tragedies of unparalleled scope and power, Shakespeare turned to tragicomedy for the first time in 1607, six years before his retirement. Donne, the sceptical libertine, became a profoundly original devotional poet. In the 1620s and 1630s the ageing Jonson wrote a sequence of love poems, a romantic comedy, an English grammar, an unfinished pastoral play, and other works that little resemble the pointed epigrams and satiric urban comedy for which he had first become famous.

So, 'Jacobean' writing (so called after *Jacobus*, the Latin for James) may differ from 'Elizabethan' writing less because the culture has shifted than because its writers want to do something new. If the Elizabethans had preferred Cicero and Ovid as models, the Jacobeans would prefer Tacitus and Horace. If Spenser had developed a self-consciously archaic English poetic idiom in order to manufacture a tradition for himself, Jonson and Donne would embrace the rhythms of contemporary speech: for, as Jonson opined, 'Spenser, in affecting the ancients, writ no language'.[3] If Elizabethan comedy had been largely 'romantic', Jacobean comedy would be satiric, even cynical, about sexual motives. Writers in the early decades of the seventeenth century experiment with new literary forms or resurrect old ones that had been neglected: epigram, satiric comedy, tragicomedy, masque, the country house poem. In the epistle to the reader in *The Roaring Girl* (1611), Thomas Middleton half-facetiously compares 'the fashion of playmaking' to changing tastes in clothing:

> For in the time of the great crop-doublet, your huge bombasted plays, quilted with mighty words to lean purpose, was only then in fashion; and as the doublet fell, neater inventions began to set up. Now, in the time of spruceness, our plays follow the niceness of our garments: single plots, quaint conceits, lecherous jests ... Such a kind of light-color summer stuff, mingled with diverse colors, you shall find this ... comedy.

Not merely the form but also the substance of the play is new. A 'light-color summer stuff' is what was called, in the cloth-making industry, 'new drapery'. *A la mode* among wealthy Jacobeans, new draperies were fabrics produced by technologically novel weaving processes: they were lighter in weight and capable of being more colourfully dyed than the traditional

---

[3] *Timber, or Discoveries*, lines 1281–1282, ed. Lorna Hutson, *The Cambridge Edition of the Works of Ben Jonson*, vol. 7, p. 559.

heavy English broadcloths. Middleton claims that literary techniques, like changes in clothing fashion, are continuously adapting to new possibilities and to contemporary stylistic preferences. They are open to invention and modernization, for not only are the present tastes new but they are, Middleton's language implies, the better for their newness: sprucer, neater, nicer.

In Middleton's epistle the past tends to look, well, *passé*, like yesteryear's outmoded garment. Middleton thus celebrates 'single plots' as typical of contemporary drama, even though *The Roaring Girl* itself, like most of Middleton's plays, interlaces several storylines just as its predecessors had ten or fifteen years earlier. Given the emphasis on being up-to-date in the first years of the seventeenth century, to revive an 'old' genre, such as the revenge tragedies so popular in the late 1580s and 1590s, was necessarily to revive it with a new self-consciousness and irony. When, late in Elizabeth's reign, Shakespeare turned his attention to the Hamlet story, he most likely wrote something pointedly different from Thomas Kyd's now-lost original—it is certainly very unlike Kyd's only surviving play, *The Spanish Tragedy* (1592) or Shakespeare's own early revenge tragedy, *Titus Andronicus* (1594). Moreover, when an anonymous author, probably Middleton, wrote *The Revenger's Tragedy* (1606) in the wake not only of early revenge tragedy but of Shakespeare's *Hamlet*, he had to devise a way cleverly to differentiate his work from both prototypes. Much early seventeenth-century writing, particularly in the fast-moving, closely knit world of the theatre, is edgily self-conscious in this way, intensely aware of the past, but aware of it in an often irreverent, innovating spirit. When Jonson's Volpone or Epicure Mammon speak blank verse obviously indebted to Marlowe's grandiloquent iambic pentameters, they do so as a fraud and a dupe, respectively. High language has become a sign of lowmindedness, magnificence is recycled as pomposity or self-absorption, and the element of parody is unmistakable. To work more seriously in an 'old' genre such as sonnet sequence or Spenserian allegory—as did Mary Wroth and Phineas Fletcher—was pointedly to reject the modish pretensions of Jacobean literary culture, at least for one's own artistic purposes, and to insist on the continuing pertinence of familiar forms in the face of cultural change. Likewise, to revisit and revise the work of one's youth, as William Camden or Michael Drayton did, was itself to make a statement about the value of tradition.

Yet, unlike Dryden in 1694, Jacobean writers rarely saw their predecessors in the sixteenth century as impossibly distant and alien. Middleton's image for literary change, in the preface to *The Roaring Girl*, is not Noah's

Flood but changing clothing styles: not a universal cataclysm but an ongoing, inevitable series of relatively minor adjustments. Indeed, the jokey tone of his comments seems to imply that literary change is a rather frivolous topic. Still, it is difficult for a literary critic, trained to find profound significance in small details, to see any such shift, whether in literary practice or, for that matter, in clothing preferences, as truly superficial. As already noted, many Jacobeans preferred Tacitus' terse, oblique Latin over the orotund Ciceronian periods, partly, no doubt, because the change from Cicero's familiarity was piquant, cutting-edge. Yet a shift from Cicero to Tacitus, like a taste for 'spruceness' over 'bombast', also registered new ways of seeing the world. The public-spirited, self-consciously high-minded, long-winded defender of Roman republican *nobilitas* was superseded by a sceptically analytical, worldly wise student of the Roman empire in its later, decadent stages.

Likewise, and more generally, although Jacobean writers' commitment to stylish novelty was arguably an attempt to compensate for an underlying continuity of literary practice, the choice of novelty itself is significant. These were people convinced that innovation is a positive good—not a heretical violation of a revered tradition. Their openness to newness and change set the stage for important changes in sensibility that eventually occur in tandem with important changes in the social and political climate. For the literary historian these transformations become visible not immediately, in 1604 as opposed to 1602, but slowly and incrementally, over the course of several decades. Yet their cumulative effect is very large indeed. Comparing the greatest poet of the beginning of the period, William Shakespeare, with John Milton, the greatest poet of its end, gives some hint of its direction and magnitude. Shakespeare dramatized complex confrontations with a famous evenhandedness: between Richard and Bolingbroke in *Richard II*, between Hal and Falstaff in *Henry IV Parts 1 and 2*, between Shylock and Portia in *The Merchant of Venice*, between Brutus and Cassius in *Julius Caesar*, between Antony and Augustus in *Antony and Cleopatra*. Shakespeare has thus been construed as a staunch monarchist and a republican; as a thoroughgoing snob and a champion of the common man; as a crypto-Catholic, devoted son of the Reformation, and religious sceptic toying with atheism. For Milton, this kind of detachment, or reserve, is impossible. Milton was a committed revolutionary with a long career as a propagandist and strongly held, strongly argued polemical views on highly controversial topics: divorce, press censorship, the Trinity, monarchy, the organization of the church and its relationship to the state. Milton's positions on the issues of the day might indeed be intricately nuanced and, at times, conflicted or ambivalent. He might even be, as William Blake would later put it, 'of the devil's party without knowing it' in *Paradise Lost* (1667). Yet no one imagines him to be a secret Catholic or a closet royalist. He does not achieve, and just as importantly does not wish to achieve, Shakespeare's magnificent reticence. This difference has often been ascribed to a difference in temperament between the two authors: Shakespeare the master of what John Keats called negative capability, the capacity to accept 'uncertainties, mysteries, doubts, without any irritable reaching after fact and reason'; Milton the great prophet-preacher, with explicit didactic and reformatory aims on his reader. Yet the difference between the two great writers is also the consequence of a different sense of the poet's ethical responsibility, an altered sensibility arising in response to a changed culture. Not only Milton but all the writers in his generation found themselves obliged to take a stand on the burning issues of their day, whether they might like to or not.

In order to have a sense of how and why the culture changed, one must have a grasp of what happened in England between 1603 and 1660. Early seventeenth-century writing is deeply enmeshed in the milieu in which it was produced, and is best understood in that context. The remainder of this chapter will provide a brief account of some of the issues and events that loomed large to contemporaries. Some of these matters may seem far removed from literature; in fact, their implications for literary history will largely be deferred to later chapters in this volume. In some cases, too, I have postponed a more detailed historical account to a point in the book where it will seems more relevant (for instance, I will discuss the period's increasing consumer culture in the chapter on city comedy, and some of its religious controversies in the chapter on devotional poetry). Still, I hope that the following pages will serve as helpful orientation. At the end of this chapter, I will return to the topic of literary history more specifically, because the particular problems posed by that history help determine the shape of the volume that follows.

Jacobean and Caroline England

In March 1603, Queen Elizabeth, the last of the Tudor monarchs, died at the age of sixty-nine, after a reign of almost forty-five years. The Virgin Queen had no children of her own, of course, and had refused to publicly name an heir; many of her subjects fretted that the end of her long reign would produce a violent struggle for power among her would-be successors. But, in fact, clandestine preparations for engineering a smooth transition had been underway for some time.

Arguably, the man with the best hereditary claim on the throne of England was James Stuart, already ruling Scotland as James VI.[4] James was the great-grandson of Henry VII via his eldest daughter, Margaret. James did not trust the lustre of his pedigree alone to ensure his right; he had spent the past two and a half decades cultivating, by letter, a relationship with the woman he called 'madame and dearest sister', choosing to overlook the awkward fact that Elizabeth had executed his mother, Mary Queen of Scots, in 1587. Elizabeth's chief ministers, Robert Cecil and Henry Howard, were also prudent men. In the last years of Elizabeth's reign they inaugurated a secret correspondence with James, and negotiated discreetly with James's agents in London. Elizabeth's councillors further forestalled any unpleasantness by claiming that Elizabeth had named James her heir on her deathbed, which may well have been true.

As a result, when the thirty-six-year-old James rode south from Edinburgh in April 1603, he was widely embraced as Elizabeth's natural replacement. Many welcomed the idea of a male ruler in his prime after so many years of subjection to a queen; moreover, the fact that James had three children by his wife, Queen Anne, seemed to secure a future free of succession concerns. Those with literary ambitions were especially heartened by the fact that their new king was a writer and an intellectual, having produced a volume of poetry and treatises on monarchy and on witchcraft. After a brief flurry of activity in which James attempted to endear himself to his new subjects by freely bestowing honours and titles, he largely continued many of Elizabeth's policies and retained her advisors. James saw himself as a peacemaker and, to the extent that he innovated, it tended to be in a spirit of reconciliation. He brought back into favour several prominent noblemen who had been convicted of involvement in the Essex rebellion several years earlier. In 1604 his ministers negotiated a peace treaty with Spain, thereby ending decades of hostility, in which Spain recognized England's Protestant government and England promised to withdraw its support for the Dutch, who were rebelling against their Spanish overlords.

---

[4] Alan Stewart, *The Cradle King: The Life of James VI and I*, is a good biography; Christopher Durston, *James I*, summarizes the major issues of his reign.

There were no official censuses in England until 1801, but modern demographers have managed to piece together, by the painstaking examination of birth and death records, population estimates for the nation James was entering in 1603.[5] Their research suggests that after the terrible shock of the Black Death in the fourteenth century—which killed between a third and a half of the population—and the destruction wrought by the Wars of the Roses in the fifteenth century, England's population had expanded steadily. By the turn of the seventeenth century, it had probably reached between 4 and 4.5 million people—that is, finally about where it had been on the eve of the Black Death. It would grow again by about a third before the middle of the century.

Given these statistics, the historian Keith Wrightson has argued that one of the most telling features of the period was something that *didn't* happen.[6] As the population expanded, arable land that had been abandoned to plague and war was cultivated once again. But the supply of land was, of course, limited, even though forests were cut down in the Chiltern Hills and fenland was drained in the east of the country in an attempt to create more. So, as the population increased past its previous high watermark, severe food shortages might have been expected. And yet, despite regular crop failures and local periods of dearth throughout the seventeenth century, widespread famine did not occur. The reason, Wrightson explains, is that over the course of the sixteenth and seventeenth centuries, farmers were figuring out how to use the land more efficiently. They invented better equipment, such as ploughshares specifically adapted for particular soils; they manured the land more carefully; and they deliberately cultivated the crops for which each microclimate was best suited. As a result, they could wrest more productivity from a given acreage. These efficiencies in turn encouraged a more active market economy and a wider use of transport, for as each locale developed its own specialties, it had to trade its surplus for the other things it required and no longer produced itself. Throughout the early seventeenth century a dense mercantile network intensified, not only between the towns and the countryside around them, but also among the different regions of England. The commodities thus exchanged were not merely agricultural products.

---

[5] For the demographic estimates, see E. A. Wrigley and R. S. Schofield, *The Population History of England, 141–1871: A Reconstruction* and Vanessa Harding, 'The Population of London, 1550–1700: A Review of the Published Evidence', *London Journal* 15 (1990): 111–128.

[6] Keith Wrightson, *Earthly Necessities: Economic Lives in Early Modern Britain*, pp. 159–167. See also L. A. Clarkson, *The Pre-Industrial Economy in England 1500–1750* and Joan Thirsk, *The Rural Economy of England: Collected Essays*.

Once trade networks were established, all kinds of goods could move along them: knives from Sheffield, tin and copper from Cornwall, lead from Derbyshire, wool from Gloucestershire, salt from Tynemouth. So many people now lived in southern England, and used wood for heating and cooking, that the region was soon deforested. By the early seventeenth century, it had become profitable to ship large quantities of coal in barges from Newcastle in northern England to southern England via routes along the seacoast, to be used as fuel in London and its environs. In the 1605 city comedy *Eastward Ho* the snobbish Gertrude, dreaming of leaving her native London for her new husband's country estate, demands that he 'presently carry me out of the scent of Newcastle coal' (1.2.118).

Sometimes the most profitable use of land was not the most socially propitious. Especially problematic was the practice of 'enclosure', in which landowners fenced off land that had previously been used for labour-intensive grain cultivation in order to pasture sheep. Enclosure threw long-time tenants off the land they had, in many cases, worked for generations, depopulating whole villages and creating an underclass of desperately impoverished vagrants. Another hated practice was the hoarding of grain, keeping it off the market to create scarcity in the hope of getting a better price. Both enclosure and grain-hoarding were widely decried in sermons and satires, but they continued anyway, eventually contributing to uproarious controversies over land proprietorship in the middle of the century as 'Levellers' and 'Diggers' attempted to squat on and cultivate wasteland to which they had no legal claim. There were other disquieting effects of population growth as well. Increased demand relative to supply produced intransigent inflation, which affected people of all economic stations. The poor were squeezed because the rise in prices was not matched by a corresponding rise in wages. The rich were squeezed because land rents, which generated much of their income, were set for long terms and relatively inflexible.

Although the economy remained largely agrarian, and although four-fifths of English people lived in provincial villages that contained, on average, several hundred people,[7] the growth of cities was much remarked upon by contemporaries. The burgeoning of London was especially explosive and socially disruptive—a matter we will return to several times in later chapters, as its rapid expansion had profound effects on the literary scene. The cities were critical nodes of trade and consumption, especially

---

[7] Peter Laslett, *The World We Have Lost: Further Explored*, p. 54.

if they were seaports or located, like London, on a major navigable river. Improved shipbuilding and navigation techniques in the sixteenth and early seventeenth centuries made feasible extended oceanic voyages, and the English were quick to realize the benefits of international sea trade for their island nation. Investors pooled their resources to finance expeditions to 'Muscovy' (Russia), Virginia, the East Indies, the Mediterranean, Africa, and the Baltic States. The Crown extended to each trading syndicate a monopoly on their routes and the profits thereof. These ventures brought in exotic cargoes: sherry and fine swords from Spain, Parmesan cheese from Italy, damask from Flanders, carpets from Turkey, spices from the East Indies, porcelain from China, tobacco from Virginia. These items, stimulating a taste for luxury, encouraged domestic manufacturers to provide versions of such goods as lace or knit stockings.[8] The explosion of merchandising and the new availability of many commodities left its mark on a variety of literary genres, most especially perhaps those comedies set in contemporary London, prominently featuring a new consumer culture.

Centres of manufacture were mostly based in the home: thus, for instance, most weaving was done on a piece-rate basis in labourers' cottages, permitting a family to participate simultaneously in agriculture and in manufacturing. Likewise, shoemaking, metalworking, and baking were crafts practiced by households consisting of a nuclear family and their servants and apprentices, who typically lived in the same quarters. Distinctions between the home and the workplace, between family and employment relationships, between domestic and wage labour, make little sense in such settings, and distinctions between toil and leisure may well also have been blurrier than they would eventually become. Full-fledged industrial capitalism would have to await technological changes in the eighteenth and nineteenth centuries that made large-scale factory production possible: big, fast machines, and new ways of powering those machines by water, coal, and steam. These expensive innovations in turn encouraged new modes of business investment and, eventually, radical changes in the workplace and in the organization of ordinary people's lives. Yet at the beginning of the seventeenth century, or even at its close, most of those changes were still far in the future.

---

[8] Joan Thirsk, *Economic Policy and Projects: The Development of a Consumer Society in Early Modern England* and 'England's Provinces: Did They Serve or Drive Material London?' in Lena Cowen Orlin, ed. *Material London, ca. 1600*, pp. 97–108.

In the early seventeenth century, the increasing importance of England's international mercantile enterprises influenced its foreign relations. Between 1615 and 1619, James sent his ambassador, Thomas Roe, to the Mughal court in Agra, India, to obtain permission to establish a trading alliance; in 1621 Roe led a similar delegation to the Ottomans in modern Turkey. In the late sixteenth and early seventeenth centuries, England had supported Protestant co-religionists in the Netherlands in their war of independence against the Catholic Habsburg dynasty. But the Dutch, like the English, were able seafarers and entrepreneurs, and by the mid seventeenth century the Dutch and the English had become fierce commercial rivals. They would end up at war with one another in the 1650s and after.

The expansion of trade was tightly connected to England's growing efforts at colonization. After the peace treaty with Spain made transatlantic shipping safer, England established its first durable colony in North America at Jamestown, VA, in 1607. Others soon followed: Plymouth Colony in 1620, Massachusetts Bay in 1628, Maryland in 1632, Connecticut in 1636. The English were also aggressively expanding into the Caribbean, establishing colonies on St Kitts in the 1624; Barbados, Antigua, and Montserrat in 1627; and Nevis in 1628. In 1655, the English invaded Jamaica and took it from the Spanish. In Africa and India, what were originally trade relationships would eventually end in colonization, but in the early seventeenth century England's only base in India was a modest trading outpost in Surat, established in 1615. Later it would expand its foothold, so that by the eighteenth century the East India Company would control much of the Indian subcontinent. The development of sugar plantations in the West Indies and tobacco plantations in Virginia stimulated a dark chapter of England's mercantile endeavour: its increasing involvement in the transatlantic slave trade. The first English slave voyages had taken place in the 1560s, when Sir John Hawkins transported and sold several thousand Africans to the Spanish and the French in Hispaniola and St Domingue. But in those years Portugal was still the major slave power, transporting human cargo between Angola and Brazil, and English voyages to Africa were more likely to be in search of ivory or gold. After the 1640s, however, England played an increasingly significant role in the slave trade, and by the early eighteenth century it was by far the dominant player. The increasing global reach of English shipping and English travel leaves many traces in the literature of the period, in particular in its romances and tragicomedies, often set in exotic locales.

A major flashpoint for controversy in the period—not just in England, but all over Europe—was religion, in an age in which religion permeated many aspects of political, social, and domestic life. I will discuss the religious complexion of early seventeenth-century England in more detail in Chapter 6: Forms of Devotion, but since it is impossible to comprehend the historical developments in the period without reference to these issues, I will also broach them briefly here.

By the time Elizabeth came to the throne in 1558, England had been reeling from the effects of the Reformation for about twenty-five years. Under Elizabeth's father, Henry VIII, and then under the short reigns of first her Protestant brother Edward, and then her Catholic sister Mary, the state religion, to which all subjects of the monarch were supposed to adhere, had changed abruptly with each change of ruler. In other words, laypeople and clergy alike were commanded to comply with the ruler-du-jour's religious preferences while, at the same time, they were told that their faith must be founded upon deep interior conviction.

Waves of lethal rebellion and persecution resulted from the attempt to impose religious unanimity. When Elizabeth came to the throne in 1558, her government sensibly attempted to calm the waters by making the Church of England as palatable as possible for a majority of believers. The Book of Common Prayer, used in all English churches, deflected doctrinal controversy through strategically ambiguous language, allowing for theological latitude provided it did not interfere with or challenge state power. Attendance at Church of England services was legally mandated, but those who conformed outwardly despite their private reservations were not aggressively pursued. Some would argue, in retrospect, that Elizabeth's temporizing merely made the eventual conflagration worse by failing to deal with genuine problems in a forthright manner as they arose. 'Some compare Queen Elizabeth to a sluttish housewife', wrote one John Rogers in 1658, 'who swept the house but left the dust behind the door'.[9]

At the time, however, the Elizabethan balancing act seemed largely successful, and to a great extent James would continue and even extend it. In 1604 James engaged the Puritan wing of the Church of England by convening the Hampton Court conference, encouraging prominent Puritans to present arguments for reforming the church hierarchy. These arguments he eventually rejected, perceiving that the Crown's control over that hierarchy helped secure his own power. 'No bishop, no king', he was famously

---

[9] Edward Rogers, ed., *Some Account of the Life and Opinions of a Fifth-Monarchy-Man: Chiefly Extracted from the Writings of John Rogers, Preacher*, p. 49: this passage comes from a letter John Rogers addressed to Oliver Cromwell in 1653.

supposed to have said. So, the upshot was that James kept the elements of the Elizabethan religious settlement largely intact, maintaining the same ecclesiastical institutions. One momentous outcome of the Hampton Court conference, however, was the creation of a commission to produce a new translation of the Bible into English—a version that became known as the 'King James Bible'. This 'authorized' version was deliberately less tendentious than the one most widely used during Elizabeth's reign, which had been made during Queen Mary's reign by committed Protestants who had fled to exile in the rigorously Calvinist theocracy of Geneva.

Even as he attempted, or at least pretended to attempt, to mollify the Puritans, James also considered easing the onerous penalties imposed upon English Roman Catholics. This initiative faltered, however, after the discovery of the 1605 Gunpowder Plot, in which a small group of Catholic terrorists planned to blow up the House of Lords on the day in which the King and the Prince of Wales were ceremoniously calling Parliament into session. If the plot had succeeded, it would have eliminated virtually the entire English ruling class, leaving the nation open to foreign conquest. Critics have argued that the trauma of the Gunpowder Plot leaves its mark on several Jacobean tragedies, most notably Shakespeare's *Macbeth*, probably written in 1606, and Jonson's *Catiline*, first performed in 1611.[10] For many years thereafter, leniency towards Catholics would seem perilously risky.

There had always, however, been those who had trouble reconciling themselves even with the rather blurry doctrines of the Church of England. Some had never abandoned their loyalty to the Roman church and continued to hear Mass in secret, sometimes going abroad to study with other English Catholics in seminaries in Rome, Douai, and Rheims. When Elizabeth had been on the throne and the Pope and Catholic Spain were militantly challenging her legitimacy as queen, Catholics had seemed potentially subversive: being a Jesuit priest, or harbouring one, was declared de facto treason in 1585. At the other end of the religious spectrum, some Puritans conceived that the Church of England had not taken the Reformation far enough. They objected to the top-down ecclesiastical organization of the English church and its retention of ceremonies and doctrines that they did not believe were scripturally based. This group tended to take

---

[10] For *Macbeth*, see Antonia Fraser, *The Gunpowder Plot: Terror and Faith in 1605*; Gary Wills, *Witches and Jesuits: Shakespeare's Macbeth*; and Rebecca Lemon, 'Scaffolds of Treason in *Macbeth*', *Theatre Journal* 54 (2002): 25–43. For *Catiline*, see B. N. DeLuna, *Jonson's Romish Plot: A Study of Catiline and Its Historical Context*.

inspiration from the Protestants in Geneva, modern Germany, and the Netherlands. In the early seventeenth century, after Elizabeth's death and England's peace treaty with Spain, Protestant malcontents slowly came to seem potentially more damaging for the stability of the monarchy than the erstwhile Catholic threat. Like their Catholic contemporaries, some English Protestants moved abroad for religious reasons in the years between 1610 and 1640, initially to the free states of the Netherlands and later to the New England colonies. Many, however, would return during the Civil War and Commonwealth years.[11]

Even for conforming members of the Church of England, simmering controversies over religious doctrine were difficult to ignore. The contours of these debates inform much of the devotional poetry of the period, and in their most radical form, they foster a scepticism about some of the fundamental grounds of religious faith. Some of the finest tragedies of the period—*King Lear*, *The Revenger's Tragedy*, *The Duchess of Malfi* (1613)— come close to implying that God or the gods may not exist or, if they do, may not take much interest in human affairs.

In the 1620s, an increasing English involvement with the religious conflicts that continued to roil the Continent had the effect of exacerbating problems at home. James saw England as potentially playing an important mediating role in European affairs, and reasoned that if he married his daughter into a Protestant royal family and his son into a Catholic one, he might position himself as an influential peacemaker.[12] At first this plan ran into some difficulties, because James's eldest son, the ardently Protestant Prince Henry, declared that he would never accept a Catholic bride. Given his own court from 1610 onward, the vigorous and self-assured Henry cultivated his image in pointed contrast to that of his pacific father.[13] He favoured the iconology of Arthurian legend rather than his father's imperial Roman imagery, and openly admired the military heroes of the Armada generation—most notably Walter Ralegh, whom his father kept imprisoned under a suspended sentence of death in the Tower of London.

---

[11] For an account of this reverse migration, much less well known than the 'Great Migration' of English Puritans to the New England colonies, see William Sachse, 'The Migration of New Englanders to England, 1640–1660', *American Historical Review* 2 (1948): 251–278.

[12] For a sympathetic account of these efforts, see W. B. Patterson, *King James VI and I and the Reunion of Christendom*.

[13] For Henry's significance to England's cultural life in the early seventeenth century, see Roy Strong, *Henry, Prince of Wales and England's Lost Renaissance*.

Prince Henry was not only a champion of Protestantism but a generous supporter of the arts: his activities as a patron will receive some discussion in Chapter 2: Literature and Social Systems. But in 1611, at the age of eighteen, he died suddenly of typhoid fever. Only a few months later, the first phase of James's marital scheme clicked into place when his daughter, Princess Elizabeth, wed the Protestant Elector Palatine Frederick, whose realm consisted of lands in modern Germany and the Czech Republic. About seven years later, Henry's younger brother Charles, now heir to the throne, came of marriageable age, inaugurating the second phase. Extended negotiations to marry the Spanish Infanta foundered in 1623, but those for the French Catholic princess Henrietta Maria were more successful and Charles wed her in 1625.

In the event, James's grand plan backfired, and not only because his death, also in 1625, permanently precluded his dreams of mediation. In 1619 his son-in-law Frederick was offered the crown of Bohemia by a group of Protestant nobles who had rebelled against their Catholic overlord, Ferdinand II. When Frederick accepted it, he enraged the Catholic powers, who saw this territory as part of the Holy Roman Empire. A few months later, in the Battle of White Mountain near Prague, they defeated Frederick, who fled with his family to The Hague, touching off the Thirty Years War. Throughout the 1620s and 1630s, the exiled Frederick and Elizabeth implored Elizabeth's countrymen to come to their aid. Meanwhile, in England, Charles's new queen, Henrietta Maria, was permitted not only to retain her religion but to bring a large Catholic entourage with her from France. The open practice of Catholicism at court during the 1620s and 1630s enraged fervent Protestants, especially given the ongoing suffering of 'their' branch of the royal family.

In the 1630s, tensions over religious questions became even more evident. Under Charles I and his Archbishop of Canterbury, William Laud, the English church veered in a much more ceremonial direction than had been the case under Elizabeth and James. In a major rebuilding programme, churches were renovated and fitted with elaborate altars and elevated pulpits. The prescribed service was retooled, as well, to centre on ritual elements rather than on preaching or improvised prayer. The Calvinist doctrines of predestination and the innate depravity of human beings, which had tended to prevail in the Elizabethan and Jacobean Church, were played down in favour of 'Arminianism': the doctrine that human beings might, by their own free will, choose to accept God's gift of grace. All these trends met stiff opposition from the Puritan wing of the established church, not to mention from those 'separatists' who no longer believed they could coexist religiously with their countrymen and broke entirely with what was supposed to be the universal Church of England. But those who dared challenge the new dispensation openly were savagely repressed. When the firebrand lawyer William Prynne published his interminable treatise *Histriomastix* (1632), railing for more than 1,000 pages against holiday revelry, stage plays, and other practices he considered idolatrous, he was considered to have insulted the Queen, who enjoyed performing in masques. His book was publicly burnt by the hangman, and Prynne was sentenced to be disbarred, to pay a fine of 5,000 pounds, to have both his ears cut off in the pillory, and to serve life imprisonment. When, from prison, he defiantly published another treatise—this time attacking bishops—he was fined again, his ears were trimmed even closer to his head, and he was branded on the face.

In the Jacobean Church, ceremonialists and anti-ceremonialists, Calvinists and Arminians, had negotiated a tense coexistence; but, increasingly, in the 1620s and 1630s many devout Christians came to feel that this expedient *via media* was an abdication of their spiritual commitments. Those who would reject moderate conformism could point to a passage in scripture: 'I would that thou wert cold or hot. So then because thou art lukewarm, and neither cold nor hot, I will spew thee out of my mouth' (Revelation 3:16). At least the religiously ardent were willing to take a firm stand for what they believed in. Faced with division, sectarians prefer the integrity of their own group to preserving the unity of the whole, especially if that unity can only be achieved by compromises that seem intolerable. Middle-of-the-road English thought in the early seventeenth century remained strongly attached to the concept of an established, state-sponsored church to which everyone belongs; but 'schism', once the dirtiest of dirty words, began to seem a less appalling prospect. Even so loyal a supporter of the Church of England as George Herbert, with his ties to the Anglican community of Little Gidding, could appreciate the resolve of those who would emigrate to one of the Puritan colonies recently established in New England rather than compromise their faith commitments. 'Religion stands on tiptoe in our land, / Ready to pass to the American strand', he wrote in 'The Church Militant' (235–236).

In the first four decades of the seventeenth century, politics underwent a similar slow tendency towards polarization and the hardening of the boundaries between positions or claims that came to seem flatly incompatible rather than simply different. Already King of Scotland when he came to the throne as King of England, James initially dreamed of combining the two kingdoms under a single administrative entity, 'The Empire of Britain'.

The aspiration is celebrated in a number of the period's court masques, and may leave its mark as well upon Shakespeare's *King Lear*, set in a prehistoric 'Britain' that seems to comprise Albany, a Scottish territory in the north, as well as Cornwall in the far southwest and Kent in the southeast. Yet this project of unification and synthesis foundered on the recalcitrant differences between the two nations: their disparate legal and religious traditions, the relative poverty of Scotland compared to England, the local customs and prestige markers that each was unwilling to give up. By 1607 the project was dead, though James continued to style himself the King of Britain and gave orders for a flag that combined the English St George Cross with the Scottish St Andrew's Cross. But the administrative entity of a 'United Kingdom' would not come into existence until the eighteenth century. In retrospect, the failure of the union of the kingdoms was an early symptom of what would become an increasing cultural tendency, across political and aesthetic as well as religious realms, towards fragmentation into segments each one of which seemed purer and more consistent in itself, but was correspondingly more alienated from its fellows than it had previously seemed. The copula 'and' increasingly seemed a pusillanimous mystification of logic; it seemed to demand replacement with a more rigorous, and inevitably more polemical, 'or'.

In addition to, and entangled with, controversies over religion were controversies over the nature and extent of royal authority. In the late sixteenth and early seventeenth centuries the grounds and extent of monarchical power were hotly debated, not only in England but all over Europe. Was sovereignty delegated 'from above', by God, or conferred 'from below', by the people? Or was it inherited from an ancestor, like any other estate? Elizabeth, at various points during her reign, made all three claims. And though James's sense of his role and his importance may not in fact have differed very much from Elizabeth's, he, and his son Charles after him, stated their views on the divine right of kings much more strongly than Elizabeth had done. With a queen on the throne, there had always been something paradoxical or askew about the performance of power. Elizabeth played up her femaleness even while asserting her royal exceptionality. But her gender remained a problem to be negotiated within a strongly patriarchal cultural and legal framework, one that denied ordinary women formal political roles and subordinated them within the family. James could, and did, make more straightforward claims to rule, most notably in two treatises he wrote before coming to the English throne: *The True Law of Free Monarchies* (1598) and *Basilikon Doron* (1599). The effect was to magnify claims of royal authority and to minimize the significance of alternative forms of legitimacy, like popular consent, traditional practice, or the rule of law, all of which arguably contributed to a 'mixed polity' that consisted of the monarchy, the hereditary aristocracy, elected members of Parliament, and local officers. The role of common law and the judiciary became a particular point of controversy in the second decade of the seventeenth century. In James's view, 'kings were the authors and makers of the laws, and not the laws of the kings';[14] in other words, the king's judges were merely his delegates. But James's Lord Chief Justice, Edward Coke, retorted that 'the king in his own person cannot adjudge any case'.[15] Instead, Coke claimed, 'this ought to be determined and adjudged in some court of justice' according to the precepts of the common law, an adjudication which required expertise that James lacked. For Coke, common law provided guard rails which the king had to respect; in other words, the king was subject to the law, not the law to the monarch. Coke's views led to conflict with James and his eventual loss of his position in 1616.[16]

Unfortunately for James, and later for Charles, their exalted theory of kingly supremacy was difficult to sustain in practice. Despite the efforts of the Tudor rulers, over the course of the sixteenth century, to bolster the power of the monarchy, the English crown remained weak in critical respects. In an age of slow travel and communication, it was challenging for the Crown to stretch its authority into the more far-flung parts of the realms. By necessity, it needed to delegate administrative tasks to local officials, but neither Elizabeth nor her successors could afford a corps of properly compensated government agents. Instead, they depended upon unpaid gentry to serve as justices of the peace in the countryside. Especially in the places far from the seat of Crown power in Westminster, such local dignitaries often had to use their own discretion. They could tacitly ignore royal policies with which they were unsympathetic or pursue their own agenda unhindered by outside interference. Meanwhile, more important figures in the central administration were rewarded with shipping and import monopolies and other perquisites that could be quite lucrative to the individual who held them, but which had the effect of distorting the economy. The lack of a regular, adequate salary for government officials was an invitation

---

[14] James VI and I, *True Law of Free Monarchies, or The Reciprock and Mutual Duty Betwixt a Free King and his Natural Subjects* in *King James VI and I: Political Writings*, ed. Johann Somerville, p. 73

[15] Sit Edward Coke, "Prohibitions del Roy", *The Reports of Sir Edward Coke, Knight, in Thirteen Parts* (London: John Butterworth, 1826) vol. 6, p. 280. The opinion was issued in 1607-1608 and included in the twelfth book of the Reports, first printed in 1656.

[16] For a detailed history of the controversy, see Glenn Burgess, *The Politics of the Ancient Constitution: An Introduction to English Political Thought, 1603–1642*.

to bribe-taking, the only way to prosper or even to meet the expenses of holding the office. Under such circumstances corruption was endemic and inevitable, rising to spectacularly extortionate levels in the late 1610s and 1620s.

In other respects, too, the Crown's lack of financial resources served as a brake on absolutist ambitions. In theory the Crown was supposed to 'live from its own'—that is, pay the expenses of governing out of the income from its extensive landholdings. It was expected to request a 'supply' or permission to tax from Parliament only in times of national emergency, such as a war: England had no standing army but, of course, if a military force was assembled for a particular purpose, it would need to be paid. The assumption was that such adventures were exceptional and that the monarch's estates ought to provide the funds for his normal operation. Elizabeth's parsimoniousness, and her unwillingness to involve herself in expensive foreign entanglements, allowed her to barely manage within her income. But James, whose family and entourage were larger and whose financial acumen was shaky, soon ran up gigantic debts. In fact, the Crown was caught in an increasingly tight financial vice. Inflation ate into the real value of land rents, a primary source of crown revenue. At the same time, the increasing sophistication of military technology made the monarch's traditional responsibility to defend the realm dramatically more expensive. Yet the situation was ill-understood at the time, and it was only too easy to blame the problem on the obviously abusive monopolists and the conspicuous consumption habits of a deliberately magnificent Renaissance court. Parliament, in which was traditionally vested the power to raise taxes, thus consistently refused to vote for sufficient 'supply' to provide even for the Crown's minimal needs, even while, especially in the 1620s, its more fervent Protestant members were urging King James, and later King Charles, to intervene militarily on behalf of the Protestant cause on the Continent.

Naturally the Crown responded to these pressures by attempting to maximize those sources of revenue that it did control. For instance, it could raise money by selling titles of honour. When he came to the throne, James required every man with an estate of more than forty pounds to present himself to be knighted (and to pay the associated fee), whether he wanted the title or not. Once this revenue stream was exhausted, a new title was created—'baronet'—in an attempt to bring in more income. But titles of honour were supposed to be just that—conferred for worthy service in war or peace—and their open commodification scandalized many and became a popular topic of Jacobean satire. As a result, the title of baronet, initially priced at more than a 1,000 pounds, quickly plummeted in value as people realized that it was simply available for purchase. Another source of funds was the monarch's control of the estates and marriages of those whose parents died before they came of age. 'Wardship' was originally designed to protect aristocratic orphans from exploitation by fortune-hunters, but by the early seventeenth century it had evolved into a cruel system in which the forced marriages of the young wards were bought and sold by wealthy investors as a strategy of estate planning. Yet another Crown prerogative was the right of 'purveyance', in which the king's officials could seize goods without paying their market value, on the excuse that they were using them to supply the royal court. Not surprisingly, this system of legalized theft was no more popular than wardship or the sale of titles.

To impose taxes in the modern sense, however, the monarch required the consent of Parliament. Because the day-to-day work of governance was vested in the Crown and its officers, Parliament traditionally had been imagined as an advisory body, meeting irregularly at the monarch's request, generally only every few years, and for a few weeks or months at a time. Indeed, Parliament was traditionally imagined to include the monarch as one of its elements. The conception of a Parliament that not only cooperated with the ruler but cooperated within itself persisted late into the 1620s; the House of Commons would routinely postpone a vote in order to try to achieve consensus on controversial measures. True adversary politics would not develop until the 1640s, and the idea of a 'loyal opposition', in which conflict is considered an inevitable and healthy aspect of political life, would take much longer to emerge.[17] Yet harbingers of such a system were beginning to show even in James's reign.[18]

The 1610 / 1611 Parliament was, in some respects, a watershed. Customarily, when a Parliament came into session, the monarch would hear and redress the grievances of his subjects and, in response, Parliament would indicate its gratitude by voting a 'supply' to the ruler. Because James desperately needed 'supply', members of Parliament realized they had him over a barrel and could press their concerns aggressively as a condition of their grant—attempting, in James's opinion, inappropriately to dictate Crown policy. As Lord Treasurer, Robert Cecil attempted to negotiate an end to what seemed to be disintegrating into distasteful quid pro quo horse-trading.

---

[17] Mark Kishlansky, 'The Emergence of Adversary Politics in the Long Parliament', *Journal of Modern History* 49 (1977): 617–640.
[18] Conrad Russell, *King James I and his English Parliaments: The Trevelyan Lectures Delivered at the University of Cambridge 1995*, ed. Richard Cust and Andrew Thrush.

He proposed a 'Great Contract' in which James would relinquish his unpopular rights to wardship and purveyance in return for a predictable grant of 300,000 pounds a year, raised by taxation. But this proposal foundered both on the king's reluctance to curb the royal prerogative and on Parliament's unwillingness to tax. When James dissolved Parliament in 1611, the matter was dropped, and Cecil died the following year with the underlying problem unaddressed.

Under James, those who troubled themselves over the potentially unbridled power of rulers often framed their concerns as a critique of the sexual immorality at court. Indeed, James's court differed from Elizabeth's in this respect. Elizabeth held her ladies-in-waiting to scrupulous standards of behaviour and would dismiss male courtiers for marrying without her permission or for fathering children out of wedlock. James was much more tolerant of irregularity; his own marriage to Anne of Denmark had been troubled from the start, and he preferred the companionship of handsome men, lavishing gifts, titles, and public demonstrations of affection upon those he cherished. From a modern standpoint, the rigidities of aristocratic marriage seem much to blame: such alliances were typically arranged for financial and dynastic reasons, sometimes between very young partners, but divorce was virtually impossible. Given these circumstances it is unsurprising that otherwise privileged and powerful people should feel themselves entitled to create their own happiness without regard to conventions of propriety. Be that as it may, a much franker and more cynical treatment of sexuality is evident in much of the writing of the Jacobean period, combined with a moralism that made sexual expression a subject for dark satire rather than for a joyful vindication of pleasure or a platform for social reform. Yet, arguably, the real bone of contention was not 'immorality'. In the late 1620s and 1630s, King Charles, unlike James, grew deeply attached to his wife: the celebration of the love between them, and of chaste romantic love in general, was the theme of many a Caroline masque, play, and poem. Still, sceptics continued to take a jaundiced view. Whereas James neglected his queen, Charles was thought to be overly entranced by his. The Puritan and republican Lucy Hutchinson, writing after the Restoration, blamed the entire Civil War on Charles's uncritical adoration of his Catholic wife:

> This lady being by her priests affected with the meritoriousness of advancing her own religion . . . applied that way her great wit and parts, and the power her haughty spirit kept over her husband, who was enslaved in his

affection only to her, though she had no more passion for him than what served to promote her designs.[19]

What connected the criticisms of both the Jacobean and the Caroline court, in fact, was not whether the sexual behaviour of kings or aristocrats was properly restrained or honoured the marriage bond. The fundamental concern was the evident liability of the monarch to attachments and preferences that could interfere with governing in the common good. The more power a king was granted, the larger his personal caprices potentially loomed, and the less easily they could be counteracted or neutralized.

This problem was crystallized in the position of the royal favourite in the reigns of both James and Charles. Between 1607 and 1615 James lavished affection and gifts on young Robert Carr, raising him to the rank of viscount, then—after the death of Robert Cecil—Privy Councillor and eventually Lord Chamberlain. When Carr fell in love with the married Frances Howard, Countess of Essex, James arranged for the annulment of her marriage (overruling the objections of the Archbishop of Canterbury), created Carr the position of Earl of Somerset so that Frances would suffer no diminution in rank, and helped celebrate their elaborate court wedding. A mere two years later, however, the Somersets were implicated in, and eventually found guilty of, the murder of Carr's erstwhile friend and private secretary, Thomas Overbury. Though James commuted their death sentences, he banished them from court. James's next favourite was tall, blond George Villiers, called 'the handsomest bodied man of England'.[20] From relatively modest gentry origins, Villiers was raised to the rank of earl in 1617 and marquess in 1618; in 1619, despite his lack of seafaring experience, he was named Lord High Admiral. In 1623 he was made Duke of Buckingham, although the title of duke was normally reserved for the brothers of the king. Unlike Carr, Villiers was politically ambitious and sophisticated. He quickly befriended Prince Charles as well as James, and in 1623 the two young men bonded during a madcap expedition to Spain in which Charles hoped to meet and court the Infanta.[21] Increasingly, as James aged and became ill, he

---

[19] Lucy Hutchinson, *Memoirs of the Life of Colonel John Hutchinson*, ed. James Sutherland, p. 49.

[20] Godfrey Goodman, Bishop of Gloucester, *The Court of King James I* (printed in London, 1839 from a manuscript written around 1650), cited in Alan Stewart, *The Cradle King: A Life of James VI and I*, p. 265.

[21] For Charles I's reign, see Richard Cust, *Charles I: A Political Life*.

delegated more and more authority to Buckingham, who seemed to many to be operating as de facto monarch.

The king's favourite, apparently, could attain almost unlimited wealth and sway despite a lack of birthright or ability, and he was all the more effective insofar as he appealed to the weakness of the ruler's character rather than his strengths. What Curtis Perry calls a 'dual perspective, in which favouritism is both commonplace and monstrous',[22] therefore pervades a great deal of the politically engaged literature of the period, in particular tragedy, which, as we shall see, is intensely concerned with problems of arbitrary rule. Especially after Charles came to the throne, Parliament viewed Buckingham's power with increasing alarm—alarm that was only exacerbated when Buckingham was associated with a series of expensive but disastrous military campaigns in France and Spain, purportedly in defence of Protestantism. In 1626 Parliament—called to provide the funding needed for these enterprises—instead began impeachment proceedings against Buckingham. Charles flatly refused to repudiate Buckingham, dissolved Parliament, resorted to a scheme of 'forced loans' to raise the money Parliament refused to grant him, and imprisoned those who declined to pay up. But since the forced loans were likely to be ruled illegal, Charles eventually needed to recall Parliament. This time, Parliament devised a Petition of Right which insisted that the prerogative to tax was Parliament's alone, and that nobody could be detained for failing to provide a 'gift or loan' that had not been authorized by an act of Parliament. Charles had little alternative but to accede to the Petition at the time, though in the event he refused to respect its terms. When a discontented soldier named John Felton assassinated Buckingham in 1628, he was widely regarded as a hero and, after his execution, a martyr.

Between 1629 and 1640, Charles avoided conflict with Parliament simply by refusing to call it into session. This strategy bought him peace in the short term, but left him dangerously isolated, unaware of his subjects' range of opinions, and oblivious to the wisdom of negotiation and compromise. And, despite his attempts to economize, it also forced him to resort once again to controversial ways of raising money. Charles had the sound idea of modernizing the English navy, but no way to pay for new vessels out of Crown resources. So he raised money by a special tax—'Ship Money'—to be levied throughout the realm without the consent of Parliament. Though

---

[22] Curtis Perry, *Literature and Favouritism in Early Modern England*, p. 15.

the court case that resulted was eventually decided in Charles's favour, the measure was widely unpopular and many stubbornly refused to pay.

However, it was religious conflict that finally demonstrated the limits of Charles's 'personal rule'. In the late 1630s, Charles decided that the standardization and ritualization of religious practice that he and Archbishop Laud had previously introduced throughout the English church would be extended to Ireland and Scotland as well. In Ireland, Charles's deputy, Thomas Wentworth, Earl of Stafford, was already violently unpopular with both Catholic and Protestant lords. And Scotland had its own national 'kirk' organized along Presbyterian lines: that is, the professional clergy rather than the Crown appointed church officials. Although James had nominally brought Scotland under the umbrella of the Church of England, appointing bishops to Scotland in 1621, he had in actual fact allowed the kirk to go its own way. Now Charles—who, unlike his father, had little actual experience with his northern realm—attempted to make ecclesiastical organization more consistent and to impose a more ritually oriented church service and prayer book. From the Scots point of view, these measures constituted not only an insult to national pride, but a devious attempt to reintroduce popery. In 1637, in Edinburgh's Church of St Giles, when Dean James Hannay attempted to conduct the new service, the congregation shouted him down, and when the Bishop of Edinburgh ascended the pulpit to calm the people, they rioted, throwing Bibles and stools. Although they were quickly evicted from the cathedral itself, violence continued in the streets outside. In Glasgow, a clergyman was nearly killed. In Brechin, the bishop led the service with two loaded pistols on the desk beside him and attended by a security force of armed family members, but he was nonetheless attacked by a mob on his way home from church and his palace was plundered. In 1638, the Scots drew up a National Covenant demanding that the prayer book be withdrawn. Soon, a Scottish army of 'Covenanters' was marching upon England's northern counties in what became known as the First Bishop's War, overrunning the poorly paid, poorly trained English force. Charles signed a peace treaty with the Scots, but, instead of conceding defeat, he called Parliament into session in order to obtain the money he needed to continue fighting. Once assembled, however, Parliament refused to grant him any money unless he provided redress of their grievances, as they had been building up over the past decade. Disgusted, Charles dissolved Parliament after only a few weeks but then—in the Second Bishops' War—suffered another crushing defeat when the Scots seized the northern English town of Newcastle. Charles was forced to call Parliament back into session, at which point Parliament proved even more intransigent. It passed statutes preventing the dissolution of Parliament without the consent of the members, inaugurating a 'Long Parliament' that would remain continuously in session for more than a decade.

Civil Wars and Commonwealth

Because many members of Parliament shared the Scots' complaints about the direction of the Church of England, Charles's most important quarrel was soon not with the Scots but with his own countrymen. Paranoia about the king's 'Popish' tendencies was only exacerbated by events in Ireland, where in 1641, under the leadership of Phelim O'Neill, Catholics attacked Protestant settlements in Ulster and elsewhere, a revolt some Parliamentarians suspected was countenanced or commissioned by Charles. The House of Commons passed 'bills of attainder' to execute Charles's advisor Strafford and to imprison and, several years later, execute his Archbishop of Canterbury, William Laud (Laud's prosecution was facilitated by his old enemy, William Prynne, now released from prison.) Parliament also abolished the Star Chamber, a court comprised of the king's privy councillors and common-law judges, which Charles's government had used extensively in the 1630s to prosecute and punish religious dissenters. In 1642 Charles tried to stymie Parliament's hostile measures by coming in person, with a force of 400 soldiers, to arrest the leaders of the House of Commons for treason. But those individuals, tipped off regarding his plans, departed earlier in the day, so the attempt only stimulated further outrage. Charles demanded that the City of London yield the fugitives, but instead City officials declared their support for Parliament. Charles and Queen Henrietta Maria were forced to leave London, first for Hampton Court and later for Oxford, a royalist stronghold.

By 1642 the Civil War was underway—or, more accurately, two periods of conflict punctuated by an interval of uneasy truce and negotiation.[23] The first phase of the conflict, between 1642 and 1646, aligned the Scots Covenanters with the English parliamentarians against the king. Although both groups rejected the Caroline version of the Church of England, the English were split between Presbyterians who, like the Scots, wanted a

---

[23] For a sweeping but succinct account of the events of the Civil War decade, see Diane Purkiss, *The English Civil War: A People's History*.

rigorously Protestant state church, and 'Independents' who rejected ecclesiastical hierarchy and the conception of a state church altogether, arguing that individual church congregations should be self-governing. In other words, the Presbyterians, who seemed radical in the 1630s, were soon outflanked by more radical reformers, who rejected the measures the Presbyterians advocated for ensuring conformity and censoring heretical opinions. By 1645 the Independents predominated in the New Model Army, the parliamentarian force ably led by Thomas Fairfax and Oliver Cromwell.

The first phase of the conflict ended in 1646 with the defeat of the royalist forces. However, Charles formally surrendered to the Scots, not the English. Attempts to hammer out an agreement between King, Parliament, and the army came to naught when Charles escaped house arrest in Hampton Court Palace, fled to the Isle of Wight, and proceeded to make common cause with both Irish Catholics and the Scottish Covenanters against the parliamentary English forces. After about a year of further violence, the New Model Army decisively defeated the royalists and re-imprisoned Charles.

Most of the royal family had succeeded in fleeing to the Continent, as had some committed supporters of the monarchy, such as the writer Margaret Cavendish and her husband William, and William's former tutor, the philosopher Thomas Hobbes. The poet Edmund Waller, accused of participating in a plot to restore Charles to power, was at first imprisoned and then exiled. Royalist clergy, including the poet Robert Herrick, were deprived of their livings, and supporters of the king, such as the poet Richard Lovelace, had their estates 'sequestered' or confiscated so that they would be unable to contribute to the war effort. But what to do about Charles? In the minds of his enemies, he represented an ongoing threat. His previous behaviour showed that he was not likely to observe the conditions of any treaty he agreed to, since he did not believe that a king ought to be bound by his promises to mere subjects. Still, the majority of Parliament shrank from bringing a rightful monarch to trial. So, in December 1648 a regiment of the New Model Army, led by Thomas Pride, occupied the House of Commons and refused entry to most members of Parliament, leaving a 'Rump' of fewer than eighty men remaining. Over the continuing objections of the House of Lords, this small group voted to put Charles on trial for treason—a charge that Charles argued was absurd, because treason had been defined since time immemorial as a crime against the king. Yet Charles, in what was a foregone conclusion, was convicted after a week-long public trial, and was beheaded in January 1649. His erstwhile allies, however, fought on. The Scots, objecting to being governed by an English parliament, recognized

King Charles's eldest son, Prince Charles, as heir to the throne of Scotland. On similar grounds, the Irish made a league with the prince as well. In 1650, the redoubtable Oliver Cromwell led campaigns first to Ireland, then to Scotland, crushing their resistance. His subjugation of the Irish was especially ferocious, not only slaughtering many non-combatants but also confiscating land from Catholics and reassigning it to Protestant supporters.

The human suffering that attended upon all this violence was extraordinary. Combat deaths in England and Wales alone are estimated at 85,000, and there were perhaps twice as many deaths from disease or from civilians caught in the crossfire. The war was even more lethal, proportional to the population, in Scotland and Ireland, and throughout the British Isles the destruction of property was also immense. Yet the turmoil of this period unleashed enormous levels of political, religious, and social innovation, some of which is tracked in an explosion of printed books. Under the Tudor and Stuart regimes, the Stationers' Company—which controlled the printing of books—and officials appointed by the Crown administered a system of pre-publication censorship. But with the disintegration of Crown control, this arrangement collapsed, opening the floodgates to new kinds of polemical writing. The number of printed tracts exploded, with a 140 per cent increase between 1640 and 1641 and another 98 per cent on top of that between 1641 and 1642, many of them devoted to highly controversial topics. The Long Parliament passed laws attempting to regulate the printing trade in 1643 and 1647, as did the Rump Parliament in 1649; Cromwell's government would pass even stricter laws in 1655. But even these measures could not completely stem the tide. Sects proclaiming the primacy of individual conscience and claiming direct inspiration from God proliferated in these years—Baptists, Quakers, and less durable movements such as the Ranters, who rejected even the authority of Scripture, and claimed that sin was merely an illusion. Many 'millenarians' believed that the civil turmoil they were living through prefigured the second coming of Christ as foretold in the Book of Revelation, and prepared for the End Times. Religious radicalism often went hand in hand with social radicalism, for early Christians had shared their property in common and redistributed wealth to the poor. In the New Model Army, these ideas spread quickly, spawning the Levellers and the Diggers, who argued for an extension of the franchise to non-wealthy males, an end to imprisonment for debt, and a redistribution of land along socialist principles.

The rapidly changing ideological landscape throughout the 1640s and early 1650s, and the lack of a clear-cut trajectory for the conflict, means that many individuals found their loyalties and alliances shifting as the situation changed. Some members of Parliament, such as Lucius Cary and Edward Hyde, who had been critical of Charles in the late 1630s thought, by 1642, that the House of Commons had taken things too far and joined the royalist side. As already mentioned, the Presbyterian Scots who first initiated conflict with Charles become his allies several years later. And in 1648 a majority of those on the 'parliamentary' side, as we have already seen, nonetheless hoped to leave Charles on the throne, and only wanted to reduce his arbitrary exercise of power. On the other hand, the millenarian 'Fifth Monarchists' believed that the execution of Charles I would inaugurate the reign of the saints, and in the early 1650s they spearheaded resistance to government by the Rump Parliament they had previously supported, on the grounds that it had not in fact furthered the cause of godliness. In 1650 Thomas Fairfax, the general of the New Model Army that had achieved some of the most impressive military victories for Parliament, refused to accede to Cromwell's plan for invading Scotland; he resigned his command and retired to his estate. John Hutchinson, one of the judges who signed Charles I's death warrant, thought Cromwell eventually betrayed the republican values Hutchinson championed. In other cases, men who were in some respects radical took conservative positions in others. For instance, Cromwell's son-in-law Henry Ireton was one of the most avid proponents of putting King Charles on trial, but he strongly opposed the Levellers' egalitarian social views. Perhaps the most eloquent statement of what must have been the ambivalence of many of those living through these conflicts is Andrew Marvell's 1650 poem 'An Horatian Ode Upon Cromwell's Return from Ireland.' The poem represents the doomed Charles sympathetically even while endorsing the 'industrious valor' of Cromwell, who will 'ruin the great work of time / And cast the kingdoms old / Into another mold' (33–36).

> Though justice against fate complain
> And plead the ancient rights in vain,
> But those do hold or break
> As men are strong or weak.
>
> (37–40)

The poem celebrates Cromwell's success as a military and political leader even as it marks the distance between his effectiveness and traditional conceptions of right and wrong. And it ends on an ominous note: Cromwell must 'march indefatigably on' (114), since 'The same arts that did gain / A power, must it maintain' (119–120). Rest or respite will, apparently, never be an option.

The end of civil war did not mean the end of institutional turmoil. The army was increasingly at odds with Parliament, and Cromwell finally dismissed Parliament in 1653. From 1653 until his death in 1658, Cromwell would rule over England and the annexed Scotland and Ireland as Lord Protector, essentially as a military dictator as autocratic as the Stuarts he had replaced.[24] His power was reinforced by the persistence of the standing army he had originally commanded—a novelty in England. Soldiers and military officers were entrusted with many of the administrative duties that had previously been delegated to the gentry or hereditary aristocracy. The ecclesiastical hierarchy of the Church of England was dismantled, and congregations chose their own clergy in accordance with Cromwell's Independent convictions. Although a version of the state church remained, attendance was no longer required. Even Quakers and Catholics could worship freely provided they did not advocate for the overthrow of the state, and some Jews were permitted to settle in England for the first time since 1290. But Cromwell did not support the Levellers' social agenda and he believed, counter to the more radical republicans in Parliament, that effective government required a single person vested with strong executive powers.

When Cromwell died, the assumption was that his son, Richard Cromwell, would succeed him just as the eldest sons of kings had done in the past. But Richard lacked his father's military experience and was unable to command the respect of the powerful army faction. In 1659 he resigned as Lord Protector, and in 1660 he went into exile on the Continent. Meanwhile, some members of Parliament, many of whom had been dismissed in Pride's Purge a decade earlier, began negotiating with King Charles' eldest son, Prince Charles, who was living in France. In 1660, Charles was invited to return to England as King Charles II. Charles II quickly re-established the Church of England, executed some of the men responsible for his father's death (exhuming Cromwell's corpse in order to hang it in chains), and otherwise attempted as much as possible to revert to the status quo ante. Legal documents even stated the year of his reign as if he had seamlessly succeeded his father in 1649. But Charles II returned to an England so profoundly

---

[24] Biographies of Cromwell include Barry Coward, *Oliver Cromwell*; Michael O. Siochru, *God's Executioner: Oliver Cromwell and the Conquest of Ireland*; and Ronald Hutton, *The Making of Oliver Cromwell*.

changed, both politically and religiously, that, as we have seen, John Dryden imagined that the old order had been decisively swept away.

History, Literature, Literary History

Looking at the earlier decades of the century with the benefit of hindsight, none of the sources of the strife at mid-century seem new: most of them had been brewing at least since the time of Henry VIII. It is easy, therefore, to see England as, for decades, drifting unstoppably towards violent confrontation. Yet in the 1620s and earlier, few seem to have regarded their society as exceptionally dysfunctional, and even in the late 1630s few imagined that England was on the brink of war. It is very difficult to know, in retrospect, whether there was really more conflict in the 1620s and 1630s than earlier, or whether a readiness to acknowledge discord made it, eventually, more likely to occur. What changed between, say, 1590 and 1640 was a cultural willingness to accept rather than evade open confrontation—an acceptance that may, ironically, have been predicated upon the relative stability of England under Elizabeth and James, which deprived most people of the bitter experience of serious conflict. Arthur Wilson, a royalist writing in 1658, blamed the war on poets who, spoiled by tranquillity, did not realize that their own obstreperousness would destroy the grounds of their comfort: 'peace begot plenty, and plenty begot ease and wantonness, and ease and wantonness begot poetry, and poetry swelled to that bulk in [James'] time, that it begot strange monstrous satires against the King's own person.'[25] Early seventeenth-century England might be imagined as a supersaturated solution—stresses were slowly added as salt, say, is added to water, until the limits of what will dissolve are reached and exceeded. The supersaturated solution is still a liquid, but the slightest addition of more salt, or even merely the jostling of the container, will cause the solids to suddenly clump and separate. The Civil War might be thought of on analogous principles. It was surely not somehow fated, and events might easily have turned out otherwise; still, rather to the surprise of contemporaries, what had been almost unthinkable forty years earlier eventually came to pass. Yet the movement from a monarchy that claimed to rule by divine right to a parliamentary form of government was hardly a linear one. The move towards greater political

---

[25] Arthur Wilson, *The History of Great Britain, Being the Life and Reign of King James I*, pub. 1653, p. 792. Cf. the roughly contemporaneous royalist view of William Sanderson, *Reign and Death of King James* (1656).

participation mooted in the 1640s seemed stymied first by Cromwell's virtual dictatorship and the inability of his government to manage the transfer of power, and then by the restoration of Charles II.

The rationale for the traditional literary periodization, breaking at 1660 with the reversion to monarchy, was already, as we have seen, prevalent in the late seventeenth century. And it gains plausibility from the account of the seventeenth century provided by some recent historians who argue that the English Civil War was the decisive event of the age. In other words, without necessarily sharing Dryden's royalist sympathies, they agree with him that the war was a historic watershed: 'the first "Great Revolution" in the history of the world', as Lawrence Stone writes, 'and therefore an event of fundamental importance in the evolution of Western civilization'.[26] The calamitous events of the mid-seventeenth century, these historians argue, brought abruptly to the fore new ideas that would, over the course of the next century and a half, set England upon a course of political modernization. The dispute between the king and the parliamentary leaders who opposed him was a profoundly significant struggle between conceptions of government. Was the monarch the source and maker of the law, or was he subject to the laws? What role ought elected officials play, and who ought to have a say in electing them? What ought to be the relationship between religious and secular authorities? Did 'freeborn' Englishmen have what would later be called inalienable rights, or were those rights conferred by, and taken away by, authorities? Such questions were not only of fundamental concern in England but would influence the political development of other Anglophone nations as well. In the late eighteenth century, the founders of the United States looked back to the English Civil War and its aftermath as both a source of inspiration and, in some respects, a cautionary example. These questions were also, as we shall see, multiply addressed in much of the literature of the period.

In the past fifty years, however, this view of English history has been challenged as too 'Whig', too teleological, to provide a satisfactory account of the period. The criticism has come from two rather different directions. 'Revisionist' historians of the civil wars tend to emphasize their contingent, almost accidental, quality, seeing them as tied up with personalities and factional manoeuvering rather than with a clash of incompatible ideologies. Conrad Russell, a leading revisionist, argues that

---

[26] Lawrence Stone, *The Causes of the English Revolution, 1529–1642*, p. 147.

hindsight has grossly distorted the story we have hitherto been told . . . There was a very wide measure of agreement [between the supporters of the king and the supporters of parliament] on the principles on which the country ought to be governed when the system was working well.[27]

And even Lawrence Stone has no illusions about widespread popular participation in the political turmoil of the period, remarking on 'the almost total passivity of the rural masses . . . the wage-earners in the towns were equally passive, even in London' (54–55). Another important challenge to the traditional view comes from historians who examine aspects of social life that seem not to dovetail neatly with the political events of the period. Economic historians note that many of the trends that made possible England's eventual ascendancy as an imperial power—increased prowess at sea, scientific and technological advances, a shift to proto-capitalist forms of wealth-creation, the explosive growth of London as a major centre of trade— were already underway well before James came to the throne, and would continue long after the Stuart dynasty came to an end with the death of Queen Anne in 1714.[28] The Civil War did not derail, or even apparently much affect, these developments, though troubled times did accelerate the flight of capital and of human beings to English colonies in North America. Social and demographic historians argue that for most English people, day-to-day life did not alter very much between the late middle ages and the late eighteenth or early nineteenth centuries: their institutions, customs, social structures, and habits persisted basically intact from generation to generation until the Industrial Revolution, which fundamentally changed social organizations and work patterns for rich and poor alike.[29] In this kind of history the early seventeenth century figures merely as part of a much

---

[27] Conrad Russell, *Unrevolutionary England, 1603–1642*, pp. ix and xv. See also *The Causes of the English Civil War: The Ford Lectures Delivered in the University of Oxford 1987–1988*. For a rejoinder to Russell's views, see Richard Cust and Ann Hughes, eds., *Conflict in Early Stuart England: Studies in Religion and Politics 1603–1642*. Ann Hughes, *The Causes of the English Civil War*, provides a useful overview of the scholarly debate.

[28] Keith Wrightson, *Earthly Necessities: Economic Lives in Early Modern Britain*.

[29] For instance, Peter Laslett, in *The World We Have Lost*, p. 158, writes: 'The truth is that changes in English society between the reign of Elizabeth and the reign of Anne were not revolutionary. The impression left by this first attempt to survey the fundamental framework during these generations is of how little, not how much, evolution seems to have taken place. Nothing in economic organization or in social arrangements seems to have come about which would have led of itself to political crisis, and the changes that did go on seem to have been gradual over the whole period rather than sudden.'

longer pre-industrial epoch: a *longue durée* so extremely *longue* that particular events tend to recede in importance, much as mountains appear small when viewed from the window of a jet plane.

These objections to the traditional historical narrative deserve the scrutiny of literary historians because it is on the validity of that traditional account—or, at least, its explanatory power for literature—that our standard period divisions rest. What happens to Dryden's notion of a 'giant race before the Flood' if the Flood was merely a rain shower? If his simple equation between the wit of writers and the clash of the battlefield seems implausible, what alternative might we propose? If the political issues that led up to, and were fought over, in the Civil War did not much engage the passions of ordinary people, then why do so many of the period's writers seem so profoundly gripped by them?

The following pages will address—though, of course, not definitively resolve—a number of these large topics, while at the same time trying to provide an overview of the literary world of early seventeenth-century England. As I try to forecast who might read this book, I imagine several audiences. One possible reader is the well-read person who is not an academic specialist in seventeenth-century literature but who would like a guide through the period and a sense of what is worthwhile in it. Another possible reader is the advanced undergraduate or graduate student who needs to get a useful sense of the main literary developments in the period. Another possible reader is the professional scholar—one reading either outside her area of specialization or inside it.

The desires of these various readers do not neatly coincide. The well-read amateur may gravitate towards something that is helpful and interesting without much caring whether it is unassailable by scholars. The undergraduate, the graduate student, and the scholar from another field may want clear, reliable information in a well-organized format. The specialist scholar might prefer something more tendentious and groundbreaking. My primary aim in writing this book is to provide an introduction to the period for those who are not already deeply versed in it. Despite the beauty and power of early seventeenth-century literature, relatively few people read it for sheer pleasure any more. Its language is often difficult for the uninitiated, many of its characteristic forms are unfamiliar, and the culture in which it arose differs profoundly from our own. Making this gorgeous heritage accessible to a larger audience is a worthwhile enterprise.

This goal helps determine how I have written and organized the volume. I shall provide helpful background information where I think it necessary, though it might seem unnecessary to a specialist. The dating of many early seventeenth-century texts—especially of individual lyric poems—is unclear, for reasons I shall discuss in Chapter 1, and some texts exist in multiple revisions. But in cases where we know, or can surmise, a date of composition, first performance, or publication—whichever seems most pertinent to the work in question—I will provide it in parentheses the first time the work is mentioned. I shall also modernize seventeenth-century spelling and punctuation in quoted passages even if the scholarly editions of the texts I rely on do not.

Part I of this book will describe the 'social rules of writing': who was able to become a writer in the early seventeenth century, and the various ways in which a literary career might be pursued. In Part II of the book, I will write about several developments that are new or that seem especially salient in the period. Genre will be a crucial organizational term for these latter chapters, as it was for Renaissance writers and readers, who typically organized the literary spectrum not by chronological 'period' but by generic categories: comedy, tragedy, epic, satire, tragicomedy. One such development is the interesting and suggestive proliferation of new genres concerned with the description of a particular place, such as city comedy, 'country house' poetry, and chorography, which combined detailed local maps with written descriptions of those areas. Other genres that develop quickly in this period are tragicomedy and court masque. I want to focus special attention as well on the genres that, while not new or unique to this period, seem especially gloriously represented in these years: tragedy, for instance, which reached a peak of subtlety and sophistication in the first two decades of the seventeenth century; devotional poetry; and poetry of love and friendship. Finally, I will discuss the increasing prestige of prose as a medium of literary expression, a development that lays the groundwork for the emergence of the novel and the periodical essay in the later seventeenth and eighteenth centuries. As this summary suggests, the two sections of my book construe 'literary history' in somewhat different ways. Part I concerns external circumstances which bear upon literary production, while later chapters discuss literary development 'internally', from poem to poem, play to play, writer to writer.

A project like this one tends to raise definitional problems and problems of scope. While we ordinarily use the term 'literature' to refer to poems, plays, and certain prose works, in the early seventeenth century the word 'literature', drawn from the Latin *litera* or letter, meant 'book-learning' more generally. It included scholarly and theological treatises, and writing in

Latin, as well as works of the imagination composed in the vernacular language. A narrower category, 'poetry', did emphasize fiction-making and creativity: Philip Sidney, in *The Defense of Poesy* (1595), describes the Poet as one who

> lifted up with the vigour of his own invention, doth grow in effect into an other nature: in making things either better than nature bringeth forth, or quite anew, forms such as never were in nature: as the Heroes, Demigods, Cyclops, Chimeras, Furies, and such like; so as he goeth hand in hand with nature, not enclosed within the narrow warrant of her gifts, but freely ranging within the zodiac of his own wit.[30]

Sidney includes both non-dramatic and dramatic verse in his purview, but his definition would presumably exclude such works as Bacon's *Essays* (1625) or Thomas Browne's *Religio Medici* (1642).

In addition, the modern concept of 'literature' contains a prestige factor. These are, we imagine, texts that *matter*: especially creative, impressive, or influential works of art, still worth reading centuries after their composition. The seventeenth century also made such distinctions, though once again those distinctions correlate imperfectly with our own. Sir Thomas Bodley, who founded the great Bodleian Library at Oxford University in 1602, excluded what he called 'riff-raff books'. He explicitly excludes ballads, pamphlets, almanacs, and proclamations, most of which remain marginal to our canon of important seventeenth-century texts. But also, startlingly for us, he excludes 'play-books', among which are some works we now consider supreme literary accomplishments of the period.

So 'literature' is, to some extent, an anachronistic category when applied retrospectively to the writing of the seventeenth century. Anachronism does not automatically invalidate its usefulness: most of our critical terminology, after all, would be unfamiliar to Ben Jonson, John Donne, or William Shakespeare. Our categories of analysis serve our own needs as readers and scholars. Yet it is important to acknowledge at the outset that our category, 'literature', is a multiply determined one and therefore always fuzzy around the edges in ways that complicate the writing of literary history. Formal or generic criteria matter: a sonnet sequence or a tragedy, for instance, is 'literary' writing; a scientific treatise, sermon, or diary might or might

---

[30] Philip Sidney, *The Defence of Poesie* (London, 1595), in *Sir Philip Sidney: The Defence of Poesie, Political Discourses, Correspondence, Translation*, ed. Albert Feuillerat, p. 8.

not be; a royal statute, tavern reckoning, or shopping list is usually not. 'Seventeenth-century literature' for us includes the period's vast panoply of verse forms, as well as plays and masques, which if not always considered significant literary accomplishments at the moment of their composition have been long enshrined in the literary canon. 'Literature' is partly a question of authorial intention: some works, such as Bacon's *Essays*, Browne's *Religio Medici*, Michael Drayton's *Poly-Olbion* (1612, 1622), and Margaret Cavendish's *Blazing World* (1666), explicitly announce their ambition to be considered notable contributions to the world of letters. 'Literature' is partly a question of author. The sermons of John Donne interest literary scholars more than the sermons of William Perkins, even though Perkins' sermons were famous in his own day—not just because of the intrinsic quality of Donne's sermons, but because of what they reveal about the poet's mind. The construction of a literary canon, of a group of texts considered 'literature', also inevitably involves questions of judgement and taste: if 'literature' is a canon of texts that matter, then what matters to us helps determine which texts we find important. John Donne and Ben Jonson, once widely deprecated authors, now loom large in any discussion of early seventeenth-century literature. In recent years, feminist scholars have generated interest in a number of texts by women writers that previously received little or no attention. Aemelia Lanyer's poem *Salve Deus Rex Judaeorum* (1611), Elizabeth Cary's play *The Tragedy of Mariam* (1613), and Lady Mary Wroth's romance *Urania* (1621) are now routinely considered part of the period's 'literature'.

My approach, which may seem tautological but which seems reasonable given my aims for this volume, is to treat as literary those texts that have routinely been treated as literary in recent years by other readers and scholars. That consensus-driven definition, however, still leaves an enormous swathe of writing to consider, especially given the indistinct and contested periphery around what counts as literary writing. Inevitably, in a wide-ranging survey that is struggling not to become too unwieldy, I have had to be very selective in the topics and works I discuss. Especially in Part II of this book, I have generally preferred to focus my attention on a limited set of striking examples, rather than trying to cover everything in a cursory fashion. That means, perforce, that many interesting works and writers will go unmentioned. And it also means that occasionally I draw the boundaries of 'English literature' in ways that could be disputed. For instance, I will not discuss translations, or sermons, or political polemic, or controversial theological writing, or ballads, or writers based in England's new colonies in North

America, though another person tasked with writing this book might construe any of these topics as falling within the volume's purview. I have tried to emphasize the kinds of writing that are at the core of what most people consider 'literary', and to discuss works that people nowadays might still enjoy reading. Naturally I will gravitate towards those works and authors that I admire most, or about which I have something interesting to say. But I have no ambition to remake the canon in this book. Accurately to delineate some of its features will be task enough.

PART I
LITERATURE AND SOCIAL SYSTEMS

1
Who Were the Writers?

Discussing literary production in demographic or sociological terms may seem reductive. Some argue that literary inspiration wells up from within the poet, its sources inexplicable even to the writer herself and neither determined nor limited by her situation in life. True, understanding the social circumstances in which literature is produced, in the seventeenth century as in any period, does not help us foresee specific artistic accomplishments. No matter how much one knew about how, or how much, the King's Men paid Shakespeare, one could not deduce that he would write *King Lear* or *The Tempest*. Moreover, literary ambition cannot be conflated with ambition for worldly power and wealth. Few writers, then or now, are likely to be motivated primarily by a desire to get rich or to wield authority over others.

Yet it is important to comprehend how writers and their work fit into a larger society. The 'social rules for writing' enable some individuals to write and discourage others, and can either facilitate or abort a writer's career. In the seventeenth century, these rules demonstrably help shape the nature of literary enterprise: who writes, how prolifically, and in which genres. Aspects of seventeenth-century literature that seem strange to us—for instance, the fact that drama looms so large, or that some poets deliberately avoid print publication, or that so many writers spent so much effort composing fulsome praise poems to rich and powerful people—all are traceable to systems for rewarding writers which differed markedly from modern ones.

As I mentioned in the Introduction, there was no census in England until the nineteenth century, so all demographic figures for the early seventeenth century are based on estimates— but those estimates are grounded in painstaking empirical research. Keith Wrightson estimates the number of aristocracy and gentry, traditionally the politically empowered group, at 2 per cent of the total population; Peter Laslett puts it at 4–5 per cent. Laslett estimates that another 10–15 per cent were reasonably well to do: yeoman farmers with a secure lease upon their own land, or, among townsmen, skilled craftsmen and artisans.[1] In the countryside, there were far greater numbers of tenant farmers and landless labourers living at subsistence levels, often cobbling together a living by a combination of farm work, casual wage employment, and by-employments within the home (poor cottagers toiled part-time as weavers, knitters, or needleworkers). Vast numbers of men and women were employed, typically on annual contracts, as live-in servants. The cities were also full of the poor, working as porters or messengers, removing 'night-soil' (human excrement), or selling fish, apples, and other foodstuffs.

These statistics may look more depressing to us in retrospect than they would have to many of those living in it. What we tend to notice about early seventeenth-century society is its robust exclusivity: its attempts to exclude women from most positions of authority, younger sons from the family property, poor people from practically any standing at all, and the corresponding, apparently arbitrary, and unembarrassed exaltation of a privileged few. Yet while elite groups remained small in the period, they were growing in numbers. The peerage at the very top of the social hierarchy, always a tiny group, expanded modestly, though in aggregate they declined in real wealth and power during the period from 1550 to 1660. The numbers of gentry or 'gentry-equivalents' grew much more rapidly. In England, gentry status had traditionally been bestowed not merely upon substantial landowners but upon those in the learned professions: lawyers, medical professionals, and the clergy. More aspirants came from the commercial classes, especially in London, by far the wealthiest of English towns: 'our merchants ... often change estate with gentlemen, as gentlemen do with them, by a mutual conversion of the one into the other'.[2] And the visibility of the gentry class accelerated in the early seventeenth century when James raised money for the crown by conferring knighthoods on anyone who could afford to pay for one.

Most poets in seventeenth-century England derive from the groups closer to the top than to the bottom of the social pyramid: from the aristocracy or gentry, or from rather prosperous citizen's or artisan's families. I will call this combined group, taken together, the 'relatively elite'. Early modern dramatists were a somewhat more varied group than the poets, yet even many of the writers who were regarded as *arrivistes* in their own time, such as Ben

---

[1] Keith Wrightson, *English Society 1580–1680*, p. 17; Peter Laslett, *The World We Have Lost*, p. 20, p. 54. For the complex and sometimes conflicting criteria for 'gentility', see Felicity Heal and Clive Holmes, *The Gentry in England and Wales, 1500–1700*, pp. 6–42.
[2] William Harrison, *The Description of England* (1587), ed. Georges Edelen, p. 115.

Jonson or William Shakespeare, came from locally prominent families of skilled tradesmen and were upstarts only compared to those even higher on the social scale. The 'writers' demographic' was further restricted by location and gender. Most writers resided, for at least part of their lives, in teeming London, in a period in which about four-fifths of English people lived in provincial villages that contained, on average, several hundred people.[3] Moreover, a disproportionate number of writers were male. There are exceptions to these broad generalizations, to which I shall attend in due course, but first I want to discuss the reasons for the general pattern.

The elite, urban bias of literary culture was hardly new in 1603, nor would it vanish by 1660. In 'Elegy Written in a Country Churchyard', Thomas Gray, writing more than a century after the period with which this book is concerned, connects impoverishment and rural origins to an enforced exclusion from the life of high culture:

> Perhaps in this neglected spot is laid
> Some heart once pregnant with celestial fire;
> Hands that the rod of empire might have swayed,
> Or waked to ecstasy the living lyre.
>
> But Knowledge to their eyes her ample page
> Rich with the spoils of time did ne'er unroll;
> Chill Penury repressed their noble rage,
> And froze the genial current of the soul.
>
> (45–52)

Universal, compulsory schooling—the most efficient way to unroll the ample page of Knowledge to a large and geographically dispersed population—would not be mandated in England and Wales until the Education Act of 1870, although Scotland authorized a comprehensive system of parish schools as early as 1696.

The most thoroughgoing attempt to gauge rates of literacy in the early seventeenth century is by David Cressy.[4] Cressy examined the surviving records of the 1641–1642 Protestation Oath: an oath of loyalty to King Charles I and the Church of England which was supposed to be administered to every male in the kingdom over the age of eighteen. Since oath-takers were required to subscribe either with their signature or with a mark, these documents offer a socially comprehensive cross-section. Cressy

---

[3] Peter Laslett, *The World We Have Lost*, pp. 59–60.
[4] David Cressy, *Literacy and the Social Order: Reading and Writing in Tudor and Stuart England*.

supplemented his statistical analysis of the Protestation Oath data with a survey of some surviving parish records—a valuable source for women because each member of a couple would 'sign the book' upon their marriage. Cressy's research revealed that one in three adult English males was apparently capable of signing his name to a document, although this statistic conceals important differences among social ranks and from one region of the country to another. While virtually 100 per cent of gentry-class men were capable of signing their own names no matter where they lived, only 15 per cent of Norwich labourers could do the same, and only 2 per cent of labourers in the Diocese of Durham. The ability to sign one's name was higher in cities, and especially in London, than in the agrarian areas; 72 per cent of craftsmen in London and Middlesex could do so, as compared to about half of the craftsmen in Exeter and Norwich, and 35 per cent in Durham. Everywhere, women's ability to sign their names lagged far behind men's, tending to be on a par with the lowest classes of males in the same locality.

Cressy's methodology has been criticized on various grounds. Keith Thomas, Juliet Fleming, Margaret Ferguson, and others have pointed out that 'literacy' actually involves a number of different proficiencies, and that persons could possess some but not all of them: for instance, a person might be able to read blackletter typeface, but not manuscript, or might be able to draw letters with a brush on a wall, but not with a quill pen on paper.[5] The latter was a difficult fine-motor skill that was typically taught to children a year or more after they learnt to read, so conceivably some fraction of the people that Cressy classes as 'illiterate' actually had had some schooling and could have deciphered some kinds of documents. Because the Protestant Reformation emphasized the individual's personal acquaintance with the scriptural text, many religiously serious individuals, even from humble backgrounds, sought out reading instruction so as to be able to study the Bible in English. They could acquire this knowledge at 'dame schools' that taught both boys and girls the rudiments of reading in English, but that rarely offered more than basic schooling to its pupils.

In fact, though, reading and writing were dispensable for many people in early modern England. Without mechanized agricultural equipment, the

---

[5] Keith Thomas, 'The Meaning of Literacy in Early Modern England', in *The Written Word: Literacy in Transition*, ed. Gerd Baumann, pp. 97–131; Juliet Fleming, *Graffiti and the Writing Arts of Early Modern England*; Margaret Ferguson, *Dido's Daughters: Literacy, Gender, and Empire in Early Modern England and France*. For the complex ways in which oral and literate forms of expression interpenetrated in the early modern period, see Adam Fox, *Oral and Literate Culture in England 1500–1700*.

ploughing, planting, harvesting, and milling of grains and the care of livestock required massive commitments of manpower. All textiles needed to be spun and woven by hand, and hand-sewn into garments, home furnishings, and ship sails. Housework—preparing and preserving food, cleaning, laundering—was also highly labour-intensive, as were the skilled trades. Performing such tasks required specialized expertise—the trades were traditionally called 'mysteries' because their techniques baffled those outside them. Yet those techniques were acquired not from books or at school but by imitation and practice, in formal or informal apprenticeships.

A life without literacy did not equate to a stupid one, in other words. Nor was it a life barren of artistic creativity. Early modern England was home to a lively popular culture and a rich oral tradition of tales, songs, and proverbs. Folk cultural practices have left their traces in William Shakespeare's *Midsummer Night's Dream* (1595), *Merry Wives of Windsor* (1602), and *Winter's Tale*, Ben Jonson's *Bartholomew Fair* (1614) and *Tale of A Tub* (1633), Francis Beaumont's *Knight of the Burning Pestle* (1607), and many of Robert Herrick's poems in *Hesperides* (1648). Unfortunately, these forms of creativity remain largely invisible to posterity, except as they filter into the textual record.

Yet however well much of early modern society may have been able to function with minimal literacy skills, the ability to write is not dispensable for a writer. Thus, even if, as some persuasively argue, Cressy considerably understates the number of people who possessed a basic, or 'abecedarian', ability to decipher written language, his research remains important for the literary historian, for whom widespread illiteracy or minimal literacy is even more of a constraint than the statistics compiled by social historians might suggest. As the modern parent of any kindergartener knows, being able to write one's own name hardly entails being able to read sophisticated texts easily and with understanding. Moreover, the ability to *produce* texts, especially the sorts of complex imaginative literature that still engage readers centuries later, obviously requires a much higher level of expertise.

In short, the reason that early seventeenth-century writers mostly came from the higher social strata is that social status is a proxy for advanced literacy skills. Indeed, many who did manage to receive an education thus considered themselves part of an elite, whatever their original family background. The slippage between class status and educational attainment is important because although, as Cressy writes, 'there appears to be no steady, cumulative progress in the eradication of illiteracy' among the general population in the early modern period,[6] an appreciation for the advantages of literacy seems to have become considerably sharper within a slender but influential subset of people between 1500 and 1600. As successive members of the Tudor dynasty aggrandized power to themselves in the sixteenth century, forming a stronger nation-state out of what had been fairly disjunct localities, they needed individuals with the skills to administer their sprawling realm. As a result, book-learning, once considered necessary only for the clergy, had increasing utility for ambitious laymen. The families of the nobility, gentry, and the more prosperous yeomen, artificers, and tradesmen—the group that I am calling the 'relatively elite'—began to regard a grammar school and university education as a good preparation for their sons' secular careers. In the later sixteenth and seventeenth centuries universities expanded dramatically, producing the educated clergy demanded by a properly Protestant Church, as well as numerous aspirants to government positions which now required university-level training. The effect was to enlarge enrolment at England's two universities, while also drawing a more socially privileged student body.[7] During the same period young men flooded into the study of the law, for as the English economy expanded and litigation expanded with it, legal expertise became both useful and potentially lucrative. In London, the Inns of Court, or law schools, grew rapidly during the Tudor period and continued to thrive under the early Stuarts.

The numbers of students were small by modern standards. Combined, enrolment at Oxford, Cambridge, and the Inns of Court totalled several thousand. Nonetheless, the concentration of literary interest and ability was such that these educational institutions constituted fertile grounds for the invention and circulation of poems, and produced eager audiences for plays and masques. By the 1590s the universities and Inns of Court were producing more well-educated individuals than could be put to work in church, state, or law courts. The employment bottleneck, historian Mark Curtis has convincingly argued, produced a culture of 'alienated intellectuals' whose frustrations fed the development of satiric genres in the early seventeenth century.[8]

Fuelling the expansion of higher education were better educational opportunities for younger children in the social group just below the apex of the social pyramid: gentry, yeoman farmers, merchants, and artisans.

---

[6] David Cressy, *Literacy and the Social Order: Reading and Writing in Tudor and Stuart England*, p. 142
[7] Mark Curtis, *Oxford and Cambridge in Transition: 1558–1642*.
[8] Mark Curtis, 'The Alienated Intellectuals of Early Stuart England', *Past and Present* 23 (1962): 25–43.

WHO WERE THE WRITERS? 49

In the 1530s and 1540s, under the influence of some Continental humanist thinkers, boys' day schools had been established in London and in some of the larger market towns, such as Canterbury and Stratford-upon-Avon. These schools accepted pupils from about the age of seven to about fourteen—the age at which a boy would normally either proceed to university studies or undertake an apprenticeship. The curriculum emphasized the learning of Latin and fostered a close acquaintance with Latin poetry, oratory, and drama in the original language. These 'grammar schools' were not free or state-subsidized, and poor children whose labour was required to support their families would not have attended; however, they were much less expensive than the private tutors hired by aristocratic and wealthy families. Grammar schools made education in the Latin classics available to children who would likely not have had the opportunity in a previous generation, such as the young Christopher Marlowe, Edmund Spenser, William Shakespeare, and Ben Jonson. Keith Wrightson's figures for two such schools in the mid-seventeenth century indicate that in one, at Bury St Edmunds, more than half the pupils were from gentry families, while the rest were the sons of clergymen, prosperous merchants, or professionals. At the other school, in Colchester, 31 per cent were gentry, 20 per cent were clergy or professionals, 37 per cent were prosperous merchants, and 12 per cent were prosperous farmers. Only a few pupils came from 'middling' families, and none at all from the labouring classes.[9]

With no attention to mathematics, science, the visual arts, or vernacular tongues, a grammar-school education was a restricted one, but for a future poet it had powerful advantages. It gave him a grounding in another language, naturally heightening his awareness of the structure and character of his own. It introduced him to the major literary genres: epic, comedy, tragedy, lyric, and history. It taught him ancient Roman history, and made him conversant with pagan myths and customs. Literary scholars have devoted special attention to two features of grammar-school education that seem especially important for writers. One was training in rhetorical 'copiousness', which encouraged students to develop fluency in Latin by inventing as many ways as possible to express the same thought, and by expanding a kernel of information into a wide variety of more elaborate accounts.[10] Another was an exercise for advanced grammar-school students drawn from classical oratorical training, in which they were assigned a

---

[9] Wrightson, *English Society 1580–1680*, p. 189.
[10] Terence Cave, *The Cornucopian Text: Problems of Writing in the French Renaissance* and Patricia Parker, *Literary Fat Ladies: Rhetoric, Gender, Property*.

morally ambiguous situation and asked to debate its merits, in Latin, 'on both sides of a question': this exercise, some critics have argued, conduced to the kind of ethical complexity we see in Renaissance drama, especially tragedy.[11]

All of these new educational opportunities were restricted to males. Only boys could attend grammar school, and only young men could attend universities or the Inns of Court. It should hardly be surprising, then, that most early seventeenth-century writers were men. The handful of women who did write in the early seventeenth century were disproportionately the daughters of affluent families who could afford to hire private tutors to educate them: Mary Sidney Herbert, Countess of Pembroke; Elizabeth Cary, Viscountess Falkland; Margaret Cavendish, Duchess of Newcastle; Anne Clifford, Countess of Pembroke and Montgomery; Lady Mary Wroth, the daughter of Robert Sidney, Viscount Lisle and later Earl of Leicester. Though the scope of their education may not have matched that afforded similarly situated boys, it could suffice to nurture talent and ambition. Anne Clifford's father, the Earl of Cumberland, refused to allow her to learn classical languages— he believed they were a male prerogative—but he did hire the poet Samuel Daniel as her tutor, and she became fluent in French and Italian. Elizabeth Cary was 'put ... to learn French'[12] at the age of four and eventually taught herself Spanish and Italian. One of her tutors was John Davies, the author of *Nosce Teipsum* [*Know Yourself*] (1599).

For some of these women, indeed, rank trumped sex, permitting them to resist to some degree the strong prejudice against women's speaking in public or occupying positions of authority. Anne Clifford and, later in the century, Margaret Cavendish, in particular, are extremely status-conscious—in Cavendish's case, despite the fact that she was not born to the aristocracy but married into it. Their wealth and position allowed them to think of themselves as 'special' despite their gender disability, convincing them that the restrictions imposed upon most women did not necessarily, or wholly, apply to them. Nor, to some extent, did they. The circle of highly born women in Queen Anne's court included a number of women who were important literary patrons and who were apparently also proficient poets themselves: our sense of their productivity is hampered by the fact that in many cases, none of their work is now extant. Thus, although

---

[11] T. W. Baldwin, *William Shakespeare's Small Latine and Lesse Greeke*; Joel Altman, *The Tudor Play of Mind: Rhetorical Inquiry and the Development of Elizabethan Drama*.

[12] Barry Weller and Margaret Ferguson, eds., *The Tragedy of Mariam the Fair Queen of Jewry: With the Lady Falkland: Her Life*, p. 186.

we have Lady Mary Wroth's sonnet sequence *Pamphilia to Amphilanthus* (1621), nothing survives by her cousin, Elizabeth, Countess of Rutland, even though Jonson praises both of them as poets. Lucy, Countess of Bedford, was also celebrated as a poet in her own time but, once again, only one of her poems survives.[13] The relationships among these women, who served at court together and whom in many cases were related by blood or marriage, would have provided a sustaining context for their creativity.

Some women writers, too, seem to have been empowered by their connection to a family tradition of involvement in the arts. Cavendish's husband wrote plays and, she assures her readers, actively encouraged her literary endeavours as well. In the 1590s, Mary Sidney Herbert, Countess of Pembroke, brought out a version of her brother Philip's *Arcadia*—and some scholars have suspected her own hand in what she represents as his work. She combined the roles of editor and collaborator more openly in a translation of the Psalms, begun by Philip but finished by Mary after his death. In both cases she plays a stereotypically female supporting role, supplementing her brother's work rather than competing with him. By assimilating her writing to family piety and to the memorializing of a lost family member, she sidesteps some of the negative associations of female authorship. In the next generation, the importance of family origin for Mary Wroth's work is likewise obvious. The daughter of Philip and Mary's brother Robert Sidney, she explicitly models her prose romance *Urania* upon the *Arcadia*, reviving and revising some of its characters and narrative lines. Her sonnet sequence similarly advertises its connection to Philip Sidney's sonnet sequence, *Astrophil and Stella* (1591)—a connection likely made all the tighter by the fact that the sequence obliquely refers to Wroth's love affair with her first cousin, William Herbert, Mary Sidney's son.[14]

Doubtless, though it's impossible to prove, the converse is also true: that for women who lacked a sense of family entitlement, the idea of writing poetry could seem impossibly exotic or daunting. Even in many 'literary'

---

[13] For the literary women in the Queen's circle, see Leeds Barroll, *Anna of Denmark, Queen of England: A Cultural Biography*. Margaret Hannay writes of Elizabeth, Countess of Rutland: 'Had she lived longer, or had her works survived, we would have a very different sense of the Sidney women and of their literary community'; *Mary Sidney, Lady Wroth*, p. 164. In *Mediatrix: Women, Politics, and Literary Production in Early Modern England*, Julie Crawford argues that courtly women, as patrons and readers, played an important co-creative role in many texts generally considered solely authored by male poets.

[14] Treatments of the Sidney family dynamic include Mary Ellen Lamb, *Gender and Authorship in the Sidney Circle* and Gary Waller, *The Sidney Family Romance: Mary Wroth, William Sidney, and the Early Modern Construction of Gender*.

families, the female members refrained from setting pen to paper. Magdalen Herbert, friend and patron of John Donne, was renowned for her intelligence, piety, and wit. She took great care over the education of her abundantly gifted sons, among them the poets George, Edward, and Thomas, and Henry, who became Master of the Revels. Yet she apparently never wrote poetry or other imaginative literature herself, nor, so far as we know, did any of her three daughters.

As I have already indicated, the population of writers was also skewed regionally. The majority of early seventeenth-century writers either spent their formative years in London, or migrated there as young adults in order to seize upon the city's unique opportunities. Once again, this is not a hard-and-fast rule: John Kerrigan, in *Archipelagic English*, has adduced evidence for regional hotspots of literary activity, such as Dublin, though most of his examples date from later in the seventeenth century.[15] Despite these exceptions, the centralization of English literate culture in London is one of the most significant phenomena of the early modern period. London was, as we have already noted, home to more literate people than the provinces. By the mid-sixteenth century it was already one of the largest cities in Europe. It continued to burgeon as England's commercial sector prospered; as state power was increasingly consolidated in the national government, based in nearby Westminster; and as the London courts, located between the City and Westminster, handled much of the nation's increasingly complex litigation. In 1538, Henry VIII made the printing of books a monopoly of the London Stationers' Company; confining most printing to the capital city made it easier for the Crown to censor print materials and to keep the disruptive potential of the Reformation in check. It was no accident that this statute seemed necessary soon after Henry VIII controversially broke with the Roman Catholic Church. Yet Henry's disquiet at the potentially explosive religious and political implications of the new technology of print were not his alone. Mainz and Frankfurt had censored print materials since 1486; beginning in 1515, Catholic authorities required the imprimatur, or ecclesiastical seal of approval, on all books printed in Catholic Europe; and in 1530s France, King Francis I also severely censored printed materials.

Once in place, Henry's system of pre-publication censorship for printed materials remained intact for more than a century, until Charles I's government collapsed in the 1640s. During this period, the only legal printers

---

[15] John Kerrigan, *Archipelagic English: Literature, History, and Politics 1603–1707*.

outside of London were the university presses, which largely confined themselves to publishing religious and scholarly texts. Even after the enforcement mechanism restraining printing to London disintegrated, printed book production remained a London-centred endeavour: a printing press constituted a large capital investment, the people who knew how to operate presses were mostly Londoners, and a large reading public was concentrated there.

Theatrical creativity converged in London over the course of the later sixteenth century. Starting in the 1560s, London saw the building of a number of purpose-built theatres, each of which housed a repertory company and employed playwrights and other theatre workers. London remained, throughout this period, the only city with a population large enough to sustain such theatres on an ongoing basis. The professional theatre industry, in which Shakespeare, Jonson, Fletcher, Middleton, Webster, and other major Renaissance dramatists worked, thus became another manifestation of the consolidation of literary talent and audiences into a metropolitan hub. Its productions were regulated by a system of pre-performance censorship by the Master of the Revels, a royal appointee, so that the constraints upon theatrical representations may be seen as roughly parallel to those imposed upon printed texts.[16]

Meanwhile, over the course of the sixteenth century, the once-thriving, guild-sponsored miracle play productions in York, Coventry, and elsewhere withered and died, the casualties of a decline of the traditional guilds and of Reformation religious controversies which made the staging of Bible stories a highly fraught and in some cases legally proscribed matter. Strict Tudor-era laws restricting itinerant actors and minstrels further suppressed indigenous theatrical activity in the provincial towns. By law, each theatre company was required to have a noble or royal patron, and the companies that had access to such sponsorship were those situated close to the court. The London-based theatre companies sometimes went on tour, playing at the great houses of aristocrats and even venturing to the Continent on occasion; but when they did so, their repertory consisted of plays originally performed before London audiences. By 1603, for those living away from London, the prospect of attending plays on a visit to the metropolis became one of the city's distinctive attractions.

The centring of such enterprises in London had important consequences for the development of the vernacular as a literary language. In the

---

[16] For a discussion of the way plays were licensed for performance, see Richard Dutton, *Mastering the Revels: The Regulation and Censorship of Early Modern Drama*.

seventeenth century, throughout the British Isles, writers continued to write poetry and prose in Latin. George Herbert and John Milton wrote Latin poetry that was admired throughout Europe. Abraham Cowley produced an entire epic in Latin: *De Plantis* (1668). Latin also remained the preferred language for scholars aiming at an international audience: William Camden's influential historical-topographic survey *Britannia* (written in the 1580s and revised in numerous editions thereafter), Bacon's *Novum Organum* (1620), James Barclay's political romance *Argenis* (1621), and William Harvey's groundbreaking treatises on the circulatory system and on the formation of embryos were all published first in Latin and later translated into English. Yet the Renaissance on the Continent had made a powerful case for the superiority of vernacular tongue as a literary vehicle, and the Reformation demanded that worshippers have direct access to the Bible in their own language. Both these intellectual movements swept England during the sixteenth century, with the result that by the early seventeenth century, writing in English, instead of in Latin, was no longer an idiosyncratic or surprising choice for English writers.

Yet, while it was possible to speak of an 'English' literature by 1603, what 'English' consisted in was still unclear. Even if one excluded at the outset the tongues still spoken widely in some regions of the British Isles, such as Cornish, Welsh, and Gaelic, the spoken language still varied enormously from one part of Britain to another. A version of southern English had been the norm in administrative documents since the middle of the twelfth century, however, and for literary purposes George Puttenham, in *The Art of English Poesy* (1589), recommended that writers adopt an idiom modelled on 'the usual speech of the court and that of London and the shires lying about London within sixty miles, and not much above.'[17] After 1603, 'the usual speech of the court' was itself a problematic touchstone, since King James and his entourage spoke, and on occasion wrote, a Scots dialect that sounded outlandish to southern English ears. Moreover, the southern, metropolitan version of English was in the process of rapid change, importing thousands of words from Latin and French and accepting untold new coinages between 1550 and 1650.

Despite these instabilities, a conception of a literary vernacular, and implicitly a norm for cultivated speech as well, developed rapidly in the

---

[17] George Puttenham, *The Art of English Poesy: A Critical Edition*, ed. Frank Whigham and Wayne Rebhorn, p. 229.

sixteenth century and gained momentum as the seventeenth century progressed. The concentration of printing, bookselling, and theatre in the metropolitan area must have made the use of 'London English' seem more natural than it would have if writers and readers had been evenly distributed throughout the British Isles. Late sixteenth- and early seventeenth-century plays stage, again and again, a confrontation between 'standard' English and what standard English was not: northern and southern dialects, French, Dutch, Welsh, Spanish, the underclass patois called 'canting'. In the late Elizabethan plays *Henry IV Parts 1 and 2* (1596–1598), Shakespeare's Prince Harry frequents the taverns of London to study

> his companions
> Like a strange tongue, wherein, to gain the language,
> 'Tis needful that the most immodest word
> Be looked upon and learned.
> (*Henry IV, Part 2*, 4.3.68–71)

After he ascends the throne, in *Henry V* (1599), he proves himself a leader of men, not least in managing to inspire an army that includes the Irish Macmorris, the Scots Jamy, the Welsh Fluellen, and the lower-class Londoners Pistol, Bardolph, and Nym, each of whom, unlike their king, speaks in some accented or extravagant way. This fascination with linguistic variety was not a Shakespearean idiosyncrasy. Jonson returns to the topic of appropriate language again and again: in *Poetaster* (1601) forcing bad poets to vomit their neologisms into a basin; in *Volpone* (1606) satirizing Italianate English; in *Epicene* (1609) staging a mock debate in incompetent Latin; in *The Alchemist* (1610) sending up the jargons of alchemy and Puritan zealotry; and in *Bartholomew Fair* (1614) including the dialect speakers Whit, Puppy, and Northern for comic effect. *The Roaring Girl*, by Thomas Middleton and Thomas Dekker, features a scene in which courtly characters are taught the elements of 'canting', a lower-class idiom associated with criminals and tramps.

In some ways, as James Simpson argues in *Reform and Cultural Revolution*, the centralization of literary life was doubtless limiting and impoverishing, sucking artistic creativity out of the provincial market and cathedral towns and diminishing the variety that would naturally flourish among writers working independently in distant regions of the country.[18] One clear

---

[18] James Simpson, *The Oxford Literary History: Volume 2: 1350–1547: Reform and Cultural Revolution*.

casualty was Scots, the dialect of English spoken in the Scottish Lowlands, which had begun to develop as a literary language in the fifteenth and sixteenth centuries. While James I had, in his years as prince and king of Scotland, written poetry and prose treatises in Scots, once he came to the English throne, and began trying to unify the two kingdoms, it suited his interests to minimize the differences between the two dialects: the brotherhood of the Scots and the English, he claimed, could be seen in their possession of a common tongue. After arriving in England in 1603, James steadily purged his writing of Scottish dialect words and distinctive spellings, and other writers followed suit. It would not be until the eighteenth century that Scots reasserted itself as a form of literary expression.[19]

Yet the concentration of literary life in London also had advantages, especially for some genres of writing. The writers of the early seventeenth century had plenty of interaction with one another, and with the potential for creative synergy that proximity entails. The writers themselves testified to the importance of literary collegiality: Donne and Jonson, Jonson and Shakespeare, Shakespeare and Fletcher, Fletcher and Massinger, Jonson and a younger group of poets he called his 'sons'. Many plays were collaboratively written. Men with literary interests formed clubs, a word first used in this period to mean a fraternal assembly: these semiformal organizations were often associated with particular London taverns, such as the Mermaid, the Mitre, or the Apollo Room of The Devil and St Dunstan.[20] Hostility could also prove inspiring: just before the accession of James, 'the War of the Theatres', a literary feud involving Ben Jonson, Thomas Dekker, John Marston, and possibly Shakespeare, stimulated the composition of, by James Bednarz's count, ten plays over the course of about two years.[21]

Proximity matters for some genres more than for others. The theatre is the clearest beneficiary, because the medium coordinates the skills of many persons in order to achieve the performance. It was important for playwrights that the actors who performed their plays were experienced, full-time professionals. John Stow's *Annals of England* remarks that 'comedians and stage-players of former time were very poor and ignorant', but that

---

[19] Paula Blank, *Broken English: Dialects and the Politics of Language in Renaissance Writings*.
[20] Timothy Raylor, in *Cavaliers, Clubs, and Literary Culture*, traces this phenomenon in some detail for the 1620s to the Restoration, but also documents its existence much earlier, in the first years of the seventeenth century. He also shows that Jacobean and Caroline gentlemen drew a distinction between the more literary and intellectual clubs, and mere drinking fraternities.
[21] James P. Bednarz, *Shakespeare and the Poets' War*.

by 1583 they had 'grown very skillful and exquisite actors for all matters'.[22] The vastly more complex characterization and the subtle poetic effects so striking in late sixteenth- and seventeenth-century drama were not merely ascribable to the unassisted genius of the playwrights, but were phenomena partly driven by the talents of the acting companies.[23] Moreover, even after the theatres had become well established, what seem to be literary changes might actually reflect new performance modes. For instance, the eclipse of the grandiloquent, ornate soliloquies of Marlowe, Lyly, and Kyd by the less obviously patterned, 'psychological' poetry of Shakespeare, Middleton, and Webster may reflect the rise of a generation of actors who favoured more subdued playing styles. The development of demanding, nuanced female roles, all played by adolescent boys or young men, may also owe something to the theatre's London home base. The playwrights must have benefited from access to a large pool of talented youth in the metropolis, who could receive expert training from full-time, professional adult actors in the companies.

For non-dramatic poetry, much of which circulated in manuscript, the urbanity of seventeenth-century literary culture mattered too. Although the restrictions that hedge printing in the period did not apply to manuscripts, so that they could in theory be created and circulated anywhere, nonetheless urban crowding facilitated their physical conveyance from person to person, and helpfully clustered potential readers and patrons at the Inns of Court, or in the households of the King, Queen, or Prince. Yet a London domicile was less important for a devotional poet, who typically regarded his work as private, akin to prayer, and circulated poems infrequently, if at all. George Herbert probably wrote much of his religious poetry at his relatively remote parish of Bemerton, near Salisbury, after abandoning a promising career as a courtier; a collection of his poems was published only after his death. Henry Vaughan, who worked as a physician in Wales, thrived on isolation, often using the Welsh countryside as a spur to religious meditation. The Catholic poet Richard Crashaw wrote much of his poetry in exile on the Continent. None required access to London in the same way that a playwright did.

---

[22] John Stow, *The Annals or General Chronicle of England* (1615), p. 697. This edition of the *Annals* appeared after Stow's death; the observation may be not Stow's but his editor's, Edmund Howes, since Howes silently made some emendations to Stow's text.

[23] I am not arguing that actors actually collaborated with dramatists in the writing of plays, but rather that playwrights wrote for the actors they knew would be performing their work, much as composers writing for particular musical performers keep their technical skills in mind and are often inspired by the awareness of their virtuosity.

There were other exceptions to the rule that writers were generally elite urban males. Occasionally a writer would emerge from a humble background: John Taylor, a prolific if clumsy versifier, was called the 'Water-poet' because he made his living ferrying passengers by rowboat across the Thames. However, most such outliers were acutely aware of their exceptional status. 'Vouchsafe to view that which is seldom seen / A woman writing of divinest things', requests Aemelia Lanyer at the opening of her long religious poem, *Salve Deus Rex Judaeorum* ('To the Queen's Excellent Majesty', 3–4). Likewise, writers who for some reason inhabit geographically remote regions—gentry with estates or ministers with clerical postings in distant regions of the realm—often portray themselves as outsiders or exiles, based on an implicit norm of London residence.

Interestingly, though, while these writers were out of the ordinary in one respect, and were often sensitive to their own oddity, none of them entirely broke the mould. Thus Taylor, despite his humble origins, had the advantage of a London domicile, which enabled him to come into contact with leading writers of his time, as well as with the printers and booksellers through whom he published his verse. William Drummond, on the other hand, who lived far from London, was a Scottish laird whose wealth and leisure permitted him to maintain correspondence with fellow intellectuals all over Europe. As we have already seen, women with literary ambitions were even more likely than their male counterparts to derive from affluent backgrounds or to have a family connection to the royal court. We do not find any woman writer at all who hailed from a lower-class, provincial background until the 1640s, when some of the traditional handicaps are temporarily lifted. At that point, encouraged by the radical Protestant emphasis on personal testimony, a few such women produce texts. Their writings are typically short memoirs, not ambitious works of literature, but the fact that they are writing at all is a significant breakthrough.

What we might call the 'entry requirements' for becoming a writer in the seventeenth century of course affects what gets written. Given the relatively elite background of most seventeenth-century writers, it should not surprise us that their typical perspective is what might be called 'top down'. Sometimes this perspective is perfectly explicit, as in Robert Herrick's poem 'The Hock Cart', which addresses rural labourers at a harvest festival as members of a separate, exploited caste:

> Come sons of summer, by whose toil
> We are the lords of wine and oil.
>
> (1–2)

'We' in this poem are the landlord and his family and friends, who include the clergyman-poet. 'We' do not ourselves cut and bind the wheat or cart it home, but use the profits from its sale to purchase wine and oil—which are, of course, not the products of an English harvest but imported luxury items. Herrick is not without sympathy for the harvesters' drudgery, and he is clear-sightedly aware of the ways in which the harvest festival deludes them into celebrating their lord's generosity—a generosity only made possible by their labour. Yet Herrick does not see himself as one of them, nor, apparently, does he fret over the injustice of their plight—as, say, Thomas Gray will do about a century later in 'Elegy Written in a Country Churchyard'. 'Feed him ye must, whose food fills you', Herrick tells the harvesters (52): that is just the way things are.

In other works, an elite point of view leaves subtler traces. At the beginning of his great love poem, 'The Good Morrow', Donne marvels:

> I wonder, by my troth, what thou and I
>   Did, till we loved? Were we not weaned till then,
> But sucked on country pleasures, childishly?
>
>   (1–3)

The poem describes the lovers awakening, literally and metaphorically, into a new perception of one another and of their relationship; in retrospect, they seem in the past to have been as ignorant as unweaned children. 'Sucked on country pleasures' refers to the practice, routine among well-off families but unavailable to the poor, of hiring a wet-nurse, typically a farmwoman, to breastfeed their newborn infants. Donne can afford to be wittily oblique here because he and his original readership took the custom of wet-nursing for granted.

If we take seventeenth-century literature as an accurate guide to 'what life was like in those days', we may assume that some concerns were more widespread than they actually were. For instance, if one's only evidence is literary, one might reasonably conclude that primogeniture, or the bequeathing of virtually the entire family property to the eldest son, was universally practiced in early modern England. And, indeed, large estates in land were typically 'entailed'—that is, their inheritance was legally restricted so that the current proprietor could not easily alter the next beneficiary, who was generally the eldest living 'heir male of the body' or biological son. The advantage of primogeniture is that it maintains the resources, and hence the power and prestige, of a socially prominent family by vesting it in a single recipient per generation, even while it disadvantages other possible claimants—for instance, the heir's sisters and younger brothers. The strain primogeniture produces within families is fodder for numerous dramatic plots, from Shakespeare's *As You Like It* to Fletcher's *The Elder Brother* (1625) to Middleton's *A Chaste Maid in Cheapside* (1613). In fact, as historians Joan Thirsk, Jack Goody, and Amy Erickson have shown, those below the gentry, less invested in the perpetuation of the family name and less likely to possess their wealth in the form of land, often divided their property fairly evenly among their children.[24] Yet this less prestigious inheritance practice receives little literary mention.

If seventeenth-century literature exaggerates some issues, it ignores others. For instance, throughout the early seventeenth century declining real incomes among the labouring classes in the countryside made marriage prohibitively expensive for an increasing number of young people, with the effect that many of them were forced to remain permanently single and 'in service', in a society in which marrying and setting up one's own household was the passport to full adulthood.[25] This phenomenon must have been emotionally costly for those who had to endure it, but it receives no attention from writers, either because the kinds of people who became writers did not consider it a 'literary' topic or because they simply failed to notice it.

The most pervasive instance of what I have been calling 'elite bias' is, however, the almost universal assumption among early seventeenth-century writers that there was an important distinction to be made between a small group of meritorious individuals and a large 'rabble' of stupid, uneducated, undiscerning, and unworthy ones. In sixteenth- and early seventeenth-century England, among those who reflected in writing upon the status classifications in their society, there is an overwhelming consensus on the important distinction between two groups: the 'gentle'—those who did not make a living by manual toil—and everybody else: those whom William Harrison, writing in the 1570s, calls 'low and base persons [who] . . . have no voice or authority in our commonwealth and no account is made of them, but only to be ruled and not to rule other'.[26] The reader of Renaissance literature comes constantly upon this distinction in poems and plays.

---

[24] Joan Thirsk, 'Younger Sons in the Seventeenth Century' and 'The European Debate on Customs of Inheritance, 1500–1700', in *The Rural Economy of England: Collected Essays*, pp. 335–373; Amy Erickson, *Women and Property in Early Modern England*; Eileen Spring, *Law, Land, and Family: Aristocratic Inheritance in England 1300–1800*; Jack Goody, *Family and Inheritance: Rural Society in Western Europe 1200–1800*.

[25] Stephen Greenblatt, *Shakespearean Negotiations: The Circulation of Energy in Renaissance England*, p. 149.

[26] William Harrison, *A Description of England*, ed. Georges Edelen, p. 118.

In Shakespeare's *Twelfth Night* (1602), the love-struck Olivia asks Viola, disguised as a servant boy, 'What is your parentage?' Viola replies, 'Above my fortunes . . . I am a gentleman'. After Viola leaves, Olivia exclaims:

> 'I am a gentleman'. I'll be sworn thou art.
> Thy tongue, thy face, thy limbs, action, and spirit
> Do give thee five-fold blazon.
>
> (1.5.261–263)

Unable to discern Viola's true sex, Olivia has no trouble at all accurately assessing her gentility, a trait that apparently leaks from her every feature and gesture. Likewise, the distinction between 'gentle' and the 'ungentle' is reinforced in the plots of Shakespeare's romances, in which noble children grow up in ignorance of their birth and often separated from their parents. Despite their rustic or secluded upbringing, the 'natural' gentility of Guiderius and Arviragus in *Cymbeline*, Perdita in *The Winter's Tale*, and Miranda in *The Tempest* manifests itself unmistakably in their deportment: the women are cultivated and chaste, and the men valiant and honourable. In *The Winter's Tale*, when Polixenes, King of Bohemia, encounters the lost princess Perdita, brought up as a shepherd's daughter, he marvels:

> Nothing that she does or seems
> But smacks of something greater than herself
> Too noble for this place.
>
> (4.4.186–188)

The conviction that the gentle sort are sharply distinguished from the common sort pervades even John Caius's enumeration of dog breeds of the British Isles: he divides noble dogs—hunting breeds and ladies' lap dogs—from dogs with humbler owners—'shepherds' curs', mastiffs, and the 'confused company' of turnspit dogs, beggar's trick dogs, and so on.[27]

With such texts as these in mind, Stephen Greenblatt calls 'the distinction between those who labour and those who rule . . . the economic and ideological center of Elizabethan and Jacobean society'.[28] Yet this simply cannot

---

[27] John Caius's *De Canibus Britannica* (1570) has a long afterlife, being translated by Abraham Fleming in 1576 under the title *Of English Dogs, the Diversities, the Names, the Natures, and the Properties*, which translation was then incorporated nearly verbatim into William Harrison's *Description of England*, itself included in the 1577 edition of Holinshed's *Chronicles*, as well as into Topsell's *History of the Four-Footed Beasts* (1607).
[28] Stephen Greenblatt, *Shakespearean Negotiations*, p. 149.

be right, in the sweeping terms in which Greenblatt puts it. The 'gentle sort' were a tiny minority, and it strains credulity to imagine that the vast majority of England's populace spent much of their energy contemplating a divide that was supposedly 'at the economic and ideological center of Elizabethan and Jacobean society'. More accurately, the difference between the labouring and ruling classes looms large for us, as readers, because it was indeed critical for the people who have left most of the textual records, the relatively elite group who usually saw themselves just barely on one or the other side of a boundary that they construed as highly significant, even constitutive of their identity. When William Harrison claims that 'no account is made' of the poor, his passive construction only half conceals the implication that it is the gentle sort, his own sort, who make no account of such humble people. The humble people themselves might well demur.

Some writers modify the standard gentle / rabble distinction, retaining its basic form but significantly changing the standard of differentiation. Ben Jonson, for instance, distinguishes between the worthy and intelligent individuals who understand and appreciate his works, and 'the unskillful', a category that includes not merely 'the sordid multitude, but the neater sort of our gallants: for all are the multitude; only they differ in clothes, not in judgment or understanding'.[29] John Milton, like many of the other religious writers of the period, sought a 'fit audience . . . though few' from among God's elect (*Paradise Lost*, 7.31). God's criteria, according to Milton, are not wealth and social position but purity of heart and uprightness of character, not to mention a willingness to agree with Milton's positions on divorce and regicide. In Jonson's and Milton's cases the criteria for merit do not openly conflict with the usual criteria for gentility; they are merely somewhat shifted, making allowances for the existence of some wise and sober poor men, and some rich fools. For other poets, the different criteria of selectivity seem in greater tension with one another. The well-born George Herbert, for instance, must renounce aristocratic magnificence and ambition if he is to receive God's favour, and the difficulty of that task leaves its traces in 'The Collar' and his 'Affliction' poems. Yet even in Herbert's renunciation, the division of elect few from cast-off 'others' persists. This division is the product of—even when it is a reaction against—a society in which power, wealth, and prestige were concentrated in a small minority rather than dispersed among many.

[29] *Timber, or Discoveries*, ed. Lorna Hutson, lines 465–467 in *The Cambridge Edition of the Works of Ben Jonson*, ed. David Bevington, Martin Butler, Ian Donaldson et al., vol. 7.

At the same time, the people who, statistically speaking, constituted the 'relatively elite' in early modern England were hardly a monolithic group. Just as the 'gentle dogs' are divided by John Caius into greyhounds, water-spaniels, setters, bloodhounds, and so on, the category of the 'gentle' as it appears in Renaissance writing is a multiply striated one. It includes not only peers of the realm and landed gentry but, William Harrison declares, anyone who:

> studieth the laws of the realm, whoso abideth in the university (giving his mind to his book), or professeth physic and the liberal sciences, or, beside his service in the room of a captain in the wars or good counsel given at home, whereby his commonwealth is benefited, can live without manual labour, and thereto is able and will bear the port, charge, and countenance of a gentleman, he shall for money have a coat and arms bestowed upon him by heralds ... be called master ... and reputed for a gentleman ever after.[30]

Gentility is, in other words, a status that is determined partly by family origin, partly by wealth, partly by education, partly by occupation, and partly by lifestyle: obviously, these factors may overlap, but they are not entirely congruent. Although traditionally gentlemen were not supposed to exhibit too avid an interest in making money, the absolute recoil from 'trade' that typifies many aristocratic cultures was not characteristic of early modern England: 'our merchants', as Harrison remarks, 'often change estate with gentlemen, as gentlemen do with them, by a mutual conversion of the one into the other'.[31]

Not only were there multiple paths to gentility, but there were enormous disparities in wealth, prestige, and mode of life between a parish priest or a minor member of the gentry, and a prominent courtier or a peer of the realm. Moreover, the consciousness of these status and wealth discrepancies may well have been more acute than they are today. While a twenty-first century professional probably associates mostly with others of the same ilk, and has few interactions with the super-rich, the custom of primogeniture in elite families forced younger brothers to notice the difference made in their circumstances by accident of birth. While as children younger sons typically

---

[30] William Harrison, *A Description of England*, ed. Georges Edelen, pp. 113–114.
[31] Ibid., p. 115.

received good educations and acquired a sense of themselves as gentlemen, they did not inherit the means that would allow them to maintain this lifestyle without work. The result could be a robust sense of entitlement that was not matched by the available prospects. Richard Helgerson has described the defiance and guilt of the 'Renaissance prodigal' in these terms, Louis Montrose the plight of the younger brother, and Mark Curtis that of the 'alienated intellectual'.[32] Such people, hovering on the edge of wealth and power, able to witness them but not fully to possess them, tended to envy their 'betters' and to aspire for preferment, rather than to give thanks for their comparative good fortune. Such figures are rife in early seventeenth-century tragedy and comedy: Vindice in *The Revenger's Tragedy*, Tharsalio in *The Widow's Tears* (1612), Touchstone Junior in *A Chaste Maid in Cheapside*, Bosola in *The Duchess of Malfi*, De Flores in *The Changeling* (1622), Wellborn in *A New Way to Pay Old Debts* (1626). Insecure gentlemen or near-gentlemen, persons of 'good family' nonetheless worried about their potential to slip down the social scale: these are characters with whom many writers and their audiences found it easy to identify.

The history and literary record of early modern England is full of instances in which differences among sorts of gentlemen are importantly at issue. When Sir Philip Sidney, for instance, who was well born but not noble, quarrels with the Earl of Oxford at a tennis match, Queen Elizabeth rebukes Sidney by 'lay[ing] before him the difference in degree between earls, and gentlemen.'[33] In this case, at least, the status degrees are clear-cut; in other cases, different kinds of elitism come into conflict. Thomas Dekker's *The Shoemaker's Holiday* (1599) opens with a conversation between the Earl of Lincoln and the Lord Mayor of London, Sir Roger Oatley; the earl's nephew has fallen in love with the Lord Mayor's daughter. Both men, by William Harrison's criteria, count as 'gentle', but they move in different spheres: the earl is a landed aristocrat, the Lord Mayor a wealthy merchant. Each despises the other: in an aside, the earl calls the Lord Mayor a 'churl' or lower-class person (1.78), while the Lord Mayor considers the earl's nephew a wastrel and 'scorn[s] to call him son-in-law' (1.44), hoping to match his daughter with another wealthy citizen instead. Of course, this being a comedy,

---

[32] Richard Helgerson, *The Elizabethan Prodigals*; Louis Montrose, 'The Place of a Brother in As You Like It: Social Process and Comic Form,' *Shakespeare Quarterly* 32 (1981): 28–54; Mark Curtis, 'The Alienated Intellectuals of Early Stuart England,' *Past and Present* 23 (1962): 25–43.

[33] John Guows, *The Prose Works of Fulke Greville, Lord Brooke*, p. 40.

the two lovers are joined in marriage at the end of the play, but only after considerable travail and a king's strategic intervention.

Status distinctions are an especially fraught issue in Renaissance drama. For reasons I shall discuss in Chapter 2, dramatists were more likely than other writers to be drawn from the lower fringe of the group I have been calling 'relatively elite', and they wrote for acting companies whose personnel were largely artisanal in origin. Yet the commercial theatre had rapidly (though unsteadily) gained prestige in the last decades of the sixteenth century, and by the turn of the seventeenth century the prosperity of such theatre company shareholders as Richard and James Burbage was difficult to ignore. By 1603, the theatre was a much more secure and ambitious enterprise that it had been only a decade earlier. More and more in the Jacobean and Caroline period, it not only pretended to be elite, it was elite: more closely tied to the court by royal patronage, and more inclined to profit from niche marketing to wealthy individuals willing to pay extra for indoor performances in comfortable surroundings.

As a result, Renaissance dramatists are capable of seeing themselves both as persons of prestige and gentility, as compared with the 'rabble', and as socially disadvantaged, as compared with those above them. Their liminal positioning, and the liminal position of the theatre companies for which they write, result in plays that manifest strong and apparently contradictory impulses towards exclusivity and wide accommodation. On the one hand, Jacobean plays savagely satirize citizens who have bought their knighthoods, goldsmith's sons who dare to attend Cambridge, and shopkeepers' wives who dress like court ladies—even when those plays are written by Ben Jonson and Thomas Middleton, both the sons of bricklayers. Likewise, William Shakespeare's plays, as we have seen, often imply that gentility is not an acquired trait, but 'runs in the blood'—although Shakespeare himself attracts criticism for purchasing, from the College of Heralds, a coat of arms that designated his family as 'gentle'. Yet even as Shakespeare and his fellow dramatists encourage audiences to 'identify up' with kings and princes, and freely make fun of artisans, tavern hostesses, servants, foreigners, and country bumpkins, they also offer, as one of the distinctive pleasures of the theatre, the ability to encourage empathy across lines of class, ethnicity, and gender. The distinctively English habit of combining several plot lines in the same play, and of mixing comic with tragic elements, did not originate with the professional dramatists; they adapted it from their medieval forbears. But in their hands the multiple plot, juxtaposing characters from different walks of life, very often has the effect of representing class boundaries as mutable and easily crossed, or of emphasizing analogies between the experiences of the upper classes and those of the low.

Shakespeare, in both his Elizabethan and his Jacobean plays, is particularly eloquent on the subject of a common experience of embodiment that links all human beings. Henry V muses that 'his ceremonies laid by', the king 'in his nakedness . . . appears but a man' (*Henry V* 4.1.101–102). 'Let husbands know / Their wives have sense like them', remarks Emilia, in *Othello*. 'They see, and smell, / And have their palates both for sweet and sour, / As husbands have' (4.3.88–91). 'Hath not a Jew eyes?' asks Shylock in *The Merchant of Venice* (1598). 'Hath not a Jew hands, organs, dimensions, senses, affections, passions? . . . If you tickle us do we not laugh? If you poison us do we not die? And if you wrong us, shall we not revenge?' (3.1.49–55) The mention of revenge, jarring in the context of Shylock's speech, is a reminder that, like empathy, revenge depends upon a sense of shared bodily vulnerability—and, like empathy, revenge is a social leveller. Revenge tragedies, in which apparently weak and marginalized victims nonetheless prove capable of annihilating their highly placed tormentors, were perennial favourites on the Renaissance stage.

The reason to note the restricted social range of seventeenth-century writing is not to deplore the snobbery of great writers, nor to fulminate against the presumed injustices of a long-ago social system, but to facilitate our better understanding of early seventeenth-century literature. On the one hand, because writers were by and large drawn from a relatively narrow social stratum and many of them gathered in a geographically constricted area, their works are unreliable guides for those whose primary intention is to comprehend English seventeenth-century society as a whole. (Thus, Patricia Fumerton, for instance, can describe her work on the itinerant poor as 'an act of scholastic penance' for her previous focus on 'the select, refined bread of canonical Renaissance literature'.[34]) On the other hand, if we are interested in Renaissance literature, we do not necessarily care how everybody—even the vast majority—of people lived and thought. We are interested, perforce, primarily in those people who wrote and, secondarily, in their readers and audiences. In other words, while Stephen Greenblatt may be wrong to suggest that the difference between 'those who labour and those who rule' was at

---

[34] Patricia Fumerton, *Unsettled: The Culture of Mobility and the Working Poor in Early Modern England*, p. xi.

the centre of early modern consciousness, he is certainly right that in the segment of society that represented itself in written texts, that difference looms large. So do the fine distinctions between the different varieties of the gentle and the near-gentle.

This focus, in turn, helps determine the kinds of history that bear most directly upon the literature of the period. 'Politics' in the early seventeenth century is not the large-scale phenomenon that it is, or at least has the potential to become, in an age of universal suffrage and mass media. As I have already mentioned, a relatively small per cent of the population was in the gentry class or above—that is, held the status in whom various functions of government were traditionally vested. Half of this group, however, were women, and though they may have had strong and informed political opinions, they were almost wholly excluded from formal political participation. An additional group—perhaps another 10 per cent—were substantial enough property owners to take part in Parliamentary elections and occasionally to play important roles in their localities. Yet this leaves almost 85–90 per cent of the male and virtually 100 per cent of the female population with little or no voice in public affairs and no expectation on anybody's part that they ought to be consulted on matters of common concern. Despite changes in regime and the disruptions of Civil War, the mechanisms of government remained throughout the seventeenth century in the hands of a minority of the population.

Social historians, and revisionist historians who tend to minimize the importance of the Civil War, point out that the political upheavals of the mid-seventeenth century did little to alter the life circumstances of most English people. Yet they did profoundly and disproportionately affect the people who were reading and writing literary texts. Most writers and readers were drawn from the ranks of the relatively politically empowered even if they themselves did not personally wield much authority. Many of them, as we shall see in Chapter 2, depended for their livelihood upon the support of powerful men. So, we should not be surprised that what happened in the courts of King James or King Charles, or in struggles between King and Parliament, take on intense importance in those texts. The restriction of political power to the 'relatively elite' group from which writers came may also have fostered in those writers a sense of personal investment in political affairs: to have authority and the responsibilities of authority was arguably their birthright. Despite censorship, it is obvious even in the more or less quiet Jacobean period that Ben Jonson, Samuel Daniel, Michael Drayton, and other poets have strong political opinions; Shakespeare takes a keen interest, too, in the drama of public affairs, though his own political commitments are hard to discern. As the nation slid towards violent confrontation and eventual civil war, no mid-century writer remained politically neutral or disengaged. John Milton was a propagandist for the commonwealth, and Andrew Marvell eventually one of its public servants, while Robert Herrick, Richard Lovelace, Katherine Phillips, Henry Vaughan, and Margaret Cavendish were strongly identified with the royalists. That is why the subdivision of this literary period by political markers—the 'Jacobean, 'Caroline', and the civil war / interregnum period—makes a good deal of sense.

2
Literary Careers

So far I have been discussing what might be called literary 'entry criteria': the traits early modern writers generally had to possess in order to begin writing. It is also helpful to understand how different kinds of writers might pursue their endeavour once they were, so to speak, underway. In the late sixteenth and early seventeenth centuries it became possible, for the first time in England, to write as a full-time occupation rather than as an avocation. At the same time, the modern concept of the author was in the process of emerging.[1] A number of writers came to occupy positions of considerable cultural and social prestige—Jonson, Donne, and Milton during their lifetimes, and, to some extent in retrospect, Sidney, Spenser, Shakespeare, and Herbert. Their biographies began to interest those who enjoyed their literary productions—a change that suggests a new concern with the relationship between a writer's life and works. The attribution of literary works to particular writers became more important as notions of intellectual property begin to develop. Although writers continued to circulate their work in manuscript into the eighteenth century, print publication for plays as well as for poetry and prose works became ever more routine. Such publication was increasingly likely to be supervised by the writer him or herself, rather than handled posthumously by friends or literary executors.

Yet if the author 'rose' in the early modern period, his ascent was neither smooth nor predictable. Different sectors of the literary world elaborated different components of what would eventually be folded into a single author-concept. Thus, as we shall see, the professional theatre companies of Renaissance London made writing a paying, full-time proposition for a few gifted and industrious men. Many of the glories of 'Renaissance literature' are attributable to the expansion of opportunity made possible by the actors' steady demand for new plays. Theatre companies, however, usually had little reason to put a premium on the individual genius. Many plays

---

[1] For a detailed overview of these developments, see the two related monographs by Joseph Loewenstein: *The Author's Due: Printing and the Prehistory of Copyright* and *Ben Jonson and Possessive Authorship*.

were commissioned from teams of collaborators and, as far as the actors were concerned, the playscript was merely instrumental to the eventual goal: a successful performance. The conception of the writer as a precious and distinctive spirit, so important to the development of literary history in the eighteenth century and afterward, originated not in the theatre world but among amateurs and patronage poets. Because their connection to their audience was typically more intimate, their individual personality tended to factor more largely in the reception of their work.

To complicate the picture further, the various support systems for writers, already in a state of flux in the Jacobean and Caroline periods, altered irretrievably in mid-century, when civil war eliminated both court patronage and professional theatre and ruptured the mechanisms of censorship. In other words, what seems from a twenty-first-century perspective to be an alien, mutable collection of early seventeenth-century practices collapses and eventually reconfigures itself—sometimes in surprising ways—in the tumultuous decades between 1640 and 1660. The pattern is one of steady evolutionary change followed by a period of more radical upheaval. Thus, this discussion will deal first with the institutions of literary support typical of the Jacobean and Caroline years, emphasizing the ways in which Elizabethan modes persisted into the seventeenth century or were superseded by new ones. Then it will go on to consider the quite different problems writers faced during the war years and in the Commonwealth. These period boundaries must, however, remain rough and permeable. Many writers born under an older regime of literary support survived into a new one. Moreover, throughout the period, the generalizations that hold true for male writers very often fail to apply to their female contemporaries.

Amateurs

In a passage to which I shall return several times, Ben Jonson, the most versatile freelance professional of his day, observes:

> Poetry, in this latter age, hath proved but a mean mistress to such as have wholly addicted themselves to her, or given their names up to her family. They who have but saluted her on the by, and now and then tendered their visits, she hath done much for, and advanced in the way of their

own professions (both the law, and the gospel) beyond all they could have hoped, or done for themselves without her favour.²

Jonson here distinguishes between people like himself, who 'have wholly addicted themselves' to poetry, and those 'who have but saluted her on the by' and do not depend on her for day-to-day support. He distinguishes, in other words, between those who frankly depend upon remuneration from their writing for their day-to-day support, and those who do not. I shall call these two groups 'professionals' and 'amateurs'. I use the term 'amateur' to refer not to an inferior or unambitious writer—as Jonson suggests, the amateur was often more successful both as a writer and in worldly terms than his professional contemporary—but rather to designate a writer who does not aim to be paid, or to be paid much, for his or her efforts. The distinction is important because these two groups bring different expectations to their endeavours, and typically occupy different institutional settings. Not only, however, are the categories themselves blurry, but a single writer may cross from one category to another in the course of a lifetime. Moreover, that 'border crossing', when it occurs, not only alters the writers' economic situations and assumptions, but eventually, as we shall see, the nature of the categories themselves.

A few writers in the period inherited substantial fortunes. Fulke Greville, Lord Brooke (1554–1628) controlled extensive landholdings, including Warwick Castle, his country seat. Edward Herbert (1583–1648), First Baron Herbert of Cherbury, had an estate in Wales and powerful court connections. The Anglo-Scots poet William Drummond (1585–1649) was laird of Hawthornden. Mildmay Fane (1601–1666) was Earl of Westmoreland. Such affluent people, most of whose income came from land rents, were not necessarily members of what we now think of as a 'leisure class'. In the early modern period a large landholder would typically have administrative and political responsibilities in his own county, and might serve in Parliament, seek appointment at court, or work abroad in a diplomatic post. Still, such people typically had a great deal of discretion over how they managed their own time. They tended to deem themselves significant because they had

---

² *Timber, or Discoveries*, lines 450–458, ed. Lorna Hutson, in *The Cambridge Edition of the Works of Ben Jonson*, ed. David Bevington, Martin Butler, Ian Donaldson et al. vol. 7, p. 520.

been treated as such from birth, an assumption that may well have encouraged them to commit their thoughts to paper by convincing them that those thoughts would naturally interest others.

Yet while Edward Herbert, Fulke Greville, William Drummond, and Mildmay Fane are all worthy writers, when one thinks of the glories of Renaissance literature they are hardly the first names to spring to mind. In fact, few major male writers come from the very highest social classes. Statistics make that fact unsurprising. In 1603, there were fewer than 60 English peers. In 1641, after a period in which King James and King Charles had bestowed honours—far too liberally, many believed—there were about 150 families in the aristocracy and upper gentry combined: a scanty population indeed from which to expect major literary talent to emerge. Even the tier of gentlemen just below that was, as we have seen, a relatively small category.

A little lower down on the social scale, many people who characterized themselves as literary amateurs, and who seem to have been categorized as such by their contemporaries, were in fact regularly employed in jobs which required a high degree of literacy and a good deal of writing. They merely did not live on income received from their literary works. Many university faculty in the humanities today are in a comparable position. Although they may be hired for their scholarly accomplishments and secure their reputations by academic or creative publication, their most significant income generally derives from their teaching position, not from book royalties.

In the seventeenth century, these amateurs tended to cluster in a couple of fields—what Ben Jonson, in the passage I quoted above, succinctly called 'law, and the gospel'. A career in law appealed to men with literary and rhetorical talents. Lawyers needed to know how to dispute and persuade, how to attend to textual detail, how to weigh likelihoods and evaluate evidence. These are what career counsellors now call 'transferable skills': forms of general competence necessary for legal endeavours but also indispensable for literary pursuits. Although the mental acuity Francis Bacon brings to his *Essays, Advancement of Learning* (1605), and *Novum Organum* was doubtless a natural gift, surely his years as one of the most successful, politically prominent attorneys in England honed his analytical rigour.

Attorneys could make a very good living: 'all the wealth of the land doth flow unto our common lawyers', noted William Harrison.[3] In addition, many gentlemen who did not intend to proceed to the bar saw the advantages of possessing at least a basic knowledge of England's complex laws of property

---

[3] William Harrison, *A Description of England*, ed. Georges Edelen, pp. 173–174.

and inheritance. These practical considerations, however, do not altogether account for the attraction of legal training in the period. For early modern England, the legal system was the secular partner of the church in ensuring a just and orderly society, and as such seemed a worthy subject of study for its own sake. Many of the large-scale institutions that today negotiate economic transactions, manage risk, and organize collective endeavours did not yet exist—there were no deposit banks, credit agencies, insurance firms, or limited-liability corporations. In consequence, as the economy became more complex in the sixteenth century, the courts performed an expanded range of functions, playing an extraordinary role even in the lives of ordinary English people. The historian Craig Muldrew shows that in the provincial towns of King's Lynn, Great Yarmouth, Bristol, Shrewsbury, Exeter, Coventry, Chester, and Carlisle, the average household was involved in at least one lawsuit *per year* in the late sixteenth and early seventeenth century.[4] Closer to London, the annual caseload of the King's Bench in Westminster increased eightfold between 1560 and 1640, and business in the other central courts kept pace.

Although it was possible to study law at Oxford and Cambridge, most would-be lawyers got their practical legal education at the Inns of Court—originally boarding houses adjacent to the London civil and ecclesiastical courts. During the sixteenth and seventeenth centuries, scions of the gentry flocked to the Inns in great numbers (in fact, gentry status was supposed to be a prerequisite for admission, though the rule was sometimes flouted.) The combined population of Gray's Inn, Lincoln's Inn, the Middle Temple, and the Inner Temple has been estimated at above 1,500—thereby exceeding the population of either of the universities or of the royal court. Unlike the universities, which often accepted students in their early or mid-teens, the Inns of Court students were typically men in their twenties, some of whom already possessed university degrees. They were, in other words, at an age in which poets typically begin to come into their own.

In the sixteenth century the Inns had proven fertile breeding grounds for literary talent. Philip Finkelpearl points out that 'during the period between Wyatt and Surrey and the appearance of Spenser and Sidney all the poets, in fact almost all writers of any value, were connected with the Inns of Court'.[5] Although by the Jacobean period the literary world was larger and more

---

[4] Craig Muldrew, *The Economy of Obligation*, pp. 199–271.
[5] Philip Finkelpearl, *John Marston of the Middle Temple: An Elizabethan Dramatist in His Social Setting*, p. 24.

diverse, the Inns continued to provide a congenial environment for literary and intellectual people. John Harington, Thomas Campion, John Donne, Francis Bacon, John Davies, John Marston, John Ford, Francis Beaumont, John Fletcher, James Shirley, George Wither, Thomas Carew, John Suckling, and others were students there in the 1580s and 1590s, or in the first couple of decades of the seventeenth century. Others, such as John Webster, whose plays display an intimate acquaintance with legal issues, may have attended as well.

Study of the common law was a slow, painstaking endeavour. Since so little law in the period was statutory, an attorney needed a vast knowledge of precedents, which were written up in Norman French and largely unavailable in a systematic, easy-to-reference form. He also needed to memorize the exact wording for contracts and other legal documents, since even a trivial variation could invalidate them. It is not surprising that a large majority of 'Inns of Court men' failed to proceed to the bar. Jonson's *Every Man in His Humor* (1598) and *Poetaster* feature protagonists who want to be poets and are studying law only at the insistence of their practical fathers—a dramatic dilemma perhaps familiar to many a member of his audiences for these two plays. Still, for a writer, the Inn's educational activities were not entirely beside the point. 'Mooting'—the formal arguing of deliberately convoluted hypothetical cases—was basic to training at the Inns.[6] Mooting and associated exercises were a baroque extension of a pedagogical tactic routinely employed among younger students in the grammar schools, who were set to debating *in utramque partem*, arguing first one, then the opposite side of an ethical dilemma as a way of developing fluency in Latin and ability in public speaking. Because the situations argued in the moots were so obviously fantastic, their usefulness as moral pedagogy would have been limited. Still, their farfetched intricacy must have helped foster an appreciation for sophistical argumentation and ostentatiously witty, preposterous comparisons. Donne's early poems, such as the satires, the elegies, and some shorter love poems (for instance, 'The Flea') display this facility to a luxuriant degree. Donne's poetic daring and intellectual restlessness were (alas) hardly an inevitable consequence of an education at the Inns of Court: plenty of aspiring poets there wrote banal, derivative verse. But the atmosphere was one in which Donne's novel imagery and startling lines of argument could be understood and applauded.

[6] Karen Cunningham, *Imaginary Betrayals: Subjectivity and the Discourses of Treason in Early Modern England*, pp. 23–39.

The Inns had the great advantage over the universities of being located in England's great metropolis. Just to the west was Westminster, England's political capital; just to the east was the commercial heart of London. Some of the public theatres were across the Thames to the south, and during the first decade of the seventeenth century the theatre companies began opening smaller indoor theatres north of the Thames, even closer to the Inns whence they clearly derived many of their best customers. Sometimes the professional playing troupes would perform in the Inns themselves, for an audience of law students: in the winter of 1601–1602 John Manningham saw *Twelfth Night* at such an occasion. The assiduous playgoing of Inns of Court men receives much comment during the period. Ben Jonson dedicated the 1616 Folio version of *Every Man Out of His Humour* to the Inns of Court, calling them 'the noblest nurseries of humanity and liberty in the kingdom'. The anti-theatricalist lawyer William Prynne took a less sanguine view, complaining that 'the Inns of Court men ... are [the player's] chiefest guests and employment ... one of the first things they learn as soon as they are admitted, [is] to see stage-plays'.[7] Poets at the Inns of Court, in other words, could easily be intimately acquainted with the theatrical innovations of the period, an acquaintance that may have had the effect of narrowing the gap between dramatic and non-dramatic writing. Some Inns of Court students themselves wrote quasi-dramatic entertainments to be performed at the Christmas revels, an important rite at the Inns, though celebrated with varying degrees of pomp and expense from year to year.

The most congenial feature of the Inns of Court was doubtless simply the sheer concentration of intelligent, well-educated young men. By and large, Inns of Court poets wrote for their friends: physically proximate individuals similar to themselves in age, social class, experience, and vocational ambitions. Several critics have noted how Inns of Court writers tend to dwell on topics in which elite young men might be expected to interest themselves: sex and sexual desire, the inadequacy of established institutions, the pleasures and perils of worldly ambition.[8] Inns of Court poets could assume that their readers were able to appreciate wit, to grasp literary and historical allusions as well as up-to-date references to current events, geometry, and the new science. The coterie quality of much Inns of Court writing was doubtless enhanced by the vocational prejudices inculcated by specialized training

---

[7] William Prynne, *Histrio-Mastix*, fol. 3v.
[8] See Philip Finkelpearl, *John Marston of the Middle Temple* and Arthur Marotti, *John Donne, Coterie Poet*.

in the common law. Lawyer's rhetoric was not designed to appeal to a lay audience, but used deliberately arcane vocabulary and forms of argument to separate those in the know from those beyond the vocational pale. Poetry commonly circulated in manuscript, both because the audience for it was, in fact, initially imagined as a small one, and because the manuscript carried with it desirable connotations of personal contact between poet and reader. The Inns-of-Court readership tends to imagine itself not as a group of consumers distinct from the poetic producers, but as a community in which the roles of reader and poet may overlap and alternate. Inns-of-Court poets thus favour genres that emphasize an interactive poetic life: verse epistles are popular, and so are 'answer' poems that reply to or imitate a well-known model.

As Jonson suggests, 'the gospel' is the other leading career choice for young men of literary inclination. Indeed, the law and the ministry appealed to some of the same individuals: John Donne, John Marston, and Robert Herrick received legal training but eventually took holy orders. Though clergymen did not, of course, make as much money as lawyers did, their vocation could be considerably more appealing to the idealistic, did not require so tedious a course of study, and offered unimpeachable respectability. If clergymen were not gentry born, taking orders effectively gentrified them and placed them in the local elite.

Unlike the lawyers, who were trained and often continued to practice in the close-knit world of the Inns of Court, clergymen-writers did not form a tight social network, or even a loose one. Educated, by and large, at various Oxford or Cambridge colleges, they did not necessarily meet one another as young men, and in later life they were scattered across the countryside. Because clergymen, as a group, do not obviously form a coterie, there's been little scholarly work on the way a clerical vocation constrained literary output. But constraints there certainly were.

For the 'lawyers'—actually, in many cases, merely law students—their training and the setting in which they received it, rather than their on-the-job experience, was typically crucial in forming their literary ambitions. For clergymen, by contrast, their pastoral function profoundly influenced the nature of their literary enterprises. Many clergymen conceived of their writing as an extension of their devotional practices or of the cure of souls. For those who publish sermons, devotional tracts, or theological treatises— William Perkins or Lancelot Andrewes, for instance—the connection is clear enough. Sermons were, in fact, the best-selling printed materials of their day, but writing less closely connected with the administration of religious service could fall into the same category.

For George Herbert, his clerical vocation becomes the subject of several poems—'Affliction I', 'The Priesthood', 'The Collar'—as well as the topic of his prose treatise, *The Country Parson*, written in the late 1620s or early 1630s, but not printed until 1652. An outline of the ideal rural minister's education, manner of life, and approach to his work, *The Country Parson* takes as its model the guides to behaviour so popular in the period, such as Thomas Hoby's oft-reprinted 1561 translation of Castiglione's *Courtier*, or Henry Peacham's 1622 *The Complete Gentleman*. Just as Herbert himself had eschewed his original worldly ambitions for a priestly vocation, in *The Country Parson* Herbert turns a worldly genre to a religious use. In his poetry he performs a similar manoeuvre. Several of his poems imitate, or reply to, love poems by Philip Sidney, Edward Herbert, and the Earl of Pembroke. In 'The Forerunners' Herbert addresses the 'sweet phrases, lovely metaphors' of erotic poetry:

> When ye before
> Of stews and brothels only knew the doors,
> Then did I wash you with my tears, and more,
>
> Brought you to church well dressed and clad.
> (lines 13–17)

In these lines Herbert describes himself as having undertaken a literary version of the minister's primary task, converting wayward parishioners from a life of sin to a life of service to the divine.

The preacher, as Herbert says, must make himself an exemplar of the holy life. His sermons and behaviour should express the sensibility of a representative worshipper not vaingloriously to display his own piety, but to model for his flock the habits of religious faith. In many of his devotional poems therefore, certainly in the majority, Herbert's ministry is only implicitly evident, as he performs with special intensity and eloquence acts of worship incumbent upon every worshipper in the Church of England. Thus, Ramie Targoff argues that Herbert realizes his subjectivity not by drawing distinctions between himself and other people, but by immersing himself in a common ritual practice.[9] He typically builds his poems upon experiences he can presume he shares with his reader: celebrating the festivals of the Christian year, for instance. His fascination with emblems may

---

[9] Ramie Targoff, *Common Prayer: The Language of Public Devotion in Early Modern England*.

proceed from the same misgivings about personal uniqueness, for, whatever its ingenuity and polyvalency, the emblem's meaning is traditional and collectively acknowledged. Herbert's contemporaries immediately recognized the inextricability in his work between poem and ministry. *The Temple* was published posthumously in 1633 not by the usual purveyors of imaginative literature, but by Cambridge University Press, which normally restricted itself to publishing devotional and theological materials.

Though their engagement with the special demands of their vocation is rarely so direct and powerful as George Herbert's, other clergymen were likewise prolific authors. The brothers Giles and Phineas Fletcher, who wrote allegorical poetry in the tradition of Spenser, were both churchmen: Giles was the author of *Christ's Victory and Triumph in Heaven and Earth Over and After Death* (1610), and Phineas of *The Purple Island* (1633), a heavily moralized allegorical description of the human body. Even the sometimes mildly risqué Robert Herrick seems often to have conceived his poetic persona as a function of his clerical role. He shares with Herbert a deep commitment to the emotional and social power of ritual, although unlike Herbert he typically emphasizes the continuity between pagan and Christian observances, joining them almost seamlessly in such poems as 'Corinna's Going A-Maying', 'The Hock-Cart', and 'To the Reverend Shade of His Religious Father'. Likewise, seamless is the segue from his secular poetry, *Hesperides*, to the devotional poems of *Noble Numbers* bound in the same 1648 volume. In 1809, 135 years after Herrick's death, a member of his parish in the village of Dean Prior was found to be using some of his *Noble Numbers* as prayers. Herrick apparently taught some of his own religious lyrics to his largely illiterate congregation, after which they were passed down orally from one generation to the next. Herrick, celebrant of folk religion, thus arranges for his own inventions to become a part of it.

Because clergymen most often assimilate the relationship between poet and reader to the relationship between preacher and congregant, their conception of their relationship with their readership is rather different from that of the Inns of Court poets. When clergy preach, they typically address issues that, they claim, are fundamentally the same for all members of their audience, regardless of the social rank, sex, or age of the persons addressed. That doesn't mean that a clergyman-writer is unaware of human variety, but that he believes the answer to one's needs, the solution to one's dilemmas, is contingent not upon one's particular circumstances but instead must be sought in reference to a cosmic drama of sin and redemption. In consequence, most early modern clergymen write from what might be called the perspective of the 'Christian universal'—not only stressing, as Herbert and Herrick do, their own participation in the common human lot, but also what their readers share with the poet and with one another. This emphasis even holds when the topic under discussion is itself the variable and heterogeneous nature of human affairs. The popular casuist writer William Perkins, who is interested in the ways particular circumstances alter moral judgements, delineates many different ethical dilemmas or 'cases of conscience'.[10] But he differentiates those cases formally, by their diverse moral structures, not in terms of the kinds of people who are likely to suffer them.

The difference between 'clergymen's rhetoric' and 'lawyer's rhetoric' is visible in the difference between the deceptively simple devotional poetry of George Herbert and Robert Herrick and the religious writing of John Donne, who took orders relatively late in life, and whose poetic style was decisively formed in his Inns of Court years. When Donne began to write devotional poetry around 1608, he was not yet a minister, and he did not attempt to shed his highly individual manner, although he does make some attempts at generalization. Underlying many of the Holy Sonnets are familiar, even routine Christian topoi, but Donne characteristically exploits the most shocking, paradoxical possibilities lurking within those apparently tame metaphors. Holy Sonnet 14, 'Batter my heart', meditates upon the irresistible power of God's grace, a universally acknowledged truth in devotional poetry, but one that in Donne's poem elicits a fantasy of homosexual rape. In Holy Sonnet 18, 'Show me, dear Christ, thy spouse so bright and clear', the Church is the Bride of Christ, a traditional Biblical figure of speech. But as the poem continues, Donne asks that Christ pimp his bride to crowds of the faithful, for she is, Donne claims, 'most pleasing to thee then / When she is embraced and open to most men' (lines 13–14). It's debatable whether Donne ever made the transition between the deliberately exclusive manner of an Inns of court poet to the typical clergyman's more expansive sense of audience. King James I was said to have joked of one of Donne's sermons that 'like the peace of God, it passeth all understanding'. Still, in his sermons Donne does attempt to develop a less idiosyncratic persona, to emphasize what he shares with his audience, and to speak for the congregation as a collective. Indeed, the classic statement of what I'm calling the Christian universal is, perhaps, Donne's formulation in *Devotions Upon*

---

[10] William Perkins, *The Whole Treatise of the Cases of Conscience, Distinguished into Three Books.*

Emergent Occasions, 17: 'No man is an island, entire of himself; every man is a piece of the continent, a part of the main'.

Another common thread in the works of clergymen is a professed interest in the moral or spiritual improvement of the audience. Thus, Phineas Fletcher's *The Purple Island* includes prefaces from both the poet Frances Quarles, testifying to its literary quality, and Daniel Featly, a doctor of divinity, who assures the reader that 'thou shalt find here *philosophy* and *morality*'. Mandatory uplift threatened to put certain kinds of writing beyond the pale for clergymen. Of course, successful self-censorship leaves no trace, but the power of the norm shows itself in the attempts of the imperfectly inhibited to apologize in retrospect for their deviations. 'Jocund his muse was, but his life was chaste', Herrick assures us in *Hesperides* ('Upon Himself', 6)—apparently concerned that a poem such as 'The Vine', about a voluptuous sexual dream, fails to stay within the bounds of clerical propriety. After he was ordained, John Donne professed to be embarrassed by the lusty and sceptical writings of his youth. In a letter to Sir Robert Ker, he distinguished between 'Jack Donne', libertine layman, and 'Dr. Donne', preacher at St Paul's. He found for his trajectory a worthy pattern in the career of St Augustine, whose autobiographical *Confessions* describe his conversion from scapegrace to devout Christian.

Donne's search for a sanctified precedent was hardly unique: it was as pervasive for most clergymen-writers as was their mandate to improve their audience. The ultimate precedent, of course, for creative authorship was God, though none were presumptuous enough to model their originality explicitly on the divine source. Still, the mysterious, outside-of-consciousness source of poetic creativity gave it obvious connections to religious aspirations and feelings. Moreover, the Scriptures, a heterogeneous group of sacred texts, provide a variety of generic prototypes—of history, of biography, of lyric and devotional poetry. Allegory had particularly strong religious connotations, given the typological interpretation of Biblical narrative endlessly elaborated in the Middle Ages and Renaissance. Fable was also, apparently, divinely favoured, since Jesus' parables suggested that God loved fictions, at least those that edified their audience. As Philip Sidney pointed out in the *Defense of Poesy*:

> our saviour Christ could as well have given the moral commonplaces of uncharitableness and humbleness as the divine narration of Dives and Lazarus; or of disobedience and mercy, as that heavenly discourse of the lost child and the gracious father; but that his through-searching wisdom

knew the estate of Dives burning in hell, and of Lazarus in Abraham's bosom, would more constantly (as it were) inhabit both the memory and the judgement.[11]

The prophetic books—Isaiah, Jeremiah, Revelations—provided yet another influential, and in many cases quite liberating, model. The prophets were monitory or visionary authorities whose mandate came directly from God, unmediated by normal social institutions. They were typically fiercely critical of contemporary mores. The example of the prophets freed seventeenth-century clergy from serving merely as bland proponents of the more tedious virtues. Moreover, since part of their recognized function was to awaken their hearers to a consciousness of their sins—obviously sometimes an uncomfortable experience—clergymen were supposed to avoid cosseting their audiences. Provided that their spiritual convictions authorized their dissent from the status quo, clergymen could become powerful voices of admonition and social critique, whether conservative or radical. Traditionally, though they could be severely punished after the fact for seditious speeches and could lose their living if they expressed heretical opinions, preachers were not to be interrupted in the course of delivering a sermon. This clerical privilege, called 'freedom of the pulpit', permitted a scope of unfettered public expression unusual in the period, at least to a man sure of his own conscience and heedless of consequences. William Drummond records of the audacious satirist Ben Jonson: 'he hath a mind to be a churchman, and so he might have favour to make one sermon to the King, he careth not what thereafter should befall him, for he would not flatter though he saw death'.[12]

The clear expectations associated with the writing of clergy—that it will conceive its audience in 'universal' terms, that it will be spiritually improving, that it will be aware of sacred precedents, that it will tell the truth unflinchingly—means that the stance of the clergyman-writer can be occupied by one who does not fulfil all its normal requirements. In the later 1630s, John Milton decided against ordination because he disliked the path that the Church of England had taken under Charles I and Archbishop Laud. But in *Lycidas* (1638) he makes a clear connection between the role of the

---

[11] 'The Defense of Poesy', in *The Prose Works of Sir Philip Sidney*, ed. Albert Feuillerat, vol. 3, p. 15.

[12] Ian Donaldson, ed., *Informations to William Drummond of Hawthornden*, lines 254–256 in *The Cambridge Edition of the Works of Ben Jonson*, ed. David Bevington, Martin Butler, Ian Donaldson, et al., vol. 5.

poet and the role of the pastor; indeed, given the decay of the established church, the poet is the purer religious guide. Almost thirty years later, when he announces in *Paradise Lost* that he aims to 'justify the ways of God to men' (1.26), Milton claims for himself even more openly a ministerial role outside the established religious hierarchy, in the tradition of Old Testament prophets. His claim that he, as epic narrator, performs and models the religious life for the benefit of his readers, adapts to his own circumstances the pastoral role imagined by Herbert or Donne earlier in the century.

Of course not every amateur writer in the period was a landed aristocrat, a lawyer, or a clergymen. William Camden, the author of important works of English history and linguistics, was the headmaster of Westminster School. Richard Burton, author of *The Anatomy of Melancholy* (1621), was a don at Christ Church Oxford, and the sometimes self-parodying scholarly apparatus of the book is visible on every page. When Thomas Browne calls his latitudinarian essay *Religio Medici*, 'the religion of a physician', he implies that his vocational self-definition, in a field that increasingly relied on empirical inquiry and eschewed received authority, influences not only his views on medicine but his spiritual life as well. In all these cases, vocational commitments to scholarship and to medicine affect the way the author represents himself, and the way he imagines his audience.

Some amateur literary works were produced in circumstances of enforced leisure. Walter Ralegh spent seven years of a fourteen-year imprisonment in the Tower of London working on his *History of the World* (1614), and was reported—probably falsely—to have composed a poem, 'The Lie', on the night before his execution. After he was forced out of office on corruption charges, Francis Bacon revised his *Essays*, wrote *The History of Henry VII* (1622) and a Latin version of the *Advancement of Learning*, and laboured on his *Instauratio Magna*, or *Great Instauration*, left unfinished at his death. In 1642 Richard Lovelace, imprisoned for his activities on behalf of King Charles, wrote 'To Althea: From Prison' from his cell at Westminster:

> Stone walls do not a prison make,
>   Nor iron bars a cage.
> Minds innocent and quiet take
>   That for a hermitage.
>   (25–28)

Imprisoned again on political grounds in 1646, he spent the time preparing his collected works, *Lucasta: Epodes, Odes, Sonnets*, for the press. Many years later, the blind John Milton, a vigorous polemicist for the Parliamentary side in the civil war and later foreign secretary under Cromwell, completed *Paradise Lost* and wrote *Paradise Regained* (1671) after he was forced first into house arrest and then into retirement upon Charles II's restoration to the throne. During the same bleak period, many scholars surmise, he wrote *Samson Agonistes* (1671), a poem about a blind, self-doubting prisoner who nonetheless possesses God-given powers to smite his heathen oppressors.

These writers draw upon a traditional connection between inspiration and misfortune that harks back to Socrates, Ovid, and Boethius. For seventeenth-century writers, Philip Sidney provided a fresher precedent: when Queen Elizabeth's displeasure forced him to withdraw from court in 1580, he took refuge in his sister's country house, wrote the prose romance *Arcadia*, and began the translation of the Psalms later finished by his sister. Even more recently, John Davies may have written *Nosce Teipsum* during an extended period of rustication; after assaulting a colleague in the Inns of Court in 1597 / 8, he was disbarred and forced to retire to his estate in the country for more than four years. Like Sidney and Davies, seventeenth-century prisoners turned despair into creative opportunity. Their personal setbacks both forced reflection and created an occasion to put those reflections into writing as they attempted to reconcile their once-grand worldly ambitions with their disastrously diminished prospects. Writers under such circumstances naturally gravitate to several genres: lament, consolation, devotional poetry, and works that celebrate the 'innocent' contemplative delights of retirement or inveigh against the corruption of courts.

Just as Milton, though he never took orders, could appropriate the well-defined stance of clergyman-poet, so the stance of poet-as-prisoner was adaptable to a range of circumstances. Robert Herrick, for instance, regarded himself as sentenced to life in the country even though no furious queen condemned him to Devon; his exile was merely the consequence of his taking a job there:

> More discontents I never had
>   Since I was born, than here,
> Where I have been, and still am, sad
>   In this dull Devonshire.
> Yet justly too I must confess
>   I ne'er invented such
> Ennobled numbers for the press
>   Than where I loathed so much.
>   ('Discontents in Devon')

Like his predecessors, Herrick finds isolation and boredom a spur to literary productivity; for the same reasons that Sidney did, he had to resort to the consolations of his own imagination.

The livelihoods of amateur writers, whatever their literary ambitions, did not depend upon audience approval. Their independence from audience demands could be enabling. Because amateurs did not necessarily require access to London's printers and playhouses, they could live almost anywhere. George Herbert wrote poetry at Bemerton, Robert Herrick in Devon, Katherine Phillips in Wales. William Drummond rarely left his estate in Scotland and sent his poems by post in manuscript to friends. Amateurs were free to define their audience, if they wished, in narrow or eccentric ways. Or they could convince themselves that they were not really bidding for others' notice at all—a conviction that could be especially helpful for female writers, in an age which normally proscribed a public role for women. Anne Clifford, for instance, kept a diary for her own use for decades, describing her long fight to wrest the lands that were her birthright from her male kin. She also produced materials apparently intended for others eventually to read, researching and describing her family history in great detail, and in 1651 writing an autobiography. She did not, however, court attention for herself as a writer during her own lifetime. Rather, this highly family-conscious woman hoped that her posterity—in particular, her female posterity—would read her work and take heart from her struggle. This dream was posthumously fulfilled when, in the twentieth century, her descendant Vita Sackville-West—herself stripped of Knole, her estate, by patriarchal inheritance law—finally published Clifford's diary.

But if isolation from, or restriction of, audience could be liberating in one way, it could be detrimental in another. The seasoned professional Ben Jonson told the isolated amateur William Drummond that his poems 'smelled too much of the schools, and were not after the fancy of the time'[13]—that is, they were the products of a literary sensibility acquired largely through solitary reading, not through contact with the vital literary currents of his own day. Likewise, Jonson worried that Donne, an author he extravagantly admired, had defined his audience in overly exclusive terms: 'Donne', he told Drummond, 'for not being understood would perish.'[14] And, indeed, Donne's reputation languished for many years, until in the early twentieth century he was rehabilitated at the hands of modernist writers, who were

[13] *Informations to William Drummond of Hawthornden*, lines 76–77.
[14] Ibid., line 147.

engaged in comparable struggles to define a readership adequate to their innovative, intellectually demanding, explicitly elitist artistic project.

Among poets less powerfully original than Donne, the tightness of the coterie often conduced not to a surplus of wit, but rather to a certain conformism. The satiric scepticism of much of the work associated with 'Inns of Court men' in the 1590s and early seventeenth century is perhaps a relic of their legal training; the tough-but-subtle intellect and agonistic persona of 'metaphysical' poetry is likely influenced by the Inns' cultivation of analytical argument as a basic professional skill. But it is also a matter of literary fashion among poets who share a youthful alertness to the prestige of the cutting edge, and a similarly youthful tendency to rebel in predictable ways, in lockstep with other members of their generational cohort.

For women, the double bind of amateurism can be especially confining. In 'The Dream', published in 1621, Rachel Speght imagines the allegorical figure of Dissuasion telling her that a mere woman is too incompetent to write poetry. Speght responds by refusing, like Jesus in Matthew 7:6, to throw pearls before swine:

> regard not vulgar talk
> For dunghill cocks at precious stones will spurn,
> And swine-like natures prize not crystal streams.
> Contemned mire, and mud will serve their turns.[15]

Good poetry requires good readers, and those who belittle her ability, Speght claims, are merely betraying their own inadequacies. This sturdy contempt for detractors is, of course, a stock-in-trade of any writer who feels neglected or underappreciated. After the failure of his late play, *The New Inn* (1629), Ben Jonson similarly recalls the dietary preferences of the pigs:

> Say that thou pour'st them wheat,
> And they will acorns eat:
> 'Twere simple fury still thyself to waste
> On such as have no taste.
> ('On the New Inn: Ode.
> To Himself', lines 11–14)

---

[15] Rachel Speght, 'The Dream', in *Mortalities Memorandum, with a Dreame Prefixed, Imaginarie in Manner; Real in Matter*.

Likewise Milton writes in disgust about the Presbyterians, his erstwhile allies in ecclesiastical disputation, when they object to his position on divorce:

> But this is got by casting pearls to hogs
> That bawl for freedom in their senseless mood,
> And still revolt when truth would set them free.
> (Sonnet 12, lines 8–10)

But whereas the men react angrily to actual censure, Speght fearfully anticipates it before it occurs. 'Dissuasion' is as much a projection of one aspect of her own mind as it is a depiction of her readers' sentiments. Not only do her inhibitions come from within as well as without—a crippling self-doubt familiar to many minority writers—but in Speght's case a dream vision itself suggests a certain solipsism about her entire poetic enterprise. Scorned, she knows, by much of her potential readership, she is simultaneously both relieved to be talking to herself, and afraid that she is merely doing so.

In mid-century, Margaret Cavendish, Duchess of Newcastle, lives out the paradigm rather differently. Cavendish cultivates a stance of extreme originality, not merely in her writing but in her dress, speech, and demeanour. A bemused Samuel Pepys writes of her in his diary: 'The Duchess hath been a good comely woman: but her dress so antic and deportment so unordinary, that I do not like her at all' (26 April 1667). Essentially Cavendish translates into female terms the 'self-fashioning' which Stephen Greenblatt has shown to be so important for aristocratic men in the early modern period[16]—a strategy which implicitly emphasizes the importance of her elite social rank. Far from shunning publication, as many amateurs did, Cavendish has her works printed in folio volumes at her own expense, and sends them to libraries at Cambridge and Oxford. She not only invades the male domain of the university, but does so in a way that simultaneously emphasizes her capacity to afford such extravagances.

By inventing herself as a sometimes outrageous 'character', Cavendish deliberately defies the force of social norms. It is easy to sympathize with her creative response to censure that might otherwise have crushed her. At the same time, when Cavendish deliberately reduces her capacity to take other people's reactions—however unjust—into consideration, she risks being dismissed as a crank. Until the recent surge of academic interest in women's writing, almost nobody took Cavendish seriously. Several centuries of contemptuous dismissal of 'mad Madge' by mostly male critics were surely

---

[16] Stephen Greenblatt, *Renaissance Self Fashioning*.

in part mere chauvinism. Yet that dismissal also testifies to the ways in which constraints on women in the early modern period forced them to adapt in ways that did not necessarily conduce to readability and broad acceptance.

Remunerated Writing

Now we turn from the world of the amateur to that of the professional writer. That anyone might make a living as a writer was a relatively new prospect in Jacobean England, and in fact very few people actually managed to do so. The handful of writers that did, however, set a highly visible, enormously influential example. Prolific by necessity, exclusively dedicated to literary endeavours, and keenly aware of the novelty of their situation, they pioneered changes that would revolutionize the way in which literature would be imagined in future generations.

Two ways in which people now write for pay were unavailable in Jacobean England. No one made a good living writing best-sellers, although such a career was not entirely unimaginable. In the early sixteenth century, the works of the humanist Desiderius Erasmus were so popular that publishers offered him generous payment for them, and his printer purchased a garden for him to contemplate and write in. Yet Erasmus was an international phenomenon. Even though he lived in England for several years, where he wrote his famous *Praise of Folly* while a guest of his friend Thomas More, Erasmus composed his works in Latin, the universal language, and shrewdly consigned his works to publishers in Paris and Frankfurt, with their superior ability to disperse books throughout Continental Europe. Printers in London, by comparison, had a limited and insular customer base. Early seventeenth-century English stationers did pay authors a fee for the manuscript copy of their works, which could then be prepared for printing, and a number of writers—most notably Dekker and Middleton—sold them entertaining and informative pamphlets. Unfortunately, this writing was not very remunerative; in the cases we know about, the payments writers received consisted of a small flat fee—forty shillings for a pamphlet manuscript, for instance—rather than a royalty arrangement that might have rewarded the authors of especially successful books. Sometimes the author was paid in copies of his books, which he then had to peddle himself to make a profit. Copyright law in Jacobean and Caroline England, insofar as it existed, was designed to protect the financial interests of publishers and printers, rather than authors.

Nor could writers make their livings as journalists. Occasionally, freelancers would write a prose account of an exciting contemporary event—a murder, a case of treason or witchcraft, a monstrous birth—but in Jacobean and Caroline England writers could not support themselves on this kind of writing alone. Because printed materials were censored, there were no newspapers in the modern sense until after the collapse of censorship in the 1640s. A few people did attempt to develop a market for news or to satisfy the hunger for information about current events. In the 1630s and 1640s, John Pory and Edward Rossingham circulated manuscript newsletters to paid subscribers; the newsletter's status as a supposedly 'private' epistle permitted some evasion of the censorship rules. Even earlier—in his 1620 masque, *News from the New World Discovered in the Moon*, and his 1625 play, *The Staple of News*—Ben Jonson, always acutely aware of new and interesting social developments, satirizes similar attempts to market information in the wake of the outbreak of the Thirty Years War. But these endeavours did not much engage the major writers of the period, except in Jonson's case, as an item of curiosity.

There were, however, two ways for an author to support himself by writing. One could supply plays to one of the several profitable London theatre companies, or one could seek the support of one or more wealthy patrons—someone willing either to support a writer on the basis of his literary skill alone, or willing to employ him on the promise of his fine qualities more generally. A number of versatile individuals—Ben Jonson, Thomas Middleton, William Shakespeare, George Chapman, John Fletcher, and Samuel Daniel—made their mark both as professional dramatists and as patronage writers. As a result, these two systems of support, though they seem, as we shall see, to operate on very different principles, actually overlap rather than compete. In the Jacobean and Caroline periods, the existence of literary patronage influences the patently commercial world of the professional theatre and, conversely, the availability of a market for theatrical writing profoundly affects the way the literary patronage system functions. But in order to understand those interactions it is first necessary to comprehend how one went about writing for the theatre, and how for a patron.

Writing for the Commercial Theatre

Professional repertory theatre companies had been operating profitably in London since the late 1560s. By James's accession the thriving London theatrical scene was, for many observers, one of the most distinctive traits of the city. In about the year 1620, Fynes Moryson wrote:

> The City of London ... hath four or five companies of players with their peculiar theatres capable of many thousands, wherein they play every day in the week except Sunday ... as there be in my opinion more plays in London than in all the world I have seen.[17]

Each of these theatre companies required lots of plays and was willing to pay for them, especially early in the period when there was no suitable inherited repertory to fall back upon. A travelling company might perform *Everyman* (c. 1530) or *Doctor Faustus* (1594) in town after town after town, but a company with a fixed location required repeat business from the same playgoers, so it needed to offer a continual parade of novel theatrical fare. Theatre historians calculate that in the 1580s and 1590s, a successful company bought a new play on an average every three weeks. By the Caroline period, companies of longer standing—particularly the King's Men, the most durable and successful company of the period—needed new plays less urgently, since plenty of old, already-paid-for plays were available for revival. It is no coincidence that most of the great plays of the English Renaissance were written between 1588 and 1625—that is, after the commercial theatre had had time to establish itself, but before the sheer weight of precedent and available repertoire had begun to oppress creative initiative.

By their own account, playwrights were scantily paid. The induction to Thomas Goffe's *The Careless Shepherdess* (1638) describes playwrights as 'poor ... even to a proverb'. Francis Beaumont and John Fletcher, in the period of their dramatic collaboration, were rumoured to share a single cloak between them. George Chapman was committed to debtor's prison, and Thomas Dekker spent years therein; Thomas Middleton died in poverty. Ben Jonson told William Drummond that 'of all his plays he had never gained two hundred pounds'. Most of our evidence of playwrights' actual compensation derives from the diary of Philip Henslowe, the man in charge of procuring scripts for the Lord Admiral's Men in the 1590s. Henslowe's job required him to keep records of his financial transactions with the men who supplied the company with plays. The years of Henslowe's Diary of course predate James's reign, but it seems unlikely that the methods of obtaining or paying for plays shifted drastically in the next couple of decades. In addition to the Diary, there are also occasional references to the compensation of playwrights in prologues, epilogues, and letters. Much later in the period, a lawsuit provides detailed information about contracts

---

[17] Charles Hughes, ed., *Shakespeare's Europe: Unpublished Chapters of Fynes Moryson's Itinerary. Being a Survey of the Condition of Europe at the End of the 16th Century*, p. 476.

between the King's Men and Richard Brome, a dramatist associated with them, in 1635 and 1638.

Henslowe's records suggest that at the beginning of the century plays fetched a price of five to eight pounds each. The price for a new play rose steadily during the first three decades of the century; by the Caroline period ten pounds or more was not an uncommon price, although by these years the companies were commissioning fewer plays than before. It was routine, in addition, for the author or authors to receive the profits from the second or third night's performance. Since when old plays were revived, they were typically 'refreshed' with new scenes, songs, prologues, or epilogues, revisions constituted another source of income. Thus, in 1601 Henslowe records paying Ben Jonson two pounds for 'additions' to a revival of Thomas Kyd's *Spanish Tragedy*.

The theatre historian G. R. Bentley has calculated that freelance playwriting had the potential to bring in rather more money than the fifteen or twenty pounds a year paid to a schoolmaster or a curate.[18] This level of compensation makes sense given that the theatre companies had to make a profit: on the one hand, they would go out of business if they paid excessively, but, on the other hand, they needed to offer a sum sufficient to attract adequate talent. Of course, many fewer people are able to write successful plays, over and over again, than are able to teach grammar school competently or conduct religious services. When early modern playwrights describe their financial precariousness, they may well be testifying to the sheer difficulty of surviving in a brutally demanding 'gig economy', not complaining about the level of remuneration the few successful practitioners did achieve.

It comes naturally to us to think of entertainment as a business, but the idea was still rather new in the early seventeenth century—and it encouraged playwrights in a self-conception quite unlike that of the literary amateurs. Jacobean and Caroline playwrights often see themselves, accurately, as participants in a commercial system, selling poetry for money just as others sell bricks, fish, or oranges. In *The Gull's Hornbook* (1609), Thomas Dekker writes: 'The theatre is your poet's Royal Exchange upon which their Muses—that are now turned to merchants—meeting, barter away that light commodity of words.'[19] Since the Royal Exchange, founded by Sir Thomas Gresham

---

[18] G. R. Bentley, *The Profession of Dramatist in Shakespeare's Time 1590–1642*.
[19] Thomas Dekker, *The Gull's Hornbook* in *Thomas Dekker*, ed. E. D. Penry, p. 98. For the marketing of literary expertise, see Douglas Bruster, 'The Representation Market of Early Modern England', *Renaissance Drama* 41 (2013): 1–23

in 1566, was the financial centre of England's manufacturing and mercantile sector by Jacobean times, Dekker's metaphor suggests both the novelty and the irresistibility of a comparison between muses and merchants. The playwright, on this view, is aligned with the values of the emerging mercantile order and a participant in its newly sophisticated economy. In this economy, the basic principle is apparently 'free trade': anything might be exchangeable for anything else. Even something so ephemeral as poetic genius can have a cash value, if the buyer and the seller can agree upon a price.

The number of professional playwrights was small. A mere 22 men provided about half of the 1,200 plays known from the period, and only a small subset of this tiny group made their living for extended periods mainly as playwrights: William Shakespeare, John Fletcher, Philip Massinger, Richard Brome, Thomas Middleton, Thomas Dekker, James Shirley, and Thomas Heywood. Other writers, such as Ben Jonson, John Marston, and George Chapman, spent some years writing for the theatre, but simultaneously or successively cultivated other fields of literary endeavour.

Some playwrights—Dekker, Middleton, and Jonson among them—sold plays to a wide variety of companies. Others—Shakespeare, Fletcher, Massinger, Brome, and Heywood—wrote exclusively, over and over again, for the same company of actors. Of this latter group, Fletcher, Massinger, and Brome apparently worked on a salary basis, with their pay and work requirements most likely contractually stipulated by the company that employed them. Shakespeare and Heywood, by contrast, were shareholders of the acting companies for which they wrote, and so their fortunes were tied not merely to their playwriting but to the overall success or failure of the company to which they belonged.[20] Thus, the immense popularity of Shakespeare's plays, by enhancing his company's general prosperity, in turn contributed to his relative affluence: unlike his playwriting colleagues, languishing in debtor's prison, Shakespeare bought a spacious house in his home town of Stratford-upon-Avon, purchased his family a coat of arms, and retired from the theatre at about fifty years of age. Yet the relationship between his company's good fortune and his own is a matter of his institutional position in the theatre company, not the automatic consequence of his gifts as a playwright. A freelance or 'salaried' dramatist, whatever his talent, would not have had any claim on company profits.

---

[20] For Shakespeare's unique situation in the world of early seventeenth-century theatre, see Bart Van Es, *Shakespeare in Company*, especially 124–162.

Whether they were freelancers or regularly attached to a company, playwrights most often worked on commission. That is, either the playwright or the theatre company would suggest a topic for a play, and the playwright might subsequently offer an outline or some sample scenes. Henslowe's Diary indicates that he typically advanced money to writers upon acceptance of a proposal, and dispensed the rest in instalments as they delivered parts of the promised play. One consequence of this system is that the dramatists typically knew in advance which repertory company they would be writing for: the number of the actors and their strengths and weaknesses, the nature of their usual playing space, and the preferences of their audiences.

Presumably the acting companies display such a marked preference for dealing with the same playwrights over and over again because a close knowledge of playing conditions would naturally have conduced to better performances, on average, than plays written without such knowledge. For instance, Brett Gamboa has demonstrated that Shakespeare's plays are closely tailored to the personnel resources of the specific theatre company for which they were written. If parts are doubled, all of them can be performed by twelve people, the number of regular shareholders in the King's Men. Plays Shakespeare wrote in the period around the turn of the seventeenth century, when the number of shareholders temporarily dipped below twelve, can be staged with even fewer actors.[21] It is probably no coincidence that the most successful company of the period, the King's Men, relied especially heavily on continuing exclusive arrangements with playwrights, both to secure the best talent for themselves and to prevent their competitors from availing themselves of it. Shakespeare, as shareholder in the company, served as its first 'house dramatist', to be succeeded by Fletcher, Massinger, and Brome. The existence of such affiliations suggests both the tight connection between the dramatists and the theatre companies and the way that the connection served their mutual interests.

Playwrights needed to be able to collaborate skilfully with other writers as well. Many plays were jointly written, often by a team assembled by the theatre company: an understandable strategy, given the urgency with which new plays were required. Two, three, or four people write a play more quickly than one. The work could be split up in various ways. Middleton wrote the tragic 'main plot' of *The Changeling* while the former clown

---

[21] Brett Gamboa, *Shakespeare's Double Plays: Dramatic Economy on the Early Modern Stage*.

William Rowley contributed a structurally almost independent comic subplot, an arrangement that would have entailed an agreement about how to allocate scenes and some thematic coordination, but not necessarily close partnership. The collaboration of John Marston, Ben Jonson, and George Chapman on *Eastward Ho* (1605) must have required more elaborate teamwork, since in some cases all three writers seem to have contributed to a single scene. The emotional temperature of collaboration varied as well: Beaumont and Fletcher were famously compatible, while Jonson quarrelled with Marston both before and after their work together on *Eastward Ho*.

The custom of revising old plays for revival performances led to a good deal of what might be called 'retrospective collaboration', in which one playwright rewrote the work of another. There are signs of Middleton's hand in Shakespeare's *Macbeth* and *Measure for Measure*: apparently he reworked both plays for productions mounted after Shakespeare's death in 1614, but before the printing of the plays in 1623. Philip Massinger, writing for the King's Men in the 1620s and 1630s when they staged many such revivals, seems to have contributed to several plays published as *The Works of Beaumont and Fletcher* in 1647. Many of these plays in this volume, moreover, do not contain the work of Beaumont, since he retired from playwriting and died young, before the majority of them were written. What remains unclear in many instances is whether the printed text represents a play on which Fletcher and Massinger collaborated from the outset, or an after-the-fact revision of a Fletcher play by the younger dramatist.

Because collaboration was so frequent, the authorship of many Renaissance plays is unknown or disputed. Some scholars have argued that the concept of authorship that reigned in the theatres is alien to a modern literary sensibility which is still, despite the anti-authorial rhetoric of poststructuralism, dominated by narratives of solitary creativity.[22] Yet there are plenty of analogies to the collaborative practices of seventeenth-century playwriting in the modern world. Screenwriters, for instance, frequently write movie and television scripts as teams; moreover, there is nothing sacred about a screenplay once a production company has purchased it, and it is often drastically revised in the course of filming and subsequent editing. In architecture, a field in which the ideology of heroic individualism has at

---

[22] See, for example, Jeffrey Masten, *Textual Intercourse: Collaboration, Authorship, and Sexualities in Renaissance Drama*.

times held sway, actual practice is often much more collaborative than architectural histories sometimes imply: a team of people works on a project that, in the end, is formally credited to the head of the firm.[23]

If a talent for collaboration was a useful trait for a professional playwright, compositional fluency was an absolute requirement. At the theatre companies' rates of pay, a 'blocked' writer would soon be a starving one. In 1633, Thomas Heywood, in his address to the reader in *The English Traveler*, claims that he wrote or 'had a main finger' in 220 plays; he was to write at least 2 plays and 4 pageants after that publication. Fletcher wrote or collaborated on at least 69 plays; Dekker 34, while simultaneously churning out non-dramatic treatises of all kinds for whatever money he could get from the printers. Massinger wrote all or part of at least 54 plays; Henry Chettle 50, Shakespeare more than 38, James Shirley 38, and Thomas Middleton at least 31. Ben Jonson, taunted by his peers for his sluggish muse, nonetheless wrote at least 28 plays and collaborated on others while producing numerous court masques and a good deal of non-dramatic poetry and prose as well. For some of these writers, moreover, these figures understate their actual productivity, because so many plays have been lost and the attribution of others is unclear.

Not surprisingly, then, unlike the amateur writers who associate their literary endeavours with their leisure pursuits, playwrights typically characterize their writing as labour—what John Webster, in his preface to *The White Devil* (1612), calls 'right happy and copious industry'. Ben Jonson is particularly fond of emphasizing the affinity between writing and the manual crafts. In his prefatory poem to Shakespeare's First Folio (1623), Jonson praises its author as a blacksmith labouring at the forge.

> he
> Who casts to write a living line must sweat
> (Such as thine are) and strike the second heat
> Upon the Muse's anvil; turn the same
> And himself with it, that he thinks to frame.
>
> (lines 58–62)

---

[23] Denise Scott Brown, 'A Worm's Eye View of Recent Architectural History', *Architectural Record* (Feb 1984) and 'Room at the Top? Sexism and the Star System in Architecture', *Architecture: A Place for Women*. Scott Brown, wife and collaborator of the celebrated postmodernist Robert Venturi, knows whereof she speaks.

This passage has often been read as a self-portrait, not a description of Shakespeare, since Jonson's compositional methods were careful and self-consciously artful, while Shakespeare was reputed (falsely) never to have blotted a line. Less frequently noticed is the way Jonson associates writing 'living lines' with hot, dirty, useful toil—precisely the kind of endeavour that gentlemen typically considered beneath them. Jonson, although a snob in some respects, never shrank from hard work himself and admired the capacity for it in others. He portrays Shakespeare as a blacksmith not to insult his memory but in order to pay a compliment to a colleague. Strenuous effort and application not merely eventuate in fine poetry, but enable self-creation. 'He who casts to write a living line' must hammer not only his writing but himself on the Muse's anvil.

The professional dramatist's attitudes may reflect not only his heavier workload but his somewhat different family origins, a topic we have already touched upon in Chapter 1. While their non-remunerated contemporaries tend to hail from the gentry and to cluster in a few learned professions, playwrights—especially those that came of age before 1610—often came from social classes that could not afford to scorn manual labour. Thomas Middleton was a mason's son and a grocer's stepson; Ben Jonson was the stepson of a bricklayer and was himself apprenticed to the trade. Shakespeare's father was a glover, Christopher Marlowe's a shoemaker. Nobody knows what Dekker's father did for a living, which itself indicates that he did not occupy one of society's top echelons. Artisans were by no means necessarily poor—Marlowe's father owned a fine house in Canterbury; Shakespeare's father, during his childhood, was a substantial Stratford citizen; and Middleton's father left money sufficient for his Cambridge education. Neither, however, were they members of England's tiny aristocracy. Professional playwrights had a very variable level of schooling. Some were educated at the universities or the Inns of Court, but others, including Jonson and Shakespeare, had no formal education past grammar school. As we saw in in Chapter 1, grammar school was itself available only to a minority in early modern England. As a group the playwrights, in other words, look privileged in their backgrounds relative to most of their compatriots, so many of whom were illiterate and economically precarious, but déclassé relative to the amateur poets among their contemporaries.

The influx of such people into English literary culture introduced a wider range of social experience and a wider sense of the kinds of events appropriately represented in literary form. These differences are so marked that the traditional English curriculum makes a sharp distinction between 'the drama of the English Renaissance' and its 'non-dramatic' writing. As a group, for instance, the playwrights were typically far more interested than were most non-dramatic poets in the representation of contemporary urban life, and relatively less interested in the georgic and pastoral that seemed, to the often more sheltered amateurs, to be a natural form of literary expression. Ben Jonson regales his friend William Drummond with a revealing anecdote. When an unnamed 'gentleman' read him a poem that began 'Where is that man that never yet did hear / Of fair Penelope, Ulysses' queen?', Jonson called in his cook and asked him whether he had ever heard of Penelope. The cook answered 'no', and Jonson quipped 'Lo, there the man that never yet did hear / Of fair Penelope, Ulysses' queen'.[24] Jonson foregrounds here not only his wit but his social knowledge: unlike the 'gentleman', he knows what cooks are likely to know. Jonson's origins are less exalted than the gentleman's, but his upbringing gives him a more realistic conception of the range of human experience.

Although women attended the theatre in great numbers, and although a few amateur women wrote closet dramas or country house entertainments, all the professional playwrights of the period were men. The absence of women seems not to have involved direct prohibition, but instead a combination of work customs and social prejudice that together militated against their participation. The members of the acting companies that bought the plays were entirely male, and a lone woman may well have found this environment difficult to learn about and negotiate, especially given its highly collaborative nature. Moreover, the typical professional playwright's combination of down-to-earth commercial savvy with literary sophistication was, if demonstrably rare in men of the period, probably entirely unattainable for a woman. There were some highly educated women in seventeenth-century England, and a large number of women worked for wages or participated in the running of businesses, but they were not generally the same women. The typical professional playwright in the early modern period possessed social attributes and attitudes markedly different from the typical woman writer's. The male playwrights, with good reason, tended to minimize the significance of their origins and to see themselves as belonging to a cohort of talented individuals. The women writers, by contrast, were by and large members of an aristocracy of birth, and derived their sense of entitlement from their family background and social status.

---

[24] *Informations to William Drummond of Hawthornden*, lines 410–416.

Unlike an Inns of Court poet or an independently wealthy amateur, who could conceivably write purely for his or her own purposes and pleasure, the commercial playwright could not afford to ignore his audience. It was a truism in the period that successful theatrical performances required not merely a good script and fine actors, but an audience willing to participate imaginatively in the creation of an illusion. The Chorus in Shakespeare's *Henry V* encourages the playgoers to supply what the relatively constrained technology of the early modern stage cannot provide:

> Think, when we talk of horses, that you see them,
> Printing their proud hoofs i' th' receiving earth,
> For 'tis your thoughts that now must deck our kings.
> (lines 26–28)

In *Midsummer Night's Dream*, Theseus voices a similar sentiment when he discusses plays with Hippolyta: 'the best in this kind are but shadows, and the worst are no worse if imagination amend them' (5.1.208–209).

On severely practical grounds, too, the playwright needed, as Ben Jonson wrote in the prologue to *Epicene*, 'not to please the cook's taste, but the guest's' (9). Theatre companies did not want plays that failed to attract an audience. In the induction to *Bartholomew Fair*, Jonson offers a telling, if tongue-in-cheek, contract between dramatist and playgoer. The playwright, he admits, has 'parted with his right' to judge his own work when he offers his play for public performance, just as any seller yields ownership rights to the buyer. Jonson specifies only that the playgoers calibrate their 'censure' in some proportion to the price of admission. The frankly commercial quid pro quo, in which the dramatist exchanges his talent for cash, could hardly be more obvious.

The apparent straightforwardness of the transaction between playwright and audience did not necessarily make it an easy one. Playwrights often chafe against the need to please playgoers defined as customers. If the pitfall of the coterie writer was a narrowly defined audience, the pitfall of the professional dramatist could be an ignorant or impatient audience or an acting company unwilling to decipher an unfamiliar dramatic scenario. Some of the plays we now consider most daringly innovative, such as Beaumont's *The Knight of the Burning Pestle*, Fletcher's *The Faithful Shepherdess* (1608), and Jonson's *Epicene*, were unsuccessful in first performance, apparently because their novelty baffled either the acting company or the audience.

Compounding the difficulty of the playwright's task was the fact that playwriting, unlike a good deal of amateur writing, was not typically implicated in face-to-face encounters with well-known individuals. Instead, the playwright had to produce work that would seem compelling to playgoers with whom he might well have little in common. The concept of addressing an 'unknown' audience is basic to our own conception of authorship: one of the important distinctions between an 'author' and someone who keeps a diary or writes letters to friends is that the author presumes to interest people who do not know him or her personally. Clearly, this 'address to unknown persons' requires an act of imagination on the part of the writer, and the more diverse those unknown persons are, the more daring the act of imagination has to be.

Although modern critics disagree about how socially various the theatre audience actually was,[25] the number and capacity of the theatres operating simultaneously in London during the first third of the century suggest that a large cross-section of the urban population attended at least occasionally. In a society in which literacy was not universal, theatrical performances were accessible to people unable to read works that circulated in print or manuscript. Moreover, all but the very poor would have been able to afford the penny charged for the cheapest places in the large outdoor playhouses—a price that, despite inflation, remained unchanged throughout the period. The theatre historian Andrew Gurr calculates that in the late Elizabethan and Jacobean period, some 25,000 people per week attended theatrical performances, and estimates a total of about 50 million visits between 1580 and 1640.[26] Moreover, these crowds did not always sort themselves out by traditionally recognized status markers such as birth or education. One gained access to theatrical performances not because one belonged to a particular guild, had inherited a title, or had been favoured by the monarch, but merely because one had paid the price of admission. The playhouse, as Thomas Dekker observes, 'allow[s] a stool as well to the farmer's son as to your templar [barrister]'[27]—a shock to contemporaries accustomed to rigid, vividly displayed hierarchies of rank.

---

[25] Alfred Harbage, *Shakespeare and the Rival Traditions*, argues that the outdoor, 'public' theatres at least attracted a socially heterogeneous audience with a large artisan component. Ann Jennalie Cook, *The Privileged Playgoers of Shakespeare's England*, argues that the public-theatre audience was more restricted and elite in character. Andrew Gurr, *Playgoing in Shakespeare's England*, reviews the evidence on both sides, eventually supporting Harbage's view, albeit with some reservations.

[26] *Playgoing in Shakespeare's England*, p. 4, and 'The Shakespearean Stage', *The Norton Shakespeare*, ed. Stephen Greenblatt et al., first edition, p. 3285.

[27] Dekker, *The Gull's Hornbook*, in *Thomas Dekker*, ed. E. D. Penry, p. 98.

The size and variety of the theatre audience forced playwrights to think about its tastes in an abstract, collective way, but the results of their thinking were very different from the deliberately universalizing strategies favoured by clergymen-poets like George Herbert, Phineas Fletcher, and Robert Herrick. In the commercial theatre, the playwright's effort to anticipate audience responses often led to a consideration of features that divide the audience as well as those that draw it together. In the epilogue to Shakespeare's *As You Like It* (1599), Rosalind jocularly suggests that the play contains something to please both men and women, but for different reasons:

> I charge you, O women, for the love you bear to men, to like as much of this play as please you. And I charge you, O men, for the love you bear to women—as I perceive by your simpering none of you hates them—that between you and the women the play may please.
>
> (10–14)

In the prologue to *Epicene*, Jonson compares the playwright's job to that of a cook at a public feast, who must satisfy people of different classes and occupations:

> For to present all custard or all tart,
> And have no other meats to bear a part,
> Or to want bread and salt, were but coarse art.
> The poet prays you, then, with better thought
> To sit; and when his cates are all in brought,
> Though there be none far-fet, there will dear-bought
> Be fit for ladies; some for lords, knights, squires,
> Some for your waiting wench, and city-wires,
> Some for your men and daughters of Whitefriars.
>
> (16–24)

In a similar vein, the closing speeches in Fletcher's *Beggar's Bush* (1622) recommend the play to various cadres among the spectators: ladies, gentlemen, honest merchants, lawyers, gamesters, drunkards, wives, maids, and midwives. All three playwrights assume that plays do not appeal in equal measure, or in the same fashion, to every playgoer, but 'catch' various members of the audience in different ways, depending upon his or her background and expectations.

Throughout the 1590s, when the only theatrical venues available were the large, socially inclusive outdoor amphitheatres, playwrights had to attempt to provide 'something for everyone' in the same play. In the early seventeenth century, however, the theatre companies' acute awareness of differentiated audience response increasingly led them to appeal to specialized market niches, a tactic that worked counter to, though never entirely eliminated, the socially levelling conception of the theatre as a marketplace open to all. Beginning in 1600, the adult theatre companies associated with large amphitheatres encountered competition from two newly established children's companies, in which the actors were prepubescent and adolescent boys. The boys performed in intimate indoor theatres that accommodated several hundred playgoers to a public amphitheatre's 2,000 or more. The indoor theatres were more comfortable physically: every audience member received a seat, and a roof kept out inclement weather. They also charged high prices for admission—about six times what it cost to attend the larger open-air theatres on the South Bank. Modern theatre historians thus call these indoor venues 'private theatres', not because they were restricted to members in the manner of a private club, but because their much higher admission fees effectively created a socially exclusive alternative to the tightly packed, heterogeneous crowds at the Globe or the Fortune.

The children's companies appealed to an affluent, well-educated, probably largely male audience. As I have already noted, the Inns of Court were home to some of London's best-heeled and most avid playgoers, ideal customers for this new medium. It is not surprising that playwriting for the private theatres shows much closer affinities to amateur non-dramatic writing than does the playwriting for the public theatres. In particular, the vogue for satire, begun in verse at the Inns of Court in the 1590s, soon emerges in the repertoire of the boys' companies. Nor is it surprising that a few Inns of Court poets, John Marston in particular, should write plays calculated to appeal to the tastes of the private theatregoers. In the first decade of the seventeenth century, some of the most important plays were written for the boys' companies: Marston's entire dramatic oeuvre; Jonson's *Cynthia's Revels* (1600), *Poetaster*, and *Epicene*; Middleton's *Michaelmas Term* (1604) and *A Trick to Catch the Old One* (1607), Beaumont's *The Knight of the Burning Pestle* (1607), Lording Barry's *Ram Alley* (1608), the collaborative plays *Westward Ho* (1604) and *Eastward Ho* (1605), and many of Chapman's plays. The boys' companies were most often associated with comedy of manners, but they performed tragedies as well: among them Marston's revenge plays, and Chapman's *Bussy d'Ambois* (1603) and its sequel, *The Revenge of Bussy d'Ambois* (printed 1613).

The adult companies were quick to notice the departure of their highest-paying customers to the more intimate environs of the private theatres. By 1609 The King's Men, the dominant theatrical troupe of the period, had developed a strategy to regain its lost market share. It secured permission to perform not only at the Globe, its big, open-air theatre on the South Bank, but also at an indoor theatre in Blackfriars, north of the Thames and close to the Inns of Court. Until the closing of the theatres in 1642, the King's Men continued to maintain this double venue. During the summer, when the weather was mild, long days afforded plenty of light for outdoor productions, and the court was on progress in the countryside, the company acted in the Globe. It moved to Blackfriars during the colder months, when London and Westminster were full of affluent courtiers and provincial visitors conducting legal business. Soon other companies followed suit on a lesser scale. The professionalism of the adult troupes, and their sheer stamina—they performed five or more times per week to the boys' one performance—meant that they soon regained their dominance. After 1609 the boy's company that had previously played at Blackfriars struggled on at a new location, but it was no longer in the market for important plays, and by 1613 its remnants were absorbed into an adult troupe.

For playwrights, the King's Men's Blackfriars theatre combined the social and performing advantages of an intimate, exclusive playing space with the highly developed acting skills of a professional adult repertory company. Numerous important Jacobean plays were written for first performance at Blackfriars, and some reflect the special features of this theatre in either physical or conceptual ways. Ben Jonson's *The Alchemist*, though performed at the Globe as well, is highly conscious of its location: set in 'a house in Blackfriars', it maps the theatre space onto the immediate neighbourhood outside. The class tensions of *Coriolanus*, one of Shakespeare's first plays for Blackfriars, may reflect his awareness of the way the new theatre, unlike the Globe, divided the well-to-do from their less affluent neighbours.

The increasing stratification of the theatre audience no doubt gave playwrights more choice over which subsection of theatregoers they wished to address, even while it heightened their already highly attuned sense of the various ways in which their work might be received. Ben Jonson satirizes the adequation of play to audience capacity in *Bartholomew Fair*, in which the story of Hero and Leander is retold for supposedly plebeian fairgoers as a puppet show about a Thames waterman and his whore brawling in an alehouse. Significantly John Littlewit, the author of the puppet-play, is a relatively affluent Londoner, and, so it happens, are most of the members of the puppet-show's audience—but they have gone to the Fair in a slumming spirit, and expect to see something appropriately demotic and crude. Francis Beaumont's *The Knight of the Burning Pestle* is equally sophisticated. A play about a grocer and his wife incongruously attending a private theatre performance, it dramatizes the clash of expectations that ensues when different 'taste groups' make incompatible demands upon the same playing space. Just as Dekker had noted in *The Gull's Hornbook*, the grocers, having paid admission, are as fully entitled to their seats as the gentlefolk who habitually attend performances. Once there, however, they find the theatrical fare on offer not to their liking because it 'girds at citizens'—that is, exploits to satiric effect the sense of social superiority the gentry feel to artisans and shopkeepers. The grocers insist upon interleaving 'their' naively heroic play, as improvised by their apprentice, with the painfully conventional city comedy the actors have been planning to perform. *The Knight of the Burning Pestle* stages and interrogates the way in which audience desire collaborates with the skill of actors and playwrights to produce the theatrical fare presented before them.

The frankly commercial nature of the playhouse and the less-than-exalted social rank of the people who worked there as actors or as playwrights combined to consign playwriting to a relatively low status, especially early in the period. As I mentioned earlier, when Thomas Bodley established a library at Oxford at the turn of the seventeenth century, he arranged with the Stationer's Company that they would send to his library in perpetuity a copy of every book they published—with the exception of plays. As he explained to his head librarian, Thomas James:

> Were it so ... that some little profit might be reaped (which God knows is very little) out of some of our playbooks, the benefit thereof will nothing near countervail the harm that the scandal will bring unto the library, when it shall be given out, that we stuff it full of baggage books ... This is my opinion, wherein if I err, I think I shall err with infinite others.[28]

In fact, the status of playwriting did rise steadily during the Jacobean and Caroline period—partly, no doubt, because of the extremely high quality of the best plays, and partly because the success of relatively expensive venues like Blackfriars tended to push the theatre upmarket and lend it greater social cachet. While the playwrights who came of age in the 1580s and 1590s came

---

[28] G. Wheeler, ed., *Letters of Sir Thomas Bodley to Thomas James, Keeper of the Bodleian Library*, pp. 219–222.

from artisanal backgrounds, by the beginning of the seventeenth century individuals from more distinguished families were beginning to be attracted to playwriting as a profession. John Marston's father was a wealthy lawyer, and John Beaumont, John Fletcher, and John Ford hailed from the gentry. By the 1630s James Shirley's plays frankly addressed an upscale audience culturally little different from the courtiers and prosperous citizens who would return to the theatre after the Restoration in 1660. It is not surprising that Shirley, along with Jonson in his writing for the private theatres, should become such powerful models for Restoration playwrights.

Still, throughout the period playwriting continued to be a profession with relatively low entrance requirements. The modest rise in status accorded to playwriting had little to do with its intrinsic appeal as a career to members of the elite. Instead, it came about because some of the playwrights themselves were re-imagining the nature of their work and reconceiving its value. The writers who were the most likely to participate in that re-imagination were those who already had one foot in another kind of literary marketplace, the rules and assumptions of which were rather different. It is to that marketplace that we now turn.

Patronage

Although the theatres provided a living for a small number of writers, they obviously had no use for lyric poetry or epic, for translated poems, for prose narratives, for devotional works. Much of this work, as we have seen, was not explicitly renumerated—and thus I have called it 'amateur'—but some non-dramatic writers in the period did receive compensation from patrons: wealthy individuals, families, or, occasionally, corporate entities such as a craft guild or one of the Inns of Court. The patron's social eminence and affluence enabled him or her to bestow prestige, employment, and material benefits upon the poet. The poet, in exchange, could provide a flattering written reflection of the patron's power and virtue. An excellent poet could even offer the prospect of literary immortality:

> 'Gainst death and all oblivious enmity
> Shall you pace forth; your praise shall still find room
> Even in the eyes of all posterity
> That wear this world out to the ending doom.
> (William Shakespeare, Sonnet 55, 9–12)

In other words, patronage was a two-sided transaction, though it may seem a lopsided one, with the poet receiving the more substantial and immediate rewards. On the other hand, if Lucy, Countess of Bedford, William, Earl of Pembroke, and Henry, Earl of Southampton are remembered today, it is primarily as patrons—because such writers as Jonson, Donne, and Shakespeare celebrated them in their poetry.

Patronage confronts modern scholars with historical and conceptual challenges rather different from those presented by the playwriting system. The economic rationale of the profit-oriented Renaissance theatre was novel at the time, but the organization of literary production on a commercial basis has become familiar in the centuries since. Patronage, by contrast, seems strange to us but was a familiar aspect of medieval and early modern life. Aristocratic support of the arts had a long history in England: Geoffrey Chaucer, for instance, worked in the household of John of Gaunt; John Skelton was a tutor and ecclesiastic in the court of Henry VIII. Under Elizabeth I, Leicester, Cecil, Oxford, and Essex all provided patronage to writers.[29] Yet when writers sought patronage, they were not doing something vocationally specific, as artists and scholars do today when they apply for grants from nonprofit foundations to support their work. Both the kinds of full-time writers I am calling 'professional' and those non-full-time writers I am calling 'amateurs' might seek patronage, though the kinds of rewards they were seeking might well be different, for all of them were participating in a socially ubiquitous institution. Literary patronage was a special case, or extension, of the quasi-feudal bonds that organized society at all levels and in all occupational categories, tying individuals to those above them, to whom they offered allegiance and service, and to those below them, whom they rewarded for usefulness and loyalty.[30] As we shall see, the system was beginning to change in the early seventeenth century, but the old pattern of assumptions persisted, governing the behaviour of poets and of patrons and influencing the ways in which they imagined their roles.

'Patronage' was a very loose category. If a rich man sent a writer a small sum of money in appreciation for having a book dedicated to him, that was called 'patronage', but so was a close, longstanding connection between artist and patron based upon similarity of interests and tastes. The late Elizabethan and Jacobean periods offer several instances of such ongoing patronage,

---

[29] For a discussion of literary patronage in England under the Tudors and James I, see Richard A. McCabe, *'Ungainefull Art': Poetry, Patronage, and Print in the Early Modern Era*.

[30] For the way political patronage functioned, and failed to function, in Jacobean and Caroline England, see Linda Levy Peck, *Court Patronage and Corruption in Early Stuart England*.

which was obviously much more valuable to a writer than a one-off contribution. In 1593, Shakespeare dedicated his narrative poem *Venus and Adonis* to the young, artistically inclined Earl of Southampton; in 1594 he dedicated *The Rape of Lucrece* to the same individual. The warmth of the second dedication suggests that the first poem had been well received, especially since if Southampton had been unforthcoming Shakespeare would presumably have chosen a different dedicatee second time round. Indeed, circumstantial evidence suggests that Southampton's interest in Shakespeare, or at least in Shakespeare's theatre company, persisted for a number of years, since the Lord Chamberlain's Men got in trouble in 1601 for performing a play (possibly *Richard II*) at the request of the Essex conspirators, of whom Southampton was one. Some critics believe that Southampton was the beautiful young man addressed in Shakespeare's sonnets. And the two men's connection possibly persisted to the end of Shakespeare's career, because *The Tempest*, Shakespeare's last solely authored play, includes material drawn from supposedly confidential documents provided to the Virginia Company, in which Southampton was deeply involved as an investor. Other examples of such sustained relationships between poet and patron are a bit less conjectural. Ben Jonson often acknowledged the help he received from the Earl of Pembroke and from other members of the Sidney / Herbert family over a period of at least two decades. Lucy, Countess of Bedford gave ongoing support of various kinds to Ben Jonson, Samuel Daniel, John Florio, George Chapman, and John Donne. Magdalen Herbert, Lady Danvers extended financial help to Donne. Michael Drayton lived first in the household of Sir Henry Goodere, then in the household of Lucy, Countess of Bedford, and finally was affiliated with the household of Sir William Aston.

Many of the details even of these longstanding patronage relationships, extending over years or decades, remain unclear to us. Of course, writers are much more likely to have left a record of their supplications than their benefactors are of the gifts they bestowed. Many poems are addressed to aristocrats in the most effusively panegyric terms. In 'To the Countess of Huntingdon', Donne marvels:

> You are at first hand all that's fair and right,
> And other good reflects but back your light.
> You are a perfectness.
>
> (81–83)

He describes the Countess of Bedford in a similar vein:

> Madam, Reason is our soul's left hand, faith her right,

> By these we reach divinity, that's you,
>
> ...
>
> You are then God's masterpiece.
> ('To the Countess of Bedford', 1–2, 33)

In 'To William, Earl of Pembroke', Ben Jonson declares:

> I do but name thee, Pembroke, and I find
> It is an epigram on all mankind,
> Against the bad, but of and to the good.
> (1–3)

Of Mary Wroth, he fantasizes:

> Madam, had all antiquity been lost
> All history sealed up and all fables crossed
> That we had left us, nor by time nor place
> Least mention of a nymph, a muse, a grace,
> But even their names were to be made anew,
> Who could not but create them all from you?
> ('To Mary, Lady Wroth', [*Epigrams* 105], 1–6)

Printed books routinely carry equally hyperbolic dedications to wealthy and prominent individuals. Obviously such blandishments constitute attempts to curry favour, but it is usually hard to know what a writer is commemorating or hoping to induce by means of a dedication. Some poems seem to be slightly veiled begging letters, while others are thanking a benefactor for support already rendered. Some dedications to printed books apparently solicit patronage rather in the spirit of a celebrity endorsement that might encourage humbler customers to purchase a book. Usually, however, we do not know how the patrons or prospective patrons responded, if they responded at all. We rarely know how much a patron typically offered a writer and for what kind of work, or even if there was any 'typical' relationship at all, as opposed to entirely improvisatory, individual arrangements.

The breadth of what counted as patronage doubtless helps to obscure how patronage relationships worked, and the difficulty is compounded by the fact that few records have survived. Still, our vagueness about exactly what literary patronage involved is not merely a matter of lack of documentation. In most circumstances, both poet and patron deliberately left the precise terms of the patronage transaction unspecified. The patron is supposed to reward talent and loyalty, not pay by the line or the stanza. The client is supposed to admire the patron's generosity and taste, not demand a set remuneration. Even while they seek benefits, patronage poets typically disclaim their self-interest and their lack of concern for personal self-enrichment, pretending to be merely so dazzled by the patron's excellence that versified praise spontaneously escapes from them.

To people accustomed to a more 'businesslike' way of doing things, the patronage mode can seem obfuscatory and the poets' protests of disinterestedness obviously hollow. Thus, Stanley Fish writes incredulously of Ben Jonson, who continually emphasizes the distance between the true poet and a mere flatterer or parasite: [He writes] a poetry which declares unreal the network of dependencies and obligations that to all appearances directs and regulates his every action. It is an extraordinary project . . . for it involves a quite brazen denial in the midst of what seems irrefutable evidence.[31]

Perhaps patronage is not to be understood, however—or at least sympathetically understood—as an occluded form of market relationship. Literary patronage closely resembles those non-market transactions that Marcel Mauss and other anthropologists and historians after him have classified under the name of the 'gift economy'.[32] Natalie Davis has demonstrated the pervasive importance of the gift mode for people at all social levels in sixteenth-century France, and her argument could easily be extended to seventeenth-century England.[33] A gift economy typically shies away from strict quid pro quo arrangements. One gives a gift out of hospitality, affection, charity, or noblesse oblige, not because one is delivering upon a contract. While in the marketplace the exchanged objects are of commensurable material value—indeed, their very exchange points to their commensurability—in gift exchange the emphasis falls not on the equivalent desirability of the exchanged objects themselves, but on the love or alliance symbolized by those objects. As we still say about presents, 'it's the thought that counts'. In fact, not only must the exchange of gifts be

---

[31] Stanley Fish, 'Author-Readers: Jonson's Community of the Same', *Representations* 7 (1984), pp. 26–58.
[32] Marcel Mauss, *The Gift: The Form and Reason for Exchange in Archaic Societies*, trans. W. D. Halls.
[33] Natalie Davis, *The Gift in Sixteenth-Century France*.

technically free, but that freedom has to be strongly asserted, otherwise the gifts cannot perform their symbolic function of properly testifying to love, alliance, or respect. At the same time, and apparently paradoxically, the pointedly non-commensurate character of the gift-giving does not necessarily make it *optional*, for suitable reciprocation is often socially required. The important difference between the gift exchange and the commercial transaction is not in the degree to which the participants feel compelled to observe its terms. Rather, it lies in what the exchange means to them and how they describe it, to themselves and to others.

Because both patrons and poets shrank from delineating their transaction too exactly, they might offer one another a very wide variety of services and rewards. The 'favour' poets accepted from patrons often took in-kind forms rather than a monetary gift. Patrons might, for instance, offer their favourite poets clothing, a valuable gift in an age in which textiles were labour-intensive to produce and therefore very expensive. Sir James Hay bought Donne his clerical robes when he was ordained. Patrons often permitted writers to stay at their houses, either as a private secretary or tutor, or as a house guest. Francis Townsend, Esmé Stuart, Sir Robert Cotton, and Sir Robert Sidney provided room and board to Ben Jonson for long periods; the Countess of Cumberland apparently extended similar hospitality to Aemelia Lanyer. The Druries, for whom John Donne wrote the *Anniversaries*, took him with them on an extended European tour, and later leased him a house on their property at a nominal rent.

The heterogeneous compensation accepted by patronage poets is unsurprising given the financial circumstances of the Jacobean and Caroline aristocrats, who were land- and house-rich but typically strapped for ready money. While it was relatively cheap for them to add retainers to their large households, coming up with substantial cash payments would have been much more difficult. In fact, given the severe shortage of coin throughout England in this period, the reliance upon credit and non-monetary payment was routine not only in literary patronage situations but in many other transactional relationships as well: household servants, for instance, ordinarily received part of their wages as clothing, room, and board, and merchants often had to accept in-kind, barter-style reimbursement from their customers and from fellow merchants.[34] Still, the kinds of support patrons offer contrasts strikingly with the fully monetarized literary marketplace

---

[34] Craig Muldrew, *The Economy of Obligation The Culture of Credit and Social Relations in Early Modern England*, pp. 3–7.

of the London playhouses, which had clear, often contractually specified expectations of writers, and predictable rates of cash payment.

If the rewards patrons offered writers were diverse, the 'service' writers offered patrons was even more various. The most clear-cut, but the rarest, form of literary service was the sort Ben Jonson provided, writing the annual Christmas masque for James's court. Jonson provided the poetry while the architect Inigo Jones designed the sets, and they each received a fee for their labours. From the writer's point of view, there must have been little difference between this form of patronage and the public theatres' straightforward compensation arrangements. Far more often, however, the poet's service to a patron took a more miscellaneous form. A poet with an ongoing affiliation with a patron would not only compose poems remarking on his patrons' fine qualities, but would also typically commemorate marriages, promotions, or deaths in the patron's family. These tasks could be delicate at times. When Frances Howard, the mistress of George Chapman's patron Robert Carr, successfully sued for an annulment of her marriage to the Earl of Essex, Chapman celebrated the occasion with a narrative poem, 'Andromeda Liberata' (1614). In this retelling of the mythical story Frances figured as the beautiful Andromeda, chained to a rock and threatened by a sea-monster, but rescued by Carr, in the role of the hero Perseus. Essex's supporters were outraged that he was, by implication, the rock, and Chapman hurriedly produced a 'Justification' that rather lamely insisted that the rock was not meant to be Essex at all, and that the sea-monster was 'the base, ignoble, barbarous, giddy multitude' that was liable to misinterpret his poem. In happier circumstances, a patron might subsidize not only the poems that celebrated him- or herself, but other projects as well, which could reflect glory on the patron at least as effectively. Prince Henry may have offered support to Chapman for his Homer translations not only because the project was a highly visible one, but because it suited the persona Henry wanted to project, as a future king who possessed military ambitions as well as serious scholarly tastes.

Indeed, in many cases the patron did not expect a writer to produce any particular kind of poetry at all, because although a poet's literary skill may well have brought him to the attention of the patron, the poet did not receive compensation for the poetry per se. In the early modern period, the Crown and nobility dispensed all kinds of employment. Aristocrats needed assistance in managing their lands, handling their correspondence and legal affairs, and educating their children. Those who held government offices employed skilled underlings to help execute their charge. Many large landowners controlled seats in the House of Commons, which, despite the rhetoric of freely elected representation, was actually packed with candidates chosen by local magnates. In addition, since Henry VIII had transferred former church lands into the hands of the laity, members of the aristocracy also controlled appointments to many ecclesiastical positions.

The kinds of people who became writers were prime candidates for such posts. Unlike painters or musicians, who required costly equipment and underwent long, specialized training, writers did not require any unusual apparatus, and the non-technical education that fitted them for their art also made them eligible for any job requiring general intelligence and an ability to read and write. Thus, aristocrats with literary tastes as often subsidized writers by putting them to work in their households as by making a straightforward payment for literary services. In the 1590s, Mary, Countess of Pembroke employed Samuel Daniel as her eldest son's tutor; later Daniel worked for the Earl of Cumberland in a similar capacity, tutoring Cumberland's daughter, Anne Clifford. John Florio was made Groom of the Privy Chamber to Queen Anne, probably at the intercession of the Countess of Bedford. Likewise, in the 1650s Andrew Marvell worked in the household of Thomas Lord Fairfax, as his secretary and as a tutor to his daughter.

As a result, by the first decade of the seventeenth century, a variety of motives are distinguishable among the crowd of writers who pressed their services upon patrons. For many, the goal was a position of trust and responsibility and, in an era before standardized testing and civil service exams, a display of literary skill could suggest one's fitness for the task. Among major writers in the period, John Donne, Francis Bacon, George Herbert, and Andrew Marvell seem to have imagined their writerly ability as the efflorescence of some more general form of competence: their many talents included the writing of essays or poems. In the first decade of the seventeenth century Donne, for instance, found it frustrating that he was well-known for his writing, but could not obtain a diplomatic post or employment in high-level government administration. When his friend Henry Goodere suggested that he ingratiate himself with a patron—possibly the Countess of Huntingdon—by writing a panegyric poem, he was reluctant to do so, because 'that knowledge which she hath of me, was the beginning of a graver course, than of a poet, into which (that I may also keep my dignity) I would not seem to relapse'.[35]

---

[35] For a discussion of Donne's relationship with his patrons, see Arthur Marotti, 'John Donne and the Rewards of Patronage', in *Patronage in the Renaissance*, ed. Stephen Orgel and Guy Fitch Lytle, p. 223.

If such a writer succeeded in obtaining the kind of position he desired, he became the kind of author I have put in the 'amateur' category. Writers of this persuasion were only 'professionals' if they failed at their primary aim and were forced to make do with whatever they could earn from their writing alone. In contrast, some of their contemporaries—Ben Jonson, George Chapman, Michael Drayton, and John Fletcher—thought of their vocations as writers as primary, not ancillary. A writer in the latter category sought and accepted patronage *as a poet* who was willing to take other kinds of employment if necessary. Thus, Ben Jonson accompanied Sir Walter Ralegh's son on a tour of the Continent, as a sort of literary chaperone, but he did not for that reason consider himself to have become a tutor.

One might imagine, therefore, that there were two distinct patronage 'tracks' in the late sixteenth and early seventeenth centuries: one for those who aspired to some non-literary position, and one for those who characterized themselves as artists. But since the kind of reward given to a fine writer was so often in the form of congenial employment, and because getting congenial employment of any kind, literary or not, typically demanded recourse to the patronage system, the line I have suggested between the 'professional' and the 'amateur' writer could sometimes become a very blurry one. In some instances, moreover, the patron's understanding of the relationship may have differed from the writer's. Michael Drayton, who spent virtually his whole life in service to wealthy members of the gentry and nobility, considered himself a poet by vocation, but his patrons probably employed him as a tutor or secretary. Samuel Daniel's own account leaves it unclear whether his position as tutor in Mary Sidney Herbert's artistically inclined household encouraged him to try his own hand at poetry, or whether she offered him that position originally in recognition of his literary talents.

It is also true, of course, that the same person who at one point in his life is hoping that his talent as a writer will help him achieve a lucrative and interesting employment might at another point depend more frankly on revenue from his writing alone. John Donne's career, to which I've already alluded briefly, testifies to this kind of mutability of fortune. Donne made a name for himself as a gifted poet at a very young age; in 1618 Ben Jonson was still telling William Drummond that in his opinion, Donne had 'written all his best pieces ere he was twenty-five years old'—that is, before 1597.[36] In that year Donne obtained a position as secretary to Thomas Egerton Lord Keeper of the Great Seal, considered the harbinger of a brilliant future.

---

[36] *Informations to William Drummond of Hawthornden*, lines 82–83.

But Donne's impetuous clandestine marriage to Egerton's teenage niece in 1601 resulted in his dismissal, and Egerton's refusal to hire him back ruined his employment prospects for years. In the decade that followed, Donne behaved less like the amateur he had once been and more like a professional patronage writer. He produced the controversial works *Pseudo Martyr* (1610) and *Ignatius His Conclave* (1611) in hopes of attracting the attention of King James, and wrote *The Anniversaries* for the Drury family as memorials to their daughter Elizabeth. His verse epistles from this period suggest that he was also receiving help from the Countess of Bedford, Magdalen Herbert, the Countess of Hertford, and the Countess of Salisbury. Although Donne continually sought non-literary employment, his path to preferment was blocked by no less than King James himself, who was convinced that Donne would make a good clergyman. James flatly refused to allow Donne any position of responsibility until he finally acceded to James's wishes and took holy orders, after which his promotion was swift.

As Donne's vicissitudes indicate, one important characteristic of the early modern employment system was its unembarrassedly high degree of personalization. Nowadays—whether or not they actually do—universities, businesses, and other employers are supposed to base employment and promotion decisions on 'objective criteria', and many such decisions are made by committees rather than by individuals precisely in order to reduce the element of personal arbitrariness. In the early seventeenth century, on the other hand, favouritism, nepotism, and the use of 'connections' were entirely open and unashamed, and many practices that now seem to us unethical were customary. Thus, in 1656, when Anne Clifford went to court against her Westmoreland tenants, she noted with satisfaction that the panel of judges included 'my cousin Oliver St. John, Lord Chief Justice of the Common Pleas' (she won her case).[37] In such a system, connections that involved kinship obligations could be especially helpful for writers. John Fletcher was most likely introduced to the Earl and Countess of Huntingdon, his patrons, by his playwriting collaborator Francis Beaumont, who was a relative and friend of the earl. Thomas Carew worked as secretary to Sir Dudley Carleton, his cousin by marriage, on diplomatic missions to Venice and the Hague, though he eventually lost this position for some unspecified indiscretion, possibly a satiric poem about Carleton's wife.

---

[37] *Anne Clifford's Autobiographical Writing 1590–1676*, ed. Jessica Malay, p. 138.

George Herbert's career offers telling evidence of the way such kinship networks operated. A younger brother of Edward Lord Herbert of Cherbury, George received a fine education and had excellent prospects despite the fact that Edward, by the laws of primogeniture, inherited title and estate. George asked his stepfather, Sir John Danvers, and probably also his distant relative William Herbert, Earl of Pembroke, for help obtaining the office of Cambridge University Orator, a position which required him to welcome all distinguished visitors to the university. One attraction of the post was the chance it gave its holder to display his rhetorical talents before powerful individuals who might offer further advancement. Indeed, James I and the Marquis of Richmond both noticed Herbert's talents as Orator, and seemed inclined to promote his career. But when these potential benefactors died in 1624 / 1625, and the Herbert family found itself out of favour in the court of the new King Charles I, George's dreams of secular preferment were thwarted. His eventual decision to take orders comprised a clear disavowal of his earlier worldly ambition—'the way that takes the town', as he calls it in 'Affliction I'. But in his new walk of life, he did not repudiate the patronage system. Instead he sought patronage once again, but for different reasons. Philip Herbert, who had succeeded to the earldom after his brother William's death, employed George as a chaplain and helped him obtain his rectorship at Bemerton; George asked Anne Clifford, Philip's wife, for funds to help renovate the church there. Both William and Philip Herbert were important patrons of the arts, but it is not clear that they had any idea that George Herbert wrote poetry: they were helping him out because he was a kinsman. It is not surprising that, as Michael Schoenfeldt has noted, Herbert characteristically translates divine authority and beneficence into a patronage relationship between a powerful authority figure and his dependent.[38]

> Having been tenant long to a rich lord,
> Not thriving, I resolved to be bold
> And make suit unto him, to afford
> A new small-rented lease, and cancel th'old.
> ('Redemption', 1–4)

When Herbert's poetry is posthumously published in 1633, the printer asks rhetorically in the prefatory epistle: 'The dedication of this work having been

---

[38] Michael Schoenfeldt, *Prayer and Power: George Herbert and Renaissance Courtship*.

made by the author to the Divine Majesty only, how should we presume to interest any mortal man in the patronage of it?' The effect is less to repudiate the patronage transaction than cosmically to magnify it, imagining God functioning as a kind of super-patron in his relations with human beings.

How does the patronage system determine the sorts of people who write poetry and the kinds of poetry that gets written? Obviously, some people had easier access to patrons and were better able to take advantage of whatever opportunities they offered. In this way the nature of literary patronage could shape the talent pool in ways that are hard to trace in retrospect because of the invisibility of the people excluded. One consequence of the often personal quality of the relationship between poet and patron was that the social character of the poet could become an important aspect of his appeal. John Donne and Ben Jonson, whose patrons were sophisticated courtiers, were witty men with strong personalities and a flair for conversation, unabashed at the tables of the great. Michael Drayton, by contrast, better known for his sweetness and virtue than for clever repartée, found more sympathetic support among the provincial gentry.

Despite the fact that aristocratic women such as the Countess of Bedford and the Countess of Montgomery were important patrons, women writers were once again at a serious disadvantage. It was much more difficult for most women to take advantage of the in-kind benefits that many patrons extended to their favoured poets. Jonson lived apart from his wife and son in the households of various noblemen for years on end, but his separation from his family caused no scandal. Nor did Donne's, when he left his pregnant wife and numerous children to accompany Sir Walter Chute and, later, Robert Drury on long European tours. For a married woman, to abandon her domicile and children would have been legally problematic and socially almost impossible.

The only woman poet in the period who seems to have sought patronage was Aemelia Lanyer. Lanyer was the daughter and wife of court musicians, and her family background presumably made her more aware than most women of how the patronage system worked. Yet her options were limited by the fact that she could not affiliate herself with the household of a male aristocrat without inviting the suggestion that she was his concubine. (As a young women she was, in fact, mistress to Henry Cary, Lord Hunsdon, who married her off to Alphonso Lanyer when she became pregnant.) In her 1610 collection of poetry, *Salve Deus Rex Judaeorum*, Lanyer therefore addresses an audience she carefully specifies as female: 'I have written this small volume, or little book, for the general use of all virtuous ladies and gentlewomen of this kingdom; and in commendation of some particular persons of our own sex.' The 'particular persons' are, of course, the potential patrons, the subjects of the complimentary poems that take up more than half the volume: Queen Anne, Princess Elizabeth, Lady Arbella Stuart, Mary Dowager Countess of Pembroke, Lucy Countess of Bedford, and others. In 'At Cookham', Lanyer describes time spent at a country estate in the company of the Countess of Cumberland and her daughter, Anne Clifford. The Countess was in litigation with her male relations over Anne's estate, which her late husband, on his death, had bestowed upon his brother in order to avoid settling lands and title on a female heir. The Countess's bitter experience of patriarchy may have inclined her to the gesture of female solidarity implied by the support of a woman poet. Still, the Countess of Cumberland's defiance of the male establishment was not merely highly unusual, but by definition tenuous. In due course her daughter was married to the Earl of Dorset, effectively breaking the little circle of female companionship, and eventually the King upheld the right of the male kinfolk to inherit the disputed property. By the time Lanyer published *Salve Deus Rex Judaeorum*, the idyll at Cookham was already described nostalgically. Lanyer's attempts to conjure forth longer-term support from her 'worthy ladies' evidently failed, because although she lived until 1645, she apparently wrote no more poems.

Patronage not only helps determine which people have the opportunity to write, but also what they write about. Because the great patrons of early seventeenth-century poetry were also, very often, important figures in the state, some literary scholars have claimed that the institution of patronage, especially in conjunction with censorship of the press and theatres, effectively silenced literary dissent. In this view, opposition to authority, if it were voiced at all, had to be recuperated and incorporated into the dominant order, in a way that reinforced rather than challenged existing social arrangements. Other critics claim that the patrons were either less demanding that a single line be followed, or less attentive to nuance than one might expect, so a fair amount of poetic latitude was possible.[39]

---

[39] Those emphasizing the way Renaissance literature reflects hegemonic viewpoints (though they do not base their claim solely on the existence of patronage) include Jonathan Goldberg, *James I and the Politics of Literature* and Stephen Greenblatt, 'Invisible Bullets' in *Shakespearean Negotiations*. Those who argue for the possibility of genuine protest, even in patron-sponsored writing, include Annabel Patterson, *Censorship and Interpretation: The Conditions of Writing and Reading in Early Modern England* and David Norbrook, *Poetry and Politics in the English Renaissance: Revised Edition*. Malcolm Smuts argues for the heterogeneity

In fact, the effects of the patronage system on literary output were quite complicated. The Tudors and the Stuarts were not entirely unaware of the utility of quasi-literary propaganda. In the 1530s Thomas Cromwell employed writers willing to justify Henry VIII's reorganization of the English church, and Mary Tudor's government employed a polemicist, Miles Huggarde, who had a special gift for explaining the advantages of Catholicism in simple, vivid vernacular. Some propaganda subsidy continues in the seventeenth century. In 1626, when Charles, desperate to stave off bankruptcy, extorted a forced 'loan' from taxpayers in lieu of the levy Parliament had refused to grant him, one of his loyal clergymen, Roger Manwaring, preached eloquently on the subject's financial obligation to support God's deputy on earth. Charles arranged to have the sermon printed and distributed under the title 'Religion and Allegiance'. This limited use of writers willing to defend royal policy or actions on particular issues falls well short, however, of a sweeping policy on the political uses of the arts. Both James and Charles believed that their power derived from God's mandate, not from the will of the people; in consequence, they tended to slight the importance of public opinion. While Elizabeth had encouraged a kind of royal pageantry open to large, heterogeneous groups of people—progresses, jousts, and so on—James, Charles, and other members of the royal family fostered the court masque, restricted in attendance to members of the court, foreign ambassadors, and relatively few onlookers. These events often involved close collaboration between the patron of the masque and its poet and designer. In the first years of James's reign, the motif of the Christmas masque was generally selected by Queen Anne, who performed in the masque with her entourage of ladies, so that she was arguably not merely commissioning the performance but co-creating it. Ben Jonson, Thomas Carew, and William D'Avenant might use the occasion of the masque for dramatizing the king's, queen's, or prince's perspective on current events, but the practical reach of these spectacles did not extend beyond the circle of admittedly influential and powerful people who witnessed them. By the 1630s, when opposition to Charles's policies was largely emanating from groups outside the court, the masques were ineffective as propaganda because they were not witnessed by those segments of the population who most needed convincing of the wisdom of their king's policies.

---

of viewpoints among James's courtiers in 'Cultural Diversity and Cultural Change at the Court of James I', *The Mental World of the Jacobean Court*, ed. Linda Levy Peck, pp. 99–112.

Throughout the period, government control of the arts tended to take a negative form: censoring books and plays before they were printed and performed, and punishing expression deemed defamatory or seditious. In the early 1590s, the boys' theatre for which Lyly wrote his plays seems to have been closed down, possibly because its satiric comedy was cutting too close to home. In 1599, the Bishop's Ban prohibited satires, epigrams, and histories that had not been approved by the Privy Council, and works by a variety of controversial authors, including the young Joseph Hall, John Marston, Thomas Middleton, and John Davies. In the Jacobean and Caroline period punishments were more limited and sporadic. Ben Jonson and George Chapman landed in prison for some anti-Scottish humour in *Eastward Ho*; Thomas Middleton got in trouble for the transparent political satire, *A Game at Chess* (1624). In the 1630s, as the culture wars between the court and their Puritan opponents heated up: William Prynne, as already noted in the Introduction, had his ears cut off for insulting Queen Henrietta Maria in his anti-theatrical treatise *Histrio-Mastix*. Perhaps overt encouragement of more acceptable forms of expression was deemed unnecessary, given that patronage poets had little reason to turn on those who rewarded them. For obvious reasons, motives are hard to read in this case; when a Spenser, Jonson, Donne, or Chapman praises powerful people, it is difficult to know whether he does so because he sincerely approves of them, or because flattery serves his personal advantage, or both. One's benefactors, after all, are likely to seem wiser and more virtuous than those who spurn one's talents.

The probability that the patronage system muted some kinds of literary dissent is increased by the fact that the circle of potential patrons was not only relatively small, but multiply interconnected by blood, marriage, and friendly association. William Herbert, Earl of Pembroke—one of the richest men in England and the most important literary patron of his day—provides as good a starting point as any for exploring the ramifications of this genealogical web. More than 100 literary works were dedicated to him, including Shakespeare's Folio of 1623. Pembroke paid for the architect Inigo Jones's study-tour of Italy, gave Ben Jonson an annual book allowance, and was a major donor to the Bodleian Library in Oxford. He may have been a patron of Philip Massinger as well, whose father had been his own father's estate manager.

On the paternal side, Pembroke was kin not only to Edward and George Herbert but also to Walter Ralegh; after Walter's execution, Pembroke tried to help his son to some preferment by bringing him to court, but to no avail,

King James objecting that the young man 'looked like his father's ghost'. William had equally illustrious literary connections on his mother's side of the family. His mother was Mary Sidney, Philip Sidney' sister—not only a fine writer herself but a patron of such writers as Edmund Spenser and Samuel Daniel, William's boyhood tutor. Robert Sidney, William's maternal uncle, wrote some poetry and was also an active patron despite his relatively straitened circumstances; he was the father of the accomplished writer Mary Wroth. After the death of her husband, Mary moved to her first cousin's estate, eventually becoming William's lover and bearing him two illegitimate children. Wroth's sonnet sequence, *Pamphilia to Amphilanthus*, and her prose romance, *Urania*, make veiled references to this affair.

William's younger brother Philip, named after his famous uncle, was more interested in art and architecture than literature; he was a major patron of Van Dyck and amassed a large collection of paintings. Nonetheless, he received many dedications from poets and presumably responded to at least some of them. In 1604 Philip married Susan De Vere, daughter of the major Elizabethan patron Edward de Vere, Earl of Oxford, and grandniece of Arthur Golding, the translator of Ovid, who had been her father's tutor. Like the marriage in the previous generation between the Herbert and Sidney families, the Herbert / De Vere marriage brought together two families with longstanding interests in the arts. In 1630, after Susan's death, Philip married Anne Clifford, the daughter of the Countess of Cumberland, Aemelia Lanyer's erstwhile patron. Anne Clifford was a niece of Lucy Russell, Countess of Bedford, another generous Jacobean literary patron. Lucy herself was William and Philip's second cousin on the Sidney side, through her father, Sir John Harington, tutor to James's daughter, Princess Elizabeth.

These multiply interwoven ties of blood, friendship, dependence, and intermarriage, of which both patrons and poets in the period were so keenly aware, quickly become confusing to many modern readers of seventeenth-century literature. Fortunately, comprehending their precise details is less important than understanding some of their general consequences for writers. Since the group of patrons was so small, having access to one of these individuals most likely enabled access to others. It may have also encouraged a certain amount of 'group think' on the part of patrons. The fact that Chapman, Donne, Jonson, Daniel, and a few others successfully obtain patronage over and over again may merely testify to their pre-eminent literary quality. Yet it also implies a certain degree of shared taste on the part of aristocratic patrons, and perhaps, too, the social inertia that tends to keep favouring those who have received benefits in the past. The dark obverse, of course, is the possibility that alienating one of these individuals might damage one's prospects with other potential supporters.

Nonetheless, despite all these interconnections, patrons were not a monolithic group, nor did they fall solidly behind their king on matters of policy. Several of James's leading courtiers—the Earls of Pembroke, Montgomery, Southampton, and Bedford gave little credence to their new monarch's authoritarian theory of kingship. Indeed, the royal family itself was hardly a happy unanimous clan. When James came to the English throne, many writers looked forward eagerly to a golden age: James himself, as I have already noted, wrote poetry and had published prose works on various subjects as well. In the event, James, like his predecessor Elizabeth, proffered little direct support to poets. The only imaginative writer to whom he showed significant favour was Ben Jonson and, despite his own literary endeavours, he took a greater personal interest in theology and political philosophy than in poetry. Early in his reign he authorized the massive work of translation and textual scholarship that produced a new translation of the Bible, the 'King James' version, in 1611—a work that was enormously influential for the later development of English poetry and prose, but which made little practical difference to poets at the time.

Fortunately for writers, the relationships among James, Queen Anne, and the heir apparent Prince Henry were distant. Anne almost immediately established a separate household from her husband, with a separate entourage, and Henry too acquired his own court after being installed as Prince of Wales in 1610. Born in 1594, Prince Henry matured into a charismatic, self-confident young man, the antithesis of his cautious, socially inept father. While James cultivated diplomatic relations with Catholic Spain, Henry favoured aggressive English colonial expansion and military intervention on behalf of Protestants on the Continent. These policy differences had strong personal overtones, and the rivalry between father and son received comment from many quarters.

Unlike his father, Henry gave direct financial support to poets, painters, and scientists. He attracted his own circle of writers, such as Daniel, Drayton, and Ralegh. Some have argued that the writers associated with the court of Prince Henry constituted a group of proto-republicans, suspicious of James's assertion of royal prerogative, and anticipating in some respects the opposition to royal absolutism that would eventually become violent in the late

1630s.[40] Yet Henry was also a patron of George Chapman, whose *Revenge of Bussy D'Ambois*, dedicated to the Catholic Earl of Arundel, defends the notoriously ferocious persecution of Protestants in France. The unprecedented torrent of literary grief that followed upon Henry's premature death in 1612 might have reflected not only many writers' sense of England's loss, but their sense of their own personally diminished prospects. Chapman, for instance, claimed that Henry had promised him the large sum of 300 pounds upon completion of his Homer translation, but in the event he had no way of collecting on this pledge.

Queen Anne, as Leeds Barroll has persuasively argued, was possibly the most significant royal patron.[41] She was an important supporter of the masque—often a chief player, and most likely more involved as well in the design of the performances than her easily distracted husband. As her ladies-in-waiting and intimate companions, she brought together women with a marked interest in the arts. These women were on friendly terms with one another, and related by blood or marriage; their husbands and male relations were often possessed of similarly artistic and literary tastes.[42] Mary Wroth, Lady Rich (in younger days, Philip Sidney's Stella), and the Countesses of Bedford, Derby, and Montgomery were part of this circle.

Further widening the range of opinions that writers could safely express, some artistically inclined aristocrats disliked either the atmosphere or the politics of James's court. The Earl and Countess of Huntingdon dwelt resolutely on their country estates, ignoring royal pleas for their attendance at court. They did not even show up for the 1613 wedding of Princess Elizabeth to Frederick, the Elector Palatine. The Huntingdons were patrons to Thomas Roe, John Donne, and John Fletcher; Fletcher's critics have detected strong anti-courtly sentiments in the poetry Fletcher addressed to the Huntingdons.[43] Michael Drayton, who writes movingly of the English provinces as pointedly opposed to court and city, obtained support from Sir William Aston, a Warwickshire gentleman with a similar aversion to the Jacobean court. Likewise, in the 1630s the Earl of Bridgewater, who commissioned *Comus* from John Milton, was well known for his Parliamentarian

---

[40] David Norbrook suggests some of the forms this opposition could take, as well as its limitations, in *Poetry and Politics in the English Renaissance: Revised Edition*, pp. 140–154 and 173–223.

[41] Leeds Barroll, *Anna of Denmark, Queen of England: A Cultural Biography*.

[42] For the creative role played by these and other women patrons in the period, see Julie Crawford, *Mediatrix: Women, Politics, and Literary Production in Early Modern England*.

[43] Philip Finkelpearl, *Court and Country Politics in the Plays of Beaumont and Fletcher* and Gordon McMullan, *The Politics of Unease in the Plays of John Fletcher*.

and Puritan leanings, as well as for the integrity of his family life. Milton did not have to compromise his principles to accept Bridgewater's patronage.

Moreover, in a society in which aristocratic rank no longer reliably bespoke great wealth, and vice versa, some members of the commercial classes were beginning to vie with the aristocracy as magnanimous dispensers of bounty. The wealthy aldermen of London were strongly defensive of the City's ancient privileges and self-government, and sometimes found themselves at odds with the royal government based in Westminster. They also had patronage to dispense—perhaps not on the scale of the Earl of Pembroke or the Countess of Bedford, but patronage nonetheless. Just as Jonson received, over and over again, a commission for the Christmas masque at court, Thomas Middleton received the City's patronage for the pageants that accompanied the investiture of the Lord Mayor. Eventually he was awarded a position as city chronologer.

The London aldermen hold different views than King James or, after him, King Charles on the role of commoners in the government of the nation and on the dangers of tyranny. Many of the tragedies attributed to Middleton—*The Revenger's Tragedy*, *The Second Maiden's Tragedy* (1611), *Women Beware Women*(1623?)—fiercely satirize courtly superficiality, competitive consumption, moral corruption, and sexual licence. Although he sets his plays in Italy, the pertinence of the criticism to locales closer to hand was not likely to be lost on English spectators. While Middleton's *A Game at Chess* offended James, it would hardly upset Middleton's habitual patrons, who probably shared his low opinion of Spain, Roman Catholicism, and the prospect of a Spanish match for Prince Charles.

Still, these patronage circles were hardly mutually exclusive. Jonson, for instance, was on good terms with Pembroke, James, and the circle around Queen Anne, and received benefits from all of them. He was capable of inveighing against the superficiality of court life when writing to Sir Robert Wroth or Lady Aubigny, while at the same time praising its beauty and sophistication in masque after masque. Thomas Middleton, despite his strong ties to the City, also wrote masques for court patrons. He contributed *The Masque of Cupid* (1614) for the marriage of James's favourite, the Earl of Somerset, to the recently divorced Countess of Essex—a relationship nearly as scandalous as anything in *Women Beware Women*.

This fluidity of alliances reflects not only the professional poet's need to cultivate a variety of options, but also the fact that, as we have already seen, the world of the patrons was a small and interlaced one. In the first two decades of the seventeenth century, moreover, political factions were loose and oft-changing, and had not yet hardened into the oppositions that were eventually to go to civil war. As a practical matter, too, since powerful men generally held their positions by birthright or indefinite tenure, it was difficult to distinguish the individual from his office, so disagreements tended to be construed as matters of personality rather than as matters of long-range policy or grand principle. Though the London alderman, with their strong sense of the City's traditional prerogatives, could at times set themselves counter to the Crown, they were certainly not as a group or in principle opposed to monarchy, nor, until well into the reign of Charles I, to most of the monarch's political and religious objectives. Likewise, William, Earl of Pembroke, despite his differences from James, was a senior courtier and an advisor in Crown affairs for nearly his entire adult life.

In short, the evidence cuts in two apparently contradictory directions. On the one hand, there weren't very many potential patrons; often they were blood relatives, and socially intimate, in a way that one would think would encourage a narrow collective taste. Moreover, from the patrons' point of view, the options were sometimes constrained as well. In 1610 Prince Henry and Queen Anne employed Samuel Daniel instead of Ben Jonson to write the Christmas masque—a move, Roy Strong speculates, inspired by their desire to distance themselves from the King and thus from Ben Jonson, perceived as the King's poet.[44] Alas, Daniel's masque was apparently a flop, and Ben Jonson received the commission again the following year. On the other hand, the available patrons did have different political views, and those variations doubtless gave poets more expressive options than a centralized, top-down patronage system would have done.[45]

The effect was most likely to permit certain limited kinds of dissent and to quell others. Certainly, whatever their differences on specific policy issues, the various elites in early seventeenth-century English society shared an interest in protecting their own position. Many Renaissance literary forms gravitate to the highborn: tragedies, histories, and tragi-comedies typically centre on royalty, chivalric romance on the adventures of knights and ladies, pastoral on princes and princesses in rustic disguise. Patronage undoubtedly exaggerates this tendency to dwell on the experience of the privileged classes and to magnify its importance. Undoubtedly, too, patronage mutes

---

[44] Roy Strong, *Henry, Prince of Wales and England's Lost Renaissance*, pp. 155–157.
[45] For the way aristocratic patrons used the court masque to promote their own policy agendas, see Martin Butler, *The Stuart Court Masque and Political Culture*. The matter will be more fully discussed in this volume in Chapter 5.

really radical criticism of the role of elites in early modern society. The London aldermen who supported Middleton might have shared his distaste for corrupt courts, but would have been as outraged as James himself by, say, an anarchist tract. Middleton's works satirize Anabaptists and separatist Puritans quite as savagely as they do courtly vice. Nor do 'anticourtly' nobles such as Huntingdon or Bridgewater support fundamental social change of the kind that would later be advocated by the Levellers and the Diggers. Historians argue, in fact, about whether the radicalism of mid-century, in which some argued for doing away with private property and 'degree' altogether, was invented on the spot in response to new social possibilities or had been circulating orally long before. What is significant for literary historians is that if those views existed in the first decades of the seventeenth century, there was little impulse to record them, no literary form to accommodate them, and no venue in which they could safely circulate.

Although the political consequences of patronage have received the majority of scholarly attention, most patronage poetry does not conceive itself, at least explicitly, as a statement on a matter of political policy, but rather as the poet's address to an individual patron. Even when, as often seems to have happened, the poem got written first and the patron selected afterwards, the poet had an interest in presenting the finished work as a form of homage from one person to another. Since the praise of rich benefactors can strike a modern reader as unbearably sycophantic and repetitive, we often read past it in an attempt to find something in the poems that interests us more. It's in these purportedly individual-to-individual moments of direct address, however, that patronage poetry most often and most richly becomes a forum for authorial self-representation—for the conceptual work that underlies 'the rise of the author'.

The patronage system depended, as we have seen, upon the idiosyncrasies of the rich and the powerful, and did not even pretend to erect standards of objectivity or merit. Poets were painfully aware that the support of great literature depended upon the weak reeds of a few rich people's generosity and good taste. Boorish patrons were as free to shower bounty upon dreadful writers as tasteful patrons were to support good ones. In Jonson's *Volpone*, the wealthy protagonist applauds doggerel composed by his parasite and recited by freaks. In *The Alchemist*, Sir Epicure Mammon, in a delirious fantasy about the luxuries he will possess once he acquires the philosopher's stone, imagines himself as, among other things, a patron of the poet 'that writ so subtly of the fart, / Whom I will entertain still for that subject' (2.2.63–64).

Jonson's distinction, quoted earlier, between full-time poets and occasional ones is pertinent again here because it reveals a telling pattern of assumptions about the workings of the patronage system:

> Poetry, in this latter age, hath proved but a mean mistress to such as have wholly addicted themselves to her, or given their names up to her family. They who have but saluted her on the by, and now and then tendered their visits, she hath done much for, and advanced in the way of their own professions (both the law, and the gospel) beyond all they could have hoped, or done for themselves without her favour.

Jonson personifies 'Poetry' specifically as a patron, dispensing bounty to the poets that are her dependents. Yet she does so capriciously, rewarding the occasional visitor more than the faithful lifetime attendant. She is as inconstant, as unpredictable, and as little susceptible to correction as that other imperious mistress, Lady Fortune. In case the reader doesn't catch his drift, Jonson makes the analogy between Poetry and the whimsical patron explicit in the next sentence:

> Wherein she [that is, Poetry] doth emulate the judicious but preposterous bounty of the time's grandees, who accumulate all they can upon the parasite, or fresh-man in their friendship, but think an old client, or honest servant, bound by his place to write and starve.
>
> (*Discoveries* lines 450–458)

'Judicious' here means not 'intelligently discriminating' but 'unreasonably finicky', and refers to judgements that might well be ill-informed but were in any case beyond appeal. Jonson's sense of the system's shortcomings need not preclude his sincere gratitude towards his own patrons. Just the opposite—it's precisely because the system is so rickety that a writer feels especially surprised and relieved when he receives some deserved benefit from it.

Jonson's bitter comment comes from the best-rewarded patronage poet of the day. To those who were less successful, it often seemed as if virtue and talent had been passed over in favour of flashy, insubstantial rivals. Lucy, Countess of Bedford extended patronage to Michael Drayton in the first years of James's reign but then withdrew her support. In 1606, revising and reissuing his eclogues, the poet inserted a new passage into the eighth eclogue, apparently analogizing his own situation to that of the mistreated suitor in his pastoral fiction:

> So once Selena seemed to regard
> That faithful Rowland her so highly praised
> And did his travail for a while reward
> As his estate she purposed to have raised,
> But soon she fled him and the swain defies;
> Ill is he stead that on such faith relies.
>
> And to deceitful Cerberon she cleaves
> That beastly clown too vile of to be spoken,
> And that good shepherd willfully she leaves
> And falsely all her promises hath broken.
> . . .
> Let age sit soon and ugly on her brow,
> No shepherd's praises living let her have
> To her last end no creature pay one vow,
> Nor flower be strewn on her forgotten grave.
> And to the last of all devouring time,
> Ne'er be her name remembered more in rhyme.
>   (85–94, 103–108)

Seduced and abandoned, Drayton systematically undoes the promises of the patronage poem—to celebrate and enshrine the patron, now and after death—and turns them into curses.

It's hardly surprising, then, that when a loyal, generous patron did come along, he or she should strike poets both as nearly miraculous and as highly individual. Nor is it surprising that the poets should so often work a mention of this individuality into their flattery, defining and understanding the paragon in terms of the potential rivals he or she surpasses. The evocation of lesser rivals helps the flattery along by indicating that the poet is not one to marvel indiscriminately at just any rich and powerful person, but fully understands the patron's unique excellence.

As a result, the poet often praises the patron for deviating from an implicitly or explicitly maligned norm. In 'To the Countess of Bedford', Donne, for instance, argues that the virtues of Lucy, Countess of Bedford, a prominent figure at court, shine out radiantly from the moral murk of a court 'which is not virtue's clime' (7). In his *Epigrams* (1616), Ben Jonson addresses by name the great men and women he praises—King James, Pembroke, Salisbury, the Countess of Bedford, and so on—while, in different but juxtaposed poems, attacking unnamed but obviously courtly figures like Sir Voluptuous Beast, My Lord Ignorant, Fine Lady Would-Be, and Courtling. In *The Forest*

(1616), Jonson's country house poems not merely thank his patrons but disparage court life: 'To Sir Robert Wroth' particularly singles out for criticism, as a sign of courtly vice and triviality, the 'short bravery' of the extravagant masques Jonson had himself written (10). In many Jonson poems, the technique of praise-through-disparagement takes the form of a series of negations:

> Thou art not, Penshurst, built to envious show
> Of touch, or marble, nor canst boast a row
> Of polished pillars, or a roof of gold.
> $\qquad\qquad\qquad\qquad\qquad$ (1–3)

This strategy juxtaposes the praise of the patron with a critique of all those things that he or she might be, but isn't. The rhetorical ploy partly accounts for the apparently weirdly bifurcated view of court life, luridly overstated in the direction of both praise and blame, evident in so much early seventeenth-century writing.

Yet the desire to enhance the vividness of one's praise is surely only part of the story. Many Jacobean patronage poets really do seem to have had an intense love–hate relationship with the system of rewards upon which they depended, and even with the individuals upon whom their wellbeing depended. For writers simultaneously engaged in writing for the theatre and writing for court patrons, animosity often emerges most clearly in the plays, which were not, at least initially, written to please patrons. George Chapman's *Bussy D'Ambois* and *The Revenge of Bussy D'Ambois* portray a lethal jockeying for favour at a court carefully designated as French, therefore safely removed from overt criticism of its English counterpart. In 1609, Ben Jonson's *Masque of Queens* celebrated a bevy of powerful, beautiful, wise court ladies; in the same year, his comedy *Epicene* satirized a group of oversexed, pseudo-intellectual viragos who bear a suspicious resemblance to the circle around the Countess of Bedford—the same women who performed in *The Masque of Queens*. Although Jonson always claimed that he eschewed satire directed at particular persons, it is not surprising that few believed him.

Whence comes this intensity of feeling, this tendency for idealization to slide so easily and rapidly into cynicism and satire? Courts typically are receptive places for the arts because they are full of people who possess the education, leisure, and financial resources to constitute an audience for them. The question of financial resources was, however, a tricky one in the Jacobean court. Unlike the close-fisted Queen Elizabeth, King James was a big spender and his courtiers followed suit. William, Earl of Pembroke died 80,000 pounds in debt despite the enormous income of 22,000 pounds per year; Richard, Earl of Dorset is calculated to have spent 100 pounds every day in the years between his father's death in 1609 and his own in 1624. England's newly powerful trading companies and her increased exposure to foreign goods allowed unprecedented possibilities for elite consumption and opportunities for competitive display: large and beautifully appointed houses, opulent clothing, expensive delicacies elegantly served on imported porcelain dishes. High-stakes gambling on horse-races, cockfights, and card games was popular too.

The habit of conspicuous consumption in the Stuart court had a double and apparently contradictory effect on artistic patronage. On the one hand, the imperative for display theoretically reduced the amount of money available for writers by redirecting it to other kinds of expenditure—an effect exacerbated by rampant inflation. Under financial pressure to streamline their affairs, many noblemen cut back on the size of their households and the munificence of their hospitality. When Shakespeare's King Lear, after his abdication, argues with his appalling daughters over the size of his retinue, their resistance displays not merely their filial ingratitude, but also a generational change in the way the nobility calculated expenditure and prestige. Perhaps in response to this trend, many writers, even while deploring 'newfangled' spending on material luxuries, tend at the same time to celebrate an 'old-fashioned' freehandedness in the rewarding of followers (which includes, of course, people like themselves). Ben Jonson's 'To Penshurst' represents the patronage of the poet as a morally healthy alternative to empty competitive expenditure, and associates that patronage with Robert Sidney's harmoniously traditional relationship to his land, his tenants, and his guests.

On the other hand, a milieu that encouraged free spending increased the probability that courtiers—even if they felt poorer than they used to be—would nonetheless direct some of their bounty to writers and artists, whose products, after all, present themselves as one kind of luxury good among many. In Shakespeare's and Middleton's *Timon of Athens* (1607), the Poet and the Painter take their place with the Jeweler, the Merchant, and the Mercer in a long line of greedy clients who bankrupt the compulsively generous hero of the play. More optimistically, many of Jonson's masques depict the potential tension, but finally harmony, between courtly splendour and good rule. The difference between extravagance and 'magnanimity' or proper courtly greatness is partly in the eye of the beholder.

In fact, there were no fewer patrons in Jacobean and Caroline England than there had been in earlier decades, and there was no golden age of artistic patronage to which Jacobean and Caroline writers could easily look back. Still, as we have seen, even the relatively successful Jonson can deplore the parsimony and lack of discrimination of patrons 'in this latter age'. Though in 1603 most writers were looking eagerly towards the accession of James as offering them new patronage options, by 1610 they were increasingly inclined to exalt the bygone days of Gloriana.[46] These implausible expressions of nostalgia are symptomatic of a system under strain. As noted earlier, early modern patronage relationships tend to be conceived not as market transactions but as gift exchanges. Yet since the difference between gift and commodity is always a matter more of the participants' attitudes than of the objective character of the transaction, the distinction often proves tenuous and unstable.

There are reasons why this instability may have been particularly challenging for the Jacobean poet. Historians have long emphasized the way in which early modern England is in transition between a late-feudal system and a more commercial, contract-based, proto-capitalist mode of social organization. The patronage support available to non-dramatic writers seems to hark back to the old system, in which an individual's horizon of opportunities was largely dependent upon his social status and his position in kinship networks, and in which wealth was largely based on control over land resources. Meanwhile, the system of literary support available through the public theatre seemed to be the product of a dawning age, as England began to evolve into a great commercial and manufacturing power.

If the literary system was split between older and newer modes, many individual authors straddled the divide. In the later years of Elizabeth's reign, a number of writers for the theatre saw non-dramatic poetry as an additional or supplemental source of income. In the early 1590s, when the theatres were closed on account of a plague epidemic, William Shakespeare turned his hand to narrative poems, dedicating them to the Earl of Southampton. This tendency for playwrights to 'cross over' into patronage environments much accelerated in the reign of James. Ben Jonson, George Chapman, John

---

[46] For the legacy of Elizabeth in Jacobean and Caroline England, see Curtis Perry, 'The Politics of Nostalgia: Queen Elizabeth in Early Jacobean England', in *The Makings of Jacobean Culture: James I and the Renegotiation of Elizabethan Literary Practice*, 153–187; Anne Barton, 'Harking After Elizabeth: Ben Jonson and Caroline Nostalgia', *ELH* 48 (1980): 706–731.

Fletcher, Philip Massinger, and Thomas Middleton all begin their careers writing plays but on occasion, or as a later career development, wrote for patrons even while continuing to pursue a playwriting career.

The professional playwright's quest for patronage was not merely a matter of developing new opportunities alongside the older ones. Instead, the nature of the patronage transaction began to change under the pressure of assumptions imported from the theatre world. The commercial theatres, as we have seen, had stimulated an expanded writers' market, encouraging men to pursue literary careers even if they did not have an inheritance or an income from other employment. Not only did the number of writers increase much faster than the number of patrons, in other words, but those writers were on average needier, requiring more than token rewards.

As a result, competition for the attention of those who did dispense largesse was fierce. Arguably, in fact, the routine gesture of the Jacobean patronage poem, which, as I have noted flatters the patron by distinguishing him or her from other aristocrats, might be seen as a form of wishful displacement. The real need for differentiation is not among patrons, but among poets. Thus, the poet praises the patron as absolutely unique in the hopes that the patron will perceive the poet as absolutely unique in turn. When a Jacobean poet solicits patronage, he lays the flattery on with a trowel, but attempts to deploy the trowel with his own inimitable flourish. Jacobean poets pay increased attention to individuality of style and display a new resentment about forms of literary appropriation that had, in early decades, seemed an intrinsic aspect of the writer's art. Terence Cave has argued that sixteenth-century humanists make a close connection between 'copia', or imaginative fertility, and 'copying' from prior authors.[47] But by the first decade of the seventeenth century, Jonson is complaining about plagiarism and writing epigrams against 'Old End Gatherer', who steals jests from other people's conversation and lines from other people's plays. Competition encourages writers to differentiate themselves from all others—to stake a claim to 'originality'—and also to insist on a tighter connection between the person and his writing, so that the proper attribution of poem to writer becomes increasingly important. Eventually, in the eighteenth century, major changes in copyright law will define the literary work as the author's property, but the intellectual groundwork for this shift begins to be laid down more than a century earlier.

---

[47] Terence Cave, *The Cornucopian Text: Problems in Writing in the French Renaissance.*

Since this conception of imagination-as-territory arises from a competition for scarce resources, it's not surprising that it so often coexists with the conviction that writers ought to be rankable from best to worst, from genius to hack. There's no reason to believe that literary talent is like soil in a field, so that a hill at one spot implies a hollow in another—that because one person is a fine writer, the next person can't possibly be any good, or that one individual might engross all the available talent and leave everybody else impoverished. Yet in the early seventeenth century, poets begin to pit themselves, or be pitted, against one another in imagined, if not actual, combat. Thus, Jonson writes of Shakespeare in 1623:

> [I should] tell how far thou didst our Lyly outshine,
>> Or sporting Kyd, or Marlowe's mighty line.
> And though thou hadst small Latin, and less Greek,
>> From thence to honour thee I would not seek
> For names, but call forth thundering Aeschylus,
>> Euripides, and Sophocles to us,
> Pacuvius, Accius, him of Cordova dead,
>> To life again, to hear thy buskin tread
> And shake a stage; or, when thy socks were on,
>> Leave thee alone for the comparison
> Of all that insolent Greece or haughty Rome
> Sent forth, or since did from their ashes come.
>> ('To the Memory of My Beloved, The Author,
>> Mr William Shakespeare', lines 28–42)

John Sucklng's 'A Session of the Poets', in which numerous poets of the day gather at a tavern to compete (unsuccessfully) for laureate honours, bespeaks a similar impulse to 'rank' poets, to 'crown' the best one and dismiss the rest as insolent or haughty failures.

That competitive impulse survives in our own author-concept, as we see in Harold Bloom's *The Anxiety of Influence*, Peter Schaffer's *Amadeus*, or those lists of 'Best Books' devised by various literary authorities. Ben Jonson, who pioneered this idea in the course of his aggressive attempts to secure patronage, has ironically been the most heavily penalized by it, since the reception of his work has been, since the late seventeenth century, so entangled with comparison to the superior genius of Shakespeare. In Jonson's own time, however, the cultivation of competitive distinctiveness gave his work a kind of brand-character: each poem's importance depends not only upon its intrinsic merit but upon its association with his other work, and with him, as the personality that speaks through his works. By 1657, when Humphrey Moseley publishes Middleton's *Women Beware Women* and *More Dissemblers Besides Women* (1615) together in the same volume, the idea was thoroughly familiar. In a short preface to the reader, Moseley writes: 'when these ... of Thomas Middleton's excellent poems came to my hands, I was not a little confident but that his name would prove as great an inducement for thee to read, as me to print them'.

Not only the writer's self-conception but also his sense of his relation with his patron changes in the first few decades of the seventeenth century. The commercial milieu of the public theatre imbued its practitioners with an entrepreneurial attitude towards their own talents, even while, perhaps, encouraging a certain restlessness about the rewards to be found in playwriting alone. Inclined, by their experience as writers for the theatre, to think of themselves as professionals, they naturally saw non-dramatic writing as another potential field to exploit. But both their motives and their expectations hardly resembled those who imagined the patronage relationship in terms of feudal allegiance. Since literary patronage, unlike the commercial playhouses, was a venerable institution, Jacobean writers inherited models for representing the patronage relationship, but they had to modify them to reflect the new realities of their situation.

What were these inherited models? During Elizabeth's long reign as an anomalously female head of state, courtiers had adapted the conventions of the Petrarchan love lyric as a way of expressing their political ambition. The lyric situation, in which a yearning supplicant addresses an inaccessibly chaste beloved, proved a serviceable vehicle for describing the relationship of Elizabeth's courtiers to their queen. Petrarchan topoi show up not only in poetry, but in apparently prosaic, political contexts; for instance, in letters from her privy councillors requesting favours or advising her on policy matters. Some critics have gone so far as to argue that love is merely the pretext of many Elizabethan erotic poems, which are actually thinly disguised allegories of political manoeuvring.[48] Indeed, the lover's inferiority and social distance from the beloved was part of the tradition of Provençal *fin amor* from which Petrarch himself had drawn inspiration: the lady was not merely an object of desire but a potential benefactress, sexually inaccessible because

---

[48] Arthur Marotti, '"Love is Not Love": Elizabethan Sonnet Sequences and the Social Order', *ELH* 49 (1982): 396–428; Ann Rosalind Jones and Peter Stallybrass, 'The Politics of Astrophil and Stella', *SEL: Studies in English Literature* 24 (1984): 53–68.

she was one's employer, or one's employer's wife or daughter. So the connection to a patronage situation was, one might say, built into the form well before the Elizabethans got their hands on it.

Some relatively high-ranking poets—for instance, Walter Ralegh or Philip Sidney—may have self-consciously deployed Petrarchan topoi in their direct dealings with the queen. After Sidney had angered Elizabeth, to assuage her wrath and as a sign of his penitent submission he presented her with a New Year's gift of 'a whip garnished with small diamonds'. Others, like Samuel Daniel, adapted Petrarchan devices to a slightly less exalted social sphere, presenting his sonnet sequence Delia as a form of clientage to Mary, Countess of Pembroke. Some scholars have argued that the beautiful youth to whom Shakespeare addresses the majority of his sonnets is in fact a patron—suggesting as candidates Southampton or Pembroke, amongst others. It is impossible to know for certain; the plausibility of the theory lies in the fact that Shakespeare's sonnets offer the young man exactly the trade-off poets generally offer patrons. The poet is ageing, socially inferior, unable either to match or to resist the young man's glamour. Nonetheless, he commands powers that the young man does not; while the young man's natural beauty will wither, the poet has the capacity to fix it forever in verse. The beloved thinks he is too dear for the poet's possessing at his own peril.

Whether or not the love-fiction ever becomes quite as thin as some critics imagine, Elizabeth's deliberately virginal royal style surely made Petrarchism a natural choice for those who hoped for benefits from her or her delegates. Moreover, especially in allegorical modes, the same beloved can simultaneously represent a whole panoply of desirable objects, so that the tendency of erotic supplication to bleed into the rhetoric of more general bids for favour means that a single poem can perform a variety of emotional transactions at the same time. Michael Drayton writes a sonnet sequence to 'Idea', who incarnates both the queen's virginal ideal and the equally inaccessible charms of a woman closer to home: the daughter of Drayton's patron, Henry Goodere. Sidney's 'Stella' may be, in the first instance, Penelope Rich, but the poet uses the conventions of Petrarchan frustration to explore his social and political disappointments as well.

In the Jacobean period, however, the Petrarchan sonnet sequence languishes. When Michael Drayton revises *Idea's Mirror* in 1619, he does so as a way of celebrating the lost virtues of the Elizabethan age. For Drayton at this point in his career, Petrarchanism hovers on the edge of satire, contrasting the present with the past in a highly unflattering way. Mary Wroth's sequence, *Pamphilia to Amphilanthus*, is similarly backward-looking; her relationship to her late uncle, the famous Elizabethan poet-warrior Philip Sidney, helps authorize her own enterprise.

'Political' critics generally attribute the decline of Petarchanism in the Jacobean period to the accession of James, since a married man can hardly inspire a cult of female chastity. But Elizabeth's demise cannot by itself explain the change in poetic styles. Elizabeth herself, after all, had not functioned directly as a patron for most poets, instead delegating the support of the arts to such courtiers as Leicester, Oxford, and Burleigh. Especially given the prominence of female patronage in the Jacobean court, Petrarchan supplication could have been as plausible in the Jacobean period as in the Elizabethan one. But its increasingly problematic quality is suggested by the case of Anthony Stafford, an Oxford theologian who dedicated *Niobe, or his Age of Tears* to the twenty-one-year-old Anne Clifford in 1611, two years after her first marriage to the Earl of Dorset. Stafford wrote in the old-fashioned love-struck style:

> I could tell you, madam, that Virtue wanted a beautiful lodging, and therefore commanded Nature to build you; and that Nature was content to fulfil her command, with this condition, that Virtue should make you her principal palace. But I will spare those praises, as needless ... you have amazed and distracted me, by attracting the best parts of my mind from me, to honour the true honour which is in you. I beseech your ladyship then to let my ecstasy excuse me.

As Clifford's biographer points out, this 'is the kind of thing that might well have been addressed, ten years earlier, to the elderly Elizabeth—who would have considered it a very proper style for the author to adopt, without for one moment believing that he meant it'.[49] In the event, Stafford's dedication scandalized either Clifford herself or her kinfolk. The dedication was torn out of the books that had already been printed, and omitted thereafter; it survives in a single copy. Perhaps Anne's youth made her more vulnerable to gossip, or perhaps the greater licentiousness of James's court made such gossip seem more plausible, or perhaps several decades of theatre that routinely dramatized cross-class love affairs had made the social distance between a scholar and a countess seem less unbridgeable than before. At any rate, language that would previously have seemed unexceptionable now seemed presumptuous.

---

[49] Martin Holmes, *Proud Northern Lady: Lady Anne Clifford 1590–1676*, p. 24.

If Petrarchan topoi could embarrass a patron, they also had the potential to embarrass a poet. Although John Donne does not preserve the stanzaic form of the sonnet sequence in his epistles to patrons, he does have a strong affinity for Petrarchan hyperbole and for the absolute centrality it grants erotic experience. Thus, he expresses his gratitude towards female patrons in a number of extravagant quasi-love poems. Read together—as, of course, they would not have been when they were originally written— Donne's poems testify less to the transcendent worth of the women who are their purported addressees than to Donne's almost all-purpose sense of a flaw in the world. He yearns for something irresistible and overwhelming to remedy that flaw—variously imaged as a phoenix, a magnet, a sun—be it a lover, a patron, or, in the religious poems, a gracious God. Of course, in the individual poems, the virtual interchangeability of Donne's 'phoenix candidates' cannot be acknowledged. Each needs to seem, for the time being, utterly unique and irreplaceable. Thus, Donne was understandably nervous about how the Countess of Bedford would react when he accepted the patronage of the Drury family in equally rapturous terms.

Donne's dilemma suggests why, for others, Petrarchism seemed obsolete as a way of describing the patronage transaction, and also why it seemed most obsolete to those writers who were most fully professionalized. Petrarchism posits a relationship between lover and beloved that is lifelong and obsessive even in the absence of reward. It adapts nicely to arrangements in which the poet depends, or hopes to depend, for a long time upon a single individual. Petrarchism seems much less suitable when many patronage relationships are patently temporary. For full-time, professional writers, any implicit conflation of patronage to monogamous romantic love will make the necessity of cultivating a variety of supporters seem indecent.

In the case of Ben Jonson, the break with tradition is obvious. Unlike Donne, who persistently sought permanent employment in a non-literary capacity, and unlike Shakespeare, who was ensconced for life as a shareholder in the profitable King's Men, Jonson spent his entire career as a freelancer whom no individual patron, even the king, required on a full-time basis. His relation to his noble benefactors, in other words, though not as transitory and obviously commercial as the relation between dramatist and acting company or theatregoer, was very remote from feudal vassalage. Because Jonson knew from the start that he would need to appeal simultaneously to numerous patrons, the drawbacks of Petrarchism far exceeded its rhetorical advantages.

Jonson therefore developed a different model of the patronage relationship: one based not on erotic attraction but on friendship between people who share a common set of values and are perceptive enough to recognize virtue when they see it. The advantage of construing patronage as a kind of friendship, rather than as a kind of love affair, is that one can have more than one friend with perfect propriety. Jonson can praise everybody who deserves it without giving offence to any one of them. In Jonson's Jacobean poetry, published as *Epigrams* and *The Forest*, he praises numerous worthy individuals. In no case does he suggest that the relationship is an exclusive one. Moreover, he mixes poems to benefactors with poems to people from whom he did not receive financial support, such as William Camden, John Donne, and Thomas Roe.

Jonson did not invent this way of thinking about patronage entirely from whole cloth, but adapted it from Roman writers he admired, especially Horace, Martial, and Seneca. His attraction to the classical model is obvious early in his career. In the late Elizabethan *Poetaster*—when Jonson was still writing exclusively for the commercial theatre and had not yet obtained any court recognition—he celebrates the literary world of Augustan Rome. Augustus is the admiring patron of Horace and Virgil, listening respectfully to Virgil's recitation of a passage in the *Aeneid*, a poem that, in turn, glorifies the Roman imperium. Yet Augustus is not an indiscriminate dispenser of bounty. He exiles Ovid, an excellent poet, after Ovid has an affair with his daughter, and he punishes the hacks Crispinus and Demetrius for their literary presumption. Horace and Virgil do not always agree with Augustus: poetic merit weighs more heavily with them than with their patron, and they try unsuccessfully to obtain a pardon for the gifted Ovid. Nonetheless, Augustus' priorities are represented as comprehensible for a ruler in his position, and the relationship between him and his court poets is a mutually respectful one.

While the Petrarchan lover is an emotional, and often a social, supplicant, the kind of friendship Jonson evokes in *Poetaster*, and later in his patronage poems, implies a certain parity on moral if not financial grounds. By construing patronage as a form of friendship, Jonson tendentiously eliminates the social boundary between highborn patron and lower-born, relatively poor, but gifted poet. 'To Penshurst' compliments Sir Robert Sidney for a hospitality so thorough that Jonson, the bricklayer's stepson, makes himself at home in Sidney's country house 'as if thou, then, wert mine, or I reigned here' (74). At the same time, Sidney's hospitality is properly discriminating; while Jonson sits at high table, the waiter Sidney employs to serve him 'knows *below* he shall find plenty of meat' (70, my italics). Jonson flatters Sidney by implying that Sidney's own sense of aristocratic identity is secure enough not merely to tolerate Jonson's presumptuousness, but to recognize a brilliant writer as a natural aristocrat, not a quasi-servant who dines in the kitchen. While Jonson's project is doubtless in the first place to secure patronage, he also aims to eliminate the sense of social disparity and inequality of emotional investments that comes with the Petrarchan territory.

In fashioning a solution to one problem, however, Jonson creates several others. Someone who claims to be besotted by love is not required to exercise good judgement. But Jonson describes his relation to his patrons as frankly evaluative. They need, he claims, to earn his praise. The conflict of interest that arises from pretending to judge, and find worthy, those who are offering you benefits generates in Jonson's poetry pervasive worries about his own poetic integrity. In 'To My Muse' he berates her for having 'betrayed me to a worthless lord' (2); the name of the lord is, of course, left unmentioned, but the poem is tellingly printed just after an especially fulsome tribute to the Earl of Salisbury. Jonson's situation is further strained by the increasing tendency, in the course of the sixteenth century, for humanist writers on friendship to segregate affectionate respect quite rigorously from money concerns.[50] While the word 'friend' was still a very loose one, applied to neighbours, kinfolk, and especially benefactors, as well as to companions of the same rank, writers such as Erasmus and Montaigne argued that true friendship transcended such worldly concerns and was not to be sullied by them. In consequence, the necessary mixture of motives in the patronage system could easily seem sordid. Jonson spends a good deal of energy convincing others, and probably himself as well, that he is not a mere flatterer of the rich. It is no coincidence that the unscrupulous parasite Mosca, in *Volpone*, is one of Jonson's most intelligent and most memorable characters. The ferocious punishment Mosca receives at the end of the play suggests the intensity of Jonson's desire to exorcise the possibility he represents.

Despite these difficulties, 'friendship' provided Jonson with a powerful model for the kind of patronage he solicited and received. His approach to patronage suggests the effect that the commercial market for playwriting, and its accompanying mindset, has on patronage literature. Neither in

---

[50] Lorna Hutson, *The Usurer's Daughter: Male Friendship and Fictions of Women in Seventeenth-Century England*.

his dealings with the professional acting companies nor at court does Jonson seek or receive exclusive attachments, but instead cultivates profitable short-term arrangements. His willingness to refashion a poetic idiom to describe this more mutable and temporary state of affairs is perhaps one reason why Jonson can, for almost four decades, subsist, however precariously, upon income from his writing without taking clerical orders, working as a schoolmaster, or serving as a secretary or a gentleman-in-waiting.

Jonson is not, of course, not the only writer who needs to cope with the tendency for patronage arrangements to become shorter-term and more ad hoc. One increasingly common strategy was to interleave personal dedications in printed books, instead of dedicating the entire work, or print run, to a single patron; that way, each patron or potential patron could receive a personalized presentation copy, and the poet could collect benefits from several addressees. Like Jonson, other writers openly cultivated multiple sources of support. In *The Scourge of Folly* (1610), John Davies of Hereford, rather than commit himself to a single patron, produces a long list of poems 'to worthy persons'; Aemelia Lanyer does the same in *Salve Deus Rex Judaeorum*. The epigrammatist George Wither experimented with publication by 'subscription', a crowdfunding arrangement that became popular in the eighteenth century, especially for longer projects. From the patron's point of view, subscription schemes have the benefit of affordability. Instead of depending upon a single munificent benefactor, the writer would solicit relatively smaller amounts of support from a wide variety of people, whose help would be publicly acknowledged when the work was eventually finished. Subscription publication, like multiple dedications, is yet another intermediate stage between a quasi-feudal patron–client relationship and the thoroughly commercial arrangement common in the public theatres. Wither's experiment was unsuccessful, however, and he was forced to refund the money he had collected.

At the same time as playwrights were pushing the protocols of patronage in more entrepreneurial directions, patronage support was becoming increasingly important to the profit-oriented theatre companies—and thus, by extension, to the playwrights they employed. In fact, the acting companies had never been entirely estranged from the patronage system: under Elizabeth, acting companies were obliged to affiliate with noblemen in order to avoid arrest for vagrancy, and acting companies often performed at court or in noble households for the same combination of remuneration, lodging, and meals that a patronage poet might expect. One of James's first acts as king was to consolidate the major theatres under the direct patronage of the royal family. The Lord Chamberlain's Men, the company to which Shakespeare belonged, was renamed the King's Men; the Earl of Worcester's Men became the Queen's Men; the Lord Admiral's Men came under Prince Henry's auspices; and the boys' company at Blackfriars became 'the Children of the Queen's Revels' (though after repeated scandals they were demoted to mere 'Children of the Revels'). In later years, Princess Elizabeth and Prince Charles also served as theatrical patrons. The court was increasingly prone to use professional players rather than in-house performers for its own entertainment, partly for financial reasons, for a play was much cheaper to produce than a court masque. Moreover, as the masques became more ambitious, they also required the assistance of professional players.

Since the theatres were profitable business ventures, some have argued that their association with courtly or royal patrons was a mere convenience—a fiction designed to get around obsolete laws defining 'masterless' actors as vagrants. Some contemporaries held this view: for instance, John Cocke, who argued of the professional actor 'howsoever he pretends to have a royal master or mistress, his wages and dependence prove him to be the servant of the people'.[51] In the Elizabethan period, the association with the noble patron indeed tended to be fairly nominal. In the Jacobean and Caroline period, however, despite the independent commercial success of several leading theatre companies, royal patronage had significant consequences. Appearing regularly at court, the theatre companies had frequent opportunities to display their work before the most powerful people in the kingdom. In addition, the theatre companies received tangible benefits. The company was paid for a guaranteed number of court performances; every two years, each member of the company was allocated four yards of scarlet cloth for a cloak and one quarter-yard of crimson velvet for a cape. During a plague epidemic in 1636, the King's Men received 20 pounds per week from the royal coffers to sustain them while the theatres remained closed.

More important for the dramatists, and thus for the literary historian, was the changed outlook that came with a closer connection to the court. Royal patronage, especially in conjunction with the new availability of upscale 'private' theatres, leads the more successful companies increasingly to specialize

---

[51] Quoted in Kathleen McLuskie and Felicity Dunsworth, 'Patronage and the Economics of Theatre', *A New History of Early English Drama*, ed. John D. Cox and David Scott Kastan, p. 423. See also Paul Whitfield White and Suzanne Westfall, eds., *Shakespeare and Theatrical Patronage in Early Modern England*.

in plays for elite clientele and that therefore reflect an elite viewpoint. Shakespeare's Jacobean plays are more closely associated with the court than his Elizabethan ones had been—his company performs there more frequently, and the topics important in James's court life feature more largely there. *Macbeth*, 'the Scottish play', is clearly written with the Scots monarch in mind. Many have also seen traces of James in *Measure for Measure*'s Duke, and have read Lear's disastrous division of his kingdom through the lens of James's ambitious plan to unite England and Scotland. *The Tempest*—another play in which a father-king features largely—was performed at Princess Elizabeth's wedding to Count Palatine: possibly the masque Prospero stages for Miranda and Ferdinand was added for that occasion. After 1610, playwriting, which, as I've mentioned, is originally the preserve of artisan-class men, increasingly appeals to more genteel individuals such as Fletcher and Ford, and the drama loses some of its distinctive populism.

The systems of support for writers that I have outlined above helps determine how the works they produced have come down to us, and the way they come down to us complicates our efforts to determine their histories. Nowadays we take it for granted that most 'literary' works will appear in print soon after they are written. Of course, the existence of a work in print form does not guarantee its survival, but it vastly increases the odds, simply because the technology multiplies the number of copies produced. But print publication was not necessarily the rule in the early seventeenth century. Long works—epic poems, histories and other extended narratives, treatises, and so on—were typically printed soon after they were written, because copying them by hand was so unwieldy. But this was not the case with plays and shorter works. Plays were purchased by the theatre companies, who were thenceforth considered their owners, and the theatre companies generally had little material incentive to have them printed since the lack of legal intellectual property protections meant that another, rival company would then be able to use the script to generate its own performance of the play. Especially early in the period, plays were considered to find their primary audience in performance, not on the printed page. As a result, the majority of plays never found their way into print; their manuscripts did not survive either, and as a consequence they are almost entirely lost to us, though their titles appear in the Stationer's Register. Sometimes playing companies would sell their scripts to printers to raise some money, such as in times of plague when the theatres were closed, and sometimes especially popular plays found their way into print; others, contrarily, might be printed if they were hopeless flops in performance, or after their early theatre run was complete. Still, when Ben Jonson printed a selection of his plays, with his masques and poetry, in his 1616 *Works of Ben Jonson*, some derided what they considered an indecently brash form of self-promotion.[52] Nonetheless, Jonson's sense that printing, and especially printing in expensive folio formats, was a means to enshrine a writer's career for future ages to appreciate was a prescient realization, and seems to have been influential. In 1623 John Heminges and Henry Condell, two of Shakespeare's colleagues in the King's Men, brought out a folio collection of thirty-six of his plays, including eighteen that had never been printed at all and others that had been available only in cheaper quarto formats. The First Folio, as it is commonly called, has proven critical for securing Shakespeare's reputation as the premier writer of the English language, providing what is in some cases the only, and in others the best, version of his plays that we have. Our awareness of the work of several other prominent playwrights, for example Thomas Middleton and John Fletcher, is likewise dependent upon the ministrations of editors and printers working after their deaths to preserve their work in printed form. Of course, in the case of posthumous publication, the unavailability of the authors means that there is no one to check the accuracy of the scripts used to produce the printed version. As a result, the actual authorship of many plays is disputed, and in other cases there are obvious textual corruptions that some authorial supervision presumably would have been able to clear up. Still, the example of such projects as the Jonson and Shakespeare folios makes it more likely, as the period goes on, that plays will be printed shortly after their performance. We have a more complete record of plays performed in the 1620s and 1630s than we have of those performed in the 1590s because attitudes towards print and its relationship to performance were changing.

The material fate of non-dramatic works, both those supported by patronage and those produced by amateurs, was likewise tenuous. Some short lyric poems—especially devotional poems—were not designed for circulation at all, and others (for instance, many love poems) were meant to be read only by the beloved recipient or by a small coterie. When one's likely readers were locally contiguous—for instance, at court or at the Inns of Court—it was easy to circulate short lyrics in manuscript among all those who might wish to read them. The labour required to copy a short poem was minimal, and poetry aficionados could compile their favourite pieces in collections designed for their own use; numerous instances of such manuscripts have

---

[52] For a detailed discussion of Ben Jonson's innovative attitude to print publication, see Richmond Barbour, 'Jonson and the Motives of Print', *Criticism* 40 (1998): 499–528.

survived, and they are vital for our knowledge of such poets as Donne and Ralegh. Harold Love comments that 'in the early years of the seventeenth century . . . the communication of manuscripts became so widespread a practice' that printing such works was unnecessary, or even scorned as attempting to draw attention to oneself in an unseemly way.[53] Some time after consenting to the printing of the *Anniversaries* in 1611 / 1612, Donne writes in some embarrassment to his friend George Garrard:

> Of my *Anniversaries* the fault that I acknowledge in myself, is to have descended to print anything in verse, which though it have excuse even in our times by men who profess and practice much gravity, yet I confess I wonder how I declined to it, and do not pardon myself.[54]

But such manuscript collections have their drawbacks for the literary historian. Often poems will be unattributed or misattributed, and they rarely come with dates attached. In many cases, too, a poem will mutate in the course of transcription, either because the transcriber mistook a word or phrase, or because he or she decided to introduce an emendation into what was, after all, a personal copy of the poem; such deviations can proliferate as the poem passes from hand to hand.

After the Fall

The coming of civil war brought drastic changes to the multifarious ways in which Jacobean and Caroline writers had sustained themselves and found time for their writing. When the King fled his London residence in 1642, the normal routines of court broke down entirely. At this point, if not somewhat earlier, the flow of court patronage effectively ceased: there were neither funds nor occasions for the production of masques and other court entertainments. In September 1642, the London theatres were closed by an act of Parliament, and further statutes, in 1646 and 1648, provided for the demolition of the theatres and the punishment of actors. As the Parliamentarian side prevailed, royalist estates were sequestered and some writers and their patrons imprisoned; even those who survived relatively unscathed had more

---

[53] Harold Love, *Scribal Publication in Seventeenth-Century England*, pp. 50–51.
[54] John Donne, *Selected Letters*, ed. P. M. Oliver, p. 62.

pressing demands upon their resources than literary patronage. Eventually, as Cromwell's protectorate established itself in the 1650s, some modest literary patronage re-emerged, although the short duration of the protectorate, and its different structure, means that it did not regain its previous significance as a form of support for writers.[55]

The near-simultaneous collapse of both patronage networks and the theatre companies temporarily closed off all of the avenues by which writers had previously received remuneration for their work. The effect was to diminish many of the incentives for producing imaginative writing and to force literary endeavour into new channels. When the rule of the monarch broke down, so did the censorship regimes that had operated under the auspices of the king. While censorship rules were eventually reimposed by the Cromwell regime, their temporary abeyance opened a space for some new kinds of writing, notably religious and political polemic and journalism. During the 1620s and 1630s a few entrepreneurs, as already noted, had evaded the restrictions on news reporting by having their reports sent out as manuscript letters to subscribers. The printed newsbook of the 1640s and after, by contrast, was aimed at a much larger audience. Although this kind of writing does not much influence the canonical texts of the early seventeenth century, the best examples of this kind feature a precise description of quotidian events and an eye for telling detail that will later figure in the early novel. It is not a coincidence that one of the first to distinguish himself in this new genre is the journalist Daniel Defoe.

Earlier in the period, as I have already noted, literary clubs had begun to meet in some London taverns. In the Civil War and Commonwealth eras, there were self-conscious efforts to cultivate such groups as nodes of mutual support.[56] Thomas Stanley founded the 'Order of the Black Riband' and Katherine Philips the 'Society of Friends'. These groups could not, of course, replace the court or its resources, but they could offer a way for poets and lovers of poetry to come together, either in person or by letter, and possibly for the more affluent members of such groups to assist the indigent. Meanwhile, without a theatrical outlet for their talents, some writers experimented with adjacent forms. In 1656 and 1657, William D'Avenant, who

---

[55] Edward Holberton, *Poetry and the Cromwellian Protectorate: Culture, Politics, and Institutions*.

[56] For the social relationships fostering the creation and circulation of poetry in the 1640s, see Lois Potter, *Secret Rites and Secret Writing: Royalist Literature 1641–1660* and Nicholas McDowell, *Poetry and Allegiance in the English Civil Wars*.

after the Restoration would spearhead the reopening of the commercial theatres, wrote a two-part 'opera', *The Siege of Rhodes*, which claimed to be 'recitative music' and so permissible despite the ban on plays. Another possibility was to import the plots and techniques of drama into non-dramatic verse. D'Avenant's epic poem in decasyllabic quatrains, *Gondibert* (1651), borrows heavily from Fletcherian drama, just as Fletcherian drama had, in earlier decades, borrowed from prose romances. Yet in such tumultuous times, it was difficult to commit to writing long, ambitious poems. John Milton put his poetic career on hold as he entered the fray as a political polemicist, and later assumed a demanding position in the Cromwell government. D'Avenant, a royalist imprisoned on the Isle of Wight and sentenced to capital punishment (he was eventually freed at Milton's intercession) abandons *Gondibert* in the midst of the third of five planned sections:

> I am here arrived at the middle of the third book; . . . and I was now by degrees to present you (as I promised in the preface) the several keys of the main building; which should convey you through such short walks as give an easy view of the whole frame. But 'tis high time to strike sail, and cast anchor (though I have run but half my course) when at the helm I am threatened with Death; who though he can visit us but once, seems troublesome, and even in the innocent may beget such a gravity as diverts the music of the verse.

Abraham Cowley, too, is unable to complete his Biblical epic, the *Davideis* (1656). The difficulties may have been, as D'Avenant asserts, starkly practical: a dead man cannot write, and a man who fears imminent death may have trouble writing well. But surely a contributing factor was the moral disorientation of these years, to which Andrew Marvell's *Horatian Ode* also bears witness. Time-honoured institutions and structures of authority had crumbled, it was not clear what would take their place, and to many 'the world turned upside down', as a broadside ballad of the mid-1640s put it. John Denham repeatedly revises his landscape poem, *Cooper's Hill*, after events make a mockery of his confident predictions of the king's triumph in the first version of 1641.

The disintegration of the previous systems of literary support does not merely affect how writers might support themselves, but decisively changes how their work is disseminated. Already, as we have seen, longer poems, too unwieldy to be copied easily, had long been printed; in the first few decades of the seventeenth century the increased propensity to bring out plays in print as well had begun to erode what J. W. Saunders calls 'the stigma of print'.[57] So, once the pre-war communities of readers and writers shattered, making manuscript circulation difficult, print publication began to seem an effective alternative way to reach an audience. Lyric poets who in previous decades might have shied away from printing their works, such as Robert Herrick and Richard Lovelace, now edited them for the press. This development did not merely reflect the desires of writers, but also the enterprise of printers. The printer Humphrey Moseley was especially active in this regard, printing, in the course of the 1640s, not only contemporary work by Milton, Cowley, Crashaw, Suckling, and Vaughan, but also recovering the work of past decades—particularly plays, since the theatre companies that had jealously guarded playscripts as their private property were now disbanded. Mosely collected manuscript playscripts by Middleton, Massinger, Shirley, and Brome, and had many of them printed; in 1647, he brought out a folio version of Beaumont and Fletcher's plays.

At the time, reading such plays may have consoled those who missed attending performances, but the printed versions also preserved this work for future generations. And the printing of plays and love poetry, both associated in different ways with the culture of the court and the days of monarchy, may also have seemed like a political intervention of sorts. Thomas Calhoun argues in his commentary on Abraham Cowley's collection, *The Mistress* (1647), that 'the love lyric of the 1640s was recognized as a royalist genre',[58] and it is, in his view, no coincidence that so much of this work was printed in the late 1640s, when open war had temporarily ceased and negotiations between the royalists and their opponents were ongoing. In that case, the printed dissemination of love poetry could be a way of garnering sympathy for the king's position among a non-courtly reading public. Work that may have originally been intended for limited, ingroup consumption now solicited a wider audience. Circulation in manuscript did not die out after the 1640s: Harold Love has documented its continuing vitality well

---

[57] J. W. Saunders, 'The Stigma of Print: A Note on the Social Bases of Tudor Poetry', *Essays in Criticism* 1 (1951): 140–165. For more recent and detailed work on Tudor and Stuart manuscript culture and its relationship to print, see Wendy Wall, *The Imprint of Gender: Authorship and Publication in the English Renaissance*; Arthur Marotti, *Manuscript, Print, and the English Renaissance Lyric* and *The Circulation of Poetry in Manuscript in Early Modern England*.

[58] *The Collected Works of Abraham Cowley, volume 2 (1656) part 1: The Mistress*, ed. Thomas O. Calhoun, Laurence Heyworth, and J. Robert King, p. 226.

into the eighteenth century, especially for controversial or obscene material, or in settings where a coterie of readers already existed.[59] Yet, by the Commonwealth period, the notion that print was somehow a violation of gentlemanly decorum was gone with the wind.

---

[59] Harold Love, *Scribal Publication in Seventeenth-Century England*.

PART II
IMPORTANT LITERARY GENRES
1603–1660

3
Thinking About Genre in Seventeenth-Century England

In early modern Europe, the habit of subdividing literary territory by genre was very thoroughly ingrained, authorized since ancient times by the example of Aristotle in *The Poetics* and Horace in *The Art of Poetry*. The great neo-Latin critic Julius Caesar Scaliger devotes the first book of his immense 1561 overview, *Poetices libri septem* [*Poetics in Seven Books*], to chapters on a wide variety of 'kinds', from tragedy and comedy to Latin satiric plays, dirges and epithalamia, songs of good cheer and foreboding, rowing-songs, and proverbs. In *The Art of English Poesy* (1589), George Puttenham, like Scaliger, spends most of his first book on these 'sundry forms',[1] with descriptions of hymn, tragedy, comedy, satire, pastoral eclogue, elegy, epigram, and so on. Similarly, Sir Philip Sidney, writing *The Defence of Poesy* around 1580 (it was not printed until 1595), distinguishes hymns and philosophical or scientific works from fictional genres, and subdivides the last category into pastoral, elegy, comedy, tragedy, lyric, and heroic poetry.[2]

So organizing a discussion of early seventeenth-century literature by 'kind', by its generic characteristics, is compatible with the way the creators of that literature would have conceptualized their work. Yet how those 'kinds' are constituted in the first place is a difficult question. The available generic lists—even Scaliger's—are not meant to be exhaustive, and their criteria are heterogeneous. In some cases, as Sidney notes, the subject area of literary works, 'the matter they deal with', determines their genre; in other cases, a 'sort of verse'—that is, stylistic or technical features— distinguish one genre from another. In addition, Renaissance genres are not rigid categories or

---

[1] George Puttenham, *The Art of English Poesy: A Critical Edition*, ed. Frank Whigham and Wayne A. Rebhorn, p. 115.
[2] Scholarly discussions of Renaissance genres and genre theory include Rosalie Colie, *The Resources of Kind: Genre-Theory in the Renaissance*; Lawrence Manley, *Convention 1500-1700*; Heather Dubrow, *Genre*; Barbara Lewalski, ed., *Renaissance Genres: Essays on Theory, History, and Interpretation*; Alastair Fowler, 'The Formation of Genres in the Renaissance and After', *New Literary History* 34 (2003): 185-200 and *Kinds of Literature: An Introduction to Genres and Modes*.

lists of rules. Rather, genres provide rough templates for the aims of writers and for the expectation of audiences. Taken together, the various genres deal with the multifarious forms of human experience and endeavour: tragedy with the fall of princes and nobles; epic with the adventures of heroes; comedy with the interactions of ordinary people, often in urban settings; pastoral with the lives of shepherds. Genre thus works as a filtering device, focusing on some phenomena and implicitly excluding others. The way tragic characters speak and the values they represent are different from comic or pastoral speech-patterns and values. The kinds of things that can happen in satire are different from the kinds of things that can happen in romance. Different genres accept different reality principles as axiomatic.

Consequently, genre is closely associated with the concept of 'decorum' or suitability. In twenty-first-century parlance, the word 'decorum' often denotes something primly polite, but in early modern literary usage 'decorum' is relativistic and context-dependent. Unity of time and place might be desirable in a play, but not in an epic. Obscene humour might be appropriate in a comedy or a satire, but improper in an elegy. Nonetheless, the decorum of different genres remains hard to pin down exactly, both because distinctions between genres are hardly clear-cut, and because hybrid forms are welcomed—'If severed they be good', Sidney opines, 'the conjunction cannot be hurtful'.[3] Tragicomedies include distressing events, even deaths, but the ending is typically joyful. In romantic comedy, the main characters are often highborn, as in tragedy, but the plot deals mainly with courtship and marriage, not wars or affairs of state. In other words, the rules of genre, and the conventions of decorum that accompany them, often seem honoured as much in the breach as in the observance.

The title page of Ben Jonson's 1616 Folio *Works* suggests both how genre was imagined and how the rules could be bent or ignored. The title of the book is centred within an engraving of an elaborate classical façade, in the architectural niches of which stand five figures: Tragedy, Comedy, Satire, Pastoral, and Tragicomedy. Each figure is labelled in Latin and appropriately attired. Tragedy, for instance, is outfitted with a crown and sceptre, suggesting tragedy's focus on royal characters, and wears buskins, the distinctive footwear of tragic actors on the classical stage. Pastoral is rustically clad and equipped with a shepherd's hook. Satire is a satyr with goat's legs and a panpipe. Tragicomedy combines the attributes of Comedy and Tragedy. The five genre-figures are positioned as monumental components

---

[3] Sidney, *The Defense of Poesy, Sir Philip Sidney: Works*, ed. Albert Feuillerat, vol. 3, p. 22.

of an elaborate architectural composition, suggesting Jonson's versatility as a writer and tying his works to a glorious classical past. Yet the genres are not exactly statues. They step out of their niches, peer at one another around the columns and pediments. There is no contradiction, for Jonson, in representing genres as simultaneously inherited and contemporary, universal and local, architectonic and vigorously alive. Generic conventions enable his creativity rather than constricting it.

Renaissance commentators attribute etymologies and origin stories to the different genres, asserting that each genre captures the *modus vivendi* of a particular juncture in human development. The crudeness and aggression of satire is laid at the cloven feet of the satyrs who were allegedly its first practitioners, while pastoral exemplifies the simple, uncorrupted tastes of the shepherds who supposedly invented it. To us, these stories often seem fanciful. Epic heroism is clearly visible only in retrospect, not in the moment when it is being performed; and as William Empson points out,[4] affluent urban people are more likely than poor rural ones to romanticize the sheep-keeping life. Yet the insight that various literary genres arise out of particular social configurations is nonetheless a plausible one; certainly, genres that predominate in a given literary period give important clues to the function of literature in that particular culture.

One of the striking features of early seventeenth-century literature, therefore, is how boldly its major practitioners innovated with respect to genre. Genres that had captivated the writers in the latter part of the sixteenth century—chronicle history plays, sonnets, chivalric romances—were not entirely eclipsed. Some scholars believe Shakespeare wrote or revised some of his sonnets close to their date of first printing in 1609—though others argue he completed the sequence earlier. Mary Wroth publishes a prose romance, *Urania*, including an important sonnet sequence, *Pamphilia to Amphilanthus*, in 1621, explicitly harking back to her uncle Philip Sidney's *Arcadia* and *Astrophil and Stella* from the 1580s. But work in these genres seemed less central than it had only a decade or two before. By contrast, tragicomedy and satiric city comedy were self-consciously innovative developments; revenge tragedy, which had a short burst of popularity at the end of the 1580s and then seems to have fallen out of fashion, came roaring back at the turn of the seventeenth century after a revival of Kyd's *Spanish Tragedy* and the first performances of Shakespeare's *Hamlet*. Of course, in the fast-moving theatre world such changes occurred much more rapidly than they

---

[4] William Empson, *Some Versions of Pastoral*.

did in the quieter domains of non-dramatic writing, but those areas, too, are characterized by the restless trial of new forms: Francis Bacon and Thomas Overbury experiment with the short prose forms of the essay and the 'character'; Ben Jonson and others develop the epigram and the country house poem. Devotional lyric was not new to the period, but the quantity and quality of such writing reached unprecedented heights in the work of John Donne, George Herbert, Richard Crashaw, Henry Vaughan, and John Milton. The following pages will discuss some of the new and revived genres that are most important in the literature of the early seventeenth century, describing their typical features and speculating about the reasons for their popularity.

4
A Sense of Place

A surprising number of what we now think of as distinctive new genres of the Jacobean and Caroline periods are ones that evoke particular rather than generalized settings—indeed, that make such an evocation one of their distinguishing characteristics. 'Country house' poetry, loosely modelled on classical models, is one of these genres: poems describing and celebrating an aristocratic house and grounds. Country house poetry originated in the first decade of the seventeenth century with Aemelia Lanyer's 'The Description of Cookham' and Ben Jonson's 'To Penshurst' and 'To Sir Robert Wroth'; examples of the genre later in the century include Thomas Carew's 'To Saxham' and 'To My Friend G. N. From Wrest', Edmund Waller's 'At Penshurst', and Andrew Marvell's 'Upon Appleton House'. John Denham's influential 'Cooper's Hill', although it does not celebrate a nobleman's estate, nonetheless shares the country house poem's interest in specific, named topographical features. In what may be a related development, Richard Helgerson has noted that what he calls 'chorography'—the verbal and pictorial mapping of the English countryside—flourished in the reigns of James I and Charles I, though it originated earlier. Michael Drayton's long poem *Poly-Olbion* (1612, 1622) was the most ambitious literary attempt of this kind, offering a comprehensive delineation, in almost 15,000 hexameter lines of poetry, of the counties of England and Wales.

Meanwhile some dramatists began routinely to set their comedies in familiar London neighbourhoods, evoked in considerable detail, rather than in the generalized Italian or French cityscapes common in 1590s comedy, and to depict urban life in a satiric light. Satiric city comedy seems a distinctively Jacobean genre. It was a sign of the times when, some time between 1605 and 1616, Ben Jonson extensively revised his 1598 comedy *Every Man in His Humour*, turning a play originally set in Florence into a London comedy strongly infused with local colour. None of Jonson's comedies written before 1608 are set in London; after 1608, all of them are, until the 1629 experimental romance *The New Inn*. Similarly Shakespeare, less attracted to the genre, nonetheless apparently revised his only comedy set in England, *The Merry Wives of Windsor*, sometime after 1602 in ways that render it more topographically specific and evocative.[1] Other writers who set their plays in familiar London locales include Thomas Middleton, Thomas Dekker, and Richard Brome.

The circumstances under which country house poems, city comedies, and 'chorography' got written, and the motives for writing them, seem so wildly different that these genres have rarely (if ever) been considered together, as a group of related literary kinds. Yet, as we shall see, the connections among them were in fact manifold, and occasionally too they defined themselves against one another—so that, for instance, the values articulated by country house poems often seem expressly poised against the ethos of city comedy. More tenuously, problems of place and its representation can become important in writings in other genres as well. Jacobean and Caroline court masques often, though not invariably, make the literal and symbolic location of the court central to their proceedings, drawing eclectically upon the techniques of exotic and domestic travel narrative, of country house poems, and, in the antimasque, of city comedy. A related genre—the entertainments and shows commissioned by the Lord Mayor of London or the Inns of Court to celebrate holidays or inaugurate new officeholders—seems similar to the antiquarian chorography in the way it deploys lore about local history and customs.

What motivated this concern for place in several apparently disparate literary kinds? The patronage system made it inevitable that a great deal of seventeenth-century non-dramatic poetry was occasional, and therefore perhaps inevitably focused on local concerns. Written for particular people in particular situations, it often circulated, by manuscript or private performance, among a small audience acquainted with the original circumstances of its creation. In such circumstances, evoking a specific, familiar milieu becomes a technique for creating intimacy between the poet and the audience. Indeed, what is surprising is not that patronage poetry should be local and specific, but that poets should so often insist that its topicality is a vehicle for more permanent and general concerns. Ben Jonson claimed of his masques that 'though their voice be taught to sound to present occasions, their sense or doth or should always lay hold on more removed mysteries'.[2]

---

[1] For the significances of the differences between the 'fuzzy' relationship to place in Q *Merry Wives*, and the 'topographically anchored' F versions, see Adam Zucker, 'Shakespeare's Green Materials: Windsor Forest and *The Merry Wives of Windsor*', pp. 23–53 in *The Places of Wit in Early Modern English Comedy*, and Leah Marcus, *Unediting the Renaissance: Shakespeare, Marlowe, and Milton*, pp. 84–87.

[2] *Hymenaei*, ed. David Lindley, lines 13–14 in *The Cambridge Edition of the Works of Ben Jonson*, ed. David Bevington, Martin Butler, Ian Donaldson, et al., vol. 2.

Our experience of reading seventeenth-century poetry must often be almost the opposite of what it was for its original addressees. For the readers or auditors to whom the poet dedicated his work, the contemporary milieu was obvious, for they were immersed in it, and the trick of interpretation was, as Jonson implies in his comment on the masque, to discover the 'more removed mysteries', the deeper significance behind the in-jokes and local references. The modern reader, by contrast, often finds a poem's 'more removed mysteries' easier to intuit than its long-vanished original circumstances of production and reception. Even if the patient labour of scholars reconstitutes a tissue of local references, the references matter less to us than they did to the original audience. As people say about jokes that fall flat, 'you had to be there'.

Yet if the demands of patronage help explain why, say, Jonson writes poems about Penshurst, or Lanyer writes about Cookham, they do not explain why Jonson, or Middleton, or Dekker, or Brome write about London for public theatre audiences, or what generates the supply and demand for information about the counties and monuments of England. Nor can the patrons' taste explain the appeal of such writing to contemporaries who were somewhat far removed from the original situation of composition. Why, for instance, could Jonson imagine that the general public would want to read 'To Penshurst'? What attracts seventeenth-century writers to the depiction of specific places, not merely as a set of geographical coordinates but as sites pregnant with meaning?

We are often inclined to imagine the England of the past as a settled world, in which families occupied the same neighbourhood, even the same house, for untold generations. Yet historians of the early modern period have discovered a society on the move.[3] In the late sixteenth and seventeenth centuries, significant percentages of people, both poor and rich, died in parishes other than the one in which they were born. Motives for relocation varied widely, of course, for different social groups. Changes in agricultural practices, particularly the enclosing of cropland for sheep and the consolidation of small parcels into larger ones, displaced large numbers of the rural poor, who wandered from town to town in search of work or alms despite the heavy penalties for vagrancy. Domestic servants often changed employers on a yearly basis, venturing considerable distances in search of higher wages

---

[3] For internal migration within seventeenth-century England, see Peter Spufford, 'Population Movement in Seventeenth-Century England', *Local Population Studies* 4 (1970), 41–50, and the essays in *Migration and Society in Early Modern England*, ed. Peter Clark and David Souden.

or better working conditions. Both male and female adolescents migrated from rural hamlet to market town in search of work or apprenticeship opportunities. Many of these relatively humble migrants did not live far from the place of their birth. On the other hand, in an era when twenty miles was a day's journey, even a modest transplantation could drastically alter one's social surroundings.

Higher on the social scale, some landowning families prided themselves on their long-established ties to a particular locale: the Sidneys in Kent, the Cliffords in Cumberland, the Corbetts in Shropshire. Yet family ties to a county or neighbourhood did not mean that the members of the family spent their entire lives there. Adolescent children from elite families routinely boarded for years with other families of a similar class, a custom of fostering-out that often took them far from home. As university-level education became more common for affluent males, time spent in Oxford or Cambridge, or in London at the Inns of Court, became an expected phase of their late adolescence and early adulthood. For some, the exile from the family land and house would be permanent, since the estate typically passed undivided to the eldest brother. The professional careers open to younger sons rarely required returning home, and sometimes precluded it. Aspiring lawyers often remained in London; those who hoped for court employment made their way to Westminster and accompanied the king on his annual progresses through the southern counties; military men and those assigned to diplomatic posts travelled internationally. Church of England clergymen often ended up in far corners of the realm. John Donne, who became a priest in middle age and held out for a clerical position in London, seems to have been an exception. George Herbert, brought up in Wales, lived for years in Cambridge, and after taking orders was granted a living near Salisbury in the gift of his distant cousin, the Earl of Pembroke. The London born and bred Robert Herrick found himself a vicar in Devonshire.

For women of all classes, marriage incorporated her into the husband's family, and typically entailed residence at the husband's domicile. Since the higher the position one occupied on the social scale, the smaller the pool of appropriate mates, the marriage market for aristocratic women was essentially a national rather than a local one. In consequence noblewomen—who, as we have already seen, made up a disproportionate number of the period's female writers—could end up far from their birth home and family. Upon her marriage to the Earl of Pembroke, Mary Sidney moved from Kent to Salisbury. Anne Clifford, whose birth family hailed from northern England, found herself isolated from her friends and effectively under house arrest on one of her estranged husband's estates in Devon.

No matter what one's station in life, a removal to a new place of abode, temporary or permanent, affects the psyche in profound ways: one cannot comprehend what is distinctive about one's home except by contrast. Moreover, once one has experienced those differences, one has a harder time assuming that all places are essentially the same. In other words, the new appetite for 'place genres' in early seventeenth-century England was likely stimulated by the marked increase in geographical mobility across all levels of society after 1550.

   Early seventeenth-century political vicissitudes helped expand the significance of place for early modern readers and audiences. Perez Zagorin has identified and chronicled the presence, in the early seventeenth century, of an oppositional 'Country' faction: not a full-fledged political party in the modern or even Restoration sense, but an identifiable group of noblemen and gentry with a set of values and policy preferences at odds with those of the Jacobean and Caroline courts.[4] Richard Helgerson has argued that an efflorescence of local antiquarian research and mapping likewise entailed a subtle challenge to the absolutist claims of King James and King Charles, by locating the essence of English nationhood not in its consolidation under a sovereign power, but in its enduring topographical features and the history associated with them.[5] Curtis Perry has traced an emergent sense of political differentiation in London, too, in the early part of the seventeenth century, as urban merchants distinguished their interests, and the interests of their city, from the aims of the Crown and the landed aristocracy.[6] As we shall see, these political categories do not necessarily correspond very closely to the interests of playwrights and poets. Nonetheless, a heightened awareness of the political significance of these divisions may well have had the effect of sensitizing their readers and audiences to the importance of place more generally.

Satiric City Comedy

The most commonly remarked-upon kind of geographical mobility in the early seventeenth century was an apparently unstaunchable flow of migrants—about 10,000 a year throughout the early seventeenth century—from provincial towns and villages to London. Already the third-most

---

[4] Perez Zagorin, *The Court and the Country*.
[5] Richard Helgerson, *Forms of Nationhood: The Elizabethan Writing of England*.
[6] Curtis Perry, *The Making of Jacobean Culture: James I and the Renegotiation of Elizabethan Literary Practice*, pp. 188–210.

populous city in Europe, London mushroomed from about 100,000 in the mid-sixteenth century to an estimated 200,000 at James's accession, and to 375,000 fifty years later. The metropolis swelled well beyond its old boundary walls on the north of the Thames River, extending to the entertainment centres south of the river and stretching westward and upriver to the Inns of Court, then to the king's palaces, and then to the Houses of Parliament at Westminster, originally a separate town. London's growth rate was especially impressive considering that the city's death rate always exceeded its birth rate; virulent diseases such as plague, typhoid, and smallpox flourished in its overcrowded, unsanitary neighbourhoods. Despite the risks, people poured in to take advantage of the city's higher wages and greater economic opportunities. By some estimates, one in eight people in early modern England spent at least part of their lives in the metropolis. 'Soon London will be all England', remarked James I. In a speech to Parliament in 1640, Sir Thomas Roe characterized London as a 'fat head', and the rest of England as 'thin guts and lean members'.[7] Especially alarming to the government was the new fashion among the affluent for spending a good deal of the year in London, socializing and transacting legal business. James and Charles counted on substantial landholders to serve as unpaid justices of the peace and as patrons of local churches, functions that required their presence in the countryside. Yet lucrative court appointments commonly went to those physically in attendance at Westminster, giving noblemen and others ambitious for state employment additional reason to frequent the metropolis.

As has already been suggested in Chapter 1, the demographic centripety of early modern England had a profound impact on the writing of the period. Increasingly, many English writers lived in London, or at least spent part of their lives there. All licensed printers, except for the two university presses, were located in London. The authorized public theatres, too, were uniquely London institutions, although their repertory companies frequently toured the provinces. It is not surprising, then, that the immediate London environment should become a compelling literary topic.

Relocation to London was not merely a matter of miles but involved a radical alteration of social scale and expectations. Most migrants to London hailed not from towns such as Norwich or Canterbury, which were home to thousands of people, but from small villages and hamlets, where the average

---

[7] 'Sir Thomas Roe's Speech in Parliament, wherein he sheweth the cause of the decay of coin and trade in this land', dated 1640, printed 1641, and reprinted in *Seventeenth-Century Economic Documents*, ed. Joan Thirsk and J. P. Cooper, p. 45.

population was about 200 persons.[8] These new citydwellers had to learn to manage not merely a larger quantity of interactions but a wider spectrum of familiarities, from fleeting interactions with unknown persons, to casual acquaintances, to intimate relationships. Moreover, London did not merely have more people, but it had more different kinds of people—migrants from all over the British Isles, as well as significant numbers of religious refugees from France and the Netherlands, and some immigrants from more distant places like Africa, Turkey, and Russia. In the absence of a trained police force, maintaining order among this heterogeneous population was challenging. English villages, from which so many internal migrants came, had for centuries relied heavily upon the informal policing effect of mutual neighbourly scrutiny. Local church courts, for instance, which handled cases of defamation, spousal abuse, or sexual misbehaviour, paid careful attention to the reputations of the plaintiff and the defendant when assessing the guilt of the parties that came before it; moreover, the shaming punishments they typically meted out were effective because they involved humiliation before one's entire social universe. But because the city was so large and because many of its residents had only lived there for a short time, social mechanisms based upon close mutual acquaintance inevitably degenerated.

Seventeenth-century London comedy thus depicts what happens when a community grows so large and various that social and legal sanctions dependent upon cultural consensus, and upon the discipline imposed by care for one's reputation, begin to break down. The collapse creates new hazards, but also new pleasures and opportunities. On the one hand, new Londoners had to master difficult social and conceptual skills in order to succeed in the urban world. On the other hand, early modern London seemed to liberate its inhabitants from many of the bonds of kinship and neighbourhood that both nourished and constrained the inhabitants of England outside the metropolis.

As is usual in this period, literary taxonomies do not neatly coincide with the change of reign in 1603. The late 1590s saw the development of a line of plays that celebrate the lives and accomplishments of London citizens. A good example of this subgenre is Thomas Dekker's 1599 comedy, *The Shoemaker's Holiday*. This play, loosely based on the life of the fifteenth-century Lord Mayor Simon Eyre, charts Eyre's rise to civic prominence and

---

[8] Many of Steven Rappaport's observations about migration to London in *Worlds Within Worlds: Structures of Life in Sixteenth-Century London* hold true for the early seventeenth century as well; see especially pp. 76–81.

his erection of Leadenhall, the city granary. Yet its regard for historical fact is slight—in actuality, Eyre had been a draper, not a shoemaker—and the appeal of the play lies in its sympathetic, vivid depiction of a proud artisan community. Thomas Heywood writes plays of the same romantic type, featuring apprentices sallying forth on exotic adventures and imaginative citizens endeavouring deeds of civic virtue. Satiric city comedy, more ironic and 'sophisticated' in tone than the plays of Heywood, is often considered a distinctively 'Jacobean' form. In fact, however, at least as far as we can tell from the printed plays that survive, 'citizen's comedy' and 'satiric city comedy' originate at about the same time, or at least within a few years of one another, around the turn of the seventeenth century. Yet citizen's comedy seems, in its general atmosphere of festive good cheer, to be of a piece with earlier comedy of the 1590s—for instance, some of Shakespeare's romantic comedies, though they are not set in London. Satiric city comedy, by contrast, is the heir of classical New Comedy and Latin satire, as filtered through the pungent English verse satire of the 1590s.[9]

The two masters of satiric city comedy were Ben Jonson, who set a brilliant series of plays in London—*Epicene*, *The Alchemist*, the revised *Every Man In his Humour*, *Bartholomew Fair*, *The Devil is an Ass* (1616), and *The Staple of News*—and Thomas Middleton, who wrote prolifically in the genre—his city comedies include *Michaelmas Term*, *A Mad World, My Masters* (1605), *The Puritan* (1606), *Your Five Gallants* (1607), *More Dissemblers Besides Women*, *The Roaring Girl*, *A Trick to Catch the Old One*, and *A Chaste Maid in Cheapside*. Yet other playwrights wrote satiric city comedies, too. John Webster and Thomas Dekker collaborated on *Westward Ho* and *Northward Ho* (1605); John Marston wrote *The Dutch Courtesan* (1604) and collaborated with Jonson and George Chapman on *Eastward Ho*. Lodowick Barry wrote *Ram Alley*; Francis Beaumont wrote *The Knight of the Burning Pestle*, a play that both deploys and parodies city comedy conventions.

The Knight of the Burning Pestle, first performed in 1607, is particularly interesting because it makes clear the distinction, in contemporary theatregoers' minds, between satiric city comedy and the 'citizen's comedy' of the kind produced by Heywood and Dekker. As the play is about to begin, a

---

[9] Book-length treatments of Jacobean and Caroline satiric city comedy include Brian Gibbons, *Jacobean City Comedy: A Study of Satiric Plays by Jonson, Marston, and Middleton*; Alexander Leggatt, *Citizen Comedy in the Age of Shakespeare*; Theodore Leinwand, *The City Staged: Jacobean Comedy 1603–1613*; Wendy Griswold, *Renaissance Revivals: City Comedy and Revenge Tragedy in the London Theatre 1576–1980*; Jean Howard, *Theater of A City: The Places of London Comedy 1598–1642*; Heather Easterling, *Parsing the City: Jonson, Middleton, Dekker, and City Comedy's London as Language*; and Dieter Mehl, Angela Stock, and Anne-Julia Zwerlein, eds., *Plotting Early Modern London: New Essays on Jacobean City Comedy*.

grocer in the audience—actually an actor in the playing company—objects to plays that 'have still girds at citizens' (1.1.8)—that is, jokes at the expense of people like himself. The grocer demands instead something 'notably in honour of the commons of the city' (1.1.26–27), such as *The Legend of Whittington* or *The Life and Death of Sir Thomas Gresham, with the Building of the Royal Exchange*—the last the subject of Heywood's 1605 play, *If You Know Not Me, You Know Nobody Part 2*. The grocer and his wife insist on interpolating episodes of romantic derring-do, featuring their apprentice Rafe in the role of hero, in between scenes from the play the actors have intended to stage: *The London Merchant*. As *The Knight of the Burning Pestle* continues, the two plots, each hackneyed and ridiculous in its own way, begin to collide and interpenetrate with hilarious results, possibly implying that the differences between the romantic 'Elizabethan' kind of London comedy and satiric city comedy is less stark than it might seem. In a less elaborately ironic vein, the collaboration between Thomas Dekker, a 'citizen's dramatist', and Thomas Middleton, a playwright of satiric city comedy, produces *The Roaring Girl*, which combines aspects of both modes.

The majority of satiric city comedies were written in the first two decades of the seventeenth century. A few Caroline dramatists produced such plays as well: Philip Massinger's *The City Madam* saw its first performance in 1632; Richard Brome and James Shirley wrote satiric city comedies right up until the closing of the theatres in 1642. These later plays owe a great deal to patterns established by Ben Jonson and Thomas Middleton, but they draw their characters and plot situations from a narrower, more affluent social spectrum. They constitute a bridge between the satire typical of the first decade of the Jacobean period, in which the aim of city comedy is partly to display a wide swathe of different human types, and the socially restricted comedy of manners that will flourish in the works of such playwrights as John Dryden, William Wycherley, and William Congreve after the Restoration. The 'upward drift' may be partly due to the opening of expensive indoor theatres, which attracted affluent audiences in the 1620s and 1630s. But it is also due, as we shall see, to the way satiric city comedy defines its project as depicting the social and psychological ramifications of a newly significant, distinctively urban economic order.

A salient characteristic of Jacobean city comedy is an extraordinary proliferation of local references, far in excess of what is apparently required to move the plot along: references to the substantial houses in Blackfriars and the luxurious ones in the Strand; to the shops in Cheapside and the New Exchange; to the 'Garden' in Southwark where bears were baited in sport; to Bedlam, where madmen were on display; to the courts at Westminster;

to the whorehouses in Whitefriars and Turnbull Street; to Brentford and Ware outside the city, where adulterers arranged to meet; to the livestock markets at Smithfield; to the mustering grounds at Mile End Green; to the debtors' prisons, the Counter and the Fleet—the latter hard by a stinking open sewer, the Fleet Ditch. In Jonson's *Epicene*, Truewit suggests a variety of ways by which a London resident might kill himself: 'the Thames being so near, wherein you may drown so handsomely; or London Bridge at a low fall, with a fine leap to hurry you down the stream; or such a delicate steeple i' the town as Bow to vault from; or a braver height, as Paul's' (2.2.20–24).

In Webster and Dekker's *Westward Ho*, the citizen Honeysuckle, just returned from France, inquires about what has happened in London in his absence:

> *Que nouvelles*? What news flutters abroad? Do jackdaws dung the top of Paul's steeple still? ... They say Charing Cross is fallen down, since I went to Rochelle, but that's no such wonder, 'twas old, and stood awry, as most part of the world can tell.
>
> (2.1.30–37)

In Middleton and Dekker's *The Roaring Girl*, the rake Laxton awaits the arrival of Moll, whom he thinks he has hired for sex:

> *(The clock strikes three.)* Hark? What's this? One, two, three, three by the clock at Savoy. This is the hour, and Gray's Inn Fields the place, she swore she'd meet me. Ha! Yonder's two Inns o' Court men with one wench, but that's not she; they walk toward Islington out of my way.
>
> (3.1.28–32)

A rich tissue of local references is a potent means of establishing fellowship in the playhouse. Knowing where Moorfields or 'St. Pulchre's' is, or having seen a particularly striking shop sign, 'him o' the saddler's horse in Fleet Street' (*Epicene* 4.1.23), is information shared between the playwright and the members of his audience. As Wendy Griswold remarks, 'everyone likes to have the inside dope, and city comedy dramatists flattered their audiences by implicitly assuming that they had it'.[10]

That local colour feeds audience enjoyment is a point Jonson makes explicitly in *Bartholomew Fair*. John Littlewit, the author of a puppet play,

---

[10] Wendy Griswold, *Renaissance Revivals*, p. 35. See also Daryll Grantley, *London in Early Modern English Drama: Representing the Built Environment*.

discusses his adaptation of the Hero and Leander story for the plebeian spectators he expects to draw at the Fair. Christopher Marlowe's Elizabethan retelling of the classical story being 'too learned and poetical for our audience', the playwright makes it 'a little easy and modern for the times':

> As, for the Hellespont I imagine our Thames here; and then Leander I make a dyer's son, about Puddle Wharf, and Hero a wench o' the Bankside, who, going over one morning to old Fish Street, Leander spies her land at Trig Stairs and falls in love with her.
>
> (5.3.120–126)

Notably, the adaptation does not merely move a Greek story to London, but it moves an ancient story into the present moment. When *Westward Ho*'s Master Honeysuckle inquires '*Que nouvelles*? What news flutters abroad?', he asks a question virtually every Jacobean city comedy undertakes to answer. In these plays, London is invariably imagined as the place of the present. This was not merely a Jacobean conceit; in the 1590s the notionally medieval Londoners of Shakespeare's *Henry IV Parts 1 and 2* or Dekker's *The Shoemaker's Holiday* had commented upon such modern problems as syphilis and gunpowder warfare, and quoted freely from plays of the 1570s and 1580s. Yet seventeenth-century city comedy much more pointedly highlights its up-to-the minute credentials. If London is like no other place, city comedy insists, London right now is like no other time—even though the play's characters and situations may ultimately derive from morality plays or Roman new comedies.

So the detailed evocation of place in city comedy has a temporal dimension, coinciding with, and reinforcing, a heightened sensitivity to novelty: new habits, slang expressions, current events, trendy clothing fashions, new forms of business transaction. City comedies register the rise of an urban leisure class, a new phenomenon in the first decade of James's reign; comment on the selling of honorific titles, another Jacobean innovation; depict the expansion of a credit economy and warn against its excesses; and portray on stage the city's boisterous 'roaring boys' or urban hooligans. Beginning around 1622, a few London entrepreneurs undertook to print 'corantos', periodical reports of information and rumours from the Continent, where war was raging. In 1625, Jonson wrote *The Staple of News*, a play that satirically portrays the 1620s equivalent of a newsroom. Indeed, in an era in which censorship laws prevented the printing of domestic news or of opinion on current events, Jonson may rightly have seen the corantos not merely as an emergent but as a rival form. City comedy professed to offer the kind of cultural commentary that would in a later age become the specialty of journalists.

City comedy, then, claims to provide an analysis of local modernity, circa 1600 or 1610 or 1620. What does that modernity entail? In London, at least according to Jonson or Middleton, Dekker or Marston, the markers of wealth and status have shifted decisively and with profound social consequences. In the agrarian provinces, where the majority of the population still lived, the most important criterion for social prestige had long been proprietary rights over land. Gentlemen and aristocrats ideally lived off the rents they collected from subletting acreage to small farmers, or by managing their land directly to produce foodstuffs, wool, timber, or minerals.

In London, too, of course, real estate was an important form of wealth. Yet urban landholding rarely figures as such in city comedies, which typically feature such communal locations as open streets, parks, or fairs, or public gathering places such as taverns. Some scenes in *The Roaring Girl* take place in 'three shops, open in a rank': in other words, the characters circulate through an apothecary, a feather-shop, and a sempster-shop lined up next to one another. *Bartholomew Fair* revives a medieval staging technique in which the plays' various locations—the pig booth, the toy stall, the stocks, the puppet tent—all remain on stage simultaneously while the action circulates through them. The effect is to evoke a setting potentially inhabited by everybody, exclusively possessed by nobody. Even when the action of a city comedy takes place in a private residence, as it does for much of *Epicene* or *The Alchemist*, the owner of the house has often failed to maintain his control over it, so that it becomes, scandalously, a place of public resort. Nor is one's house or shop a means of asserting one's distinctiveness, or one's superiority to others. In *The Alchemist*, Abel Drugger consults Subtle, a fake wizard, for advice on how best to arrange the interior of his apothecary:

> And I would know by art, sir, of Your Worship
> Which way I should make my door, by necromancy,
> And where my shelves, and which should be for boxes
> And which for pots.
>
> (1.3.10–13)

Drugger's request is absurd, the play implies, because even if, as Subtle suggests, he writes '*Mathlai, Tarmiel*, and *Baraborat*' (65) high on the east wall of his shop, it will inevitably resemble every other apothecary in London.

Instead, in city comedies, social distinctions are typically predicated upon differences in the amount or quality of one's personal chattels: furniture, silver plate, jewellery, clothing, and the like. Of course, such items tend to loom large in Renaissance drama regardless of genre, because the public theatres, lacking moveable scenery, relied heavily on costumes and props: Bel-imperia's glove in The *Spanish Tragedy*, Hamlet's black cloak and Yorick's skull in *Hamlet*, the embroidered handkerchief in *Othello*. Yet in city comedy even more than in other Renaissance plays, portable property, especially luxury items worn upon the body, become particularly fraught with significance. In the opening scene of *Bartholomew Fair*, John Littlewit prattles in fetishistic ecstasy at the sight of his wife's velvet cap; later in the play, the wife's transformation into a prostitute is signalled when she appears in a green gown with a crimson petticoat. In *The Roaring Girl*, Jack Dapper's delight in spangled feathers suggests flashy bad taste, while Moll Cutpurse proves her virtue by declining to purloin a watch, a gold chain, and a ruff with a diamond in it when she has the opportunity. In *Epicene*, a prospective bride signals extreme meekness by suggesting that her husband select her clothes for her, whereas the more assertive Madam Otter recalls in horror the times when she burnt a black satin gown while standing by the fire, when melting wax from a chandelier candle dripped on her ruff, and when the hooves of a passing carthorse spattered mud onto her crimson satin doublet and black velvet skirts. As Jonson's original audience would well have known, it was a bit unseemly for Madam Otter to have been wearing these garments in the first place. In Jacobean England, luxury fabrics such as satin and velvet were supposed to be reserved for the highest classes of society, but the 'sumptuary laws' were widely flouted by the rich and socially aspiring. Madam Otter enacts not merely her own social competitiveness, but an upheaval in the way the community around her sorted itself into status groups.

The researches of economic historians suggest that Jacobean playwrights were responding to recent social changes. The wealth of London was built on trade, not on agriculture—on chattel wealth, in other words—so it is not surprising that chattels took on an importance there that they did not have in the countryside. Among the affluent classes, luxury consumption, much of it funded by debt, shot up during the reign of King James, and opportunities to display such commodities were naturally concentrated in the cosmopolitan metropolis.[11] Moreover, the teeming London marketplace

---

[11] For a fuller account of these developments, see F. J. Fisher, 'The Development of London as a Center of Conspicuous Consumption in the 16th and 17th c.' in *Transactions of the Royal Historical Society*, 30 (1948), reprinted in *London and the English Economy, 1500–1700*; Lena Cowen Orlin, ed., *Material London*; Linda Levy Peck, *Consuming Splendor: Society and Culture*

was the site where the greatest variety of these enviable appurtenances might be acquired. 'Shopping'—whether in the traditional retailing streets, such as Cheapside, or in the upscale New Exchange on the Strand, or in the plebeian environs of Bartholomew Fair—was a new pastime in Jacobean London, and one frequently represented or referred to in city comedy.

To a modern reader, the difference between a social order based upon landholding and one based upon chattel property might seem negligible. But in fact, in early modern England chattel property was sharply distinguished from 'real' property—land, houses, and barns—both in common law and in the social imagination. Land is imagined as permanent and as productive, since, if well managed, it can produce a predictable stream of income into the indefinite future. Not only does it resemble a family in its capacity for continuous self-renewal, but it is also typically linked to a family by laws that classify it as a patrimonial entitlement, not alienable outside the kin group. The legal device of 'entailment' was meant to assure that landed estates succeeded to the heir of the body, to heirs male, or to other specified kin, regardless of the wishes of the current possessor. In effect, then, lands attached not to an individual but to a dynastic line and their current occupant served merely as a generational placeholder. This conception of land as more a dynastic appurtenance than an individual possession was in part an early modern idealization. In fact, Alan MacFarlane and other historians have shown that an active land market flourished in medieval and early modern England.[12] Yet in city comedy, if not in Jacobean society more generally, landed property is never legitimately bought or sold as part of a sensible business transaction. Instead it has been inherited by its rightful owner, though sometimes he may willfully mortgage it, or a shyster may pry it away from him by dubious legal means.

Chattel ownership rose rapidly among all classes in early modern England, as Craig Muldrew's analysis of wills and probate inventories has revealed.[13] All but the very wealthiest people in early modern England owned far fewer items than first-world people of comparable social status own today: thus, a poor person might possess ten or twelve individual

---

in *Seventeenth-Century England*; and Amanda Bailey, *Flaunting: Style and the Subversive Male Body*.

[12] Alan MacFarlane, *The Origins of English Individualism: Family, Property, and Social Transition*.

[13] See Craig Muldrew's study of probate inventories in *The Economy of Obligation: The Culture of Credit and Social Relations in Early Modern England*, pp. 15–36.

objects (a mattress, a table, a chair, several wooden dishes), while a substantial yeoman might possess several hundred, including more elaborate furniture and tableware, and the tools of his trade. On the other hand, persons in all social groups owned more in the early seventeenth century than their parents had; for instance, even quite a poor man in Jacobean England might have a painted cloth with which to decorate his wall. Yet the difference between these kinds of belongings and landed wealth remains clearly marked. Chattel property does not normally produce income for its owner, changes hands often, and is easily destroyed or superannuated—Mistress Otter's experience of sartorial ruin echoes many similar disasters in city comedy. For these reasons, chattels were originally classified as a minor byproduct or adjunct to land, not the form in which one's wealth might predominantly reside.

In other words, the kind of situation the city comedies depict, in which chattel wealth is primary rather than ancillary, involves a significant deviation from—even an inversion of—an original hierarchy of value. Yet what from one perspective seem to be the chattel's grave drawbacks may, from another, add to its allure. Because the chattel has traditionally been considered of secondary importance, it has something of the quality of a signifier. It is desirable not (or not only) because it is intrinsically valuable, but because it gestures towards a more 'substantial' prosperity that can be presumed to lie unseen behind it but which is always elsewhere. Easily carried about, chattels thus provide a quick way of signalling affluence in a crowded environment—albeit an unreliable one, as city comedies never tire of pointing out, since it is possible in any particular instance that chattel display has spun free of, and is unsupported by, 'real wealth'.

In a culture that routinely purports to value stability and clear distinctions between social classes, the chattel's dangerous lack of fixity seems tied up with fakery and ephemerality. Yet this feature, too, is an ambiguous one. Precisely because they are impermanent, chattels are normally not inherited but acquired by individuals, whose right to purchase, keep, sell, bestow, or bequeath them exactly as they wish is legally unconstrained. As a result chattels manifest, or seem to manifest, personal choices—especially in early modern London, where the proliferation of different kinds of goods dramatically widens their expressive potential. For better or worse, Jacobean city comedy suggests, a satin jerkin, a French hood, or a gold-handled sword are basic means by which one asserts a social identity and announces one's membership in a community of taste. 'I think this suit / Has made me wittier than I was', opines Pennyboy Junior in *The Staple of News*, to which his tailor, aptly named Fashioner, replies:

> Believe it, sir,
> That clothes do much upon the wit, as weather
> Does on the brain; and thence comes your proverb,
> 'The tailor makes the man'. I speak by experience
> Of my own customers.
>   (1.2.109–113)

The inseparability of chattel and 'self' becomes even more vivid in a moment in *Epicene*, when Otter describes his wife as literally assembled from a series of purchased materials:

> All her teeth were made i' the Blackfriars, both her eyebrows i' the Strand, and her hair in Silver Street ... She takes herself asunder still when she goes to bed, into some twenty boxes; and about next day noon is put together again, like a great German clock.
>   (4.2.93–100)

Mrs Otter is not described as attaching supplements to her body, but as compiled of prostheses. Just as the chattel has the potential not merely to augment, but to stand in for, substantial wealth, so it can also entirely replace substantial persons.

In this setting, the chattel's short shelf-life can become its strong suit. If individuals define themselves in acts of purchase, then the more frequent the necessity for purchase, the more vivid a chattel's expressive potential. Indeed, the ideal urban chattel might even be said to be one that announces its own ephemerality: food or drink that will spoil if not consumed immediately, like the fresh cherries recommended as an appropriate lover's gift in *Epicene*; or new clothes or accessories bound to wear out quickly or soon go out of fashion:

> My shirts
> I'll have of taffeta-sars'net, soft and light
> As cobwebs ...
> My gloves of fishes' and birds' skins,
> Perfumed with gums of Paradise and Eastern air.
>   (*The Alchemist*, 2.2.88–94)

A number of scenes in Jacobean city comedy take place in tobacconists' shops, not only because tobacco, a New World novelty, bred a whole variety of intriguing new social rituals, but also because tobacco literally goes up in smoke.

City comedy, then, portrays a world in which what seems to count as wealth, and what apparently determines status, is in a state of disconcerting flux. Not surprisingly, then, it tends to reshuffle, in ingenious combinations, character types and plot situations that register in some particularly interesting way the social and psychological ramifications of the new wealth paradigm. For instance, goldsmiths figure in a number of city comedies as socially liminal figures. As artisans and tradesmen, they did not rank among the traditional elites, yet as retailers of valuable, gaudy ornaments, and as moneylenders in an era still devoid of deposit banks, they were close to the top of the urban pecking order: in early seventeenth-century England goldsmithing was the most expensive apprenticeship option for young men and was beginning to be considered appropriate for gentlemen's sons. *Eastward Ho* contrasts the fates of the wastrel gentleman-apprentice Francis Quicksilver, who considers himself too fine to work and ends up in debtor's prison, with that of the equally gentle but more humble Golding, who applies himself to his trade, gains his master's trust and the love of his master's daughter, and ascends to the position of alderman's deputy. The prosperous goldsmith himself, Touchstone, is rough, canny, and goodhearted. A 'touchstone' is a piece of black jasper used to test the genuineness and purity of gold; as Touchstone's name suggests, he is a spokesman for soundly bourgeois values and sturdy pride in his craft. *The Devil is an Ass* offers a less flattering depiction: the goldsmith Gilthead claims that by cozening borrowers, he amasses the wealth that will set up his son as a gentleman, to which the son sensibly replies: 'I do not wish to be one, truly, father. / In a descent or two we come to be / Just i' their state, fit to be cozened like 'em, / And I had rather ha' tarried in your trade' (3.1.27–30). *A Chaste Maid in Cheapside* likewise features a goldsmith with social aspirations: the crass Master Yellowhammer and his wife send their son to Cambridge and ineptly attempt to arrange financially and socially propitious marriages for both their children.

Another routine character type in Jacobean city comedy is the provincial who has 'come up' from the country to London; many plays follow the ways in which such characters' moral coordinates change under the pressure of their new situation. As we have seen, because land is 'permanent' and because it is likely to have been inherited, its distinctive characteristic, as a form of property, is its link to the past. According to the dramatists, many of the social features of the countryside are thus associated with memory. In a small community, integrity and the ability to trust others are capacities that serve an individual's long-term social and financial aims—and all aims, in the countryside, are assumed to be long term. In the city, on the other hand, where (at least according to the dramatists) relationships are typically fleeting, the calculus of self-interest changes. One can more easily pretend to be something one is not, and one has less incentive to honour one's obligations to other people, especially if those obligations are not contractually or legally specified.

Conventionally, this difference between country and city is signalled as a moral degeneration. In Thomas Middleton's *Michaelmas Term*, a play that follows the fortunes of three different migrants to London, the Prologue changes his 'whitish cloak', signifying an innocent conscience, to a gown of 'civil black' as he approaches the city from the countryside. Yet the provincial's vulnerability is not always the consequence of his integrity, or even his slow-wittedness; often it is merely a matter of working within a distinctive 'rural' set of social assumptions that turn out to be maladaptive in the city. In an amusing twist, Middleton repeatedly shows provincial migrants exploiting the ingrained stereotype of the trusting, honest country bumpkin for their own advantage. In *Michaelmas Term*, the naïve gentleman Easy, just come to town from Essex, is convinced to cosign a bond, after which the bondholder aggressively enforces the terms of the bond in order to seize Easy's lands. But, by the end of the play, Easy retrieves his fortunes by a clever counter-manoeuvre. In *A Trick to Catch the Old One*, two grasping London usurers, hearing rumours circulated by an apparently ingenuous country servant, simply credit them without any evidence: 'There's more true honesty in such a country serving-man than in a hundred of our cloak companions', opines Pecunius Lucre (2.1.155–157), as he swallows the 'country serving-man's' lies hook, line, and sinker. In *A Chaste Maid in Cheapside*, the similarly gullible Yellowhammer and his wife marry their son to a 'Welsh gentlewoman' with motives of her own for wanting a swift marriage.

Because memory is so short in London, city comedy after city comedy features at least one, and often several, social climbers who, like the Yellowhammers, try to repudiate their humble backgrounds. Sir Petronel Flash of *Eastward Ho*, whose name suggests transient splendour, and Sir Andrew Lethe of *Michaelmas Term*, whose name connotes forgetfulness, are examples of this type. Exploiting the fact that, in London, most people one meets are relative strangers, the social climber adjusts, to the extent of his ability, the details of his social presentation. Usually this adjustment involves misleadingly deploying chattel property in order to 'pass' as rich. Andrew Lethe arrives in the city resplendent in a white satin suit; Sir Petronel Flash commands a coach and horses. As we have already seen, the chattel is supposed to function as a marker of wealth, not as its 'essence', but the social climber drives a wedge between the signifier and the signified, so that again and again, city comedy warns, the chattel signifier may prove unreliable. If men can dress elegantly without being gentlemen born, then silk jerkins do not necessarily signify affluence or high social status. If women can enhance their appearance with cosmetics and false hair, then beauty does not necessarily signify youth.

Another standard character type in city comedy is the prodigal. Unlike the social climber, the prodigal is typically a well-born young man who mortgages his inherited lands to finance his self-indulgence, improvidently trading away a capital asset in order to participate in a ruinously present-oriented urban form of self-fashioning. 'All's gone!' Witgood tells himself at the opening of *A Trick to Catch the Old One*. 'What milk brings thy meadows forth now? Where are thy goodly uplands and thy downlands? All sunk into that little pit, lechery' (1.1.1–4). The prodigal's moral and temperamental opposite—and, often, his opponent in the action of the play—is thus the rich and powerful usurer, who subordinates present pleasure to the expectation of future gains, and who lends money to the prodigal on predatory terms that the prodigal is too feckless to investigate closely. The animus against the usurer in city comedies rarely has much to do with religious strictures; rather, he is a suspect character because it is in his interest to exacerbate the temptations of the urban social system for those who—perhaps unwisely, but understandably—feel they need to participate in it. In *Michaelmas Term*, for instance, the usurer Quomodo makes it only too effortless for the heedless Easy to cosign a bond for a 'friend' and then uses the bond in an attempt to ruin Easy.

As this panoply of character types suggests, city comedy is fascinated by strategic planners and those who fall prey to them. While success in provincial society requires exploiting one's ties to the past, to memory, custom, and tradition, the city favours those oriented towards the present and the future. City comedy plots typically interweave several complex attempts at deceit and manipulation and pit schemers of greater and lesser expertise against one another. In *Epicene*, Morose plots to find a silent woman, marry her, beget an heir, and thereby disinherit his hated nephew, Dauphine. But he is trumped by Dauphine's plot to marry Morose to a boy in drag. Likewise, in *The Alchemist* the conventional strategic thinker, Surly, whom the routine dynamics of city comedy plot seem at first to favour, loses out to the quirky Lovewit, who snatches the prize away from him at the last moment. In *Michaelmas Term*, as we have already seen, Quomodo initially outwits Easy, but then Easy turns the tables by a counterplot; likewise, Onesephorus Hoard, in *A Trick to Catch the Old One*, learns at the end of the play that his frantic attempts to undermine his rival, Lucre, has merely played into the hands of his erstwhile victim, Witgood, who has plotted against them both. Like many successful schemers in the city comedies, Witgood is a reformed prodigal. His capacity for cool, goal-oriented thinking is the mark of his reformation, evidence that he has now renounced the pell-mell pursuit of immediate gratification and his present-oriented fixation upon chattel display.

A fascination with the ingenious plotter is not uniquely characteristic of Jacobean city comedy, of course—it's a staple of revenge tragedy, for instance, as well. Yet city comedies bourgeoisify the calculated, wary self-promotion earlier imagined as confined to court and Italianate settings, and to elite actors. It's difficult not to connect the triumph of the schemer in city comedy with new forms of proto-capitalist enterprise that rewarded calculated risk-taking and ingenuity among the middling sort. Satiric city comedies typically stage 'triumphalist', entrepreneurial fraud, as compared to the world-shattering frauds in such Shakespearean tragedies as *Hamlet*, *King Lear*, and *Othello*. They remain comedies, after all, though often bitter ones. The reduplicated conspiracies and counter-conspiracies in these plays—all of which are 'multiplot' dramas with a variety of protagonists—suggest, on the one hand, that a competition for pre-eminence pervades the crowded urban environment; on the other hand, by attending simultaneously to many connivers with a wide range of motives and aims, satiric city comedy implicitly diminishes the grandeur of any one particular struggle. Just as no one seems to own the settings of city comedy, no single protagonist dominates the action.

Yet the conception of the city as a place of ephemerality is in some tension with the conception of the city as a place especially suitable for schemers. In order for a plot to succeed, plotters need to be able to make accurate predictions, but if the setting is constantly changing, such forecasts become unworkable. The two masters of city comedy, Thomas Middleton and Ben Jonson, diverge on just this issue. Middleton delights in elaborate schemes that slowly unfold over the course of five acts. In *The Roaring Girl*, a play jointly written with Thomas Dekker, a young man feigns romantic interest in the wildly unsuitable transvestite, Moll Cutpurse, because he correctly foresees that his father, recoiling with horror, will then reconcile himself to the young man's original choice of bride. In *A Trick to Catch the Old One*, the trickster-figure introduces information about a supposed rich widow not directly to the man who might marry her, but to the man's professional rival, knowing that the jealousy between the two will eventually make them both his prey. The successful characters in Middleton's comedies are like skilled billiards players who can accurately foresee and control not merely the direction of a shot but the angle of the ball's rebound.

Jonson occasionally centres his plays on a sophisticated schemer: Dauphine in *Epicene*, for instance. Yet Dauphine's success seems predicated less on his own cleverness than upon the pathological rigidity, and hence unusual predictability, of his antagonist Morose. More often in Jonson's London comedies, unlooked-for occurrences prevent even the most intelligent protagonists from anticipating the future. Jonson's successful characters thus tend not to be those who set an elaborate conspiracy in play, but those who successfully improvise in response to abruptly changed circumstances. In *The Alchemist*, for instance, the 'winners' are neither the criminal connivers Subtle, Face, and Doll, nor the man who attempts, in a counterplot, to expose them. Instead, the homeowner Lovewit, fortuitously arriving home at the end of the play, immediately sees how to exploit a surprising situation and seizes the prizes of victory: a rich young widow and the 'alchemists'' accumulated booty. Lovewit's erstwhile butler, one of the three false alchemists, benefits as well, because, upon his master's return, he changes course in a flash and betrays his two collaborators.

The most extreme Jonsonian portrayal of London's unpredictability and novelty-seeking is *Bartholomew Fair*, a play in which an astonishing multiplication of incident and character threatens to overwhelm any vestige of a plot. The carnivalian Fair epitomizes and exaggerates the ephemerality of London as satiric city comedy more generally portrays it. Space is rented on short leases, not owned, at the Fair, and its nomadic workers' possessions consist entirely in moveable chattels: easily disassembled booths, cooking equipment, puppets. What they sell is designed for extraordinarily short-term enjoyment: pork, pears, ale, gingerbread, hobby-horses, ballads, puppet plays. Relationships are provisional, too, at the Fair: between seller and buyer, employer and employee, prostitute and client, performer and auditor, shark and gull, who constantly reshuffle themselves into new configurations. The long term is so irrelevant here that conversation degenerates into the 'game of vapors, which is nonsense: every man to oppose the last man that spoke' (4.4.25 s.d.), so that each participant is soon denying what he himself violently asserted only moments before. In this chaotic environment the elaborately calculating Justice Overdo, bumbling around with his head full of heroic precedents, merely makes a fool of himself. The canny Quarlous, on the other hand, prospers both maritally and financially by capitalizing upon unforeseen circumstances, paying no heed to principle or to consistency.

Some of the knottiest and most interesting difficulties with which city comedy must deal involve the disruption of family ties, and of the sex and gender system, in the chattel-oriented world of London. Chattels, as we have already seen, have the effect of elevating the power of the individual over the power of the family, and the power of the present over the power of the past. The emphasis on consumption as an index of status also has the effect of empowering women; shopping as a mode of self-fashioning is an equal-opportunity activity, and already in Jacobean London tends to be imagined as feminine or effeminizing.[14] Although under English common-law married women could not own anything in their own names, feminine 'paraphernalia' suitable to their rank, such as clothing and jewellery, were de facto their own property: their husbands could not sell them, and women could bequeath them in their wills. In the modest sphere of the elite woman's chattel acquisition, her husband's authority suffers an eclipse. 'The air of London / hath tainted her obedience already', complains a husband newly come to town of his spirited wife, in Richard Brome's *The Antipodes* (1638) (2.1.285–286).

Parents' authority, too, is frequently disclaimed. In *Michaelmas Term* Andrew Lethe, refusing to acknowledge his mother, employs her as a drudge, while the Country Wench disavows her father; in Phillip Massinger's *The City Madam*, two presumptuous daughters come nearly to ruin when they flout their father. Since respect for parents on the part of adult children is an effect of memory and a gesture of gratitude for past benefits, the neglect of this duty is one upshot of the city's invitation to the pleasurably present-oriented consumption. For similar reasons, widows mourn little in London comedy; the prospect of one or more new liaisons quickly overpowers any tender recollection of their husbands. Moreover, covetousness or self-gratification at the expense of one's relatives is not a vice confined to the young or the subaltern. Weakened kin relations leave junior family

---

[14] Karen Newman, 'City Talk: Women and Commodification in Jonson's *Epicoene*', *ELH* 53 (1989), 503–518.

members in satiric city comedy vulnerable to the whims of their elders, who are often more interested in amassing wealth for themselves than in assuring the success of the family line. Comedies of all kinds, of course, tend to feature a generational struggle between youths and their oppressive elders; yet, again and again in city comedies, this struggle takes a particular configuration, in which a 'bad uncle' attempts to alienate his property from the nephew who feels entitled to be his heir, but does not possess a son's right to inherit.

The relationship between the chattel economy and marriage seems particularly problematic. On the one hand, marriage among the affluent was openly treated as a property transaction in early modern England, yet, in a world of temporary market alliances and ephemeral goods, marriage seems an anomalous institution insofar as it constitutes not a contract for a limited term but an unbreakable lifelong commitment. City comedy plays again and again on the pitfalls of entering into a permanent union based on unreliable rumours of landed property far from London, rumours sometimes reinforced by an equally unreliable display of chattel property. In *Eastward Ho*, the penniless Sir Petronel Flash packs his new wife and mother-in-law out of town on a coach trip to his non-existent castle in the countryside, while he himself attempts to flee to Virginia. When, in *A Trick to Catch the Old One*, Walkadine Hoard impetuously marries a woman he believes is wealthy, but who turns out to be penniless, he is stuck with the bargain. So is the Yellowhammer family in *A Chaste Maid in Cheapside*, who marry their son to a woman they suppose to be a Welsh heiress, although she is actually Sir Walter Whorehound's cast-off mistress.

Prostitution, more than marriage, seems to approximate the fluid market alliances of mutual self-interest that thrive in the city. Satiric city comedy is ambivalently fascinated with the sex trade. Many city comedies juxtapose a plot involving a marriageable virgin with one involving a prostitute—a technique that naturally encourages the spectators to consider the similarities as well as the differences between the two kinds of sexual arrangements. Often, too, the play compares prostitution with other forms of commercial activity, implicitly asking why sex-for-pay should seem to fall into a different moral category than other forms of compensated labour. In Thomas Middleton's *Michaelmas Term*, the Courtesan, arguing against her scandalized and moralizing father, makes explicit the market rationale for her actions:

> Why, thou art an unreasonable fellow i'faith. Do not all trades live by their ware and yet called honest livers? Do they not thrive best when they

utter most and make it away by the great? Is not wholesale the chiefest merchandise?

(4.2.10–13)

Middleton's whores are often good businesswomen who collaborate intelligently with the heroes' strategic plans and typically profit through their own foresight. In *A Mad World, My Masters*, the Courtesan carefully saves up the money she earns to serve as a marriage portion; she may encourage impulsiveness in her customers, but she does not exhibit it herself. Like other Middleton whores, this one continually recycles herself as a virgin. The obliviousness to the past typical of the metropolis, as portrayed in city comedy, works to the prostitute's advantage; in her case 'experience' ought to lower her value, but no one can reliably recall whether she has it or not.

At the end of Middleton's plays, the clever prostitute generally snares an unsuspecting bridegroom. In these marriages, her past haunts her to some degree, since she does not get to wed the desirable young heir but is allotted a less attractive partner, a young dolt or an old usurer. Given the double standard pervasive in Renaissance culture, it is not surprising that her assimilation to respectable society is never as complete as the male prodigal's. On the other hand, she insists that even an unprepossessing husband renders her entirely respectable: 'If your logic cannot prove me honest', asserts the newlywed whore in *A Chaste Maid in Cheapside*, 'there's a thing called marriage, and that makes me honest'. 'So much for marriage and logic!' agrees her bridegroom cheerfully; 'I'll love her for her wit' (5.4.110–115). Middleton's accepting attitude contrasts markedly with that of, for instance, William Shakespeare in *Measure for Measure*: Lucio, compelled to marry the mother of his bastard child, complains that he would prefer the penalty of death by torture.

Even while critiquing the institution of marriage, Thomas Middleton typically ends his plays when his reformed prodigal or similar well-born hero finally weds his true love, albeit often accompanied by more mercenary couples. Jonson's city comedies tend not to include even this perfunctory gesture towards romance: *Epicene* ends with a mock divorce trial, *The Devil is an Ass* with a legal separation. Yet for Jonson, too, the line between whore and wife is a thin, even invisible one. Jonson's prostitutes, like Middleton's, are typically enterprising and intelligent: the difference between Doll Common in *The Alchemist*, or Ursula Pig-Woman in *Bartholomew Fair*, and the married or marriageable women in the plays is a difference of social status, not of moral principle. Yet while Middleton's plays tend to 'elevate' prostitutes into married life, Jonson's tend to 'degrade' wives into prostitutes. In *The*

Alchemist, the marriageable widow Dame Pliant substitutes without complaint for Doll Common, and in *Bartholomew Fair* both of the respectable married women, Win Littlewit and Dame Overdo, are easy prey for pimps.

Thomas Middleton's *A Chaste Maid in Cheapside* displays with particular thoroughness and wit the collision of a newly vigorous market-based social norm with traditional conceptions of sexual morality and marriage. Indeed, the collision is suggested in the title, which implies that chastity in Cheapside is a marvel, or an oxymoron. One of the comic 'problems' in *Chaste Maid* is that children, the legitimate fruit of marriage, are not distributed equitably even though there are more than enough to go around. The wealthy Sir Oliver Kix and his wife long for a child but cannot produce one, while Touchwood Senior and his loving wife separate because they cannot afford to support their rapidly expanding brood: 'Some only can get riches and no children, / We only can get children and no riches' (2.1.11–12). Though the inflexibilities of monogamous marriage would seem to make these couples' difficulties insurmountable, the urban marketplace efficiently matches up supply with demand. Setting himself up as a fertility doctor, Touchwood Senior induces pregnancy for Lady Kix; in gratitude, Sir Oliver offers to support Touchwood's large family. The coexistence of marriage and prostitution is even more blatant in another subplot; Allwit welcomes Sir Walter Whorehound as his wife's lover, and the true father of her children: 'I thank him, he's maintained my house this ten years, / Not only keeps my wife, but a keeps me / And all my family' (1.2.16–18). Meanwhile, Walter Whorehound has brought to town another of his mistresses, representing her as his niece, and marries her off to Tim Yellowhammer, the goldsmith's son. Not only is the actual difference between wife and whore eroded, but the rationale for making the distinction begins to seem mysterious when intimate relations are so completely subordinated to the workings of the market.

Whether a city comedy exposes the chicanery of a usurer, scoffs at the heedlessness of a prodigal, uncovers the hypocrisies of an adulterer, or mocks the pretentious upstart, it professes to initiate audiences into knowledge. The urbanite's main weapon against being imposed upon is an awareness of how the new mechanisms for social presentation and interactions operate. This awareness perhaps compensates for the lack, in London, of the social controls that had defended people against the aggressions of their neighbours in rural villages and small towns. Yet the knowledge proffered by satiric city comedies is not merely utilitarian and defensive. An important precedent for these plays are the tremendously popular tavern scenes in the Shakespeare's 1597–1598 *Henry IV Parts 1 and 2*. In these scenes, the comedy of urban life is played out not only for us but for the ambivalently playful Prince Harry, who temporarily immerses himself in the gritty world of the Boar's Head Tavern while retaining, as he tells us in his first soliloquy, ironic detachment from his role as royal prodigal. Harry tastes the pleasures of a knowledge that estranges the familiar in order to explain it.

Prince Harry's knowingness is part of the appeal of satiric city comedy as well. In a moment of mock chauvinism, Jonson writes:

> Our scene is London, 'cause we would make known
> No country's mirth is better than our own.
> No clime breeds better matter for your whore,
> Bawd, squire, imposter, many persons more.
> (*The Alchemist*, prologue, 5–8).

The playwrights stage scams for the sake of pleasure, while at the same time warning that fraudulence is rife in the London outside the theatre. But their very expertise calls their own motives, not to mention the sources of their knowledge, into question. So they revel in the ideal of detached observation, insisting that their own awareness of how to negotiate the complexities of urban life is not a guilty proficiency. 'Must you have / A black ill name, because ill things you know?' (5.2.343–344), asks Moll Cutpurse, a little plaintively, in *The Roaring Girl*, after demonstrating an impressive but suspicious facility in canting, the jargon of the criminal classes.

The fraudulence that London enables—the fraudulence of the chattel as a possibly empty sign of wealth and status, and the fraudulence of untrustworthy individuals—attracts moral condemnation in satiric city comedies, but frequently the delighted rehearsal of clever stratagems overwhelms the disapproval. The ironies of the plays are produced in the gap between modern, urban modes of life and a traditional moral code that, on the one hand, now seems inadequate but, on the other hand, also seems impossible to discard. The same gap produces a marked inconsistency of tone in many city comedies: acts one through four revel in clever opportunism and oneupmanship, and then, in the fifth act, the playwright exposes and punishes the 'bad', rewards the 'good', and closes on a flourish of conventionally high-minded sentiment. *Eastward Ho* ends with a panorama of repentance and just deserts: 'the careful father, thrifty son', 'the usurer punished', and 'the prodigal child reclaimed'. *A Mad World, My Masters* concludes with a warning to schemers: 'Who lives by cunning, mark it, his fate's cast; When he has gulled all, then is himself the last' (5.2.315–316). *The City Madam* ends with the vain and aspiring women of citizen origins confessing to their folly in seeking matches above their station: they must learn 'to move / In their own spheres'—that is, to know their proper place, and to acknowledge 'A distance 'twixt the city and the court' (5.3.162–164) *The Roaring Girl*, a comedy that provides an indulgent portrait of London's variety and in particular of a highly eccentric transvestite, ends with the marriage of a young, loving, entirely conventional couple; the bridegroom's father, previously characterized as a greedy urban chiseller, bestows upon them the deeds to land, which he calls 'the keys of wealth': 'The best joys / That can in worldly shapes to man betide / Are fertile lands and a fair fruitful bride' (5.2.205–209). In Middleton's city comedies, especially, an estate in the country often remains the ultimate object of aspiration, even for the wealthiest and most urbane citizen—an objective that suggests the residual appeal of the 'old order' even in the bustling heart of London. On the one hand, satiric city comedy tends both to celebrate and to ridicule London's distinctiveness: what it represents as the city's drastic differences from provincial England. On the other, the conventional morality of the endings suggest ambivalence, to say the least, about whether the new social situation of the city brings with it a workable new ethics of human interaction.

The Country House Poem

Pastoral—a genre with roots in Greek and Roman prototypes—was a literary kind of paramount importance to the Elizabethans. Philip Sidney's *Arcadia*, Edmund Spenser's *Shepherd's Calendar* and *Faerie Queene*, and William Shakespeare's *As You Like It* are only the most distinguished examples of an efflorescence of such writing in the 1580s and 1590s. As William Empson argued long ago, pastoral is an elite, not a rural genre, produced not by country shepherds but by citydwellers or courtiers, and it therefore sees rustic life in terms of a comparison to the more familiar urban or courtly world.[15] Depicted as natural, moderate, simple, and sincere, the pastoral countryside could offer a rebuke to more sophisticated, artificial modes of life. Duke Senior, in Shakespeare's *As You Like It*, exiled to a forest with some of his loyal followers, exclaims:

---

[15] William Empson, *Some Versions of Pastoral*, 1–22.

> Hath not old custom made this life more sweet
> Than that of painted pomp? Are not these woods
> More free from peril than the envious court?
>
> (2.1.2–4)

At the same time, pastoral—a genre ostensibly devoted to the depiction of a retired and humble life far from centres of power—could comment obliquely on exactly the matters it pretends to eschew. In the 1589 *The Art of English Poesy*, George Puttenham wrote that pastoral poets are accustomed 'under the veil of homely persons and in rude speeches, to insinuate and glance at greater matters, and such as perchance had not been safe to have been disclosed in any other sort'.[16]

Pastoral in the Elizabethan mode did not entirely vanish in 1603, but the Jacobean examples of the genre were often pointedly nostalgic. Mary Wroth's pastoral romance, *Urania*, advertises itself as a continuation of her uncle Philip Sidney's *Arcadia*. Many critics have read Fletcher's pastoral play *The Faithful Shepherdess* as deliberately evoking ideals of magical virginal authority reminiscent of the cult of Elizabeth.[17] Yet there is an efflorescene of a distinctively new kind of rural poem that, since G. R. Hibbard's seminal essay delineating the genre, has usually been called 'the country house poem'.[18] Alastair Fowler collects about fifty such poems, written between 1603 and 1660, in his anthology *The Country House Poem*;[19] the genre continued to be popular in the Restoration and eighteenth century with such major writers as John Dryden and Alexander Pope. Unlike earlier pastoral, with its deliberately fictive and generalized settings—Arden, Arcadia, Faerieland—the country house poem aims to depict a particular, identifiable English setting. Though they draw on English precedents, such as the detailed description of Kalender's house and garden in Sidney's *Arcadia*, country house poems are in general less indebted to Elizabethan pastoral than to Augustan Latin models—in particular, Virgil's *Georgics* and Horace's famous *Epode 2*, 'beatus ille', in praise of rural life.

---

[16] George Puttenham, *The Art of English Poesy: A Critical Edition*, ed. Frank Whigham and Wayne A. Rebhorn, p. 128.

[17] Curtis Perry, *The Making of Jacobean Culture: James I and the Renegotiation of Elizabethan Literary Practice*, pp. 59–66.

[18] G. R. Hibbard, 'The Country House Poem of the Seventeenth Century', *Journal of the Warburg and Courtauld Institutes* (1956), 159–174. Book-length discussions that treat the country house genre include James Turner, *The Politics of Landscape: Rural Scenery and Society in English Poetry, 1630–1660*; Don Wayne, *Penshurst: The Semiotics of Place and the Poetics of History*; and Anthony Low, *The Georgic Revolution*.

[19] Alastair Fowler, *The Country House Poem: A Cabinet of Seventeenth-Century Estate Poems and Related Items*.

The country house poem, as written by Jonson, Lanyer, Carew, Flecknoe, Fane, Randolph, Waller, Fane, Herrick, Marvell, and other poets, generally examines, in the course of describing and celebrating an estate, a mode of life structured around land proprietorship. This mode of life is typically opposed, implicitly or explicitly, to London's chattel economy and its associated ethical priorities, as depicted in satiric city comedy. In other words, not only do both city comedies and country house poems oppose country to city, but they oppose them in the same way, using the same criteria. It is not entirely surprising, then, that the two genres should emerge more or less simultaneously, nor that the same writer, Ben Jonson, should have written the most distinguished and varied satiric city comedies and perhaps the first—certainly, the most influential—country house poem. It is worth looking at this poem, 'To Penshurst', in some detail to see how this opposition works.

Jonson wrote 'To Penshurst' for one of his patrons, Robert Sidney, who had permitted him to sojourn on his estate in Kent, in southern England, for a time during the first decade of the seventeenth century. The poem was first printed in Jonson's *Works* of 1616, but was likely written between eight and ten years previously. Jonson intended the poem to thank his host for the hospitality he has already experienced and also, perhaps, to encourage him to extend similar invitations in the future. Not surprisingly, then, the circulation of favours and gifts is a central preoccupation in this poem, and this circulation is sharply distinguished from venal commercial transactions.

'To Penshurst' begins by repudiating exactly the order of value that city comedy ambivalently celebrates, a bid for status based on the display of bought luxuries:

> Thou art not, Penshurst, built to envious show
> Of touch or marble, nor canst boast a row
> Of polished pillars, or a roof of gold;
> Thou hast no lantern whereof tales are told,
> Or stair, or courts: but stand'st an ancient pile.
>
> (1–5)

The building of sumptuous 'prodigy houses', upon which some affluent Jacobeans had embarked, threatens the distinction between land and chattel by making the house an item purchased expressly to show off the new owner's wealth and personal taste. Penshurst Place, by contrast, is 'an ancient pile', unfashionably immutable. Indeed, Jonson focuses, as many critics have noticed, not on the house itself but on the land around it: Penshurst's 'better marks, of soil, of air, / Of wood, of water' (7–8). Jonson's gaze wanders over the varied, harmonious landscape: its copses, walks, mount, lowland pastures, and riverbanks.

Whereas the city's reliance upon chattel property correlates with competitive rapacity—one man's gain is another's deprivation—the world of 'To Penshurst' pours forth an apparently endless array of edible and renewable homegrown bounty: deer, pheasant, cattle, fish, and fruit. This abundance eliminates competition for resources. Unstinting generosity thus characterizes the land, the land's proprietor, and every inhabitant of Penshurst. Even the game birds and fish of Penshurst ardently offer themselves up to be eaten. As the lord offers sustenance to his guests, so the lord's tenants offer capons, cakes, cheeses, and apples to their beloved lord and lady. The tenants, Jonson pointedly remarks, expect nothing in return for their homely gifts—'they have no suit'(50)—and Sidney treats rich and poor guests alike to 'the same beer and bread, and selfsame wine' (63), not calculating the likelihood of having his favours returned. Significantly, abundance does not produce equality in Jonson's poem: the lord's status is superior to his tenants, and Jonson, the lord's guest, can give orders to the waiter who takes his meal 'below' (70) in the servant's quarters. Yet abundance keeps the hierarchy from seeming exploitative: even the poor and lowly have a surplus.

Because Sidney's role is to authorize generosity, not merely to perform it himself, he is best praised in his absence. The tenants converge upon the manor house, yet sitting in the great hall we encounter not the noble proprietor but, in an almost comic substitution, Jonson himself. He depicts himself eating hugely, enabled by Sidney's munificence to enjoy a benign fantasy of role reversal: 'as if thou, then, wert mine, or I reigned here' (74). Later in the poem, King James and Prince Henry arrive unexpectedly at Penshurst when the Sidneys are away, but, because the routines of hospitality are so well established, the linen, plates, and guest rooms are all at the ready to welcome them. At Penshurst, aristocratic magnanimity is on autopilot.

The significance of place in 'To Penshurst' is thus quite different from its significance in city comedy. The spaces of the multi-plotted city comedy, as we have seen, are largely public ones, in which competing initiatives unfold simultaneously, unpredictably colliding and interpenetrating. In 'To Penshurst', the estate is a metonymy of its proprietor, whose sensibility pervades and organizes its every aspect. Indeed, by addressing a patronage poem not to his patron but to his patron's estate, Jonson implies that in some sense Penshurst might substitute or stand in for its lord. This very tight connection between place and person is in part a heritage of feudalism, in which status depended upon control over land. Indeed, at the highest levels of society, one's name was originally the domain over which one exerted authority: Essex, Salisbury, Southampton, Buckingham. Significantly, too, the 'person' here was not an individual but the current head of a family, in what was ideally an unbroken dynasty of fathers and sons.

Yet, at the same time Jonson also evokes another, newer and nonfeudal, way in which Penshurst may figure forth its owner. In the early modern period, domestic spaces were beginning to become places of privileged retirement, the places most closely connected with, and thus most profoundly revelatory, of one's character.[20] Robert Sidney's refusal to deck out Penshurst with the latest in lanterns or pillars, his contentedness with the 'pile' of a house he has inherited, thus makes a statement about his personal ethical priorities. Significantly, however, this newer mode of domestic self-expression is itself a function of the flourishing 'chattel economy' that Jonson seems to repudiate in 'To Penshurst': if expensive, temptingly gaudy decorating choices were not there to be made, then Sidney could get no credit for resisting their allure. As it is, however, just as Sidney's generosity is best demonstrated in his physical absence, his integrity and taste are best illustrated not in what he buys, but in what he declines to buy.

Still, the sense in which Penshurst can manifest Robert Sidney's virtues remains mysterious, since it might seem to reveal the love and skill not of the lord of the manor but of those who actually perform the hospitality: the husbandmen, fishers, cooks, waiters, and so on. Thus, as Raymond Williams has indignantly noted, Jonson suppresses the toil of Penhurst's labourers—the fact that the pikes do not actually leap onto plates but must be fished for, that the cattle must be fed and slaughtered, the peaches gathered.[21] Jonson does so, I think, not—or not merely—out of contempt for or ignorance of manual labour. He had himself, after all, served an apprenticeship as a bricklayer, so he could not have imagined that the wall around the estate had simply erected itself. Rather, the presence of workers has the potential to threaten the smooth operation of Jonson's metonymy between person and place. He cannot assert an identity between Penshurst and Robert Sidney if the estate's beauty and abundance is multiply mediated by a large staff of employees with, presumably, some independent initiative. The apparently

---

[20] Don Wayne discusses the relevance of this cultural development to Jonson's poem in *Penshurst: The Semiotics of Place and the Poetics of History*.

[21] Raymond Williams, *The Country and the City*.

happy submission of the tenants suggests both that the landlord's superiority is a moral trait, not merely a social accident, and that social inequality serves the interests of both high and low. Not surprisingly, as we shall see in other contexts, this view of the social order is attractive to writers and readers of early modern England, who tend to be elite or elite-identified, and have more to gain than to lose from a social ethic that emphasizes willing loyalty to a superior.

In Jonson's poem, Robert Sidney's agency is constrained not by the interference of tenants and servants, but by the history and future of his family and the land they occupy. As we have already seen, satiric city comedy depicts London as a place of forgetfulness and aggressive present-orientation. At Penshurst, by contrast, the landscape testifies to the landowners' long connection to it. Copses memorialize the ancestral surnames Gamage, Ashore, and Sidney. The tree under which Lady Leicester fell into labour is henceforth called My Lady's Oak, and another oak had been planted upon the birth of Philip Sidney. Moreover, since Robert Sidney and his 'noble, fruitful, chaste' (90) wife are careful to inculcate their children in 'the mysteries of manners, arms, and arts' (98), the intimacy between family and estate will presumably perpetutate itself indefinitely. The word 'dwells', with which 'To Penshust' ends, means both 'lives' and 'remains': Jonson not only praises Robert Sidney, the virtuous individual, but glorifies the permanence of the Sidney lineage and their enduring tie to a particular location. The terms of this opposition between urban and rural places may suggest why the Jacobeans did not write 'country house plays'. Stripped of intrigue, competition, or inventiveness, Penshurst resists narrative presentation and 'plot' and virtually demands a descriptive mode.

It goes without saying that Jonson's depiction of Penshurst in particular, and rural England in general, is highly idealized and selective. The connection between a noble family and its land was not nearly as durable as Jonson represents it. Many of the great estates of the Jacobean and Caroline periods had been created in the mid-sixteenth century, from land seized from the Catholic Church. Penshurst was no exception; the 'ancient pile' had been bestowed by Edward VI upon his steward and tutor, Robert Sidney's grandfather, about a half-century previously. Moreover, Sidney 'dwelt' at Penshurst rather rarely, spending much of his career abroad as governor of Flushing in the Low Countries, and later at James's court. And he was poor for his station in life: his unrenovated house and his reliance on homegrown foodstuffs may reflect necessity, not virtue.

The contrast Jonson implies in 'To Penshurst' between urban market calculation, based on an assumption of scarcity and competition, and spontaneous rural generosity, based on an assumption of abundance and social harmony, is likewise more poetic fiction than objective description. In early modern England, agricultural practices were rapidly changing under the pressure of a newly rigorous profit orientation, bringing enormous changes to the countryside, enclosing what had once been common lands, draining fenlands, and developing more specialized techniques of cultivation in order to wring optimum production from different kinds of land. Jonson's contemporaries vigorously debated these developments, and Jonson's own awareness of them is suggested in his portrayal of the grain-hoarding farmer, Sordido, in his early play *Every Man Out of His Humour*.

What, then, motivates Jonson's idealized, and even counterfactual, account of conditions in the countryside? Both 'To Penshurst' and 'To Sir Robert Wroth', a related poem addressed to Robert Sidney's son-in-law, explicitly mark out an exception, not a rule. 'How blest art thou, canst love the country, Wroth', exclaims Jonson in the second poem's opening line; the unstated corollary is that most similarly situated gentlemen did not. Jonson details the richness of country life so lavishly because that richness is so unintuitive, in a culture in which remaining in London or at court was widely desired and practiced among the affluent. In his country house poems Jonson not only praises the patrons to which the poems are explicitly addressed, but lends his rhetorical aid to King James's attempts to cajole landowners to reside on their estates and devote themselves to local governmental tasks. This is one reason why Jonson's country house poems describe rural life in terms of a point-by-point comparison with an urban alternative. At the same time, as Leah Marcus has noted, the politics of 'repastoralizing' England's aristocracy is a tricky one from a monarch's point of view, since fostering the independent authority of aristocratic estate proprietors might well have the effect of undermining a strong central government.[22] Indeed, towards the end of 'To Penshurst', having praised the estate's self-sufficiency, Jonson apparently feels the need to affix it securely into the larger structure of the nation-state. The hospitality extended to King James and Prince Henry suggests that the fostering of social harmony within the walls of Penshurst is not at odds with—indeed, ought to be a prop for—a healthy monarchy.

---

[22] Leah Marcus, *The Politics of Mirth: Jonson, Herrick, Milton, Marvell, and the Defense of the Old Holiday Pastimes*.

Aemilia Lanyer's 'The Description of Cookham', printed in 1611, may have been written before or after Jonson's 'To Penhurst': certainly, it did not have the fame or influence of Jonson's poem, but it considers many similar issues. Lanyer's poem describes a period in which she stayed at Cookham Dean, an estate in Berkshire, with the Countess of Cumberland and the Countess's daughter, Anne Clifford. Like Jonson, Lanyer uses the poem both to celebrate the virtues of her patrons, and to commemorate her intimacy with them. And, like Jonson, Lanyer delights in a panoramic view of the estate. The ladies' 'prospect' suggests their benign mastery of the surroundings. As at Penshurst, the landscape provides a seemingly natural endorsement of the aristocrats' superiority, a superiority simultaneously physical, social, and ethical:

> you might plainly see
> Hills, vales, and woods, as if on bended knee
> They had appeared, your honour to salute,
> Or to prefer some strange unlooked-for suit.
> (67–70)

Yet the Countess and her daughter do not 'dwell' at Cookham with the same security that the Sidneys occupy Penshurst. They are merely passing through, and while the first part of the poem describes their arrival there in summertime, the second half of the poem depicts the ladies' autumn departure. Whereas Sidney, whether at Penshurst or away, authorizes the estate's continual bounty, at Cookham the coming and going of the ladies coordinates with the changing of the seasons.

Lanyer is silent on the reasons for the ladies' peregrinations, but they may have resulted from a complex family situation. Anne Clifford was the only child of the late Earl of Cumberland, and would in the normal course of things have been expected to inherit his massive estate, yet the Earl had bequeathed his land and title to his brother, despite the terms of an entailment that seemed to designate his daughter as heir. The widowed Countess sued to overturn the will in favour of Anne. When Lanyer was writing 'The Description of Cookham', the matter was still in litigation, eventually to be decided in favour of the late Earl's brother; the fact that it was disputed at all highlights the disadvantages for women of a patriarchal system that preferred male heirs. While in this legal limbo, unable to lay claim to the lands Anne and her mother thought were rightfully hers, the two women lived either on the properties her mother had brought to her marriage to the Earl or on the estates of relatives: Cookham was a crown estate leased to the Countess's brother. Since the two ladies are not at home at Cookham, the poem cannot pay tribute to their hospitality. The productivity of the estate, so prominently featured in other country house poems, therefore does not engage Lanyer's attention. Instead, she focuses on picturesque features with little use value, such as songbirds, oak trees, brooks, and bramble patches, which encourage aesthetic enjoyment and religious meditation. Cookham, in Lanyer's account, reminds the ladies not of their roots but of their rootlessness: their real home is not on earth but in heaven.

For Robert Sidney as Jonson portrays him, Penshurst's abundance correlates neatly with his fatherly prowess: Lady Sidney pours forth children as the land pours forth food, under the benevolent aegis of the paterfamilias. Neither Anne Clifford nor her mother can occupy this authorizing position. Even if Anne were eventually re-installed as her father's heir, she would become part of her husband's family upon marriage, as would any children of their union. Indeed, by the time Lanyer writes the poem, young Anne has already married the Earl of Dorset and is, therefore, no longer living with her mother.

Moreover, Lanyer's own situation at Cookham is even shakier than her patrons'. Despite the noblewomen's legal difficulties, they are privileged compared to Lanyer: there are worse misfortunes than having to spend a summer at one's brother's estate instead of one's own. The daughter and wife of court musicians, Lanyer spent much of her life on the margins of court life, but she did not herself possess high social status or independent means. The conditions under which she stayed at Cookham are unknown. She was likely employed as Anne's companion, or perhaps retained for her poetic gifts or artistic acumen. Whatever her role, once Anne was married, her services were apparently no longer required.

The female friendship Lanyer describes in 'The Description of Cookham'—unprotected by social and legal customs and existing, as it were, between the cracks of patriarchy—seems profoundly unstable and impermanent. Indeed, the poem is explicitly one of retrospection and mourning, beginning with the word 'farewell' and returning again and again to the theme of irreparable loss: 'Never shall my sad eyes again behold' (9) ... 'And yet it grieves me'(99) ... 'I evermore must grieve / Hating blind fortune' (125–126) ... 'This last farewell to Cookham here I give' (205). Seduced and abandoned, as it were, by her noble patrons, Lanyer finds herself in the position of the rejected lover, and behaves much as such lovers do in Renaissance poetry, contenting herself perforce with highly mediated forms of intimacy—stealing a kiss, for instance, from a tree that Anne had kissed upon her departure.

In 'The Description of Cookham' Lanyer's expressions of gratitude for the generosity her patrons showed her in the past are shot through with passive-aggressive neediness, because her patrons apparently do not continue to be generous. In the poem's last line, Lanyer asserts that she remains tied for the rest of her life by 'rich chains' to the Countess of Cumberland. Yet the poem's progress from blooming summer to wintry desolation hardly bodes well for the future. Apparently Lanyer desires just what Jonson desires: a secure relationship with a generous, sympathetic patron. Yet whereas Jonson—perhaps wishfully—shores up his friendship with Sidney by aligning it with durable social and legal arrangements, Lanyer foregrounds the precariousness of her own position, and her social and emotional dependence upon the whims of a patron.

Thomas Carew wrote 'To Saxham', a close imitation of 'To Penshurst', in the early 1630s. The poem reflects some of the political and social changes that mark the Caroline period. Miraculously warm and bounteous even in the depths of winter, Saxham's prime characteristic, according to Carew, is its radical separation from its environment:

> The season hardly did afford
> Coarse cates unto thy neighbour's board;
> Yet thou hadst dainties, as the sky
> Had only been thy volary.
> (15–18)

Under these circumstances Saxham's hospitality becomes not a model for other estates to emulate, but a refuge for the poor and the pilgrim who, cold and starving, stumble in from outside its walls. In 'To Penshurst', Jonson fantasizes that animals offer themselves to be consumed merely because they love the lord of the manor; in 'To Saxham', the animals are fleeing a worse fate elsewhere (though what might that be?).

> the birds, fearing the snow
> Might to another deluge grow,
> The pheasant, partridge, and the lark,
> Flew to thy house, as to the Ark.
> (19–22)

In 'To Penshurst', as we have seen, Jonson differentiates Sidney's estate from inferior, showy alternatives, but eventually folds Penshurst into a larger community. 'To Saxham', by contrast, has no hint of a presiding monarchical presence, nor of a society into which the estate might fit. Carew instead emphasizes Saxham's isolating difference. The allusion to the story of Noah and the Ark—of a tiny virtuous remnant saved from otherwise universal destruction—implies that while Saxham may keep its gates open to all, pointedly refusing to examine the worthiness of those who claim its hospitality, the world outside those gates is nonetheless dangerous, sinful, and doomed.

Thomas Carew is a loyal servant of Charles I, not a partisan of the 'Country' faction from which opposition to the King's policies was beginning to arise, so it is highly unlikely that he means 'To Saxham' to empower individual landowners at the expense of the monarchy.[23] In fact, the poem employs a way of dealing with unpleasant or chaotic situations that would become fatally attractive to many royalists, including the king himself: the drawing of a tight boundary around a small manageable area of influence, and a concomitant refusal to engage with what lies without.

The country house poem changes markedly under the pressure of the war years. In the 1640s and 1650s, the alternative to life on the estate is no longer life at court or even life in the city, but life in a military camp. These later poems typically contrast the peace and retirement of rural life with the struggle of participating in public affairs in a strife-torn nation. Written in 1639, when England was battling Scotland, Carew's 'To My Friend G. N. from Wrest', like his earlier 'To Saxham', models itself closely on 'To Penshurst'; once again Carew lauds the estate's small size, lack of architectural ostentation, agricultural bounty, and commitment to hospitality. Yet what impresses him most is not a contrast between Wrest's simple bounty and the empty showiness of other estates, but the contrast between Wrest's 'temperate air' with 'cold nights ... by the banks of Tweed', a river in northern England where soldiers (including Carew) had been fighting the Scots (1–3). As in 'To Saxham', Wrest is precious partly because it is cut off from its hostile surroundings, in this case literally isolated by streams that meander twice around it, creating a natural double moat. The author of the Caroline masque *Coelum Britannicum*, Carew redeploys tropes of cosmic harmony that in the 1620s and 1630s he and others had associated with the court: the originally neo-Platonic conception that the glittering assembly of splendidly garbed, dancing courtiers constituted an earthly incarnation of the stars circulating harmoniously in the heavens. But here the relationship between the

---

[23] John Kerrigan discusses the complexity of Carew's allegiances, and his continued connection to provincial society, in 'Thomas Carew', *On Shakespeare and Early Modern Literature: Essays*, pp. 181–216.

earthly and the heavenly is inverted. The mundane inhabitants of Wrest's streams have it better than the 'barren' constellations who yearn to participate in Wrest's generativity, a trait that seems obscurely linked to its 'narrow' size:

> Our fishes, swans, our waterman, and boat,
> Envied by those above, which wish to slake
> Their star-burnt limbs in our refreshing lake.
> But they stick fast nailed to the barren sphere,
> Whilst our increase in fertile waters here
> Disport, and wander freely where they please
> Within the circuit of our narrow seas.
>
> (81–87)

In royalist poetry of the mid-century, Carew's celebration of abundance and freedom within a confined circuit will evolve into a repudiation of the necessity of the estate at all, as the king's followers, under the pressure of defeat and penury, learn to sustain themselves without external resources. Thus, the royalist Richard Lovelace, his fortunes ruined by the war, preserves the values asserted by the country house poem after its material occasion has vanished. The prison cell, or the private room in which friends gather to toast the king, or even the loyal heart of the defeated cavalier, becomes the cherished walled location that resists incursion and honours hospitality. As we shall see in Chapter 6 on the poetry of love and friendship, for those whose material and social worlds have shrunk, such a retreat is more searchingly explored in poetry about intimate relationships than in celebrations of the landed estates many of them no longer possess.

The most remarkable of the later country house poems, however, is Andrew Marvell's 'Upon Appleton House', written in the early 1650s, which appropriates and radically revises many of the genre's typical features. Like Jonson and Lanyer, Marvell writes as a poet whose patron, Thomas Lord Fairfax, had permitted him to live on his estate, Nun Appleton, where Marvell served as tutor to Fairfax's daughter. Like Carew, Marvell contrasts the peaceful agrarian routines at modest Nun Appleton with the violence of civil war. Fairfax, the relatively moderate Lord General of the New Model Army, disputed Cromwell's insistence upon putting Charles I on trial for treason and, in 1650, resigned his commission rather than lead a pre-emptive invasion of Scotland. Not surprisingly, then, Marvell dwells at length upon both the obvious contrasts and the surprising similarities between Fairfax's previous life of military engagement and public service, and his current life as gentleman farmer:

> See how the flowers, as at parade,
> Under their colours stand displayed:
> Each regiment in order grows,
> That of the tulip, pink, and rose.
>   (309–312)

The garden, laid out in the shape of a fortress and manned with flower-soldiers, both compliments and consoles Fairfax, who in Marvell's poem has not so much relinquished a professional military career as redirected his efforts in peaceful directions.

The relation between garden and battlefield seems closer than it might otherwise because Marvell's vision of nature is not the quietly harmonious, submissively bounteous nature of Jonson, Lanyer, and Carew, but one which incorporates mutability, sudden reversals, and even violence. Also, unlike Jonson's Penshurst, Lanyer's Cookham, or Carew's Saxham, Nun Appleton is full of workers—in particular mowers, whose traditional association with death Marvell emphasizes:

> With whistling scythe, and elbow strong
> These massacre the grass along:
> Whiles one, unknowing, carves the rail
> Whose yet unfeathered quills her fail.
> The edge all bloody from its breast
> He draws, and does his stroke detest;
> Fearing the flesh untimely mowed
> To him a fate as black forebode.
>   (393–400)

In other respects, too, 'Upon Appleton House' insists upon pointing out, even celebrating, what its predecessors had denied or suppressed. The estate is not the ancestral home of the Fairfaxes, Marvell frankly admits, but was acquired by marriage at the dissolution of the monasteries, and its future will not lie with a Fairfax either, since the family heir is a daughter, not a son. Marvell's answer to the 'prospect moment' featured in so many country house poems is a witty reversal that puts insects in the position of power and prestige:

> And now to the abyss I pass
> Of that unfathomable grass,
> Where men like grasshoppers appear,
> But grasshoppers are giants there;
> They, in their squeaking laugh, contemn
> Us, as we walk more low than them.
> (369–374)

A similar upside-down image ends the poem, a vision of salmon-fishers walking home in the evening carrying their boats aloft:

> And, like Antipodes in shoes,
> Have shod their heads in their canoes.
> (771–772)

Whereas Jonson denies that change matters, Lanyer deplores its effects, and Carew defiantly celebrates what he suspects to be a fast-vanishing way of life, Marvell, who comes to maturity during the civil war years and eventually sides with the Parliamentarians, not the royalists, seems convinced that disorienting change is inevitable and that a totalizing perspective upon one's world is impossible to achieve. In consequence, the scope of the landholder's power, as the poem imagines it, is dramatically diminished. The task of the Fairfaxes, as Marvell sees it, is to 'make destiny their choice' (744) by gracefully accepting life circumstances which are impossible to anticipate or control.

Chorography and Landscape

Chorography or 'map-writing'—the mapping and description of local places, their landmarks, history, and customs—first became popular in the sixteenth century, as part of a surge of an antiquarian interest in English history. As Richard Helgerson has influentially argued, chorography was initially conceived as a national, royally sponsored project under the Tudors, and its energies originally derive from a widely shared desire to incorporate the various regions of the British Isles into a newly powerful nation-state. But the implicit politics of the genre change, Helgerson argues, in the first part of the seventeenth century. Helgerson detects in Stuart chorography a veiled challenge to the claims of absolute royal power promulgated by James I. In these years, chorographers' attention to local interests and authority defines the essence of 'Englishness' not in terms of subjection to a monarch or in the national state, but in terms of a connection between the land and the people who live on it.[24] Moreover, contra James's stated ambition of folding England, Wales, and Scotland into a single 'empire of Great Britain', the chorographers' focus on local phenomena, legends, customs, and history implicitly undermines the sweeping, homogenizing paradigms of political and cultural union.

Most Jacobean chorographical works are works of antiquarian research that do not present themselves as ambitious works of literature. Some, such as John Speed's *Theatre of the Empire of Great Britain* (1611) are collections of maps with short descriptions attached, and others, such as Richard Carew's *Survey of Cornwall* (1602) are straightforward antiquarian accounts in prose, accompanied by a map of the locale described. There are a few noteworthy exceptions. William Camden's magisterial *Britannia*, a comprehensive work of scholarship first published in Latin under Elizabeth, was revised and reissued under James, and translated into English in 1610 by Philemon Holland; his *Remains Concerning Britain*, first published in 1605, is a shorter English companion to *Britannia*. More self-consciously artful, Michael Drayton's long chorographical poem, *Poly-Olbion*, presents itself as a work of a high order of literary ambition.[25] Written in alexandrines, Drayton's county-by-county chorographical description of England and Wales was sumptuously published in two folio instalments, complete with maps and detailed notes, in 1612 and 1622.

Poly-Olbion aspires to both variety and comprehensiveness. Its name means 'many Albions', and the poem is dedicated to celebrating the distinctiveness of each of the different parts of the British Isles and to recounting their long histories. These aims partly determine the poem's structure. If its narrator is to describe all of England, Wales, and Scotland, he cannot remain in one place, however enticing, celebrating the way the lord 'dwells' on his inherited property and passes it on to his descendants. So, accompanied by his Muse, Drayton moves through his landscapes tour-guide fashion, neither host nor guest but pilgrim. Like a tour guide, he is most arrested by what is unique about each locale he visits, not what it shares with the others, and, like a tour guide too, his aims are strongly didactic.

---

[24] Richard Helgerson, 'The Land Speaks', *Forms of Nationhood: The Elizabethan Writing of England*, pp. 105–148.
[25] For recent scholarship on Drayton's *Poly-Olbion*, see Andrew McRae and Philip Schwyzer, eds., *Poly-Olbion: New Perspectives*.

For the country house poem, as we have seen, the beauty and fruitfulness of the landscape testifies to the virtues of the land's proprietor. Penshurst is fruitful because Robert Sidney is generous. Cookham is idyllic because the Countess of Cumberland is devout. Saxham is plenteous because Sir John Croft is hospitable. Chorography tends to reverse this relationship between land and person quite explicitly. For instance, William Camden, in *Remains Concerning Britain*, remarks that

> I cannot yet see why men should think that their ancestors gave names to places, when the places bare those very names before any men did their surnames. Yea, the very terminations of the names are such as are only proper and applicable to places, and not to persons in their significations, if any will mark the local terminations ... Who would suppose hill, wood, field, ford, ditch, pool, pond, tower, or tor, and such like terminations, to be convenient for men to bear their names, unless they could also dream hills, woods, fields, fords, ponds, pounds, etc. to have been metamorphosed into men by some supernatural transformation? And I doubt not but they will confess that towns stand longer than families continue.[26]

While Jonson, Carew, Lanyer, and Marvell poetically imagine the land as subordinate and responsive to a landlord, Camden sees the land as prior and the people who live there as taking their identity from it.

Both out of personal conviction and because Camden is the source for much of Drayton's antiquarian lore in *Poly-Olbion*, Drayton much amplifies this conceit. As we have seen, the country house poem contrasts the customary life of rural folk with the fashion-driven, chattel-cluttered urban lifestyle—but, possibly deliberately, the country house poem fails to scrutinize the actual antiquity of what it represents as timeworn custom. Drayton, on the other hand, attempts to look back to the earliest settlement of the British Isles. He portrays successive waves of invaders—Romans, Celts, Saxons, Normans—sweeping over Britain, as they war, settle, war again, and often are displaced in their turn. In other words, while the country house poem's relatively short-term historical imagination consolidates the landlord's control, Drayton's longer-term view tends to undermine it, by suggesting the ephemerality of all human arrangements, and thus implicitly of proprietary authority over land. While individuals and groups of human beings come and go over the aeons, only the land persists—land

---

[26] William Camden, *Remains Concerning Britain*, ed. R. D. Dunn, p. 104.

often allegorically personified by Drayton as resenting its despoliation by human beings.

Drayton was one of a number of writers who maintained their distance from James I, or failed to receive patronage from his court.[27] It was a group that grew sadder and bitterer after the death of the Crown Prince Henry in 1611 robbed those disenchanted with James of an alternative upon which to pin their hopes. Drayton's political and ethical preferences are especially clearly marked in 'The Thirteenth Song', the Warwickshire book—arguably the high point of *Poly-Olbion*, because Drayton grew up in Warwickshire and is drawing upon his own experience rather than merely channelling Camden. Drayton's account of Warwickshire and its history focuses upon the defiant, the victimized, and those marginal to the workings of power. He praises Lady Godiva, who memorably challenges the political and marital authority of her husband to champion the people oppressed by an unjust tax. He depicts the Forest of Arden from the point of view of a hunted stag; the princely sport notoriously relished by James here seems vicious, motiveless persecution. Drayton's ideal figure is a gentle hermit who lives alone in the forest and knows how to use the healing power of its herbs without exploiting it aggressively or making any claim of ownership. In such moments Drayton seems closer to contemporary environmentalists, who celebrate the primacy of the natural world, than to most Jacobean writers, who accept that God has given man dominion over the earth and its creatures.

Richard Helgerson argues that Drayton's egalitarian impulses are a reaction against theories of royal absolutism; yet they might also be seen as a more thoroughgoing critique of subordination in a variety of settings. In his description of a Warwickshire sunrise, Drayton gives the conventional pride of place to Philomel, the nightingale, but nonetheless what catches his ear is not the nightingale's song alone but the 'mirthful choirs' (51) of many bird species singing at once: the throstle, the woozel, the merle or blackbird, the linnet, the woodlark, reed-sparrow, nope, red-breast, wren, yellow-pate, goldfinch, tydie, hecco, and jay. The birds do not, of course, intentionally harmonize with one another: the pleasant soundscape is merely a collection of independent efforts. All 'singers' contribute to the distinctive sound of the forest—the modest as well as the virtuosic, the jay as well as the nightingale. Possibly there is an element of self-justification in this description: certainly the anti-elitist aesthetic suggested here contrasts with Ben Jonson's view that poets naturally rival one another

---

[27] David Norbrook, *Poetry and Politics in the English Renaissance: Revised Edition 2002*, pp. 173–198.

for artistic pre-eminence, with the result that great artists, like Jonson, triumph over and silence lesser ones, like Drayton. Elsewhere, competition is hardly absent in *Poly-Olbion*; again and again, Drayton concocts little narratives of strife between allegorized features of his landscapes: rivalries between neighbouring mountains, for instance. Yet these antagonisms are typically unresolvable, since one geographical feature cannot 'defeat' the other.

To Drayton's bitter disappointment, *Poly-Olbion* was unpopular in its own day, and it failed to found a tradition of similar poems. Drayton's insistence that the land persists while its proprietors vanish was hardly a flattering message for potential patrons. More seriously, although Drayton's quasi-egalitarian sentiments are perhaps politically appealing, the result for the poem is equivocal. They seem to prevent him from settling on an overarching narrative that would hold the poem's elements together—a narrative that would inevitably have forced him to subordinate some aspects of its presentation in the interests of others. On the small scale, Drayton's refusal or inability to be selective results in interminable lists. On a larger scale, the 'songs' tend to turn into list-equivalents that merely juxtapose tale after tale, rambling on with little trajectory or sense of coherence.

John Denham's *Cooper's Hill* draws both on the tradition of the country house poem and chorography to produce a new kind of poem, inaugurating a genre of philosophical landscape poetry that would continue to thrive in future centuries: Pope's 'Windsor Forest', John Dyer's 'Grongar Hill', Wordsworth's 'Tintern Abbey', and Matthew Arnold's 'Dover Beach' are distinguished examples of this mode. The narrator describes himself standing atop Cooper's Hill, a rise of land in Surrey that comprised part of an estate Denham had inherited from his father, and that offers sweeping views of the surrounding countryside. The poem, however, makes little account of the poet's legal proprietary claim to this hilltop—or, rather, reformulates that property relationship as an artistic prerogative. Whereas in Drayton's *Poly-Olbion* people come and go, while the anthropomorphized landscape persists forever, Denham's poem opens by asserting that landscape derives its significance from the meanings human beings affix to it.

> Sure there are poets which did never dream
> Upon Parnassus, nor did taste the stream
> Of Helicon, we therefore may suppose
> Those made not poets, but the poets those.

> And as courts make not kings, but kings the court,
> So where the Muses and their train resort,
> Parnassus stands.
>
> (1–7)[28]

The presence of a poet makes Cooper's Hill a Parnassus, the seat of classical poetry, as the presence of a king makes the court—not reciprocally. The poet's job is not to discover meanings intrinsic in the land but to use the land to incite his own reflections.

As the analogy between poet and monarch suggests, the poem that follows will be deeply concerned with political relations. And the complicated textual history of the poem reflects the turmoil of these relations in mid-century. The first version of the poem was published in 1642, just before the outbreak of war between Charles and the forces of Parliament, then reprinted with small changes in 1643 and 1650. A second, much revised, version was first printed in 1655; in 1668 the poem was printed again, with some minor changes from the 1655 version, and with four added lines.[29] In other words, Denham kept tinkering with his poem over the course of more than twenty years and rewrote it extensively to accommodate new political realities.

In the first version, the height of Cooper's Hill offers philosophical distance from and perspective upon both the landscape and its inhabitants. Denham's viewpoint is literally lofty:

> So raised above the tumult, and the crowd
> I see the city.
>
> (27–28)

As in the city comedies, London is the place of venal commerce and consumption:

> Men like ants
> Toil to prevent imaginary wants;

---

[28] This is the wording in the revised, 1655 version; in 1642 the sentiment is similar but the wording is slightly different: 'Sure we have poets that did never dream / Upon Parnassus, nor did taste the stream / Of Helicon, and therefore I suppose / Those made not poets, but the poets those.'

[29] All the versions, plus extensive commentary on the revisions, are available in Brendan O'Hehir, *Expans'd Hieroglyphics: A Critical Edition of Sir John Denham's Cooper's Hill*.

Yet all in vain, increasing with their store,
Their vast desires, but make their wants the more.
(30–33)

In the later version of *Cooper's Hill*, this sense of personal invulnerability has vanished—not surprisingly, as Denham was forced into political exile during the Civil War and, when he returned to England, his lands had been confiscated. Still, in both versions of the poem, the view of the landscape sweeping before him—including London, Windsor, and the Runnymede meadow—evokes reflections upon tumultuous events that had transpired over centuries. Like Drayton, Denham portrays England as an active participant in global activities—the Crusades, the Reformation, the exploration of East and West Indies—but his primary concern is the relationship between the monarch and his people. Again and again Denham poses two extreme alternatives and suggests that the best state is a moderate one in which conflicting impulses balance one another out. Thus, while Catholics are too idle and too rich, Puritans are too ardent and too violent; the Anglican way offers a happy medium. Similarly, the relationship between king and subject is ideally reciprocal and harmonious, yet often—historically and in the present moment—disordered and competitive. Although Denham is a royalist, he does not support unlimited royal prerogative. He criticizes Henry VIII's confiscation of church property and King John's intransigence with the barons, the first contrasting with Charles's renovation of St Paul's Cathedral, the latter appropriately countered by the barons' assertions of the subject's right in the Magna Carta. Yet if overly aggressive assertion of monarchical power leads to tyranny, rule by the people leads to anarchy. In the first version of the poem Denham represents Charles, the modern monarch, as the embodiment of the true *via media*, harmoniously uniting a variety of potentially competitive impulses. He is both pious and courageous, and his loving union with Queen Henrietta Maria blends Mars and Venus. In its early version, 'Cooper's Hill' foretells a royalist victory in which monarchical supremacy will be reasserted, but in a legal and appropriate way.

When the first version of Cooper's Hill was published in 1642, it was not unreasonable to hope for the compromises Denham suggests at the end of the poem between royal and parliamentary power. By the 1650s, of course, the political situation seemed much different. Although the 1655 printing of 'Cooper's Hill' purports to be 'the only true copy' of a poem that was supposedly previously printed in a corrupt form, in fact the revised version reflects the situation in the 1650s, when (counter to the confident prediction of the king's eventual victory in the first version) the royalists had been defeated, Charles executed, and Cromwell installed as Lord Protector. Denham remains loyal to his memory of Charles as the hero of Windsor: soldier, saint, and friend. One passage in the 1642 version dealt with a stag hunt: as Earl Wasserman noted many years ago, the episode alludes allegorically to the trial and execution of Charles's close advisor Thomas Wentworth, Earl of Strafford, to which Charles reluctantly acceded in an attempt to appease his enemies.[30] In the 1655 version the stag-hunting episode is much extended and there is more sympathy for the hunted animal, who now seems more analogous to Charles I than to the long-dead Strafford. There is likewise a less sanguine sense that things will eventually turn out for the best. In the first version of the poem, Denham expects custom and institution to prevail: 'may the law, which teaches kings to sway / Their sceptres, teach their subjects to obey' (353–354). In the later version there is no clear political, institutional solution to the struggle between the king and the people; the landscape itself must provide whatever solace is to be had. The Thames River, which runs through the entire breadth of the diverse landscape Denham is describing, provides a natural model of balanced harmony, in lines later commended by Dryden for their elegance and poise:

> O could I flow like thee, and make thy stream
> My great example, as it is my theme!
> Though deep, yet clear, though gentle, yet not dull;
> Strong without rage, without o'erflowing full.
> (189–192)

Attempts to control such a river, by enclosing it too tightly or damming it up, are counterproductive, for then the river rages and overflows: 'Stronger, and fiercer by restraint he roars / And knows no bound, but makes his power his shores' (357–358). Yet properly used and respectfully managed, the Thames is a lifegiving source of abundance.

Denham's view of the political world as the restless play of opposites has some similarities to Marvell's, but the differences are just as striking. For Denham the political and aesthetic ideal is one in which disparate, even potentially contradictory, tendencies might potentially be harmonized, but the tendency to 'excess' in either direction is always ruinous. For Marvell,

---

[30] Earl Wasserman, 'Denham: Cooper's Hill', in *The Subtler Language: Critical Readings of Neoclassic and Romantic Poems*, pp. 45–88.

while the play of opposites is just as extreme and unsettling, it is also dynamically invigorating and potentially restorative.

Outlandish Spaces

In some moods, early modern English writers liked to think of their island nation as a place set apart, geographically and morally. This literal isolation could be a good thing: in Shakespeare's *Richard II*,[31] John of Gaunt imagines England as

> This happy breed of men, this little world,
> This precious stone set in a silver sea,
> Which serves it in the office of a wall,
> Or as a moat defensive to a house,
> Against the envy of less happier lands.
> (2.1.40–44)

Or England could stand out from other nations for its corruption: 'no clime breeds better matter for your whore / Bawd, squire, imposter', as we have seen Ben Jonson claiming in *The Alchemist* (prologue, 7–8). But, in fact, the British archipelago had always been strongly tied politically, religiously, and culturally to Continental Europe. And as England's trade networks, exploration and colonizing enterprises, and diplomatic initiatives multiplied through the late sixteenth and early seventeenth centuries, its citizens were increasingly exposed to a wide variety of non-English people and experiences, both from other European locales and from further afield, in Africa, India, the Middle East, and the New World. English voyages of exploration to the New World in the sixteenth century had been chronicled in Richard Hakluyt's *Principal Navigations, Voyages, and Discoveries of the English Nation* (1598–1600), and colonizing activity began to take hold in Virginia and New England in the first decades of the seventeenth century. In 1616 one of the Jamestown settlers, Thomas Rolfe, returned to the English court with his native American wife, Pocohantas, the daughter of the chief, Powhatan, who had converted to Christianity and taken the name Rebecca.

Professional theatre, from its outset in the late Elizabethan period, had capitalized on its audience's fascination with foreign places, strange customs,

---

[31] Shakespeare, William. The Norton Shakespeare, Third Edition. Ed. Stephen Greenblatt et al. New York: W. W. Norton, 2015.

and alien religions. Christopher Marlowe's *Tamburlaine* plays (1587–1588) are set in regions that, from the English point of view, seem at the periphery of the familiar European world: Persepolis, Scythia, Damascus, and Babylon. As a result, of course, Christian Europe seems marginal to the characters. *Tamburlaine Part II* begins on the eve of a confrontation between the Muslim Orcanes of Natolia and the Christian Sigismund of Hungary, but Orcanes makes peace with Sigismund in order to confront the more serious threat posed by Tamburlaine. In both plays, Christianity figures minimally and England not at all: the important religious difference of the play is between Islam and a form of paganism. In Thomas Kyd's *Spanish Tragedy* (1592), too, the English figure as the foreigners: Hieronimo presents a masque to the Portuguese and Spanish kings that (rather improbably) shows the English defeating armies of both nations. In *The Merchant of Venice* (1597) the beautiful heiress Portia, courted by suitors from all over Europe, lists an English contender among them, notable for his inability to speak Italian and his odd attire. It was, in fact, a common jibe about the English that they did not possess a national costume but instead adopted their clothing styles from others, so this depiction is just as stereotypical as Portia's characterization of the German suitor as a hopeless drunk, the French one as a volatile twit, or the Neapolitan as a horse-crazy monomaniac. Still, the scene purports to present an Italy for whom England is a marginal and distant place.

The imaginative engagement with remote places is characteristic of much seventeenth-century drama as well. Tragedies are often set in foreign places—partly because their plots are often drawn from non-English source texts, and partly because commenting too pointedly on contemporary English politics would trigger censorship. Reference to exotic locales is especially common in masque and tragicomedy. Both of these genres, unlike city comedy or country house poetry, traffic in the marvellous, and both develop quickly in the early seventeenth century. We will turn to these genres in Chapter 5.

5
Authority, Obedience, and Defiance

Who gets to govern whom, and with what justification? What are the sources, the proper uses, and the limits of authority? Obviously such questions dominate the consciousness of the English nation in the war years of the mid-seventeenth century, but, in a less overtly contentious form, they loom large in the earlier decades as well. In the domain of literary writing, the struggle over these issues is especially well manifested in three disparate genres: court masque, tragedy, and tragicomedy. In slightly altered form, it pervades devotional poetry as well. Not coincidentally, the first half of the seventeenth century sees the flowering of all of these forms.

Questions of rule and allegiance are so omnipresent in the period because they are not narrowly political questions, but constitute organizing principles of the entire culture—what E. M. W. Tillyard calls 'the utter commonplaces . . . essential as basic assumptions'.[1] These commonplaces are, however, more complicated than they first seem. Most early modern writers—who, as we have seen, typically come from relatively elite backgrounds—routinely dismiss the possibility that egalitarian social arrangements are desirable. They prefer clear, predetermined lines of command and obedience. Even people who may not have themselves uncritically endorsed the standard view were certainly familiar with it. Although Shakespeare's work, as Stephen Greenblatt argues, may suggest that he was 'allergic to the absolutist strain so prevalent in his world',[2] nonetheless, in *Troilus and Cressida* (1602) he puts into the mouth of Ulysses an unusually eloquent defence of the ideal of hierarchical order. Ulysses is something of a charlatan, and his motives for making this speech are patently self-interested, so there is no reason to conflate his views with his author's. However, his speech is worth quoting at length because it rehearses so many of the truisms of Shakespeare's culture:

---

[1] E. M. W. Tillyard, *The Elizabethan World Picture: A Study of the Idea of Order in the Age of Shakespeare, Donne, and Milton*.
[2] Stephen Greenblatt, *Shakespeare's Freedom*, p. 3.

The heavens themselves, the planets, and this centre
Observe degree, priority, and place,
Insisture, course, proportion, season, form,
Office and custom, in all line of order.
And therefore is the glorious planet Sol
In noble eminence enthroned and sphered
Amidst the other, whose med'cinable eye
Corrects the ill aspects of planets evil
And posts, like the commandment of a king,
Sans check, to good and bad. But when the planets
In evil mixture to disorder wander,
What plagues and what portents, what mutiny,
What raging of the sea, shaking of earth,
Commotion in the winds, frights, changes, horrors,
Divert and crack, rend and deracinate
The unity and married calm of states
Quite from their fixture. Oh, when degree is shaked,
Which is the ladder to all high designs,
The enterprise is sick. How could communities,
Degrees in schools and brotherhoods in cities,
Peaceful commerce from dividable shores,
The primogenitive and due of birth,
Prerogative of age, crowns, scepters, laurels,
But by degree stand in authentic place?
Take but degree away, untune that string,
And hark, what discord follows: each thing meets
In mere oppugnancy; the bounded waters
Should lift their bosoms higher than the shores
And make a sop of all this solid globe;
Strength should be lord to imbecility,
And the rude son should strike his father dead.
Force should be right—or rather, right and wrong,
Between whose endless jar justice resides,
Should lose their names, and so should justice too.
Then everything includes itself in power,
Power into will, will into appetite,
And appetite, an universal wolf,
So doubly seconded with will and power

>   Must make perforce an universal prey
>   And last eat up himself.
>   (1.3.84–123)

Two features of Ulysses' conception of 'degree' are remarkable. The first is its reliance upon analogy. The structure of the human community, organized in status ranks from high to low, echoes the structure of the heavens, in which the planets themselves 'observe degree, priority, and place'. Conversely, the Sun, or Sol, behaves as a good king does, correcting errant subordinates when necessary. This hierarchical order of nature was often described as obvious to every observer, as plain to a pagan like Ulysses as it was to a Christian with access to the divinely revealed Word of God. Nonetheless, scriptural texts were taken to reinforce this emphasis. In Paul's letter to the Romans, he declared that 'The powers that be, are ordained of God. Whosoever therefore resisteth the power, resisteth the ordinance of God, and they that resist, shall receive to themselves damnation' (Romans 13:1–2). The catechism issued with the Book of Common Prayer in 1552, expanded and reissued in 1604, construed the fifth commandment, 'honour thy father and thy mother', to cover all human relationships of superiority and subordination:

> My duty... is... to honour and obey the King and his ministers. To submit myself to all my governors, teachers, spiritual pastors, and masters. To order myself lowly and reverently to all my betters.

A different passage—God's decree in Genesis, after the Fall, that Eve should obey her husband—gave a scriptural basis for the subordination of women in marriage.

In a society in which few people participated formally in the political process, and in which the workplace and the home were generally one and the same, power relationships tended to correlate closely with familial intimacies. Authority was not, therefore, conceived as an abstract institutional force exerted upon atomized 'free' individuals, but as inhering in a concrete network of personal relationships. One consequence of the continuity between domestic and political realms is that a superior tends to be considered a superior, as it were, across domains, and often those domains overlap. A king, writes James in *Basilikon Doron*, is both 'a little God' and 'the natural father and kindly master' of his people.[3] The common practice of daily

---

[3] *Basilikon Doron*, in *King James VI and I: Political Writings*, ed. Johann Somerville, pp. 12, 20.

family prayers supported the authority of the father and master in the home by enlisting religious piety in the service of domestic order: the paterfamilias, in charge of supplicating the deity on behalf of his wife, children, servants, and apprentices, acquires some of the deity's charisma. In such works as Shakespeare's *King Lear*, *The Winter's Tale*, and *The Tempest*, the protagonists' political and paternal powers are tightly enmeshed with one another. One form of authority tends to reinforce the other, and a failure in one sphere is a failure in them all.

Another remarkable feature of Ulysses' vision of hierarchical order is its link with its apparent opposite, a phobic vision of utter disintegration: 'Take but degree away, untune that string, and hark, what discord follows'. In his magisterial *Laws of Ecclesiastical Polity*, published the decade before the accession of James, the Church of England theologian Richard Hooker similarly argues for the indispensability of divine law: conjuring up, like Shakespeare's Ulysses, a nightmarish fantasy of its opposite:

> Since the time that God did first proclaim the edicts of his law upon it, heaven and earth have hearkened unto his voice, and their labour hath been to do his will: He *made a law for the rain*. He gave his *decree to the sea, that the waters should not pass his commandment*. Now if nature should intermit her course, and leave altogether, though it were but for a while, the observations of her own laws; if those principal and mother elements of the world, whereof all things in this lower world are made, should lose the qualities which now they have; if the frame of that heavenly arch erected over our heads should loosen and dissolve itself; if celestial spheres should forget their wonted motions and by irregular volubility, turn themselves any way as it might happen; if the prince of the lights of heaven which now as a giant does run his unwearied course, should as it were through a languishing faintness begin to stand and to rest himself; if the moon should wander from her beaten way, the times and seasons of the year blend themselves by disordered and confused mixture, the winds breathe out their last gasp, the clouds yield no rain, the earth be defeated of heavenly influence, the fruits of the earth pine away as children at the withered breasts of their mother no longer able to yield them relief, what would become of man himself, whom these things now do all serve? See we not plainly that obedience of creatures unto the law of nature is the stay of the whole world?[4]

---

[4] Richard Hooker, *Of the Laws of Ecclesiastical Polity*, vol. 1, ed. Arthur Stephen McGrade, p. 49.

The chain of command, from God to heaven and earth, to nature and earthly creatures, needs constantly to be clarified and restated as a defence against the possibility of chaos. Hierarchical order is paradoxically both completely obvious to anyone who looks and, at the same time profoundly fragile, susceptible to the ravages of 'appetite, an universal wolf' a rapacious self-aggrandizement heedless of the individual's place in a network of relationships. Few sixteenth- or seventeenth-century writers think of rivalry or competition as a productive force in social life—as, for instance, such Enlightenment philosophers of the free market as Adam Smith would begin to do in the eighteenth century. Instead, social harmony is imagined as being the consequence of everybody accepting his or her place and duties within a larger scheme. Yet because this knowledge is weak and easily overridden by envy and self-interest, the sense of duty and decorum must be constantly policed.

How did this policing work in practice? The crime of treason, defined as killing or planning to kill an authority figure, was considered the most heinous of offences in the early modern period, since it struck not only at an individual but at the hierarchical principle upon which social thriving was thought to be organized. While ordinary felons were merely hanged, female traitors were sentenced to be burnt alive, and male traitors were hanged only until partly dead, then cut down, castrated and disembowelled while still conscious, beheaded, cut in quarters, and parboiled. These penalties were not merely meant to torture the offender to death, but to demonstrate in the most vivid possible terms his or her complete physical obliteration. Significantly, these penalties were exacted not merely for 'high treason'— killing or planning to kill a king or member of the royal family—but also for 'petty treason'—killing or conspiring against a husband or master. In fact, the petty traitor was more likely to suffer the full force of the law than the high traitor, because many of those with designs on the monarch were of exalted rank and their sentences were commuted to simple beheading. In these cases, the impulse to punish treason severely—to reinforce the importance of the social hierarchy by marking out deviations as especially monstrous—conflicted with the impulse to exempt prominent individuals from public degradation, because that degradation might itself call into question the logic and naturalness of hierarchy.

In less sanguinary situations too, custom and the law robustly endorsed both social and domestic hierarchies. Gentlefolk were ordinarily exempt from the humiliating physical punishments frequently visited upon the lower orders, like whipping, stocking, or branding. Peers of the realm could not even be arrested for debt (though their servants could be, and were held as hostages until their masters ransomed them from prison.) The authority of the husband, father, or master in the home was reinforced by common law: he could physically 'chastise' his subordinates in ways that nowadays would be classified as assault or domestic abuse. If such discipline failed, the legal system could step in to reinforce him, whipping servants and punishing wives who defied their 'lords' by 'bridling', stocking, or ducking them. The law enforced dependency in other ways as well, by putting practical obstacles in the way of an inferior's self-sufficiency. A married woman could not own property or execute contracts in her own name, and if she worked for wages, the wages belonged to her husband.

When thus flatly stated, Renaissance tenets of authority and obedience sound intolerably oppressive to a modern inhabitant of a first-world democracy, but they were somewhat more flexible and contested than they might first appear. Some of these complications derived from an inevitable gap between theory and lived experience. Nowadays, when most of us claim to favour the ideals of equality before the law and near-universal political participation, the actually domineering behaviour of parents, teachers, bosses, or political leaders often belies their egalitarian pretensions. Similarly in early modern Europe, the ideal of harmoniously ordered social structure was often imperfect and fractured in practice. In fact, as the persistent fears of a descent into chaos might suggest, a vigorous assertion of hierarchical privilege tended to be necessary not because all accepted it without question, but because so many, so often, defied or disregarded that hierarchy. For instance, Tudor-era sumptuary regulations, which attempted to regulate the garments of different status groups in order to make social standing visible at a glance, were widely flouted and eventually abandoned by James as impossible to enforce. 'What age, what place ever was there, which hath not just cause to complain of subjects' rebellion, servants' stubbornness, children's disobedience, wives' presumption?' asks the minister William Gouge in his popular handbook *Of Domestical Duties* (1622), complaining in particular of 'the opinion of many wives, who think themselves every way as good as their husbands, and no way inferior to them'.[5] The women in his own congregation, he admits, derided his sermons on wifely obedience despite his conviction that his claims were grounded in the Bible. Indeed, the pervasive interest in 'shrews' in many Renaissance plays suggests not only that female assertiveness and cunning were a source of male anxiety

---

[5] William Gouge, *Of Domestical Duties*, p. 23, 272.

(and sometimes male appreciation), but also that many women were hardly the meek, compliant creatures that their cultural conditioning was supposed to ensure. When, in Ben Jonson's *Epicene*, the elderly Morose wishes to marry a silent, submissive virgin, the worldly wise Truewit ridicules his ambition as hopelessly anachronistic:

> Alas, sir, do you ever think to find a chaste wife in these times?... If you had lived in King Ethelred's time, or Edward theConfessor's, you might perhaps have found in some cold country hamlet then a dull, frosty wench would have been contented with one man. Now they will as soon be pleased with one leg or one eye.
>
> (2.2.32–40)

The patriarchal ideal to which Morose aspires, Jonson implies, is a casualty of modern life, and in particular of modern urban life.

Apart from grumbling or 'grudging', there were more subtle and theoretically sophisticated articulations of dissent. One important complication for the doctrine of hierarchy and obedience was that in early modern England there were several sources of authority, which sometimes seemed to limit or compete with one another. A strong constitutionalist strain of thought lodged ultimate authority not in the person of the monarch but in the system of laws and precedent which bound ruler and subject alike, and which dispersed power among the king, Parliament, the judiciary, and the local authorities. The relationship between these governing agents was imagined as a collaboration, not as a system of checks and balances, but, in fact, the government of England was a 'mixed' one, not an autocracy. Both James and Charles clashed with Parliament, as we have seen, eventuating in Charles attempting to govern without Parliament altogether. James came into conflict as well with his Chief Justice, Edward Coke, who insisted that although judges were technically servants of the king, the judges and not the king were solely possessed of the expertise needed to interpret and administer the law.

Also complicating the practical assertion of authority is that the duty of subordinates to submit, and an awareness of one's place in the hierarchy, was never equated with slavery. A king's power over an English subject was not unlimited; moreover, the allegiance of the subordinate imposed obligations of care upon the superior. The English were proud of insisting that they were 'free subjects', protected by customary and statutory privileges, and by rights over their private property. In the countryside, under the prevailing system of semi-feudal landholding, the same landed estate that bound the landholder to his lord via a vow of homage also provided him with an independent living and place of refuge from the lord. In the cities, and in London especially, an increasingly powerful commercial and professional class was beginning to flourish, with political values and cultural priorities rather different from those of the landed elites. The result, among the affluent, was not only a space for free agency, but the availability of a variety of prestige claims. Noble birth, wealth, practical competence, and intellectual distinction might all provide the basis for exercising some form of power over other men, but these forms of distinction did not necessarily coincide in the same individual, and when they did not, it was unclear which should take precedence.

Further down the social scale, another such refuge from domination could be provided by specialized forms of expertise. Many practical and artisanal skills could be, and often were, declared 'base' forms of knowledge by the elite, compared with the 'noble' arts of war, statesmanship, philosophy, and so on. As a result, few people in positions of power shared a servant-women's domestic proficiency, a peasant's practical farming know-how, or a craftsman's handiness. (Thus, in *Hamlet*, the university-educated Hamlet becomes the student of the gravedigger, who knows better than a prince how long it takes a corpse to decay.) These specialized domains of knowledge and action could offer a space for the subordinate's agency, because for a superior to invade them was normally a derogation of his dignity. In *The Merry Wives of Windsor*, Shakespeare shows a middle-aged bourgeois woman, theoretically subject to her husband's authority, operating with almost complete impunity despite his jealous attempts to supervise her. She packs a would-be lover off in a basket of dirty laundry that it does not occur to the husband to search; when he belatedly realizes his error and returns to investigate a second (lover-free) laundry basket, he is ridiculed by his friends: 'Why, this is lunatics. This is mad as a mad dog . . . 'Tis unreasonable: will you take up your wife's clothes? Come, away' (4.2.110, 124). Similarly, in *Bartholomew Fair*, Ben Jonson portrays the carnival folk easily and comically evading those who attempt to impose religious, educational, or juridical discipline upon them; the 'judges' all eventually make ridiculous spectacles of themselves. Their attempts to supervise petty criminality demonstrates only their presumption and lack of street-smarts. The real queen of Jonson's *Bartholomew Fair* is the 'Pig Woman' Ursula: fat, unscrupulous, foulmouthed, and slatternly. Yet, like Shakespeare's merry wives, Ursula is not leading a movement for revolutionary change, merely making a space of operation for herself and her immediate compatriots, without disturbing the larger order. A great deal of Jacobean and Caroline comedy—in fact, of comedy more generally, going back to the classical period—displays a similar insouciance about the structures of control, with clever servants, indigent younger sons, rebellious daughters, and other inferior persons outwitting their betters, to the delight of audiences.

There was a similar, and overlapping, multiplicity in the domain of religious authority. Because the Christian God is omnipotent, omniscient, and omnipresent, He has none of the defects of attention or capacity that placed practical limits upon human authority figures. Nor, because He is perfectly good, is rebellion against Him ever justified. Yet, as the turmoil of the Reformation made painfully clear all through the sixteenth and seventeenth centuries, the translation of God's will into human terms was a fraught enterprise. A few radical sects put special emphasis on the Christian doctrine of the equality of souls, and strove to emulate the communitarian social arrangements practiced by early Christians. But the established Church of England strongly asserted the God-given nature of the social hierarchy, and with it the sanctity of property rights. In 1562, the thirty-eighth of Elizabeth's Thirty-Nine Articles asserted that 'The riches and goods of Christians are not common, as touching the right, title, and possession of the same, as certain Anabaptists do falsely boast'. The *Homily on Obedience*, issued shortly after the death of Henry VIII in 1547, expands upon the thought:

> Almighty God hath created and appointed all things in heaven, earth, and waters in a most excellent and perfect order.... Some [people] are in high degree, some in low, some kings and princes, some inferiors and subjects, priests and laymen, masters and servants, fathers and children, husbands and wives, rich and poor ... Take away kings, princes, rulers, magistrates, judges, and such estates of God's order, no man shall ride or go by the high way unrobbed ... no man shall keep his wife, children and possessions in quietness, all things shall be common.

In this view, religion does not break down but reinforces social hierarchy, and endorses differences of privilege and status. 'The strength of all government is religion', declared Sir John Eliot in a speech at the opening of Charles I's first parliament in 1625. 'Religion it is that keeps the subject in obedience, as being taught by God to honour his vicegerents'.[6] The impetus to Civil War eventually came less from radical communitarians than from those convinced that the King Charles had tyrannically usurped upon his

---

[6] Sir John Eliot, *Negotium Posterorum*, ed. A. B. Grosart, pp. 70–71.

subjects' god-given property rights with his unorthodox means of taxation, and from those who resented his innovations in religious matters.

The Protestant Reformation had privileged scripture, the 'revealed' Word of God, as the ultimate authority in religious matters. However, not only was scripture subject to multiple interpretations, but the relationship between scripture and the rituals and organizational structure of the Church became hotly contested. As a result of these interpretive differences, what purport to be the same principles of reverence for authority and respect for religious tradition can play out in flatly opposed ways. The ornate ceremonies that for William Laud, Archbishop of Canterbury under Charles I, signified 'due and seemly reverence' to the Deity appeared to Laud's Puritan critics to be the tawdry rags of popery and superstition.

None of the parties to these disputes imagine themselves to be discarding the principle of authority in the abstract, but they are willing vigorously to reject what they consider false or subordinate authorities when their directives apparently contradict those of an even higher power. The various parties in the English Civil War are each fully convinced that they are acting according to the Will of God, and that they uphold the laws and traditions of the English people. But the relationship of royal authority to divine mandate as well as to the consent of the governed is under dispute. The question, apparently, was not 'is authority good and necessary?'—everybody, apparently, thought so—but 'what authority is the relevant one, and in which situation'? This way of framing the debate may seem to make no practical difference, since Royalists and Republicans, Catholics and Protestants, Arminians and Puritans were coming to blows regardless. Actually, however, the fact that they shared an important tract of common ground has important consequences for the literature of the period.

Writers, especially ambitious writers, tend to be drawn to situations of conflict and to unresolved social and political problems because that is where ethical and narrative interest is generally to be found. This proclivity makes them prone to discern potentials for disruption that, to another sensibility, might seem hardly worth noticing. The traditional 'Whig' view of the English Civil War—that it grew out of longstanding and principled rifts among opposed groups—may well be overstated, applied to 'England' in general or to the great majority of people living at the time. Yet the traditional view might very well capture a *writer's* sense of the social milieu, hypersensitive as he or she typically is of its fault-lines and incongruities. Many Jacobean revenge plays, for instance, pit the interests and rights of oppressed subjects against those of despotic rulers in ways that seem vaguely premonitory of the issues that would dominate the grievances of mid-century. Is it anachronistic to read these works in this way? Beaumont and Fletcher, writing *The Maid's Tragedy* around 1610, or Middleton, writing *The Revenger's Tragedy*, are unlikely to be commenting directly, or even indirectly, on the workings of the Stuart court. But they are picking up on a widely recognized structural weakness in a monarchical system—that it is unclear what legal remedy might be had against a tyrannical ruler. In the 1640s, their thought-experiments might have seemed prescient.

The following sections will first discuss some of the genres most obviously concerned with relationships of authority and submission, rule and subjection: court masque, tragedy, and tragicomedy. In chapter 6, I will go on to discuss religious lyric and narrative poetry, which broach many of the same issues from a different angle. I will also consider the poetry of love and friendship, which locates itself both within and without the debates about authority and allegiance in complicated, interesting ways.

Court Masque

No literary genre was more tightly associated with court culture and with the representation of royal authority than the masque.[7] A multimedia theatrical artform combining music, poetry, extravagant costumes, and opulent sets, masque reached the zenith of its development in England in the reigns of James and Charles. Generally performed only once or twice for an audience of courtiers, ambassadors, and other favoured persons, a masque formed the ceremonial frame for an evening of dancing. It was an honour to be invited to attend a masque, and an even greater honour to be invited to perform in one: contemporary accounts attend at least as avidly to the guest list, to the roster and ordering of dancers, and to the placement of spectators in the chairs and galleries, as they do to masques' artistic merits.

Masque was not an entirely new genre. Invented in Italy and long fashionable in France, it was imported to England in the reign of Henry VIII. In Queen Elizabeth's time, ambitious courtiers had sought her favour by staging entertainments in her honour on pastoral or classical themes. But

---

[7] Scholarly discussions of the Stuart court masque include Stephen Orgel, *The Jonsonian Masque* and *The Illusion of Power*; Joseph Loewenstein, *Responsive Readings: Version of Echo in Pastoral, Epic, and the Jonsonian Masque*; Karen Britland, *Drama at the Courts of Queen Henrietta Maria*; and Martin Butler, *The Stuart Court Masque and Political Culture*. The surviving drawings of Inigo Jones's masque costumes and sets are reproduced and discussed in Stephen Orgel and Roy Strong, *Inigo Jones: The Theater of the Stuart Court*.

because Elizabethan masques were individually commissioned by a variety of patrons, there was little formal consistency among them, and none of them required much in the way of staging apparatus.

During the Jacobean and Caroline periods, prominent noblemen, the Inns of Court, and the wealthier guilds, such as the Merchant Taylor's Company, continued to provide entertainments for royal guests, as they had in Elizabethan times, as a sign of hospitality and a bid for favour. Masques became a customary part of the festivities for an aristocratic wedding, the celebration of which could go on for days—a trend already visible at the end of Elizabeth's reign. However, with the accession of James, the royal family itself began to commission masques. To celebrate King James's first Christmas season in England in 1604, eight of his close associates—four Scots and four English—performed *The Masque of Indian and China Knights*, while about a week later *The Vision of the Twelve Goddesses* featured Queen Anne and her ladies-in-waiting. The following year, when Anne commissioned *The Masque of Blackness*, James's Privy Council, shocked by the expense of the production, noted that in the past the masque had been an occasional feature rather than a regular part of Yuletide festivities: 'many Christmases pass without any such note, dancing, comedies, plays and other sports having been thought sufficient marks of mirth'. Yet masques quickly became an expected part of Christmas and Shrovetide celebrations at court, and Charles continued and expanded upon this tradition after succeeding to the throne in 1625.

For the Venetian ambassador, witnessing *The Masque of Beauty* in 1608, the glorious spectacle of the royal masque exhibited the power of the English monarchy:

> The apparatus and the cunning of the stage machinery was a miracle, the abundance and the beauty of the lights immense, the music and the dance most sumptuous. But what outdid all else and possibly exceeded the public expectation was the wealth of pearls and jewels that adorned the Queen and her ladies, so abundant and splendid that in everyone's opinion no other court could have displayed such pomp and riches.[8]

In Renaissance courts the open, even reckless display and dispersion of wealth, especially upon festival occasions, was an important signal of the

---

[8] Quoted in David Lindley's introduction to *The Masque of Beauty* in *The Cambridge Edition of the Works of Ben Jonson*, ed. David Bevington, Martin Butler, Ian Donaldson, et al., vol. 3, p. 230.

ruler's strength and magnanimity. As Martin Butler has pointed out, the splendour of the Stuart royal masques amplified the discrepancy between revels at court and the more modest holiday observances in the homes of noblemen or gentry.[9] This was an effect consistent with the absolutist ideology of the early Stuarts, who tried—not always successfully—to distinguish strongly between the power of the king and the power of his subjects. Masque was a vehicle for, and celebration of, the exercise of royal dominion.

Yet these elaborate performances did not always proceed according to plan. In 1606, James celebrated the visit of his brother-in-law, King Christian of Denmark, with a banquet followed by a masque, *Solomon and the Queen of Sheba*. Both Christian and James were heavy drinkers and the rest of the company followed the royal example. The courtier Sir John Harington describes the occasion:

> But alas! as all earthly things do fail to poor mortals in enjoyment, so did prove our presentment hereof. The Lady who did play the Queen's part, did carry most precious gifts to both their majesties; but, forgetting the steps arising to the canopy, overset her caskets into his Danish majesty's lap, and fell at his feet, though I rather think it was in his face. Much was the hurry and confusion; cloths and napkins were at hand, to make all clean. His Majesty then got up and would dance with the Queen of Sheba; but he fell down and humbled himself before her, and was carried to an inner chamber, and laid on a bed of state which was not a little defiled with the presents of the Queen which had been bestowed on his garments; such as wine, cream, jelly, beverage, cakes, spices, and other good matters. The entertainment and show went forward, and most of the presenters went backward, or fell down, wine did so occupy their upper chambers. Now did appear in rich dress Hope, Faith, and Charity: Hope did assay to speak, but wine rendered her endeavours so feeble that she withdrew, and hoped the King would excuse her brevity. Faith was then all alone, for I am certain she was not joined with good works, and left the court in a staggering condition. Charity came to the King's feet, and seemed to cover the multitude of sins her sisters had committed ... She then returned to Hope and Faith, who were both sick and spewing in the lower hall ... Now did Peace make entry, and strive to get foremost to the King; but I grieve to tell how great wrath she did discover unto those of her attendants; and, much contrary

---

[9] Martin Butler, *The Stuart Court Masque and Political Culture*, p. 69.

to her semblance, most rudely made war with her olive branch, and laid on the pates of those who did oppose her coming.[10]

Harington may have been exaggerating the disaster for comic effect, but in this case, the association of the masque with occasions of revelry and excess seems to have eclipsed its artistic ambitions.

Staging a masque required the collaboration of a variety of artists and a coordination of their talents. The 'poetic' part of the masque was relatively brief—a few hundred lines could suffice for a whole evening of dancing—but the poet was typically the source of the masque's 'invention' or device (although sometimes, as in the case of *The Masque of Blackness*, he was elaborating upon a theme suggested by the masque patron.) Composing the poetry for masques became an important source of employment for Jacobean and Caroline poets: Samuel Daniel, Ben Jonson, Thomas Campion, Thomas Middleton, Francis Beaumont, George Chapman, Thomas Carew, Aurelian Townshend, Walter Montagu, James Shirley, and William D'Avenant, among others. Jonson's accomplishments as a masque writer were particularly remarkable: he wrote more than thirty masques over three decades, originating many of the genre's formal innovations. Jonson also argued strongly for the significance of the masque as a poetic form. The texts of many masques were printed shortly after the performance, often with a detailed description of the scenery and costumes; Jonson added copious marginal notes citing the scholarly sources for his classical and allegorical references. For though a masque might seem ephemeral, even frivolous, he insisted that it ought to contain something more profound and thought-provoking as well.

Yet the visual splendour of the masque was at least as important as its poetic excellence. In contrast to the relatively bare stages of the public theatres, the masque featured elaborate sets, some of which slid to the side or turned on an axis in the midst of the performance to provide a spectacular 'reveal'. The *Masque of Blackness* featured an artificial sea with waves that seemed to move, over which 'a great concave shell' in which the masquers were placed, was 'curiously made to move on those waters and rise with the billow'. In *The Masque of Beauty*, the Throne of Fame rotated clockwise, while a series of steps ascending to the throne rotated in the opposite direction, adorned by 'a multitude of Cupids chosen out of the best, and most

---

[10] John Harington, *Nugae Antiquae: Being a Miscellaneous Collection of Original Papers, in Prose and Verse*, p. 66

ingenuous youth of the kingdom'. In the middle of the *Masque of Queens*, which opened in 'an ugly hell', 'the whole face of the scene altered, scarce suffering the memory of such a thing. But in the place of it appeared a glorious and magnificent building.' In *The Haddington Masque* (1608), a 'cliff parted in the midst and discovered an illustrious concave filled with an ample and glistering light'; similarly, in *Oberon, the Fairy Prince* (1611), a rugged crag opened to 'discover' the front of a 'glorious palace', and shortly thereafter the 'whole palace opened', disclosing a 'nation of fays' and their prince, Oberon, advancing in a chariot 'drawn by two white bears'. In fact, stony landscapes that concealed dazzling displays behind them were such a familiar contrivance that in George Chapman's *Memorable Masque* (1613) one of the characters complains 'Nothing but rocks in these masquing devices? Is Invention so poor she must needs ever dwell amongst rocks?' Later masques featured multiple sliding flats that enabled swift changes of scenery, and introduced flying machines. In *Tempe Restored* (1632), 'Jove, sitting on an eagle', appears 'hovering in the air with a glory beyond him', while 'at that instant Cupid from another part of the heaven comes flying forth, and having passed the scene, turns soaring about like a bird'. Marvellous effects could also be achieved by special lighting: candlelight augmented by reflectors or refracted through coloured liquids. Such complex devices required the services of highly skilled designers and carpenters, primarily among them Inigo Jones, an Italian-trained architect who also, in many cases, planned the masquers' lavish costumes. Music was also needed, and therefore composers, singers, instrumentalists, and choreographers. As the masque became more elaborate, some of its parts became too complex, or too unbecoming, to be executed by aristocratic amateurs, so professional actors were employed. In some cases the teamwork among these various artists and craftsmen could become strained. The collaboration between Ben Jonson and Inigo Jones grew especially tense, as Jonson insisted that poetry was the 'soul' of the masque while Jones strove to maximize the visual impact of the performance.

While the court masque's opulence implicitly flaunted the monarch's magnificence and power, its rhetoric glorified him explicitly. Masques deployed, sometimes in dizzying combinations, the resources of classical mythology and Arthurian legend, the iconology of imperial Rome, and the costumes and the imagery of 'exotic' times and places, in order to present an homage to the king. During the Jacobean period, while Anne and her sons, Prince Henry and Charles, danced in the masque, James did not. However, his role as the masque's primary spectator was critical: the masque was performed to him, for him, as he sat front and centre and sometimes conversed with the masquers. The masque represented James as he wished to seen: a scholar, a peacemaker, a wise and beloved father of his people, bringing together the kingdoms of Scotland and England in a harmonious imperial union. James was 'a god o'er kings', Jove, Pan, Neptune, or the Sun. He achieved impossibilities: 'turning an Ethiop white'; quelling storms, restoring men who had been magically changed into flowers to their human shape.

> 'Tis he that stays the time from turning old,
> And keeps the age up in a head of gold;
> That in his own true circle still doth run,
> And holds his course as certain as the sun.
> He makes it ever day and ever spring
> Where he doth shine, and quickens everything
> Like a new nature, so that true to call
> Him by his title is to say: he's all.
> (*Oberon, The Fairy Prince*, 264–271)

The design of the Jacobean masquing space reinforced this focus upon the power and centrality of the king. Inigo Jones's innovative perspectival sets were designed to be viewed from front and centre, where James was seated, so that the royal line of sight was the perfect and authoritative one, while the other spectators had a more or less oblique view depending upon their proximity to the monarch.

However, the masque was not simply a festival of sycophancy. Masques often addressed, however obliquely, topics of current political concern. Not surprisingly, masques commissioned by the guilds, or by the Inns of Court, were inclined to press their constituency's interests, even while they swathed their requests in a heavy blanket of deference and compliment. The royal masque, too, often became a site where competing objectives could be (tactfully) displayed, for in order to celebrate the achievement of harmony and unity it had first to conjure up the possible threats to that harmony. The Stuarts asserted rights over the ethnically and linguistically distinct territories of Wales, England, Scotland, and Ireland, and many of James's masques, in particular, acknowledge this heterogeneity. *The Indian and China Knights*, the first of his masques, obliquely addresses the friction between English and Scots courtiers in the early years of his reign. *The Irish Masque at Court* (1613) and *For the Honour of Wales* (1618) raise even while they attempt to minimize the threatening possibilities in these remote regions, presenting the Irish and the Welsh as comically bumptious, uncourtly intruders nonetheless eager to submit themselves to James's benevolent authority. In addition to these large-scale national differences, the Jacobean and the Caroline court saw inevitable conflicts between ambitious individuals and between groups with competing agendas. For instance, in the first years of James's reign, the court was split between those who favoured rapprochement with Spain, aligned with the Catholic Howard family, and those allied with the Essex family, who preferred a Protestant alliance. In 1606, the marriage of the fifteen-year-old Frances Howard to the fourteen-year-old Earl of Essex opened the possibility of a rapprochement between these groups. In Jonson's *Barriers at a Marriage*, one of the masques performed during the wedding celebration, courtiers in the Howard faction squared off in a mock tournament against courtiers in the Essex faction. But just before combat was supposed to begin, 'a striking light seemed to fill all the hall, and out of it an angel or messenger of glory' emerged to reconcile them.

Ideological tensions were also sometimes perceptible. In the Jacobean court, even those masques that purportedly lauded James's pacifism often invoked elite chivalric and martial ideals that were championed by many members of his court, but that were in some tension with his ethic of non-violence. Although the king was the formal patron and *raison d'etre* of the royally commissioned masques, Queen Anne generally took the lead in planning and performing in them—and Anne was semi-estranged from her husband, living in her own household surrounded by a circle of female friends. Several of Anne's masques—*The Masque of Blackness, the Masque of Beauty, The Masque of Queens*—celebrate strong women and imply their qualified independence from male control.[11] Of these masques, *The Masque of Blackness*, performed on Twelfth Night in 1605, is perhaps the most interesting, and its complicated discourse of racial difference has made it an important recent focus of critical discussion.[12] On the face of it, *The Masque*

---

[11] Leeds Barroll, *Anna of Denmark, Queen of England: A Cultural Biography*.
[12] See, for example, Yumna Siddiqi, 'Dark Incontinents: The Discourses of Race and Gender in Three Renaissance Masques', *Renaissance Drama* new series 23 (1992): 139–163; Mary Floyd-Wilson, 'Temperature, Temperance, and Racial Difference in Ben Jonson's "The Masque of Blackness"', *English Literary Renaissance* 28 (1998): 183–209; Bernadette Andrea, 'Black Skin, The Queen's Masques: Africanist Ambivalence and Female Author(ity) in the Masques of "Blackness" and "Beauty"', *English Literary Renaissance* 29 (1999): 246–281. For more general discussions of race and race discourse in seventeenth-century England, see Margo Hendricks and Patricia Parker, eds. *Women, 'Race', and Writing in the Early Modern Period*; Kim Hall, *Things of Darkness: Economies of Race and Gender in Early Modern England*; Mary Floyd-Wilson, *English Ethnicity and Race in Early Modern Drama*; Sujata Iyengar, *Shades of*

of Blackness is an over-the-top celebration of James. Twelve daughters of the river god Niger—the queen and her ladies, in blackface—hear that poets attribute the dark skin of Africans to their being burnt when Phaeton's sun chariot ran amok and came too close to the earth. The daughters of Niger become convinced that they will not be truly beautiful until they are somehow transformed to white, even though, as one of Aesop's fables holds, it is impossible to 'wash a blackamoor white'. In a vision, the moon goddess Ethiopia tells them to make a pilgrimage to a land that ends in '-tania', but 'black' Mauritania, 'swart' Lusitania, and 'rich' Aquitania, each apparently paler than the last, disappoint them. Finally, evidently journeying north and west, they come a place that seems a citadel of whiteness:

> This land, that lifts into the temperate air
> His snowy cliff, is Albion the fair.
>   (164–165)

Here, Ethiopia tells Niger, 'Thy daughters' labours have their period', because the island of Albion (a word derived from the Latin word for 'white') is now called 'Britania', the renamed 'Empire of Great Britain' created by James's attempt to unify England and Scotland. Whereas the sun that scorched the Africans was destructive, the 'sun' that rules Britania is temperate; his

> beams shine day and night, and are of force
> To blanch an Ethiop and revive a corse.
> His light sciential is, and, past mere nature,
> Can salve the rude defects of every creature.
>   (207–211)

In other words, in the fiction of the masque, James, the temperate sun of Britain, can perform miracles, redressing the harms caused by excessive sunlight elsewhere. Strangers are divinely inspired to come from the ends of the earth to seek his aid. Yet the celebration of James's power is more than a little equivocal. The masque obviously trades in English stereotypes associating black skin with the ugly and undesirable, and 'fair' whiteness with beauty and purity. But it also critiques those stereotypes. Niger argues that his black daughters already possess 'the perfect'st beauty' since their complexion is supposedly unalterable by care, age, or even death, its fixity manifesting

---

Difference: Mythologies of Skin Color in Early Modern England; Kimberley Ann Coles, *Bad Humor: Race and Religious Essentialism in Early Modern England.*

> How near divinity they be,
> That stand from passion or decay so free.
> (113–114)

By his accounting, his daughters are simply deluded by liars who 'envy . . . their graces' (107), and do not need the change they seek. At the end of the masque, the daughters of Niger are promised that they will eventually become white, but not, apparently through the intercession of James. Instead, they must bathe themselves in rosemary-water; and, since the treatment will take an entire year, the ladies remain black for now. As Andrea Stevens has pointed out, the queen chose to paint herself and her ladies with an oily pigment that was difficult to remove quickly, preventing the instant performance of a 'miraculous' change.[13] She and her entourage remain, throughout an evening of dancing, visibly unassimilated sojourners in 'fair Albion'.

'Within the masque', writes Hardin Aasand, 'Queen Anne transmogrifies the typical allegorical representation of royalty into a grotesque mockery of orthodox ideology'.[14] 'Grotesque' may be an overstatement, but certainly the unexpected vision of a queen in blackface complicates its paean to James's power. The mixed messages of this masque possibly account for the disquiet expressed by one member of its audience, the courtier Dudley Carleton, who complained in a letter to his friend John Chamberlain that the performers' costumes were 'rich, but too light and courtesan-like; their black faces and hands, which were painted and bare up to the elbows, was a very loathsome sight, and I am sorry that strangers should see our court so strangely disguised'.[15] In other words, Anne's blackface and skimpy attire violated conventional notions of beauty and decorum. The spectacle of a queen in blackface, fretted Carleton, potentially embarrassed the English before the foreign dignitaries who were James's guests, even while Niger's praise of blackness suggested that English beauty standards might be culturally and ethnically myopic.

The Masque of Blackness was not unique in the way it implied fault-lines in its celebration of James's purportedly serene and effortless dominion. The teenage heir apparent, Prince Henry, espoused interests and political views

---

[13] Andrea Stevens, *Inventions of the Skin: The Painted Body in Early English Drama, 1400–1642*, pp. 84–89.

[14] Hardin Aasand, '"To blanch an Ethiop, and revive a corse": Queen Anne and *The Masque of Blackness*', *SEL* 32 (1992): p. 272.

[15] *Dudley Carleton to John Chamberlain, 1603–1624: Jacobean Letters*, ed. Maurice Lee.

quite different from his father's. *Oberon the Fairy Prince*, the 1611 masque that celebrated Henry's investiture as Prince of Wales, divides its attention between the supposedly omnipotent but immobile King and the gracefully dancing Prince, cynosure of all eyes. Henry as 'Oberon' threatens to eclipse James as 'Pan', although the son derives his legitimacy from his father, and the father needs the son to perpetuate his dynasty. The masque both suggests the rivalry between them and insists upon their mutual love and interdependence. In the last years of James's reign, as his grand plans to serve as a moderator between warring religious groups in Europe came to grief, some masques tried to put the best possible face on a disappointment or a policy reversal. *Neptune's Triumph for the Return of Albion* (1624), written after the failure of Prince Charles's embassy to Spain to woo the Catholic Infanta, recasts rejection as victory, possibly channelling some of the relief that many English people felt when the nuptial plans collapsed. Even so, the topic was a difficult one and the masque performance was cancelled at the last moment, though some of its material was recycled in the following year's masque, *The Fortunate Isles and their Union*.

In addition to the complex personal and political dynamics that many masques had to attempt to finesse, they risked a drawback inherent in a complimentary form: unadulterated celebration tends to be a pretty static affair, no matter how beautiful the sets and how gorgeous the costumes. Because, as Jonson notes in the preface to *The Masque of Queens*, 'a principal part of life in these spectacles lay in their variety', he invents a means of providing that desideratum by adding an 'antimasque' to precede the entrance of the masquers: a prologue meant both to contrast with and to clarify the nature of the masquers' particular excellence. The introduction of the antimasque immediately gives the masque a simple bipartite structure. In his early masques, Jonson uses the antimasque to display the dark, anarchic, or dangerous energies that are countered and dispelled by the ideal personages of the main masque. *The Masque of Queens* begins with an antimasque of witches: grotesque, wickedly powerful women, against whom King James had warned in his *Demonology* (1597). But then

> in the heat of their dance, on the sudden, was heard a sound of loud music, as if many instruments had made one blast; with which not only the hags themselves, but the hell into which they ran, quite vanished, and the whole face of the scene altered, scarce suffering the memory of such a thing. But in the place of it, appeared a glorious and magnificent building, figuring the House of Fame. (319–322)

Enthroned in the House of Fame are twelve queens, beautiful and virtuously powerful women played by Queen Anne and her ladies, apparently the antitheses of the banished witches. The annihilation of the witches and their world is swift and complete, suggesting the overwhelming power of the monarch to defeat and triumph over any challenge to his authority.

As years go by, however, Jonson develops the antimasque considerably, showcasing his talent for comic dialogue, so that the antimasque becomes a sort of satiric playlet with an independent charm of its own. The antimasque in *Mercury Vindicated From the Alchemists at Court* (1615) returns to material Jonson had first explored in *The Alchemist*, and *News from the New World Discovered in the Moon* (1620) broaches a topic he will dramatize more fully in a city comedy, *The Staple of News*. In some cases, too, the line between antimasque and masque becomes blurred in interesting ways. In *The Vision of Delight* (1617), the figure of Fant'sy presents both the grotesques of the antimasque and the splendid masquers, 'the Glories of the Spring': they are equally the products of imagination and wonder. In *Lovers Made Men* (1617), the transition from antimasque to masque involves not a banishment of the villains and an exaltation of their opposites, but a transformation of 'fantastic' and deluded lovers into wise and constant ones, and a truce between Cupid, the god of love, and Mercury, the god of wit.

Of course, if the change from antimasque to masque is marked by a transformation, rather than by banishing a lowly or debased group and replacing it with a more exalted alternative, then the connection between antimasque and masque worlds becomes more continuous. In *The Gypsies Metamorphosed* (1621), one of the most Jonson's most sophisticated masques, James's favourite, the Duke of Buckingham, much excoriated for his voracious self-enrichment, plays a gypsy pickpocket and fortuneteller, eventually casting off his gypsy mantle to reveal himself in all his courtly splendour. The playfulness of the masque acknowledges, even while it humorously disarms, the criticisms of Buckingham's behaviour and James's tolerance of it. This double gesture reminds us that the tradition of masquing has its roots in times of revelry when status hierarchies are relaxed or temporarily overturned. For James, tolerating this licensed foolery was a sign of his serene dominion; he enjoyed *The Gypsies Metamorphosed* so much that he asked for two repeat performances. Similarly, in our time presidents and prime ministers attend celebrity roasts. Laughing along with the comedian—provided he does not go too far—is a sign that the powerful man is strong enough not to worry about frisky ridicule.

Jonson's invention of the antimasque was widely copied, but other poets took his innovation in different directions. Some, such as Thomas Middleton, saw the antimasque not primarily as a 'foil' or contrast to the main masque but merely as introductory—an 'ante masque' (ante = 'before'). Others focused on the grotesque or comic element: the text of *The Masque of Flowers* (1614), a masque sponsored and perhaps written by Francis Bacon,[16] spells the word 'antic-masque'. The popularity of the antimasque encouraged writers to create more of them; by the end of the Jacobean period a masque typically included several antimasque interludes, increasing the variety of the performance but also tending to mute the thematic connections between its parts. In the Caroline masque, the number of antimasques proliferates wildly; they often seem simply to be series of contrasting dances. *Tempe Restored* (1632), for instance, features '7 Indians adoring their pagol' [idol], followed by '1 hare, 2 hounds', followed by '4 lions', then '3 apes, an ass like a pedant', then '6 barbarians', then '5 hogs', then a dance, presumably combining some previous performers, of '2 Indians, 2 hounds, 2 apes, 2 lions, 1 ass, 2 barbarians, and 2 hogs'. *Salmacida Spolia* (1640) lists twenty antimasques, among them '3 young soldiers', 'a nurse and three children', 'an ancient Irishman', 'an ancient Scottishman', 'an old-fashioned Englishman and his mistress', and 'Doctor Tartaglia and two pedants'.

The changed nature of the antimasque was not the only alteration introduced at the Caroline court. The new queen, the French princess Henrietta Maria, imported fashions from her native country, where masque conventions were somewhat different, blurring the difference between a court entertainment, pastoral play, and a ballet. Of Henrietta Maria's first masque in England, in 1625, the noblewoman Katherine Gorges wrote to her brother-in-law: 'I saw the masque acted by the queen's servants all French, but it was disliked of all the English for it was neither masque nor play, but French antic.'[17] For the first few years of Charles's reign, however, masquing was in abeyance: Charles was in serious financial straits, attempting to pay off his father's enormous debts while simultaneously waging war on both France and Spain. After peace was concluded in 1629 / 1630, masquing resumed, even more lavishly than before. Like his father, Charles believed that traditional festive rituals, provided they were decorously performed,

---

[16] For an analysis of this masque and a discussion of the evidence pointing to Bacon's authorship, see Christine Adams, 'Francis Bacon's Wedding Gift of "A Garden of a Glorious and Strange Beauty" for the Earl and Countess of Somerset', *Garden History* 36 (2008): 36–58.
[17] Quoted in Karen Britland, *Drama at the Courts of Queen Henrietta Maria*, p. 32.

undergirded the authority of the monarch and the state. In 1633 he reissued the 'Book of Sports', or list of lawful holiday and Sabbath recreations, that his father had first proclaimed in 1617 / 1618.

Caroline masques differed from their Jacobean counterparts both in the circumstances of their production and their characteristic preoccupations and imagery. While the ungainly James simply watched the masque, Charles—who had danced in masques since childhood—often participated in them as one of the performers, along with his wife. Unlike his father, Charles was deeply in love with his queen, and after the assassination of Buckingham in 1628 he did not cultivate male favourites as his father had done so notoriously. Henrietta Maria was an avid proponent of the doctrine of neo-Platonic love, which encouraged the virtuous sublimation of sexual desire into the chaste male adoration of lovely women. These new personal and performing circumstances accordingly changed the emphasis of the masques, which now represented the harmonious and fertile union of the royal couple as not only a model for marital relations, but an analogy of the proper relationship between king and kingdom. Whereas James had used the masque as a tool of diplomacy, inviting selected ambassadors as guests or staging masques in honour of their visits, masques in the more inwardly focused Caroline regime make fewer references to foreign affairs and are more invested in portraying Charles and his court as a place apart, ensconced in an island kingdom blessedly free of turmoil.

By the 1630s Ben Jonson was ill and elderly, though he wrote *Love's Triumph Through Callipolis* and *Chloridia* for the court in 1631, and *The King's Entertainment at Welbeck* (1633) and *Love's Welcome at Bolsover* (1634) for noble patrons entertaining the monarch. But, after a fierce quarrel with Inigo Jones, he was largely succeeded by a new generation of masque poets: Aurelian Townshend, William D'Avenant, and Thomas Carew. None of these dominated the genre as Jonson had done, perhaps because, from a literary point of view, the most important difference between Jacobean and Caroline masques was a change in the relative importance of the elements of the production. Charles was an art connoisseur and collector, profoundly receptive to visual beauty. The Caroline masque, reflecting these tastes, tended to subordinate the poetry of the masque to its ever more astounding spectacle. The text of *Tempe Restored* celebrates the unprecedented nature of these spectaculars:

> This sight altogether was for the difficulty of the engining and number of the persons the greatest that hath been seen here in our time. For the

apparitions of such as came down in the air, and the choruses standing beneath, arrived to the number of fifty persons all richly attired, showing the magnificence of the court of England.

Such displays were, not surprisingly, expensive. Whereas *The Masque of Queens*, in 1609, shocked contemporaries by its extravagance, costing 3,000 pounds, the staging of *The Triumph of Peace* in 1634, funded by the Inns of Court, required the stupendous sum of 21,000 pounds.

The wastefulness of the court masque had long been a topic of criticism. In the first decade of the seventeenth century, William Farington wrote to his father that 'the commonalty do somewhat murmur at such vain expenses, and thinks that that money worth bestowed other ways, might have been conferred upon better use'.[18] Even those who participated fully in masque culture could sometimes express ambivalence. Francis Bacon, who wrote entertainments for the Earl of Essex to present to Queen Elizabeth in the last years of her reign, and who bankrolled the performance of *The Masque of Flowers* in 1614, dismisses masques as 'but toys' in an essay that describes in detail how to stage one properly. Jonson, too, the most vigorous defender of the masque's conceptual and literary sophistication, nonetheless often uses masquing as a synecdoche for the court's obsession with empty show and its preference for style over substance. In 'To Sir Robert Wroth', Jonson praises Wroth for preferring the quiet blessings of country life over the 'vice' and 'sport' of city and court:

> Nor throng'st (when masquing is) to have a sight
> Of the short bravery of the night;
> To view the jewels, stuffs, the pains, the wit
> There wasted, some not paid for yet!
>   (9–12)

To many Puritans, the masque seemed unnervingly akin to pagan orgies or, worse, the 'idolatrous' Catholic Mass championed by Henrietta Maria and the ornate liturgy being imposed upon the Church of England by Archbishop Laud. Lucy Hutchinson, whose husband would become colonel in the Parliamentary forces during the civil war, recalled during the 1660s that in the reigns of James and Charles

---

[18] Letter dated 7th Feb. 1608 / 9, in *Records of Early English Drama: Lancashire*, ed. David George, p. 152.

The generality of the gentry of the land soon learnt the court fashion, and every great house in the country became a sty of uncleanness. To keep the people in their deplorable security till vengeance overtook them, they were entertained with masques, stage plays, and sorts of ruder sports. Then began murder, incest, adultery, drunkenness, swearing, fornication and all sort of ribaldry to be no concealed but countenanced vices, favored wherever they were privately practiced because they held such conformity with the court example.[19]

In the culturally polarized atmosphere of the 1630s, as the masque grew ever more extravagant, it attracted even more negative attention; the erotically charged neo-Platonic fictions of the Caroline masque, despite their high-minded veneer, arguably remained merely provocations to sexual misbehaviour. In the introduction to this volume, I mentioned the severe punishments meted out to William Prynne for his claim that masque actresses, including by implication the Queen herself, were 'notorious whores'. Because the culture of court festival was so tightly intertwined with the prestige of the king, an attack on the masque was an attack on the monarchy itself.

Given these fraught circumstances, it is interesting that what is nowadays the best-known masque of the 1630s was not a production at Charles's court, but *A Masque Presented at Ludlow Castle*, otherwise known as *Comus*, by the young poet John Milton. Milton's religious sentiments were strongly Protestant and he had little affinity with Caroline court culture. What was Milton doing writing a masque? He was probably invited to do so by the composer Henry Lawes, who wrote the music for *A Masque Presented at Ludlow Castle* as well as for many of Charles's masques, and who may have become acquainted with Milton through musical circles in London. Whereas the more stringent Puritans, like Prynne, regarded the masque, and indeed all kinds of shows and dramatic performances, with deep aversion, Milton took a different view throughout his lifetime. He attempted not to repudiate the literary and dramatic genres invented in pagan or Catholic cultures but, literally, to re-form them to make them suitable for expressing Protestant convictions. Decades later, in *Paradise Lost*, he would refashion classical and chivalric epic conventions to retell the Fall of Adam and Eve, and in *Samson Agonistes* would recast the scriptural story of Samson as a Greek tragedy.

---

[19] Lucy Hutchinson, *Memoirs of the Life of Colonel Hutchinson*, ed. James Sutherland, p. 42.

Similarly, in *A Masque* the young poet adapts a form typically used to glorify earthly rulers to very different ends. In this project he probably had the support—or at least, not the objection—of his patron, John Egerton, Earl of Bridgewater, a moderate Puritan who kept his distance from the Caroline court. In 1634, the year of *A Masque*'s performance, Egerton was Lord President of Wales, based in Ludlow on the Welsh–English border.

Milton's masque employs many of the common conventions of the Jacobean and Caroline masque. For instance, the masquers undertake a journey, encountering the grotesque figures of the antimasque, meant to serve as a foil to the ideal virtues celebrated in the masque, on their way to a festive conclusion. The influence of Aurelian Townshend's *Tempe Restored* is especially pertinent. Townshend's masque, performed at court in 1632 under the auspices of Henrietta Maria, is one of a long tradition of literary works that employs the myth of the seductive Circe, who magically turns her lovers into beasts, as an allegory of intemperate sexual desire. Townshend's Circe, who is surrounded by her grotesquely transformed lovers, is initially enraged when one of them escapes her clutches. But at the Palace of Harmony, awed by Divine Beauty (Henrietta Maria) and Heroic Virtue (Charles), she voluntarily resigns her magical power. Milton echoes, but reframes, the earlier masque's use of the Circe myth and its concern with sexual continence. In Milton's *Masque*, a virginal Lady and her two brothers are travelling through a wood on their way to their father's house, but the Lady has become separated from her brothers. She is soon beset by the sorcerer Comus, a son of Circe, who like his mother transforms men into bestial monsters. Disguised as a shepherd, Comus offers the Lady shelter nearby, but after she accepts his hospitality he traps her by magic in a chair and attempts to convince her to taste a delicious potion. When his true intentions become clear, the Lady refuses to drink, sternly refuting his invitation to pleasure.

The simple setting for Milton's masque—it requires unpretentious scenery and no special effects—was no doubt partly a matter of Egerton's restricted budget, But it is also ideologically consistent with a work that showcases the talents of the poet and the composer, not the set designer. The text of Milton's masque is more than twice as long as the typical Stuart masque, prominently featuring beautiful and metrically varied songs, lengthy philosophical speeches by each of the main characters, and spirited debates about morally complex issues. The neo-Platonic masques of Queen Henrietta Maria tended to identify physical and spiritual beauty, as *Tempe Restored* explains: 'Corporeal beauty, consisting in symmetry, colour, and certain unexpressible graces, shining in the Queen's majesty, may draw us to the contemplation of the beauty of the soul, unto which it hath analogy.' Milton, by contrast, draws a sharp distinction between 'corporeal beauty' and 'the beauty of the soul'. In the world of Milton's *Masque*, appearances cannot be trusted and courtly values are estranged from genuine courtesy:

> Which oft is sooner found in lowly sheds
> With smoky rafters, than in tapestry halls
> And courts of princes, where it first was named
> And yet is most pretended.
> (323–326).

This suspicion of visual allure, and a preference for auditory and intellectual stimulation, is a typical Protestant attitude; so is the appreciation for 'lowliness' and the aversion to pretence.

Milton, then, undermines masque values not by rejecting but by embracing and redirecting masque conventions. His characteristic method is neatly illustrated at the midpoint of *A Masque*. The first scene, 'a wild wood', gives way to 'a stately palace, set out with all manner of deliciousness; soft music, tables spread with all dainties'. This is the moment when, in a typical Stuart masque, the antimasque yields to the masque proper and idealized royal power unmistakably manifests itself in all its glory. Yet in Milton's masque, the stately palace turns out to be the locus of supreme moral danger, in which the Lady's chastity, and even her humanity, are sorely beset by Comus, the lord of the palace. Whereas in *Tempe Restored* the Stuart rulers stymie Circe, promising to reform the desires of her bestial lovers, in *A Masque* Comus, standing in for the ruler, incarnates the court's degrading potentials. And that degradation includes not merely the 'fornication' and 'ribaldry' of which Lucy Hutchinson would later complain, but sensual pleasure more generally, including the pleasure associated with the masque genre. In her reply to Comus the Lady defiantly points out not merely the moral dangers to the individual inherent in wasteful consumption and display, but their hidden social costs. 'Do not charge most innocent nature / As if she would her children should be riotous / With her abundance', the Lady declares:

> If every just man that now pines with want
> Had but a moderate and beseeming share
> Of that which lewdly pampered luxury
> Now heaps upon some few with vast excess,
> Nature's full blessings would be well dispensed

In unsuperfluous even proportion.
(762–773).

Aristocratic magnificence, she argues, requires rapaciously depriving the poor.

In Milton's masque, as in its court counterparts, virtue triumphs and the performance ends on a note of celebration and social reincorporation. Yet the route to this happy conclusion is once again atypical. Most court masques represent the triumph of good as miraculously effortless: the powerful emanation of royal charisma swiftly dispels or converts troublesome threats to good order. But in Milton's masque, the exercise of worldly power is irrelevant since, as Victoria Kahn remarks, 'we are no longer dealing with obvious questions of political sovereignty but ... with sovereignty over the self'.[20]

The achievement of the happy ending—the freeing of the Lady and her reunion with her family—involves an arduous three-step process. First, the Lady engages Comus in a strenuous debate over principle, in which she maintains that, despite her lack of physical resources, her firm resolve is enough to protect her virtue from Comus's importunity: 'Thou canst not touch the freedom of my mind / With all thy charms', she stoutly insists (663–664). The Lady's neo-stoic distinction between the impregnable fortress of her mind and her 'corporal rind' still leaves her body vulnerable to Comus, however; he is about to force her to drink his potion, and perhaps to rape her, when her brothers and a heaven-sent Attendant Spirit rush in to rescue her. They have protected themselves against Comus's dark magic by means of a 'small unsightly root' (629) that, consistent with the counterintuitive logic of the Miltonic masque, possesses a potency belied by its completely unassuming appearance. Yet, even after Comus flees, the Lady remains trapped in her chair. Her complete liberation requires the help not of the monarch, her earthly ruler, nor of her father, her domestic superior, nor of a pastor, but the supernatural aid of the nymph Sabrina, an allegory of divine grace. Not earthly hierarchies but heavenly entities—the Attendant Spirit, the magical herb, the divine nymph—intervene to support the virtuous individual who must, at the same time, strive to stay fast to her commitments. The reformed wing of the Protestant Church insisted that God's grace, not merely human effort, was necessary for salvation, and that every believer had direct access to God without the necessity of intervening human systems. Whereas the court masque locates its ultimate values

[20] Victoria Kahn, *Machiavellian Rhetoric: From the Counter-Reformation to Milton*, p. 196.

in the power and virtue of earthly rulers, Milton insists that real power and virtue emanate from a heavenly order that transcends and, to some extent, contravenes worldly hierarchies of value.

The last masque of the Caroline regime, William D'Avenant's *Salmacida Spolia*, was danced in 1640. After the defeat of the royalists, the form died out in England and was not revived at the Restoration in 1660. However, many of its conventions persisted in the related forms of opera and ballet. In fact, D'Avenant incorporated some aspects of *Salmacida Spolia* in his 1656 *The Siege of Rhodes*, considered the first English opera, for which the Caroline masque composer Henry Lawes wrote some of the music. Moreover, many of the masque's novelties—the proscenium stage, its use of splendid moveable scenery, and its employment of female actors—became commonplace in the public theatres when they reopened after the Restoration in 1660. However, the link between these spectacles and the celebration of royal power was gone forever.

Tragedy

In the first two decades of the seventeenth century, tragic dramaturgy reached a pinnacle unmatched in English—and, arguably, world—literature. These are the years of Shakespeare's tragedies, unprecedented in the complexity of their characterization and in their astonishing poetry—*Julius Caesar* (1599) and *Hamlet*, written before the accession of James, followed by *Othello*, *King Lear*, *Macbeth*, *Antony and Cleopatra*, and *Coriolanus*, all performed between 1602 and 1608. Ben Jonson bases two ambitious tragedies on Roman history: *Sejanus*, written in 1603 shortly before James's accession, and *Catiline*, performed in 1611. Between 1606 and 1622, Thomas Middleton writes *Women Beware Women*, *The Bloody Banquet* (1608) in collaboration with Thomas Dekker, and *The Changeling* in collaboration with William Rowley. John Webster produces two important tragedies: *The White Devil* and *The Duchess of Malfi*. George Chapman sets his tragedies in France: *Bussy d'Ambois*, *The Conspiracy and Tragedy of Charles, Duke of Byron* (1608), *The Revenge of Bussy d'Ambois*, and *The Tragedy of Chabot, Admiral of France*, probably written before 1622 but not printed until 1639, in a version revised by James Shirley. Although John Fletcher is better known as a prolific writer of tragicomedy, he also wrote several tragedies, most notably *The Maid's Tragedy*, a collaboration with Francis Beaumont.[21]

---

[21] Book-length discussions of English Renaissance tragedy (often including late sixteenth-century as well as seventeenth-century examples) include: Fredson Bowers, *Elizabethan*

Although it was slowly becoming more common to print plays, the often significant gap between first performance and printed edition can lead to dating difficulties and to cases of disputed authorship. The anonymously published *Revenger's Tragedy*, once attributed to Cyril Tourneur, is now thought to be by Thomas Middleton, who also probably had a hand in Shakespeare's *Timon of Athens* and contributed to the text of *Macbeth* printed in Shakespeare's First Folio. John Marston appears on the title page as the author of *The Insatiate Countess* (1613), although the actual authors may have been William Barkstead and Lewis Machin. While all these plays were written for performance in the commercial theatres, a few tragedies were designed for reading, not performance, most notably Fulke Greville's *Mustapha* (1609) and Elizabeth Cary's *Tragedy of Mariam* (1613), the only surviving tragedy of the period written by a woman.

Well before the end of James's reign, this remarkable tragic efflorescence begins to wither. But there are a few important tragedies from the later Jacobean and Caroline years: among them, Philip Massinger's *The Roman Actor* (1626), John Ford's *Tis Pity She's A Whore*, *The Broken Heart*, and *Perkin Warbeck*—all first performed between 1624 and 1634—and James Shirley's *The Cardinal* (1641). The tragedies of these decades are not merely fewer in number but intensely, self-consciously derivative and nostalgic. *The Roman Actor* draws heavily on Jonson's *Sejanus* but also borrows extensively from other predecessors, so that, as Jonathan Goldberg remarks, 'it reads at times as if it were an anthology of the best-loved moments of Jacobean drama'.[22] *Perkin Warbeck* is an *hommage* to the kind of English history plays Marlowe and Shakespeare had written three or four decades earlier. *The Cardinal* reprises Webster's luridly corrupt Catholic Italy. *Tis Pity She's a Whore* channels moments from *Doctor Faustus*, *Romeo and Juliet* (1597), and *The Revenger's Tragedy*.

Revenge Tragedy 1587–1642; Robert Ornstein, *The Moral Vision of Jacobean Tragedy*; Irving Ribner, *Jacobean Tragedy: The Quest for Moral Order*; Muriel Bradbrook, *Themes and Conventions of Elizabethan Tragedy*; Jonathan Dollimore, *Radical Tragedy: Religion, Ideology, and Power in the Drama of Shakespeare and His Contemporaries*; Catherine Belsey, *The Subject of Tragedy*; Thomas McAlindon, *English Renaissance Tragedy*; Dymphna Callaghan, *Women and Gender in Renaissance Tragedy: A Study of King Lear, Othello, The Duchess of Malfi, and The White Devil*; Rebecca Bushnell, *Tragedies of Tyrants: Political Thought and Theater in the English Renaissance*; Naomi Conn Liebler, *Shakespeare's Festive Tragedy: The Ritual Foundations of Genre*; Frank Whigham, *Seizures of the Will in Early Modern English Drama*; Michael Neill, *Issues of Death: Mortality and Identity in English Renaissance Tragedy*; John Kerrigan, *Revenge Tragedy: Aeschylus to Armageddon*; Naomi Liebler, ed., *The Female Tragic Hero in English Renaissance Drama*; Emma Smith, ed., *The Cambridge Companion to English Renaissance Tragedy*; Peter Holbrook, *English Renaissance Tragedy: Ideas of Freedom*; Daniel Cadman, Andrew Dufield, and Lisa Hopkins, eds., *The Genres of Renaissance Tragedy*.

[22] Jonathan Goldberg, *James I and the Politics of Literature*, p. 203.

Unlike the masque, frequently criticized even by its authors as risking triviality, tragedy was a high-prestige form, generally placed at or near the top of the hierarchy of genres by Renaissance commentators. Its stature derived partly from its antiquity. Sixteenth- and seventeenth-century writers had access to classical tragedy through the Latin plays of Seneca, which were part of the grammar school curriculum; in the course of the sixteenth century some Greek dramas had also become available in the original language.[23] Aristotle's *Poetics*, with its detailed analysis of Greek tragic form, had been translated into Latin in 1498 and Italian in 1549, stimulating considerable discussion among sixteenth-century Italian commentators. Some playwrights, especially Ben Jonson, George Chapman, John Fletcher, and John Ford, demonstrate a keen awareness of classical prototypes, and of the thriving contemporary theatre scene on the Continent. But their most important precedents, by far, were Elizabethan tragedies, written to be performed on the English stage in the fifteen or so years immediately prior to James's accession. Plays of the late 1580s and 1590s such as *The Spanish Tragedy*, *Doctor Faustus*, *Titus Andronicus*, *Romeo and Juliet*, *Richard II*, and *Richard III* were available in printed editions by the turn of the seventeenth century and remained popular in revival, continuing to exert a powerful influence in the decades that follow. The line of demarcation between 'Elizabethan' and 'Jacobean' literature is, as we have already seen, an indistinct one, and this is particularly true in the case of tragedy: although there are some stylistic differences between seventeenth-century tragedy and their Elizabethan predecessors, there is no discernible break with James's accession in 1603. The great burgeoning of tragic achievement, in fact, really began several years earlier, at the turn of the century, as Shakespeare finished his series of English history plays and wrote *Julius Caesar* and *Hamlet*. As Rowland Wymer has convincingly argued, many of what are thought to be the distinctive features of 'Jacobean tragedy' actually originate in the last years of Elizabeth's reign.[24]

What are these features? If court masque attempts to show authority in its best possible light, celebrating the triumph of benevolent rule and

---

[23] For a detailed discussion of the influence of classical tragic rhetoric on particular Jacobean plays, see Charles Osborne McDonald, *The Rhetoric of Tragedy: Form in Stuart Drama*. Excellent discussions of the Senecan influence include Gordon Braden, *Renaissance Tragedy and the Senecan Tradition: Anger's Privilege* and Curtis Perry, *Shakespeare and Senecan Tragedy*.

[24] Rowland Wymer, 'Jacobean Pageant or Elizabethan Fin-de-siecle? The Political Context of Early Seventeenth Century Tragedy', *Neo-Historicism: Studies in Renaissance Literature, History, and Politics*, pp. 138–151.

glorifying the persons in whom that dominion is invested, early modern English tragedy does just the opposite. George Puttenham, writing in the 1580s—that is, prior to the great flowering of Elizabethan and Jacobean drama—asserts that, since ancient times, tragedy has been a genre that showcases disenchantment with rulers—a disenchantment that is the flip side of adulation:

> Whereas... in their great prosperities, [kings] were both feared and reverenced in the highest degree, after their deaths, when the posterity stood no more in dread of them, their infamous life and wicked tyrannies were laid open to the world, their wickedness reproached, their follies and extreme insolencies derided, and their miserable ends painted out in plays and pageants to show the mutability of fortune and the just punishment of God in revenge of a vicious and evil life.[25]

Tragedy, by this account, dramatizes stories in which authority lurches into crisis and becomes malignant. The nature and severity of this disaster vary from play to play, but because a virtuous ruler is, as we have seen, the linchpin of a hierarchically organized community, failure at the top can eventuate in a collapse of the entire social structure.

Often, one or more characters draw a sharp contrast between their own situation and an ideal of harmonious security imagined as situated elsewhere or in the past. *The Duchess of Malfi* begins with Antonio's description of the wise French king and his well-organized court, so different from the reality in Italy where the tragedy will take place. And, towards the end of the play, Antonio and his friend Delio find themselves in a derelict abbey, reminiscent of those which, after the Reformation, remained roofless and abandoned all over seventeenth-century England. Antonio's tone is one of elegiac lament:

> I do love these ancient ruins.
> We never tread upon them but we set
> Our foot upon some reverend history;
> And questionless, here in this open court,
> Which now lies naked to the injuries
> Of stormy weather, some men lie interred

---

[25] George Puttenham, *The Art of English Poesy: A Critical Edition*, ed. Frank Whigham and Wayne Rebhorn, p. 123.

> Loved the church so well, and gave so largely to't,
> They thought it should have canopied their bones
> Till doomsday. But all things have their end,
> Churches and cities, which have diseases like to men
> Must have like death that we have.
>
> (5.3.9–19)

The death of virtuous individuals—of the Duchess, who is already dead, and of Antonio himself, which will soon ensue—is both an analogy to and a consequence of the demise of institutions that once appeared impregnable. The Church, which in the past seemed to underwrite the mutual obligations between rulers and subjects, husbands and wives, brothers and sisters, parents and children, the living and the dead, is desolate now; the ruined courtyard in which Antonio walks with his friend is hard by the palace of the murderous Cardinal, the embodiment of the Church in the present day.

Although Antonio's tone seems gently nostalgic, he suggests that degeneration is inevitable, both for individuals and for societies: 'all things have their end'. In Chapman's *The Revenge of Bussy d'Ambois*, Renel, in similarly parlous straits, seems less resigned, voicing greater outrage at what he sees as the moral failures of rulers and subjects:

> things most lawful
> Were once most royal; kings sought common good,
> Men's manly liberties, though ne'er so mean,
> And had their own swinge so more free, and more.
> But when pride entered them, and rule by power,
> All brows that smiled beneath them, frowned; hearts grieved
> By imitation; virtue quite was vanished,
> And all men studied self love, fraud, and vice.
>
> (1.1.19–26)

In days of yore, according to Renel, the king kept the wellbeing of the entire community in mind ('sought common good') and his prudent use of power had the effect of freeing his subjects to occupy their proper roles, enjoying what Renel calls their 'manly liberties'. In the here-and-now, however, 'self love, fraud, and vice' prevail. Renel describes a causal relationship: the king's greedy and tyrannical behaviour leads to first his subjects' suffering, and then to their imitation of his signal excesses. Ironically, when either kings or subjects attempt to assert themselves beyond their proper compass, their 'swinge' or scope of power is actually constrained because they no longer possess the self-restraint or spirit of cooperative endeavour necessary to maintain a thriving society.

Both *The Duchess of Malfi* and *The Revenge of Bussy d'Ambois*, as in Jacobean and Caroline tragedy more generally, depict worlds in which the ethical and religious precepts that ought, and apparently used to, govern the behaviour of virtuous people have given way to an amoral self-aggrandizing that pays no heed to the larger dynamics of relationships or to the health of the community. In this diagnosis of social breakdown, Jacobean tragedy is closely akin to satiric comedy, which likewise, as we saw in chapter 4, depicts egoists who have little regard for a larger temporal or social context, or for the constraints of a prescribed social role. So it is not surprising that many Jacobean and Caroline tragedies contain a strong satiric component, or that the topics they choose to satirize are often the same ones obsessed over in the comedies. Women's cosmetics, for instance, become a theme of complaint in plays as varied as *Hamlet, Sejanus, The Revenger's Tragedy*, and *The Duchess of Malfi*. In *The Revenger's Tragedy*, Vindice comments sarcastically:

> It was the greatest blessing ever happened to women
> When farmers' sons agreed and met again
> To wash their hands and come up gentlemen.
> The commonwealth has flourished ever since.
>
> (2.1.221–224)

These parvenus, he continues, assert their prestige by turning their 'solid' landed wealth into flauntable but ephemeral chattel property:

> Lands that were mete by the rod, that labour's spared;
> Tailors ride down and measure 'em by the yard.
> Fair trees, those comely foretops of the field
> Are cut to maintain head-tires.
>
> (2.1.225–228)

Vindice's acerbic commentary on ruinous conspicuous consumption would not be out of place in one of Middleton's city comedies. Yet in comedy, social consensus is often reimposed, at least shakily, by the end of the play, so the pushy, manipulative characters can still seem amusing. In tragedy, the world seems catastrophically disordered, and the corrupt present seems impossibly distant from an evoked conservative ideal.

There are two related but distinct ways to imagine this distance. It is possible to retain a commitment to the idea of a divinely ordained hierarchical social order, and simply believe that the current situation is a painful deviation. In Cyril Tourneur's *The Atheist's Tragedy* (1611), the virtuous Charlemont is betrayed and disinherited by his wicked uncle, the aptly named D'Amville. Even after he learns that D'Amville has killed his father, Charlemont steadfastly refuses to take revenge but, despite his forbearance, he is unjustly convicted of murdering a man D'Amville has sent to assassinate him, and is sentenced to death. D'Amville insists upon serving as executioner but, as he raises the axe, he accidentally clubs himself in the head and 'strikes out his own brains'. Although mortally wounded, D'Amville still has time to make a long speech confessing his crimes; upon his death, Charlemont not only recovers his own patrimony but inherits his uncle's estate as well. A judge comments:

> The power of that eternal providence
> Which overthrew his projects in their pride
> Hath made your griefs the instruments to raise
> Your blessings to a greater height than ever.
> (5.2.269–272)

Even in plays less ridiculously contrived than this one, the final lines of a tragedy sometimes look forward to a more hopeful future in which order might be restored. *Macbeth* ends with Duncan's rightful heir, Malcolm, hailed as king of Scotland by his loyal thanes, whom he promptly makes earls of the realm and invites to his coronation ceremony. Pointedly declaring his dependence upon the grace of God, he promises to restore the 'measure, time, and place'(5.7.103) that have been lacking for the duration of the play. There is a similar emphasis on the re-establishment of stability at the end of *The Duchess of Malfi*. 'Let us make noble use / Of this great ruin', Delio proposes, holding the Duchess's child in his arms: 'and join all our force / To establish this young hopeful gentleman / In's mother's right' (5.5.128–131).

Alternatively, however, a tragedy might call into question the very ideal of a functional, just society, since that ideal seems nowhere instantiated. Perhaps God, who is supposed to ordain and preserve proper order, is absent or asleep at the switch; perhaps human beings are actually at the mercy of malevolent divinities; perhaps concepts like duty, justice, and fidelity are merely pious fictions. In many early seventeenth-century tragedies, not only the villainous blasphemers—from whom such sentiments might be expected—but also the 'good' characters evince a radical scepticism about any transcendental guarantee. In *King Lear* the Earl of Gloucester, betrayed by his bastard son and then blinded and cast out by people whom he had welcomed as guests into his home, comments bitterly: 'As flies to wanton boys are we to th' gods / They kill us for their sport' (4.1.38–39). Similarly, in *The Duchess of Malfi* the equivocal villain Bosola laments, after accidentally killing Antonio, 'We are merely the stars' tennis balls, struck and banded / Which way please them' (5.4.56–57). The bleakest, most memorable occasions in early seventeenth-century tragedies tend not to be those in which people suffer—because people are, after all, always suffering—but those in which their suffering no longer makes sense, no longer seems connected to a larger pattern of cosmic justice and oversight. The spectacular 'mad scenes' in so many early seventeenth-century tragedies often mark those moments when the conceptual apparatus that makes the world cohere seems to have disintegrated. Few Jacobean tragedies take an explicit stand on religious issues, but they often seem to echo the profoundly sceptical and interrogatory intellectual currents of the age, and of past ages: the shrewd, darkly ironic historical vision of Tacitus, the rigorously materialist philosophy of Lucretius, and the unsentimental political commentary of Machiavelli.

Spectators, readers, and critics of early seventeenth-century tragedy in the centuries since have therefore debated how seriously and deeply these forms of scepticism cut. Some argue that Jacobean and Caroline tragedy remains fundamentally Christian, others that it becomes a vehicle for an anti-religious, anti-providentialist outlook, exploring the fissures in early modern systems of social ordering and subjecting established patterns of thought to searching ironic critique.[26] In Jonathan Dollimore's view, the

---

[26] G. Wilson Knight, *The Wheel of Fire: Interpretations of Shakespearean Tragedy*, Robert Ornstein, *The Moral Vision of Jacobean Tragedy*, and Irving Ribner *Jacobean Tragedy* discuss the Christian resonances of early seventeenth-century tragedy; so does Arthur Kirsch in *Jacobean Dramatic Perspectives*. On the other side, William R. Elton, *King Lear and the Gods*, explores that play's radical scepticism; Jonathan Dollimore, *Radical Tragedy*, argues that early modern tragedy 'undermined religious orthodoxy' (p. 4). Catherine Belsey, *The Subject of Tragedy* and Peter Holbrook, *English Renaissance Tragedy: Ideas of Freedom* similarly emphasize the sceptical and unorthodox aspects of the form. William Hamlin, *Tragedy and Scepticism in Shakespeare's England*, discusses the way tragedy refracts some of the concerns of philosophical scepticism, as inherited from the Greeks and Romans and elaborated by early modern philosophy. In a somewhat different key, Jeffrey Knapp, in *Shakespeare's Tribe*, argues that early modern theatre people saw themselves—not just as tragedians but in all their writing and performance—as engaged in a performative activity that encouraged the virtues of charity, empathy, and community that were the traditional purview of the Church; Peter Lake argues that 'the denizens of the popular stage ... were engaged in a struggle with the godly clergy both for the same audience or at least for massively overlapping audiences and for great swathes of the same cultural, moral, and intellectual terrain' (*The Antichrist's Lewd Hat: Protestants, Papists, and Players in Post-Reformation England*, xxxi.)

tragedy of the period 'interrogates ideology from within, seizing on and exposing its contradictions and inconsistencies and offering alternative ways of understanding social and political process'.[27] Rather obviously this subversive, critical strain may be more fully manifested in some tragedies than in others. And, in some cases, the subversive point is dependent upon the very system it seems to challenge. This is a technique pioneered in the early 1590s by Christopher Marlowe in *Doctor Faustus*, a play in which a purportedly loving God is remote and silent while the apparently solicitous devil Mephistophilis spends the play at Faustus's elbow. Yet despite God's absence the story of the hero's damnation is inconceivable outside a religious world view. In Stephen Greenblatt's words:

> Marlowe's protagonists rebel against orthodoxy, but they do not do so just as they please; their actions of negation not only conjure up the order they would destroy but seem at times to be themselves conjured up by that very order ... Faustus' whole career binds him ever more closely to that Christian conception of the body and the mind, that divinity, that he thought he was rejecting... the blasphemy pays homage to the power it insults.[28]

Many Jacobean tragedies seize on and elaborate this backhanded acknowledgement of an order that is only perceptible in its negative manifestations. For instance, the plot of *Macbeth* seems to subvert the distinction between the loyal adherent and the traitor, between foul and fair, between witch and devoted spouse, depicting a world of moral confusion in which the connections between king and subject, guest and host, husband and wife, parent and child no longer pertain. Yet, soon after the murder of King Duncan, the remarks of an Old Man suggest a different perspective:

> Threescore and ten I can remember well,
> Within the volume of which time I have seen
> Hours dreadful and things strange; but this sore night
> Hath trifled former knowings.
>
> (2.4.1–4)

The Old Man and his interlocutor, Ross, discuss disturbing, topsy-turvy events: the day is as dark as night, an owl has hunted and killed a falcon,

---

[27] Dollimore, *Radical Tragedy: Religion, Ideology and Power I the Drama of Shakespeare and his Contemporaries*, p. 8.
[28] Stephen Greenblatt, *Renaissance Self Fashioning*, pp. 210, 212.

and the King's horses, 'contending 'gainst obedience' (17), have broken out of their stalls and eaten one another. These prodigies, uncannily amplifying the regicide, are inexplicable except in a resonantly connected universe in which a political crime is 'naturally' attended by analogical disruptions, such as freakish weather and the misbehaviour of beasts. In the world of *Macbeth*, a transcendent ordering principle cannot easily be perceived; but neither, on the other hand, can it be ruled out, and violations of hierarchy still seem monstrous. Some have theorized that the efflorescence of tragedy in late sixteenth and early seventeenth-century England is a response to the trauma of the Reformation, which had profoundly altered the metaphysical coordinates by which Christian society had oriented itself. In particular, by dismissing Purgatory as a fiction and by insisting that salvation came solely by God's grace and not by 'works' or by living a virtuous life, the Reformation disrupted the ways in which God had been imagined to redress worldly wrongs by meting out justice in the afterlife.[29]

Unsettling ironies trouble the conclusions of many Jacobean and Caroline tragedies, which often end with a sentential warning that purports to sum up the story's moral. For instance, Terentius, in the final speech of *Sejanus*, intones:

> Let this example move th'insolent man
> Not to grow proud and careless of the gods.
> It is an odious wisdom to blaspheme
> Much more to slighten or deny their powers.
> For whom the morning saw so great and high,
> Thus low and little, 'fore th' even, doth lie.
> (5.880–885)

This advice sounds appropriately pious and definitive; unfortunately it is inapposite to the action we have just witnessed. Although shortly before his downfall the 'insolent' Sejanus did unwisely ridicule several omens of disaster, he would have been doomed even if he had attended to them respectfully. Moreover, the tyrannical system that produced Sejanus is still in place, and Sejanus has merely been superseded as Tiberius' henchman by the even more ruthless Macro. The inadequacy of the play's moral summary suggests that the 'lessons' of Sejanus' fall are more complicated than Terentius acknowledges.

---

[29] Stephen Greenblatt, *Hamlet in Purgatory* and Michael Neill, *Issues of Death: Mortality and Identity in English Renaissance Tragedy.*

There is a similar disjunction at the end of John Ford's *Tis Pity She's a Whore*. Just moments earlier, the protagonist, Giovanni, has murdered his pregnant sister, Annabella, with whom he was having an incestuous affair, and rushed onstage with her heart skewered on his dagger; their father, Florio, has collapsed with grief and horror; Giovanni has stabbed Annabella's treacherous husband Soranzo and has himself been killed by a team of hired assassins; meanwhile, Soranzo's servant reports that he has gratuitously blinded Annabella's maidservant. After this spectacular bloodbath, the summary lines go to a corrupt Cardinal, who—after seizing the property of the dead for the Church, and condemning the blinded maidservant to be burnt at the stake—marvels at Annabella's unchastity:

> never yet
> Incest and murder have so strangely met.
> Of one so young, so rich in nature's store,
> Who could not say, tis pity she's a whore?
> (5.6.156–159)

The 'whoredom' of Annabella seems hardly the most remarkable outrage in this carnival of mayhem. As in *Sejanus*, the inadequate attempt at closure suggests that the flawed system that produced such atrocities is going to endure beyond the play.

Why should tragedy be the genre in which authority is challenged, in which ethical certainties are destabilized, in which godly pieties are subjected to critique? The answer probably lies in what early seventeenth-century writers thought a tragedy to be. Ben Jonson, in his introduction to *Sejanus*, succinctly lists what he considers the characteristics of a tragedy: 'truth of argument' (a story based on fact), 'dignity of persons' (royal or aristocratic protagonists), 'gravity and height of elocution' (serious and elevated diction), and 'fullness and frequency of sentence' (memorable maxims and vivid figures of speech).[30] Jacobean and Caroline tragedy focuses upon elite characters—there are no 'tragedies of common life' of the kind pioneered in the late nineteenth century by Theodore Dreiser, Thomas Hardy, Henrik Ibsen, and others. Even largely domestic tragedies, such as Heywood's *A Woman Killed With Kindness* (1603), Middleton and Rowley's *The Changeling*, or Ford's *Tis Pity She's A Whore*, feature affluent gentry and

---

[30] Ben Jonson, 'To the Readers', ll. 13–14, *Sejanus*, ed. Tom Cain, *The Cambridge Edition of the Works of Ben Jonson*, p. 213.

mercantile protagonists. Such characters seem, to seventeenth-century playwrights, better suited for high-stakes existential dilemmas than are ordinary people whose freedom is hemmed in by lack of resources and limited authority over others. Shakespeare makes this difference plain in the opening scenes of *Hamlet*. The watchmen, and later Horatio, cope with the disturbing appearance of the dead king's ghost by alerting his son, the prince: 'we did think it writ down in our duty / To let you know of it'(1.2.222–23). But Hamlet must speak with the ghost directly, and personally confront all the questions about death, justice, and the afterlife that the ghost ambiguously raises. If the world is, as Hamlet laments, out of joint, he is the person 'born to set it right' (1.5.190): there is no higher-up to whom he can deflect the responsibility for action.

Tragedy's focus on powerful characters brings with it a concern with the appropriate deployment of that power. And since tragedy by definition concerns misfortune and disaster, it is not surprising that, again and again, Jacobean and Caroline tragedy shows power abused, and a hierarchical society gone badly off the rails. In other words, the deviation from an ideal of order and harmony, and thus potentially the challenges to that ideal, are, as it were, baked into the form. What registers as 'subversiveness', however defined, may therefore be a consequence of tragedy's particular generic niche, as interpreted through the pressing concerns of the early seventeenth century—a formal imperative, in other words, and not necessarily a sign of the playwrights' personal political opinions or ethical commitments. Occasionally, indeed, tragic playwrights found themselves in trouble for treading on precarious ground. Samuel Daniel's *Philotas* (1604) came under suspicion for its possible references to the Essex conspiracy; Ben Jonson was called in for questioning about *Sejanus*; the French ambassador formally complained about George Chapman's depiction of the French court in his Byron plays. Yet many of the major tragic writers of the period—including Jonson and Chapman, but also Middleton and Webster—were accomplished writers of masques that glorified the powers-that-be, deftly suiting the sentiments expressed to the decorum of the genre.

Despite the elite orientation of early seventeenth-century tragedy, the cast of characters was not necessarily entirely restricted to noblemen and women, as would be the case in, say, French neoclassical drama later in the seventeenth century. A great deal of Jacobean tragedy traffics in abrupt changes in register, deliberately juxtaposing scenes of nobility and pathos with comic grotesquerie, melodrama with levity, and princes with fools and beggars. Shakespeare's King Lear endures the storm on the heath in the company of a court jester and a man who seems to be a mad vagrant; in *Antony and Cleopatra* the defeated Cleopatra, on the brink of suicide, banters with the rustic clown who brings her poisonous asps hidden in a basket of figs. Middleton and Rowley, in *The Changeling,* pair a psychologically searching tale of lust and murder with a darkly comic story of two courtiers who disguise themselves as madhouse inmates in order to seduce the elderly keeper's luscious young wife. Moreover, although the 'main characters' in a seventeenth-century tragedy are typically highborn, it is often a subordinate or outcast character who provides the most trenchant commentary on the action.

Many Jacobean and Caroline tragedies skilfully exploit the way dramatic performance provides a give-and-take among an array of competing perspectives, none of which is definitive. Of course, the dialogic form of all kinds of drama makes the policing of hierarchy hard to enforce, but the effect is particularly marked in tragedy both because the ethical stakes are higher and because so many seventeenth-century tragedies concern extreme situations in which an appropriate course of conduct is simply unclear. In these plays, the breakdown of a customary way of life or form of social order produces characters who refuse to obey, or who violate, or are for some reason uncertain about, the precepts by which they are supposed to live. The hero might be the victim of somebody else's disruptions, like Hamlet, or, like Macbeth, he may have generated them wholly or in part. Often, like Shakespeare's King Lear, Antony, and Coriolanus, Chapman's Bussy d'Ambois, or *The Revenger's Tragedy*'s Vindice, the tragic hero both suffers and perpetrates wrong. In all cases, the stress of political and social instability—a revolution, a usurpation, a civil war, a transgressive marriage—complicates the lives of the protagonists in a way that brings them to heightened consciousness. In tranquil times one might cope with and conceptualize the world in terms of habits, stereotypes, and precedents, but disruption requires improvisation. And this improvisation both reveals unique characters and creates them, as individuals respond to the pressure of extreme circumstances without a model to go on. So, while part of the pleasure of watching a comedy is the recognition of familiar characters and plot devices cleverly redeployed, tragedy tends to emphasize instead the distinctiveness of the characters and their suffering. Indeed, the titles of many Jacobean tragedies are simply the names of their protagonists: *Sejanus, Othello, Macbeth, Bussy d'Ambois, Charles Duke of Byron, King Lear, Antony and Cleopatra, The Duchess of Malfi, Coriolanus, Perkin Warbeck.*

Not everyone agreed with Jonson (and Aristotle) that tragic stories needed to be based upon fact (or what passed for fact), and a number of influential Elizabethan plays were patently fictional. Yet the link between tragedy and history remained significant. In the late 1580s and 1590s, Marlowe's *Tamburlaine* plays (1587–1590), *Edward II* (1592), and *The Massacre at Paris* (1593) all had some basis in fact; Shakespeare's *Richard II* and *Richard III* were called 'tragedies' in the first printed versions but grouped with the 'histories' in the Folio. Even Shakespeare's generically mixed Elizabethan 'history' plays, such as the *Henry VI* series or *Henry IV Part 1*, present the stories of the Duke of York or of Hotspur as tragedies set within a larger national narrative.

In the seventeenth century, as he moved into a period in which he wrote one great tragedy after another, Shakespeare continued to rely upon historical accounts, although now he drew upon Roman, Danish, Scottish, and Greek materials, not just English ones. George Chapman brought the turbulent politics of sixteenth-century France to the stage in *Bussy d'Ambois*, *The Revenge of Bussy d'Ambois*, and *The Conspiracy and Tragedy of Charles, Duke of Byron*. Philip Massinger derives the basic elements of *The Roman Actor* from Suetonius' life of the emperor Domitian, and John Ford bases *Perkin Warbeck* on English history in the time of Henry VII. Elizabeth Cary consulted Josephus' *Wars of the Jews* and *Antiquities of the Jews* as sources for The *Tragedy of Mariam*. Jonson based both his extant tragedies, *Sejanus* and *Catiline*, on events in Roman history, even annotating the printed editions of the plays with citations to his sources. Jonson's scholarly scrupulosity was not the rule, however; in both tragedies and in 'history' plays, Renaissance dramatists did not hesitate to tailor the story to fit the demands of the stage, compressing events, adding or omitting characters, and freely combining 'historical' plots with material taken from romance. Often, indeed, the line between fact and fiction was already pretty thin in the sources. Shakespeare derived the main plot of *King Lear* from Holinshed's (supposedly) historical *Chronicles*, but that plot strongly resembles an old folktale; its 'legendary' quality is highlighted by its juxtaposition with a frankly invented subplot adapted from Sidney's *Arcadia*. John Webster's *The White Devil* and *The Duchess of Malfi* each have some historical basis, but his immediate source is William Painter's *Palace of Pleasure* (1575), a vast collection of sensational stories, mostly translated from Italian, that served as a treasure trove of plots for Elizabethan and Jacobean dramatists alike.

In general, tragedies that foregrounded sex and domestic conflict, whether by Shakespeare (*Othello*), Middleton (*Women Beware Women*,

The Changeling), Heywood (*A Woman Killed With Kindness*), Beaumont and Fletcher (*The Maid's Tragedy*), or Ford (*Tis Pity She's a Whore*) were more likely than 'tragedies of state' to involve entirely invented plots. Moreover, the connection to historical incidents becomes more tenuous in the later Jacobean and Caroline period: these plays, featuring highly stylized characters and extreme situations, virtually demand a fabricated plot. Shirley's *The Cardinal* piles melodramatic plot devices one on top of another to produce a fast-paced drama of unceasing retaliation. Fletcher invents all his plots or adapts them from fictions by such writers as Cervantes and Sidney. Although John Ford's *Perkin Warbeck* is based on an episode in English history, it is hard to imagine that anyone believed the prologue to his patently fantastic *Broken Heart*:

> What may be here thought a fiction, when time's youth
> Wanted some riper years, was known a truth.
>
> (15–16)

The Broken Heart features three interconnected couples, with allegorically appropriate names, whose unions are proscribed by family members. The interest of the drama lies in how the characters cope with the complex mixture of empathy, vengefulness, and schadenfreude provoked by their closely parallel situations.

The linguistic resources for Jacobean tragedy were likewise more expansive and flexible than Jonson's phrase 'gravity and height of elocution' might suggest. By the beginning of the seventeenth century, the accepted norm for elevated language on the stage was unrhymed iambic pentameter, with occasional couplets at the ends of scenes or to mark sententious or witty utterances. But most Jacobean playwrights resort to prose at least occasionally in their tragedies, especially in 'low' episodes or scenes of repartee. Moreover, their verse is markedly less orotund than its Elizabethan precedents, with plenty of enjambment, caesuras, and off-stresses to complicate the aural pattern of the line. The effect is to blur the distinction between prose and poetry, and to suggest the impulsive spontaneity of thought and conversation. Peter Holland has argued that this evolution in blank verse style reflects a shift towards a less highly rhetorical, more naturalistic acting style on the late Elizabethan and Jacobean stage.[31] It is also likely connected to the development of a new fashion, among such poets as Jonson and

---

[31] Peter Holland, '*Hamlet* and the Art of Acting', *Themes in Drama* 6 (1984): 39–61,

Donne, for verse modelled upon colloquial speech rather than upon music or public oratory. Yet, whether the direction of influence is from stage to page or vice versa is hard to determine.

As we have seen, tragedy emphasizes the individuality of its protagonists, but nonetheless most Jacobean and Caroline tragedies, including Shakespeare's, ingeniously ring changes upon three sturdy plot scenarios. These may be dramatized alone or, more usually, in combination:

1) A ruler suffers a disaster, generally of his own making.
2) An ambitious subordinate asserts himself in ways that bring ruin on himself and others.
3) A sexual relationship between a man and a woman, often one that cannot be comprehended within the institution of marriage, ends in catastrophe.

Early modern tragedy concerns itself with episodes of social breakdown generally, not necessarily with the ruination of individual monarchs. Tragedies like *Julius Caesar*, *Catiline*, or *Coriolanus*, set in republican Rome, ask searching questions about the nature of authority, the obligations of citizenship, and the necessity of hierarchy without dramatizing the missteps or downfall of a king. Yet, since most western European societies were monarchies or quasi-monarchies, the emphasis on a single powerful ruler—a king or the duke of a city-state—is not surprising. The perennial fascination of the king, in classical and Continental tragedy as well as in its English variant, is that, apparently, he does not need to answer to anybody. It is plausible for him to imagine that his choices determine what will happen (though he often turns out to be mistaken). Moreover, plays are always better at portraying conflicts among a restricted group of characters than at conveying complex or large-scale social patterns.

For all these reasons, early seventeenth-century drama generally depicts rulers, whether virtuous or vicious, as absolutists who wield their power with little institutional interference. Few Jacobean tragedies feature a functional parliament or judiciary. The lack of obvious constraints upon the ruler's power means that the distinction between a king and a tyrant becomes a thin and shaky one. As Rebecca Bushnell has pointed out, although on one hand the categories of 'king' and 'tyrant' are opposed to one another in both classical and early modern political theory, in fact the criteria for doing so are uncertain. Is a tyrant a morally monstrous king, or merely one who in some respects exceeds his mandate? Must he be a usurper who assumed his office illegitimately?[32] Who gets to decide at what point properly kingly power has veered into tyrannical overreach? What, in fact, is the difference between 'right rule' and 'tyranny'? For the mid-century political theorist Thomas Hobbes, writing in the immediate aftermath of the English civil wars, the difference between tyranny and right rule no longer seems a matter of the conduct or piety of rulers, but merely registers subjective perception: 'the name of tyranny signifieth nothing more nor less than the name of sovereignty, be it in one or many men, saving they that use the former word, are understood to be angry with them they call tyrants.'[33] To supporters of Parliament, Charles I is a tyrant; to royalists, Cromwell is a tyrant—Hobbes suggests that 'tyrant' is merely a term of invective that fails to point to a genuine ethical distinction. However, if the ethical distinction between tyranny and right rule disappears, so does the supposedly harmonious relationship between a just and merciful God and the human delegates in whom power is vested. Hobbes's line of political thinking tends to undermine the entire intellectual framework on which the traditional notion of a harmonious hierarchy depends.

Tragedies about bad rulers insistently pose questions about how power is constituted, what its limits might be, to what extent it ought to be vested in a single individual, and how and in what circumstances it might be resisted. These were problems that generated a good deal of dispute among political theorists in the sixteenth and seventeenth centuries, as rulers across Western Europe attempted to consolidate their authority and as religious conflict divided loyalties among many of their subjects. Understandably, most, unlike Hobbes, wanted to differentiate between a good ruler and a tyrannical one even if they were not sure exactly how to draw that distinction. In years when James I, and then his son Charles, were making strong authoritarian claims, the representation of tyranny has potentially powerful political implications. Yet stage tyrants were not necessarily remote or displaced portraits of Queen Elizabeth or King James or King Charles personally (in fact, *Sejanus* incorporates into the show-trial of the historian Cordus a warning against interpreting historical writing, and presumably also plays based on historical events, as commentary upon contemporary politics). Many tragedies were performed at court, and some of the most horrendous tyrants were depicted in plays written in the last years of Elizabeth's reign or the

---

[32] Rebecca Bushnell. *Tragedies of Tyrants: Political Thought and Theatre in the English Renaissance*, pp. 42–49 and *passim*.

[33] Thomas Hobbes, *Leviathan*, ed. J. C. A. Gaskin, p. 470.

first years of James's, when he was still a popular ruler. The political point, if there was one, could well be a distinction between the unfortunate Italians, French, or imperial Romans, and the happier English. Shakespeare's Jacobean tyrant play, *Macbeth*, was likely conceived with performance at court in mind: it appeals to a new interest in Scots history stimulated by the arrival of James and his courtiers from the north, and incorporates some of James's personal preoccupations, such as his longstanding interest in witchcraft. While the play unsparingly exhibits the brutality of Macbeth's rule, it alters the historical account to exonerate James's ancestor, Banquo, from the assassination of Duncan, and it celebrates the mysterious healing powers of the (rightful) English king. Monarchy per se is not the problem here, only monarchy achieved by treason and sustained by murder.

Early seventeenth-century plays are especially preoccupied with the most important weakness in the monarchical scheme: there is no sanctioned method for removing even an obviously incompetent or evil ruler. Playwrights can depict abuses of power from various perspectives. In the 1590s Shakespeare had written a successful 'tyrant play', *Richard III*, in which melodrama was tempered by a subtle psychological depiction of a killer eventually torn by conscience and self-loathing. Shakespeare's late Elizabethan and Jacobean tyrants are similarly complex. *Hamlet*'s Claudius is a traitor, a poisoner, a fratricide, and a machiavel, but Shakespeare gives him an agonized soliloquy of attempted repentance; Hamlet's stark contrast between Claudius and the brother who preceded him on the throne reveals more about Hamlet's neuroticism than about Claudius's actual demeanour. In *King Lear*, Lear's imperious demand that his daughters publicly declare their love for him as a condition of receiving their inheritances seems more foolish than wicked. Even Macbeth is not simply rotten to the core, but is, as Maynard Mack writes, 'an heroic and essentially noble human being who, by visible stages, deteriorates into a butcher'.[34]

The disasters of failed rule have obvious dramatic interest not only because a ruler's plummet from the pinnacle to the depths is sensational to watch, but because he never suffers alone. While Shakespeare often focuses on the tyrant himself, revealing his intricate mental life in extended, reflective soliloquies, Middleton, Fletcher, Jonson, and Chapman are more interested in the lives of those who must struggle to cope with the effects of misused power. Their plays depict nightmarish courts in which a vastly wicked or deranged despot makes life hellish for his subjects. In Beaumont

---

[34] Maynard Mack, *Everybody's Shakespeare: Reflections Chiefly on the Tragedies*, p. 183.

and Fletcher's *The Maid's Tragedy*, the lecherous king who forces his mistress to marry a naïve courtier is a shadowy figure; the foci of dramatic attention are Evadne, the mistress; her brother, Melantius; her husband, Amintor; and Aspatia, Amintor's rejected fiancée. Likewise, the Duke and his five awful sons, in Middleton's *The Revenger's Tragedy*, are stock villains and the interest of the play lies in the way their neglected vassal, the witty, abused Vindice, comments upon and exploits their vice and stupidity for his own ends. Chapman's *Bussy d'Ambois* is the story of a courageous warrior whose integrity is compromised and who is finally ruined, by the vicious French prince he is compelled to serve.

The fate of the ruler, then, is necessarily tied to the fate of his subjects. As Renel comments in the passage I have already cited from Chapman's *Revenge of Bussy d'Ambois*, when the subordinate is injured by a tyrannical ruler's presumptuous overextension of his 'swinge', he might—cut loose from constraint, just as his king is—try to enlarge his own smaller sphere of power in equally illegitimate ways. In Renel's account the tyrant functions both as an oppressor and as a nefarious model for his subjects to imitate. And the easiest way to imitate the tyrant is often to offer to serve him, for no ruler, good or bad, can carry out his wishes by himself—he requires helpers and agents of enforcement. In *The Duchess of Malfi* Antonio, just returned from foreign travels, describes the policies of the virtuous King of France:

> In seeking to reduce both state and people
> To a fixed order, their judicious king
> Begins at home, quits first his royal palace
> Of flatt'ring sycophants, of dissolute
> And infamous persons.
>
> (1.1.5–9)

The French court, one of those ideal but unavailable alternative worlds so commonly evoked in Jacobean tragedy, aspires to a 'fixed order'. To achieve it, the king flushes out criminals and the 'dissolute'—those who enjoy the pleasures of the court without performing its duties—as well as social climbers who will only tell him what he wants to hear. Instead, the French king relies upon 'a most provident council, who dare freely / Inform him the corruption of the times' (1.1.17–18). In place of servile adulation the French king prefers honest service and fearless advice. That's a pointed contrast to the dystopian Italian here-and-now. Antonio has no sooner finished his account than the opportunist Bosola enters, followed moments later by the corrupt Cardinal who will employ Bosola as a spy and assassin, and by the Cardinal's unhinged brother, who viciously upbraids his entourage for failing to laugh at his (unfunny) jokes. Ben Jonson's *Sejanus* is perhaps the most chilling survey of the relationship between an unchecked autocrat and his savagely ambitious enforcer, charting the career of Sejanus as the henchman, and eventually the victim, of the sinister and secretive Roman emperor Tiberius.

Thus, the counterpart to the bad ruler is the frustrated subject. Thwarted subordinates are so common in Jacobean tragedy that Mark Curtis has argued that they exemplify a common dilemma for many of the spectators, a significant proportion of whom were men with dubious prospects, courtiers dissatisfied with their chances for advancement, or younger brothers shut out of the family patrimony.[35] The frustrated subject may be disgruntled in his prescribed role and ambitious to change it, like Edmund in *King Lear*. Alternatively, like Kent in *Lear*, he may embrace his role as loyal follower but find it difficult to thrive in an unfavourable environment without resorting to subterfuge. Sometimes, as in *Othello*, the ambitious subordinate is a bitterly malicious schemer whose sense of grievance seems all out of proportion to any wrong he has actually suffered. Sometimes, as in Chapman's *Bussy d'Ambois*, the subordinate is admirably independent, but eventually tarnished by the environment in which he is forced to operate, or, as in *The Tragedy of Byron*, he is an impressive but arrogant nobleman aspiring above his station. Sometimes he is criminally dangerous, like De Flores in *The Changeling*. *The Duchess of Malfi* pairs two such aspirants: the virtuous Antonio, conservative in his social instincts but a participant in a marriage that transgresses class boundaries, and the intelligent, murderous Bosola, fully aware of his master's vileness but determined to 'rise' at all costs, who first betrays Antonio and the Duchess and then attempts to save them. *The Revenger's Tragedy* likewise juxtaposes a variety of strategies by which a subject might respond to a corrupt regime. The righteously aggrieved Vindice, bent on avenging the Duke's crimes against his family, insinuates himself into the Duke's good graces by impersonating two different, equally unprincipled social climbers: first an obsequious pimp, and later an impoverished law student easily suborned to homicide.

Closely related to the problem of the subject's prospects in life is the problem of how to give counsel to a flawed superior. Typically, the tyrant

---

[35] Mark Curtis, 'The Alienated Intellectuals of Early Stuart England', *Past and Present* 23 (1962): 25–43. For treatments of the problematic relationships between monarchs and their subject counsellors, see Laurie Shannon, *Sovereign Amity: Figures of Friendship in Shakespearean Contexts* and Curtis Perry, *Literature and Favoritism in Early Modern England*.

prefers flattery, retaliating cruelly against candid truth-tellers. In *King Lear* the king's frankest, most loyal advisors—Cordelia, Kent, and the Fool—are the least prepossessing, and Lear reacts to them—Kent and Cordelia especially—with fury and incomprehension. In *Lear*'s subplot, too, Gloucester is unable to distinguish good counsel from bad, outlawing his loyal son on the advice of the treacherous one. Meanwhile, the bad counsellors—Goneril, Regan, Edmund, Oswald—profit, at least in the short term, from their sycophancy and their unscrupulous pursuit of self-interest. Many Jacobean and Caroline plays obsess over this injustice: a bad ruler promotes and rewards bad followers, while ignoring or persecuting good ones. *Sejanus* contrasts the downtrodden, doomed Germanicans, who attempt to sustain their traditional Roman integrity, with the slavish spies associated with Tiberius and his favourite, Sejanus. *Othello* presents a variation on this pattern: a bold, forthright, but gullible leader fails to discern the perfidy of an apparently dutiful subordinate:

> The Moor is of a free and open nature,
> That thinks men honest that but seem to be so,
> And will as tenderly be led by th' nose
> As asses are.
>
> (1.3.377–380).

Iago is perhaps the period's pre-eminent example of a dangerous counsellor, proffering advice that he knows is false in a plot to ruin his credulous commanding officer.

One of the commonest ways to combine the drama of the inordinate ruler with the drama of the aggrieved subject is the revenge plot.[36] Revenge tragedy in its early modern incarnation generally concerns a subject who has been wronged but who cannot employ institutional means of achieving redress because the ruler who ought to punish the crime is himself a party to it. In order to obtain justice, the revenger must work outside the established justice system, and generally outside the bounds of religion as well, since Christianity strictly prohibits revenge.

There had been a flurry of sensational revenge tragedies in the late 1580s and early 1590s, and then the genre apparently lay fallow for a while (although, since many plays never made it into print, we cannot be entirely sure). About ten years later, a successful revival of Thomas Kyd's *The Spanish Tragedy*, with significant passages added to the part of the revenger,

---

[36] Surveys of revenge tragedy include John Kerrigan, *Revenge Tragedy: Aeschylus to Armageddon*, Stevie Simkin, ed., *Revenge Tragedy*, and Katharine Eisaman Maus, 'Introduction', in *Four Revenge Tragedies of the English Renaissance*.

seems to have stimulated new interest in the genre. Shakespeare's *Hamlet*, probably itself inspired by a lost *Hamlet* by Kyd, and John Marston's *Antonio's Revenge* were both written just at the turn of the seventeenth century. The years following saw Henry Chettle's *Tragedy of Hoffman* (1602), *The Revenger's Tragedy*, probably by Middleton, Beaumont and Fletcher's *The Maid's Tragedy*, Middleton's *Women Beware Women*, and Chapman's *Bussy d'Ambois* and *The Revenge of Bussy d'Ambois*. In addition, many plays that are not normally classified as revenge tragedies, such as *King Lear, The White Devil, The Duchess of Malfi, The Changeling*, and *Tis Pity She's A Whore*, incorporate plenty of tit-for-tat violence into their plots and subplots. Often several individuals are pursuing revenge simultaneously, sometimes collaborating against a common enemy and sometimes pursuing one another. In *The Revenger's Tragedy*, so many people are plotting against the Duke and his horrid sons that they end up unintentionally, and sometimes laughably, obstructing one another's plans. Shirley's *The Cardinal* features no less than five revenge plots, each a response to the one that has gone before. The fascination, in revenge tragedy, with getting one's own back is yet another connection with the ethos of satiric comedy, where retaliation is likewise often a central aim. Yet, while the plots of comedy generally successfully redress injustice and restore equilibrium, in revenge tragedy the only way to get a semblance of justice is to commit more injustice. Although the revenger's moral authority derives from his righteous outrage, he cannot remain uncontaminated by the crime he seeks to avenge, for the law not only mandates the punishment of crimes, but restricts that punishment to what is appropriate and no more. Working outside the law, and therefore without any sense of limit or proportion, the revenger's violence spirals out of control.

Many revengers want not merely to slaughter their enemies but to do by some unique, cleverly appropriate means and, ideally, while forcing the victim to know who is killing him and why:

> I would have our plot be ingenious,
> And have it hereafter recorded for example
> Rather than borrow example.
> 			(*The White Devil*, 5.1.74–77)

The Revenger's Tragedy revels especially luxuriantly in the pleasures of inventive retribution. The hero, Vindice, wants revenge for his fiancée, Gloriana, who was poisoned nine years previously by the lecherous Duke when she rejected his sexual overtures. Pretending to be a pimp, Vindice arranges an assignation between the Duke and a 'lady' who is actually a scarecrow featuring Gloriana's skull anointed with a toxic drug; when the Duke kisses it, he is fatally poisoned in his turn. Vindice declares triumphantly:

> The very ragged bone
> Has been sufficiently revenged. 3.5.153–54

In fact, however, the tit-for-tat poisoning is not entirely 'sufficient', for while the Duke slowly, painfully expires, Vindice forces him to watch his duchess and his bastard son cuckolding him—an adultery which the duchess and the bastard have arranged as their own form of vengeance on a hated husband and father. Later in the play, Vindice kills his other great enemy, the Duke's son and heir Lussurioso, by performing a deadly masque at the banquet that celebrates Lussurioso's installation as the new Duke. (Using a masque as a vehicle to deliver vengeance is, of course, a generic joke, repurposing the dramatic form invented to glorify authority to destroy it; not surprisingly, the 'revenge masque' becomes a commonplace device in Jacobean and Caroline tragedy.) In both cases, the revenger takes pains to let his victim know who has killed him: "twas Vindice murdered thee... Murdered thy father... And I am he' (5.3.94–96.) In the end, Vindice's desire for recognition proves his downfall: after committing these two perfect crimes, he cannot restrain himself from boasting about them, and is forthwith condemned to death.

Another important tragic scenario involves a disastrous connection between a man and a woman. Some of the most memorable Jacobean and Caroline tragedies put sexual catastrophe front and centre: Shakespeare's *Othello*, Beaumont and Fletcher's *A Maid's Tragedy*, Webster's *The Duchess of Malfi* and *The White Devil*, Middleton's *The Changeling* and *Women Beware Women*, Ford's *Tis Pity She's A Whore*. Of course, the two modes— the political and the sexual—often overlap; one of the distinctive features of Jacobean tragedy is its constant linking of dark erotic energy to sinister political power. The tyrant's hunger for unlimited dominion entails his outrageous flouting of rules, especially sexual ones. Jacobean and Caroline tyrants are typically adulterers, rapists, paedophiles, committers of incest, seducers of other men's wives, fathers of bastards. These excesses signify not merely their absence of self-regulation but their cavalier lack of respect for their subjects' rights. In *The Maid's Tragedy*, the King breaks the betrothal of one of his courtiers in order to arrange a marriage between the courtier and the king's mistress; he then prohibits the courtier from sleeping with his new wife. In *The Revenger's Tragedy*, the Duke sexually propositions Vindice's fiancée and poisons her when she does not submit to him; one of his sons rapes the wife of a lord, and another son seeks to prostitute Vindice's sister. In *Women Beware Women*, when the Duke catches sight of a beautiful married woman, he summarily sends for her, rapes her, and makes her his concubine. The Duke in *The White Devil* is similarly unbridled, arranging for the murder of both his own wife and the husband of his inamorata.

The range of female tragic characters somewhat resembles the range of thwarted counsellors and courtiers, and for similar reasons: these are characters who experience their agency as constrained and may frankly mutiny against those constraints or re-interpret them in some creative way. In the case of women, the constraints in question always have to do with their sexuality. To what extent are they obliged, as women, to submit to the orders of their male relatives? To what extent they are bound by a double standard that mandates, for women but not necessarily for men, virginity before marriage and sexual fidelity during it?[37]

When women do rebel, their defiance is sometimes presented as a scandalous, even dangerous flouting of moral standards. In *The Insatiate Countess*, Isabella, the nymphomaniac title character, behaves as rapaciously as any male tyrant, marrying a second husband without observing a period of mourning for the first, then conceiving a passion for one of the wedding guests and fleeing with him, then seducing the guest's friend, then—when her two lovers fall out—entrapping yet another man in order to induce him to murder both the wedding guest and the friend. The Duchess in *The Revenger's Tragedy* is another unprincipled slut, aggressively courting her husband's bastard son in order to cuckold her despised husband. Less marauding in their sexual style, but still deploying their charms in ways calculated to advance their interests, are such characters as Isabella in *The White Devil*, Bianca in *Women Beware Women*, and Evadne in *The Maid's Tragedy*. When propositioned and, in Bianca's case, raped by their rulers, they have little alternative but to accede to the demands of their physically and socially more powerful suitors. Yet the women become complicit, using their status as concubines to advance themselves. Such characters are essentially female versions of the ambitious subordinate, who may well be initially victimized but who is eventually neither innocent nor merely pathetic. And,

---

[37] Important work on women in English Renaissance tragedy includes, in addition to Callaghan, Belsey, and Liebler cited above, Linda Bamber, *Comic Women, Tragic Men: A Study of Gender and Genre*; Lisa Jardine, *Still Harping on Daughters: Women and Drama in the Age of Shakespeare*; Mary Beth Rose, *The Expense of Spirit: Love and Sexuality in English Renaissance Drama*; Karen Newman, *Fashioning Femininity and English Renaissance Drama*.

like such characters, they are conscious of their transgressions and therefore sometimes liable to regret them. In *The Maid's Tragedy*, Evadne, at first mocking Amintor's naiveté in having been induced to marry her, repents of her scorn and helps her husband revenge his wrongs by murdering her lover, the king. *Women Beware Women* includes a remarkable scene between Bianca, who has left her husband to live as the Duke's mistress, and her husband, who has become the gigolo of the Duke's sister. Their edgy confrontation, mingling boasting and resentment, unsuccessfully conceals their mutual yearning for their irretrievably lost romantic innocence.

In other cases, however, female rebellion is coded as virtuous. Desdemona's stolen marriage with Othello is initially presented as disgraceful: she 'hath made a gross revolt, / Tying her duty, beauty, wit, and fortunes / In an extravagant and wheeling stranger' (1.1.130–132). But when she defends her conduct before the Venetian Senate it becomes clear that she is not challenging the principle of patriarchy:

> Brabanzio.   Come hither, gentle mistress.
>   Do you perceive in all this noble company
>   Where most you owe obedience?
> Desdemona.   My noble father,
>   I do perceive here a divided duty.
>   To you I am bound for life and education;
>   My life and education both do learn me
>   How to respect you. You are the lord of duty;
>   I am, hitherto, your daughter. But here's my husband.
>   And so much duty as my mother showed
>   To you, preferring you before her father,
>   So much I challenge that I may profess
>   Due to the Moor my lord.
>   (1.3.177–188)

Marrying idealistically for the love of a man she unreservedly admires, Desdemona assumes that marriage entails accepting her husband's authority over her and welcomes that eventuality. The tragedy of the play is that her purity of motive is insufficiently appreciated, not least by her new spouse. Iago encourages Othello to regard Desdemona's eagerness to wed him as a sign of her faithlessness and lustful nature, in effect reprising the accusation that she seemed to have rebuffed successfully in her speech before the Senate.

The Duchess of Malfi is an even clearer instance of a woman victimized by her own virtues. The Duchess's assertion of her right to marry is consistent with her assertion of her rights as an aristocrat to govern herself and her domain without the interference of her powerful brothers; she is, after all, a widow, not a never-married maiden, and thus legally under her own control rather than subject to a male guardian. Nevertheless, her brothers make unreasonable demands for her celibacy. 'Why might not I marry?' she asks. 'I have not gone about in this to create / Any new world or custom' (3.2.112–114). The Duchess's aims, indeed, are traditionally feminine ones: she wants a loving marriage, a contented husband, thriving children. Facing a violent death, she frets about whether someone will give her child its dose of cough syrup. 'Hers is a heroism not of grandeur but of dailyness', as Linda Woodbridge puts it.[38] Still, given her ferocious brothers, her course of action requires tremendous audacity. She echoes Marlowe's world-conqueror Tamburlaine, who ascends to a throne by literally trampling his vanquished enemies underfoot, when she exclaims:

> If all my royal kindred
> Lay in my way unto this marriage
> I'd make them my low footsteps.
> (1.1.342–344)

Plays like *Othello* and *The Duchess of Malfi* create scenarios in which women are slandered, abused, and eventually killed merely for being sentient beings who legitimately desire their own happiness.

John Ford's women characters, too, find themselves in tragic dilemmas not because they resist the constraints of their culture, but because they embrace them with tremendous enthusiasm. In *The Broken Heart*, Penthea has been forced to break a betrothal to Orgilus and marry the hated Bassanes. Her only hope for happiness, ever, would be if Bassanes died, leaving her free to marry again. But even if that were to transpire, she announces, her erstwhile fiancé deserves better than a recycled bride. She tells Orgilus:

> The virgin dowry, which my birth bestowed,
> Is ravished by another. My true love
> Abhors to think that Orgilus deserved

---

[38] Linda Woodbridge, 'Queen of Apricots: The Duchess of Malfi, Hero of Desire', in *The Female Tragic Hero in English Renaissance Drama*, ed. Naomi Conn Liebler, p. 179.

> No better favors than a second bed ...
> Should I outlive my bondage let me meet
> Another worse than this, and less desired,
> If of all the men alive thou shouldst but touch
> My lip or hand again. (2.3.99–107)

'Widowed by lawless marriage' (4.2,147), her true love permanently beyond reach, she goes mad and starves herself to death.

In *Perkin Warbeck*, Perkin's wife Katherine Gordon, kinswoman to the King of Scotland, continues true to him even after Perkin, who claims to be the rightful king of England, has been convicted of being a baseborn pretender and sentenced to death for treason:

> Oxford. Remember, lady, who you are; come from
>   That impudent imposter.
> Katherine.   You abuse us:
>   For when the holy churchman joined our hands,
>   Our vows were real then; the ceremony
>   Was not in apparition, but in act.
>   (5.3.110–114)

Even Annabella, the 'whore' in *Tis Pity She's A Whore*, is no sexual predator: her sheltered life, which has protected her from contact with men outside the family, leaves her susceptible to her narcissistic and grandiose brother, the only male she has been allowed to know well. The play implies that the ideals of a passionate, companionate love marriage so often celebrated both in early modern comedies and in such tragedies as *The Duchess of Malfi*, might logically be best served by incest.

Not surprisingly, Shakespeare develops some of the most interesting variants. In *Macbeth* and *Coriolanus*, the savagery of Lady Macbeth and Volumnia seems both transgressively 'unfeminine' and strongly inflected as female. Lady Macbeth is, in her way, a faithful helpmeet, cold-bloodedly ambitious on her husband's behalf. Volumnia likewise fashions herself as a model of Roman maternity, channelling an aggressive nature not all that different from her son's into a tigerish parenting style that effectively produces a prodigious military hero. 'Thy valiantness was mine, thou suck'st it from me', she proudly tells her son (3.2.129). Perhaps the most challenging of these portraits is Cleopatra in *Antony and Cleopatra*. Cleopatra incarnates many of the stereotypical traits of the 'whore' and yet seems to transfigure them as a form of greatness. As Enobarbus puts it:

>   vilest things
> Become themselves in her, that the holy priests
> Bless her when she is riggish.
>
> (2.2.250–252)

What ought to be condemnation swerves, in Cleopatra's case, into wonder and applause. This is partly a response to Cleopatra's charisma and performative skill, which differentiate her from 'other women' who 'cloy / The appetites they feed, but she makes hungry / Where most she satisfies' (2.2.248–250) But it also reflects Egypt's alien cultural priorities, its celebration of fecundity and indulgence, coded as 'exotic' to the Romans.

All of these portraits—favourable, unfavourable, or ambivalent—are the productions of male playwrights. *The Tragedy of Mariam*, a unique case of a Jacobean tragedy written by a woman, instantiates some of the familiar topoi with an interesting difference of emphasis. The tyrant Herod—insecure, unstable, and dangerous—and his licentious sister Salome are character types familiar from other Jacobean tragedies. Yet the play focuses primarily upon Mariam, who is both Herod's wife and his oppressed subject. Mariam knows that a wife ought to submit to and honour her husband, but she cannot countenance Herod's crimes, which include the slaughter of her beloved brother, and she is too forthright to conceal her opinions successfully. Although Mariam is repeatedly described as incomparably beautiful, the impossibility of reconciling her duty and her moral convictions is less a sexual than a political problem: her story is paired, in the play, with the dilemma of Constabularus, Herod's subject and brother-in-law, who has saved his friend Babas' two sons from Herod's violence by hiding them for twelve years. When Constabularus' actions are discovered, and Mariam is falsely accused, Herod condemns them all to death—Constabularus and Babas' sons for their supposed treason, Mariam for an adultery she has not committed. On the way to her execution, despite her innocence of the crime for which she is about to be beheaded, Mariam nonetheless chides herself—and is faulted by the Chorus—for her lack of submissiveness. Herod, who immediately repents of having sent Mariam to her death, laments her loss at length but of course cannot bring her back; in this play, the only way power manifests itself is to kill and, in his stupidity and passion, Herod kills the wrong people. Meanwhile, the unscrupulous Salome, who revolts against feminine constraint much more aggressively than Mariam, arrogating to herself such male prerogatives as the right to divorce, survives unscathed and unpunished to the end of the play. Cary depicts a world essentially without recourse, and the Chorus oscillates between pitying the victims of Herod's injustice and blaming them for their doomed attempts at resistance.

Tragicomedy

According to classical literary theory, as first formulated by Aristotle and elaborated by Horace and others, tragedy and comedy are distinct and opposite genres. Tragedy deals with highborn characters, uses elevated diction, and ends badly, while comedy deals with middling to lower-class characters, uses familiar language, and ends joyfully. Even in ancient drama, though, these categories are not entirely exclusive. Euripides' *Ion* seems in most respects a tragedy, but ends happily, while his *Alcestis* ends with the resurrection of the dead heroine. Plautus' *Amphitryon* introduces a god into a comedy while playfully commenting on the indecorum of doing so. Still, the classical definitions of tragedy and comedy were widely circulated and discussed throughout Renaissance Europe, and English writers were cognizant of them: Ben Jonson's description of tragedy, quoted in the preceding section, echoes the Aristotelian definition; and in *The Defense of Poesy* Philip Sidney deplores the practice of 'mingling kings and clowns' onstage (even though his own prose romance, the *Arcadia*, does exactly that in a nondramatic genre). Yet in England a penchant for hybridity had a long native history. *The Second Shepherd's Play*, probably written in the first half of the fifteenth century, begins with a rowdy farce about a stolen sheep hidden in a manger before segueing into a serious retelling of the Visitation of the Shepherds after the birth of Jesus. And, as the commercial theatres get underway in the late sixteenth century, dramatists freely lace their tragedies with comic subplots and with satiric commentary that tempers, contrasts with, or intensifies the loftiness of the tragic action. They adapt many of their plots from Italian, French, Spanish, and English prose romances, works heedless of the generic strictures of classical drama. The anonymous *Clyomon and Clamydes*, probably written around 1570, follows two wandering knights and a much-beset heroine through a fabulous series of adventures, including a combat with a flying serpent and a shipwreck. Robert Greene's *Alphonsus King of Aragon* and *Orlando Furioso*, written in the early 1590s, and the anonymous *Mucedorus*, written between 1588 and 1598, similarly adapt the conventions of chivalric romance to the stage. Further muddying a clear distinction between tragedy and comedy in the 1590s is the popularity of plays based on English history. Shakespeare's *Henry IV* plays, for instance, interlace the elevated plot of rebellion and conquest with comic scenes dominated by Falstaff. *Henry V*, a play about an epic military campaign in France, likewise includes funny episodes and ends like a comedy, with a courtship scene and a promised wedding. In the early seventeenth century, the practice of juxtaposing comic and tragic material continues unabated, and in some ways becomes more deliberately daring and artful. The jarring combination of blood and farce in *The Revenger's Tragedy*,; the punitive end of *Volpone*; the episodes of foolery in *Hamlet*, *Macbeth*, and *King Lear*; the exploration of sexual predation and punishment in *Measure for Measure*; the satiric treatment of romantic love and martial heroism in *Troilus and Cressida*—all combine 'tragic' and 'comic' effects in new and interesting ways.

So, is tragicomedy a new genre, or merely an intensification of what English dramatists were doing all along? In 1608 John Fletcher gives a stab at a definition in his preface to *The Faithful Shepherdess*: 'A tragicomedy is not so called in respect of mirth and killing, but in respect it wants deaths, which is enough to make it no tragedy, yet brings some near it, which is enough to make it no comedy.' Yet this is not very helpful, given that Elizabethan and Jacobean comedies routinely include near-death experiences: *The Merchant of Venice*, *Much Ado About Nothing*, *As You Like It*, *Measure for Measure*, *A Chaste Maid in Cheapside*. Moreover, although by classical precept comic characters were supposed to be drawn from the lower and middling orders, many Elizabethan and Jacobean comedies, like the prose romances from which they derive their plots, feature kings, dukes, princesses, and countesses.

Jacobean and Caroline dramatists tend to combine tragic and comic elements in one of several ways. One kind of hybrid play is 'tragicomic' simply in the sense that it dramatizes wildly varied episodes in the adventurous life of its characters; plays of this kind include William Shakespeare and George Wilkins' 1607–1608 *Pericles* and Thomas Heywood's *Four Prentices of London*, written in the 1590s but not printed until 1615. Another popular kind of hybrid play ends in a 'dual outcome',[39] in which some characters benefit but others suffer. These might represent themselves as either comedies or tragedies but are in fact in-between artefacts. For instance, Cyril Tourneur's *The Atheist's Tragedy*—usually considered, as its title suggests, a tragedy—shares many plot similarities with Massinger's *A New Way to Pay*

---

[39] The phrase is Marvin Herrick's in *Tragicomedy: Its Origin and Development in Italy, France, and England*.

Old Debts (c. 1625), usually classified as a comedy. Both plays centre on a grasping, utterly amoral man who victimizes his nephew financially, violently disrupts traditional protocols of inheritance, and attempts to force the virtuous heroine into an unsuitable marriage. Eventually these nefarious plots come to light, the villain goes mad, his beleaguered nephew is restored to his estate, and the heroine marries the man she loves. Both plays feature rollicking farcical scenes among the subsidiary characters. At the end of Tourneur's 'tragedy', however, the villain accidentally brains himself with an axe, while in Massinger's 'comedy' he is hustled off to the madhouse. Both *The Atheist's Tragedy* and *A New Way to Pay Old Debts* celebrate the triumph of the virtuous and the punishment of the wicked, but a dual outcome does not always reflect a moral judgement: in Shakespeare and Fletcher's *Henry VIII* (1613) and *Two Noble Kinsmen* (1612), the disparate fates of the characters have little to do with their worthiness or lack of it. A third kind of hybrid is a plot that seems headed for catastrophe but ends with a turn for the better, sometimes because of a trick, a revelation, or a change of heart. Marston's *The Malcontent* (1603), Wilkins's *The Miseries of Enforced Marriage* (1607), Shakespeare's *Cymbeline* and *Winter's Tale*, Beaumont and Fletcher's *Philaster* (1608–1610) and *A King and No King* (1611), Fletcher and Massinger's *The Custom of the Country* (c. 1620), and Massinger's *The Renegado* (1625) are examples of this pattern. This last sort of play is the kind most often considered 'tragicomedy' both on seventeenth-century title pages and by modern critics and scholars. It seems paradigmatic because it is not merely an unusually dark comedy, or tragedy with a comic subplot. Instead, it is a new and distinctive kind of drama featuring elite central characters and melodramatic love plots in which, in Eugene Waith's words, 'imitation of the familiar world is counteracted by extreme improbabilities and distortions'.[40] Over the course of the Jacobean and Caroline periods, its conventions stabilize and it becomes extremely popular.

Still, the different flavours of tragicomedy are never very fully demarcated one from another, partly because the plot blueprint does not emerge immediately. The first Jacobean play to call itself a tragicomedy is John Marston's *The Malcontent*, listed as 'tragicomoedia' in the Stationer's Register in 1604 and initially performed by the Children of the Queen's Revels, a private boys' company. *The Malcontent*'s lurid plot, involving tyrannous usurpation, adultery, murderous intrigue, and betrayal in a corrupt Italian court, is typical of revenge tragedy, as is its alienated antihero, the displaced duke

---

[40] Eugene Waith, *The Pattern of Tragicomedy in Beaumont and Fletcher*, p. 42.

Altifronto, disguised as a misanthropic court hanger-on, Malevole. But the play does not end with the usual bloodbath. Instead, the victims of *The Malcontent*'s primary villain all survive his attempts to kill them, and at the end of the play the rightful ruler is restored to his throne, the usurper repents and is reconciled with his straying wife, and the murderous villain is merely humiliated and exiled. If, in tragedy, bad things often happen to good people, in *The Malcontent* good things happen to bad people.

The Malcontent was a durably popular play, eventually entering the repertory of the King's Men in the second decade of the seventeenth century. It was also, apparently, an influential model. *The Revenger's Tragedy*'s insouciantly satiric, shape-shifting Vindice owes much to Marston's Malevole, and Shakespeare may have borrowed the idea of the disguised duke for *Measure for Measure*.[41] Yet the next important self-declared tragicomedy is wholly different in conception from *The Malcontent*: more a comedy bereft of humour than a tragedy deflected. The title of John Fletcher's *The Faithful Shepherdess* recalls the famous Italian tragicomedy, Battista Guarini's *Il pastor fido* [*The Faithful Shepherd*], which had been translated into English in 1602, probably by Tailboys Dymock. Like its prototype, *The Faithful Shepherdess* features an idealized pastoral setting, lengthy declamations, and highly stylized characters and situations. Its central figure is Corin, a virgin with magical healing powers—a figure that Gordon McMullan and Curtis Perry see as a nostalgic revival of the cult of Elizabeth, and perhaps as a veiled critique of the notoriously libidinous Jacobean court.[42] *The Faithful Shepherdess* concerns the fate of several pairs of lovers, with variously deranged desires, whose relationships Corin must adjust by the end of the play: tempering lust in one case, renewing trust in another. Yet the action seems strangely suspended because none of these relationships are, as they would be in a conventional comedy, teleologically oriented towards marriage. At the end of the play Corin remains virginal, perpetually mourning a betrothed lover who has died; the other characters simply resume their amours on a more emotionally sound footing while remaining, apparently, indefinitely celibate. *The Faithful Shepherdess* was a failure in its first performance, a miscarriage Fletcher and his admirers, who included Ben Jonson, Francis Beaumont,

---

[41] Carolyn Asp, *A Study of Thomas Middleton's Tragicomedies*.
[42] Gordon McMullan, *The Politics of Unease in the Plays of Beaumont and Fletcher*; Curtis Perry, *The Making of Jacobean Culture: James I and the Renegotiation of Elizabethan Literary Practice*; Lee Bliss, 'Tragicomic Romance for the King's Men, 1609–1611: Shakespeare, Beaumont, and Fletcher', in *Comedy from Shakespeare to Sheridan*, ed. A. R. Braunmuller and J. C. Bulman, p. 153.

and George Chapman, attributed to the audience's ignorance of its poetic form and aims. The play was successfully revived at court, however, in 1634, by which time Henrietta Maria's introduction of French pastoral comedy to the English court, and the concurrent development of the masque, had presumably made the idiom of *The Faithful Shepherdess* more intelligible. The play's celebration of romantic chastity not as a temporary, premarital phase but as a permanent ideal, jibed well with the Caroline court's neo-Platonic aspirations; its near-allegorical characters, pastoral setting, and poetic style influenced Milton's *Comus*.

Fletcher's next venture into tragicomedy, *Philaster or Love Lies a-Bleeding*, was written around 1609 / 1610 in collaboration with Francis Beaumont, the first fruits of what became a storied collaboration. A highly original play, *Philaster* was much more successful in the theatre than *The Faithful Shepherdess* had been. It established the pattern of many of the plays that Fletcher would thereafter write both by himself and in collaboration with Beaumont and, later, Massinger; after Fletcher's death in 1625, Massinger would continue to write plays along the same general lines. At the beginning of *Philaster* the eponymous hero, the rightful heir to the kingdom of Sicily, has been displaced by a more powerful king, but he remains uneasily at court, too popular with the common people to be eliminated by the current ruler. Yet, like most of the tragicomedies that follow it, *Philaster* is less concerned with the hero's political fortunes than with his love life. Philaster and the usurper's daughter, Arethusa, commit to one another in secret, but their relationship is maliciously disrupted by false accusations of her unchastity. Confronting Arethusa in a forest, Philaster attempts to kill her; although he is captured and condemned to death, Arethusa defies her father and weds him, and is therefore herself subject to the same sentence. But in the end a group of citizens rescues them, Arethusa is cleared of suspicion when it turns out that her supposed paramour is actually a woman in disguise as a man, and Philaster is restored to his throne.

Many 'Fletcherian'[43] tragicomedies work from what initially seems to be a tragic premise: Philaster's situation at the beginning of his play echoes Hamlet's, and his jealousy later in the play recalls Othello's. Sometimes they begin with a ruler pursuing, as the tyrants of tragedy so often do, an outrageously

---

[43] The question of how to attribute authorship in the 'Beaumont and Fletcher' canon is a difficult one, with many scholars attempting to figure out which plays are collaborative and which by Fletcher alone, who his collaborators are, how they distributed the work between them, and the order in which they were written. Since it is not really important for this discussion to settle the question of authorship, but on the other hand it is simply inaccurate to attribute them to Fletcher alone, I will follow the practice of several prior critics and call these plays 'Fletcherian'.

oppressive course of action. In *The Custom of the Country*, the duke is in the habit of deflowering every bride on her wedding night; in *A Wife for a Month* (1624), the king decrees that a loving couple can only be married for a month before the bridegroom's execution—an arrangement they willingly accept—but then adds the proviso that the bridegroom may not consummate the relationship, and may not tell his bride why he is refusing to do so. In other cases, the nature of the dilemma seems less capriciously imposed. In *A King and No King*, Arbaces, the accomplished but braggadocious ruler of Iberia, falls violently in love with his sister, whom he has not seen since childhood. His behaviour to her, to his wise counsellor Mardonius, and to the man whom he had originally intended to be his sister's husband becomes increasingly erratic, as despite his compunctions he behaves in many ways like the deranged autocrats so common on the tragic stage. It looks as if Arbaces may be heading straight for ruin, especially after his modest and chaste sister suddenly declares her reciprocal desire: 'I feel a sin growing upon my blood / Worse than all these, hotter, I fear, than yours' (4.4.157–158). Finally, Arbaces' supposed mother reveals that he was switched in the cradle as an infant, and that the princess is therefore not his sister at all. Arbaces can marry his true love and, because she is also the heiress to the kingdom, he thereby recovers his throne as well.

As even these abbreviated plot summaries might suggest, the problem for the tragicomic dramatist is how to yoke violently heterogenous material into the same play, and, for critics and audiences, how to interpret the inevitable disjunctions. In *Philaster* and the tragicomedies that follow, Fletcher and his collaborators frequently seem more interested in exploiting the immediate emotional effects of particular situations than in integrating them into a psychologically coherent overall scheme. As John Dryden, a great admirer of these plays, remarks in his *Preface to Troilus and Cressida* (1679), the characters 'are either good, bad, or indifferent, as the present scene requires it'. Andrew Gurr describes the same phenomenon rather differently: 'instead of a plot serving as vehicle for the 'personation' of character in splendid verse, the characters are set in patterns to serve the plot ... the individuality of the situation overrides in importance the individuality of the characters in it'.[44] The 'noble' Philaster, for instance, who wrongly suspects his beloved of infidelity, first stabs her nearly fatally in an unreasoning fury, and then creeps into a bush to hide himself—hardly the behaviour of a hero. Yet within a few

---

[44] *The Works of John Dryden* vol. 13, ed, Maximilian Novak and George Robert Guffey, eds. pp. 237-238; Francis Beaumont and John Fletcher, *Philaster, or Love Lies a-Bleeding*, ed. Andrew Gurr, xxix-xxx.

scenes, his atrocious behaviour seems to have been forgotten. In *A King and No King*, Arbaces is even more volatile, rebuked by the wise Mardonius for wildly careening from mood to mood. But the ethical dilemma posed by his incestuous desire turns out to be the result of a misprision, and his other personality flaws seem to vanish without a trace as soon as his true identity is revealed. The end of *The Queen of Corinth* (c. 1617) is similarly amnesiac: with apparent equanimity, the heroine proposes marriage to a man who has brutally raped her twice, content, apparently, in the knowledge that her honour is thereby saved. Unexpected conversions are common, particularly in the denouements. In *Philaster*, the usurper repents of his unkindness to the hero: 'I have heaped a world / Of grief upon his head which yet I hope / To wash away' (5.5.6–7). He blesses the union of Philaster to Arethusa and relinquishes the throne he had unjustly seized. In *The Custom of the Country*, the wicked Duke Clodio, impressed by the spotless virtue of a beautiful woman he wants to rape, abruptly abandons his designs on her, while the lustful Hippolita, rejected by the heroine's husband, aborts her plot to murder the heroine and instead marries a long-time suitor. In Massinger's 1624 play *The Renegado*, the atheist pirate who begins the play as its chief villain undergoes a crisis of conscience, embraces religion, and daringly rescues the virtuous characters from certain death in the exciting finale.

Many tragicomedies were the work of two or more playwrights, and perhaps the tendency to elevate the emotional intensity of single episodes over the whole design is a consequence of collaborative authorship. Early modern playwrights for the commercial theatre generally divided up the work by scenes, and a collaborator might naturally be more attentive to the shape of the segments over which he had immediate control than to an overall design. When Fletcher partnered with Massinger, Cyrus Hoy points out, Massinger tended to write the opening and closing scenes and Fletcher the ones in the middle, suggesting perhaps that Fletcher was more invested in elaborating complex situations than in devising their plot resolutions.[45] Often, too, both plot and characters seem manipulated to permit occasions for extended flights of eloquence: as Eugene Waith remarks, 'the tirades, the laments, the defenses of honour ... contain the very life of Fletcherian tragicomedy'.[46] But the main reason for the primacy of the immediate context

---

[45] Cyrus Hoy, 'Massinger as Collaborator: The Plays with Fletcher and Others', in Douglas Howard, ed., *Philip Massinger: A Critical Reassessment*, pp. 51–82.

[46] Eugene Waith, *The Pattern of Tragicomedy in Beaumont and Fletcher*, p. 170.

over a longer-term objective is that emotional states in Fletcherian tragicomedy are conceived in extreme, all-or-nothing terms. Love, especially, is an overwhelming compulsion, obliterating any considerations of self-preservation or expediency. Heroines unjustly accused of infidelity beg their outraged lovers to kill them rather than defending themselves; heroes cheerfully accept the prospect of imminent capital punishment in order to spend a single night with their brides. The near-suicidal constancy of the heroic lovers is typically set off by contrast with satirically portrayed cowards, fools, drunkards, and sluts. In *Philaster*, Arethusa's comically cloddish suitor complains that 'the constitution of my body will never hold out till the wedding; I must seek elsewhere' (1.2.204–205); he finds relief in the wanton Megra, who then accuses Arethusa of unchastity in order to cover up her own misconduct. In *A King and No King*, Arbaces' passion for his supposed sister is stoutly rebuked by his noble counsellor, Mardonius, but another court hanger-on, the servile Bessus, is eager to facilitate their union: 'Oh, you would have a bout with her ? . . . and when this is dispatched, if you have a mind to your mother, tell me' (3.3.150, 169–170). Arbaces' moral salvageability is signalled by his recoil from Bessus' unscrupulousness, which—he has the self-awareness to recognize—merely reflects and augments his own sinful yearnings: 'If there were no such instruments as thou, / We kings could never act such wicked deeds' (3.3.185–186). He banishes Bessus from his presence and resolves to resist his passion. But, of course, he cannot do so for long.

If the force of strong emotion helps to rationalize the extravagant crosscurrents of the Fletcherian tragicomic plot, however, it is also in some tension with the plays' elevation of constancy in love and friendship as primary virtues. Some tragicomedies deliberately exacerbate this incongruity. In *The Two Noble Kinsmen* (c. 1613), jointly authored by Fletcher and Shakespeare, a couple of imprisoned male friends swear unending loyalty to one another in touching and passionate speeches. But no sooner have they completed their vows then they catch sight, out of the window of their cell, of a women with whom they both fall instantly in love. Within moments they are threatening to kill one another and, indeed, given the way 'love' is imagined in this and other tragicomedies, their rivalry can only be resolved if one of them perishes. The suggestion is not merely that love and friendship may be at odds, but that a profession of allegiance, although entirely heartfelt at the time of utterance, cannot be sustained given the unpredictability of events and the power of passion to cancel memories of the past or concerns about the future.

Fletcher and his collaborators were the most prolific, but not the only writers of tragicomedy in early seventeenth-century England. Although Shakespeare's friends, who assembled the First Folio in 1623, classified his plays into three categories—comedies, tragedies, and histories—those categories fit his oeuvre only inexactly. As Lawrence Danson remarks, 'virtually all Shakespeare's plays are woven with the mingled yarn of romance, or tragicomedy: the mixed mode is the Shakespearean default mode.'[47] In the first years of the seventeenth century he wrote several generically indistinct 'problem plays': *All's Well That Ends Well*, *Troilus and Cressida*, *Timon of Athens*, and *Measure for Measure*. This group of plays infuses the traditional dramatic genres of tragedy and comedy with the ethos of satire, and takes a darker, more cynical view of sexuality than had Shakespeare's earlier work. Then, starting around 1609—in other words, at about the same time that Beaumont and Fletcher were writing *Philaster*—Shakespeare began writing a distinctive series of plays that, since the late nineteenth century, Shakespeare scholars have called 'romances': *Pericles* (1608), a possibly collaborative and unfinished play which did not appear in the First Folio; *Cymbeline*, classed as a tragedy in the First Folio; and *The Winter's Tale* and *The Tempest*, classified as a comedies. In addition, Shakespeare collaborated on two tragicomedies with Fletcher, *The Two Noble Kinsmen* and the lost play *Cardenio* (1613), as well as on a history play, *Henry VIII*, that displays many tragicomic features. Of this group of plays, *The Winter's Tale*, *Cymbeline*, and *The Two Noble Kinsmen* seem particularly closely connected to Fletcher's style of tragicomedy, deliberately mixing elements that would not normally coexist in the same play, revelling in wild improbabilities, and staging remarkable reversals and surprising revelations in the denouement. *The Tempest*, too, with its exotic but indefinite setting and its evocation of revenge tragedy derailed into reconciliation, shares many features with Fletcherian tragicomedy—a resemblance that comes to seem all the stronger retrospectively when, in around 1620, Fletcher draws upon *The Tempest* for his tragicomedy *The Island Princess*.

Even by Shakespeare's experimental and freewheeling standards, the plays now classed as 'romances' seemed, to his contemporaries, a departure from his previous practice. In his induction to *Bartholomew Fair*, Ben Jonson, though he was Shakespeare's friend, ridicules his improbable 'tales, tempests, and suchlike drolleries' that 'make nature afraid'; thirteen years after Shakespeare's death, in an 'Ode to Himself', he is still fuming about the

---

[47] Lawrence Danson, 'The Shakespeare Remix: Romance, Tragicomedy, and Shakespeare's "distinct kind"', *Shakespeare and Genre*, ed. Anthony Guneratne, p. 102.

popularity of *Pericles* onstage. Like the Fletcherian tragicomedies, Shakespeare's romances are intensely self-conscious and metatheatrical, and typically make a point of highlighting the non-mimetic features of which Jonson complains. Both *The Winter's Tale* and *The Tempest* foreground complex ruminations about the relationship between 'art' and 'nature', imposture and authenticity, naiveté and refinement, and the way these apparent opposites turn out to be mutually constitutive. In *The Tempest*, Prospero's sophisticated book-learning cannot save him from disaster in courtly Milan; it only becomes efficacious, apparently, once he is marooned on an island remote from civilization. At the centre of *The Winter's Tale's* pastoral scenes—themselves part of a long literary tradition of appropriating the 'simple' natural world for urbane uses—Perdita and Polixenes debate whether art defaces nature or enhances it. While Perdita rejects all artifice as fraudulent, Polixenes takes a more expansive, dialectical view, arguing that art enriches nature by repurposing natural materials: 'Nature is made better by no mean / But Nature makes that mean', he argues, 'so over that art / Which you say adds to Nature, is an art / That Nature makes' (4.4.89–92). For example, he continues, by grafting delicate cultivated varieties on to rugged native rootstocks, a gardener can derive an improved plant, combining natural elements that would not ordinarily occur together:

> You see, sweet maid, we marry
> A gentler scion to the wildest stock,
> And make conceive a bark of baser kind
> By bud of nobler race. This is an art
> Which does mend Nature—change it rather; but
> The art itself is Nature.
> (4.4.92–97)

It is easy to read this passage as a defence of tragicomedy's hybridity and improbability in anticipation of something like Jonson's objections: the genre's eschewal of ordinary life is not a repudiation of mimesis that 'makes nature afraid', but a deliberate and meaningful transformation. And yet Polixenes' eloquent defence of art, in a typical tragicomic reversal, is almost immediately undercut by events and by human inconsistency. His theoretical approval of the 'grafting' of noble scion to base stock entirely evaporates when he is confronted with his princely son's infatuation with a girl believed to be lowborn. Polixenes' precipitous shift from indulgent, mildly flirtatious interlocutor to vengeful patriarch, like Leontes' sudden lurch into paranoid jealousy earlier in the play, recalls the similarly unexpected conversions of Fletcherian tragicomedy.

The interest of tragicomedies in remarkable transformations, the pointed contrasts they draw between idealism and satire, their emphasis on pattern rather than on character development, and their self-conscious lack of realism means that they find some of the techniques of the masque congenial: a form that, as Suzanne Gossett points out in a book-length study, was developing contemporaneously and, like tragicomedy, drew upon models from the Continent.[48] Moreover, as the theatre audience—particularly, the audience for the King's Men, for whom Shakespeare, Fletcher, and Massinger wrote—gentrified in the second and third decades of the seventeenth century, drama and masque may have been appealing to some of the same spectators. Fletcher did not write masques (though Beaumont did), but many Fletcherian tragicomedies incorporate elements of masque staging: dances, dumb shows, songs, and ritualized spectacle. Shakespeare's romances also include masque-like elements. The descent of Jupiter in *Cymbeline* in a 'god machine' to bless the beleaguered hero, Posthumus, is a bit of stagecraft more typical of the masque than of the less scenically spectacular commercial theatre. The sheepshearing festival in *The Winter's Tale* recalls an elegantly stylized masque pastoral, complete with a high-minded debate about art and nature; the unscrupulous and funny Autolycus would be at home in a Jonsonian antimasque. The finale of *The Winter's Tale*, too, in which a statue seems to come to life, evokes a quasi-magical masque transfiguration. *The Tempest* includes a masque Prospero commands his spirits to perform to mark the betrothal of Ferdinand to Miranda. The play, first performed in 1611, comprised part of the wedding festivities for James's daughter Elizabeth and Frederick in 1613, and some scholars argue that the masque was inserted at that time; if so, the effect of the revision would have been to add another level of self-reflexive, masque-like idealization of the relationship between the world of the play and the world of the audience.

Despite the generic affinities between Fletcherian tragicomedy and the plays of Shakespeare's last years, there are significant differences between them. Fletcher's heroes and heroines are invariably youthful; as Lee Bliss writes, 'Beaumont and Fletcher's subject is idealized adolescence, trembling on the brink of adult commitment and decisive action, and youth's first

---

[48] Suzanne Gossett, *The Influence of the Jacobean Masque on the Plays of Beaumont and Fletcher*.

confrontation with experience and disillusionment.'[49] By contrast, Shakespeare's romances—like many of his earlier plays—are deeply concerned with generational transition, and focus as much (or more) on the parental characters as on the young. In consequence, the action of his romances takes place over, or at least evokes, long spans of time. *Pericles* and *The Winter's Tale* each take place over about sixteen years—long enough for an infant daughter to grow almost to adulthood. The action of *The Tempest*, unusually for Shakespeare, is rigorously abbreviated, but it is intelligible only in terms of events that transpired twelve years earlier.

The end of a Fletcherian tragicomedy rescues the innocent and unites the faithful lovers, yet the relationship between the characters' goodness and their happy outcome is generally obscure because their actions have typically done nothing to bring it about. Indeed, one of the signs of virtue in a Fletcherian tragicomedy is a willingness to suffer undeserved oppression and pain: to be a martyr, not an entrepreneur. In Shakespeare's tragicomedy, too, the course of the plot often highlights the characters' vulnerability to error and accident. In *Cymbeline*, for instance, the fortuitous convergence of three separate plotlines—each of them unlikely in its own right—produces a spectacular irony of misprision in which Imogen mistakes the headless corpse of a loathsome sexual predator for her beloved husband. Sheer contingency seems more important than human effort in *Cymbeline*'s resolution as well. 'Fortune brings in some boats that are not steered', as the astute servant Pisanio observes (4.3.54)—and this is not mere metaphor, given the frequency of storms at sea and shipwreck in Shakespearean romance. On the other hand, although Shakespeare's characters are frequently 'assailed with fortune fierce and keen', as Gower puts it in the epilogue to *Pericles* (4), they retain considerable agency. In *The Tempest*, the turn from tragedy to comedy is partly a matter of a lucky coincidence: the usurpers of Prospero's dukedom happen to sail past his island on a voyage home to Italy from Tunis. But the happy ending is also a consequence of Prospero's wisdom and skill:

> By accident most strange, bountiful Fortune,
> Now, my dear lady, hath mine enemies
> Brought to this shore; and by my prescience
> I find my zenith doth depend upon

---

[49] Lee Bliss, 'Tragicomic Romance for the King's Men, 1609-1611: Shakespeare, Beaumont, and Fletcher', in A.R. Braunmuller and J. C. Bulman, eds., *Comedy from Shakespeare to Sheridan*, p. 153.

> A most auspicious star, whose influence
> If now I court not, but omit, my fortunes
> Will ever after droop.
>
> (1.2.178–184).

Fortune may hand Prospero an opportunity, but it is up to him to recognize and exploit it. And, once he does so, getting his enemies in his power, he could easily exact revenge, but resolves to forgive them instead:

> Though with their high wrongs I am struck to the quick,
> Yet with my nobler reason 'gainst my fury
> Do I take part. The rarer action is
> In virtue than in vengeance.
>
> (5.1.25–28)

The happy ending of *The Tempest* is the consequence of Prospero's skill and restraint.

In *The Winter's Tale*, Shakespeare's most elaborately self-reflexive tragicomedy, the relationship between luck and effort is similarly complex. In this play Leontes is seized with a sudden, uncorroborated conviction that his wife, Hermione, has committed adultery with Polixenes, his best friend. In the grip of this delusion, he devastates his relationships with his counsellors, his friend, his wife, and both his children. At Hermione's trial, immediately after Leontes blasphemously defies the clear testimony of the Delphic oracle to Hermione's fidelity, news comes that his young son and heir Mamillius has died 'with mere conceit and fear / Of the queen's speed' (3.2.141–142). Hermione collapses, and Leontes immediately repents of his error: 'Apollo, pardon / My great profaneness 'gainst thine oracle' (3.2.150–151). He seems to assume that he can simply change course and resume his comfortable life:

> I'll reconcile me to Polixenes,
> New woo my queen, recall the good Camillo,
> Whom I proclaim a man of truth, of mercy ...
>
> (3.2.152–154)

But the easy reversals so common in Fletcherian tragicomedy turn out to be impossible here. Paulina, the queen's lady, enters with the report of Hermione's death, and a different view of Leontes' future:

> Do not repent these things, for they are heavier
> Than all thy woes can stir; therefore betake thee

> To nothing but despair. A thousand knees,
> Ten thousand years together, naked, fasting,
> Upon a barren mountain, and still winter
> In storm perpetual, could not move the gods
> To look that way thou wert.
>
> (3.2. 208–214)

It is possible to see the remainder of *The Winter's Tale* as asking, in effect: how can someone possibly make amends after committing a wicked error with irrevocable consequences? Is there a middle way between simply recognizing and proclaiming one's mistake—which seems inadequate to the immense harm Leontes has unleashed—and endless self-mortification: 'nothing but despair'? *The Winter's Tale* concludes in lucky marvels. Not only is the lost daughter Perdita restored to Leontes, but, while her true identity was unknown, she happens to have gotten betrothed to the son of Leontes' abused best friend Polixenes, and the supposedly dead Hermione turns out to have survived after all. The joyful ending, however, seems to have required not merely the operations of chance but Leontes' arduous and extended penitence, supervised by the formidable Paulina. Apparently, he needed to earn it. And still, restoration is only partial. Mamillius is not resurrected and the 'wrinkled' Hermione is apparently past childbearing, so Leontes is permanently deprived of a male heir, and thus of the dynastic perpetuation so important in many Shakespeare plays. The end of *The Tempest* is similarly bittersweet. Prospero has arranged an advantageous marriage for his beloved daughter and reconciled with his erstwhile enemies, but the focus of the play's last lines is not the union of the young couple but the imminent death of the ageing Prospero—'every third thought shall be my grave' (5.1.312)—and the vanishing of his magical power.

The signature of both Fletcherian tragicomedy and Shakespearean romance is the 'happy ending', which, some critics have argued, presents a narrative of suffering followed by resurrection, salvation, vindication, and triumph, consistent with a Christian world view. Mimi Still Dixon writes: 'Stories of fall and repentance, despair and renewal, struggles between saint and idolator, or tyrant and martyr, are all in various ways averted tragedies, serious conflicts resolved improbably into joyful endings.'[50] Battista Guarini

---

[50] Mimi Still Dixon, 'Tragicomic Recognitions: Medieval Miracles and Shakespearean Romance', in *Renaissance Tragicomedy: Explorations in Genre and Politics*, ed. Nancy Klein Maguire, p. 62. For Arthur Kirsch, the conclusions of Fletcherian tragicomedy suggest a loss of faith in such providential outcomes: 'the play is no longer sustained by metaphysical reverberations, when Providence disappears as a principle of structure as well as belief'; *Jacobean Dramatic Perspectives*, p. 129.

had argued, in fact, in his defence of his tragicomedy *Il pastor fido*, that Christianity made tragedy obsolete: 'what need have we today to purge terror and pity with tragic sights, since we have the precepts of our most holy religion, which teaches us with the word of the gospel?' Yet apparently cutting against this claim to a quasi-religious import of the happy denouement, Fletcherian tragicomedies have frequently been accused of moral shallowness and gaudy sensationalism; in more muted terms, the same complaints have been made against Shakespearean romance as well.

Whence come these objections? While the means by which the happy ending of tragicomedy is achieved are unpredictable, it is at the same time generically expected; part of the pleasure of watching such a play is knowing that the happy ending is assured, but not knowing how the playwright will contrive to bring it about. And here Shakespeare's typical practice differs from Fletcher's. Shakespeare's romances are not only implausible; they interrogate the concept of plausibility and implausibility, suggesting that those categories are contingent upon the previous, inevitably limited experience of a perceiving individual. In *The Tempest*, for instance, Caliban seems a 'monster' to Trinculo and Stefano—something alien and perhaps not fully human—whereas Caliban is actually more at home on the island than any of the other characters. But, conversely, to Caliban, the effects of strong liquor, a European commonplace, are wildly novel, apparently a gift from the gods. Sebastian and Alonso, for their part, struggle to make sense of the banquet Ariel spreads before them, aligning it with tales of unicorns and other mythical beings, but unable to understand its 'true' magical origins. At the end of the play Miranda, after a literally isolated childhood, finds marvellous the humdrum assemblage of Neapolitan and Milanese men that, in fact, constitute her father's auld acquaintance: 'Oh brave new world, / That has such people in't!' (5.1. 183–184). The implication is surely that the world is a larger, more various space than most of us realize, with plenty of room for what seems to be wondrous and strange. Consistent with this capacious view, Shakespearean romance is comfortable drawing upon supernatural, if not explicitly Christian, resources to facilitate its denouements. Near the end of *Cymbeline*, Jupiter 'descends in thunder and lightning, sitting upon an eagle' to bless Posthumus (5.4.91); Hermione's 'resurrection' in *The Winter's Tale* deliberately goes beyond the joyous father–daughter reunion that the audience was probably anticipating for the end of the play, and is staged as a kind of miracle, shadowed forth by the mysterious prediction of the Delphic oracle. The conclusion of *The Tempest*, too, pointedly exceeds the bounds of reason and probability: 'these are not natural events', exclaims Alonso, 'they strengthen / From strange to stranger' (5.1.230–231). Of course, these spectacular endings are intensely theatrical, but in a way that emphasizes the connections between dramatic machination and a logic that exceeds human understanding.

While the endings of Fletcherian tragicomedies are also deliberately improbable, they differ from Shakespeare's in being rigorously rationalized. They typically present an exaggerated tragic dilemma only to make it suddenly vanish, and the instruments of deliverance are not gods or magical spirits but repentant stepmothers, conscious-striken usurpers, and patriotic citizens who rise up to replace a tyrant with a rightful king. Paradoxically, the lack of recourse to supernatural agency makes the fortuitousness of these happy endings seem all the more artificial. If Fletcherian tragicomedy evokes a pattern of fall and redemption, it seems at the same time to disavow those implications, or to hold them at an ironic distance by emphasizing not wondrous transcendence but the contrivance of the *coup de theatre*.

The simultaneous evocation and disavowal of momentousness in these plays perhaps reflects a fraught debate about the status of exceptional and miraculous phenomena in sixteenth- and seventeenth-century Europe, a debate that troubled both the domain of religion and the nascent physical sciences.[51] In his work on scientific method, Francis Bacon took issue with Aristotle's venerable claim that ordinary and predictable causal relationships comprised the proper purview of scientific inquiry. Rather, Bacon suggested, it was often the exceptional or aberrant instance that, carefully attended to, might lead to extraordinary insight. In other words, the anomalous instance, the apparently fortuitous event, might often be more telling than customary or common ones. In a devotional context, improbable, unforeseen, and apparently contingent events had unusual significance as well. Both Protestants and Catholics believed that God continuously intervened directly in the world to punish the sinful and reward the good. Yet how that intervention might occur, whether it had occurred on a particular occasion, and how it might be interpreted were all hotly disputed. Even while Protestants continued to see the hand of Providence determining the fates of individuals and nations, they insisted that the 'age of miracles had ceased' and poured scorn on many of the marvellous powers the Catholics had attributed to holy places and relics, dismissing them as theatrical frauds. We know little for certain about either Shakespeare's or

---

[51] For a discussion of this debate, see Michael Witmore, *Culture of Accidents: Unexpected Knowledge in Early Modern England*.

Fletcher's religious convictions, but Shakespeare may well have grown up in a family that was either Catholic or sympathetic to Catholicism, while Fletcher was the son of one of the most prominent Reformation divines of the age. Perhaps—although this must remain speculative—the difference between Shakespeare's and Fletcher's tragicomedy is rooted in a difference of religious outlook.

If the ethical seriousness of tragicomedy is equivocal, so are the politics of the genre—not surprisingly, perhaps, given that tragicomedy draws both upon masque, which tends to glorify the powers-that-be, and tragedy, which tends to critique them. Shakespeare enthusiastically deploys romance conventions with conservative implications. *Pericles*, *Cymbeline*, and *The Winter's Tale* all feature lost royal children whose 'natural' superiority uncontrollably manifests itself despite their humble surroundings, and his tragicomic plots invariably end with the re-establishment of a hierarchy that had been earlier disrupted. *The Tempest*, though, does not disguise the unpleasant coerciveness of Prospero's dominance over the recalcitrant Caliban, who has a plausible prior claim to the island. It also counterpoints Prospero's imperfect attempts to wield power benevolently with the utopian levelling fantasies of Gonzalo, and with Ariel's yearning for freedom.[52] The politics of Fletcherian tragicomedy have also been a matter of debate. Admirable characters often insist upon the necessity of obeying a ruler despite his moral shortcomings, yet those shortcomings are unsparingly depicted. As we have already seen, a repudiation of tyranny is routine in Jacobean tragic plots, and insofar as the Fletcherian tragicomedy begins with a potentially tragic situation, some critique of illegitimate power is to be expected. Recent critics, such as Philip Finkelpearl and Gordon McMullan, have convincingly linked Fletcher with anti-courtly patrons who were suspicious of James I's strong assertion of monarchical privilege.[53] In *Philaster*, for instance, the citizens who riot to rescue the hero are treated as goodhearted assistants, not as dangerous rebels; in *A Wife for A Month*, an uprising of loyal citizens similarly overthrows a tyrant. But their aims are limited: as soon as they succeed, they show themselves happy to defer to the man they

---

[52] For a fuller account of the way 'the ideal states projected by Prospero and Gonzalo...open up utopian possibilities which question complacent celebrations of natural order', see David Norbrook, '"What Care These Roarers for the Name of King?": Language and Utopia in *The Tempest*', in *The Politics of Tragicomedy: Shakespeare and After*, pp. 21–54.

[53] Philip J. Finkelpearl, *Court and Country Politics in the Plays of Beaumont and Fletcher* and Gordon McMullan, *The Politics of Unease in the Plays of Beaumont and Fletcher*.

consider a worthy ruler. This is a familiar conception in early modern England, as we have seen: a subordinate person or group withstands an injustice not by challenging the concept of hierarchy per se, but by exploiting the gap between a local oppressor and a distant, more powerful superior who can put a stop to that cruelty. In the Fletcherian tragicomedies involving a tyrant and his overthrow, the power of an oppressive ruler is eventually trumped by what seems like a higher authority, whether human or providential. The tragicomic plot seems to endorse an ultimately beneficent hierarchy, rather than sharing tragedy's sceptical, even nihilist misgivings. Its simultaneous willingness to challenge particular abuses of power, but to contain and localize those challenges, may well have proven congenial to the gentrifying audience for tragicomedy when Shakespeare and Fletcher were writing in the 1610s and 1620s. Later in the century these conservative implications may have contributed, as Lois Potter argues, to the strong royalist attachment to the genres of tragicomedy and romance during the war years and the interregnum.[54] The genre permitted anyone to interpret disaster and defeat as a temporary interval of trial, to be superseded in the future by a glorious restoration.

Another way in which some tragicomedies reflected the political concerns of the age involves their settings. As I have already mentioned, the professional English theatre often staged worlds unfamiliar to its audiences. But tragicomedy as a genre is particularly invested in exotic places because, trafficking as it does in marvellous improbabilities, it is almost never imagined as happening at home. Some plays—for example, *The Faithful Shepherdess*—are set in an abstract pastoral landscape frequented by pagan deities; some—like *Philaster, The Custom of the Country, A King and No King*, and *The Winter's Tale*—nominally in various distant parts of southern Europe. In many of these cases geographical realities seem to matter little to the playwrights: as Jonson grumbled to Drummond, *The Winter's Tale* features a memorable scene on the seacoast of the actually landlocked Bohemia. But in other cases, the setting is more carefully specified and more conceptually important. The island in Shakespeare's *The Tempest* seems to be somewhere in the eastern Mediterranean. Prospero and Miranda landed there, we learn, twelve years earlier, after a terrifying ordeal in an open boat from Milan; Ferdinand, his father Alonso, and the other courtiers and hangers-on are apparently passing by on a return trip

---

[54] Lois Potter, *Secret Rites and Secret Writing: Royalist Literature 1641–1660*.

to Naples from Tunis in North Africa, where Ferdinand's sister was married. At the same time, Shakespeare's sources of inspiration derive from the European encounter with the New World: an essay by Montaigne reflecting on an account of Amerindian 'savages'; a letter to the Virginia Company, describing the discovery of the heretofore unknown island of Bermuda, on which a resupply ship to the English settlement in Jamestown spent several months after being blown there in an Atlantic storm. The island native Caliban, despite his mother's supposed origins in Algiers, worships a South American deity, and his name is a variant of 'cariban', an indigenous West Indian word that becomes the origin for both the word 'cannibal' and for the 'Caribbean' Sea.

The play thus engages, as many critics have noted, with England's still-tentative and faltering attempts to understand and exploit the possibilities of exploring and colonizing the Americas. For the courtiers stranded there, the island inspires fantasies of social re-founding outside an established and enforceable legal framework. The goodhearted Gonzalo imagines a peaceful and harmonious community operating without recourse to coercion, whereas Antonio and Sebastian see the apparent suspension of the law as a chance to commit regicide with impunity and seize power for themselves. Prospero, Miranda, and Caliban, the only long-term human inhabitants on the island, have had to work out their relations among themselves. Caliban, we learn, initially welcomed Prospero and Miranda to the island and showed them how to survive there. He was in turn introduced to European language and culture, but he now finds himself enslaved: his experience with Prospero echoes that of the native encounter with the Europeans: often initially cordial, but rapidly deteriorating into hostility and exploitation. So too, in a different key, does his later encounter with Trinculo and Stephano, who get him drunk and fantasize about making a fortune displaying him in England as a freak, or taking him to Naples and offering him as a gift to the king. It was routine for European explorers to kidnap native inhabitants to serve as translators and guides, and, after they had served this purpose, to transport them across the Atlantic as curiosities.

The rupture in Prospero's relationship with Caliban was Caliban's sexual overture to Miranda—advances Prospero describes as a rape attempt, although, as Richard Strier remarks, Prospero has essentially facilitated this situation: 'He "lodged" an adolescent boy in his "cell" with his daughter

[and] was startled, shocked, and horrified when Caliban became sexually interested in Miranda as she reached or approached puberty.'[55] Strier perceptively connects Prospero's rage against Caliban with his fury at his usurping younger brother Antonio, whom Prospero likewise put in a tempting situation, failing to anticipate Antonio's own ambitions. The critical point here, though, is that Prospero and Miranda are castaways, not actually settlers or colonizers; during their sojourn on the island Prospero must protect Miranda's 'honor' at all costs, so that she will eventually be a suitable mate for European royalty. When Prince Ferdinand wades ashore and first encounters her, he immediately inquires 'if you be maid or no', (1.2.511) and makes his conditional infatuation with her entirely clear a few lines later: 'O if a virgin, / And your affection not gone forth, I'll make you / The queen of Naples' (1.2.538–540). The happy ending of *The Tempest*, for Prospero and Miranda, involves not the establishment of a secure colonial regime, but a prospective return to Naples and Milan and the resumption of life as Italian aristocrats.

Two tragicomedies written by Shakespeare's successors as King's Men playwrights—John Fletcher and Philip Massinger—are much more thoroughgoing in their depiction of fully developed alien societies, wherein the opportunities and threats to the European protagonists are quite differently imagined than they are in *The Tempest*. And although both plays strike a modern reader as overwhelmingly xenophobic and culturally insensitive, they are perhaps more nuanced than they first appear. Fletcher's *The Island Princess* (1621) is set in the Moluccas, or Spice Islands, in what is now Indonesia. In the seventeenth century these islands were ruled by minor princes who sometimes allied with Europeans of various nationalities who came there to trade for valuable commodities like cinnamon and cloves. In *The Island Princess*, the king of Ternate has been kidnapped by the governor of another island; his sister, Quisara, who is ruling in his stead, is beset by suitors. Enamoured of the Portuguese captain Ruy Dias, she announces she will marry whoever can free her brother from captivity, fully expecting Dias to win her hand thereby. But Dias dithers, and another European—the valiant newcomer Armusia—swoops in, swiftly rescues the king, and attempts to claim Quisara as his prize. (Ania Loomba reads Armusia as an avatar of the English, who in the second and third decade of the seventeenth

---

[55] Richard Strier, *Shakespearean Issues: Agency, Skepticism, and Other Puzzles*, p. 149.

century were displacing the Portuguese in the Spice Islands trade.)[56] Horrified by the failure of her plan to select the 'right' man, Quisara invents excuses for delay, while Ruy Dias challenges Armusia to a duel. But after Armusia pleads his case in person to Quisara, and defeats Ruy Dias in their duel (honourably sparing his life), Quisara's affections begin to change. She agrees to marry Armusia if he will convert to her religion, apparently a form of paganism. Although the issue of religious difference has not come up earlier, Armusia is outraged by this demand and furiously repudiates his interest in Quisara. His defiance, however, only serves to cement Quisara's love for him, so she embraces Christianity and marries him. 'The power of Christianity and sexual mastery are interchangeable', writes Ania Loomba.[57]

Although many critics have connected *The Island Princess* with Shakespeare's *Tempest*, it seems at least as heavily indebted to *The Merchant of Venice*. Beginning the play as an enterprising character similar to Portia, Quisara ends as Jessica, the Christian convert whose religion hinges on her submission to her husband's authority. Like *The Merchant of Venice*, *The Island Princess* trades in a fantasy in which stubborn cultural, religious, and other differences magically vanish via a process of assimilation. Despite the apparent triumph of the Europeans at the end of the play, however, the play is not merely, or entirely, propaganda. The play's ostensible villain, the Governor, who attempts to turn Quisara and her brother the king against the Europeans, makes cogent anti-colonialist arguments, and Ruy Dias's nephew, Piniero, counterpoints Armusia's romantic chivalry throughout with wryly deflating commentary. The effect is to point up the improbability and wishfulness of the play's conclusion, not to promote it as a real-life solution to the difficulties of interacting with alien peoples in distant parts of the world.

Massinger's *The Renegado* (1624) is another tragicomedy in which intermarriage and religious difference loom large. The play is set in Tunis, an outpost of the vast Ottoman empire that in the seventeenth century stretched from Persia in the east to Vienna in the west, and included much of North Africa as well. Not only had the Muslim Ottomans long been at war with Christians in eastern Europe and the Mediterranean, enslaving Europeans when they were able to capture them, but in the late sixteenth century and early seventeenth century North African pirates regularly raided the

---

[56] Ania Loomba, 'Break her will, and bruise no bone sir': Colonial and Sexual Mastery in Fletcher's *The Island Princess*', *Journal of Early Modern Cultural Studies* 2 (2002), 68–108.
[57] Ibid., p. 84.

southwest coast of England, kidnapping its residents into slavery. Most of those too poor to ransom themselves were forced into hard labour or concubinage. Nonetheless, North Africa was an attractive trading destination for English merchants and sailors, some of whom settled there and converted to Islam, and some of whom became pirates themselves. These converts were called 'renegades' because they had 'reneged' or renounced their religion.[58]

In Massinger's play, a Venetian gentleman, Vitelli, accompanied by his servant and a priest, has come to Tunis in search of his sister, Paulina, who has been kidnapped and sold into slavery by the 'renegade' Grimaldi, an Italian pirate 'gone native' who is more an atheist blasphemer than a Muslim. Paulina has been sold to a Muslim master, Asembeg, who keeps her closely confined but is, however, unable to ravish her virginity because she is protected by a sacred relic. Before he locates Paulina, however, Vitelli is seduced by the beautiful Princess Donusa, niece of the Ottoman sultan. When their affair is discovered both Donusa and Vitelli are sentenced to death, with the proviso that their lives will be spared if Vitelli becomes a Muslim. As in *The Island Princess*, however, the hero stoutly refuses to comply and ends up converting Donusa to Christianity instead. Meanwhile, Grimaldi, with the help of a Jesuit priest, repents of his apostasy, rescues all the protagonists just before their scheduled execution, and sails back with them to Europe in his pirate ship.

Although Massinger's play is rather vague on the precepts of Islam, its version of Christianity is stridently, and rather surprisingly, Roman Catholic. Massinger not only adopts many of the specifically Catholic features of his Spanish source text, but highlights them in the play. Paulina's virginity is protected by a holy relic; Grimaldi's original offence against Christianity was his sacrilegious disruption of Communion at a mass; Donusa is converted via a lay baptism (a Catholic practice); and the happy ending is due to the ministrations of the Jesuit priest, who convinces Vitelli of the wrongness of his affair with Donusa, effects Grimaldi's repentance, and masterminds the Christian characters' final escape. The play seems to make a case for a strategic alliance between Protestants and Catholics against the threat of

---

[58] For a fuller discussion of the way the Muslim world figures in early modern English theatre, see Daniel Vitkus, *Turning Turk: English Theater and the Multicultural Mediterranean, 1570–1630* and Richmond Barbour, *Before Orientalism: London's Theater of the East 1576–1626*.

Islam—a case consistent with James I's desire to mediate between and reconcile the warring forms of Christianity.[59] Indeed, in 1620 James had directed troops to participate in a joint English–Spanish raid on the north African town of Algiers in an attempt to free Christians enslaved there, and in 1624 was actively negotiating for a Catholic bride for his heir apparent.

William D'Avenant's *Siege of Rhodes* (1656) is most often discussed for its theatrical innovations, but its portrayal of a confrontation between Muslim and Christian forces is similarly original. D'Avenant, who was born in 1608 (and apparently claimed to be the illegitimate son of William Shakespeare), had been active as a playwright and masque author in the Caroline era, and after the Restoration he would become a leading impresario in the reopened theatres. In the 1650s, with the theatres closed, he wrote librettos to two 'operas' with recitative music by Henry Lawes and others. In several respects these works draw on D'Avenant's experience with the masque before the onset of civil war. His main composer, Henry Lawes, had written music for many Caroline masques and continued to collaborate with poets into the war and Commonwealth years. Visually, *The Siege of Rhodes* is also masque-like, staged with moveable scenery flats designed by John Webb, a student of Inigo Jones. In addition, like the Jacobean and Caroline masque, *The Siege of Rhodes* employs both male and female actors, featuring Mrs Coleman—the wife of one of the composers—in the role of Turkish princess Roxolanda. The musical form of the production allowed D'Avenant to evade the strict prohibition on public theatre performances during the Commonwealth.

The plot of *The Siege* draws directly on the tradition of tragicomedy as D'Avenant inherited it from Fletcher and Massinger, and more remotely from the romance tradition in general: it features dauntless womanly virtue, violent but unfounded fits of jealousy, dramatic declarations of love, exciting battle scenes, and high-minded debates about male and female honour. What is unexpected is the portrayal of Solyman, the Ottoman sultan, whose behaviour is impeccable throughout. In the play, the heroine Ianthe sails from Sicily to the Christian town of Rhodes, where her husband Alphonso is visiting, when Rhodes is besieged by Turkish forces. Solyman, who has blockaded the Rhodian port, captures Ianthe and falls in love with her. But, impressed with her devotion to her husband, he allows her to land

---

[59] Jane Hwang Degenhardt argues, additionally, that *The Renegado* anticipates some of the changes Charles I and William Laud will make to Church of England theology and ritual in the later 1620s and 1630s: 'Catholics Prophylactics and Islam's Sexual Threat: Preventing and Undoing Sexual Defilement in *The Renegado*', *Journal for Early Modern Cultural Studies* 9 (2009): 62–92.

in Rhodes with the supplies she has brought from Sicily, and offers the couple safe-passage home. However, they feel honour-bound to remain in Rhodes, fighting on behalf of the Christians. Alphonso cannot believe Solyman has simply let Ianthe go unscathed, and is beset by jealousy; Solyman's wife, Roxolanda, senses his attraction to Ianthe and is initially murderously resentful.

The plot emphasizes the indistinguishability of the Muslims and Christians on moral grounds: they are both subject to the same weaknesses and value the same virtues. The Christian Ianthe is as modest as any Muslim woman, refusing to unveil herself in the presence of Solyman; Solyman's delicate esteem for her resembles the chaste neo-Platonic admiration of beauty that Queen Henrietta Maria had promulgated in the masques of the 1630s. Solyman remains scrupulously faithful to Roxolanda despite his attraction to Ianthe, and shows his confidence in her by delivering both Ianthe and Alphonso into her power. Both Solyman and Roxolanda are prompted to revenge but renounce it: Solyman shows compassion to the defeated Rhodians, while Roxolanda befriends her supposed rival, Ianthe, frees Alphonso, and reunites the couple. The villains of the piece, if there are such, are the European powers who neglect to send troops and materiel to Rhodes, leaving it bravely but inadequately defended.

Two years later, in another opera-like work, drawing even more heavily on the staging conventions of the Caroline masque, D'Avenant performs a similar script-flipping. In *The Cruelty of the Spaniards in Peru* (1658), the Peruvians are Golden Age innocents until strife between two royal brothers engenders a civil war, which opens them up to conquest by the tyrannical Spaniards. The invading forces are described from the point of view of the native Americans:

> What dark and distant region
> For war that bearded race
> Whose every uncouth face
> We more than Death's cold visage dread?
>   (Fourth Speech, 1–4)

European disquiet at colonial despoliation was nothing new: D'Avenant gets his material from a translation of Bartolome de las Casas' 1551 Spanish account of the shocking behaviour of his fellow-countrymen in Hispaniola, Cuba, and Mexico. Yet, unlike Fletcher and Massinger, D'Avenant eschews the us–them logic implied by confrontation with a foreign society and an alien religion. Moreover, in these moments of cultural contact he tends to discriminate among different kinds of Europeans rather than letting, say, a Portuguese gentleman stand in for an English one in the action of the play. At the end of *The Cruelty of the Spaniards*, counterfactually, the English come to the rescue of the oppressed Peruvians. As in *The Siege of Rhodes*, the English, when they appear, figure as valiant and honourable, but there is little sense that religion has made them that way, or that Christians as a group are qualitatively better than those of other faiths. D'Avenant's awareness of the actual cultural practices of foreign peoples is no better informed than Fletcher's or Massinger's—he conflates Peru with the West Indies, and makes only passing reference to a few Ottoman customs. But, like many others on the defeated, royalist side in the 1640s and 1650s—Robert Herrick, John Denham, Isaak Walton—he tends to be wary of disputes over religious dogma, and to identify religious zeal with the aggressions of the Puritans in the ascendant.

6
Forms of Devotion

Religious Poetry

The long tradition of religious poetry in English reached its zenith in the early seventeenth century. John Donne, George Herbert, John Milton, Henry Vaughan, and Richard Crashaw all wrote prolifically and inventively in this vein. Robert Herrick is better known today for his secular lyrics, but they were printed bound together with his collection of religious verse, the *Noble Numbers*. Aemelia Lanyer's longest and most ambitious poem, *Salve Deus Rex Judaeorum*, tells the story of Christ's trial and crucifixion from a woman's point of view. There were a host of minor practitioners as well, including Francis Quarles, William Drummond, William Austin, George Wither, Henry King, and Patrick Cary. Other poets occasionally wrote religious poems. Ben Jonson printed 'To Heaven' in *The Forest* (1616), and his later collection, *The Underwood* (1641), opens with three 'Poems of Devotion' on the Trinity, on God the Father, and on the Nativity. He also composed a 'Garland of the Blessed Virgin Mary', presumably during his Catholic period. Even after his re-conversion to the Church of England, he admired the Jesuit priest Richard Southwell's religious lyric 'The Burning Babe' so extravagantly that he told William Drummond that 'so he had written that piece . . . he would have been content to destroy many of his'.[1] Andrew Marvell, although most of his work is not explicitly on religious topics, writes one superb devotional poem, 'The Coronet', while another, 'Bermudas', makes reference to the self-exile of Puritans under the regime of Charles I. And John Milton, whose most ambitious work appeared after the Restoration, published important, highly original religious lyrics in his 1645 *Poems of Mr John Milton*, by which time he was already developing a plan for the epic poem that would eventually become *Paradise Lost*.

---

[1] *Informations to William Drummond of Hawthornden*, l. 136, in David Bevington, Martin Butler, and Ian Donaldson, eds., *The Cambridge Edition of the Works of Ben Jonson*, vol. 5, p. 359.

The religious poetry we still read today was merely the tip of an enormous iceberg of oral and written religious practices that pervaded everyday life in the early seventeenth century. England was, at least nominally, a universally Christian nation, in which the institutions of church and state were profoundly intertwined. An ecclesiastical court system oversaw many aspects of marriage, family life, and sexual conduct. For most of the period, regular church attendance was legally mandated—and those who violated the law were suspected of secretly attending Catholic or separatist Protestant services, not of skipping religious observance entirely. Sermons by popular preachers attracted large crowds, and published sermons and aids to worship were some of the most popular printed material of the age. Not only in church but in public gatherings of all kinds, spoken prayer was ubiquitous, both 'set' and improvised for the occasion. Once or twice daily in many homes, family and servants gathered for devotions led by the head of the household. Religion—etymologically derived from the Latin word *religare*, to bind together—was conceived not merely as attaching the human believer to God, but as joining human believers to one another.

Yet by the early seventeenth century the binding function of religion seemed badly compromised. In the early sixteenth century much of Northern Europe had broken with the Roman Catholic Church, and in subsequent decades the Reformed churches had fractured further. In response to these stressors Roman Catholicism underwent its own retrenchment and resurgence, called the Counter-Reformation. The Reformed churches, emphasizing scripture rather than the authority of the church as the primary warrant for Christian practice, dispensed with dogmas considered insufficiently attested to in the Bible, such as the doctrine of Purgatory, the veneration of the saints, and the requirement of priestly celibacy. Of the seven Catholic sacraments, Protestants accepted only two—baptism and communion—although several others, such as marriage and ordination, remained 'rites of the church'. The sacrament of Communion, which was supposed to forge the participants into a society of loving care—including all Christians across time and space, imagined as members in the Body of Christ—rather ironically became a node of especially intense dispute. Was Christ's body and blood literally present in the consecrated bread and wine, or was that presence merely metaphorical or memorial? Did the ceremony embrace the whole community or only the godly part of it? These challenges to ritual practice went hand in hand with a Reformed theology that stressed the importance of the individual believer's faith in Christ, rather than good works, in effecting salvation.

In England, the sixteenth century had brought whiplash-inducing religious change. Henry VIII, initially an ardent defender of the Pope, broke with Rome in the 1530s and declared himself Supreme Head of the Church of England, but he did not renounce Catholic forms of worship or most of its doctrine. After Henry's death in 1647 the reign of his son Edward VI took the English church in a markedly more Protestant direction, but when Edward died in 1653, his successor, the Catholic Queen Mary, reversed course. Mary's attempts to return England to Roman Catholicism resulted in the burning at the stake of 284 men and women for heresy—a social trauma memorialized in John Foxe's 1563 *Acts and Monuments*, also known as *The Book of Martyrs*. When Elizabeth succeeded Mary in 1558, she returned England to the Protestant fold, but found herself confronted with the challenge of governing a confessionally diverse population. The solution her government devised insisted on uniformity of worship in the interests of preserving the peace, while allowing considerable latitude of conscience on many disputed points of doctrine.

Nowadays, when the idea of a 'catholic' or universal church has long been abandoned, differences in theological opinion generally have denominational consequences, so that a committed Baptist will naturally choose to attend a Baptist church, a Presbyterian a Presbyterian church. By contrast, the Church of England in the early modern period was a deliberately crafted compromise, designed to serve as an acceptable umbrella for people who might harbour quite different private religious convictions, but who were all obligated to attend the same church services. Seen in the context of unrelenting religious wars and bloody persecutions on the Continent, this policy can seem not a homogenizing cop-out but a means for bracketing controversy. There was, many reasoned, a domain of *adiaphora* or 'things indifferent', questions of faith or ceremonial practice that could be settled a variety of ways without affecting salvation. Perhaps, since the mysteries of religion were ultimately beyond human comprehension anyway, it was not worth rending the community of Christendom with every possible quarrel over theological detail.

Yet exactly which matters were or were not 'indifferent' was itself a matter of dispute. The devil, possibly quite literally, seemed to be in the details. Were religious paintings and statues aids to worship or idolatrous distractions? Should Communion be celebrated at an altar or at a communion table, in the middle of the church or at the front, and should participants kneel to receive it? Should the garments of the clergy be ornate or sober? Should religious service centre upon ritual elements, or upon preaching and spontaneous prayer? What sorts of music were appropriate? What ought to be the organizational structure of the institutional church, and what the relationship between ecclesiastical and secular authority? Political developments in the late sixteenth century further endangered a policy of tacit broadmindedness. In 1570, the Pope declared Elizabeth I illegitimate and released Catholics from allegiance to her. Thereafter, tolerance of Catholics began to seem dangerous because Catholicism was arguably a threat to the regime. Over the course of the following three decades, a total of about twenty Jesuit priests were captured and executed for treason, and some Catholic laypeople were imprisoned for aiding and abetting them. Nonconforming Protestants were also subject to increasingly severe measures: in 1591 the eminent Presbyterian Thomas Cartwright was briefly imprisoned, and in 1593, the separatist John Penry was executed for treason after a rough draft of a petition to the Queen was found among his private papers.

When James came to the English throne in 1603, he largely maintained Elizabethan policies. Religious dissenters were still suppressed: Roman Catholics, in particular, continued to be assessed punitive fines. Yet the only Catholics to suffer death for their faith in James's reign were those associated with the Gunpowder Plot. At the other end of the religious spectrum, some radical Protestants renounced the national church, emigrating to Holland and, beginning in 1620, to the New England colonies. Most Puritans, however, remained within the fold of the Church of England, and the disputes within the established Church, though often spirited, did not erupt into violence.

In Scotland, meanwhile, the Reformation had proceeded along lines independent of England's. The nation officially accepted the Reformation only in 1560, in a movement spearheaded by the clergyman John Knox, a Scot who had spent considerable time in exile in the Reformed theocracy of Geneva. Knox promoted a church, or kirk, along Calvinist lines, with authority over many aspects of everyday life. The kirk thus soon seemed to be interfering with matters that the monarch considered his own domain. James, prior to his ascension to the English throne, had attempted to quell the kirk's obstreperousness by gaining the power to appoint bishops, whom he saw as a bulwark of monarchical power. Yet the kirk retained its own liturgy and, below the level of the bishops, it remained largely Presbyterian in structure, governed by the decisions of church councils rather than ruled by state power. Although James initially wished to unite Scotland and England as 'the empire of Britain', and whilst between the years 1603 and 1625 he strengthened the power of the Scottish bishops, he did not attempt to alter the Scottish kirk's distinctive style of worship to conform to English practices.

In the reign of King Charles, however, contentiousness increased sharply. Charles's French Catholic Queen Henrietta Maria and her entourage elicited deep suspicion among Protestants, while his Archbishop of Canterbury, William Laud, introduced greater ceremony to parish worship and embarked upon a programme of church rebuilding and ornamentation. Whereas the Elizabethan and Jacobean church had emphasized the Calvinist doctrine of predestination, Laud promoted an 'Arminian' theology which took a more optimistic view of human agency, claiming that God offered grace to everybody and that individuals could freely accept or reject that gift. In response to these innovations, Puritans became increasingly disaffected and politically mobilized: in the 1630s several Puritans, most notably William Prynne, Henry Burton, and John Bastwick, were stocked and imprisoned for outspoken religious protests that, to the authorities, looked like sedition. As briefly discussed in the Introduction to this volume, religious disagreements eventually sparked the outbreak of civil war, the first phase of which erupted in 1639 after Charles and Laud attempted to impose the Church of England's Book of Common Prayer on a resistant Scotland. In the 1640s, with Parliament in the ascendant, the pendulum swung in the other direction. Laud was executed in 1645, and royalist clergymen, including the poets Robert Herrick, Henry King, and Henry Vaughan's twin brother Thomas, were ejected from their clerical posts. Not surprisingly, the religious poetry produced in the 1630s and 1640s reflects the turmoil of the period, as we will discuss later in the chapter.

The centrality of religion to social and political life throughout the period meant that doctrinal and liturgical differences that, to many in the twenty-first century, seem outlandishly esoteric were of burning importance in early modern England. In fact, it would be an understatement to call them matters of life and death, since resolving them correctly might determine one's damnation or salvation for all eternity. Such disputes must have sharpened a sense of difficult indecision among the population in general, and in particular among the spiritually serious people moved to write religious poetry. The roster of Jacobean and Caroline devotional poets is rich in converts for whom the interpretive dilemmas that proliferate during the Reformation and Counter-Reformation must have, at least at one point in their lives, become deeply personal. John Donne and Patrick Cary were brought up

Roman Catholic but conformed to the Church of England as adults. Ben Jonson converted to Catholicism during a stint in prison, returning to the Church of England more than a decade later. Richard Crashaw, the son of an adamantly Puritan minister, took orders as a priest in the Church of England but affiliated himself with its ceremonial, Laudian wing, and eventually converted to Catholicism, ending his life in Italy as a Catholic priest. Elizabeth Cary openly converted to Catholicism only in 1626, but some critics see signs of spiritual struggle in *The Tragedy of Mariam*, mostly likely written between 1602 and 1604, and published in 1613.[2]

In his early poem *Satire 3*, John Donne writes movingly of what it is like to be faced with several plausible but mutually exclusive religious options. The young Donne is painfully aware that he cannot allow a choice to be made for him by worldly authorities: by King Philip of Spain or Pope Gregory, champions of Roman Catholicism, or by King Henry VIII of England or Martin Luther, who had broken from the Catholic Church.

> Fool and wretch, wilt thou let thy soul be tied
> To man's laws, by which she shall not be tried
> At the Last Day? O, will it then boot thee
> To say a Philip, or a Gregory,
> A Harry, or a Martin taught thee this?
> Is not this excuse for mere contraries
> Equally strong? Cannot both sides say so?
> (93–99)

Donne trembles anxiously at the prospect of being found lacking on 'the Last Day', when souls will be summarily judged. He knows that he needs to obey God's law, not man's. Yet what is that law? 'Both sides' stridently claim to be right, but their arguments cancel one another out. The criteria by which he would prefer one creed over another remain entirely mysterious. To the wavering conscience, the high-stakes existential quandary is an agonizing one, and hard to resolve without some lingering doubt and anxiety.

In religious matters, even more than in the social and political domains treated by masque, tragedy, and tragicomedy, the questions about proper authority that dominated so much of the literature and politics of the early

---

[2] For the evolution of Elizabeth Cary's religious convictions, see Barry Weller and Margaret Ferguson's introduction to *The Tragedy of Mariam*, pp. 3–17.

seventeenth century became especially fraught. God's power was taken to be absolute, but His will was difficult to discern, especially since Scripture testifies to so many instances in which worldly afflictions turn out to be signs of God's special favour. These interpretive conundrums hardly seemed abstract or peripheral during the Civil War and its aftermath, when the attempt to read the will of God in the unfolding of contemporary events intensified and became extraordinarily problematic. After 1649, the royalists represented the executed King Charles as a sainted martyr, while Cromwell's supporters considered their victory as sign of God's approval.

Most seventeenth-century religious poetry falls into one of two broad groups. The most common kind of religious poem is a short devotional lyric modelled upon a prayer or a meditation, of the kind composed by Donne, Jonson, Herbert, Crashaw, Herrick, Vaughan, and Marvell. The second kind of religious poem is a verse narrative based on stories from the Bible: examples include Aemilia Lanyer's *Salve Deus Rex Judaeorum*, Abraham Cowley's unfinished *Davideis*, and John Milton's *Paradise Lost* and *Paradise Regained*. In the Middle Ages, religious drama had flourished, but it withered after the Reformation—in some cases, suppressed out of a fear that performances would exacerbate religious tensions. Drama based on stories from Biblical times did not entirely die out, but it was reframed as closet drama meant for reading and not for performance, and often inspired by classical models rather than as a continuation of the vernacular tradition of the miracle play. Elizabeth Cary's *Tragedy of Mariam* and Milton's *Samson Agonistes* are distinguished examples of this kind of drama. They both draw upon episodes from Jewish history—though Cary's source is not the Bible but Flavius Josephus' *Antiquities of the Jews*, translated into English by Thomas Lodge in 1602. Both closet dramas wed this Jewish material to the conventions of Greek tragedy: unity of time and place, a Chorus, physical conflicts and deaths reported rather than enacted onstage.[3]

Devotional Lyric

Religious lyricists drew, of course, on vernacular poetic traditions but claimed to look to the Bible for their primary inspiration. The Psalms, attributed to King David, provided an especially important prototype for

---

[3] Marta Straznicky, *Privacy, Playreading, and Women's Closet Drama, 1550–1700*.

a devotional lyric that is simultaneously personal and communal. The psalmist speaks as an individual, from his own experience of suffering, need, or gratitude, but also, as King of Israel, on behalf of his whole people. After the Reformation, when congregational singing became a staple of the Protestant worship service, hymns were often musical settings of the Psalms as translated into English by Thomas Sternhold, John Hopkins, or Thomas Norton in the mid sixteenth century, and later, by Philip and Mary Sidney and by George Wither. It was a short step from this kind of translation to using original religious verse as a devotional aid, whether set to music or not.[4] George Herbert, parish priest and fine lutenist and violist, arranged settings for some of his own poems, and Robert Herrick, also a parish priest, apparently taught his verses to his parishioners. In 'The Church Porch', Herbert writes: 'Though private prayer be a brave design / Yet public hath more promises, more love ... Pray with the most, for where most pray, is heaven' (397–402). Not surprisingly, then, some devotional poems, such as Donne's 'A Litany', adapt the formal features of prescribed prayers recited in church services. Whereas Donne's secular love poems experiment with idiosyncratic stanza forms, many of his religious poems, including *La Corona* and the *Holy Sonnets*, conform to established verse patterns. The implication, perhaps, is that the devotional poet does not strive primarily to showcase his own individuality or the distinctiveness of his experience, but rather aims to fit himself into a community of believers with a shared repertory of spiritual procedures.[5] Many devotional poets were clergymen; as I discuss in Chapter 2, they constructed poetic personae consistent with their vocation, imagining the audience of their poetry as a kind of congregation. Their poetic task involved asserting their common humanity with their congregants, even while using that expression of fellow feeling to model appropriate religious behaviour.

Yet the practice of Christianity could not be summed up in its communal manifestations. Pious Christians of all denominational commitments were expected to pray in private, and one's most intense spiritual experiences were assumed to transpire in one-to-one colloquy with God. Jesus had, after all, been explicit about the importance of private prayer:

---

[4] Anthony Low, *The Reinvention of Love: Poetry, Politics, and Culture from Sidney to Milton* and Ramie Targoff, *Common Prayer: The Language of Public Devotion in Early Modern England* discuss the importance of the Psalms as a model for Herbert.

[5] Ramie Targoff, *Common Prayer: The Language of Public Devotion in Early Modern England*.

And when thou prayest, thou shalt not be as the hypocrites are: for they love to pray standing in the synagogues and in the corners of the streets, that they may be seen of men. Verily I say unto you, they have their reward. But thou, when thou prayest, enter into thy closet, and when thou hast shut thy door, pray to thy Father which is in secret, and thy Father which seeth in secret shall reward thee openly.

(Matthew 6:5–6)

For Protestants in particular, as Alec Ryrie claims, 'private prayer was the lifeblood of . . . piety, the central love affair between God and the believer'.[6]

Many seventeenth-century religious lyrics take the form of such solitary prayers, or, as both George Herbert and Henry Vaughan call them, 'private ejaculations'. This privacy has consequences both for the conditions in which devotional lyric was produced and for some of its thematic and formal features. While drama, and the poetry associated with the court or country estate, was inherently social and, as we have seen, often tied to specific locales, devotional poetry could and did flourish anywhere. Nothing prevented a lone practitioner from penning a devotional poem; moreover, the English parish system, which distributed clergymen throughout the realm, had the effect of sequestering many religiously sophisticated, verbally gifted individuals in relatively remote situations. Thus, the centring of literary production on London and its environs, so evident in many other genres, is not a feature of the religious lyric tradition. George Herbert ministers to a tiny parish outside Salisbury, Herrick one in remote Devon. Richard Crashaw, after his conversion to Catholicism, lived on the Continent. Henry Vaughan (who was a doctor, not a clergyman) resided in his native Brecknockshire, Wales.

Compounding this regional isolation was a deliberate attempt to shut out external distractions and social commitments while in prayer. In one of his sermons, John Donne confesses the difficulty of doing so:

> I throw myself down in my chamber, and I call in, and invite God and his angels thither, and when they are there, I neglect God and his angels, for the noise of a fly, for the rattling of a coach, for the whining of a door . . . A memory of yesterday's pleasures, a fear of tomorrow's dangers, a straw

---

[6] Alec Ryrie, *Being Protestant in Reformation Britain*, p. 257. The book has an extensive and helpful section on private prayer, pp. 99–256.

under my knee, a noise in mine ear, a light in mine eye, an anything, a nothing, a fancy, a chimera in my brain troubles me in my prayer.[7]

As this passage indicates, the prayerful individual may seek physical solitude in the retirement of a chamber; the more affluent fitted out 'closets', small rooms designated especially for prayer and furnished with aids to devotion, such as altars, holy books, and religious pictures.[8] In addition, medieval and Renaissance believers, both Catholic and Protestant, had developed mental techniques for cultivating and sustaining devout attention. Several important studies have shown that the procedures of Christian meditation help structure religious lyrics by Donne, Jonson, and Herbert.[9]

Donne's poem 'A Hymn to Christ, at the Author's Last Going into Germany' demonstrates some these techniques in action. Donne wrote this poem in 1619, when he set sail as chaplain to the Earl of Doncaster on a diplomatic mission to Frederick, the Elector Palatine, and his wife Elizabeth, who was daughter of James I. The mission, undertaken just at the beginning of the conflict that would eventually balloon into the Thirty Year's War, aimed to shore up the Protestant cause on the Continent, and Donne's role was politically delicate, as he was expected to preach sermons to adherents of a Reformed church with some significant doctrinal differences from the Church of England.[10] But none of this context makes its way into the poem:

> In what torn ship soever I embark,
> That ship shall be my emblem of thy ark:
> What sea soever swallow me, that flood
> Shall be to me an emblem of thy blood.
> Though thou with clouds of anger do disguise
> Thy face, yet through that mask I know those eyes,
>   Which, though they turn away
>   sometimes, they never will despise.
>
> (1–7)

---

[7] Sermon preached at the funeral of Sir William Cockayne, 12 Dec. 1626, *The Sermons of John Donne*, ed. Evelyn Simpson and George Potter, vol. 7, p. 264.

[8] Richard Rambuss, *Closet Devotions*.

[9] Louis Martz, *The Poetry of Meditation: A Study in English Religious Literature*, revised edition; Barbara Lewalski, *Protestant Poetics and the Seventeenth Century Religious Lyric*. For Jonson's connection to traditions of Christian meditation, see Paul M. Cubeta, 'Ben Jonson's Religious Lyrics', *JEGP* 62 (1) 1963, pp. 96–100.

[10] For Donne's responsibilities as part of this embassy, see Hugh Adlington, 'Donne and Diplomacy', *Renaissance Troplogies: The Cultural Imagination of Early Modern England*, ed. Jeanne Shami, pp. 187–216, esp. 203–214.

The hubbub of dignitaries and the commotion of life aboard a crowded ship is excluded from the poem's view. Of import is not the aim of the mission nor its outcome, matters upon which the poem is silent, but the emblematic meaning of the ship and the sea, which signify God's saving love regardless of whether Donne lives, like Noah, or dies, like Christ. That allegory of salvation constitutes knowledge for Donne, more trustworthy than the shifting shadows of experience and appearance, which, like the clouds in a stormy seascape, only obscure the truth. Behind the 'clouds of anger', the dangers that beset the speaker, there remains, like the sun, the face of an unseen but putatively loving God. The poem continues:

> I sacrifice this island unto thee,
> And all whom I love there, and who loved me,
> When I have put our seas twixt them and me
> Put thou thy seas betwixt my sins and thee.
> As the tree's sap doth seek the root below
> In winter, in my winter now I go
>   Where none but thee, th'eternal
>   root of true love, I may know.
>   (8–14)

By surrendering his attachments to the family and friends left behind in England, Donne further strengthens his single-minded allegiance to God.

> Seal then this bill of my divorce to all
> On whom those fainter beams of love did fall;
> Marry those loves which in youth scattered be
> On fame, wit, hopes (false mistresses) to thee.
> Churches are best for prayer that have least light:
> To see God only, I go out of sight,
>   And to scape stormy days,
>   I choose an everlasting night.
>   (22–28)

For Donne, a dissociation from worldly attachments is a necessary precondition for the 'marriage' of his various loves to the single-minded love of God. In the last line of the poem, one might expect 'everlasting light' to symbolize an access to the divine, But Donne instead seeks a solitary darkness that, for him, is the most authentic way of concentrating his love and attention and experiencing an intimate connection to God.

Not every devotional poet is as worried about his own potential for distraction as Donne often portrays himself as being. Yet even a more sanguine worshipper may feel that dwelling on worldly matters is inappropriate in a devotional poem. Accolades and accomplishments—the 'false mistresses' of 'fame, wit, hopes'—are alien to the decorum of the genre. Occasionally individual poems, like Herbert's 'Affliction I', portray the costs of that renunciation: 'my birth and spirit rather took / The way that takes the town', the poet admits (37–38) but he needs to turn aside from that alluring prospect to realize his vocation as a priest. In 'The Collar', too, Herbert chafes against the restrictions his clerical position places upon him. Yet by the end of both poems the speaker accepts, even celebrates, these constraints. More often, the delimitations of subject matter are simply assumed. Even the consummately plugged-in Ben Jonson does not trumpet his social connections in his devotional poems, instead representing himself alone and trembling before a terrifying judgemental Deity.

The strategic social decontextualization of lyric, and the private uses it serves, can make charting its history complicated. Devotional poets represent themselves as pointedly or deliberately unconnected to the contemporary literary scene and, in particular, to its competitive ethos of self-display—what Henry Vaughan calls, in his preface to *Silex Scintillans*, 'a most vain, insatiable desire to be reputed poets'. Whereas the authors of narrative religious poetry generally had their works printed promptly, with the aim of reaching a large audience, many devotional lyrics, especially early in the period, remained in manuscript. They were circulated not at all or among a small group of intimates, and reached a larger public long after their original composition, or almost accidentally. Stylistic evidence suggests that Donne wrote religious poetry throughout his almost four decades of adult life, but only a few poems can be dated with any certainty. He shared some of his lyrics with friends—the sonnet 'O my black soul', for instance, survives in fifteen manuscript copies. But most of his religious verse did not become widely visible, and available to other poets to imitate, until his collected poetry was published posthumously in 1633; several of the Holy Sonnets were only discovered in a single manuscript in 1892. Herbert's poems were probably written in the early Caroline period, between the death of King James in 1625 and Herbert's own demise in 1633, but it is difficult to date them more precisely. Like Donne's, Herbert's poems were posthumously published. Shortly before his death, according to his biographer Isaak Walton, Herbert entrusted the manuscript of *The Temple* to his friend Nicholas Farrar, the founder of an Anglican religious community at Little Gidding, near Cambridge: 'if he can think it may turn to the advantage of any dejected poor soul, let it be made public; if not, let him burn it'.[11] William Austin's meditations were posthumously published, too, by his widow in 1635 under the title of *Devotionis Augustinianae Flamma*, although he apparently circulated them among his literary friends, because James Howell praised his 'precious pieces' in a 1628 letter and encouraged Austin to have them printed for a wider readership. In fact a devotional poet could think of his work as appropriately published merely by the act of composition itself, since his most significant audience was an omnisicient God who did not require the medium of a printed book.

Though these generic tendencies make the tradition of devotional lyric unfold more slowly and erratically than the domains of 'worldly' literary production, a tradition develops nonetheless. George Herbert knew Donne's poetry because Donne was a friend of his mother, Magdalen Herbert. Ben Jonson, another friend of Donne, also saw a great deal of his poetry in manuscript and doubtless was aware of his religious verse. Still, 1633 was something of an *annus mirabilis* in English devotional poetry: the year in which both Herbert's *The Temple* and Donne's collected poetry were printed for the first time. The profound influence of *The Temple*, in particular, is attested to in both of the most important religious collections of the following decades. Richard Crashaw calls his collection *Steps to the Temple*, and Henry Vaughan, in the preface to his collection *Silex Scintillans*, attributes his spiritual awakening to 'the blessed man, Mr George Herbert, whose holy life and verse gained many pious converts, of whom I am the least'. By the mid-seventeenth century, devotional poets had begun to share with their more worldly brethren an increasing propensity to arrange for their works to appear in print. In, fact the collapse of court patronage networks and the commercial theatre in the early 1640s, which had the effect of channelling other sorts of literary endeavour into print publication, also made devotional poetry available to a much wider public than before. A collection of Milton's poetry appears in 1645, followed by Crashaw's in 1646, Herrick's in 1648, Vaughan's in 1650, and Cowley's in 1656. And, as we shall see, members of the post-1633 generation of devotional poets differ not only in their acceptance of print, but, in some respects, in their conception of their poetic project from their immediate literary forebears.

The characteristic themes and tropes of Jacobean and early Caroline devotional lyric were provided by the impressive, even terrifying system

---

[11] Isaak Walton, *The Life of Mr George Herbert*, p. 109.

that was English Christianity in the early seventeenth century. The universal drama of loss and redemption begins as a story of Adam and Eve's disobedience against God's rightful authority. In consequence Adam and Eve are expelled from the Garden of Eden, they and their heirs are doomed to endure toil, pain, and death. When eventually the human race receives a partial deliverance from its punishment, that deliverance is effected not by human effort but by means of authoritative intervention: God sends down his incarnate Son to suffer in the place of sinful humanity and thus to satisfy His just demand for vengeance. The distinctive emphasis of Reformation theology was to insist upon the primacy of God's agency in this process. Christians are saved not because they live meritorious lives, but because they have faith that Jesus' sacrifice will save them regardless of their sins. In the Calvinist-tinged variety of Christianity that prevailed in the Church of England in the first three decades of the seventeenth century,[12] fallen human beings are taken to be so inherently defective that they are unable to take the least step towards their own spiritual betterment without direct divine intervention: in other words, people cannot even opt to accept the gift of salvation unless God's grace intervenes to give them the power to do so. And, of course, if God in his infinite mercy can choose to extend the gift of grace to anyone, he can also choose to withhold it. The question of who is and who is not 'elect', and how to tell whether one was oneself among the saved or the damned, was a topic of hot discussion and a source of great anxiety among conscientious Protestants throughout the Elizabethan and Jacobean periods. Moreover, even the recipients of God's saving grace are constantly falling back into their natural patterns of thought and behaviour, which are ungrateful, prideful, and selfish. In 'The Labyrinth', Henry King writes:

> Still we repent and sin, sin and repent;
> We thaw and freeze, we harden and relent.
> Those fires which cooled today, the morrow's heat
> Rekindles: thus frail nature does repeat
> What she unlearnt.
>
> (17–21)

---

[12] Discussions of the theology of the Jacobean church include Debora Shuger, *Habits of Thought in the English Renaissance: Religion, Politics, and the Dominant Culture*; Peter White, *Predestination, Policy, and Polemic: Conflict and Consensus in the English Church from the Reformation to the Civil War*; Stuart Prall, *Church and State in Tudor and Stuart England*; Tom Webster, *Godly Clergy in Early Stuart England*; Jean Shami, *John Donne and Conformity in Crisis in the Late Jacobean Pulpit*; Charles W. A. Prior, *Defining the Jacobean Church: The Politics of Religious Controversy 1603–1625*; Jessica Martin and Alec Ryrie, eds., *Private and Domestic Devotion in Early Modern Britain*; Natalie Mears and Alec Ryrie, eds. *Worship and the Parish Church in Early Modern Britain*.

Human depravity seems endemic and inescapable—the 'toils of sin' an almost unbreakable net within which a trapped animal struggles vainly to free itself.

At the same time as sinfulness is baked into human character, profoundly corrupting it, it is also central to the way the universe operates. Originally, God's creation had been entirely good. Death, disease, misfortune, animal predation, weather disasters, the changes of the season: all these are not merely accidental, or the results of natural processes, but instead are the immediate consequences of human depravity. In a curious combination of intense humiliation and extraordinary hubris, human beings are imagined to be dreadfully bad, but *momentously* bad in ways that affect the fundamental structure of the universe. In Milton's *Paradise Lost*, after Adam and Eve eat the fruit of the Tree of Knowledge, the sun, moon, and the constellations change their course to bring malign influences down upon the earth:

> Some say [God] bid his angels turn askance
> The poles of Earth twice ten degrees and more
> From the sun's axle; they with labour pushed
> Oblique the centric globe: some say the sun
> Was bid turn reins from th'equinoctial road
> Like distant breadth to Taurus with the sev'n
> Atlantic Sisters, and the Spartan Twins
> Up to the Tropic Crab; thence down amain
> By Leo and the Virgin and the Scales,
> As deep as Capricorn, to bring in change
> Of seasons to each clime; else had the spring
> Perpetual smiled on earth with vernant flow'rs.
> (X.668–679)

Given the universe-changing consequences of human transgression, no lapse can be too small to ignore. For the devout person, a habit of relentlessly critical self-regard is inextricable from the act of prayer.

The upshot of this self-analysis ought to be a conviction that as a sinner one deserves—even welcomes—punishment. For while God, as John Calvin claims, takes vengeance upon the wicked, he makes the faithful and the elect suffer as a sign of His favour. 'O think me worth thine anger, punish me', pleads Donne in 'Good Friday. 1613. Riding Westward' (39). Seventeenth-century England was a culture in which corporal punishment was a routine educational tool. Children were beaten to make them learn Latin, and adult malefactors thrashed to encourage them to mend their ways. In some communities in early modern England, devoid of maps or documents, the young boys were walked to the village boundaries and soundly whipped; the ritual was meant to impress upon them the location of those boundaries, preserving the memory of them down through the generations.[13] Rigorous chastisement, in other words, awakened one's memory and made one better. 'Th'ingenuous child, corrected, doth not fly / His angry mother's hand, but clings more nigh, / And quenches with his tears her flaming eye', writes Francis Quarles in a poem about the wrath of God ('Oh Whither Shall I Fly?', 31–33). Among devotional poets, Donne is particularly fervent in his devout masochism. In 'Good Friday 1613. Riding Westward' he demands a flogging; in the famous sonnet 'Batter My Heart', he implores God to beat, capture, imprison, and rape him. Herbert, less enthusiastic about pain, nonetheless credits God's chastening hand with making him aware of his own fallibility, vulnerability and transience, and thus his need for God.

For both poets, distressing experiences of fear, shame, and vulnerability propel the believer into a grateful and productive relationship with the divine. For, of course, their aim in these poems is not merely to cultivate self-loathing; penitence serves a purpose. Many of Donne's and Herbert's devotional poems are little narratives in which the speaker begins in a state of acute apprehension or despondency, but eventually breaks through to new insight that provides a relief proportional to the original anxiety. Herbert's 'Love (III)' shows this paradigm in action:

> Love bade me welcome: yet my soul drew back,
>   Guilty of dust and sin.
> But quick-eyed Love, observing me grow slack
>   From my first entrance in,
> Drew nearer to me, sweetly questioning
>   If I lacked anything.
>
> A guest, I answered, worthy to be here:
>   Love said: you shall be he.
> I the unkind, ungrateful? Ah my dear,
>   I cannot look on thee.

---

[13] Adam Fox, *Oral and Literate Culture in England: 1500–1700*, pp. 268–270.

> Love took my hand, and smiling did reply
>   Who made the eyes but I?
>
> Truth Lord, but I have marred them: let my shame
>   Go where it doth deserve.
> And know you not, says Love, who bore the blame?
>   My dear, then I will serve.
> You must sit down, says Love, and taste my meat:
>   So I did sit and eat.

The speaker feels profoundly unworthy of Love's hospitality, so overwhelmed with guilt that he is reluctant to accept the invitation. His bashfulness requires Love to take the initiative, as God always does in Reformed theology: pointing out that He made the speaker's downcast eyes, alleviating the speaker's fears by emphasizing that the penalty for sin has been abrogated by Christ's atonement for the sins of humankind. Love will not even let the speaker serve at table, but only 'sit and eat' (18) as a guest at Communion. Every move in this gentle poem is made by God. The speaker's fitness for the love feast, paradoxically, is his very conviction that he is unfit for it: by acknowledging with abject humility his utter dependence upon God, he finally acquires grace and power. As Gordon Braden puts it, 'Guilt and self-doubt that rationally "ought" to be endless in the infinite regress of the Protestant conscience have a way of suddenly turning over, converting themselves into unaccountable peace and confidence'.[14] Charting, and perhaps eliciting, that sudden turn is one of the typical motives of the devotional lyric.

The radical disparity between God's nature and role and man's nature and role, as these poets imagine it, compels the following question: what does it mean to 'love' a being so drastically different from oneself? Immense differences of scale between the human lover and the divine beloved preoccupy early seventeenth-century poets. In 'The Temper (I)', Herbert writes:

> O rack me not to such a vast extent;
>   Those distances belong to thee:
> The world's too little for thy tent,
>   A grave too big for me.

---

[14] Gordon Braden, 'Unspeakable Love: Petrarch to Herbert', in *Soliciting Interpretation: Literary Theory and Seventeenth-Century Poetry*, ed. Elizabeth Harvey and Katharine Eisaman Maus, p. 267.

> Wilt thou meet arms with man, that thou dost stretch
> A crumb of dust from heav'n to hell?
> Will great God measure with a wretch?
> Shall he thy stature spell?
>
> (9-16)

Ameliorating this disproportion in some respects, but in other ways exacerbating it, is the mystery of the Incarnation: the fact that God is not merely a remote, incomprehensible, unearthly being but has also taken bodily form and lived in the human community as a human being Himself. For while the Incarnation makes God more accessible, it simultaneously creates new puzzles: while God the Son may seem more approachable than God the Father, he is still a figure of extravagant pity and terror. Donne begins Holy Sonnet 11 by imagining himself in Christ's place, tortured and reviled before his execution:[15]

> Spit in my face, you Jews, and pierce my side,
> Buffet, and scoff, scourge, and crucify me.
>
> (1-2)

This torture is appropriate, however, not because the speaker resembles Jesus, but because he differs from him:

> For I have sinned, and sinned, and only He,
> Who could do no iniquity, hath died.
>
> (3-4)

Reflecting on this difference leads to the realization that the speaker has more in common with Christ's persecutors than with Christ Himself:

> But by my death cannot be satisfied
> My sins, which pass the Jews' impiety.
> They killed once an inglorious man, but I
> Crucify him daily, being now glorified.
>
> (5-8)

'O let me then His strange love still admire', Donne exclaims (9). In seventeenth-century English, the word 'admire' means not just 'approve

---

[15] The numbering of the Holy Sonnets varies in the different manuscripts and early editions. Like most modern editors and commentators, I follow the numbering suggested by Herbert Grierson in his 1912 scholarly edition of the poems.

of' but 'marvel at', as at something astonishing and hard to comprehend. God's love, like his Being, is indeed 'strange', exceeding earthly paradigms of affinity and self-interest.

Because God and His ways are so different from what human beings find intuitive, the devotional lyricist must perforce use concepts and language that, insofar as they are developed for limited human purposes, can only imperfectly communicate their subject matter. Much seventeenth-century religious poetry highlights rather than plays down this discrepancy, juxtaposing the bodily and the spiritual, the quotidian and the divine, in deliberately incongruous ways. 'I saw Eternity the other night', writes Henry Vaughan in the opening line of 'The World', paradoxically locating the experience of timelessness in a specific moment. Various writers develop a range of strategies for conveying what they admit cannot be fully conveyed. Donne often invokes an apparently routine image for the relationship between God and humanity, but then pushes it in an outrageous direction. For instance, the Church is conventionally imagined as the Bride of Christ, but in Holy Sonnet 18 Donne imagines the Bride as pimped out by Christ, a knowing cuckold:

> Betray, kind husband, thy spouse to our sights,
> And let mine amorous soul court thy mild dove,
> Who is most true and pleasing to thee then
> When she is embraced and open to most men.
>
> (11–14)

The poem teases the reader, equating or pretending to equate the welcome of the Universal Church with the spreading of the Bride's legs, and then denying that equation, defining her indiscriminate openness to 'most men' as a token of wifely submission and fidelity. Donne's slyly scandalous wit suggests that analogies between divine and earthly doings fail to match up seamlessly. Human beings need the parallel, but also need to understand that the parallel is imperfect.

Richard Crashaw pushes this technique in an even more extreme direction. The title of one poem is drawn from a story in the gospel of Luke in which a woman in a crowd who has assembled around Jesus cries out to him 'Blessed is the womb that bare thee, and the paps which thou hast sucked!' Jesus replies 'Yea rather, blessed be they that hear the word of God, and keep it'. Here is Crashaw's poem in full:

> Luke 11: Blessed Be the Paps Which Thou Hast Sucked
>
> Suppose he had been tabled at thy teats,
> Thy hunger feels not what he eats.
> He'll have his teat ere long (a bloody one)
> The mother then must suck the son.

In a vivid, even grotesque parallel, the poem identifies the wound in the crucified Christ's side with the maternal breast, but in order to assert that His blood, shed for mankind and consumed in the rite of Communion, is more truly lifegiving than the milk that once sustained the infant Jesus. The familiar image of lavishly generous mother and needy baby is thus inverted, and the human mother becomes the nursling of her divine son. The perversity of the image registers both the allure and the shortcomings of the parallel between ordinary human family relationships and the relationship between God and his worshippers.

The struggle to understand and convey a radically different divine reality often draws self-consciously upon the tradition elaborated in the parables of Jesus, which explains the Kingdom of Heaven by means of homely analogies: a master and his servants, a father with two sons, labourers hired to work in a vineyard, a wedding party awaiting the arrival of the bridegroom. Yet even as it deals in the humdrum and the everyday, the parable typically defies the expectations raised by the worldly parallel. In the parable of Dives and the Lazarus, the wretched beggar Lazarus ends up in Abraham's bosom, while the wealthy Dives writhes in the torments of hell. In the parable of the vineyard, the labourers who have been working a single hour receive the same wage as those who have been working all day. In the story of the Prodigal Son, the ruined younger son is joyfully welcomed home while the obedient elder son feels snubbed. Paradox is central to this system, in which the true, holy perspective constantly upends what seems obvious or just from a worldly point of view. Moreover, since the time of the Church Fathers, the parables had been taken to be multiply meaningful, with a variety of possible allegorical significances. For instance, the parable of the Prodigal Son may describe the career of an individual sinner, repudiating his Father but eventually returning broken and penitent to be reconciled with him. Yet the story was also commonly glossed as an allegory about the fate of nations: the elder son who remains with the

Father stands for the Jews, and the younger son who strays, repents, and then returns stands for the Gentiles. The same love of polyvalent meanings pervades the ingrained habit of typological interpretation, or Biblical interpretation by analogy and allegory. Episodes in the Old Testament were said to 'figure forth' the events of the New, so that, for instance, Abraham's sacrifice of Isaac is a figure for God's sacrifice of his Son; Jonah's three days in the whale's belly is a figure for Christ's death and resurrection. In *Devotions Upon Emergent Occasions* Donne exclaims that God is 'a figurative, a metaphorical God':

> Neither art thou thus a figurative, a metaphorical God in thy word only, but in thy works too. The style of thy works, the phrase of thine actions, is metaphorical. The institution of thy whole worship in the old law was a continual allegory; types and figures overspread all, and figures flowed into figures, and poured themselves out into farther figures. . . This hath occasioned thine ancient servants, whose delight it was to write after thy copy, to proceed the same way in their expositions of the Scriptures, and in their composing both of public liturgies and of private prayers to thee, to make their accesses to thee in such a kind of language as thou wast pleased to speak to them, in a figurative, in a metaphorical language.[16]

In other words, the poet's expression of telling resemblances in metaphor is an imitation of God's own methods. Thus, the titles of many of the lyrics in Herbert's *The Temple* are common objects—'The Bunch of Grapes', 'The Pulley', 'The Flower', 'The Collar', and so on—but over the course of several stanzas, the simple reference item develops into an emblem glowing with multivalent spiritual meaning.

In 'Hymn to God My God, in My Sickness', Donne applies this typological overlapping to his own situation:

> We think that Paradise and Calvary,
> Christ's cross, and Adam's tree, stood in one place;
> Look Lord, and find both Adams met in me.
>
> (21–23)

And he similarly deploys it in the sonnet I have already quoted, 'Spit in my face, you Jews', making the entirely traditional point that, by his own neglect

---

[16] John Donne, *Devotions Upon Emergent Occasions*, Expostulation 19, ed. Antony Raspa, p. 100.

and sinfulness, he effectively re-crucifies the Christ who has already suffered for him—committing a sin of ingratitude similar to, but much graver than, that of Jesus's original persecutors. The end of the sonnet employs another typological comparison:

> And Jacob came clothed in vile harsh attire
> But to supplant, and with gainful intent:
> God clothed himself in vile man's flesh, that so
> He might be weak enough to suffer woe.
> (11–14)

In the story in Genesis, the smooth-bodied Jacob clothes himself in goatskins in order to trick his blind father, Isaac, into giving him the blessing intended for his hairy twin brother, Esau. In Donne's poem, the incarnated God 'puts on' human flesh as Jacob puts on the goatskin, and, like Jacob, substitutes himself for another. However, as Donne points out, the resemblance between Jacob and Christ is only partial because whereas Jacob is selfishly wresting a benefit away from his brother, Christ's substitution is purely altruistic, as he sacrifices himself in order to atone for the sins of mankind. At the same time, the story of Jacob calls into question the poet's own strategies. When he imagines himself first as Christ, being spat upon by Jews, and then as Christ's persecutors, what are his motives for 'supplanting' the figures in the gospel story? Is he trying to steal something good for himself, like Jacob—the benefit of God's grace—or is he recognizing his dependence on Christ through the very failure of his *imitatio Christi*?

A complex awareness of the way similes and analogies do and do not match up demands intellectual effort from the reader. In many cases devotional poets deliberately decline to spell out the ways in which a particular quotidian paradigm fails entirely to convey its holy 'translation', instead leaving the relationship for the reader to discover and ponder upon. George Herbert is a master of this form of strategic withholding. In his sonnet 'Redemption', essentially a parable, the speaker describes himself as a tenant 'not thriving'(2) under the provisions of a lease. He resolves to ask his wealthy landlord to arrange easier terms, and tries to find him in aristocratic locales:

> I ... knowing his great birth,
> Sought him accordingly in great resorts,

> In cities, theatres, gardens, parks, and courts.
> (9–11)

But 'at length' he locates the lord, surprisingly, in a 'ragged noise and mirth / Of thieves and murderers':

> There I him espied,
> Who straight, *Your suit is granted*, said, and died.
> (12–14)

Left unspoken in this closing couplet is that the death of this unusual landlord does not merely happen to coincide with the speaker's presentation of his difficulty, but constitutes the solution to the speaker's problem, the release of the speaker from the punitive terms of the original contract. For, by his death, Jesus redeems the believer-tenant from the 'Old Law', the too-strict covenant under which he had failed to prosper, and offers him 'New Law', the grace of salvation by faith.

The representational complexities of religious lyric testify to the apparently unbridgeable disproportion between the poem's speaker and its infinite, omniscient, omnipotent addressee. Yet the mysterious otherness of God is not necessarily a literary disadvantage. Love poetry, whether sacred or profane, thrives on distance and the inaccessibility of the love object. The medieval troubadours' poems, and Dante's *Vita Nuova* and Petrarch's influential *Rime* after them, adore a beautiful but distant mistress—even, in both Dante and Petrarch's case, a mistress who has already died. In this tradition the connection between unconsummated erotic fixation and religious devotion is often entirely explicit: Dante's Beatrice is his guide to heaven in the *Divine Comedy*, and Petrarch's love for Laura spurs him to contemplate the truths of Christianity. Donne and Herbert both capitalize on the proximity of erotic and divine yearning: Donne's religious poetry, in fact, makes fuller use of Petrarchan conventions than do his love poems, in which the beloved is typically anything but distant and physically unachievable. As we have already seen, Donne freely uses sexual metaphors in devotional contexts, frequently tweaking them to make the shock of the connections more apparent. In 'The Forerunners', Herbert describes his authorial strategy as analogous to rescuing fallen women from the sex trade; he takes the 'lovely metaphors' of erotic poetry out of the 'stews' or whorehouses, and brings them 'to church well dressed and clad' (13–17). Similarly, in 'The

Coronet', Marvell attempts to fashion a poetic flower-crown for Christ by 'Dismantling all the fragrant towers / That once adorned my shepherdess's head' (7-8). The 'translation'—literally, *trans latio*, the moving from one place to another—of sexual to religious, profane to holy, contexts preoccupies all three poets. Can religious love be imagined in erotic terms? Can it be imagined otherwise? Is religious love a form of sublimated sexuality, or is religious love primary and sexual love merely its earthly and partial manifestation?[17] Either way, the relationship between poet and God may be said to offer a limit case of the form of distant adoration, to which the frankly sexual poem of longing can only aspire.

The theology that prevailed in Jacobean Protestantism, as we have seen, emphasized that human beings were saved not by their own efforts but by God's free gift of salvation. In other words, God controls everything, even whether a human being can love Him in the first place: as Donne puts it in Holy Sonnet 4, 'grace, if thou repent, thou canst not lack; / But who shall give thee that grace to begin?' (9-10). All legitimate initiative in this system is on the part of the mysterious and inscrutable authority. Human freedom is not the liberty to strive or to innovate, but to accept one's subordinate place in the scheme, remaining aware of one's unworthiness and grateful for God's love. The ardent believer does not even get credit for his own ardency. In the opening stanza of 'The Holdfast', Herbert writes:

> I threatened to observe the strict decree
> Of my dear God with all my power and might.
> But I was told by one, it could not be,
> Yet I might trust in God to be my light.
>
> (1-4)

The poem begins with a familiar Pauline distinction between the Old Law, which specifies right behaviour, and the New Law, instituted by Christ, which is based on faith not works. While the speaker's motives might be good—he is trying to serve and praise God as best he can—the unexpected word 'threatened' is a clue to the inordinacy of the speaker's ambition: he cannot observe God's law because he has, in fact, no 'power and might' of his own. So he must try another strategy:

> Then will I trust, said I, in him alone.
>
> (5)

---

[17] Michael Schoenfeldt, 'That Ancient Heat: Sexuality and Spirituality in *The Temple*', in *Soliciting Interpretation: Literary Theory and Seventeenth-Century Poetry*, ed. Elizabeth Harvey and Katharine Eisaman Maus, pp. 273-306.

But once again he is rebuked:

> Nay, ev'n to trust in him, was also his;
> We must confess, that nothing is our own.
> (6–7)

Stymied again, the speaker again endeavours to comply:

> Then I confess that he my succour is.
> (8)

Even this attempt at cooperation, however, turns out to be erroneously formulated, as the interlocutor points out:

> But to have nought is ours, not to confess
> That we have nought.
> (9–10)

By this time, the speaker is baffled: 'I stood amazed at this'. What is a worshipper to do, if even confessing one's nothingness seems presumptuous?

Of course, there is a way out of this dilemma, which the end of the poem provides:

> I stood amazed at this,
> Much troubled, till I heard a friend express,
> That all things were more ours by being His.
> What Adam had, and forfeited for all,
> Christ keepeth now, who cannot fail or fall.
> (10–14)

In other words, the speaker's original conception that right worship involves *doing* something is incorrect not merely because salvation is based on faith, not works, but because thinking that one is supposed to do anything, even something so slight and apparently innocent as to confess one's powerlessness and utter dependency, involves an invidious and false distinction between man and God, 'ours' and 'his', human and divine agency.

The pervasive suspicion of human initiative extends to poetic creativity as well. Herbert's famous poems shaped like altars or wings patently foreground their ingenuity and technical skill. Yet the substance of these poems undermines their formal premises, making them, in Stanley Fish's phrase, 'self-consuming artifacts'.[18] 'The Altar' begins with the speaker attempting to rear an altar to God, but soon it becomes clear that that the altar of the heart, the true altar, is not the work of the poet but of God:

> A HEART alone
> Is such a stone
> As nothing but
> Thy pow'r doth cut.
> (5–8)

Similarly, in 'Easter Wings' the agency of the speaker dwindles and becomes, like the poem's lines, 'Most thin', until he 'imps' or supplements his wing with Christ's, at which point his fortunes reverse, the lines expand, and the speaker soars with his resurrected saviour. The difference between the religious and the secular viewpoint becomes clear in George Herbert's recasting of Philip Sidney's famous opening poem to his sequence of love sonnets, *Astrophil and Stella*. Sidney describes himself attempting to get inspiration for his own poems by consulting prior love poems: 'Oft turning other's leaves, to see if thence would flow / Some fresh and fruitful showers upon my sunburned brain' (7–8). But this only aggravates his frustration. Sidney must stop trying to derive inspiration outside himself, and write about his own experience:

> 'Fool', said my Muse to me, 'Look in thy heart and write'.
> (14)

For the love poet, in other words, the desiring human heart is a site of authenticity. But for the religious poet, the heart is sinful and unreliable. In Herbert's 'Jordan II', the poet begins full of ideas:

> When first my lines of heavenly joys made mention,
> Such was their lustre, they did so excel,
> That I sought out quaint words and trim invention;
> My thoughts began to burnish, sprout, and swell,
> Curling with metaphors a plain intention,
> Decking the sense, as if it were to sell.

---

[18] Stanley Fish, *Self-Consuming Artifacts: The Experience of Seventeenth Century Literature*, pp. 156–223.

> Thousands of notions in my brain did run,
> Offering their service, if I were not sped ...
> (1–8)

Herbert's problem, unlike Sidney's, is not writer's block, but hyperactive creativity: unfortunately, none of his copious production is any good. And that is because the poet is injecting too much of himself into the poem:

> As flames do work and wind when they ascend,
> So did I weave myself into the sense.
> (13–14)

In order to produce good poetry, he must change tactics. Just as Sidney's Muse interrupts to give Sidney good advice, here too a 'friend' whispers in Herbert's ear:

> There is in love a sweetness ready penned:
> Copy out only that, and save expense.
> (17–18)

According to Herbert, the religious poet, in other words, needs to learn not to cultivate originality but to efface himself, to 'copy' what is already plainly there. Elsewhere in *The Temple* Herbert imagines God guiding his hand as an adult holds the hand of a child who is just learning to form letters. Yet the difficulty of knowing the difference between adoration and self-promotion remains. In 'The Coronet', Andrew Marvell attempts to replace Christ's crown of thorns with a beautiful crown of flowers:

> And now when I have summed up all my store,
>   Thinking (so I myself deceive)
>   So rich a chaplet thence to weave
> As never yet the King of Glory wore:
>   Alas, I find the serpent old
>   That, twining in his speckled breast,
>   About the flowers disguised does fold
> With wreaths of fame and interest.
> (9–16)

Like Herbert's image of the working, winding flames, Marvell's image of the serpent camouflaged within the flowers suggests the difficulty of disentangling the motives of worship and ambition. For the more extravagant the poet's profession of weakness, sin, or humility, the more it looks like passive-aggressive self-glorification and attention-seeking.

Although devotional lyric tends to represent itself as repudiating purely temporal concerns, it of course reflects the controversies in the church of the early seventeenth century. Yet the precise doctrinal commitments of the earlier poets, such as Herbert and Donne, remain topics of critical dispute.[19] Poetry permits a variety of interpretations, and particularly permits hedging about the nature of religious symbols, which is one of primary points of contention among the factions of the English church. For instance, as we have seen, Herbert begins the main section of *The Temple* with 'The Altar'. This choice might seem to align him with the ceremonialist Laudians who, beginning in the 1620s, emphasized the importance of the altar, the site of ritual, over the pulpit, the site of preaching, as the Puritan wing of the church would prefer. And yet, as Stanley Fish points out, over the course of the poem the altar is de-literalized: Herbert's is not a manmade architectural structure but an internal feature built and consecrated only by God. So, while a literal altar has ceremonial and ritual associations, the altar in Herbert's poem correlates with an invisible, interior spiritual disposition, and with a Puritan emphasis on the exclusive power of God. There is a similar strategic dematerialization in the other poems in *The Temple* that reference church architecture: floor, monuments, stained-glass windows. According to Fish, as I have already mentioned, Herbert's poems are 'self-consuming' in that they deliberately undercut what seem to be their initial premises.[20] Yet Herbert may not be taking sides in this controversy, but rather implying that there are no sides. An altar may function simultaneously as an external prompt to prayerful reflection *and* as a shrine in the hearts and minds of believers. In other words, the slipperiness of Herbert's metaphors may represent a deliberate equivocation, akin to that of the Book of Common Prayer, which tailored its language to accommodate as many worshippers as possible despite their

---

[19] Contributors to the ongoing discussion include Joseph Summers, *George Herbert: His Religion and Art*; Louis Martz, *The Poetry of Meditation: A Study in English Religious Literature*, revised edition; Barbara Lewalski, *Protestant Poetics and the Seventeenth Century Religious Lyric*; John Carey, *John Donne: Life Mind, and Art*; Richard Strier, *Love Known: Theology and Experience in George Herbert's Poetry*; Christopher Hodgkins, *Authority, Church, and Society in George Herbert: Return to the Middle Way*; Daniel Doerksen, *Conforming to the Word: Herbert, Donne, and the English Church Before Laud*; Elizabeth Clarke, *Theory and Theology in George Herbert's Poetry: 'Divinitie and Poesie Met'*; Ramie Targoff, *Common Prayer: The Language of Public Devotion in Early Modern England*.

[20] Stanley Fish, *Self-Consuming Artifacts: The Experience of Seventeenth-Century Literature*.

doctrinal disagreements. In that case, Herbert is emphasizing, insofar as it is possible to do so, what C. S. Lewis calls 'mere Christianity' over sectarian differences.[21] And in that case too, religious lyric does not merely reflect the controversies of the day, but may offer, via polysignificant metaphors and analogies, a potential solution: a way to solder competing factions back into the Universal Church.

Herbert takes a similarly balanced position on what, for many in the period, was a fraught relationship between individual and communal religious commitment. Although the poems of individual devotion that make up the central section of *The Temple* are Herbert's best-known and most celebrated, they are bookended by the long poems 'The Church Porch' and 'The Church Militant', which are less concerned with private religious experience than with the church as a social institution. The structure of the volume implies that devout individuals require the institutional church to contain and enable their piety. Donne is more inclined to segregate his private devotional life, as expressed in his poems, from his public institutional role, as elaborated in his sermons, but again and again he insists upon their mutual interdependence and on the importance of religious community. For Donne, as for Herbert, religious life demands both individual and group practice.

In the increasingly contentious, and eventually war-torn, late 1630s and 1640s, and during the Commonwealth period, the episcopal structure of the Church of England is temporarily abolished, the Book of Common Prayer is suppressed, and sectarianism flourishes. Eventually, the Elizabethan–Jacobean balancing act becomes virtually impossible, and devotional poets take more obviously polemical positions. But their strategies of accommodation to the new circumstances differ according to their politics and temperament. In 1648 Robert Herrick publishes his religious verse, *Noble Numbers*, in the same volume as his secular poetry, *Hesperides*. But many critics find these poems profoundly disappointing. John Creaser is representative:

> the depths of Herrick's imagination are rarely stirred by his simple Christian faith. Even in *Noble Numbers* that faith often seems too easily won. The

---

[21] C. S. Lewis, *Mere Christianity*. Daniel Gibbons, *Conflicts of Devotion: Liturgical Poetics in Sixteenth- and Seventeenth-Century England*, argues that not only Donne and Herbert but also Crashaw in the next generation systematically strive to make their poems readable in a variety of ways, because their multi-significance makes them minimally alienating to people with quite different religious convictions. Also see Elena Levy-Navarro, 'Breaking Down the Walls That Divide: Anti-Polemicism in the *Devotions Upon Emergent Occasions*', in *John Donne and the Protestant Reformation*, ed. Mary Arshagouni Papazian, pp. 273–292.

poems on 'affliction' early in the sequence are comfortable and effortless, especially in comparison to George Herbert. The 'loathsome sores' of his humanity are a mere gesture.[22]

A royalist and a Laudian, Herrick responds to the tumult in the church by seeming to retreat from difficult topics—but arguably this pointed deflection is in itself a way of engaging the controversies. Many of the poems in *Noble Numbers* are merely two lines long, stating accepted points of Christian doctrine without elaboration. For instance:

> That there's a God, we all do know,
> But what God is we cannot show.

End of poem. Here is another:

> God doth embrace the good with love, and gains
> The good by mercy, as the bad by pains.

The curt, axiomatic, stand-alone form of such assertions imply that what was once true is always true, and that what is true for one person is true for all. These poems seem akin to the commonsense wisdom that George Herbert offers up in 'The Church-Porch', recommending a temperate life and honest dealing. But what for Herbert is only prolegomenon seems for Herrick to constitute the core of religious life. While Donne and Herbert use the lyric to dramatize subjective struggle and the mindboggling paradoxes of human interaction with the divine, Herrick eschews idiosyncrasy and, with it, much of the high anxiety that had propelled the lyrics of the earlier poets. He drastically simplifies both his language and his religious claims. In 'His Creed' he writes:

> I do believe that die I must
> And be returned from out my dust.
> I do believe that when I rise
> Christ I shall see, with these same eyes.
> I do believe that I must come,
> With others, to the dreadful doom:
> I do believe the bad must go

---

[22] John Creasar, '"Jocund his Muse Was": Celebration and Virtuosity in Herrick', in *Lords of Wine and Oil: Community and Conviviality in the Poetry of Robert Herrick*, ed. Ruth Connolly and Tom Cain, p. 53.

> From thence, to everlasting woe.
> I do believe the good, and I
> Shall live with him eternally.
>
> (1–10)

This declaration of faith, with its repetitive structure and easy-to-remember tetrameter couplets, recalls the catechism that every early modern English child was required to memorize and recite. Yet although the poem might seem glibly orthodox, in fact Herrick's confidence in God's favour represents a marked departure from the intuitions of his predecessors: 'The good, and I / Shall live with him eternally'. Herrick equivocates about whether he classifies himself with 'the good' or rather whether he hopes he will, despite his flaws, merely end up lumped among them. But in any case he is remarkably less fearful of God's judgement—'the dreadful doom'—than Donne and Herbert had been. This difference is partly due to his Arminian convictions. In the second of two poems on predestination, Herrick argues that even if you are not among the predestined elect, you have within yourself the ability to live a good and pious life. And if you do so, God will lovingly respond to your earnest efforts at improvement:

> Art thou not destined? Then, with haste go on
> To make thy fair predestination:
> If thou canst change thy life, God then will please
> To change, or call back, his past sentences.
>
> ('Another', lines 1–4)

In other words, while the Calvinist imagined the gift of salvation as entirely God's to bestow or withhold—and some Calvinists believed that He decided the fate of each individual soul even before the human race was originally created—Arminian Herrick believes that human beings are able to 'make' their predestination and, by changing their life, persuade God to change His mind.

Not only human nature but also divine nature looks different from this point of view. Where Donne emphasized terror and Herbert distance, Herrick's God is a more reassuring figure, often imagined as the infant Jesus. In 'To His Savior, a Child; A Present, by a Child', Herrick writes:

> Go pretty child, and bear this flower
> Unto thy little saviour;
> And tell him, by that bud now blown,

> He is the rose of Sharon known:
> When thou hast said so, stick it there
> Upon his bib or stomacher,
> And tell him (for good handsel too)
> That thou hast brought a whistle new,
> Made of a clean straight oaken reed,
> To charm his cries at time of need.
>
> (1–10)

The sentimentality of the image, with its 'pretty' toddler offering a flower and a wooden whistle to an even younger, more helpless incarnate godhead, emphasizes God's familiarity and closeness to the human world. For Herrick, Christianity should be comforting and universally accessible—at least as, and perhaps more, available to the innocent child than to the sophisticated theologian. Herrick's oft-noted love of time-honoured ceremonies[23] (at least, ceremonies he takes to be time-honoured) originates from the same spiritually levelling impulse—a spiritual levelling that does not militate against, but in fact might reinforce 'degree' and 'place' in social arrangements.[24] Everyone, he suggests, knows how to participate in May Day or Christmas rituals. These shared pleasures offer the promise of universal community that is no longer, by the time *Noble Numbers* is published, plausibly embodied in what is now a fragmented and dispersed church.

Though they respond to the same political and religious developments, John Milton's mature convictions are virtually the opposite of Herrick's—and differ from Donne's and Herbert's as well. Milton did not write many short devotional poems, so his work will be treated at greater length in the next section of this chapter, which deals with religious narrative poetry. But because his outlook is so distinctive, it is worth discussing here. Coming of age in the 1630s, Milton found some aspects of the Laudian innovation attractive—he, like Herrick, holds Arminian views on human freedom and salvation—but he eventually found the institutional commitments that had

---

[23] Leah Marcus, 'Churchman Among the Maypoles', in *The Politics of Mirth' Jonson, Herrick, Milton, Marvell, and the Defense of Old Holiday Pastimes*, pp. 140–168; Aschah Guibbory, *Ceremony and Community from Herbert to Milton*, pp. 79–118.

[24] For the actually invented, politically motivated use of 'traditional carnival' rituals in the early modern period to help ensure the docility of the labouring classes, see Peter Stallybrass, '"We Feast in Our Defense": Patrician Carnival in Early Modern England and Robert Herrick's "Hesperides"', *English Literary Renaissance* 16 (1986): 232–254.

shaped the careers of Donne and Herbert impossible.[25] Although his education and inclinations prepared him to take holy orders, and although he never repudiates the pagan past as many Puritans did, Milton could not reconcile service to the Laudian Church with his conscience. In *Lycidas*, written in 1637 and reprinted in Milton's 1645 verse collection with a new headnote, the stern figure of Peter brusquely interrupts a pastoral elegy to a friend to decry 'our corrupted clergy, then in their height' and to predict their imminent ruin. By the 1640s if not earlier, Herrick's trust in ritual and custom, his principled refusal to think too deeply on religious mystery, seemed to Milton dangerously complacent.

Yet Milton—like Herrick, but for different reasons—is considerably less self-abasing than Donne and less self-effacing than Herbert.[26] In *An Apology for Smectymnuus* he defends himself against his antagonists' slanderous claims that he visits bordellos, on the claim that such behaviour is inconsistent with his sense of poetic vocation:

> he who would not be frustrate of his hope to write well hereafter in laudable things ought himself to be a true poem, that is, a composition and pattern of the best and honourablest things—not presuming to sing high praises of heroic men or famous cities, unless he have in himself the experience and practice of all that which is praiseworthy. These reasonings, together with a certain niceness of nature, an honest haughtiness, and self-esteem either of what I was or what I might be (which let envy call pride), and lastly that modesty whereof . . . I may be excused to make some beseeming profession, all these uniting the supply of their natural aid together, kept me still above those low descents of mind beneath which he must deject and plunge himself that can agree to saleable and unlawful prostitutions.[27]

---

[25] Because the young Milton does not fit neatly into any of the polemical categories of the 1630s, his biographers have interpreted his youthful commitments variously: Barbara Lewalski, in *The Life of John Milton: A Critical Biography*, emphasizes his Puritan affinities, whereas Gordon Campbell and Thomas Corns, in *John Milton: Life, Works, and Thought*, argue that, early on, he was sympathetic to many aspects of the Laudian programme.

[26] Richard Strier argues that 'Milton never praises abjection and he does not sustainedly exhort us, with Calvin, to be "consumed with the awareness" of our own ethical poverty'. 'Milton Against Humility', in *Religion and Culture in Renaissance England*, ed. Debora Shugar and Claire McEachern, p. 280; see also Stephen Fallon, *Milton's Peculiar Grace: Self-Representation and Authority*.

[27] Milton, *An Apology For Smectymnuus, with the Reason of Church-Government* (London, 1641), p. 16.

Raphael makes a similar point in Book 8 of *Paradise Lost*, when he informs Adam that 'ofttimes nothing profits more / Than self-esteem, grounded on just and right' (571–572). Throughout his career, Milton champions courageous spiritual assurance. The Lady in *A Masque*, for instance, abducted and physically immobilized by a seductive magician, defiantly proclaims her spiritual invulnerability:

> Thou canst not touch the freedom of my mind
> With all thy charms, although this corporal rind
> Thou hast immanacled, while Heaven sees good.
> (663–665)

Frozen in an enchanted chair, she nonetheless argues ably and at length against the magician; and though she eventually requires the outside aid of Sabrina, an avatar of divine grace, to free herself entirely from Comus' magic, her boldness begins to cow her would-be seducer even before she is rescued. In Books 5 and 6 of *Paradise Lost*, written decades later, Milton once again celebrates defiant firmness. Abdiel is the only angel in Lucifer's army to resist Lucifer's logic of rebellion, and he stoutly chastises his military superior although 'his zeal / None seconded, as out of season judged, / Or singular and rash'.

> Among the faithless, faithful only he;
> Among innumerable false, unmoved,
> Unshaken, unseduced, unterrified,
> His loyalty he kept, his love, his zeal;
> Nor number nor example with him wrought
> To swerve from truth, or change his constant mind,
> Though single.
> (5.897–903)

Abdiel is the model provided to Adam of a hero able to recall his true allegiance to God despite a situation that encourages him to forget it—an example which Adam, 'fondly overcome' by his love of Eve (9.999), will eventually fail to emulate.

Whereas Herrick wants to think of himself, and other people, as fundamentally ordinary and as eager to join group practices, Milton glorifies sturdy outliers. In the last two books of *Paradise Lost*, the archangel Michael foretells for Adam the history of the world, highlighting a few monitory scenes plus a string of visionary mavericks: Noah, Abraham, Moses, and eventually Christ Himself. Moreover, Milton conceives himself as a person of this type, set apart by God and gifted with special abilities. It does not follow that he approves of independent agency per se: in *Paradise Lost* Satan's sin, of course, and eventually Adam and Eve's, consists in a prideful assertion of independence, a profoundly mistaken conception that they can do without God, and that God is their rival. Rather, the righteously non-compliant individual single-mindedly privileges his allegiance to a remote, invisible God over what seem to be the immediate demands of his contingent situation. By definition, these individuals are rare. While Herrick arguably dumbs down religion so everyone can participate, for Milton the gap between the small elect and the majority of human beings yawns just as widely as it does for any Calvinist, although the criteria for election are rather different. In Milton's universe the role of the Church as it is usually understood is much diminished, and Milton argues, in *Areopagitica* and elsewhere, that the dangers of a sclerotic, coercive institutional religion far outweigh the supposed solaces of religious society. If there is a vital religious community at all in Milton's later writing, it is not defined by parish or national boundaries, but instead comprises a fellowship of likeminded exalted spirits, linked across long distances or centuries of historical time by similarity of aspiration and sympathy of views.

Although Milton never seems to have worried that he might end up in hell, or that God might abandon him, he is aware, sometimes painfully so, that he might not be living up to divine expectation. In his version of Arminian theology, the earnest believer must strive to satisfy a God whom Milton, in a sonnet written in his early twenties, calls 'my Great Taskmaster' (7.14). About two decades later, in a sonnet written in the mid-1650s, Milton returns to his concerns about falling short given his difficult circumstances at midlife when he was going blind. God has bestowed upon him a poetic gift, and, instructed by the Parable of the Talents, Milton wants to put it to good use: his soul is 'bent / To serve therewith my Maker' (19.4–5). Yet blindness seems to make his genius impossible to deploy. 'Does God exact day-labor, light denied?' (7) Milton asks querulously, invoking the unfair expectations of the Egyptian Pharaoh who required the Hebrews to make bricks without giving them the requisite materials. Yet the lesson Milton must ultimately learn is not what project he needs to perform, but rather that God is not really served by task completion.

>   God doth not need
> Either man's work or his own gifts.
>   (9–10)

Like Herbert in 'Jordan II', Milton has been misled by his own piety into misconstruing what God demands of him, which is not a great or brilliant accomplishment, but simply faithful obedience come what may. The hardest lesson, for a gifted, driven individual like Milton, is that the ambition to distinguish oneself, to become remarkable, is itself a temptation: 'that last infirmity of noble mind' (71), as he calls it in *Lycidas*. Even the steadfast servants of God must constantly be confronted with the evidence of the pointlessness of their service. In *Paradise Lost*, after Abdiel bravely defies the army of rebel angels, he rushes off to inform God's allies of the conspiracy— only to find, when he arrives in friendly territory, that the loyal angels are already fully aware of the news he had intended to deliver.

Religious Narrative Poetry

Devotional lyric poets, as we have seen, are often a bit nervous about their own ingenuity, since human cleverness can involve deviating from a divine script. Even so, the spontaneous prayer favoured by Protestants, and the meditational modes cultivated by both Protestants and Catholics, demand a certain amount of improvisation. The problem of potentially disruptive interpolation becomes more acute in narrative poetry on religious topics— especially those poems that retell Biblical stories, since they are already available in an authoritative version. The supplemental material the poem inevitably provides might well seem blasphemous, impertinent, or simply falsifying.

The potential for prideful self-assertion, moreover, is higher for the narrative poet than for the devotional lyricist. Whereas it is possible to imagine a devotional lyric for whom the primary audience is God, the storytelling function of narrative poetry only makes sense addressed to a human reader. John Milton suggests this distinction in the opening of the most famous of seventeenth-century narrative poems, emphasizing that *Paradise Lost* aims to 'justify the ways of God *to men*' (1.26). The publication history of these works suggests a similar distinction since, unlike many devotional lyrics, they were typically printed soon after composition, hoping to attract a wide readership. And as soon as a human audience becomes primary, concerns about ambition, competition for worldly prestige, the flaunting of a fallen imagination, and similar distractions follow closely. So, it is not surprising that scripturally inspired narrative poems often include, or preface their works with, a defence of their method and intentions, drawing on several unimpeachable precedents. Jesus' parables, as we have already seen, offer a powerful model for the religious poet: fictions that are simultaneously memorable and fraught with interpretive possibilities. Giles Fletcher argues that 'as none may compare [with Christ] without presumption, so all may imitate, and not without commendation'. Episodes of Biblical history offer similar opportunities for praise, reflection, and imitation. A poet, like a minister, might use Bible stories to induce piety, to instruct on points of doctrine, and to foster a harmonious Christian community. Many early modern writers gravitated to this quasi-pastoral conception of the poet's role; Jeffrey Knapp has even suggested that it influenced dramatists' self-conception as well, although their material was not explicitly religious.[28]

The prophetic books of the Bible provide another precedent for the narrative poet. While the Psalms, the Proverbs, and the Song of Songs were attributed to kings of Israel, the prophets stood pointedly outside secular and ecclesiastical institutions. Their authority derives neither from their social eminence nor from their own intrinsic merit, but solely from the direct inspiration of God. Several seventeenth-century religious poets speak self-consciously from a position that is both marginal and privileged, and perhaps privileged insofar as it is marginal. In *Salve Deus Rex Judaeorum*, Aemelia Lanyer deploys the 'last shall be first' ethos of the New Testament to make an unconventional feminist case for Eve, and for women's spirituality in general. Several decades later, John Milton likewise finds the example of the Biblical prophets inspirational. Milton cannot conscientiously take orders as a clergyman of the Church of England, but his poems give him a pulpit of sorts, bearing witness to his sense of righteous exclusion. *Lycidas* decries the corruption of the Laudian clergy; *A Masque Presented at Ludlow Castle* comments trenchantly on distributive justice and the decadence of institutions which ignore the needs of the poor. At several points in *Paradise Lost*, as I will discuss later in this section, Milton describes his process of poetic creation in detail: a complex amalgam of the concept of classical inspiration by a personified Muse, with a Biblical paradigm of the prophet as God's mouthpiece.

Religious narrative poetry in the period also draws on a variety of non-Biblical genres and prototypes. Giles Fletcher's *Christ's Victory and Triumph*

---

[28] Jeffrey Knapp, *Shakespeare's Tribe: Church, Nation, and Theatre in Renaissance England*.

in Heaven and Earth, over and after Death, published in 1610, is profoundly influenced by Edmund Spenser, the premier narrative poet of the prior generation. Fletcher not only borrows Spenser's stanzas of 'interlaced' rhyme and his division of his work into cantos, he also imitates Spenser's allegorical method. For instance, his second canto rewrites Christ's temptation in the wilderness in allegorical terms reminiscent of the encounter of the Red Crosse Knight and Archimago in *The Faerie Queene*. The first and most interesting of the cantos in *Christ's Victory*, however, is framed as a rhetorical duel between the allegorical figures of Justice and Mercy, arguing over the fate of mankind as if they were attorneys for the prosecution and the defence. Fletcher plays with the discrepancy between human time, in which events happen in consecutive order, and eternal, heavenly time, which seems to defy sequential presentation. Fletcher narrates the debate as a suspenseful courtroom drama—what will the verdict be? On the other hand, the conflict between Justice and Mercy seems to happen in a space beyond time: it anticipates the Creation, Fall, and Redemption, even while occurring simultaneously, continuously, within human history and within the life of individual believers.

Aemelia Lanyer's *Salve Deus Rex Judaeorum*, her poem on Christ's trial and crucifixion, is reminiscent of the narrative epyllia on secular topics, such as *Venus and Adonis* and *The Rape of Lucrece*, that had been widely popular in the 1590s and continued to be reprinted into the 1630s. The poem's ottava rima stanza form is well suited to an alternating rhythm of narrative and commentary, delivering a parcel of story, then following up with several stanzas of reflection and interpretation. The need to editorialize may seem particularly urgent for Lanyer, the first Englishwoman to publish a volume of original poetry with her full name on the title-page, because the question of her poetic fitness was unavoidable. Not only was her act of publication scandalously ambitious on its face, but the choice of a sacred subject might seem especially so, given Paul's admonition, in Corinthians and Timothy, that women should remain silent in church and should not instruct on sacred matters. Lanyer's response to doctrines of female inferiority is complex. On the one hand, she stoutly resists them on Biblical grounds: in Galatians, she points out, Paul develops an alternative doctrine of the equality of male and female souls. On the other hand, Lanyer embraces the aspersion of female weakness in order to make a case for her endeavour: 'The weaker thou dost seem to be / In sex or sense, the more His glory shines', she tells herself (289–290). The success of her poem will testify to its authentic source in divine inspiration.

Salve Deus Rex Judaeorum narrates the last days of Jesus' life, from his betrayal in the Garden of Gethsemane to the Resurrection—possibly the most familiar of Biblical stories for any Christian reader. Yet Lanyer foregrounds female characters that are briefly passed over in the authorized version: Pilate's wife, who encourages her husband to absolve and free the innocent Jesus; Jesus' mother, Mary, mourning at the foot of the cross; and Jesus' follower, Mary Magdalene, the first to discover the empty tomb on the day of the Resurrection. In her poem, Lanyer draws a powerful implicit connection between these figures, often dismissed or marginalized, and the apparently defeated and humiliated, but actually triumphant and powerful, Jesus. It is an analogy that becomes explicit in her preface, 'To the Virtuous Reader', in which she deplores misogynistic men 'who forgetting they were born of women, nourished of women . . . do like vipers deface the wombs wherein they were bred . . . Such as these, were they that dishonoured Christ his Apostles and Prophets, putting them to shameful deaths'. Her volume as a whole, centred on the poem about the Crucifixion but featuring as well a number of dedicatory poems to devout members of England's elite, pushes back against this persecutory, exclusionary viewpoint. In its place, Lanyer imagines a spiritual gathering of women believers: as Micheline White remarks, 'she depicts women as the true disciples and founders of Christ's healing Church, and she positions Jacobean women as the spiritual heirs of these female disciples'.[29] Female sex does not impair spiritual fitness, nor does the status difference between Lanyer and the much wealthier, titled court patrons whose support she solicits.[30] The Christian model for the egalitarian society thus created is founded in the ritual of the Eucharist, binding Christians to God and to one another—a ritual that derives its significance from Christ's sacrificial death and rebirth.[31] In other

---

[29] Micheline White, 'A Woman With Saint Peter's Keys?: Aemelia Lanyer's "Salve Deus Rex Judaeorum" (1611) and the Priestly Gifts of Women', *Criticism* 45 (2003), p. 324.

[30] For Lanyer's class positioning relative to those from whom she seeks patronage, see Ann Baynes Coiro, 'Writing in Service: Sexual Politics and Class Position in the Poetry of Aemila Lanyer and Ben Jonson', *Criticism* 35 (1993) 357–376; Lisa Schnell, 'So Great a Difference Is There in Degree: Aemilia Lanyer and the Aims of Feminist Criticism', *Modern Language Quarterly* 57 (1996): 23–35; Wendy Wall, *The Imprint of Gender: Authorship and Publication in the English Renaissance*, p. 329.

[31] Two essays that explore Lanyer's imagery of communion are Yaakov Mascetti, 'Here I have Prepar'd My Paschal Lambe: Reading and Seeing the Eucharistic Presence in Aemilia Lanyer's "Salve Deus Rex Judaeorum"', *Partial Answers: Journal of Literature and the History of Ideas* 9 (2011): 1–15, and Julianne Sandberg, 'Book, Body, and Bread: Reading Aemilia Lanyer's Eucharist', *Philological Quarterly* 96 (2017): 1–25.

words, Lanyer's narrative provides the origin story for the unity she attempts to actualize among its community of readers.

John Milton, in 'On the Morning of Christ's Nativity', plays with some of the same discrepancies between 'divine' and 'human' time that intrigue Giles Fletcher, and some of the same resulting narrative paradoxes. Milton portrays the Nativity as a fateful historical turning point, the moment at which the arrival of God, in infant human form, inaugurates a Christian era. Moreover, on a personal level, the poem represents the dawning of his own new era. Written in 1629, just as Milton turned twenty-one (the age of legal majority), 'On the Morning of Christ's Nativity' presented itself as the first fruit of the poet's maturity, the opening work in his 1645 collection. Yet within the poem the birth of Christ is almost a non-event, taking place in what seems like a moment of suspended animation:

> No war or battle's sound
> Was heard the world around;
> The idle spear and shield were high uphung;
> The hooked chariot stood
> Unstained with hostile blood;
> The trumpet spake not to the armed throng;
> And kings sate still with awful eye,
> As if they surely knew their sovereign Lord was by.
>
> But peaceful was the night
> Wherein the Prince of Light
> His reign of peace upon the earth began:
> The winds with wonder whist,
> Smoothly the waters kissed,
> Whispering new joys to the mild Ocean,
> Who now hath quite forgot to rave,
> While birds of calm sit brooding on the charmed wave.
>   (53–68)

The Nativity is significant not so much for its own sake as for what has happened earlier and will happen in the future. The angels heralding Jesus' birth sing, Milton tells us, as they have not done since the Creation; Milton fantasizes that, if they continue, 'Time will run back and fetch the age of gold' (135), but also that Time will run forward, inaugurating the last days and the reign of heaven on earth. The power of angelic music—closely aligned, of course, with the power of poetry—seems to be able to evoke universal history in a single sweeping, simultaneous revelation.[32] Milton can thus imagine himself, via his 'Heavenly Muse', 'preventing' (literally, coming before) the Wise Men who, in the poem, are still in the process of wending their way from the East, bringing their gifts.

The immediate effect of Christ's arrival, in Milton's retelling, is the flight of the pagan gods before His superior power:

> The lonely mountains o'er,
> And the resounding shore,
> A voice of weeping heard and loud lament;
> From haunted spring, and dale
> Edged with poplar pale,
> The parting Genius is with sighing sent;
>   With flower-inwoven tresses torn
>   The nymphs in twilight shade
>   of tangled thickets mourn.
>   (181–188)

As the beauty of these lines suggests, there is something melancholy in this departure despite the poem's overall posture of joyful welcome. Once again, however, Milton suggests that the banishment of the past is not a once-and-for-all expulsion. While, like Fletcher, Milton evokes Spenser in his opening stanzas, with their interlaced rhyme and final alexandrine lines, the body of the poem shifts metrically into the irregular lines of the ode—a form strongly linked to classical poetry. This formal choice suggests that the pagan past is not so much excluded as adapted and assimilated into the new Christian dispensation—a theme which Milton will elaborate decades later in *Paradise Lost*.

The most ambitious of the period's narrative religious poems are self-consciously epic in scope. Along with tragedy, epic was considered to occupy the pinnacle of literary achievement in the hierarchy of genres inherited from classical Greece and Rome. Epic was the form in which to address

---

[32] The temporal paradoxes of the *Nativity Ode* are remarked upon by many critics, including David Morris, 'Drama and Stasis in Milton's Ode on the Morning of Christ's Nativity', *Studies in Philology* 68 (1971): 207–222; David Quint, 'Expectation and Prematurity in Milton's Nativity Ode', *Modern Philology* 97 (1999): 195–219. Barbara Lewalski, *The Life of John Milton: A Critical Biography*, p. 47; Stanley Fish, *How Milton Works*, pp. 310–325.

the noblest acts of heroism, and in which to depict the events of world-historical importance. The composition of an epic was also, traditionally, thought to be the culmination of a great writer's career, produced, as Virgil's *Aeneid* was, after a thorough apprenticeship in smaller forms. What could be more appropriate than to marry this most prestigious of forms with the most exalted material? By the seventeenth century there had been numerous attempts to adapt the classical conventions of the epic, originally developed for pagan material, to the requirements of a Christian ethos, in many cases by melding it with the conventions of romance.[33] Dante toured Hell, Purgatory, and Heaven; Ariosto and Tasso depicted military and romantic struggles between Muslims and Christians; Edmund Spenser centred his allegory on questing knights who embodied such virtues as Faith, Temperance, and Justice. The late sixteenth-century French poet Guillaume Du Bartas wrote two epic poems based on stories from Scripture: one on the Creation, the other treating the lives of the Biblical patriarchs; his work was translated into English by Joshuah Sylvester and became very popular, influencing both Abraham Cowley and John Milton.

Cowley's unfinished epic *Davideis*, published in 1656, is based on the life of the Biblical David, as recounted in Samuel 1 and 2. Cowley was well versed in classical literature and powerfully conscious of epic conventions, including previous attempts to redeploy the conventions of epic for Christian purposes. He designed his epic in twelve books, he writes in the preface to the 1656 edition of his *Poems*, 'after the pattern of our master Virgil', and planned to end the poem shortly before David's anointing 'because it is the custom of heroic poets (as we see by the examples of Homer and Virgil, whom we should do ill to forsake to imitate others) never to come to the full end of their story, but only so near, that everyone may see it'. Cowley's hero has several affinities with the heroes of classical epic: he is devout and divinely favoured, he is a successful warrior who triumphs over formidable enemies, and, eventually, after considerable tribulations, he will unify his people under his leadership. In addition, he combines poetic gifts with military prowess: 'The two chief gifts Heav'n could on man bestow' (1.4). Like many religious poets, Cowley sees his task as a wresting of a profane medium to a higher use:

> Too long the Muse's lands have heathen been,
> Their gods too long were devils, and virtues sin,

---

[33] David Quint, *Epic and Empire: Politics and Generic Form from Virgil to Milton*; Colin Burrow, *Epic Romance: Homer to Milton*.

> But thou, Eternal Word, hath called forth me
> Th' Apostle, to convert that world to thee.
>
> (1.37–40)

Just as David, 'best poet, best of kings' (1.3) wrests territory for his people from the Philistines, so Cowley aims to transform 'the Muse's lands' of classical epic to consecrated use.

The four completed books of Cowley's poem treat a dangerous interval in David's youth. *Davideis* begins, in Virgilian fashion, *in medias res* or in the middle of the action, with Saul briefly repenting of his previous suspicion of David. But Saul almost immediately reverts to paranoia, a change of heart Cowley motivates via a descent into hell, also an epic mainstay. Satan calls up Envy, who incites rage in Saul; meanwhile, an angel warns David to flee. At first he sojourns with the prophet Samuel—imagined as presiding over a research institute devoted to dispassionate scientific inquiry—and then finds sanctuary in the pagan land of Moab.

As in the *Aeneid*, Cowley provides extensive backstory via episodes narrated by various characters, including the choice of Saul as king, the flourishing of David's friendship with Saul's son Jonathan, David's youthful defeat of Golias, and David's marriage to Saul's daughter, Michal. A long digression describing the historical tapestries in Moab's palace allows Cowley to retell the history of Lot, the shared ancestor of David and his pagan host. While David is on the run, the angel Gabriel brings him a dream foretelling the future of his bloodline and its culmination in the birth of Jesus Christ. Unfortunately, the poem's elaborately artful oscillations between forecasting and retrospection render David's circuitous path to the throne simply confusing, at least in the poem's unfinished condition. The tendency for *Davideis* to collapse into fragments is perhaps the reason why, although it received respectful attention in the years immediately after its publication, it soon ceased to be much read.

Davideis was printed, as already mentioned, in 1656. Shortly after Cowley's death his friend and biographer, Thomas Sprat, claimed that Cowley had written it in 1638, when he was a Cambridge undergraduate, but Frank Kermode has argued that it more likely dates from the early 1650s.[34] Kermode's dating certainly seems plausible given both the poem's style and

---

[34] Frank Kermode, 'The Date of Cowley's *Davideis*', *The Review of English Studies* 25 (1949): 154–158. Victoria Moul, 'Abraham Cowley's 1656 Poems: Form and Context', in *Royalists and Royalism in 17th-Century Literature: Exploring Abraham Cowley*, ed. Philip Majors, similarly asserts that *Davideis* 'belongs . . . specifically to the political and cultural moment of the mid-1650s'.

its concerns. *Davideis* is written in heroic couplets, a stylistic choice made as well by Cowley's friend William D'Avenant in his 1651 narrative poem, *Gondibert*. The themes of *Davideis* likewise seem characteristic of the interregnum period and in particular to reflect Cowley's own experience in those decades. At the outset of civil war, Cowley was a committed royalist who followed Queen Henrietta Maria into France and served as her secretary. He retained, however, his allegiance to the Church of England despite the Catholicism of his environs. In 1654, he returned to England and apparently accepted the authority of Cromwell's government on the grounds that its success had legitimated its claims to authority. (Possibly, however, he continued to work as a royalist spy.) The poem touches on the problem of how a devout man ought to behave in exile, where one's most helpful allies, like Moab, might not be one's co-religionists. Samuel's 'college', where David finds refuge, not only echoes the similar description of Astragon's collegiate country house in D'Avenant's *Gondibert*, but also reflects the preoccupations of some among Cowley's circle of acquaintance in the 1650s, the intellectuals who would form the Royal Society after the Restoration.

Several of the dilemmas the poem confronts may have seemed especially salient after Cowley had tentatively reconciled himself to the republic. The question of whether monarchy tends to degenerate into tyranny is a live one throughout the epic: while Moab is a wise ruler and David is clearly soon to prove one, God warns the Israelites that they would be better off governing themselves, and their subsequent history suggests that good kings are rarer than wicked ones. The story of David also tends to query, without abandoning altogether, the hereditary principle upon which monarchy in Cowley's day was founded. On the one hand, David's claim to the throne rests not upon his birthright but upon his military effectiveness and his closeness to God. On the other hand, his importance in a Christian epic, as his prophetic dream makes clear, is partly as the human ancestor of Jesus. Sue Starke notes the disparity: Cowley uses 'the epic form to comment on the futility rather than the glory of dynastic ambitions', yet, at the same time, 'David's position as neo-Virgilian hero . . . owes not to his achievements but to his bloodline: he is the ancestor of Christ, while Jonathan, for all his commendable heroism, is not.'[35] Yet *Davideis* is certainly not explicitly autobiographical, and some of the problems Cowley's characters confront

---

[35] Sue Starke, '"The Eternal Now": Virgilian Echoes and Miltonic Premonitions in Cowley's *Davideis*', *Christianity and Literature* 55 (2006): 195–219, pp. 200, 207.

are familiar ones in Renaissance tragedy and tragicomedy. What is the relationship between heredity and merit? To what extent may a subject resist an unjust ruler? If one's loyalty to a friend or spouse conflicts with one's duty to a father or a ruler, which should take precedence? How should the virtuous person behave in a world in which virtue does not seem to be rewarded?

An interesting feature of the printed text of *Davideis* is its elaborate annotation. Cowley is at pains to emphasize his scrupulous adherence to the laws of epic composition, and his story's basis in fact. His notes cross-reference his literary devices with their precedents in Virgil, cite a Biblical source for many incidents in his poem, and comment extensively on ancient customs. While most of his notes seem designed to reassure the reader that his epic is reliably 'true', a few register the dissonance between his poetic aims and what he takes to be historical actuality. When, in the poem, he calls Hell 'endless'(1.84), in note #11 he clarifies: 'This must be taken in a poetical sense; for else, making Hell to be in the center of the Earth, it is far from infinitely large, or deep'. When David reminds Saul that God helped the Israelites defeat 'twice fifteen kings' (3.479) in the time of Joshua, Cowley adds a note: 'They were 33. But poetry instead of the broken number, chooses the next entire one, whether it be more or less than the truth' (3.n51). The Biblical text, too, is subjected to critical scrutiny. Cowley draws attention to chronological discrepancies in the account of Saul's reign, and points out moments that strain credulity. The battle between Abijah and Jeroboam, he claims, is

> one of the strangest and humanly most hard to believe ... that out of a kingdom, not half so big as England five hundred thousand chosen and valiant men should be slain in one battle, and of this not so much as any notice taken in Abijah's or Jeroboam's lives in the first of Kings. (2.n56)

Sometimes too Cowley attempts to come up with scientifically plausible accounts of apparently miraculous events; he speculates that when God destroyed Sodom and Gomorrah 'it is not improbable, that this raining of fire and brimstone was nothing but extraordinary thunders and lightnings' (3.30). Cowley does not go so far as openly to doubt the veracity of the Biblical account, but the rationalizing tendency of his notes consistently cuts against a poetic form that self-consciously attempts to render history as myth.

In 1667, eleven years after Cowley published *Davideis*, John Milton published the first version of *Paradise Lost*. Strictly speaking, then, *Paradise*

Lost is a 'Restoration' work. Yet it is traditionally seen as the crowning achievement of the English Renaissance: far and away the most impressive and influential of the seventeenth-century religious narrative poems, as well as the most successfully comprehensive and assimilative. And although recent scholarship has suggested how fully the poem responds to the particular historical moment of its publication,[36] it was nonetheless a labour of many years, 'long choosing, and beginning late' (9.26), as Milton acknowledges. As erstwhile secretary of state and polemicist for Cromwell's government, attacking the concept of monarchy in print even after its restoration seemed inevitable, Milton had found himself in considerable danger after Charles II returned to England. Spared because of his age and blindness, apparently due to the intercession of Andrew Marvell, Milton wrote the latter parts of *Paradise Lost* in retirement, positioning himself as the survivor of an earlier epoch: 'On evil days ... fallen, and evil tongues' (7.26). Ironically, the poet who had foregrounded his precocity in his 1645 volume eventually funnelled the wisdom of old age into his retelling of the story of the Creation and the Fall: his experiences of war, of political disillusion, of marital love and conflict, of persecution and physical vulnerability, of hopes for the future tempered but not extinguished.

While Cowley construes the task of the religious epic poet as one of harmonizing Biblical and pagan traditions, Milton typically deploys classical epic conventions in order to critique them. Like Lanyer, he emphasizes the way a scriptural sense of significance fails to correspond with, and is in many cases at odds with, worldly glory. The epic's typical celebration of military adventuring has little to do with the important actions in the poem, which tend to be interior, fateful moments of decision or commitment. While, like Cowley, Milton apparently begins *in medias res*, the epic convention here has a twist of which his readers only slowly become aware. As the poem begins, the decisive, 'epic' battle between Satan and God has already been fought.[37] In fact, *Paradise Lost* will go on to tell two interrelated stories. The War in Heaven, and the Creation which follows it, transforms the entire cosmos. The story of Adam and Eve, two individuals enjoying the first days of their marriage within a walled garden, is both an aftermath to the 'big story' and, eventually, an enormously consequential episode in its own right. The relationship between the apparently gigantic story and the

---

[36] For example, David Norbrook, *Writing the English Republic 1627–1660*; Michael McKeon, '*Paradise Lost*: Poem of the Restoration Period', *Eighteenth Century Life* 41 (2017): 9–27; *Milton in the Long Restoration*, ed. Blair Hoxby and Anne Coiro.

[37] David Quint, *Epic and Empire: Politics and Generic Form from Virgil to Milton*.

apparently small, domestic story will turn out to be far trickier than first appears.

Paradise Lost grapples in a complex way with the notions of divinely appointed hierarchy and order that, as we have seen, permeated much of the thinking of the period. Hierarchy is baked into the created world as Milton depicts it. Seraphim are superior to cherubim; humans have 'dominion' over the animals and plants on Earth; Adam and Eve are 'Not equal, as their sex not equal seemed . . . He for God only, she for God in him' (4.296–299). All created beings ought to worship God the Father and his Son as his deputy, gratefully recognizing their utter dependence and the incomparably greater power and capacity of the divinity. God's role as Creator, of course, is particularly highlighted in a poem that massively expands upon the terse account in Genesis, revelling in the dizzying richness of the created world. Milton's Garden of Eden is no orderly parterre but a place of riotous variety, in which 'Nature boon / Poured forth profuse on hill and dale and plain' (4. 242–243), in which Adam and Eve can barely keep the paths clear of new growth, through which streams wind 'with mazy error'(4.239). Even Eve's hair is desirably 'Disheveled, but in wanton ringlets waved / As the vine curls her tendrils' (4.306–307). Milton's evocation of the beauty of unstudied irregularity has some affinities with the 'wild civility' celebrated by Robert Herrick and other cavalier poets. Yet one of the challenges of the poem will be to distinguish between the beautifully meandering and the sinfully erroneous, between the intricately complicated dances of the unfallen angels and the tortuous 'wandering mazes' (2.561) in which the fallen ones roam endlessly. For the abundance that bears witness to God's infinite creativity also problematizes the relationships among created beings, because their heterogeneity often seems to defy arrangement in a simple vertical hierarchy. Adam, speaking to the archangel Raphael of Eve, declares that 'well I understand in the prime end / Of nature her th'inferior, in the mind / And inward faculties, which most excel' (8.540–542). Yet Eve is not merely a lesser Adam but differs from him in looks, sensibility, and experience, manifesting nurturing traits and botanical talents that he does not possess himself. Adam's perception of her as 'in herself complete' (8.548), perfect in her own way and not merely a defective male, is true as well.

Milton's distinctive sense of hierarchy has political implications. For the royalists who were Milton's political opponents, monarchy simply echoes God's dominion over the universe. As James I put it in *The True Law of Free Monarchies*: 'Monarchy is the true pattern of divinity . . . Kings are called gods ... because they sit upon God his throne in the earth.'[38] Milton, though, draws a stark distinction between divine rule, which he represents as absolute and unimpeachable, and human rule, which can only lay claim to those attributes by a process of usurpation and parody. Milton's God does not rule as a wise king might. He does not, for instance, consult advisors; he merely pronounces his verdicts and judgements, in a manner somewhat reminiscent of King Lear in the opening scene of Shakespeare's play. And yet Milton's point is that God is not a tyrant, though Satan persists in trying to cast him in that role, because His authority is founded on unique characteristics of omniscience and omnipotence. When lesser beings—Satan, or earthly kings—attempt to lay claim to those attributes, they fall ludicrously short because their assertions of power founder on their personal limitations. Thus, the deeds of the fallen angels in Books 1 and 2, though they seem remarkable when we have not yet seen their heavenly prototypes, are at their best merely derivative. Even Satan's strengths often turn out to hinge on weakness. For instance, in Book 2 he convenes a consultation among the demonic peers to debate their course of action. Although the discussion seems free and the outcome undecided, Satan has cannily arranged for a sidekick to propose his preferred scheme: a point of political intelligence that Milton marks as such. But the need for manoeuvring is telling. Unlike God, who is different in kind from created beings, Satan is merely different in degree. He must constantly strategize to sustain his 'bad eminence' (2.6), disarming potential threats from below. God does not need strategy.

If the earthly monarch risks sinfully arrogating to himself, like Satan, the prerogatives of God as ruler, the epic poet risks sinfully arrogating to himself the prerogatives of God as Creator. Where Cowley takes Virgil as his master and the *Aeneid* as his model, Milton claims that, for all his consciousness of epic precedent, he must go beyond it, essaying 'Things unattempted yet in prose or rhyme' (1.16). His ambitious poem ranges through Hell, Heaven, Chaos, and Earth, and from the beginning of the universe to its predicted end. His master and precedent, then, is not a human poet or a prior poem, but God Himself, His creation, and His revealed word. The potential for failure is obviously high. Milton's poetic anxieties resemble George Herbert's, writ larger as befits the scope of his work. Like Herbert, Milton vanquishes concerns about a prideful and potentially blasphemous competition with God by disclaiming his originality: just as Herbert claims that God holds the

---

[38] James VI and I, *True Law of Free Monarchies, or The Reciprock and Mutual Duty Betwixt a Free King and his Natural Subjects* in *King James VI and I: Political Writings*, ed. Johann Somerville, p. 64.

pen while he writes his poems, Milton claims that his poem is dictated into his ear while he sleeps by Urania, the 'heavenly Muse'. Urania is not merely a literary device displacing or allegorizing his own imaginative enterprise, but a form of divine inspiration that minimizes Milton's conscious agency and turns his task into one of faithful transcription. Like the Biblical prophets, he does not speak for himself, but allows God to speak through him.[39] Moreover, he dramatizes within the poem how this kind of delegated storytelling might work. Before the Fall the 'affable' (7.41) archangel Raphael provides Adam with accounts of the War in Heaven and the Creation; after the Fall the sterner archangel Michael shows him the future course of human history. Both angels provide narrative contexts to help Adam understand his own role in a cosmic drama, and both need to adjust their accounts to allow for the conceptual and experiential limitations of their audience.

What are these adjustments? As we have seen, many narrative poems on religious subjects, including Milton's earlier 'Nativity Ode', foreground the difference between the human experience of time as sequence, and an eternal, presumably God's-eye view that cannot be conveyed in narrative. *Paradise Lost*, too, deliberately complicates the time scheme in a poem whose various events occur in Heaven, in Hell, and on Earth. Raphael allows that the War in Heaven, for instance, did not necessarily transpire in exactly the form in which he will go on to relate it. At some points he will have to resort to similes or metaphors to make himself intelligible.

> what surmounts the reach
> Of human sense, I shall delineate so,
> By likening spiritual to corporal forms
> As may express them best.
> (5.571–574)

And yet, at the same time, he deliberately refuses to stipulate the degree of difference between spiritual and corporal forms, or to clarify where he will be straightforwardly literal and where he will need to deploy 'likenesses':

> though what if earth
> Be but the shadow of heav'n, and things therein
> Each to other like, more than on earth is thought?
> (5.574–576)

---

[39] For the way Milton's characterization of Urania encapsulates both his yearning for and fear of self-loss, see Stanley Fish, *How Milton Works*, pp. 281–306.

In other words, it is wrong to imagine heaven as earth's duplicate, but also, possibly, to imagine heaven in terms other than earthly. The resemblance between these realms remains unspecified, and unspecifiable.

As well as qualifying what might be meant in Raphael's account by 'a day' or 'a night', and thus troubling the problem of time, *Paradise Lost* also troubles the problem of space: problems posed not merely by theology, but by the scientific discoveries of the sixteenth and seventeenth centuries. Like Cowley, Milton is aware of and responsive to state-of-the art scholarship in multiple fields,[40] and in some cases may have consulted the same authorities: Milton's catalogue of pagan gods in Books 1 and 2 of *Paradise Lost* and Cowley's account of pagan religious practices both rely on the polymath John Selden's *De Diis Syri* [On the Syrian Gods]. But whereas Cowley uses such information to rationalize his Biblical source and to bolster the reader's conviction that his story is factually accurate, Milton uses recent discoveries to destabilize the human knowability of the universe in which his epic action transpires. It had become clear to intellectuals in the early seventeenth century that the cosmos was much larger than previously thought, and possibly organized along different principles. At the same time, how the heavenly bodies were arranged in relationship to earth, and what their properties might be, were still matters of debate. Milton conveys this largeness and indeterminacy in the design of his epic universe: Hell is not in the centre of the earth, where (as Cowley had pointed out) it would be 'far from infinitely large, or deep', but located elsewhere, separated from Heaven and from the newly created universe by an indefinitely large expanse of Chaos. At one point in his dangerous journey across Chaos from Hell to Earth, Satan alights on the sun to reconnoitre:

> There lands the Fiend, a spot like which perhaps
> Astronomer in the sun's lucent orb
> Through his glazed optic tube yet never saw.
> (3.587–90)

Sunspots were a relatively new discovery in the mid-seventeenth century, one of the many surprises revealed via the telescope, and still a source of

---

[40] Milton's astronomy has long been a topic of critical discussion. Grant McColley, 'The Astronomy of *Paradise Lost*', *Studies in Philology* 34 (1937): 219–247, summarizes the earlier tradition of scholarship. More recent considerations include Alastair Fowler's introduction to his edition of *Paradise Lost*, John Rogers, *The Matter of Revolution: Science, Poetry, and Politics in the Age of Milton*, and Catherine Gimelli Martin, 'Milton and Donne's Stargazing Lovers: Sex and the New Astronomy', *Studies in English Literature* 54 (2014): 143–171.

controversy insofar as they seemed to suggest defectiveness and mutability in planetary bodies that had been assumed to be flawless and permanent. Milton's simile likens Satan to a sunspot, not only because he is here a dark speck on the sun's otherwise radiant surface, but because, like the sunspot, he is a blemish upon God's beautiful and good created world. Yet Satan is also *not* like a sunspot—apparently the Astronomer 'yet never saw' anything like Satan there. Milton's ambiguously placed 'perhaps' calls both the adequacy of the comparison and the negation of that comparison into question at the same time. The effect of the simile—like Raphael's warning about the veracity of his story in Book 5—is both to convey a resemblance, and to suggest that all similes will be insufficient. It forces the reader to shuttle between recognizing similarity and acknowledging difference, and to acknowledge as well the limits upon the human imagination properly to apprehend what Milton must attempt to convey.

The spatial indeterminacies of *Paradise Lost*, with their concomitant problems of scale, generate ethical conundrums by making relative importance difficult to assess. As previously noted, the poem juxtaposes two plots, each of which might seem subordinate to the other. The war between Satan and God, waged on a cosmic scale, already seems to be over as the epic begins, but Satan refuses to admit defeat. The story of Adam and Eve's experience, on the other hand, takes place entirely within the walled environs of Eden. The two plots are causally related, insofar as God the Father asserts that the created universe is a reparative response to Satan's rebellion, insofar as human sin will alter that creation for the worse, and insofar as the Son will eventually take human form and then, at some later date, defeat Satan for good. Yet the relative importance of the two plots depends upon who is assessing it. From the point of view of Satan, the earthly story is a desperate aftermath; from the point of view of the human protagonists, Satan's challenge to God is a prelude and backdrop to their more urgent concerns. As a result, Milton becomes what Eric Song calls 'the great poet of multiple perspectives', toggling dizzyingly among a variety of possible, and possibly incompatible, viewpoints.[41]

Adam explicitly addresses such problems when he asks the angel Raphael about the motions of the stars and planets, wondering about the apparent wastefulness of a universe in which so many great heavenly bodies seem to encircle and 'serve' (8.87) the little Earth. Raphael answers, equivocally, that the Earth may not be the centre of the universe after all, and that,

[41] Eric Song, *Dominion Undeserved: Milton and the Perils of Creation*, p. 4.

moreover, size is not a criterion of value: 'great / Or bright infers not excellence' (8.90–91). A heliocentric model of the universe seems to demote the earth, previously imagined as the centre of the universe, to a satellite position, but perhaps the satellite position is a place of consequence after all. The sentiment is one of Milton's favourites: in *A Masque*, written more than three decades earlier, remarkable powers had inhered in a 'small unsightly root' (629). Yet Raphael does not say, either, that the small is necessarily better than the large; and, of course, to the human observer, what is close always looms larger than what is distant. As we have already seen, the created universe is so enormous and complicated—a testimony to God's absolute superiority to any created mind—that it escapes human or angelic understanding. Since it is impossible to grasp the full picture of Creation, and easy to be overwhelmed by its complexity, it is natural to focus on, and potentially to exaggerate the importance of, a single instance of the created order that looks magnificent simply because it is close at hand. Such myopia can easily slide into idolatry, confusing an impressive nearby created being with the much more impressive, but remote, creative mind that originated it. Lucifer's legions, with the single exception of Abdiel, commit this error when they accept Lucifer, their military commander, in the place of their God. They are the first idolators—idolators who, insofar as they will eventually become the gods of paganism, aspire to be idols themselves. Eve's fall, in which she is led to attribute life- and knowledge-giving qualities to a fruit, involves a similar mistake of perspective. So is Adam's fall, in which he prioritizes his love for Eve over his duty to a distant God, succumbing not to Eve's logical arguments for eating the fruit but to her immediately present beauty: 'not deceived, / But fondly overcome with female charm' (9.998–99).

The difficulty, of course, is how to know which perspective is 'correct' when it is impossible, as a created being, to escape the limitations of one's own point of view. Milton sees his own creativity as entirely dependent upon and imitative of God's creative power, while at the same time he is aware that the divine presence in the poem originates in his own unprecedented creative, but necessarily human, enterprise, as he writes 'things unattempted yet in prose or rhyme' (1.26).[42] With one foot in the religious world of the late middle ages and Renaissance and the other in a secular Enlightenment future, Milton teeters on the brink of a profound historical transition.

---

[42] Gordon Teskey has brilliantly elaborated the consequences of this double perspective in *Delirious Milton: The Fate of the Poet in Modernity*.

Intimacies: Lyrics of Love and Friendship

In Shakespeare's *Much Ado About Nothing* (1599), Benedick is convinced by his friends that although Beatrice quarrels with him every time she encounters him, she actually loves him desperately. He immediately decides to reciprocate her supposed passion, and therefore tries to write a poem in her praise. He finds the task difficult:

> I can find no rhyme to lady but baby, an innocent rhyme; for scorn, horn, a hard rhyme; for school, fool, a babbling rhyme; very ominous endings. No, I was not born under a rhyming planet, nor I cannot woo in festival terms.
>
> (5.2.31–34)

At the end of the play, just as Beatrice and Benedick are about to be wed, they discover that their friends originally deceived them, and attempt, half-playfully, to disavow their mutual attachment. But the friends refute their denials by producing, as evidence, sonnets each of them have written to the other.

These funny moments, and many others in English Renaissance comedies, rely on a cultural assumption that wooing 'in festival terms' is such an expected phase of courtship that even an unpoetic soldier like Benedick will attempt it. And whether or not the writing of poems to one's beloved is quite as widely customary as Shakespeare, Jonson, and others imply, the practice is common enough in the period that a truly enormous amount of love poetry survives—some of it, predictably, of excellent quality. In fact, some of the best love poetry in English was written or published between 1603 and 1660. As a result, a chapter like this one, which attempts to survey decades of such writing in a short space, will necessarily have to be very selective.

The early modern period had a robust medieval vernacular tradition to draw upon, as well as temporally more remote paradigms. The Biblical Song of Solomon, although often allegorized as a parable of the love between God and Israel or between Christ and his Church, is on the face of it a dialogue between lovers exulting in one another's bodies. Love poems by Ovid, Catullus, Horace, Virgil, and other Latin poets were staples of the grammar school curriculum, although some pedagogues fretted about the effect of their sexual content on the impressionable minds of young boys. Early modern England is also heir to centuries of philosophizing about the nature of sexual desire and its relationship to religious devotion, to marriage, and to community formation. Such topics preoccupy Plato and his followers but also loom large for such Christian thinkers as Augustine, Tertullian, Aquinas, and Luther.

Intimate non-sexual friendship, too, had been celebrated since antiquity, often as the highest and most precious of human relationships. The poetry of friendship is less extensive than erotic lyric, but there are some distinguished classical examples, in particular some of the epistles of Horace and the epigrams of Martial. Seventeenth-century poets contributed enthusiastically to this form of writing as well. While sexual love was generally imagined as sudden, inexplicable, irrational, and all-consuming—'whoever loved that loved not at first sight?', as Christopher Marlowe put it—friendship was supposed to be founded on good judgement and the intuition of spiritual likeness. However, the boundary between the two categories could be blurry. In early modern English, the word 'lover' could refer to anything from a distant well-wisher to an intimate bed companion (and, for that matter, women routinely shared beds with women, and men with men, without any sexual implications.) One's 'friends' included one's neighbours and kin, especially the latter, but 'friend' could also be a euphemism for a sexual partner outside of marriage. The ambiguity of the terms might well have afforded strategic vagueness, in a period that criminalized extramarital heterosexual relationships as well as same-sex physical intercourse. Yet for the early moderns, the line between erotic and platonic association may actually have been indistinct, or at least drawn differently than it has been in recent centuries.[43] Moreover, an ideal of companionate marriage, introduced by Reformation thinkers but much elaborated during this period, has the effect of further blurring the boundaries between sexual and nonsexual love.

The connections between intimate relationships and more explicitly political obligations and alliances were complex. As we have seen, the language of orderly hierarchy was pervasive in the period, though often fractured by competing priorities. Some close relationships could easily be described in terms of allegiance and obligation. As noted, dependents or would-be dependents, including writers in need of support, often sought patronage using the rhetoric of friendship. And political relationships, such as the bond between ruler and subject, were routinely imagined in terms of mutual love and heterosexual congress. These equivalences could go both

---

[43] Early modern same-sex friendship among men, and its entanglement with sexuality, has received extensive discussion, especially from Alan Bray, *Homosexuality in Renaissance England* and *The Friend*; Bruce R. Smith, *Homosexual Desire in Shakespeare's England*; Jonathan Goldberg, *Sodometries: Renaissance Texts, Modern Sexualities*; Stephen Orgel, *The Impersonations of Gender in Shakespeare's England*; Laurie Shannon, *Sovereign Amity: Figures of Friendship in Shakespearean Contexts*. For female love and friendship, see Harriette Andreadis, *Sappho in Early Modern England: Female Same-Sex Literary Erotics* and Valerie Traub, *The Renaissance of Lesbianism in Early Modern England*.

ways: while James I imagines the king–subject relationship metaphorically as a sexual union, Donne's 'Going To Bed' characterizes the woman as the male speaker's 'kingdom, safeliest when with one man manned' (28). But, in other cases, one-on-one relationships seemed to defy the usual pecking order. Men were legally women's superiors in marriage, the state, and the church, but the conventions of courtship typically cast the man as supplicant, and the woman a ruler or goddess whose power over her admirer was arbitrary and absolute. In *Amoretti* (1594), Spenser writes:

> The sovereign beauty which I do admire,
> Witness the world how worthy to be praised:
> The light whereof hath kindled heavenly fire
> In my frail spirit, by her from baseness raised;
> That being now with her huge brightness dazed,
> Base thing I can no more endure to view;
> But looking still on her, I stand amazed
> At wondrous sight of so celestial hue.
>
> (3.1–8)

In the reign of Elizabeth, when the actual ruler was biologically female, the political aspirations of striving courtiers allegorized easily as a form of ardent wooing.[44] But after 1603, the relationship of subject to ruler was harder to describe in terms of heterosexual courtship. And sometimes the 'private', unshared quality of exclusive friendships or romantic attachments seemed to offer an escape from the public, political world, not merely an inversion or duplication of it. For John Donne, the bedroom often figures as a refuge: from the demands of daytime business in 'The Sun Rising', from colleagues advising him to get rich, or become learned, or climb the ladder of ambition in 'The Canonization'. To be sure, the 'little world' created by Donne's lovers may end up replicating the power dynamics from which they attempt to exempt themselves. Still, here and elsewhere there is a note of solace, understandable in the case of a poet whose recklessly passionate marriage was, in worldly terms, a disastrous misstep. Later in the century the defeated royalists, in a similar compensatory move, tried to substitute a tight society of supportive likeminded colleagues for the larger society from which

---

[44] Arthur Marotti, 'Love is not Love: Elizabethan Sonnet Sequences and the Social Order', *ELH* 49 (1982): 396–428. See also Peter Stallybrass and Ann Rosalind Jones, 'The Politics of Astrophel and Stella', *SEL* 24 (1984): 53–68. Melissa Sanchez, in *Erotic Subjects: The Sexuality of Politics in Early Modern Literature*, points out that not only can love language be a screen for political ambition, but also that political relationships are often eroticized in the period, so that the metaphorical equivalence can work both ways.

they now found themselves excluded. So, while in some cases the intimate relationship duplicates—or provides a pattern for—the same principles that seem operative elsewhere, in other cases it potentially offers a quasi-utopian alternative.

'In early modern England', writes Arthur Marotti, 'lyric poetry was a literary form that was basically regarded as occasional and ephemeral . . . a poet's family, friends, and social contacts were the proper recipients of what he or she wrote'.[45] And, even more than other lyric genres, love poetry offers itself as personal communication, making the question of audience especially complicated. Some intimate poems may at least ostensibly be written for an audience of one—the beloved—or even merely for the poet him- or herself, as a means to process complicated feelings. Other such poems are either addressed to, or intended to be 'overheard' by, third parties. But even in the latter cases, the group of imagined readers might be a restricted one, a social group to which the poet him- or herself belonged. In the early part of the seventeenth century most love poems circulated in manuscript within social circles at court, among members of extended families, among groups of young men at the Inns of Court, or in the literary 'clubs' that began to flourish in the early decades of the seventeenth century. If the purpose of a love poem was to communicate affection, desire, or admiration from one individual to another—or even to describe such sentiments for a circle of close acquaintances—there was no urgent reason to have it printed. Printing would merely make the poems available to a wider, but presumably uncomprehending, audience, an audience who may have appreciated the lyrics for their literary merit but would not be able to match them back to whatever social originals may have inspired them.

The fact that the readership for many love poems was initially limited, and that readers and poets moved in the same social circles, doubtless affected how the poems were written and, as a result, how we are now able to read them. The original readers of such poems presumably possessed a good deal of contextual information that is now lost to us. The habit of manuscript transmission also complicates our ability to understand the development of a literary tradition, because it is often unclear who had access to what, and when. Eventually, a good deal of early modern love poetry did find its way into print, but often long after the date of composition, and often in versions markedly different from those that still

---

[45] Marotti, *The Circulation of Poetry in Manuscript in Early Modern England*, p. 1.

survive in manuscript copies. As a result, the chronological difficulties that complicate a good deal of Elizabethan and Jacobean literary history are especially marked in the case of love poems. Shakespeare's collected sonnets, for instance, were printed in 1609, but Francis Meres remarked in 1598 that his 'sugared sonnets' were already circulating 'among his private friends'. A poetic anthology, *The Passionate Pilgrim*, printed in 1599 / 1600, includes alternate versions of Sonnets 138 and 144. Donne's collected poems were first printed posthumously in 1633—a second, expanded edition appeared in 1635—but much of his erotic verse was doubtless written much earlier. According to William Drummond, in 1618 Jonson opined that Donne had 'written all his best pieces ere he was twenty-five years old'[46]—that is, by 1597. Occasionally biographers are able to link poems to known events in Donne's life, but in many cases the dating of individual lyrics remains conjectural.

As is the case with other genres, over the course of the early seventeenth century print gradually became a default method of dissemination. Poets in the 1640s and 1650s were much more likely than their forebears to collect their work for publication and see it into print. Even in these cases, however, individual poems can be impossible to date. Robert Herrick's *Hesperides* was printed under his supervision in 1648, but the volume includes several decades of work, and we are not sure how extensively or to whom the poems circulated in manuscript beforehand. Lyrics written in the 1650s show up for the first time in the posthumous printing of *Poems by the Most Deservedly Admired Katherine Philips, the Matchless Orinda* (1667) and Andrew Marvell's *Miscellaneous Poems* (1681).

A consequence of this delay between writing and print publication is that the borders between 'Elizabethan', 'Jacobean', and 'Caroline' poetry, already blurry, become even more blurry in the case of these lyric forms. Yet despite all these difficulties in understanding how the poetry of love and friendship evolved over the first decades of the seventeenth century, it is still possible to describe a tradition. There are clear differences between the work that appears early in the century and the poetry, several decades later, of a new generation of writers.

---

[46] *Informations to William Drummond of Hawthornden*, lines 82–83, ed. Ian Donaldson, in *The Cambridge Edition of the Works of Ben Jonson*, vol. 5, ed. David Bevington, Martin Butler, Ian Donaldson, et al.

'Jacobean' Love Poetry

In late sixteenth-century England, the quintessential 'love poem' was the sonnet, a fourteen-line form invented 300 years earlier in Italy and developed over the following century by Dante in *La Vita Nuova* (1294) and Petrarch in *Canzoniere* (1327–1368). Petrarch's sonnet sequence to his beloved Laura became especially popular and inspired imitations in many vernacular languages. The compression of an individual sonnet, which captures a short burst of thought or emotion, resonates in intriguing ways with the logic of a sequence, which strings these fleeting moments of desire, ecstasy, and despair into implicitly narrative form. Over the course of the sonnet sequence the poet celebrates the perfections of the beloved while, at the same time, examining the vagaries of his own yearning: the sonnet thus becomes a vehicle for introspection and philosophical reflection, as well as a memorandum to the beloved.[47]

Yet, despite the pan-European popularity of Petrarch's example, it was not until the 1530s that a few sonnets were translated from Italian or written in English from scratch by Thomas Wyatt and Henry Surrey. And the creation of a full-fledged sequence of love sonnets had to wait until the 1580s, when Philip Sidney composed *Astrophil and Stella*, a fictionalized account of his unsuccessful wooing of the court beauty, Penelope Rich. After its printing in 1591, sonnet sequences by Edmund Spenser, Barnaby Barnes, Samuel Daniel, Giles Fletcher, Thomas Lodge, and others quickly followed. All these sequences conformed to the plot principles of their Italian prototypes, chronicling the ups and downs of a single monogamous, even obsessive relationship, whether happy or (more usually) unhappy. The relationship could be real, semi-fictional, or entirely imaginary, but the names of actual persons were typically concealed under sometimes-diaphanous pseudonyms. And the lack of biographical specificity was not merely due to discretion. As Rebecca Rush argues, the sonnet tradition is one that, by simultaneously celebrating the irreplaceable individuality of the beloved and the universality of the love experience, tends to render the beloved as a 'thin person'

---

[47] Paul Oppenheimer, *The Birth of the Modern Mind: Self, Consciousness, and the Invention of the Sonnet*, goes so far as to argue that sonnet-writing marks the birth of subjectivity.

whose significance resides purely in his or her relation to the speaker of the poem.[48]

Two distinguished sonnets sequences first saw print in the Jacobean period. *Shakespeare's Sonnets. Never Before Imprinted* appeared in 1609, and Mary Wroth's *Pamphilia to Amphilanthus* was bound with her romance *Urania* in 1621. By this time the vogue for such sequences was waning but, as already mentioned, many of the poems in Shakespeare's collection were likely composed considerably earlier. For her part, Mary Wroth was self-consciously backward-looking, fashioning herself as the literary heir of her famous uncle and aunt, Philip and Mary Sidney. Her father, Robert Sidney, had also composed an incomplete sonnet sequence which could have served as a model.

The collection of Shakespeare's sonnets, which may or may not have been printed with his permission, consists of 154 poems. The first group in the sequence encourage a beautiful young man to marry. By producing a child, the poet asserts, the young man will be able to perpetuate his magnificence in the next generation, consoling himself as he ages by contemplating his own younger self in his son. There is little attention to the prospective emotional or physical pleasures of marriage; the bride is metaphorically merely ploughland from whom a child might potentially be harvested: 'Where is she so fair whose uneared womb / Disdains the tillage of thy husbandry?' (3.5–6). But by Sonnet 18, the speaker discards his role as counsellor and presents himself as a lover. Now the young man's beauty will be immortalized not by an heir but by the poet, whose verse will last forever, or at least 'so long as men can breathe, or eyes can see' (18.13). The next 110 sonnets apparently portray one side of an emotionally intense friendship between the speaker and his glamorous beloved, who is seemingly younger and of higher social standing. The speaker's initial flush of idealized adoration is superseded by repeated disappointments, as the young man entertains a 'rival poet' and apparently seduces the speaker's female partner. Despite these setbacks, the speaker never relinquishes his attachment. Eventually, in Sonnet 127, the sequence swerves to describe a different relationship with an unconventionally beautiful, apparently unprincipled woman whom the sonnet speaker, despite his better

---

[48] Rebecca Rush, 'Like Alcestis: Milton's Twenty-Third Sonnet and Lyric Personhood', *Milton Studies* 64 (2022): 173–199.

judgement, finds sexually irresistible. Several poems in this latter series, too, bitterly berate both the young man and the 'dark lady' when the speaker suspects, or realizes, that they have undertaken a sexual relationship with one another, a relationship which the speaker experiences as a double betrayal.

Shakespeare's sonnet collection seems not to have made much of an impression immediately following its publication, but it has received an enormous amount of critical scrutiny in the centuries since, as its author became established in retrospect as the pre-eminent writer in Renaissance England. Because sonnets are composed in the first person, and because the implied narrative of *Shakespeare's Sonnets* is complex and distinctive, many readers have tried to read the volume as a quasi-memoir. A great deal of Shakespeare sonnet commentary has entailed attempts to identify the poems' personalities—the fair young man, the dark lady, the rival poet— to speculate on the author's sexual orientation, and to wonder whether the dark lady is possibly of African descent or merely a brunette in a culture that prized blonde women with pale skin. Not surprisingly, these biographical efforts have been inconclusive and contested. We have no way of knowing whether the sonnets record Shakespeare's actual experience. Nor can we be sure that the order of the sonnets as printed was prescribed by their author—while some adjacent poems are clearly connected as part of a mini-series, others seem possibly out of place.[49] But if the order of the poems is not authorial, then the narrative it suggests is questionable, and the many individual sonnets that fail to specify the gender of their addressee do not necessarily refer, as their context in the sequence suggests, specifically to the young male friend or to the dark woman. Moreover, to the extent that scholarship has been able to date the sonnets, it has cut against the idea that the sequence portrays a chronological series of events. Stylometric analysis suggests that the sonnets were not printed in the order of their composition, but that the 'dark lady' sonnets, which appear late in the sequence, were the first to be written.[50] David Schalwyck has aptly compared the reading experience of Shakespeare's sonnets to looking through photo albums of a family one does not know: faces recur, relationships are suggested, but without sufficient context it is hard to understand what may have happened, when,

---

[49] For a detailed account of the issues, see Brent Stirling, *The Shakespeare Sonnet Order: Poems and Groups*. See also Heather Dubrow, '"Incertainties Now Crown Themselves Assur'd": The Politics of Plotting in Shakespeare's Sonnets', *Shakespeare Quarterly* 47 (1996): 291–305.

[50] Colin Burrow summarizes the research to date in his edition of *Shakespeare's Sonnets and Poems*, pp. 103–106. The most rigorous uses of stylometric analysis to date of the composition of the sonnets is MacDonald P. Jackson, 'Vocabulary and Chronology: The Case of Shakespeare's Sonnets', *Review of English Studies* 52 (2001): 59–75.

and in what order.[51] Our ignorance about the social matrix in which the sonnets were written—not only their addressees, but the group of 'private friends' among whom they originally circulated—prevents us from learning anything definite from them about events and liaisons in Shakespeare's life.

These lacunae do not, however, entirely eliminate the sonnet sequence's biographical salience. Whether or not the poems refer to 'actual' people or 'actual' events, they certainly indicate some of their author's characteristic preoccupations. Thus, for instance, the sonnets are silent on whether the speaker's passionate attachment to the young man is sexual or platonic. But surely nobody goes to the trouble of writing more than 100 finely crafted poems on this topic unless the issue of same-sex love, however defined, matters deeply to him. Several of the most insightful readers of the sonnets have productively explored them by connecting them to similar preoccupations in the plays. Paul Edmondson and Stanley Wells claim that 'the Sonnets can soon seem like a collection of fourteen-line monologues, compressed character studies which, in the plays, are given fuller dramatic development'.[52] David Schalwyck argues that the performance values of theatre pervade Shakespeare's sonnet technique, even while the situations depicted in the sonnet sequence, possibly drawn from experience, likely inform his dramatic practice. Some plot points obviously recur. The emotional dynamic between an enamoured older man and an alluring, possibly heedless younger man is variously explored in the relationship between Prince Henry and Falstaff in the *Henry IV* plays, in the relationship between Antonio and Bassanio in *The Merchant of Venice*, and in the relationship between Antonio and Sebastian in *Twelfth Night*. Shakespeare's Egyptian queen Cleopatra, 'wrinkled deep in time', 'black', unscrupulous, sexually imaginative, and irresistible, seems possibly a version of the sonnets' 'dark lady'. *Two Gentlemen of Verona* at the beginning of Shakespeare's career, and *Two Noble Kinsman* at the end, each features a love triangle involving two male friends and a woman they both desire.

Throughout the sonnet collection, and in particular in the poems addressed to the young man, the speaker attempts to assert that love produces something enduring despite the ephemerality of beauty and the brevity of human life. In the early poems in the sequence, the hope of permanence is embodied by the prospective child, who will renew the beauty of

---

[51] David Schalwyck, *Speech and Performance in Shakespeare's Sonnets and Plays*, p. 27.
[52] Paul Edmondson and Stanley Wells, *Shakespeare's Sonnets*, p. 101. David Schalkwyck provides a more detailed discussion of the ways in which the sonnets rehearse some of the same preoccupations as the plays.

the father in the next generation. Later sonnets suggest that the poems themselves will confer a kind of immortality, by projecting the representation of the beloved into the consciousness of future readers. A preoccupation with time and its passage is not unique to Shakespeare, but the particular twists of his thinking are distinctive. It is striking, for instance, how scrupulously the sonnets avoid two routine ways in which early modern poets address the anxieties of evanescence. Many classical and early modern love poets write poems in which an awareness of decay encourages the enjoyment of pleasure in the fleeting present. The name of the convention, *carpe diem*, comes from one of Horace's odes, and Catullus' poems in this vein were much imitated by early modern writers, including Marlowe and Jonson. Shakespeare, too, writes such lyrics: in *Twelfth Night*, Feste sings

> What is love? Tis not hereafter,
> Present mirth hath present laughter,
>   What's to come is still unsure.
> In delay there lies no plenty,
> Then come kiss me, sweet and twenty,
>   Youth's a stuff will not endure.
>
> (2.3.43–48)

Yet the sonnets never sound this note. Instead, they privilege dogged constancy over the acceptance, even the enjoyment, of flux. In Sonnet 116, 'Love is not love / Which alters when it alteration finds': it is 'an ever-fixed mark / That looks on tempests and is never shaken' (5–6). At the same time, the persistency imagined in Shakespeare's sonnets is a decidedly this-worldly matter. For many religious poets, including Herbert and Donne, a recognition of the brevity of life, youth, health, and happiness spurs a search for something more permanent. In Herbert's 'The Flower', for instance, the heartbreaking mutability of mood and fortune leads the poet to crave an alternative: 'O that I once past changing were / Fast in thy Paradise, where no flower can wither!' (22–23) We learn that 'we are but flowers that glide', Herbert concludes, so that we will appreciate God's solution to the dilemma: 'thou hast a garden for us where to bide', a heaven beyond time and death. In 'The Canonization', Donne imagines himself and his beloved as saints of love, venerated by future lovers who pray to them for guidance. Shakespeare's sonnets, by contrast, rather rigorously eschew reference points outside secular, human time. Even the extravagant assertions of Sonnet 116 do not imagine a realm beyond the ravages of time. Love, the sonnet declares, 'alters not with [Time's] brief hours and weeks / But bears it out even to the edge of doom' (12). And presumably, no farther. What is promised the youth, therefore, is not personal immortality but memorialization. In Sonnet 106, the speaker reads old poetry, 'the chronicle of wasted time', and finds there 'descriptions of the fairest wights / And beauty making beautiful old rhyme' (2–3). These records of now-defunct beauty prefigure the splendour, in the present moment, of the beloved. But the beloved is himself doomed to die and be remembered, as Shakespeare's poems that celebrate him themselves become 'chronicles of wasted time' in their turn.

This fixation on the persistence of love in secular time means that Shakespeare's speaker is fascinated not merely by *la longue durée*—'now till doomsday'—but by smaller intervals as well—the space of a few days, a few years, a single lifetime. Again and again the sonnets consider ways in which an awareness of the past might condition one's thoughts and actions in the present. In Sonnet 30, the speaker reflects on the things and people he has lost:

> Then can I drown an eye unused to flow
> For precious friends hid in death's dateless night
> And weep afresh love's long since cancelled woe,
> And moan th'expense of many a vanished sight.
>   (5–8)

His only consolation is his relationship to the friend, which 'restores' the losses and ends his sorrows. In the next sonnet he expands upon this thought: the present relationship surpasses his previous ones by, in a sense, including them: 'Thou art the grave where buried love doth live, / Hung with the trophies of my lovers gone . . . Their images I loved I view in thee, / And thou, all they, hath all the all of me' (31.9–14). Sonnet 120 describes a situation in which the speaker has hurt his friend but is able to empathize with the friend's suffering because the friend has previously hurt him; he ends the poem hoping that he will be forgiven as he has forgiven the friend in the past. Other sonnets anxiously anticipate scenarios in which things will or might happen: absence, abandonment, ageing, death. 'These poems', as Colin Burrow writes, 'are preoccupied with the future and with how they will be read. . . . they reflect on death, decay, the 'millioned accidents' (115.5) of time, on what would happen to the young man or his estate if he were to die without issue.'[53] In Sonnet 49 the speaker prepares himself emotionally to be cast off. 'Against that time, if ever that time come, / When I shall see thee frown on my defects' (1–2), he tells himself that he never deserved the friend's love in the first place, so cannot complain of being discarded. In Sonnet 81 the speaker wonders whether he or the friend will die first: 'Or I shall live your epitaph to make, / Or you survive when I in earth am rotten' (1–2). This restless preoccupation with potential futures seems of a piece with Shakespeare's interest in strategic thinking as it manifests in his plays. His successful rulers are those who know when to strike and when to wait, who cannot necessarily control events but can nonetheless devise ways of bending time to their advantage. Thus, Prince Harry in the *Henry IV* plays deftly manages his public self-presentation, 'redeeming time when men least think I will' (1.2.195). The Duke in *Measure for Measure* plots both to clean up Vienna and to test Angelo's virtue, and improvises successfully when his initial plans do not play out as expected. Prospero in *The Tempest* knows precisely when to seize the opportunity: 'by my prescience / I find my zenith doth depend upon / A most auspicious star' (1.2.181–83). Still, the sonnet's constant playing with scenarios of mutability and loss sorts oddly, of course, with the claim that love is settled and unchangeable. One suspects that the sonnet speaker insists that 'love does not alter when it alteration finds' not because it is flatly true, but, on the contrary, because it is often false.

To the extent that the sonnets' declaration of love's unshakeable permanence comes across as compensatory or defiant, their 'meaning' includes not merely what is being directly asserted but something that is almost its opposite. In other words, many of the sonnets seem to be making two claims at once: the ostensible claim, and one that subverts it. There is a similar doubleness in the speaker's own self-presentation. Shakespeare inherits from his sonneteer predecessors a penchant for insisting upon his abjection in the presence of the idealized beloved. In the young man sonnets, this conviction of unworthiness is rooted in the implication that the speaker is older and of lower social station, and possibly debased by his theatrical profession. Yet in Shakespeare and in other sonneteers this self-abasement tends to have a passive-aggressive quality, the protestation of disability belied by the evident skill and intelligence with which it is argued. In Shakespeare's young man sonnets this dynamic is particularly pronounced:

---

[53] Colin Burrow, 'Shakespeare's Sonnets as Event', *The Sonnets: The State of Play*, ed. Hannah Crawforth, Elizabeth Scott-Baumann, and Clare Whitehead, p.102.

> Being your slave, what should I do but tend
> Upon the hours and times of your desire?
> I have no precious time at all to spend,
> Nor services to do, till you require;
> Nor dare I chide the world-without-end hour
> Whilst I, my sovereign, watch the clock for you,
> Nor think the bitterness of absence sour
> When you have bid your servant once adieu.
> Nor dare I question with my jealous thought
> Where you may be, or your affairs suppose,
> But like a sad slave stay and think of naught
> Save, where you are, how happy you make those.
> So true a fool is love that in your will,
> Though you do anything, he thinks no ill.
> (57.1–14)

It is hard to take this sonnet—or the one that follows it, which makes a similar extravagant claim of self-annihilation in the face of the beloved's agency—entirely at face value. By claiming that he has no right to accuse the young man of neglecting him, he is of course making exactly that accusation. Similarly, Sonnet 87 begins 'Farewell—thou art too dear for my possessing / And like enough thou knows't thy estimate' (1–2). 'Dear', which means both 'beloved' and 'costly', suggests both the intensity of the speaker's attachment and the possibly inflated self-esteem of the young man, as he coolly surveys his prospects and decides he might do better elsewhere. What seems to be subservience turns into its opposite: a bid to be noticed and an implicit condemnation of the shallowness of the beloved—the 'unfriendly Friend', as Heather Dubrow calls him[54]—for failing to appreciate the depth of the speaker's commitment. Finally, as Arthur Marotti argues, 'recognizing that the young man is really uneducable, morally obtuse, and generally unworthy . . . the poet discovers he is engaging in self-praise . . . celebrating a love whose constancy, growth, and worth exist in himself rather than in a beloved friend'.[55]

If the 'young man' sonnets explore the closeness—indeed, in some cases, indistinguishability—of self-abasement and self-promotion, the 'dark lady'

---

[54] Heather Dubrow, *Captive Victors: Shakespeare's Narrative Poems and Sonnets*, p. 190.
[55] Marotti, 'Love is not Love', p. 412.

sonnets elaborate upon a similarly disturbing proximity of desire and revulsion. While the typical Petrarchan mistress is chaste and unattainable, the 'dark lady' is anything but: she is 'the wide world's common place', 'the bay where all men ride'—available not only to the poet but to, apparently, anybody, including the cherished young man. The rhetoric of praise and blame, as Heather Dubrow observes, though typically imagined as opposites, thus collapse into one another in Shakespeare's sonnets: in the 'young man' sonnets because the friend often seems to fall short of lover's idealized image of him; in the 'dark lady' sonnets because the speaker finds himself compulsively attracted to exactly those traits he condemns and despises. It is this feature of the sonnets which is so reminiscent of the technique in Shakespeare's plays, in which the soliloquies, especially, often reveal facets of their speakers' character of which the speakers themselves seem only partially aware.

Mary Wroth probably wrote her collection of sonnets, *Pamphilia to Amphilanthus*, early in the second decade of the seventeenth century. It exists in two versions: a manuscript in Wroth's handwriting, consisting of 105 sonnets, and a collection of 83 sonnets printed together at the back of her 1621 romance *Urania*. *Urania* also includes 19 additional sonnets interpolated into the narrative, and Wroth incorporated several more into her continuation of *Urania*, which remained in manuscript until 1999. There are significant differences between some of the poems as they appear in the manuscript and in the printed version, suggesting considerable authorial revision. *Urania* is itself an allegory of Wroth's troubled relationship with her cousin, William Herbert, and the poems appear in the romance as the work of her heroine and avatar, Pamphilia. Thus, the collection asks to be read both in terms of the romance and in terms of Wroth's personal life. Yet *Pamphlia to Amphilanthus* does not have an obvious narrative trajectory and may well not have been designed that way: in the manuscript, it consists of groups of poems of varying size, interspersed with multi-stanza pastoral songs.[56] Often these groups experiment with formal devices: for instance, a group of fourteen sonnets late in the sequence comprise a 'corona' or set of

---

[56] For a detailed discussion of the ordering of the sonnets and the relationship between manuscript and print versions of *Pamphilia to Amphilanthus*, see Gavin Alexander, 'Constant Works: A Framework for Reading Mary Wroth', *Sidney Journal* 14 (1996–97): 5–32; Heather Dubrow, '"And Thus Leave Off": Reevaluating Mary Wroth's Folger Manuscript, V.a.104', *Tulsa Studies in Women's Literature* 22 (2003): 273–291; and Ilona Bell, 'Joy's Sports: The Unexpurgated Text of Wroth's *Pamphilia to Amphilanthus*', *Modern Philology* 111 (2013): 231–252.

linked sonnets, in which the last line of the previous sonnet is the first line of the next one.

Pamphilia to Amphilanthus flips the script on the 'standard' sonnet sequence, for the desiring, speaking lover now is female and the silent, remote, generally absent beloved is male—or, at least, is designated as male in the romance and in the title of the collection. For the poems themselves deal less with the depiction of a relationship than with the speaker struggling with uninvited emotions, often personified as the love-gods Cupid and Venus. The loving speaker, once afflicted, is obliged to remain constant even in the face of the beloved's faithlessness or inattention.

> Ah! How unkindness moves within the heart
> Which still is true, and free from changing thought
> What unknown woe it breeds; what endless smart
> With ceaseless tears which causelessly are wrought.
> (Sonnet 8, 5–8).

Of course the self-divided, tormented speaker, for whom love for an unresponsive beloved is simultaneously ecstatic and agonizing, is a well-worn Petrarchan convention; so is the conception of love as an irresistible force, victimizing the lover:

> My pain, still smothered in my grieved breast
> Seeks for some ease, yet cannot passage find
> To be discharged of this unwelcome guest;
> When most I strive, more fast his burdens bind,
> Like to a ship, on Goodwins cast by wind
> The more she strives, more deep in sand is pressed
> Till she be lost; so am I, in this kind
> Sunk, and devoured, and swallowed by unrest.
> (Sonnet 6, 1–8)

Yet even in this tradition, Wroth's sonnets are unusually inward-looking, more attuned to herself than focused upon a beloved, circling back again and again to the same problematic. In the 'Crown of Sonnets Dedicated to Love', for instance, the speaker begins in a 'labyrinth' of love, uncertain where to turn, but then, like Theseus seeking a way out of the Cretan labyrinth with the help of Ariadne, she discovers a 'thread' of love that could conceivably free her. Initially, following the thread seems like a promising way forward:

its 'line straight leads unto the soul's content'. Many of the following sonnets celebrate the glories of a chaste and constant love, not least in encouraging the lover's self-awareness:

> It doth enrich the wits, and make you see
> That in yourself which you knew not before,
> Forcing you to admire such gifts should be
> Hid from your knowledge, yet in you the store.
> (Lines 9–12)

Yet—as the logic of the 'crown' demands—the progress of the sequence is eventually circular, leading back to its origin so that at the end of fourteen poems the lover finds herself repeating the opening line of the first poem, still lost and bewildered in the 'strange labyrinth', beset by fervent love and jealousy. For Jeff Masten, the repetitive, recursive dynamic of the entire collection and the often knotty syntax of the individual poems suggest Wroth's expressive dilemma: she feels compelled to speak, but she is unable to speak freely. She is constantly aware of herself not, or not only, as the 'gazer' conventionally gendered as male, but as a subject of scrutiny aware that she is being watched, and hence of the necessity for circumspection. 'Take heed mine eyes, how you your looks do cast / Lest they betray my heart's most secret thought', she tells herself in Sonnet 34 (1–2). While she must write in order to establish her own poetic agency—otherwise, of course, there would be no poems—as soon as she does she enmeshes herself into the male-directed system of 'trafficking' which designates her not as a subject or speaker, but as an item of merchandise.[57] Even apart from the difficulties of writing in a masculinist Petrarchan tradition that would silence her, however, the practical complications of Wroth's situation are obvious. Her passion for her married cousin was a semi-concealed scandal, and publishing these poems indicates, as Line Cottegnies remarks, 'a

---

[57] Jeffrey Masten, '"Shall I turne blabbe?": Circulation, Gender, and Subjectivity in Mary Wroth's Sonnets', *Reading Mary Wroth: Representing Alternatives in Early Modern England*, ed. Naomi Miller and Gary Waller, pp. 67–87. Waller much expands on Masten's observation, connecting the gender politics of the poems to Wroth's position in the Sidney family, in *The Sidney Family Romance: Mary Wroth, William Herbert, and the Early Modern Construction of Gender*, esp. 95–131 and 191–220. See also Maureen Quilligan, 'The Constant Subject: Instability and Authority in Wroth's *Urania* Poems', in *Soliciting Interpretation: Literary Theory and Seventeenth-Century English Poetry*, ed. Elizabeth Harvey and Katharine Eisaman Maus, pp. 307–335.

certain social recklessness'[58] even if she did not entirely anticipate the furore that the printing of the romance and its attached sonnet collection would provoke among the courtier class. No wonder that Wroth feels torn by the simultaneous need to speak and to conceal speech, to guard her yearnings even while she describes them in detail. By the end of the sequence, however, even as Pamphilia declares herself done with writing love poetry, her continued commitment to faithfulness in love remains as an unshakeable element of personal integrity: 'Now let your constancy your honour prove', she tells herself. Such constancy and honour are entirely private matters, unconnected to her sexual reputation, to the beloved's reciprocation of her love, or to any institutional or familial framework for her emotional life.

After Wroth, nobody in the period attempts a sonnet sequence on the Elizabethan model, but the sonnet form itself remains available for other purposes. John Donne writes devotional sonnets, as we have seen, and John Milton one-off sonnets on an extraordinary range of topics, including his belligerent reaction to the reception of his divorce tracts, his outrage at a religious massacre in Italy, his dismay at his blindness, and his reflections upon his poetic vocation. But one of Milton's later sonnets, written in 1658 after the death of his second wife, Katherine Woodcock,[59] revives some of the traditional concerns of the love sonnet in a strikingly different context. 'Methought I saw my late espoused saint', the poet begins; he dreams of his recently deceased wife visiting his bedside, dressed 'all in white, pure as her mind':

> Her face was veiled, yet to my fancied sight
> Love, sweetness, goodness, in her person shined
> So clear as in no face with more delight.
> 							(Sonnet 23, 9–12)

As she leans to embrace him, however, his dream vanishes: 'I waked, she fled, and day brought back my night' (14). In this short poem Milton

---

[58] Line Cottegnies, 'The Sapphic Context of Lady Mary Wroth's *Pamphilia to Amphilanthus*', *Early Modern Women and the Poem*, ed. Susan Wiseman, p. 62.

[59] Some critics have argued that the poem may have been written in memory of Milton's first wife, Mary Powell, who died in 1652, rather than his second wife, Katherine Woodcock. Given the apparent unhappiness of his first marriage and the probable date of the poem, I find such arguments unconvincing. But see Rebecca Rush, 'Like Alcestis: Milton's Twenty-Third Sonnet and Lyric Personhood.' *Milton Studies* 64, no. 2 (2022): 173–199, for a discussion of the poem's strategic ambiguities.

juxtaposes a fleeting, incomplete glimpse of a wished-for heavenly reunion with the darkness of quotidian existence. The notion that dreams are a gateway to an otherwise-inaccessible transcendent realm is a very old one. Yet Milton's circumstances give the convention special poignancy. Happiness seems only accessible in a dream; the daylight, waking world is a dark and grieving one. Moreover, Milton had gone blind in middle age, several years before marrying Katherine, so that not just the woman but the seeing itself is chimerical. The phrase 'fancied sight', in other words, refers both to the dream illusion, and to a memory of a lost faculty, as irrecoverable as Milton's dead wife. She comes veiled in his dream because, in life, he would in fact have never seen her face.

Though John Donne's love poems are eventually collected, in the second posthumous edition of his poems, under the title 'Songs and Sonnets', only one of them is a sonnet in the formal sense. Nor do they at all conform, emotionally, to the patterns established by the Petrarchan tradition—even in the unconventional ways in which Shakespeare and Wroth channel and challenge that tradition. Donne's earliest surviving poems, written while he was a student at the Inns of Court in the mid-1590s, are satires on the corruption and hypocrisy of the urban and court worlds, which both fascinate and repel him. By importing the wittily colloquial language, rough rhythms, and abrupt forms of address generally thought appropriate to satiric writing into the apparently alien domain of love poetry, Donne creates an effect of startling immediacy. The innovative migration of style has an intermediate stage in Donne's Elegies, some of which are also likely among his earlier compositions. Many of these poems, loosely based on the precedent of Ovid's Elegies, treat sexual topics but, as Diana Trevino Benet has persuasively argued, they are not 'love poems'. Instead, they wittily present 'topical and often social commentary' on dramatic scenes of sexual transgression and negotiation.[60] In one elegy, a man attempts to sneak into his mistress's bedroom but is detected by the woman's father because he is wearing a telltale scent. In another, a man has lost a gold chain that belongs to his mistress, and she demands that he provide twelve coins to be melted down to fashion another chain (since Elizabethan coins were made of precious metal, this practice was a common one.) In another, a sexually aroused man watches

---

[60] Diana Trevino Benet, 'Sexual Transgression in Donne's Elegies', *Modern Philology* 92 (1994): 14–35: 'The Elegies are not bizarre, misogynistic love poems. Most of them are less interested in the inner world of emotion than in the outer world of social interactions.' In the elegies Donne shares common territory with satirists concerned with gender roles and gender non-conformity.

his partner disrobe and welcomes her into his bed. In yet another, a man dissuades his mistress from disguising herself as a pageboy in order to follow him on a trip to the Continent. As a 'great frequenter of plays', Donne-the-elegist was undoubtedly influenced not only by the tradition of verse satire, to which he himself was contributing, but also by dramatists who were developing ways of elaborating vivid incidents and characters onstage. In fact, many of the Elegies are close in tone and content to the satiric city comedies that will proliferate in the Jacobean theatre only a few years later.

   As has already been noted, there is little evidence of date of composition for most of the 'Songs and Sonnets', although most editors believe that they were largely written between the late 1590s and 1615 or so. All of the poems are one-offs, imagined independently of any longer narrative scheme, and the surviving manuscript copies indicate that they circulated as individual lyrics, not as part of a series. As a group, they depict a considerable range of different kinds of erotic experience, with a variety of partners. Some poems boastfully allude to promiscuous conquests and revel in emotional detachment: 'Changed loves are but changed sorts of meat, / And when he hath the kernel eat, / Who doth not fling away the shell?' ('Community', 22–24). Others are flamboyantly misogynist: 'Hope not for mind in women; at their best / Sweetness and wit, they are but mummy possessed' ('Love's Alchemy', 23–24). The carnal preoccupations of these poems are meant to be deliberately shocking, especially when juxtaposed to the idealizing language of most contemporaneous sonnet sequences. The implicit audience, in fact, often seems not to be a beloved woman but other young men, conceived as rivals and fellow-travellers.

   Yet this cynical, even predatory tone is far from the only one struck in *Songs and Sonnets*. We have a great deal more information about Donne's life than we do about Shakespeare's, and many critics have attempted to map the variety of Donne's love poetry on to his biography. In his youth, they suggest, he wrote precociously cynical seduction poems and boasted about his sexual triumphs to his male friends. But then, in his late twenties, having embarked on a promising career as a secretary to the Lord Chancellor, Thomas Egerton, he fell deeply in love with his employer's teenage niece, Anne More. When he eloped with her in 1601, he enraged her father and, as a result of the scandal, Egerton dismissed him. Donne's rash, 'all for love' behaviour ruined his prospects for many years, but the marriage remained emotionally satisfying until Anne's death sixteen years later, shortly after giving birth to their twelfth child. So, although there is no textual evidence to associate such tender poems as 'The Good Morrow', 'The Canonization', or

'A Valediction: Forbidding Mourning' with Donne's relationship with Anne, there is also no reason not to. In these poems, like the presumably earlier ones, bodily pleasure is hardly dismissed or minimized. Chaste yearning is not this speaker's style. 'The Good Morrow' adapts the conventions of the *aubade*, or 'dawn song', to describe an awakening to this new, physically and spiritually enthralling reality: 'If ever any beauty I did see / Which I desired, and got, 'twas but a dream of thee' (6–7). He does not pretend to have been monogamous in the past—he 'got' those earlier beauties—but now, he is dazzled by a relationship of heretofore unimagined depth. 'The Exstasie' describes two lovers lying on a bank, staring into one another's eyes and sharing an uncanny, out-of-body communion.

> So to intergraft our hands, as yet
> > Was all the means to make us one
> And pictures in our eyes to get
> > Was all our propagation.
> As twixt two equal armies, Fate
> > Suspends uncertain victory,
> Our souls (which to advance their state
> > Were gone out), hung twixt her, and me.
> > > (9–16)

Despite the lovers' mind-meld, Donne argues that the body remains necessary: 'They are ours, though they are not we' (51):

> Love's mysteries in souls do grow,
> And yet the body is his book.
> > (71–72)

Consummation remains a consummation devoutly to be wished.

What holds *Songs and Sonnets* together is not a narrative of a consistent relationship, nor a repeated formal pattern, but the distinctive personality of the poet, whose prickly individuality coexists with an intense yearning for union with another. The seductiveness of this poetry is not, as it is in the sonnet tradition, in the extravagant compliments paid to the beloved or even in the insightful self-analysis of the frustrated lover, but rather in the palpable erotic charge of wit between intelligent people. In 'The Flea', for instance, the speaker attempts, via patently absurd sophistries, to get his reluctant beloved into bed with him, claiming that because the flea has bitten them both, they are already intermingled:

> Mark but this flea, and mark in this,
> How little that which thou deny'st me is;
> It sucked me first, and now sucks thee,
> And in this flea, our two bloods mingled be.
> Thou knowst that this cannot be said
> A sin, nor shame, nor loss of maidenhead.
>
>   . . .
>
> This flea is you and I, and this
> Our marriage bed, and marriage temple is.
>   (1–13)

Between stanzas, his interlocutor suggests what she thinks of this argument by crushing the flea, an action that produces an outburst of mock horror: 'Cruel and sudden, hast thou since / Purpled thy nail, in blood of innocence?' (19–20). If, in fact, the speaker succeeds in his aim it will not be because his beloved seriously believes a flea has already married them, or that the flea is really a martyr, but because she is beguiled and amused by her lover's desperate ingenuity. Often, as here, the wit of the poem is partly at the speaker's expense. In 'The Sun Rising', for instance, the speaker, reluctant to get out of bed at daybreak, orders the 'unruly' sun to go away and shine somewhere else. Of course, it is the speaker, not the sun, who is unruly—there is little in the world more predictable than sunrise—but the poem effectively conveys the massive self-absorption of a lover whose whole consciousness is dominated by postcoital contentment. 'Shine here to us', he tells the sun at the end of the poem (clearly having failed to send it elsewhere): 'This bed thy centre is, these walls, thy sphere' (29–30). Hyberbole, routine enough in love poetry, becomes an instrument of self-characterization.

Donne's poetry is famous for its unexpected imagery—what Samuel Johnson called 'a discovery of occult resemblances in things apparently unlike ... the most heterogeneous ideas are yoked by violence together'.[61] John Carey has discussed this imagery in detail, noting not merely its variety but its

---

[61] Samuel Johnson, *The Lives of the Most Eminent English Poets: With Critical Observations on their Works*, ed. Roger Lonsdale, vol. 1, p. 201.

obsessive quality—Donne returns again and again to the hardness and ductility of metal, the absorbency of sponges, the reflective properties of eyes, the features of technological paraphernalia such as maps and compasses.[62] Two poems in *Songs and Sonnets*, 'The Funeral' and 'The Relic', imagine a lover's corpse wearing a bracelet made of his beloved's hair: in 'The Funeral' the corpse is about to be buried, and in 'The Relic' it is being dug up. Some poems are centred on a striking image, or on a familiar image pursued in a surprising direction. In 'Air and Angels', Donne begins with what seems like a routine comparison of his beloved to an angel. Yet Donne's angel manifests as a mysterious presence, at first intuited only by her influence. She must assume a bodily form in order for him to recognize her fully, just as an entirely spiritual angel must assume a body made of air in order to be perceptible by human beings. Then, unexpectedly, at the end of the poem the difference between air and angels swerves: now the man's love for the woman becomes the entirely pure 'angel', while her reciprocal love for him is the slightly inferior air, 'not pure as it, yet pure' (24). What holds the poem together is less a logical argument than a fascination with two subtly different, immaterial substances, which can be told apart conceptually but not experientially.

In 1615 Donne took holy orders in the Church of England, at which point he seems to have found the more libertine of his love poems something of an embarrassment. Yet the young John Donne was deeply religious, too, and many critics have remarked upon the inextricability of his sexual and his devotional preoccupations. For John Carey, the real subject of Donne's love poetry is apostasy. Donne was brought up in a defiantly committed Roman Catholic family—his uncle, Jasper Heywood, a Jesuit who refused to renounce his religion, had been exiled for life in 1583, and his younger brother, Henry, had died in prison, charged with a felony for harbouring a priest. But by the late 1590s, after a period of evident religious turmoil, Donne had committed himself to the Church of England. Carey argues that the residual guilt about his departure from the family faith pervades Donne's repeated concern with sexual constancy:

> The love poems display . . . a profound anxiety about the permanence of human relationships, and especially about his own ability to attract or merit stable affection. They do so with a persistence which, even if we did not know about his apostasy, we should be tempted to ascribe to some

[62] John Carey, John Donne: *Life, Mind, and Art*, passim.

major rift in his personal life. What seems to happen is that Donne, in the fantasy world of the poems, rids himself of his disloyalty by transferring it to women, and directing against them the execrations which he could be seen as meriting.[63]

Both Carey and Ramie Targoff remark on the importance, to Donne, of the Christian doctrine of the 'resurrection of the body'—the idea that at the end of the world one's soul will be reunited with one's body. For Targoff, Donne's frequent poems of 'valediction' or the parting of lovers rehearse his anxieties about the imminent, if temporary, dissolution of soul and body in death.[64] Conversely, we have already seen that the Holy Sonnets imagine a relationship with God in robustly physical terms. Donne is the heir of a long tradition, deriving directly from Augustine and more remotely from Plato, which sees sexual desire and religious devotion as part of an emotional continuum, sharing the same libidinal character. The difference between the saint and the libertine, in this tradition, is in the objects they choose to adore: not whether one loves, but what one loves. Thus, in Holy Sonnet 17, Donne surmises that God killed off his beloved Anne in order to focus Donne's emotional energies more exclusively on the domain of the sacred.

Although Donne's devotional poetry, in which he sometimes imagines himself being battered, flogged, and ravished by a domineering male God, might seem rife with homoerotic masochism, his love poetry proper celebrates exclusively female partners and the joys of heterosexual coupling. However, Donne also wrote poems to his male friends. Unlike love poems, which typically obscure the identity of the beloved and deliberately blur the line between fantasy and reality, most seventeenth-century friendship poems are patently autobiographical. In Donne's case, the friendship poems are generally framed as letters to named addressees. They participate in an tradition of literary letter-writing among male friends that harks back to Cicero, Seneca, Horace, and Pliny the Younger, and which was central to the formation of humanist sociability in the European Renaissance.[65] Donne was a dedicated letter-writer throughout his life, and his poems to his

---

[63] Ibid., p. 38.
[64] Ramie Targoff, *John Donne, Body and Soul*.
[65] Claudio Guillen, 'Notes toward the Study of the Renaissance Letter', in *Renaissance Genres: Essays on Theory, History, Interpretation*, ed. Barbara Lewalski, argues that 'epistolary literature [reaches] new peaks in Europe during the sixteenth and seventeenth centuries' (p. 70).

friends generally read as versified versions of the missives he more ordinarily composed in prose.

While the love poems tend to exclude the world and prioritize a single, intense relationship with one other person, Donne's poems to his friends embrace a masculine world of current events, advice, and transactions. An early poem, 'The Storm', framed as a letter to Christopher Brooke, vividly describes Donne's experiences aboard a ship during the Earl of Essex's expedition to the Azores in 1597; the follow-up poem, 'The Calm', was most likely also imagined as a verse epistle. And whereas many of the love poems present themselves as, more or less, transcriptions of an originally face-to-face interaction or conversation, the epistolary poem is predicated upon the physical distance between friends. 'Sir, more than kisses, letters mingle souls; / For, thus friends absent speak' (1–2), writes Donne to Sir Henry Wotton. In other words, instead of a plea for, or a celebration of, physical intimacy, Donne's friendship poems enact an imaginative traversal of geographical separation via the written word.

But the real master of friendship poetry in the early seventeenth century is Ben Jonson. Jonson structures the reception of these lyrics quite differently from Shakespeare's or Donne's. When lyrics of love and friendship circulate initially in manuscript, and emerge into print without the permission of an author, they might seem fortuitously intercepted by readers other than those to whom the poems were initially addressed, read with an almost voyeuristic interest in someone else's affairs. Ben Jonson, by contrast, arranges for his work to be printed, so that although individual poems are often addressed to a specific recipient, they are unambiguously presented for public consumption. Jonson selected and ordered the two collections of poetry, *Epigrams* and *The Forest*, included in his First Folio in 1616. It was long believed that these collections were first printed in this folio, but recently some evidence has materialized of an octavo edition of the epigrams in circulation up to four years earlier.[66] Many more poems of love and friendship appeared in a 1641 collection, *The Underwood*, which was printed posthumously.

The Forest contains a number of memorable love lyrics, largely modelled on classical originals—'Drink to me only with thine eyes' borrows material from Philostratus and Catullus, and 'Come, my Celia' loosely translates Catullus' *Carmen 5*. Interestingly, the elderly Jonson seems more interested

---

[66] Tara Lyons, 'Reading a Lost Book: Ben Jonson's *Epigrammes* (c. 1612) and Disposable Authorship', *ELR* 53 (2023): 1–34.

in writing about sexual love than he was in his youth: a development evident in his late play, *The New Inn*, as well as in his short sequence in *The Underwood*, 'A Celebration of Charis in Ten Lyric Pieces'. By this time, of course, Jonson is aware that whatever his verbal dexterity, he is a physically unpromising specimen—'a tardy, cold / Unprofitable chattel, fat, and old' (7–8), as he describes himself in 'To My Lady Covell'. These relatively late poems are notable, in fact, for foregrounding how women see men, rather than vice versa. In one poem Charis lists her criteria for a lover—nobility, youth, physical beauty, valiant demeanour—but, as Jonson's editor Colin Burrow notes, the 'erotic blazon of her ideal man sadly fails to correspond to the corpulent Jonson in any detail'.[67] In general, though, Jonson is not much of an erotic poet. Unlike Donne, whose perspective is essentially Augustinian, Jonson's most important classical influences are neo-Stoic and Aristotelian. In this philosophical tradition, sex is a relatively minor part of life, and the most significant form of relationship—the proper foundation of human community—is non-sexual mutual esteem among virtuous persons.[68] Jonson's poems can be seen as reflecting upon and helping to create this community, both among his addressees and, vicariously, among his readership.

Jonson's model for his collection of epigrams was the Latin poet Martial's epigrams: short, punchy occasional poems assembled into a powerful whole that evokes and passes judgement upon a variegated social world. Jonson's epigrams praise the historian and schoolmaster William Camden; the actor Edward Alleyn; the classicist Henry Savile; the polymath lawyer John Selden; the poets John Donne and Francis Beaumont; and prominent courtiers such as William, Earl of Pembroke, Lucy, Countess of Bedford, and Sir Henry Goodere. Jonson had military experience, and several epigrams celebrate soldiers: Horace Vere and John Roe, the latter a close friend who died of the plague in Jonson's arms. A number of the epigrams to literary figures were evidently designed as prefatory verses to literary works: Joshua Sylvester's translation of du Bartas, Alfonso Ferrabosco's book of musical airs, Clement Edmondes's *Observations upon Caesar's Commentaries*. In *The Forest*, many of the addressees are members of the extended Sidney / Pembroke family, who offered Jonson patronage and hospitality during the first decade of the seventeenth century. One witty short poem, 'That Women

---

[67] *The Cambridge Edition of the Works of Ben Jonson*, ed. David Bevington, Martin Butler, Ian Donaldson, et al., vol. 7, p. 94.
[68] For a more detailed discussion of Jonson's views on friendship, sexuality, and community formation, see Katharine Eisaman Maus, *Ben Jonson and the Roman Frame of Mind*.

Are But Men's Shadows', was, Jonson told his friend Drummond, written as a 'penance' at the command of the Countess of Pembroke, after Jonson agreed with this sentiment, as expressed by her husband the Earl. Unlike most love poems, then, and even unlike Donne's poetic letters to friends, the poems in *Epigrams* and *The Forest* eschew the intense focus on an intimate dyad, evoking instead a densely networked array of acquaintance, multiply connected not only to Jonson but to one another.

Because the bonds among these friends develop from shared values, not only the merits of the friend but the character of the poet always becomes, explicitly or implicitly, one of the topics of a Jonson friendship poem. 'To Sir Henry Neville' begins with a typical self-description: 'Who now calls on thee, Neville, is a muse / That serves nor fame nor titles, but doth choose / Where virtue makes them both' (1–3). More elaborately, 'The Epistle to Katherine, Lady Aubigny' opens with a full twenty lines of self-description. Jonson is 'in love / With every virtue, wheresoe'er it move' (7–8), is 'at feud with sin and vice' (9–10), and 'though forsook / Of Fortune, have not altered yet my look / Or so myself abandoned' (15–17). 'I, madam, am become your praiser', he pronounces grandiloquently in line 21. Only such a poet is qualified to recognize 'the beauties of the mind' (44) that radiate from Lady Aubigny, and to celebrate her 'just course' (91) and 'tried manners' (112).

It was a truism that, just as jewels glittered especially brilliantly against a 'foil' or dark background, good behaviour looked even better when contrasted with its opposite. So, in Jonson's *Epigrams* as in Martial's, encomiastic poems alternate with satiric ones that amusingly or disgustedly depict vicious types under allegorical names: Court-Worm, Brain-Hardy, Groom Idiot, Poet-Ape, Sir Voluptuous Beast, Captain Hazard the Cheater, English Monsieur, Cashiered Captain Surly, Mime, Mongrel Esquire. These satiric labels suggest that while the virtuous persons are individuals, the vicious are mere types. Not only are the named people the ones who are worthy of praise, but the name itself, in a Jonson poem, often becomes a sort of fount and vessel of praise, a succinct summation of the bearer's good qualities. 'I do but name thee, Pembroke, and I find / It is an epigram on all mankind, / Against the bad, but of, and to the good' (*Epigrams* 102 1–3). In 'On the Countess of Bedford', Jonson attempts to imagine an ideal woman, 'courteous, facile, sweet', (9) with 'a learned and a manly soul' (13). But his muse simply orders him to write 'Bedford': 'and that was she' (18). In the generally longer-form lyrics in *The Forest*, Jonson achieves the effect of contrast not by juxtaposition with other poems, but by enclosing the negative exempla within the poem itself, often in its opening. Unlike the gaudy houses recently erected by the *nouveaux riches*, 'Thou art not, Penshurst, built to envious show' (1). Robert Wroth's preference for the blessings of rural life is marked by his indifference to the evanescent splendours of the court masque: 'the jewels, stuffs, the pains, the wit / There wasted, some not paid for yet!' (11–12). Elizabeth, Countess of Rutland, scorns 'that for which all virtue now is sold, / And almost every vice, almighty gold' (2–3), and values instead the inspired poet who can confer eternal fame.

'Inviting a Friend to Supper' is perhaps Jonson's most extended early-career reflection on the significance of friendship. Some critics speculate that the poem's addressee was his former teacher, William Camden, but it is surely significant that Jonson doesn't specify the addressee. For this poem deals less with the character of the friend himself than with the ceremonies of hospitality that sustain the relationship. In both pagan and Christian traditions, the dinner-party has long been imagined as one of those ceremonies. In Plato's *Symposium*, the guests discuss the nature of love during a long night of eating and drinking; at the Last Supper, Jesus inaugurates the ritual of Communion that in the future will allow the disciples to re-enact their bond with Him and with one another. The connection between corporeal and intellectual or spiritual nourishment is thus extremely close; Thomas Greene suggests that 'Inviting a Friend to Supper', which distils material from several of Martial's poems, demonstrates and celebrates not merely the communion between individuals but a similar harmonious engagement of the classical and native traditions.[69] Jonson frequently thought of such imitation as analogous to the consumption and digestion of food: in *Discoveries*, for example, he claims that the excellent poet draws from his predecessors 'not, as a creature that swallows what it takes in crude, raw, and indigested, but that ... hath a stomach to concoct, divide, and turn all to nourishment'.[70]

Although Jonson claims that it is the guest's 'fair acceptance' of an invitation, not the food on offer, that creates 'the entertainment perfect', he nonetheless promises a supper described in mouthwatering detail: olives and capers to start, followed by mutton and a hen with 'lemons, and wine for sauce', and perhaps a rabbit, followed by cheese, fruit, and sweet wine. While

---

[69] Thomas Greene, *The Light in Troy: Imitation and Discovery in Renaissance Poetry*, pp. 278–284; see also Joseph Loewenstein, 'The Jonsonian Corpulence: Or the Poet as Mouthpiece', *ELH* 53 (1986): 491–518, for an extended and sophisticated reading of 'Inviting a Friend to Supper', focusing in particular on the significance of the analogies between the nourishments of the body and the nourishments of the mind.

[70] *Timber, or Discoveries*, ed. Lorna Hutson, lines 1752–1757, in *The Cambridge Edition of the Works of Ben Jonson*, ed. David Bevington, Martin Butler, Ian Donaldson et al., vol. 7.

consuming these items freely, but in moderation, Jonson and his guests will hear a passage of some classical author read aloud, and then discuss it. Friendship thus imagined is a relationship of trust and mutual enrichment: what Jonson calls the 'liberty' of innocent enjoyment. At the same time, this atmosphere of openness is fostered not only by what it includes, but by what is kept out. Jonson's party, he notes, will 'have no Pooly or Parrott by' (36)—no government informers, in other words, of the sort that may have tried to entrap Jonson into a criminal confession during his sojourn in prison in 1598. Despite its emotional difference from Donne's or Shakespeare's passionate attachments, Jonson's pleasant dinner party holds out a similar promise of a bounded, nurturing region of escape from zones of hostility or oppression.

According to Cicero, Seneca, and other classical theorists of friendship, true friendship was free of material self-interest or a desire for gain; ''tis virtue alone, or nothing, that knits friends', as Jonson claims in 'An Epistle to Master Arthur Squib' (12). Yet the patronage system, as we have already seen, requires the poet to deploy the language of disinterested admiration in a highly strategic form, and Jonson has been faulted for representing as friendships what are fairly obviously bids for financial support.[71] Yet Jonson's need for patronage does not, of course, pre-empt genuine warmth and admiration. Moreover, as Martin Butler has demonstrated, Jonson did not always play it safe in his choice of persons to praise: many of those he admired occupied precarious or marginal positions in the Jacobean hierarchy.[72] And even when some poems may have begun as attempts to align himself with more powerful and wealthy persons, the original aim may have eventually been eclipsed. By the time the Folio *Works* appear in 1616, quite a few of the subjects and addressees of the poems in *Epigrams* and *The Forest* were dead; in the 1641 volume—itself posthumous—even more of the writers, intellectuals, and patrons celebrated therein were long gone.

Jonson wrote some of his most ambitious poems of love and friendship in the 1620s and early 1630s—that is, when he was already in his fifties or sixties. Given the demographic realities of seventeenth-century England, it is not surprising that some of the most impressive of his later friendship poems should be memorials to the departed. His prefatory poem to the 1623 Shakespeare First Folio announces itself as a friendship poem: 'To the Memory

---

[71] Stanley Fish, 'Authors-Readers: Jonson's Community of the Same', *Representations* 7 (summer 1984), p. 56.

[72] Martin Butler, '"Servant But Not Slave": Ben Jonson at the Jacobean Court', *Proceedings of the British Academy* 90 (1996): 65–93.

of My Beloved, The Author William Shakespeare, And What He Hath Left Us'. This poem shares several rhetorical moves with the lyrics in *Epigrams* and *The Forest*. It specifies the author's qualifications to praise Shakespeare before embarking upon that praise in line 16, and comments on the unique appropriateness of Shakespeare's name:

> Look how the father's face
> Lives in his issue; even so the race
> Of Shakespeare's mind and manners brightly shines
> In his well-turned and true filed lines;
> In each of which he seems to shake a lance,
> As brandished at the eyes of ignorance.
> (65–70)

Yet 'To the Memory of My Beloved' is also the first extended and nuanced assessment of Shakespeare's importance, locating him in a native and international literary and dramatic tradition and attempting to specify his unique excellences. Jonson had always been eager to locate himself in a literary tradition reaching back to ancient Greece and Rome, self-consciously modelling his authorial persona and his sense of career on classical prototypes. Here, he does the same for Shakespeare.

As Jonson grows older, too, he increasingly sees himself not merely as the recipient of a long literary tradition but as a grey eminence now responsible for conveying that tradition into the next generation. In the 1620s and early 1630s, Jonson becomes an arbiter of poetic quality and a mentor to talented younger writers who gathered in the Devil Tavern to exchange their work and discuss literary topics. These constitute a loosely affiliated group called the 'sons' or 'the tribe of Ben', semi-jocularly named after one of the twelve tribes of Israel, the descendants of the Biblical patriarch Jacob's son, Benjamin. In 'An Epistle Answering to One that Asked to be Sealed of the Tribe of Ben', Jonson distinguishes the friendships he values from those forged in drink and quarrelling or in pretences of political gamesmanship. Characteristically, he describes his model friendship by articulating his ideals for his own conduct. He metaphorically imagines human beings as clay vessels—courtly porcelain or coarser 'earthen jars'—easily chipped and broken by life's vicissitudes:

> Well, with mine own frail pitcher, what to do
> I have decreed: keep it from waves and press;

> Lest it be jostled, cracked, made naught or less;
> Live to that point I will, for which I am man,
> And dwell as in my centre as I can.
>
> ...
>
> So short you read my character, and theirs
> I would call mine.
> (54–74)

If the supplicant finds these ideals worthy and hopes to emulate them himself, if he and his friendships are 'led by reason's flame', then he is worthy to be accepted into Jonson's 'tribe'. As in his earlier work, Jonson posits a shared ethical orientation, a mutual appreciative reading of character, as the foundation of friendship.

Perhaps the most ambitious of Jonson's late friendship poems is an ode 'To The Immortal Memory and Friendship of That Noble Pair, Sir Lucius Cary and Sir Henry Morison'. In the Cary–Morison ode Jonson imports the classical 'Pindaric' form into English to console Cary for the death of his dear friend Morison, who had died of smallpox when he was only twenty. Originally designed to be sung by a chorus, a Pindaric ode consists of 'strophes', in which the singers turn or move in one direction, followed by 'antistrophes', in which they turn in the opposite direction, and then 'epodes', in which they stand still. Jonson translates these terms as 'the turn', 'the counter-turn', and 'the stand', implicitly associating the ode's brief, circling structure with the abbreviated but 'ample, full, and round' life of Morison.

> In small proportions we just beauties see,
> And in short measures life may perfect be.
> (72–73)

Yet while the poem celebrates Morison's beautiful, if abbreviated, life—'his life was of humanity the sphere' (52)—it also suggests the raggedness of loss in its daring and witty use of enjambment or run-on lines. Enjambment makes form and substance diverge: the lineation indicates a breach, while the sense suggests a continuity. When Jonson claims that Cary and Morison are 'These twi- / Lights, the Dioscuri' (93–94), John Hollander has commented, 'the meter imitates the action of death by cutting the word apart even as death divided the two men'.[73] Yet the myth of Castor and Pollux, the Dioscuri or 'double stars', complicates this reading. Although twins, Castor was the son of a mortal, while Pollux was the son of Zeus and hence immortal. After Castor's death, Pollux asked that Castor be permitted to share his own immortality, so that the two brothers could remain together. Zeus rewarded their mutual devotion by transforming the brothers into two stars in the constellation Gemini ('The Twins'). So death divides Cary and Morison as Jonson divides 'twi-light', and yet the myth implies that death may not entail a complete or permanent rupture, but perhaps instead initiate a new perpetuity. 'Twi-light' is a particularly telling word here, since in context it seems to mean 'two-light'—the double stars of Gemini—but it also means 'half-light', referring to the borderline between day and night, or life and death, when these two different, mutually exclusive states come briefly into contact. An even more daring enjambment occurs a few lines earlier, when Jonson refers to himself in a phrase that not only runs to the next line, but that overflows the stanzaic division between the 'Counter-turn' and the 'Stand'. Morison, Jonson asserts,

> leaped the present age,
> Possessed with holy rage
> To see that bright eternal day;
> Of which we priests and poets say
> Such truths as we expect for happy men,
> And there he lives with memory, and Ben.
> *The Stand*
> Jonson, who sang this of him, ere he went
> Himself to rest.
>
> (80–87)

Jonson here divides himself between 'Ben', one of the priests and poets who intuit and celebrate the glories of an eternal life after death, and 'Jonson', who, as an old man, partially paralysed by stroke, knows that he too will soon 'leap the present age' and share Morison's fate. In *The Underwood*, the break is made the more abrupt by the period mark after 'Ben', which could signify merely that the name is an abbreviation for 'Benjamin', or which could function as a full stop, the 'Ben' with whom Morison continues to live even

---

[73] John Hollander, *Vision and Resonance: Two Senses of Poetic Form*, p. 178; see also Michael McCanles, *Jonsonian Discriminations: The Humanist Poet and the Praise of True Nobility*, pp. 77–80.

in death. The poem is poignant because it not merely commemorates the mutual friendship of two young men, Cary and Morison, but because it so effectively conveys Jonson's love for both of them.

Caroline and Interregnum Poetry of Love and Friendship

By the 1630s, a new generation of poets was coming of age, though, in fact, the writers who would dominate the mid-century, and who in a few cases would continue their careers into the Restoration, were born over a forty-year period. The oldest of them were Robert Herrick, born in 1591, and Thomas Carew, born in 1595. Edmund Waller (1606), John Milton (1608), and John Suckling (1609) were born early in the reign of James I; Richard Lovelace (1617), Abraham Cowley (1618), and Andrew Marvell (1621) towards the end; Katherine Philips in 1631, well into the reign of King Charles I. Of this group, Herrick, Carew, Waller, Cowley, Suckling, Lovelace, and Philips wrote love poems that clearly owed much to the example set by their Elizabethan and Jacobean predecessors, though their work was unmistakably distinct in tone and emphasis. Meanwhile, Marvell, in a group of strikingly original poems most likely written in the early 1650s but not published until 1681, took the love lyric in a direction rather different from that of his contemporaries. Despite Marvell's example, this generation of poets, while often continuing to circulate their compositions in manuscript, was much more likely than its predecessors to be comfortable with the printing of their poetry. Thomas Carew's *Poems* (1640) was most likely posthumous, and John Suckling's *Fragmenta Aurea* (1646) was definitely so, but Milton publishes *Poems of Mr John Milton, Both English and Latin* in 1645, Cowley *The Mistress* in 1647, Herrick *Hesperides* in 1648, and Lovelace *Lucasta* in 1649.

Herrick, Carew, Suckling, Lovelace, and several of their contemporaries are often grouped together as 'cavalier poets', bound by their shared royalist politics and the supposed similarity, even indistinguishability, of their poetic aims. There is a long tradition of condescending to cavalier poetry in general, and cavalier love poetry in particular, on the grounds of its lack of individuality or ambition and what Nicholas McDowell calls its 'taste for erotic fantasy and sensual overindulgence'.[74] This dismissal manifests early

---

[74] Nicholas McDowell, 'Classical Liberty and Cavalier Poetics: The Politics of Literary Community in Caroline England', *Yearbook of English Studies* 44 (2014), p. 125.

in John Milton's *Lycidas*, written in 1637 to mourn the death of Milton's fellow student at Cambridge, Edward King. Milton contrasts himself and the learned young man he eulogizes—both serious, pious men who 'strictly meditate the thankless Muse'—from unnamed counterparts:

> Were it not better done, as others use,
> To sport with Amaryllis in the shade,
> Or with the tangles of Neaera's hair?
> (67–69)

No, is the emphatic answer. For Milton and, by extension, for King, poetry is a sacred and prophetic vocation; for the 'others', it is a sensual diversion, for whom immediate pleasure is the only aim and *carpe diem* its quintessential poetic expression. Milton's spurning of the 'others' is echoed a century later by Alexander Pope, who condescends to 'the mob of gentleman who wrote with ease' in his *First Epistle of the Second Book of Horace Imitated*, an attitude reprised in Richard Helgerson's comment: 'Together the Caroline poets made a distinguishable contribution to our literature, but neither individually nor collectively are they illuminated by an aura of greatness.'[75] Even more recently, David Norbrook has dismissed the cavaliers as a group as 'specious'.[76]

It is true that royalist poetry of the 1630s, 1640s, and 1650s tends to reject the strenuous distinctiveness of Donne and Jonson for a common ground of shared experience. Many 'cavalier' poets not only knew one another but emphasize that sociability in their literary production. While it is common enough for works printed in the 1610s and 1620s to be prefaced by one or two commendatory poems by friends and fellow writers—some of Jonson's 'friendship poems', as we have seen, are of this type—among Caroline and interregnum royalist poets the commendations multiply. Seventeen of Richard Lovelace's friends compose prefatory poems for *Lucasta*; some fifty contribute to William Cartwright's *Comedies, Tragicomedies, With Other Poems* (1651). In other words, homosocial camaraderie is not merely the topic of many of these poems, but their occasion. The effect is that a printed volume of poetry often contains not merely the work of the 'author', but a testament to the social circle in which his work had circulated prior to its

---

[75] Richard Helgerson, *Self-Crowned Laureates: Spenser Jonson Milton and the Literary System*, p. 187.
[76] David Norbrook, *Writing the English Republic: Poetry, Rhetoric, and Revolution 1627–1660*, p. 137.

printing, sometimes in manuscript, sometimes with the intention that it be performed—read or sometimes sung—among friends or before a group.[77] Important precedents for the cavalier poets therefore include not merely Donne and Jonson but also late Elizabethan and Jacobean court musicians who composed songs for lute accompaniment, such as John Dowland and Thomas Campion. The third edition of Thomas Carew's poems (1651) indicates that his 'songs were set in music by Mr Henry Lawes, Gentleman of the King's Chapel'; Lawes also set at least four of Katherine Philips' poems to music during her lifetime. Herrick declares that 'learned musicians shall, to honour Herrick's / Fame, both set and sing his lyrics' ('Upon Himself', 3–4); indeed, settings for several of his poems survive, by Henry Lawes, William Lanier, Richard Lanier, and Nicholas Lanier. Richard Lovelace's *Lucasta* mentions the composers with whom he collaborated: John Lanier, Henry and William Lawes, John Wilson, John Gamble, Thomas Charles, 'Mr. Hudson', and others. The lyrics in Abraham Cowley's collection *The Mistress* proved especially adaptable for musical purposes: Cowley's friend, the musician William King, published settings for fourteen of the poems as a memorial to him in 1668, and settings for forty of the poems survive by later seventeenth-century composers including Henry Purcell and Pietro Reggio. The lyrics for such songs naturally tend to be more straightforward and rhythmically regular than, say, Donne poems or Wroth sonnets, since they need to be comprehensible when wedded to melodies and, in some cases, sung in rounds or complex harmonies.

For the 'cavalier' generation, moreover, the increased factionalism of the body politic, and its eventual disintegration into civil war, arguably discourages the assertion of idiosyncrasy and fosters instead a search for a shared territory of experience and affect. In other words, the model of friendship based on like-mindedness offered by their mentor Ben Jonson remains powerful even while 'like-mindedness' increasingly means not the fortuitous conjunction between two sometimes craggy personalities, but the suppression, or at least de-emphasis, of traits that might alienate a potential ally. In some cases, the hints of autobiography that animate much Elizabethan

---

[77] The Jacobean and Caroline manifestations of these literary-social groups are described in Timothy Raylor, *Cavaliers, Clubs, and Literary Culture: Sir John Mennes, James Smith, and the Order of the Fancy* and Michelle O'Callaghan, *The English Wits: Literature and Sociability in Early Modern England*. Nicholas McDowell, 'Classical Liberty and Cavalier Poetics: The Politics of Literary Community in Caroline England from Jonson to Marvell', *Yearbook of English Studies* 44 (2014): 120–136, argues that in the late 1640s and 1650s Thomas Stanley and his 'Order of the Black Riband' 'sought to preserve pre-war traditions of literary community and aristocratic literary patronage in postwar London' (p. 126).

and Jacobean poetry are either played down or actively disclaimed. 'Jocund his muse was, but his life was chaste' (6), Robert Herrick declares in 'Upon Himself', warning the reader not to take his professions of love to 'Julia', 'Perilla', 'Anthea', 'Dianeme', or any of his other 'fragrant mistresses' as literal fact. Thomas Carew's 'A Rapture', with its detailed description of foreplay and coitus, is obviously indebted to John Donne's 'To His Mistress Going to Bed', but while Donne purports to be giving a play-by-play account of an actual encounter, Carew's poem represents itself as a patently escapist erotic fantasy. In 'The Dissembler', Abraham Cowley argues that strength of emotion might even inhibit poetic skill: 'Truth gives a dull propriety to my style, / And all the metaphor does spoil' (16–17). In the poem, the speaker laments that what was initially a sort of poetic game—'unhurt, untouched did I complain'—has unexpectedly become a serious matter: 'but now I feel the mighty evil . . . I became / Lame, with counterfeiting lame' (3, 21–22). Yet, of course, the protestation of desperate sincerity is itself conventional and falsifiable: in his preface Cowley specifies that the poems in *The Mistress* describe not real events, but 'things and persons imagined by him'.[78]

Yet a suppression of idiosyncrasy does not mean that the 'cavalier' poets are in fact indistinguishable from one another. The best-known and most sophisticated among them is arguably Robert Herrick. Herrick published his collection of secular poetry, *Hesperides*, in 1648, bound with his religious verse, *His Noble Numbers*. But Thomas Cain and Ruth Connolly, in their recent edition of Robert Herrick's poetry, demonstrate that his poetry circulated widely in manuscript long before its print publication, and that some of the individual lyrics in *Hesperides* date from the 1620s.[79] *Hesperides* offers short lyrics on a wide variety of topics; as Jonson does in his *Epigrams*, Herrick deliberately juxtaposes the sublime and the ridiculous, interspersing ecstatic love poems with off-colour jokes and satiric grotesquerie. As many critics have noted, *Hesperides* locates itself, like Jonson's collections, in the tradition of the *silva* or heterogeneous collection of different kinds of poems. Yet *Hesperides* is more miscellaneous than most. The arrangement of poems within the collection is deliberately non-chronological: Herrick's

---

[78] Abraham Cowley, preface to *Poems: Miscellanies, The Mistress, Pindarique Odes, Davideis, Verses Written on Several Occasions*, ed. A. R. Waller, p. 10.

[79] The most comprehensive attempt to deduce when the individual poems in *Hesperides* were originally composed is John Creaser, 'Time's Trans-shifting: Chronology and the Misshaping of Herrick', *ELR* 39 (2009): 163–196. See also the introduction in Tom Cain and Ruth Connolly, ed., *The Complete Poems of Robert Herrick*, vol. 1.

poem welcoming King Charles and his army into the West, probably written in 1644, appears long before Herrick's poem celebrating the birth of Prince Charles in 1630. 'Come forth my book at last', Herrick writes in a poem that one could imagine naturally occurring either at the beginning or the end of the volume, but which Herrick places about a quarter of the way through. An ode to Endymion Porter mourns the death of Herrick's brother; in the following poem, the brother is still alive and Herrick is bidding him his last farewell.[80] Nor do the poems, taken as a group, promote a rigorously consistent position on the burning issues of the day—not surprisingly, given that the poems were composed over three decades, in rapidly shifting political circumstances, and that Herrick himself may have had mixed or moderate views on many of these issues.[81] 'I am sieve like, and can hold / Nothing hot, or nothing cold', he writes in 'Upon Himself' (1–2).

The ordering of the love poems follow a similar pattern, or non-pattern. Herrick mourns 'the loss of his Mistresses' only a few pages into the volume, before he addresses most of his poems to them. The poem immediately after 'Upon Julia's Clothes' is a marriage proposal to Anthea. 'His Protestation to Perilla' ends with a hyperbolic declaration of constancy:

> Shapeless the world, as when all chaos was,
> Before, my dear Perilla, I will be,
> False to my vow, or fall away from thee. (8–10)

The next poem begins

> If I kiss Anthea's breast,
> There I smell the phoenix nest
>
> . . .
>
> Hands, and thighs, and legs, are all
> Richly aromatical.
>
> (1–4)

---

[80] Ann Coiro sees the poems as artfully arranged: *Robert Herrick's Hesperides and the Epigram Book Tradition*. If so, however, the artfulness involves frustrating a reader's attempt to impose a narrative sequence.

[81] Creaser, 'Time's Trans-shifting', points out that poems written in the 1610s or 1620s ought not be read as reflections on the politics of the late 1640s. Joseph Mansky, in 'Rethinking Royalism in Herrick's *Hesperides*', *Review of English Studies* 73 (2022): 476–489, argues that Herrick generally occupies a 'constitutional middle ground' that was shared by many on both sides of the civil war conflict.

One can see why Perilla might doubt the seriousness of Herrick's vow. When short poems get sequenced in a way that can describe a relationship, or even only an obsession, as they do in the Elizabethan sonnet sequence, the effect is to hint at a poetic subjectivity unveiling itself—thus, our interest in the autobiographical resonances of sequences by Sidney, Spenser, or Shakespeare. Herrick seems deliberately to thwart just this effect by refusing to arrange his poems in a way that might suggest monogamous courtship with sexual intercourse or marriage as its goal.

Typically, in other words, Herrick's lyrics decline to represent themselves as episodes in a narrative. The poem 'Her Legs' reads in its entirety:

> Fain would I kiss my Julia's dainty leg,
> Which is as white and hairless as an egg.
>
> (1–2)

The wit here lies not just in the unexpected comparison, but in the fact that this observation, all by itself, counts as a poem—rather than, as it might in Donne, Jonson, or Shakespeare, a rhetorical flourish on the way to a more protracted argument. Instead of journeying to a destination, Herrick is, as Harold Toliver puts it, 'a poet of isolated moments'.[82] Not surprisingly, then, some of his most famous lyrics are *carpe diem* poems, such as 'Gather Ye Rosebuds While Ye May' and 'Corinna's Gone A-Maying.'

Herrick's rejection of narrative trajectory has consequences for the kind of erotic experiences he describes in his love poetry—consequences particularly striking when his poems are compared with those of his predecessors. In 'Going to Bed', for instance, Donne details his lover's piece-by-piece undressing; the slow strip-tease is itself, of course, arousing, but Donne's goal is, he proclaims, 'Full nakedness!'

> Gems which you women use
> Are as Atalanta's balls, cast in men's views,
> Than when a fool's eye lighteth on a gem,
> His earthly soul may covet theirs, not them.
>
> (35–38)

Donne draws a clear distinction between women's sparkling jewels and bright coverings, which are merely 'theirs, not them', and their substantial

---

[82] Harold Toliver, 'Herrick's Book of Realms and Moments', *ELH* 49 (1982): 432.

persons; and characteristically distinguishes too between his discerning self and the fools who mistake surface for depth, ornament for truth, appearance for reality. Along similar lines, Jonson inveighs against vapid clotheshorses and those who fetishize expensive accoutrements. Herrick, by contrast, professes himself entranced by precisely the surfaces the earlier poets want to penetrate or cast aside. He writes poems to his mistress's petticoat, to her bracelet, to her elaborate hairdo:

> Whenas in silks my Julia goes
> Then, then, methinks, how sweetly flows
> The liquefaction of her clothes.
>
> Next, when I cast my eye and see
> That brave vibration each way free,
> O how that glittering taketh me!
> ('Upon Julia's Clothes', 1–6)

Herrick celebrates the evanescent play of light on shiny fabric, not the prospect of access to Julia's body.

Herrick's concern with the preliminary and peripheral aspects of sexuality has seemed proof positive, to many critics, of his lack of seriousness. But of course this criticism prompts the question of what is 'the point' of love poetry and what is 'leading up to the point'. Herrick's playfully 'slight' love lyrics on 'trivial' topics raise the question of what is and is not significant and subsidiary, of how one might organize one's priorities. They are consistent with the many other poems in *Hesperides* that foreground small, ephemeral, and often disregarded things: cobwebs, acorns, fairies. Wendy Hyman has recently pointed out that the *carpe diem* poems for which Herrick is best known are at their core profoundly at odds with a Christian belief in a futurity in which God will pass judgement on the worth of an entire lifetime.[83] (Such obliviousness to futurity and to career is, in fact, the source of Milton's disquiet with his unnamed contemporaries in *Lycidas*.) In Hyman's view, the *carpe diem* poem can become a vehicle for a scepticism that might seem quite at odds with the deliberately simple pieties of Herrick's devotional poems, *Noble Numbers*. In fact, Herrick's pointed lack of concern for narrative and for climax, sexual or otherwise—his insistence that each moment ought to be savoured for its own sake, not for what it is

---

[83] Wendy Hyman, *Impossible Desire and the Limits of Knowledge in Renaissance Poetry*, pp. 1–26.

leading up to or away from—quietly subverts the hierarchical truisms that, as we have seen, are such important organizing principles for the period in which he lives, or at least into which he is born. For if one imagines one's life not as a career with a coherent ethical shape, capable of retrospective evaluation and summary judgement, but rather as a succession of potentially scintillating but discontinuous moments, then each moment, and each item in the world, is potentially as important as any other.

What tends to replace hierarchy as a principle of order in Herrick's worldview is a principle of repetition. In *Hesperides* his love poems are interwoven with memorable celebrations of traditional festivals: May Day, Yuletide, Pentecost, harvest-home. As Leah Marcus has shown, although Herrick typically represents these festivals as innocent diversions, they become deeply politicized in the 1630s, as under Charles the Laudian church increasingly emphasized ritual and 'traditional pasttimes' that scandalized the Puritans who saw them as pagan survivals. For Herrick, though, 'old ways' whether pagan or Catholic are benignly imagined not as a diabolical temptation but as a set of innocuous communal practices. That the Christian festivals share so many features with pagan ones is, for Herrick, a heartening fact, suggesting continuity and the satisfaction of perennial, universal human needs. These poems perhaps also express the hope that ingrained cultural habit might place invisible guard rails on behaviour, reducing the need for violence and coercion as ways of ensuring social order. In 'Art Above Nature', Herrick praises Julia's silken dress: 'those lawny films I see / Play with a wild civility' (13–14). Julia's expensive garment, a fabric marker of elite status, enacts a playful but contained disorder, a 'wildness' that nonetheless remains within the implicit boundaries set by 'civility'. It is a concept that Herrick returns to in 'Delight in Disorder', with its 'erring lace' and 'tempestuous petticoat'. The delicate sprezzatura suggested by lawny films and erring laces might seem delusional escapism in a society on the verge of, or in the midst of, civil war. Still, what might seem from one point of view non-serious might also be, more generously, seen as speculative. Herrick's apparently casual jests can permit him to tentatively or temporarily occupy the sceptical positions which Hyman discerns in his *carpe diem* lyrics—positions to which he did not necessarily want to commit fully, and which he might have wanted in other circumstances to disclaim.

Whereas Herrick creates a poetic persona who generally avoids depicting the hardships that, as his recent biographers and editors show, he inevitably encountered, Richard Lovelace puts them at the centre of some of his best poems. Lovelace came to Charles's court as a teenager in the mid-1630s and immediately turned heads, according to his biographer Anthony Wood: 'being then accounted the most amiable and beautiful person that ever eye beheld; a person also of innate modesty, virtue, and courtly deportment'.[84] But his military and financial support of the royalist cause during the 1640s led to repeated spells of imprisonment and the sale of his estates; he died in poverty in 1657. He published one volume of poetry, *Lucasta*, in 1649, and after his death his brother supervised the publication of a second, *Lucasta: Posthume Poems*.

In many of his love poems Lovelace presents himself as a man of unyielding principle. In 'To Lucasta, Going to the Wars', he bids farewell to his beloved to follow 'a new mistress': armed combat with an enemy. The poem trades on the durable notion that while a woman's exclusive devotion to her man may be wholly admirable, the man must not reciprocally devote himself to her, but must put himself in the service of some other, 'higher', and sometimes competing ideal. (We see this concept playing out in works as varied as Fletcher's *The Island Princess*, in which the dashing Armusia refuses to convert to Islam in order to marry his beloved, and in Milton's *Paradise Lost*, in which Raphael advises Adam to subordinate his infatuation with Eve to his obedience to God.) In fact, Lovelace hazards, the woman too is happiest when her swain shows himself worthy of her by committing himself to a noble purpose.

> This inconstancy is such
> As you too shall adore;
> I could not love thee, dear, so much,
> Loved I not honour more.
>
> (9–12)

Yet Lovelace's gallant principles often seem ill-adapted to his circumstances, a disappointment he describes in 'To Lucasta, From Prison: An Epode'. His love of peace, his courage in war, his sincere devotion to religion, his care for the liberty and property which he sees as his birthright, his eagerness to serve 'the public faith' and his king: none seem to avail him in a time when 'an universal mist / Of error is spread o'er each breast' (49–50).

Not surprisingly, then, Lovelace gravitates to the idea already incipient in Jonson, Shakespeare, Wroth, and Donne that intimate relationships might create an alternative to a cruel world, a space of reparation and escape. 'The

---

[84] Anthony Wood, *Athenae Oxoniensis*, ed. Philip Bliss, vol. 3, p. 460.

Grasshopper' is a friendship poem addressed to Lovelace's friend, Charles Cotton, that opens with an idyllic invocation describing the grasshopper's life:

> O thou that swing'st upon the waving ear
> Of some well-fillèd oaten beard,
> Drunk every night with a delicious tear
> Dropped thee from heaven, where now th' art reared;
>
> The joys of earth and air are thine entire.
>
> (1–5)

These lines echo an 'Ode to the Cicada' attributed to the Greek poet Anacreon in the seventeenth century—a poem Lovelace may have been introduced to by his kinsman Thomas Stanley, whose English translation of Anacreon's poetry was published a couple of years after *Lucasta*:[85]

> We pronounce thee happy, cicada,
> For on the tops of the trees,
> Drinking a little dew,
> Like any king thou singest,
> For thine are they all.

The Anacreontic poem obliquely refers to a myth also retold in Plato's *Phaedrus*: cicadas were originally men so enchanted by the Muses that they failed to eat and eventually starved to death: the gods rewarded them by transforming them into singing insects.

> The Muses love thee,
> And Phoebus himself loves thee,
> And has given thee a shrill song.

In these renditions the cicada, or grasshopper, is a figure for the inspired poet, ecstatically exercising his gift. But in the background of Lovelace's poem is also Aesop's fable about the grasshopper and the ant. In the fable the grasshopper sings and plays all summer while the ant toils to store food;

---

[85] Stanley's translation, called 'The Grasshopper', begins: 'Grasshopper thrice-happy! Who / Sipping the cool morning dew, / Queen-like chirpest all the day / Seated on some verdant spray, / Thine is all what ere earth brings'.

when winter arrives, the hardworking ant turns out to have been wiser than the improvident grasshopper. In the fable, seizing the day and valuing pleasure and poetry may not pay off in the long run. Lovelace—erstwhile wealthy and favoured—implicitly identifies himself with the musical grasshopper, glorying in beauty and ease and composing exquisite poetry. But now—imprisoned, impoverished, and his courtly ambitions in the dust—he, like the grasshopper, finds that 'Sharp frosty fingers all your flowers have topped, / And what scythes spared, winds shave off quite' (15–16).

Yet Lovelace has a resource that the frozen grasshopper lacks: a loyal friend, Charles Cotton, who can provide practical and emotional solace.

> Thou best of men and friends! we will create
> A genuine summer in each other's breast,
> And spite of this cold time and frozen fate,
> Thaw us a warm seat to our rest.
>
> (21–24)

The rituals of friendship become all the more precious in hard times because they are now untainted by the ambition and self-seeking that had always infected court poetry of praise and friendship, including Jonson's. 'The Grasshopper' finally recommends, in times of adversity, a strategic withdrawal into the resources of oneself and one's few remaining comrades: 'Richer than untempted kings are we / That asking nothing, nothing need' (37–38). Lovelace strikes a similar tone in 'To Althea from Prison', in which he describes, in the first stanza, his liberation-through-erotic bondage:

> When I lie tangled in her hair
> And fettered to her eye,
> The birds that wanton in the air
> Know no such liberty.
>
> (5–8)

In the second stanza he makes a similar claim about male friendship, evoking a group of royalist men finding solace as they drown their sorrows together:

> When thirsty grief in wine we steep
> When healths and drafts go free,

> Fishes that tipple in the deep
> Know no such liberty.
>
> ...
>
> If I have freedom in my love
> And in my soul am free,
> Angels alone that soar above
> Enjoy such liberty.
>
> (13–16, 29–32)

Notably, although Lovelace cherishes his lover and his friends, the 'liberty' thus achieved does not actually depend upon a relationship with a particular beloved: it is a state of equanimity available to the individual even in the absence of another. Lovelace draws immediately upon Jonson's praise of self-sufficiency, and more remotely upon such philosophers as Epicurus, Seneca, and Boethius, for his resolute embrace of the 'quiet mind', undaunted by misfortune and confident in its own resources.

The most thoroughgoing and imaginative poet of consolatory friendship in this period is, however, a little surprisingly, a woman: Katherine Philips. The surprise derives from the fact that classical and Renaissance theorists of friendship—Aristotle, Cicero, Montaigne, and so on—generally claimed that women were incapable of the kind of friendship so often idealized among men. Montaigne, in his influential essay on friendship, summarizes the traditional view:

> the ordinary sufficiency of women, cannot answer this conference and communication, the nurse of this sacred bond; nor seem their minds strong enough to endure the pulling of a knot so hard, so fast, and durable. . . . this sex could never yet by any example attain unto it, and is by ancient schools rejected thence.[86]

Philips, however, explicitly refutes this premise. In 'A Friend', she writes:

> If souls no sexes have, for men t' exclude
> Women from friendship's vast capacity,
> Is a design injurious or rude,
> Only maintained by partial tyranny.

---

[86] Michel de Montaigne, 'Of Friendship', *Essays, or Moral, Politic, and Military Discourses*, trans. John Florio (London, 1603), vol. 1, chapter 27, pp. 91–92.

> Love is allowed to us and innocence,
> And noblest friendships do proceed from thence.
> (19–24)

Friendship is central to both Philips' life and her poetry. Born into an affluent family in London in 1631, Philips had moved to Cardiganshire, Wales, with her stepmother in her mid-teens, and married a locally prominent magnate there. During her twenties and early thirties she cultivated a wide circle of acquaintances both in Wales and in London, assembling a 'Society of Friends' upon whose members she conferred pastoral names: she is 'Orinda', her best friends 'Rosania' (Mary Aubrey) and 'Lucasia' (Ann Owen). The Society included some men: Philips' husband is 'Antenor'; her friend's husband, Edward Dering, is 'Silvander'; and Sir Charles Cotterell is 'Poliarchus'—but the glue that holds the group together is apparently the relationships among the women. This social configuration is possibly inspired by the example of Henrietta Maria and her ladies in the Caroline court of the 1630s, or by the contemporaneous mixed-sex intellectual salons in Paris (Philips was fluent in French and sensitive to French culture: after the Restoration, her translation of Corneille's *Pompey* was the first woman-authored play performed on the English stage.) Although, given the geographical distances involved, many of its interactions must have been by letter, during the interregnum Philips' coterie constitutes an informal court-in-the-absence-of-a-court that resembled, and overlapped with, the largely male literary clubs.

In numerous poems to 'Lucasia', 'Rosania', and several other female friends, Philips boldly reworks both male friendship theory and the tropes of heterosexual erotic poetry to celebrate female emotional intimacy. For instance, in 'Friendship in Emblem, or the Seal: To My Dearest Lucasia' she redeploys John Donne's famous image, from 'A Valediction Forbidding Mourning', of lovers as halves of a compass:

> The compasses that stand above
> Express this great immortal love:
> For friends, like them, can prove this true,
> They are, and yet they are not, two.
>
> And in their posture is expressed
> Friendship's exalted interest:
> Each follows where the other leans,
> And what each does, the other means.

> And as when one foot does stand fast,
> And t'other circles seeks to cast,
> The steady part does regulate
> And make the wanderer's motion straight.
>
> (21–32)

Yet whereas in Donne's poem the two parts of the compass play different, complementary roles—the male part 'roaming' while the female remains 'fixed'—the halves of Philips' compass are identical, each reciprocally supporting the other. The aim and effect of friendship is a mirroring or merging in which the two persons effectively become one: a perfect union.

Notably, the effect of Philips' poems taken together is that the tropes of erotic poetry and of friendship poetry, so often conceptually separated in the poetry of Jonson, Donne, and most of the cavalier poets, tend to converge. Philips' poems to her husband evidence much of the same imagery as her poems to her female friends, suggesting that harmonious union is the proper aim of every human relationship. Thus, in 'Content: To Lucasia' she praises friends 'Whose minds and interests are so the same'; in 'To my dearest Antenor, on His Parting', she writes:

> Each of our souls did its own temper fit
> And in the other's mold so fashioned it
> That now our inclinations both are grown
> Like to our interests, in persons, one.
>
> (13–16)

Valerie Traub relates Philips' innovations to 'changes at the level of patriarchal alliance' that, over the course of the seventeenth century, make companionate marriage increasingly a desideratum: 'once friendship becomes a goal of marriage for men and women, female friendship begins to look a lot like companionate marriage'.[87] Still, Philips' effective conflation of marriage and same-sex friendship has made her sexuality the site of considerable critical attention.[88] Like Shakespeare, Philips declines to specify

---

[87] Valerie Traub, '"Friendship so Curst": *Amor Impossibilis*, the Homoerotic Lament, and the Nature of Lesbian Desire', *The Noble Flame of Katherine Philips: A Poetics of Culture, Politics, and Friendship*, ed. David L. Orvis and Ryan Singh Paul, p. 261.

[88] For various discussions of this issue, see Traub, 'Friendship so Curst'; Eleanor Hobby, 'Katherine Philips: Seventeenth-Century Lesbian Poet', in *What Lesbians Do in Books*, ed. Eleanor Hobby and Chris White (London: Women's Press, 1991): 183–204; Harriette

whether her same-sex relationships have a genital component, but, clearly, the emotional importance of those attachments looms very large for her.

For Philips, the contented harmony of friendship provides both counterweight and rebuke to the violence of wartime:

> we by love sublimed so high shall rise,
> To pity kings, and conquerors despise,
> Since we that sacred union have engrossed
> Which they and all the factious world have lost.
> ('To Mrs Mary Aubrey', 19–22)

> Here is no quarreling for crowns,
> Nor fear of changes in our fate,
> No trembling at the great one's frowns,
> Nor any slavery of state.
> ('A Retired Friendship:
> To Ardelia 1651', 4–8)

These poems, and many others, strike a familiar note of solace and strategic retirement that we also see in Philips' male predecessors and contemporaries, but with a gendered twist. For Philips exploits the apparent privacy and inconsequentiality of female friendship— 'so innocent a flame', as she calls it in 'To Mrs Mary Aubrey'—to open up for herself a space of independent agency. Friendship, of course, had always been lauded as a domain in which the individual's freedom reigned supreme; one cannot choose one's kin, but one does select one's friends, according to criteria known only to oneself. However, while male friendship had, at least since Aristotle, been considered an important factor in the constitution of the state, female friendships had largely been belittled and ignored because patriarchal culture tended to define a woman solely in terms of her birth family and her husband. Philips, though, forges a 'society' out of her own choice of associates, claiming simultaneously that such society is beneath the notice of the 'public' world but also that it exceeds it in perfection. This strategic 'womanly' humility can facilitate other forms of agency as well. Although her family were Presbyterian dissenters and she married a Welsh Parliamentarian, Philips' own political convictions were strongly royalist and she befriended many of the writers in the cavalier group. When one 'J. Jones'—perhaps the

---

Andreadis, *Sappho in Early Modern England: Female Same-Sex Literary Erotics 1550–1714*, pp. 295–308; and Mark Llewellyn, 'Katherine Philips, Friendship Poetry, and Neo-Platonic Thought in Seventeenth-Century England, *Philological Quarterly* 81 (2002): 441–468.

Welsh cleric Jenkin Jones—threatened to embarrass her husband by publicizing her poem lamenting the execution of King Charles, Philips insisted, in 'To Antenor, on a Paper of Mine', that despite their harmonious love for one another, Antenor's and Orinda's convictions were not identical:

> My love and life, I must confess, are thine,
> But not my errors; they are only mine .
> And if my faults should be for thine allowed,
> It will be hard to dissipate the cloud.
> But Eve's rebellion did not Adam blast,
> Until himself forbidden fruit did taste.
> (7–12)

It is typical of Philips that while she declares herself a submissive wife—her husband is, she claims in 'To My Dearest Antenor', 'My guide, life, object, friend, and destiny' (36)—and while she refers to her own opinions as 'errors', she evidently does not apologize for or repent of them. Similarly, in the 'offending' poem itself, 'On the Double Murder of King Charles', she begins by disavowing a political agenda—'I think not on the state, nor am concerned / Which way soever that great helm is turned' (1–2)—and then goes on to make a thoroughly political argument.

Philips does not use the conventional notions of female modesty merely as a stalking horse. Her conception of her role as a female poet, committed to a form of private sociability, seems to have deeply influenced her objectives for the reception of her poetry. Her work had circulated in manuscript among royalist circles during the 1650s, where it was well known and widely admired; after the Restoration of Charles II, her political views were an advantage and her literary career seemed poised to take off. Yet when an apparently pirated edition of her works appeared in print in 1664, she protested vigorously: in her view, she had written her poetry for a select group of intimates:

> That private shade, wherein my Muse was bred
> She always hoped might hide her humble head.
> ('To His Grace Gilbert, Lord Archbishop
> of Canterbury', 1–2)

Indeed, she figures the unauthorized printing of her work as a sexual violation, writing to Sir Charles Cotterell: 'I . . . am that unfortunate person that cannot so much as think in private, that must have my imaginations rifled and exposed'. The edition was hastily withdrawn, yet in 1667, three years after Philips' untimely death of smallpox at the age of thirty-two, her friends brought out an impressive folio edition of her poems, praising her demureness and womanly modesty even while they ushered her work into a fully public sphere.[89]

By far the most arresting of the mid-century love poets is Andrew Marvell. Marvell began the 1640s as a royalist sympathizer: his first published work is a friendship poem prefaced to Lovelace's *Lucasta*. But in the late 1640s, as the Parliamentarians triumphed, he re-evaluated his political views; he was less committed to the monarchy per se than to a commonwealth that encouraged free and responsible citizenship, an ideal that might be realized under the Protectorate as well as under a king. As noted in the Introduction to this volume, Marvell's 'Horatian Ode upon Cromwell's Return from Ireland', written in 1650, balances sympathy for the doomed, graceful Charles with admiration for Cromwell's military effectiveness and political energy. The subtle, dialectical play of opposing forces in this poem is typical of much of the love poetry as well. Between 1650 and 1652 Marvell worked as tutor to the daughter of Thomas Fairfax, a Parliamentary general who had resigned his commission and retired to his estate, Nun Appleton, in protest at Cromwell's proposed invasion of Scotland. It was during these years that, most critics believe, Marvell evidently wrote most of the brilliant, sometimes puzzling lyric poetry for which he is now best remembered.[90]

Marvell seems not seem to have circulated his poetry in manuscript, and it markedly lacks the sociable quality of much cavalier verse. Many of his speakers are isolated figures, admiring from a distance, and the love object is often inaccessible. In 'The Definition of Love', the lovers are imagined as permanently separated despite their complete compatibility: two parallel lines who, 'though infinite, can never meet' (28). Poems about unrequited love are, of course, a staple of the genre, but in Marvell's hands the prospect of happiness with another seems thwarted not just by circumstances but by the unsettled, unsatisfactory nature of desire itself. Sometimes the gulf between lovers is a consequence of the inappropriateness of the beloved. In 'Young Love' and 'A Portrait of Little T. C. in a Prospect of Flowers', the speaker addresses prepubescent girls, entranced by an innocence he does not share,

---

[89] For a discussion of Philips' attitudes towards publication and her conceptions of friendship, see Hilary Menges, 'Authorship, Friendship, and Forms of Publication in Katherine Philips', *SEL* 52 (2002): 517–541.

[90] For a dissenting view that dates some of Marvell's lyrics in the 1660s, see Allan Pritchard, 'Marvell's "The Garden"', *SEL* 23 (1980): 371–388 and Paul Hammond, 'The Date of Marvell's "The Mower Against Gardens"', *Notes and Queries* 53 (2006): 178–181.

and which his advances would presumably destroy. The first-person speaker in 'A Nymph Complaining for the Death of Her Fawn' is a forest maiden obsessed with a dying baby deer whom she treats simultaneously as her pet, her child, and her lover. In 'The Unfortunate Lover', the lover, or perhaps the beloved, is marooned on a rock at sea, tormented and alone:

> See how he nak'd and fierce does stand,
> Cuffing the thunder with one hand,
> While on the other he does lock
> And grapple, with the stubborn rock.
> (49–52)

Even when the dramatic situation is apparently heteronormative, Marvell tends to give it a twist. As we have seen, *carpe diem* was a popular theme among Marvell's cavalier contemporaries, and Marvell's 'To His Coy Mistress' is often considered the greatest poem of this kind in English. Yet, set next to, say, Herrick's 'Gather Ye Rosebuds', the poem is astonishingly cheerless. It expends considerably more energy summoning the bleak imminence of death, the 'deserts of vast eternity' in which, grotesquely, 'worms shall try'(27) the mistress's virginity, than it does celebrating a flowery and springlike present. And the prospect of pleasure, introduced at the end of the poem, is inflected with desperate haste, even cruelty: knowing that time will inevitably annihilate both himself and his beloved, the speaker aspires to 'tear our pleasures with rough strife / Through the iron gates of life' (43–44). What fun.

While, like his cavalier contemporaries, Marvell often writes about patently imaginary situations, he frequently takes the evocation of a fictional world one step further, writing dramatic monologues with invented speakers clearly differentiated from the poet. This technique distances the poet from the subject of the poem, and complicates our response to it, insofar as it is often unclear whether the poem endorses or critiques the claims of the speaker. Moreover, sometimes our understanding of the fictional circumstances changes over the course of the poem. In 'Daphnis and Chloe'—the names are formulaic pastoral ones—Daphnis protests his desperate love of Chloe and berates her for her refusal to yield to him. Yet when, pitying his distracted state of mind, Chloe agrees to gratify him, Daphnis flounces off anyway to sleep with Phlogis and Dorinda, maintaining all the while that his faithless promiscuity is all Chloe's fault. In other words, what begins, apparently, as an entirely conventional love plea morphs into a playlet of cynical manipulation: Daphnis turns out to be a blame-shifting jerk, more in love with his own self-dramatizing performance than with poor Chloe. In this case the critique of Daphnis, and perhaps of the well-worn poetic traditions upon which he draws, seems pretty clear. More equivocal are four poems spoken by 'Damon the mower', a rustic figure who seems by turns naïve and discriminating, powerful and vulnerable, destructive and enabling. In 'The Mower Against Gardens', the Mower deplores the sophistications of 'man, that sovereign thing and proud' (20) who develops new kinds of flowers and trees, and encloses them in formal gardens rather than the 'sweet fields . . . Where willing nature does to all dispense / A wild and fragrant innocence' (32–34). Like Shakespeare's Perdita in *The Winter's Tale*, Marvell's Mower likens selective plant breeding to perverse human sexual practices: teaching tulips to 'paint' themselves like whores, grafting 'forbidden mixtures' to produce 'uncertain and adulterate fruit' (25). The Mower's eloquently voiced affinity for wild places seems very attractive, although his disapproval of botanical calculation seems excessive, especially given that the hay he cuts is, after all, itself a cultivated crop. But in 'The Mower to the Glow-Worms', 'Damon the Mower', and 'The Mower's Song', his untroubled life in the meadows is interrupted by heterosexual passion:

> but Juliana comes, and she,
> What I do to the grass, does to my thoughts and me.
> ('The Mowers Song', 5–6)

At the end of 'Damon the Mower', the unhappy speaker accidentally cuts his ankle with his own scythe, a victim of his self-lacerating rapture. Especially because a mower is not one of the usual figures of pastoral poetry, critics have disagreed about him and his significance: is he a visionary or a bumpkin? An icon of vigorous masculinity or an avatar of death? To what extent does he voice Marvell's opinions and feelings, and to what extent is he meant to be held at an ironic distance? Even more remarkable is 'The Nymph Complaining for the Death of her Faun', which ventriloquizes a naïve girl struggling to understand the casual cruelty of her faithless lover, Silvio, and of the 'wanton troopers riding by' who have thoughtlessly wounded the pet fawn that Silvio gave her as a gift. The nymph remembers nursing the fawn on sugar-water it sucked from her fingers: 'and as it grew, so every day / It waxed more white and soft than they'. She celebrates the peaceful hours she has spent with the fawn in her garden of roses and lilies:

> For in the flaxen lilies' shade
> It like a bank of lilies laid.
> Upon the roses it would feed
> Until its lips ev'n seemed to bleed,
> And then to me 'twould boldly trip
> And print those roses on my lip.
> . . .
> Had it lived long it would have been
> Lilies without, roses within.
>
> (81–92)

The nymph describes a idyll of tender mutuality within an enclosed space, in which the 'pure virgin limbs' of the white fawn duplicate the nymph's own. Her fond obsession with the fawn seems as constricted as her small, exquisite garden.[91] And yet this very myopia seems the clue to her happiness: at least temporarily, before the cruel world intrudes, she appears to find complete fulfilment.

The enigmatic intensity of all of these poems, their perceived surplus of meaning and their habit of destabilizing the reader, has encouraged many critics to attempt to discern what might be implied or hidden under their fluent surfaces. In the mid-twentieth century, the poems tended to be allegorized in Christian terms: thus, Muriel Bradbrook argues that 'A Nymph Complaining' reflects 'the love of the Church for Christ', and Douglas Bush suggests that it registers 'an Anglican's grief for the stricken Church' in the period immediately after the Civil War.[92] Writing several decades later, John J. Teunissen and Evelyn Hinz propose that the Nymph is mourning a miscarriage.[93] Yvonne Sandstrom believes the poem is a lament for the death of Charles I, with the nymph personifying 'the grieving and apprehensive English nation'.[94] More recent critics have read the poems through the lens of psychoanalytic or queer theory. We know absolutely nothing about Marvell's sex life or the lack of it—only that he may (or may not) have been married at

---

[91] Rosalie Colie complains of the Nymph's 'narrowly confined emotional vision . . . myopically self-regarding', in *My Echoing Song: Andrew Marvell's Poetry of Criticism*, p. 89.
[92] Muriel Bradbrook and M. C. Lloyd-Thomas, *Andrew Marvell*, pp. 47ff. Douglas Bush, *English Literature in the Early Seventeenth Century*, p. 161.
[93] John J. Teunissen and Evelyn Hinz, 'What is the Nymph Complaining For?', *ELH* 45 (1978): 410–428.
[94] Yvonne Sandstrom, 'Marvell's 'Nymph Complaining' as Historical Allegory', *SEL* 30 (1990), p. 105.

the time of his death. One of his enemies, after the Restoration, characterized him as sexually indeterminate, an androgyne or eunuch:

> I shall only advise the painter if ever he draws him below the waist, to follow the example of that artist, who having completed the picture of a woman, could at any time, with two strokes of his pencil upon her face, two upon her breast, and two betwixt her thighs change her in an instant into Man: but after our author's female figure is completed, the change of sex is far easier, for nature or sinister accident has rendered some of the alteration strokes useless and unnecessary.[95]

Following the footsteps of William Empson, who hazards that Marvell 'fell in love with the Mower', Paul Hammond claims that the reason the lovers cannot unite in 'A Definition of Love' is because their love is homoerotic.[96] Derek Hirst and Stephen Zwicker suggest that the subtext of the enigmatic poem 'The Unfortunate Lover' is a childhood memory of sexual sadism at the hands of clerical pedagogues: 'a narrative of abuse, sustained and yet pleasurable and deeply guilty violation'.[97] George Klawitter argues that 'A Nymph Complaining' is a coded account of a girl's discovery of her clitoris and the pleasures of masturbation.[98] The extravagant variety of these allegorical readings suggests that their plausibility depends less on Marvell's text than upon the parameters imposed by contemporary critical fashion: Christianizing, political, psychoanalytic, or queer, as the case may be.

The most unequivocally happy of Marvell's love poems is, perhaps, not a love poem at all, since it celebrates not a beloved but the absence of a beloved. In 'The Garden', the speaker wanders alone in a garden, reinterpreting the Ovidian myths of attempted rape as a deliberate strategy for inducing botanical effects: Apollo chased Daphne because he hoped to change her into a laurel; likewise, Pan pursues Syrinx not for sexual purposes but because he wanted reeds. As the speaker ambles along, delicious fruits—apples, grapes, nectarines, peaches, and melons—offer themselves

---

[95] 'The Transproser Rehearsed', quoted in Derek Hirst and Stephen Zwicker, *Andrew Marvell: Orphan of the Hurricane*, p. 43; also Paul Hammond, 'Marvell's Sexuality', *The Seventeenth Century* 11 (1996): 87–123; Lynn Enterline, 'The Mirror and the Snake: The Case of Marvell's "Unfortunate Lover"', in *The Tears of Narcissus*, pp. 153ff.

[96] Paul Hammond, 'Marvell's Sexuality', *The Seventeenth Century* 11 (1996): 87–123.

[97] Derek Hirst and Stephen Zwicker, *Andrew Marvell: Orphan of the Hurricane*, p. 81.

[98] George Klawitter, *Andrew Marvell, Sexual Orientation, and Seventeenth-Century Poetry*, pp. 142–148.

up to him. In stanza 6 the garden becomes the site of an ecstatic out-of-body experience:

> Meanwhile the mind, from pleasures less
> Withdraws into its happiness;
> The mind, that ocean where each kind
> Does straight its own resemblance find,
> Yet it creates, transcending these,
> Far other worlds, and other seas;
> Annihilating all that's made
> To a green thought in a green shade.
>   (41–48)

Notably, the enjoyment of the garden-inhabitant does not require other people: any gratifying coupling occurs within the mind of the speaker, 'where each kind / Does straight its own resemblance find'. Marvell's garden, in fact, improves upon Eden insofar as it does not contain an Eve:

> Such was that happy garden-state
> While man there walked without a mate.
> After a place so pure and sweet,
> What other help could yet be meet?
> But 'twas beyond a mortal's share
> To wander solitary there:
> Two paradises were in one
> To live in paradise alone.
>   (57–64)

This glorification of solitude is, perhaps, testament to Marvell's sexlessness, or to his oft-noted reticence, even secrecy. But it also can be seen as a logical extension of the tradition that associates 'love' with an ecstatic, privatized intimacy that Donne evokes in poems like 'The Sun Rising'; that Herrick evokes in his poetry of momentariness, with its eschewal of goals and trajectory; that Lovelace evokes in his defiant withdrawal into his own tight circle of lovers and friends.

For Stanley Fish, this radical introversion is the distinguishing attribute of Marvell's poetry, which, he writes, 'attempts ... to perform ... the action of withholding, of keeping to oneself'.⁹⁹ Yet this withholding or withdrawal does not constitute a permanent solution for Marvell. Marvell's solitary lovers—whether contented, anguished, or abandoned—seem to resolve their dilemmas in one of two ways. In one, emotional extremity metamorphoses him or her into a dead and static, but lasting, art form. The obscurely tormented Unfortunate Lover ends up as a heraldic emblem:

> And he in story only rules
> In a field sable a lover gules.
> (63–64)

The Nymph aspires to die and be memorialized with a statue of herself weeping over her lost fawn. The other option is to emerge from erotic privacy into public life. In 'The Horatian Ode', Cromwell departs his pleasant garden to embrace his destiny as a conqueror and re-maker of England's ancient institutions. Even 'The Garden' ends not with the ecstatic oblivion of a 'green thought in a green shade' but with a description of a flower clock, which gently reintroduces time-consciousness and its attendant pressures. In due time, Marvell leaves his quiet life at Nun Appleton and pursues a government career, first as an aide to Milton and Cromwell, and later in life as Parliamentary representative for his hometown of Hull. He also, apparently, abandons love poetry, and turns to writing scathingly witty political satires that reflect his active political engagement.

---

[99] Stanley Fish, 'Marvell and the Art of Disappearance', *Revenge of the Aesthetic: The Place of Literature in Theory Today*, ed. Michael P. Clark, p. 27.

7
Intellect and Expression

Prose in the Early Seventeenth Century

Around 1580, Philip Sidney wrote a famous justification of the value of imaginative literature, published posthumously in 1595 by two different printers under the titles 'The Defense of Poesy' and 'An Apology for Poetry'. 'It is not rhyming and versing that maketh a poet', Sidney claims, 'but it is that feigning notable images of virtues, vices, or what else.'[1] What distinguishes 'poetry', in other words, is not conformity to a verse pattern but fiction-making. Nonetheless, as both titles might suggest, in the sixteenth century the 'feigning of notable images' normally entailed a presentation via 'rhyming and versing'. The late sixteenth and early seventeenth centuries witnessed vigorous debates about rhyme, metre, and stanzaic form, including treatises by George Puttenham, William Webbe, William Scott, Thomas Campion, and Samuel Daniel. These often connect the formal beauties of rhyme and metre with larger social desiderata, such as the harmony of a community and the beauty of the divinely ordered cosmos.[2]

Yet despite this preference for verse, there had long been instances of literary works in English prose. Malory's *Morte d'Arthur*, a retelling of the Camelot legends, is an early example, written in the mid-fifteenth century and first printed in 1485 by William Caxton. Over the course of the sixteenth century the increasing availability of printed books produced a flourishing of utilitarian prose: cookbooks and herbals, chronicle histories, accounts of travels and explorations, almanacs, guides to health and etiquette, legal textbooks, devotional aids, and so forth. Several ambitious, immensely long works were widely read and influential. John Foxe's *Acts and Monuments* chronicled the sufferings of Protestant martyrs with special emphasis on the recent persecutions under Mary Tudor; in 1571, a copy was installed next

---

[1] Sir Philip Sidney, *The Defence of Poesie*, in *The Prose Works of Sir Philip Sidney*, vol. 3, ed. Albert Feuillerat, pp. 10–11.

[2] For the formal and ideological consequences of this debate, see Derek Attridge, *Well Weighed Syllables: Elizabethan Verse in Classical Metres* and Rebecca Rush, *The Fetters of Rhyme: Liberty and Poetic Form in Early Modern England*.

to the Bible in every cathedral church. The collaboratively produced collection of historical narrative from the Norman Conquest almost to the present day, 'Holinshed's Chronicles', was a source from which Shakespeare, Marlowe, Spenser, and Daniel would draw. Simultaneously, the Reformation emphasis on the sermon as the centre of communal worship led to a rapid development of the art of preaching. By the seventeenth century, published sermons were some of the most popular printed material of the day.[3]

Given this larger total output, it is not surprising that towards the latter part of the sixteenth century, prose was becoming normalized in the smaller subset of texts that we now consider literary. Comedy—especially comedies with contemporary settings—often employed prose; so, occasionally, did tragedies, such as *Arden of Faversham* (1592). Long prose narratives proliferated: 'romances' such as Philip Sidney's own *Arcadia*, Robert Greene's *Pandosto* (1588), and John Lyly's *Euphues* (1588), as well as the boisterous satires of Thomas Nashe. The early decades of the seventeenth century saw an even more exuberant burgeoning of prose writing, both in these genres and in new ones, such as the essay and the 'character'. An important stimulus to the development of English prose style was the masterfully eloquent 'King James' translation of the Bible, completed in 1611 as a collaboration among the period's most distinguished scholars of Greek and Hebrew. Used in the Church of England in a period in which virtually everyone attended weekly services, and in which individual worshippers were expected to acquire an intimate knowledge of Scripture, the 'Authorized Version' would profoundly influence English writers for centuries to come.

After 1640, the turmoil of civil conflict produced yet new possibilities. Journalism was one. Reporting upon current events had long been difficult because of the Crown's strict censorship rules, which inhibited the open discussion of prominent individuals or government policies. Punishment for violating these laws could be savage. In 1579, John Stubbes' right hand was amputated with a cleaver after he wrote and published a tract objecting to one of Queen Elizabeth's marriage prospects. In 1593, the Protestant radical John Penry was hanged for sedition: the evidence against him was a harshly worded but unpublished and uncirculated petition addressed to Queen Elizabeth, found among his private papers. As I have mentioned in the Introduction, when William Prynne's 1632 anti-theatrical tract, *Histriomastix*, seemed to cast aspersions upon Queen Henrietta Maria's sexual virtue, the

---

[3] For the immense volume of printed religious texts in the period, see Alec Ryrie, *Being Protestant in Reformation Britain*, pp. 259–297.

author was disbarred, heavily fined, and pilloried; his ears were cut off, and he was sentenced to prison for life. Nonetheless, in the early seventeenth century a tiny news industry began to emerge (Ben Jonson satirized this development in his 1620 masque, *News from the New World Discovered in the Moon*, and the 1625 comedy, *The Staple of News*.[4]) To work around the censorship laws, which focused on printed or performed material, the reports were often delivered as ostensibly personal correspondence from a city dweller and courtier to a provincial friend. In the early years of James's reign these letters really circulated among groups of acquaintance, but in the 1620s, when a larger readership developed, eager for information about the religious wars on the Continent, the process began to become professionalized: 'A well-organized newsletter writer, with good sources of information, would soon build up a network of customers, who would pay a subscription to receive the letters.'[5] The 'letters to a friend' were copied and recopied by professional scribes, sometimes hundreds of times. Parliamentary speeches and other political material also circulated widely in manuscript by similar means. In the 1640s the breakdown of Crown power made censorship laws unenforceable, ending the need for subterfuge. Almost immediately, a plethora of printed 'newsbooks' began to provide readers, from a variety of political perspectives, with a steady diet of what purported to be eyewitness reports of battles, state trials, and executions, including, in 1649, the trial and execution of King Charles himself.[6]

With censorship laws temporarily in abeyance, the pressing religious and political issues of the day could also be openly addressed in print. This too was not an entirely new development. In the 1590s the 'Marprelate' tracts had taken satiric aim at the English episcopacy, but the vigilance of the censors had meant that the printing of such incendiary material had to be done surreptitiously and the author (or authors) remained anonymous. But in the 1640s and 1650s, even after Cromwell's government eventually strengthened the government's oversight of printed material, religious and political controversy could be conducted with some impunity. And conducted it was. John Milton, John Lilburne, Roger Williams, and Gerrard Winstanley promoted various radical concepts such as freedom of the press, universal male suffrage, divorce for incompatibility, the separation of church

---

[4] Paul Salzman discusses the early attempts to satisfy a demand for news in *Literary Culture in Jacobean England*, pp. 140–158.
[5] Harold Love, *Scribal Publication in Seventeenth-Century England*, p. 26.
[6] For the development of the newsbook, see Joad Raymond, *The Invention of the English Newspaper: English Newsbooks 1641–49*.

and state, and the redistribution of land. On the royalist side, Hobbes's *Leviathan* (1651) mounted a theoretically rigorous defence of a powerful authoritarian state, while Charles I's spiritual autobiography *Eikon Basilike* (1649) became, after his death, a highly effective instrument of conservative propaganda.

The expanded uses of prose in the early part of the seventeenth century heralded an even greater literary role of prose after the Restoration, when the periodical essay would become a dominant literary mode, and when a new genre, the novel, began to establish itself as heir to the social and psychological intricacy of Renaissance drama. A variety of critics have analysed the process of this emergence, focusing on the stylistic evolution of English prose between the latter part of the sixteenth century and the beginning of the eighteenth. Morris Croll and George Williamson argue that, just as humanist writers strove to develop a graceful style in Latin, they also attempted to reproduce in their vernaculars specific admired qualities of particular Latin originals. In the late sixteenth and early seventeenth centuries a distinctive group of French and English writers reacted against the rotund oratorical 'Ciceronian' periods preferred by the early humanists, replacing them with a terse, oblique, syntactically disjunct, deliberately jagged style imitative of Tacitus and Seneca.[7] The 'Senecan' or 'Tacitean' imitation often was deliberately tortuous, resulting in what Croll calls the baroque style:

> Expressiveness rather than formal beauty was the pretension of the new movement . . . It disdained complacency, suavity, copiousness, emptiness, ease . . . It preferred the forms that express the energy and labour of minds seeking the truth, not without dust and heat, to the forms that express a contented sense of the enjoyment and possession of it.[8]

Even as the 'baroque' style predominated, however, it was in the process of being superseded. In the middle decades of the seventeenth century, as Richard Foster Jones has shown, the nascent scientific community began to develop a deliberately straightforward 'plain style' emphasizing an

---

[7] Morris Croll, *Style Rhetoric, and Rhythm: Essays by Morris Croll* and *'Attic' and Baroque Prose Style: The Anti-Ciceronian Movement*, ed. J. Max Patrick et al., collects essays Croll originally wrote several decades earlier. See also George Williamson, *The Senecan Amble: A Study in Prose Form From Bacon to Collier*.

[8] Morris Croll, 'The Baroque Style in Prose', in *'Attic' and Baroque Prose Style*, pp. 207–208

unembellished statement of fact.⁹ As Jones and Perry Miller have shown, this shift towards plainness and economy goes hand in hand with a similar movement towards uncomplicated diction and lack of rhetorical ornament in Puritan and Baptist sermons.¹⁰

These accounts of seventeenth-century English prose style, while they insightfully capture some important trends in the period, are limited in several respects. By focusing so intently on sentence construction and rhetorical effect, they tend to minimize the often daring and speculative ideas being presented—ideas that would in some cases revolutionize large fields of knowledge. They are also constrained by the relatively circumscribed group of writers whom they consider significant: largely university-educated clergymen, lawyers, and physicians writing for a similar readership. Popular middlebrow writers, such as Thomas Dekker or Thomas Overbury, receive no attention; nor does Mary Wroth, whose long, two-part romance *Urania* was only rediscovered in recent decades by feminist critics.

In actuality, there is not really a single 'tradition' of English prose in this period, in the sense that seventeenth-century prose writers together form an even semi-cohesive group. In many cases, because their interests were so diverse, they are unlikely even to have been aware of one another's endeavours. In addition, for the literary historian, the prose writers of the period pose a special challenge because this sprawling array of works includes many that are sometimes considered 'literary' and sometimes not. Are Lancelot Andrews' or John Donne's sermons literature? William Camden's *Remains Concerning Britain*? John Selden's *History of Tithes* (1618)? Thomas Hobbes's *Leviathan*? John Milton's divorce tracts? This chapter will discuss a variety of prose genres and authors, but for reasons of space it will exclude histories, sermons, journalism, and political polemic. Each of these have complex, separate developmental trajectories which have received extensive scholarly treatment elsewhere.¹¹

---

⁹ Richard Foster Jones, *Ancients and Moderns: A Study of the Rise of the Scientific Movement in Seventeenth-Century England*.

¹⁰ Perry Miller, *The New England Mind: The Seventeenth Century*.

¹¹ For journalism, see Joseph Frank, *The Beginnings of the English Newspaper 1620–1660*; Joad Raymond, *The Invention of the English Newspaper: English Newsbooks 1641–49*; Jurgen Habermas, *The Structural Transformation of the Public Sphere: An Inquiry into a Category of Bourgeois Society*, trans. T. Burger, and the essays in N. H. Keble, ed., *The Cambridge Companion to Writing the English Revolution*. For sermons, see *The Oxford Handbook of the Early Modern Sermon*, and for devotional prose more generally, see Alec Ryrie, *Being Protestant in Reformation Britain*, pp. 259–314. For political writing, see David Norbrook, *Writing the*

The history of 'English' prose in this period raises questions of language as well. As we shall see, many educated writers wrote, or yearned to write, in Latin in order to address an international audience. At the same time, those less linguistically gifted, or those (like playwrights) that needed to produce at a hectic rate, routinely used English translations of prose texts originally written in foreign languages. Of course, both short and long works were translated in the period, and there were important translations both of poetry and prose, but prose works were especially likely to be long, and thus much easier for an English writer to access once they were available in translation. Shakespeare and many other dramatists took their plots from stories translated from French, Italian, and classical writers by William Painter in his 1575 collection of tales, *The Palace of Pleasure*; Shakespeare drew as well upon Thomas North's 1580 English translation of Plutarch's *Lives*—itself derived from a French translation—for his Roman plays and *Timon of Athens*. He seems to have read Montaigne's essays with interest and care, but only after Montaigne's essays were translated into English by John Florio in 1603.[12] Similarly, John Fletcher, who drew many of the plots of his tragicomedies from Cervantes, and who may have read some Spanish, nonetheless evidently relied upon the translations of *Don Quixote* by Thomas Shelton published in 1612 and 1620, and Matthew Lownes' 1619 translation of *Persiles and Sigismunda*.[13] This chapter will focus on English writers, but it will not attempt to draw a clear line between 'literary' and 'non-literary' prose, nor to draw an anachronistic distinction between English and Latin works, nor to describe a clear evolution of stylistic change. And because, even with some prose forms excluded, the field is still so enormous, the selectivity that has governed my presentation in earlier chapters of this book will become even more evident in this one. I am not attempting a comprehensive survey, but more modestly aiming to showcase a variety of early seventeenth-century prose writings, and to suggest why they still are worth reading.

English Republic: Rhetoric and Politics 1627–1660; Nigel Smith, *Perfection Proclaimed: Language and Literature in English Radical Religion 1640–1660* and *Literature and Revolution in England*; Sharon Achinstein, *Literature and Dissent in Milton's England*; John Gurney, *Brave Community: The Digger Movement in the English Revolution*; Rachel Foxley, *The Levellers: Radical Political Thought in the English Revolution*; Lois Potter, *Secret Rites and Secret Writing: Royalist Literature 1641–1660*; Quentin Skinner, *Liberty Before Liberalism*.

[12] For Montaigne's influence on Shakespeare in the latter half of his career, see Lars Engle, Patrick Gray, and William Hamlin, eds., *Shakespeare and Montaigne*.

[13] Edward Wilson, 'Did John Fletcher Read Spanish?' *Philological Quarterly* 27 (1948): 187–190, reviews the evidence, arguing that Fletcher's 'knowledge of Spanish was not profound and sometimes he used translations to save himself trouble', but that he read some Spanish texts in the original.

Intellectual Prose

The early seventeenth century witnessed considerable upheaval and excitement in the natural sciences. In its first decades, Johannes Kepler and Tycho Brahe published important mathematical refinements to the heliocentric astronomical model pioneered by Copernicus in the mid-sixteenth century; meanwhile, Galileo Galilei was bolstering its plausibility via astronomical observations made newly possible by the telescope. Challenges to the traditional view of the earth and heavenly bodies were particularly unsettling because the Copernican system, if true, suggested that what seemed like some of the most obvious and undeniable testimonies of the human senses—the fixity and centrality of the earth, the movement of the sun and moon across the sky—were not objective facts, but tricks of perspective. Simultaneous with these innovations were new discoveries about 'the little world of man'. The dissection of cadavers had revolutionized the science of anatomy in the sixteenth century and continued to offer new insights, challenging long-held medical orthodoxies based on the teachings of the late-classical physician Galen. Yet while dissection allowed a close investigation of physical structures, many of the dynamic processes of living organisms remained unobservable and mysterious. Nonetheless, in 1628, the English physician William Harvey demonstrated, through a series of ingenious experiments, that blood circulated in the body, pumped by the heart into the arteries and then returned via the veins. His discoveries were completely incompatible with the traditional understanding of the function of the heart and the behaviour of blood, and took decades to win general acceptance.

Of course, there was nothing provincially English about such scientific concerns. The community of investigators and commentators was a cosmopolitan one and, as a result, the normal scholarly and intellectual language of communication was in Latin rather than in any of the vernacular tongues. Latin not only had a much wider provenance among educated male readers all over Europe, but it was regarded as fixed and therefore permanent in a way that English was not. Thus, Francis Bacon, dedicating his 1625 *Essays, or Counsels* to the Duke of Buckingham, hopes that 'the Latin volume of them (being in the universal language) may last as long as books last'.[14] Many landmark treatises of the period were originally written in Latin, such as Bacon's *Novum Organum* or William Harvey's *De Motu*

---

[14] Francis Bacon, *The Essays or Counsels, Civil and Moral*, in Michael Kiernan, ed., *The Oxford Francis Bacon*, vol. 15, p. 5.

Cordis, and only translated into English well after the fact. The scholarly John Selden, a towering early seventeenth-century figure in legal and Biblical exegesis, wrote far more in Latin than in English. Other works, such as Bacon's *Essays* or Browne's *Religio Medici* (1643), originated in English but were made available in Latin translation shortly thereafter. Robert Burton tells the reader, in his introduction to *The Anatomy of Melancholy*, that 'it was not mine intent to prostitute my muse in English', but he could not find a local printer willing to handle a Latin version.[15] So he writes in English but often lapses into extended Latin quotations and citations: 'if the book's basic character is necessarily English', writes Joan Webber, 'it is nevertheless a macaronic English'.[16] Similarly, in the preface to *Pseudodoxia Epidemica* (1646), Thomas Browne claims that he only belatedly decided to compose his treatise in English: 'our first intentions considering the common interest of truth, resolved to propose it unto the Latin republic and equal judges of Europe'. Eventually, however, he decided patriotically that he owed 'in the first place this service unto our country, and therein especially unto its ingenuous gentry'.[17] The bilingualism of these early seventeenth-century intellectuals (indeed, multilingualism, since most of them were conversant in French, Italian, and sometimes Greek as well) is of course what facilitated their modelling their English prose on classical originals in the first place. Insofar as writers of intellectual prose considered themselves to be contributing to an international conversation, their English and Latin works need to be considered together.

One of the most important and influential early seventeenth-century English intellectuals was the polymath lawyer and courtier Francis Bacon.[18] Bacon was born into a well-connected political family: his father was Elizabeth's Lord Keeper of the Great Seal and his maternal aunt was married to Elizabeth's most important advisor, William Cecil. Under King James, Bacon had a busy, highly distinguished career as a lawyer and courtier himself, eventually becoming Attorney General and Lord Chancellor, before being forced into retirement on a charge of bribe-taking. The pressures of his political career helped shape his literary endeavours. While he began

---

[15] Robert Burton, *The Anatomy of Melancholy*, ed. Thomas C. Faulkner, Nicolas Kiessling, and Rhonda Blair, p. 16.
[16] Joan Webber, *The Eloquent 'I': Style and Self in Seventeenth-Century Prose*, p. 84.
[17] Thomas Browne, *Pseudodoxia Epidemica*, ed. Robin Robbins, p. 2.
[18] Brian Vickers, *Francis Bacon and Renaissance Prose*; Lisa Jardine, *Francis Bacon: Discovery and the Art of Discourse*; James Stephen, *Francis Bacon and the Style of Science*; Alan Stewart and Lisa Jardine, *Hostage to Fortune: The Troubled Life of Francis Bacon, 1561–1626*.

to develop his characteristic preoccupations in early adulthood, in the last years of Elizabeth's reign, a great deal of his actual writing, with a full explication of his most important ideas, was not produced until the years between his disgrace in 1621 and his death in 1626.

Although not a distinguished scientist himself, Bacon developed a powerful theoretical groundwork for scientific investigation based on systematic empirical study. Bacon's first publication on the topic was in English: *The Advancement of Learning*, printed in 1605 and addressed to King James, who had recently succeeded to the English throne. *The Advancement* is an attempt to survey all of human knowledge, jettisoning the deadwood and identifying fruitful avenues for future research. Bacon develops his vision further in *De Augmentis Scientiarum*, his 1623 expansion of *The Advancement of Learning*, and in his unfinished 1626 utopian fiction *The New Atlantis*. In an age in which experimentation was largely conducted by individuals pursuing idiosyncratic projects, Bacon understood that a disciplined, collective approach to research could dramatically amplify the power of scientific investigation. In *The New Atlantis*, science is imagined as an organized social endeavour. Practitioners serve distinct functions: some compile data, some design new experiments, some devise technological applications, and some study others' experiments in an attempt to codify natural laws. Yet these different forms of expertise conjoin to reach coherent goals. By the mid-1640s, inspired by Bacon's dicta, some scientists and mathematicians were meeting regularly in Oxford and Gresham College, London, to pool their expertise. After the Restoration, their collaborations would lead to the founding of the Royal Society.

The principles underlying Bacon's scientific method are set out most fully in *Novum Organum* ('The New Organon'), published in 1620. It was originally designed as the second part of a much larger work, *Instauratio Magna* ('The Great Instauration' or renewal), which Bacon did not live to complete. The word 'organon' means 'tool' in Greek, and the word was the traditional title for Aristotle's six treatises on logical thinking. In his *Organon* Aristotle promoted syllogism, or deductive reasoning, as a way of arriving at truth. Bacon takes aim at Aristotle's legacy, and in particular the implication that it is possible to discover truth merely by logical cogitation, without the input of experience or experiment. For Bacon, the Aristotelian method is suspect because the propositions that make up the logical syllogism are potentially untrustworthy verbal constructs:

the syllogism is made up of propositions, propositions of words, and words are the tokens and signs of notions. Thus, if the very notions of the mind (which are as the soul of words and the basis of this whole fabric and structure) are ineptly and recklessly abstracted from things, and vague, insufficiently delimited and circumscribed, and indeed rotten in many ways, everything collapses.[19]

Unfortunately, the confusion of notions is not only possible but likely. In *Novum Organum* Bacon argues that the human mind is prone to both intrinsic and acquired faults, which he calls 'idols'. The intrinsic ones are psychological flaws in the mind's operation, either shared with other people (the 'idols of the tribe') or idiosyncratic to a particular individual (the 'idols of the cave'). Other faults are the result of acculturation, and are acquired either through deceptively reifying language (the 'idols of the marketplace') or through fallacious philosophical systems (the 'idols of the theatre'). Thus, the human mind is a flawed instrument, and language both reflects and exacerbates these flaws. The investigator must do everything in his power to eradicate or at least compensate for these four kinds of idols before, and while, he undertakes his experimental inquiries.

Though Bacon excludes religious phenomena from his purview, his conviction that the human mind is profoundly defective is a familiar theme in Protestant theology. In fact, in *The Advancement of Learning* Bacon connects his campaign of intellectual renovation with the methods of reformers such as Martin Luther. The Baconian subject is a self-critical, continuously self-policing one, pessimistic about its own unaided abilities, distrustful of pleasure, chronically apprehensive of what Bacon is constantly calling 'mixture' and 'corruption', and wary of being defrauded by 'idols', 'masks and mummeries', 'enchantments', and other dangerous allurements.

> So much then for the individual kinds of idols and their trappings, all of which must be foresworn and renounced with unwavering and solemn resolve, and the intellect must be thoroughly freed and purged of them, since entrance into the Kingdom of Man, which is founded on the sciences, differs little from that into the Kingdom of Heaven, into which none enters except in the likeness of a little child.[20]

---

[19] Francis Bacon, *Novum Organum*, 'The Plan of the Work', in *The Instauratio Magna Part II Novum Organum and Associated Texts*, ed. Graham Rees and Maria Wakeley, *The Oxford Francis Bacon*, vol. 11, p. 31.

[20] Ibid., p. 109.

Bacon's metaphors for the properly prepared mind resemble the austere interior of a reformed church: scoured clean, uncluttered by distracting ornament, evenly illuminated by clear white light. In order to discover 'the very art and rule of interpreting nature', he writes in a typical passage in *Novum Organum*, 'I have purged, raked, and leveled the seed-bed of the mind'.[21] The Baconian subject is, in other words, mentally puritanical.

Yet Bacon's deviations from the spirit of the Reformation are as important as the similarities. While for the Reformers human defects are spiritual, requiring divine aid for their amelioration, for Bacon they are essentially epistemological and can be remedied by determined, self-aware efforts to counteract them. Moreover, the Baconian doctrine of the 'idols of the mind' turns the traditional idolatry concept almost on its head. The religious objection to idolatry was that it constituted a form of spiritual myopia. The idolator worships visible objects—a river, a heavenly body, a statue—without understanding the larger, less easily perceptible creative and ordering power behind these sensual manifestations. For Bacon, by contrast, 'idolatry' involved a too-swift tendency to abstract and generalize: not a dwelling in sensual particulars, in other words, but a prideful claim that, on the basis of limited and partial evidence, one was entitled to make universalizing claims. Thus, while for religious thinkers the idolator is hopelessly mired in material details, Bacon's scientist embraces these details, only cautiously hypothesizing general laws, and restraining himself from conjecturing far beyond what he can observe.

Another crucial difference between Bacon and religious reformers is his orientation towards time. Religious reformers typically located their ideals in the past, yearning for the Eden lost in the Fall, and aiming to strip away the contaminating accretions of centuries in order to restore the purity of the primitive Christian church. Bacon, by contrast, argues that 'the discovery of things is to be sought not from the shadows of antiquity but from the light of nature'.[22] He places his faith in the future, in which he expects that scientific and technological advances will dramatically improve the lot of humanity. The title-page of the *Novum Organum* shows a ship sailing through the Pillars of Hercules that were supposed to have been set up at the strait of Gibraltar in ancient times, marking the limit of the Mediterranean and the boundary beyond which it was not considered safe to voyage. By the seventeenth century, of course, trans-Atlantic travel was feasible and common;

---

[21] Ibid., p. 173.
[22] Ibid., p. 183.

the illustration suggests an analogy between the European exploration and colonization of the 'New World' and the progress of the sciences, discovering things previously unknown or thought impossible. Bacon is thus an important transitional figure between the Reformation sensibility, pervaded by religious conviction, and a secular, empirical Enlightenment worldview.

While Bacon was an influential proponent of science and the scientific method, he also produced many other kinds of writing. Perhaps most notable among these is a shrewdly analytical history of the reign of Henry VII, which showcases the author's political intelligence, and his innovative essays, the first in English. The essay form had been invented by the French writer Michel de Montaigne in the sixteenth century and swiftly became popular all over Europe. Variable in length, the essay gives the impression of recording the author's sometimes meandering thought process, rather than being organized as an attempt to narrate or persuade. John Florio's English translation of Montaigne's essays was printed in 1603, but they were widely read in England by Francophone authors before that date. Bacon was probably introduced to Montaigne's work by his brother, Anthony, who had lived in France for some years and had become friendly with Montaigne there. At any rate, Bacon begins writing essays in the 1590s, well before Florio's translation. The first edition, published in 1597, contains only ten essays; a second edition appears in 1612, with thirty-eight; and a third is published in 1625, with fifty-eight. Not only does Bacon write new essays throughout his life, but he often revises and expands the old ones, just as Montaigne had done. This revision practice is characteristic of many of the writers of intellectual prose in this period, who periodically revisit, expand, and update their work, issuing it in new printings.

What probably appealed to Bacon in Montaigne's work is Montaigne's refusal to fit his thought into any predetermined form, and his concomitant celebration of the authority of experience. As Stanley Fish points out, although Bacon's essays often begin with what seems like a confident generalization, the force of that sweeping statement tends to be overturned or even contradicted as the essay develops.[23] This provisional quality, in which theories may always be discarded or revised based upon new evidence, is, of course, very much in line with the flexibility of mind and openness to data that Bacon recommends to the aspiring scientific investigator. Like Montaigne, too, Bacon rejects philosophical systems that seem too rigorous or ascetic in favour of a nuanced scepticism. Even Biblical passages that seem

---

[23] Stanley Fish, *Self-Consuming Artifacts*, pp. 78–155.

to recommend heroic forms of self-denial receive a critical eye. In 'Of Greatness and Goodness of Nature', Bacon recalls Jesus' encounter with a wealthy young man. 'Sell all thou hast and give it to the poor, and follow me', Bacon quotes Jesus, and then adds 'but sell not all thou hast, except thou come and follow me; that is, except thou have a vocation wherein thou mayest do as much good with little means as with great. For otherwise in feeding the streams thou driest the fountain.'[24] What in Scripture might seem Jesus' demand for recklessly total renunciation becomes, in Bacon's reading, a prudent cost–benefit calculation.

In other essays, in keeping with his pragmatic sense of the variability of circumstances, Bacon comments on the useful features of traits that are ordinarily thought to be shortcomings or sins. Cruelty, for instance, has its uses: in 'On Marriage and Single Life', Bacon notes that unmarried men, who have had no occasion to develop their capacity for empathy in a domestic setting with wives and children, are 'good to make severe inquisitors'.[25] Though he condemns vainglory, he notes that it often accompanies military valour. Even more commonly, an attribute or practice might be good or bad depending upon the situation. In 'Of Suspicion', Bacon labels suspicion a defect 'not in the heart but in the brain', with many disadvantages: 'suspicions . . . cloud the mind, they leese friends, and they check with business'. Yet the remedy is not credulity, but a clear-eyed awareness that other people may not be entirely trustworthy:

> What would men have? Do they think those they employ and deal with are saints? Do they not think they will have their own ends, and be truer to themselves than to them? . . . There is no better way to moderate suspicions than to account upon such suspicions as true and yet to bridle them as false.[26]

In other words, realistic suspicion drives out the paranoid variety. Along similar lines, in 'Of Usury' Bacon begins by noting that 'many have made witty invectives against usury', but argues that 'few have spoken of usury usefully'. 'To speak of the abolishing of usury is idle', he continues: 'all states have ever had it, in one kind or rate or other'. The solution is not to deplore usury but to regulate it, 'that the tooth of usury be grinded, that it bite not too

---

[24] Bacon, *The Essays or Counsels, Civil and Moral*, in Michael Kiernan, ed., *The Oxford Francis Bacon*, vol. 15, p. 40.
[25] Ibid., p. 26.
[26] Ibid., p. 102.

much', while at the same time 'there be left open a means to invite monied men to lend to the merchants, for the continuing and quickening of trade'.²⁷

The most striking difference between Montaigne and Bacon is in their authorial self-presentation. Montaigne's essays are disarmingly self-revelatory: intermixed with his reflections upon friendship, Stoicism, liberty of conscience, and the education of children are discussions of his kidney stones, his dining preferences, his bowel habits, and his fondness for his cat. Bacon's authorial voice, by contrast, is oracular and impersonal. The difference may reflect their different situations. While Montaigne, a well-off gentleman who had retired to his provincial estate, observes the world from a position of relative security, for the first two decades of the seventeenth century Bacon had no such sanctuary, occupying a series of powerful roles at the centre of the knives-out Jacobean political establishment. He was understandably wary of self-disclosure in an environment in which his enemies might try to ruin him (as they eventually did, by instigating a trial on corruption charges). Moreover, Bacon was rumoured to be homosexual in an age in which 'sodomy' was a capital crime, so circumspection was perhaps second nature.²⁸ At any rate, Bacon imagines an essayist who is less a conversational confidante, and more a shrewd mentor and guide, giving the reader the benefit of his wide learning and experience. The subtitle of his 1625 edition, 'Counsels', suggests that Bacon conceives his essays not as confessions or ruminations, but as pithy advice implicitly addressed to other busy, practical men of affairs.

While Bacon, his career close to the centres of power, develops an authorial persona that exudes worldly acumen, Robert Burton, the author of *The Anatomy of Melancholy*, spent his entire adult life as a scholar in Oxford, immersed in the world of books. Despite these differences, he shares with Bacon a proclivity for gigantic, open-ended intellectual projects, expanded in successive revisions. *The Anatomy of Melancholy* went through five printings in Burton's lifetime, each more compendious than the last.

Also like Bacon, Burton focuses especially on the way subjective phenomena—moods, fixed ideas, emotional disturbances—can distort perceptions and behaviour. 'Melancholy' in early modern England was a term covering what would now be classified as a variety of mental disturbances: what we would call depression certainly, but also manias, delusions, anxiety

---

[27] Ibid., pp. 124–127.
[28] For a discussion of Bacon's sexuality, see Lisa Jardine and Alan Stewart, *Hostage to Fortune: The Troubled Life of Francis Bacon, 1561–1626*, pp. 17, 161–163, 437, 460–466.

disorders, phobias, obsessive compulsions, and post-traumatic stress disorders. Melancholy was imagined as simultaneously a physical disease—an imbalance of the bodily humours—and as a spiritual malady; Burton also details the ways in which social institutions might exacerbate melancholic afflictions.[29] There was some discussion of mental illness in English before Burton—Timothy Bright's 1586 *Treatise of Melancholy* and Thomas Wright's 1601 *Passions of the Mind*—but Burton's capacious understanding of his subject, combined with his enormous erudition, produces a vast, heterogenous, and often unpredictable work. The entire human race, asserts Burton, suffers from melancholy, and for the author, moreover, the writing of his book functions as a therapy.

Whereas for Bacon the 'idols of the mind' were flaws to be eradicated, Burton's attitude is much more equivocal. He deplores and ridicules human follies and extravagances, but he cherishes them too. This difference of perspective shows up in his prose style, which although it traces, according to Croll, back to the same Latin models that inspire Bacon, conveys a quite different impression. Here, for instance, is a representative sentence, in which Burton reflects upon his own compositional practice:

> I have no such authority, no such benefactors, as that noble Ambrosius was to Origen, allowing him six or seven amanuenses to write out his dictates; I must for that cause do my business myself, and was therefore enforced, as a bear doth her whelps, to bring forth this confused lump; I had not time to lick it into form, as she doth her young ones, but even so to publish it as it was first written, *quicquid in buccam venit*, in an extemporanean style, as I do commonly all other exercises, *effudi quicquid dictavit genius meus*, out of a confused company of notes, and writ with as small deliberation as I do ordinarily speak, without all affectation of big words, fustian phrases, jingling terms, tropes, strong lines, that like Acestes' arrows caught fire as they flew, strains of wit, brave heats, elogies, hyperbolical exornations, elegancies, etc., which many so much affect.[30]

Both Bacon and Burton favour semi-detached clauses, in which each element of the sentence is only tenuously attached to the one prior. Yet in Bacon's case, compression and control evoke disciplined, goal-oriented

---

[29] Douglas Trevor, *The Poetics of Melancholy in Early Modern England*, pp. 118 ff.
[30] Robert Burton, *The Anatomy of Melancholy*, ed. Thomas C. Faulkner, Nicolas Kiessling, and Rhonda Blair, p. 17.

creative endeavour, while Burton's writing aspires, as he notes, to conversational spontaneity. His sentences, therefore, wander on and on, taking unpredictable swerves and detours. Like Bacon, Burton is hyper-aware of the world's heterogeneity and wary of classifying it prematurely, as suggested by his enumeration of near-synonyms and his habit of citing, throughout *The Anatomy*, multiple telling-but-strange anecdotes illustrating each of his assertions. Yet while Bacon wants to winnow and test, and ultimately to systematize, Burton tends merely to juxtapose, apparently untroubled by contradiction or incongruity. What counts as 'truth' is different for the two writers. For Bacon, lies and misconceptions are dangerous enticements that interfere with the progress of the sciences, so falsehoods must be identified and eliminated. Burton, on the other hand, references all kinds of authorities indiscriminately, without attempting to evaluate their credibility: indeed, the wild diversity of his sources and exempla are key to the pleasure of reading his book.

Burton's preface, 'Democritus Junior to the Reader', is as long as many free-standing books. Here he introduces his persona, heir to the Greek philosopher Democritus. The original Democritus was famous for a variety of philosophical claims, among them the first recorded atomic theory, but he is compelling for Burton because he features in a famous anecdote. While his contemporary Harpocrates wept at the sight of human folly and futility, Democritus, confronted with the same evidence, reacted with laughter. Burton embraces both Democritus' reputation for eccentricity and his capacity for satiric detachment. His preface is a skilled, self-reflexive work of satire along the lines of Erasmus' ironic *Praise of Folly* (1511), skewering human craziness in all walks of life, including his own, in order to argue for the importance of his topic.

In the main section of the book Burton's presentation becomes somewhat soberer and more straightforward, cataloguing the causes, symptoms, and treatment of different kinds of melancholy, and often evincing great compassion for those suffering from mental illness. Burton writes eloquently on the plight of the suicidal, and excoriates guardians who induce despair in their charges by unreasonable demands and forced marriages. Here, too, however, a great deal of fascinating material emerges in the eccentric deviations and unexpected forays. Just after discussing whether laxatives and sexual activity might cure melancholy, and before launching into the effects of climate and locale, Burton inserts an extraordinary 'Digression of the Air', which begins with an imagined flight around the entire globe, first enumerating the many geographical questions that remained unresolved in the early seventeenth century, then proceeding through a similar cache of problems posed by the new astronomy, and then on to debates about the nature of God.

Eventually, Burton focuses on two kinds of disturbance: one caused by unreasonable sexual passion, the other by religious anxiety. The relationship between sexual love and religious worship had long been remarked upon by Augustine and other Christian writers in the Platonic tradition. In Petrarch's sonnet sequence and in Dante's *Divine Comedy*, the author's infatuation with an earthly mistress becomes, after her death, a path to divine enlightenment; a similar dynamic suffuses the poetry of Donne, Herbert, and Milton. Yet Burton problematizes the 'ladder of love' by making it less a one-way journey to transcendence and more a two-way street. If religious devotion can 'cure' erotic melancholy by sublimating sexual urges, sexual activity can equally be the cure for unhealthy religious fixation. The fluctuating and cockeyed nature of the human mind finally, in Burton's view, defeats attempts to impose upon it the systematic thinking perhaps suggested by the word 'Anatomy' in his book's title. If 'all the world is melancholy, or mad, dotes, and every member of it',[31] then there is no stable, 'reasonable' perspective from which to make an objective assessment.

John Donne, who is of course better known as a poet than as a writer of prose, is roughly contemporary with Bacon and Burton, although his interests and his intellectual orientation are markedly different. His most extensive, and most extensively studied, prose writings are the numerous sermons he delivered as Dean of London's St Paul's Cathedral between 1621 and his death in 1631; he was one of the most celebrated preachers of his age. But he authored a number of prose treatises as well, both before and after his ordination in 1615. In the first decade of the seventeenth century, he wrote several tracts against the Jesuits: having been raised in a Roman Catholic family, he was well-placed to critique their views and could deploy their own casuistical forms of argument against them. Yet he was hardly a complacent member of the Jacobean establishment. During the same period, in 1608, he wrote the startling *Bia-Thanatos* ['life / death' in Greek], a treatise on suicide. Christians had long considered suicide a profoundly sinful act. The believer does not have the right to dispose of his own life, which is a gift from God. If he does so, he declares his despair of God's mercy (itself a damnable sin) and insists, pridefully, upon taking things into his own hands instead

---

[31] Ibid., p. 109.

of waiting trustfully for God to determine his fate. English law classified suicide as a subset of murder; suicides were considered felons and, like other felons, forfeited their rights to their property, thus denying an inheritance to their heirs. They were also forbidden a Christian funeral or burial in the consecrated ground of the churchyard. (Hence the discussion, in *Hamlet*'s 'graveyard scene', over Ophelia's 'doubtful' death and the rites appropriate for her.) Nonetheless, as the classically educated were fully aware, the pagan cultures of ancient Greece and Rome considered suicide an unobjectionable, oft-times even heroic act—a cultural difference highlighted in Shakespeare's Roman tragedies and in his narrative poem, *The Rape of Lucrece*.

Donne's treatise argues that suicide may in some circumstances be acceptable. He works painstakingly through civil law and church doctrine, highlighting the cultural variability of the former and the internal inconsistencies of the latter, and demonstrates how blurred are the lines between apparently culpable suicidal behaviour and the reckless disregard for self-preservation that sainted martyrs often exhibit. Towards the end of the treatise he discusses several Biblical figures—not only problematic ones like King Saul and Judas Iscariot, but also heroes like Samson, who destroyed himself when he pulled the Philistine's temple down upon them, and who was often considered a prefiguration of Christ. Most explosively, Donne suggests that Christ himself could be considered a suicide. As God, He had the power to save himself at any moment, and indeed He took leave of life at the moment of his own choosing, not when his body gave out completely but as soon as the work of atonement was complete.

The tone of Donne's argument has been debated by critics. His editors, Helen Gardner and T. S. Healey, consider it 'a long and careful piece of casuistry', emphasizing his analytical distance from his own arguments, while John Carey stresses his personal investment in the topic, calling it 'a giant suicide note'.[32] It is perhaps telling that Donne subtitles his treatise 'a declaration of [a] paradox, or thesis'. Donne had long been interested in the genre of the 'paradox', normally an argument for a deliberately outrageous and counterintuitive claim. He had written a number of paradoxes in the 1590s: 'in defense of women's inconstancy', 'that Nature is our worst guide', 'that only cowards dare die'. These paradoxes are the kind of thing that appeal to a young law student's love of playing devil's advocate, giving him the opportunity to showcase his resourcefulness and wit. At the same time,

---

[32] Evelyn Simpson, Helen Gardner, and T. S. Healy, eds., *John Donne: Selected Prose*, p. 25; John Carey, *John Donne, Life, Mind and Art*, p. 209

the paradox is not necessarily merely a joke: it offers a kind of freedom to voice otherwise unacceptable thoughts while not actually endorsing them. *Bia-Thanatos* is far longer than Donne's early paradoxes, and the topic is considerably more daring and significant. Moreover, Donne acknowledges his personal investment in that topic, admitting to what we would now call 'suicidal ideation'—an ideation abundantly visible elsewhere in his poems and sermons—but insisting that his fantasies do not arise from despair at his own salvation or a grudge against God.[33] By calling his work 'a paradox, or thesis', he suspends his argument between believability and unbelievability, asserting a claim that many of his contemporaries would have found shocking, but at the same time partially disavowing it. Donne's ambivalence may reflect a concern about how his arguments might be received, but it more likely reveals a certain unease about their heterodoxy. He seems to have controlled the circulation of *Bia-Thanatos* closely: the treatise was not printed during his lifetime, but he sent copies to a few trusted friends. Apparently he did not want *Bia-Thanatos* widely known, but he did not destroy it or keep it entirely private either.

Devotions Upon Emergent Occasions (1624), written much later in Donne's career, was a more openly devout text, and one Donne was eager to circulate: he had it printed shortly after he wrote it, dedicating it to Prince Charles. Yet, like *Bia-Thanatos*, *Devotions* is extraordinary: 'in English literature', writes Ramie Targoff, 'there is no precedent'.[34] And, like *Bia-Thanatos*, *Devotions* can be read as an attempt not just to reconcile oneself to one's death, but in some sense to master it via a heroic effort of the will and intellect. In 1623, London was in the midst of an epidemic of 'relapsing fever', possibly typhus. Donne contracted the illness, which was often fatal. Confined to his bedchamber, he wrote—probably largely in the weeks during his recuperation—a day-by-day account of the 'several steps in my sickness' and the thoughts elicited by each of them. Each of the twenty-three chapters begins with a 'meditation' describing the 'occasion' or stage in his illness, followed by an 'expostulation' in which he wrestles with his own reaction to his plight, and then a 'prayer' in which he asks God for help. Conceptually, however, these three categories tend to merge since the addressee throughout is God, and since for Donne his spiritual and physical states are inextricable. His bodily illness is both the manifestation of his sinful spiritual condition

---

[33] Mark Allinson 'Re-Visioning the Death Wish: Donne and Suicide', *Mosaic* 24 (1991): 31–46, takes a psychoanalytic approach to Donne's obsession with voluntary death. See also John Carey *John Donne, Life, Mind, and Art*.

[34] Ramie Targoff, *John Donne, Body and Soul*, p. 130.

and, he believes, a deserved punishment for that sin. Yet at the same time it is a welcome gift, allowing him the occasion to reflect, repent, and strengthen his faith before his likely demise.

While Bacon, and later those who adopted his mode of scientific endeavour, tended to regard metaphor with suspicion as a source of falsehood, for Donne metaphor was the tissue of reality and God's ways were essentially those of the poet or the rhetorician.

> My God, my God, thou art a direct God, may I not say, a literal God, a God that wouldst be understood literally and according to the plain sense of all that thou sayest? But thou art ... a figurative, a metaphorical God too; a God in whose words there is such a height of figures, such voyages, such peregrinations to fetch remote and precious metaphors, such extensions, such spreadings, such curtains of allegories, such third heavens of hyperboles, so harmonious elocutions, so retired and so reserved expressions, so commanding persuasions, so persuading commandments, such sinews even in thy milk, and such things in thy words, as all profane authors seem of the seed of the serpent that creeps, thou art the Dove that flies.[35]

Donne was deeply familiar with typological readings of the Bible, in which many personages and incidents are interpreted as symbolic of others, so that, for instance, events in the Old Testament were said to foreshadow those in the New and to have their analogies in the spiritual life of the Christian believer. For the typological reader, the scriptural text, the course of human history, and the progress of the individual soul towards or away from God all constitute a vast web of interrelated correspondences. In *Devotions Upon Emergent Occasions*, Donne's virtuosic capacity to discover surprising connections reaches a (perhaps literally) feverish pitch. In Expostulation 13, for instance, the outbreak of a rash on Donne's body leads him to consider his spiritual blemishes in the context of the Old Testament prohibition against sacrificing blemished animals: 'My God, my God, thou hast made this sickbed thine altar, and I have no other sacrifice to offer but myself: and wilt thou accept no spotted sacrifice?' After dwelling on the impossibility of becoming 'spotless', he decides that the visibility of his skin eruptions is in fact preferable to 'hidden spots' or secret sin, connecting his spotted body with the speckled sheep born to Jacob from Laban's flocks, a sign of God's

---

[35] John Donne, *Devotions Upon Emergent Occasions*, Expostulation 19, ed. Anthony Raspa, p. 99.

favour to the patriarch of the Jewish people. Manifesting his spots—openly confessing his sinfulness—enables Donne to rely upon Christ's saving grace: 'even my spots belong to thy Son's body . . . when I open my spots I do but present him with that which is his.' Thus, Donne declares, the 'spots' of his illness may signify not a rejection of or by God, but a reminder of Him: 'these spots upon my breast, and upon my soul, shall appear to me as the constellations of the firmament'.[36] Eventually, the spots that had at first seemed to estrange him from God become hopeful tokens of His favour. The paradoxical redefinition of misfortune as divine approval is entirely orthodox: we have already seen it underlying much of the most powerful devotional poetry of the period, Donne's included. But in this instance the redefinition unfolds as a cartwheeling free association correlating skin rash to sin, sheep, and stars.

In *Devotions Upon Emergent Occasions*, this yearning to make a connection takes social as well as literary and intellectual forms. Quarantined in his sickbed—no one dares visit him but his physicians—Donne becomes acutely aware of the community outside the walls of his chamber. The most famous passage in *Devotions Upon Emergent Occasions*, in which Donne declares that 'no man is an island', is elicited by the constant ringing of funeral bells marking the deaths of his neighbours, victims of the same disease from which he is suffering. Just as the solitary devotional poet offers himself to readers as a model, so here Donne at his loneliest also is aware that his story of vulnerability and mortality is ultimately everybody's story. 'Do not ask for whom the bell tolls; it tolls for thee': the conditions of epidemic bring the common plight of humanity acutely to mind.

Thomas Browne, writing in the generation after Francis Bacon, Robert Burton, and John Donne, shares their implicitly European rather than provincially English point of view. After receiving his undergraduate degree at Oxford, Browne pursued education as a physician at Montpellier, Padua, and Leiden—three universities that not only provided distinctly different kinds of medical training, but that, in an era of intense religious strife, exposed Browne to two distinct strains of Roman Catholicism as well as to the Reformed churches of the Netherlands.[37] It is unclear whether Browne consciously followed in Bacon's footsteps, but at any rate his mindset was markedly similar in its respect for empirical evidence and his lively sense of

---

[36] Ibid., pp. 68–70.
[37] Reid Barbour discusses Browne's unusual educational formation, and its effect on his religious views, in *Thomas Browne: A Life*.

the error-prone nature of the human mind. Browne debunks 'an epidemic of false teachings', submitting traditionally accepted notions to sceptical critique, in *Pseudodoxia Epidemica*, which his biographer Reid Barbour calls his 'most considerable work . . . his personal favorite . . . and the one that would contribute most to his scholarly and philosophical reputation'.[38] The 'false teachings' Browne eviscerates, one by one, over the course of his volume range from popular racial prejudices, to misconceptions about history and scripture, to fabulous lore about animals, plants, and minerals. The book opens, as does Bacon's *Novum Organum*, with a survey of the causes of error: custom, false reasoning, over-reliance upon unreliable authorities, the fallen human imagination. But unlike *Novum Organum*, which is more concerned with establishing a process by which a diligent investigator might arrive at truth, *Pseudodoxia Epidemica* fact-checks particular propositions, debunking error by a combination of empirical data and common sense. For instance, to the myth that elephants had no joints in their legs, Browne remarks that without joints they would be unable to move; besides, when one was brought to London and put on display, it was easily observed to flex its knees. Like Bacon, Browne especially deplores the deceptions of language, remarking 'how dangerous it is in sensible things to use metaphorical expressions unto the common people, and what absurd conceits they will swallow in their literals'. He attributes the common belief that Jews 'stink naturally, that is, in their race and nation there is an evil savor' to a misunderstood metaphor of spiritual abomination, 'which ... metaphorical expression, did after proceed into a literal construction, but was a fraudulent illation.'[39]

Browne's most famous work, however, was his first effort, *Religio Medici*, 'the religion of a doctor': a spiritual autobiography that attempts to mediate between scientific scepticism and faith, and to negotiate some of the fraught religious disputes between Catholics, Anglicans, and Puritans. The first authorized edition appeared in 1643, but Browne began writing it around 1635 and several earlier manuscript versions survive. Although Browne does not call *Religio Medici* an 'essay', it is in fact closer to the Montaignean tone and spirit than Bacon's essays, with a disarming self-regard and admitted lack of consistency. Although Browne repeatedly emphasizes his adherence to mainstream Church of England teachings, *Religio Medici* presents faith as

---

[38] Reid Barbour, *Sir Thomas Browne: A Life*, p. 296.
[39] Thomas Browne, *Pseudodoxia Epidemica*, ed. Robin Robbins, pp. 324–328.

a personal, even quirky, choice, rather than a commitment to a set of doctrines. The efficacy of a religious practice might well reside, he argues, in the individual experiencing it, not in the practice itself. For instance, of the Catholic veneration of the Virgin Mary, he writes:

> I could never hear the Ave Maria bell [sounded in Catholic countries] without an elevation, or think it a sufficient warrant, because they [Catholics] erred in one circumstance, for me to err in all, that is in silence and in dumb contempt; whilst therefore they directed their devotions to her, I offered mine to God, and rectified the errors of their prayers by rightly ordering mine own. At a solemn procession I have wept abundantly, while my consorts, blind with opposition and prejudice, have fallen into an access of scorn and laughter.[40]

The implication is that one man's religious meat might be another man's poison—or even that the same man's meat might be his poison at a different time in his life, since Browne cheerfully admits that in earlier years he had found several heretical positions attractive. For that reason, he writes, 'I could never divide myself from any man upon the difference of an opinion, or be angry with his judgment for not agreeing with me in that, from which perhaps in a few days I should dissent myself'.[41]

For some readers, this grounding of religious faith in individual foible can seem profoundly un-serious. One of the first readers of *Religio Medici*, Kenelm Digby, wrote of the book to the Earl of Dorset: 'What should I say of his making so particular a narration of personal things, and private thoughts of his own—the knowledge of which cannot much conduce to any man's betterment?'[42] For Stanley Fish hundreds of years later, Browne is 'the bad physician', more interested in showing off his own bravura prose style than in facilitating his readers' spiritual improvement.[43] Yet Browne is perhaps not quite so blithely narcissistic as these critics assume. For if one's own religious convictions are intrinsically bound up with one's individual personality and unique history, so are everyone else's. If faith is partly a matter of subjective preference, then the pretexts on which bloody wars of

---

[40] *Religio Medici, The Complete Works of Sir Thomas Browne*, vol. 1, ed. Reid Barbour and Booke Conti, pp. 181.
[41] Ibid., pp. 182–183.
[42] Kenelm Digby, *Observations upon Religio Medici Occasionally Written by Sir Kenelm Digby, Knight*, p. 53.
[43] Stanley Fish, *Self-Consuming Artifacts*, pp. 353–373.

religion are waged may be largely chimerical. In this respect, *Religio Medici* can seem a bellwether text for the each-to-his-own, live-and-let-live form of religious tolerance that will eventually become normalized in the West in the centuries to come.

Ranking with these other idiosyncratic prose contributions to mid-seventeenth-century literature is Isaak Walton's *The Complete Angler*. Like some of these other works, too, it has a complicated history of ongoing revision over the course of its five editions during the author's lifetime, the last of which was published in 1676. The first version appeared in 1653, as a dialogue between Piscator, the Fisherman, and Viator, the Traveller, who becomes Piscator's disciple. In the second edition, in 1655, Walton enlarged the work by about a third, changed Viator's name to Venator, the Hunter, and added another interlocutor, Auceps, the Falconer. Over the course of the dialogue Piscator, the master angler, provides a detailed account of different species of freshwater fish, explains where to find the right kinds of worms and caterpillars for live bait, shows how to make artificial flies for trout-fishing, and demonstrates the most effective methods of luring each kind of fish to his hook. His skill is honed by long experience: despite his careful explanation of his practices, Piscator can catch six fish to his 'scholar's' one.

The Complete Angler often cites Francis Bacon as an authority and an inspiration, and Piscator's granular descriptions of fish and fish habitats suggest a Baconian attention to pragmatic skills and to real-life observation of a heterogeneous natural world. Yet much of the charm of *The Complete Angler* is the thoroughly non-Baconian way in which Walton uses the dialogue as a way of showcasing his personal priorities—in his preface, he calls the book 'a kind of picture of my own disposition'.[44] The book celebrates angling as a lifestyle that combines action and contemplation, requiring not only an 'inquiring, searching, and discerning wit'[45] but patience and the ability to remain quiet. Fishing for Walton is a leisurely, gentlemanly pursuit, not a commercial endeavour, and it encourages affability and generous reciprocity. Piscator cheerfully teaches his techniques to others, for 'we anglers all love one another',[46] and shares his catch with a couple of nearby milkmaids, who repay him by singing a song and offering him some of their milk. In Walton's view, angling promotes the religious virtues: Jesus,

---

[44] Isaak Walton, *The Compleat Angler (1653)* in *Isaak Walton: The Complete Angler 1653–1676*, ed. Jonquil Bevan, p. 59.
[45] Ibid., p. 67.
[46] Ibid., p. 64.

he notes, chose fisherman as his first apostles, and 'the primitive Christians ... were (as most anglers are) quiet men, and followed peace'.[47] Walton infuses his descriptions of the English riverbanks with the spirit of utopian pastoral, interspersing Piscator's practical advice with snatches of poetry from Marlowe, Donne, and Herbert.

In the early 1650s, after years of turmoil, Walton's devotion to practical knowledge of the natural world seems of a piece with the imagined scientific academies conjured up in Abraham Cowley's roughly contemporaneous *Davideis* and William D'Avenant's *Gondibert*, in which objective investigations into the mysteries of nature provide purpose and solace after the experience of defeat. Like Cowley and D'Avenant, Walton was a committed royalist, though a discreet one. After the Restoration it was discovered that, during the 1640s, when the royal family was on the run, he had conveyed one of the Crown Jewels to safety at considerable risk to himself, but, notably, his service to the royalist cause did not involve military service and remained a secret for years. *The Complete Angler*'s air of good cheer has sometimes elicited a certain amount of condescension from critics who take its performance of artlessness at face value, much as they scoff at Herrick's apparent naiveté. Yet in troubled times, the appearance of quiet simplicity can be strategic, and so can the claim that one's own side is the peaceful, mild one. Like John Denham in *Cooper's Hill*, who associates royal power with the mighty but generally serene Thames River, Walton tends to displace responsibility for conflict onto the urban, commercial, and military interests associated with the Parliamentary cause and with Cromwell's ascendancy.

Moreover, despite the sunny descriptions of pastoral tranquillity that dominate *The Complete Angler*, Walton is aware that the management of the fishery is not an entirely pacific undertaking. In one of the dialogue's early sequences, the interlocutors witness an otter-hunt. Piscator hates otters, which he considers rapacious killers: 'in my judgment, all men that keep otter dogs ought to have a pension from the commonwealth to encourage them to destroy the very breed of those base otters, they do so much mischief'.[48] He cheers on the hunters and their dogs as they corner and kill a 'bitch otter', and then seek out her nest of babies to destroy them. The implication is that Walton's vaunted zone of peace and leisure may need strong, even brutal measures to exclude competition and predation.

[47] Ibid., pp. 66–67.
[48] Ibid., p. 64.

A Tale of Three Romances

Superficially, the patently counterfactual fantasy worlds of romance, full of giants, witches, enchantments, and unforeseeable calamities, might seem far removed from Baconian science—though, as we shall see, they are in some respects closer than they might initially appear. The prose romance tradition had long been a pan-European phenomenon. It originated with the Hellenistic 'novel', flowering in the twelfth century and afterward with tales of chivalry written in medieval dialects of French, German, English, Portuguese, and Italian. It continued in the early modern era, with such classics as *Amadis de Gaule* (1508; originally written in Spanish, possibly from a Portuguese original, but arriving in England via a French version) attracting wide readerships of both sexes and of all nationalities. For Jacobean romance writers, the most important native precedents were two late-sixteenth-century works: Philip Sidney's *Countess of Pembroke's Arcadia* and Edmund Spenser's *Faerie Queene* (1590–1596), the latter of which although, of course, not composed in prose drew upon many of the same narrative conventions. By the early seventeenth century a great deal of French, Italian, and Spanish romance was available in translation to monoglot English readers. *Don Quixote*, in particular—the first part translated by Thomas Shelton in 1612, and the second part in 1620—which both makes fun of romance conventions and at the same time exploits them in a highly sophisticated way, was extremely popular, influencing works by Shakespeare, Beaumont, Fletcher, Jonson, and Wroth.

Early seventeenth-century prose romance draws upon many of the same plot devices as tragicomedy and masque, already discussed in Chapter 5,[49] but the effect is quite different. The practical demands of live performance require a plot that, whatever its twists and turns, winds itself up in a couple of hours. A limited cast of characters must briskly experience remarkable setbacks on their way to a surprising—but at the same time expected—happy ending. Prose romances, by contrast, are typically very long and purposely digressive. They introduce a vast array of loosely affiliated characters, each of whom has his or her own trajectory, whose careers intersect and diverge in unpredictable ways. They often include interpolated tales or extended verse interludes. The denouement is thus long delayed, and perhaps even omitted

---

[49] For some of the connections between prose and dramatic romance, see the essays in Mary Ellen Lamb and Valerie Wayne, eds., *Staging Early Modern Romance: Prose Fiction, Dramatic Romance, and Shakespeare*.

altogether. Philip Sidney, after massively expanding his original version of *Arcadia*, abandoned the new version mid-sentence and, dying young, never completed it. Edmund Spenser's *Faerie Queene* is also incomplete, since he lived to write only six of the projected twelve books.

Romance had long been a mode in which, despite or because of the threat of state censorship, it had been possible to reflect seriously on political affairs. Remote, fantastic, often magical settings could be used to pose politically intriguing thought experiments.[50] The central story of Sidney's *Arcadia* involves the secretive double courtship of two princesses by two princes; one suitor cross-dresses as a woman, and the other disguises himself as a shepherd. Yet many of its conflicts arise from the virtual abdication of a weak and superstitious king, the rebelliousness of his subjects, and the potential incompatibility between youthful military prowess and proper deference to the authority of elders. Fulke Greville, Sidney's friend, asserted that the romance was intended 'lively to represent the growth, state, and declination of princes, change of government and laws, vicissitudes of sedition, faction, succession, confederacies, plantations, with all other errors or alterations in public affairs'.[51] Spenser's *Faerie Queene* engages even more directly with contemporary politics under a veil of allegory. In Canto 1, for instance, the true beloved, Una, is associated with the Protestant Church, Queen Elizabeth I, and a chaste love that leads to marriage; Duessa, the showy imposter that temporarily supplants her, is associated with the Catholic Church, Mary Queen of Scots, and a dangerously seductive, non-procreative sexuality.

Three Jacobean romances exemplify both the different potentials of the genre and the vagaries of reception and canon-formation in constructing a literary history. Arguably, one of them is no more a work of 'English' literature than are some of Bacon's treatises, because James Barclay's *Argenis*, the most celebrated romance of the period, was published in 1621 in Latin 'in order', his editors assert, 'to appeal to an international audience, in order to gain eternal fame'.[52] Yet, as Gerald Langford claims in his survey of Barclay's influence, *Argenis* 'is easily the outstanding novel produced by an Englishman during the first sixty years of the seventeenth century'.[53] Barclay was

[50] For the relationship of *Argenis* and *Urania* to the particular political circumstances of 1621, the date when both romances were printed, see Paul Salzman, *Literary Culture in Jacobean England: Reading 1621*, pp. 64–80.
[51] Fulke Greville, 'A Dedication to Sir Philip Sidney', *The Prose Works of Fulke Greville, Lord Brooke*, p.10.
[52] Mark Riley and Dorothy Prichard Huber, Introduction to John Barclay, *Argenis*, p. 39.
[53] Gerald Langford, '*Argenis*, a Seminal Novel', *SEL: Studies in English Literature* 26 (1947), p. 76.

even more internationally minded than Bacon or Browne; born of Scots parents in France, he came to the English court after the accession of James I, where he rapidly gained respect as a Latinist and served the Crown on several ambassadorial expeditions to the Continent. King James commissioned Ben Jonson to translate *Argenis* into English, and, when the work was, apparently, almost complete the manuscript was destroyed by a fire in Jonson's study. Jonson never recommenced the translation, although possibly it was his close engagement with Barclay's work that encouraged his experimentation with tragicomedy in such late plays as *The New Inn*, so different from the satiric urban comedies for which he is best known. In the event, two different English translations of *Argenis* were soon published: Kingsmill Long's in 1625 and Robert de Gruys' in 1628.

Barclay's decision to write in Latin not only suggests his cosmopolitan European outlook, but also, since classical learning was normally only afforded to boys and men, implicitly frames the intended readership for his romance as male. The plot concerns two heroic young men, Archombrotus and Polyarchus, who rescue King Meleander of Sicily from a nefarious coup attempt and a foreign invasion. They both fall in love with Meleander's daughter, Argenis, but their potentially deadly rivalry is precluded when it turns out that Archombrotus is Argenis' long-lost half-brother. Although the romance's title comes from the name of the heroine, she plays a relatively minor and passive role in the fast-paced and exciting action. The narrative leans much more heavily on themes of male friendship and competitiveness, military alliance and political ambition. In fact, many of the episodes are lightly allegorized versions of French sixteenth-century political and religious struggles, with some interpolation of more recent events suggested by Barclay's sojourn at the Jacobean court. A 1627 Latin edition even provides a key to the allegory, linking each character to a particular historical personage. The events of the romance give rise to extended dialogues on political and ethical dilemmas.

It is easy to see why King James would have appreciated *Argenis* and wanted it widely available in English as well as Latin. The central political dilemma involves a benevolent but overly lenient king, a bit too given to hunting, undermined by a scheming faction of ambitious aristocrats who are eventually aided by powerful and unscrupulous outside forces. The romance makes an unsubtle case for the desirability of absolutist monarchy: 'Barclay wishes to demonstrate that without union a country inevitably falls into ruin, that order and submission to authority are essential for political stability, and that such authority is divinely appointed and may not rightfully be resisted by subjects'.[54] The politics of *Argenis* make it popular, later in the century, with supporters of King Charles I. Barclay's work provides a template for several royalist romances published during the interregnum: William Sales' *Theophania* (1655), the first part of Percy Herbert's *Princess Cloria* (1653), and Richard Brathwait's *Panthalia* (1659). Lois Potter has convincingly described the appeal of tragicomedy and romance for interregnum supporters of the monarchy: 'the assimilation of contemporary history to literary models was a way of making sense of the disturbing and unprecedented nature of much that was happening in 1640–1660'.[55]

Argenis remained popular for more than 150 years and was reissued in more than fifty editions in many of the languages of Europe. It was a favourite of Leibniz, Richelieu, and Coleridge. Thereafter, it was virtually forgotten. The fate of Mary Wroth's *Countess of Montgomery's Urania* has been quite different. The first part of *Urania*, probably written between 1615 and 1620, was printed in 1621; the second part, probably written between 1620 and 1630, remained in manuscript until 1999. When the first part was printed—the first romance published by an Englishwoman—it caused something of a stir, but there is little evidence that it was widely read between the early 1620s and the 1990s. Yet in the past several decades feminist scholars have begun to rediscover seventeenth-century women's writing, of which Wroth's ambitious, multifaceted work is one of the most impressive examples. There is now a magnificent scholarly edition of *Urania*, which has in turn stimulated a substantial body of criticism and a scholarly biography. An abridgement of the work has been prepared for student use, and excerpts from *Urania* are routinely included in literary anthologies.[56]

Mary Wroth was the niece of Philip Sidney and his sister Mary Sidney, Countess of Pembroke—both renowned writers of the previous generation—and her aunt's namesake. In the early years of King James's reign she was a member of Queen Anne's circle of ladies, many of whom had literary interests, and consorted with the poets and playwrights associated

---

[54] Ibid., p. 62. For further discussion of Barclay's influence, and a discussion of the Latin style of *Argenis*, see J. IJselwiin, 'John Barclay and his *Argenis*: A Scottish neo-Latin Novelist', *Humanistica Lovaniensia* 32 (1983): 1–27.

[55] Lois Potter, *Secret Rites and Secret Writing: Royalist Literature 1641–1660*, p 107.

[56] The scholarly edition of the Urania is Mary Wroth, *The First Part of the Countess of Montgomery's Urania*, ed. Josephine Roberts and *The Second Part of the Countess of Montgomery's Urania*, ed. Josephine Roberts, Suzanne Gossett, and Janel Mueller. The biography is Margaret Hannay, *Mary Sidney, Lady Wroth*. The student edition is *The Abridged Countess of Montgomery's Urania*, ed. Mary Ellen Lamb. For Wroth's reception, see Naomi Miller, *Changing the Subject: Mary Wroth and Figurations of Gender in Early Modern England* and Paul Salzman, 'Mary Wroth: From Obscurity to Canonization', in *Reading Early Modern Women's Writing*, pp. 60–89.

with the Jacobean court. Just as Sidney dedicated *Arcadia* to his sister, so that the book came to be called *The Countess of Pembroke's Arcadia*, Wroth included the name of her dedicatee, her sister-in-law and fellow lady-in-waiting Susan, Countess of Montgomery, in the title of her work. The elaborate title-page of *The Countess of Montgomery's Urania* prominently features Wroth's illustrious family background, describing her in a heavily ornamented top-centre rondel as 'the right honourable the Lady Mary Wroth, daughter to the right noble Robert Earl of Leicester. And niece to the ever famous, and renowned Sir Philip Sidney, knight. And to the most excellent Lady Mary Countess of Pembroke late deceased.' Moreover, the *Urania* is named after, and prominently features, a character who appears fleetingly at the beginning of her uncle's romance, and then disappears. Thus, the opening establishes the *Urania* as, in a sense, a continuation or prolongation of *Arcadia*, even as Wroth herself furthers the notable tradition of a famous literary household.

The preoccupation with Wroth's birth family does not stop there. Wroth puts at the centre of her romance a hero, Amphilanthus ('lover of two'), royal, valiant, and handsome, and his first cousin Pamphilia ('all-loving'), a beautiful, wise, and poetically gifted princess. They seem a natural match for one another, and unsurprisingly fall deeply in love, but despite their profound mutual attachment they are separated again and again, not only by the buffets of fortune but also by Amphilanthus' temperamental inability to commit fully to Pamphilia. As the narrator rather acidly addresses him, 'I cannot say but thou art constant in love, for never art thou out of love. But variety is thy stain.' Wroth's modern critics have explored the way the relationship between Amphilanthus and Pamphilia tracks Wroth's relationship to her own first cousin, William Herbert, Earl of Pembroke. Pembroke was a powerful Jacobean courtier and patron of the arts (a dedicatee of Shakespeare's First Folio and of Jonson's *Forest*) as well as a notorious womanizer who exploited to the full the sexual liberty afforded to a man of his wealth and status. Although Mary and William were close from childhood, they were disposed in arranged marriages, as was common for Jacobean aristocrats. After the death of Mary's husband and toddler son, she might have been expected, as the still-young and reputedly beautiful daughter of an earl, to remarry. Instead, she embarked upon an affair with the married Pembroke, eventually bearing him two illegitimate children.

What is interesting here is not so much that Wroth uses romance conventions to reflect on 'real life', but that she uses it as a way to refract *her own life*. Barclay—or, for that matter, Spenser in *The Faerie Queene*—mainly depicts people who are safely dead or who are remote acquaintances. In *Argenis* the author's avatar is the court poet Nicompomus, who plays a minor role as an occasional commentator on the action; Wroth's avatar, by contrast, is the heroine, Pamphilia. Once again, there was a family precedent for Wroth's self-representation—Philip Sidney's sonnet sequence *Astrophil and Stella* had riffed on his doomed courtship of Penelope Rich—but Wroth's use of her own experience is much more elaborate and sustained. Not only does the central relationship echo the circumstances of Wroth's life, but several of *Urania*'s subplots provide alternate versions of a similar narrative and emotional dynamic.

Nor does Wroth merely mine her own experiences. When the first part of *Urania* was published it produced an uproar among Jacobean courtiers who thought themselves or one of their family members depicted within it. In one interpolated story, a father attempts to murder his daughter after her husband, Sirelius, suspects her of adultery. Sirelius intervenes to prevent the honour killing, and husband and wife reconcile. After the publication of *Urania*, Sir Edward Denny wrote a poem 'To Pamphilia from the Father-in-Law of Sirelius', protesting that Wroth had slandered him and thus essentially outing himself as the homicidal father. Although Wroth replied that 'not one word of that book' referred to 'his lordship's person or disgrace', Denny continued to sulk: 'the whole world conceives me to be meant'.[57] And Denny was not alone in taking offence; the courtier John Chamberlain writes to his friend Dudley Carleton that 'many others she makes bold with, and they say she takes great liberty or rather license to traduce whom she pleases, and thinks she dances in a net [i.e. invisibly]'.[58] For her part, Wroth complains, possibly disingenuously, of the 'strange constructions which are made of my book contrary to my imagination ... my purpose no way bent to give the least cause of offense'. Yet the scandal of the book's perceived topicality may have been the reason the second part of *Urania* remained in manuscript.

Many critics of romance have discussed the way its postponed endings create an especially sharp yearning for closure, a yearning exacerbated by its frustration.[59] Wroth elevates indefinite deferral to an existential principle.

---

[57] For a full discussion of the contretemps between Wroth and Denny, see Margaret Hannay, *Mary Sidney, Lady Wroth*, pp. 233–242.
[58] *The Letters of John Chamberlain*, ed. Norman Egbert McClure, vol. 2, p. 427.
[59] Jonathan Goldberg, *Endlesse Worke: Spenser and the Structures of Discourse*, and Patricia Parker, *Inescapable Romance: Studies in the Poetics of a Mode* and *Literary Fat Ladies: Rhetoric, Gender, Property* discuss the deferred conclusions of romance.

The through-line of most romances is the dogged fidelity of true lovers, loyal to one another through calamity after calamity—kidnappings, enchantments, impersonation by imposters, shipwrecks. Fletcherian tragicomedy, in some ways close in spirit to Wroth's romance, is, as we have seen, especially emphatic in its portrayal of love as making absolute and exclusive demands upon the heroic lovers. The eventual union of those lovers, then, provides an appropriate denouement. But in *Urania*, many characters—the males, especially—are flighty and unreliable. In one important plot strand, Parselius and Urania fall in love, but Parselius forgets her and marries Dalinea instead; then, after some time has passed, he remembers Urania in a dream and goes in search of her. Parselius and Urania are cured of their love by being immersed in magical sea-water off the island of Maura. For both parties, achieving freedom from a destructive passion comes as a relief. Parselius is delighted to return to Dalinea and lives with her happily until her death; Urania also finds contentment with someone else. And while Parselius' behaviour is not applauded, it is not a fatal character flaw, either; he continues to play a heroic role as Amphilanthus' friend and sometimes accomplice in great endeavours.

Wroth's heroine, Pamphilia, never stops loving Amphilanthus, but Wroth's narrative sometimes critiques the absolute desirability of her dogged fidelity. An interpolated story of Pelarina, who falsely idealizes her beloved and unwisely dedicates herself wholly to him despite his hostility and contempt, suggests that uncritical devotion can border on madness. Elsewhere, the wise Urania, who is Amphilanthus' sister and Pamphilia's confidante, counsels Pamphilia to cast her brother off:

> If he be false, will you vex yourself, when you may rather be glad you discover it before too far misfortune assailed you, as longer engagement would produce? If cruel, were it not better he matched elsewhere, than that you had fallen into that unhappiness?

Pamphilia rejects her advice:

> To leave him for being false would show my love was not for his sake but mine own: that because he loved me, I therefore loved him, but when he leaves, I can do so. Oh no, dear cousin, I loved him for himself, and would have loved him had he not loved me, and will love though he despise me . . . Pamphilia must be of a new composition before she can let such thoughts fall into her constant breast.

'Tis pity', replies Urania, 'that ever that fruitless thing constancy was taught you as a virtue.'[60] Indeed, while Urania questions if constancy in love is always a virtue, Pamphilia's language suggests, more radically, that that the terminology of virtue and vice may simply be inapposite—that constancy, or a penchant for erotic variety, may rather be ingrained traits of personality, unsusceptible to moral suasion. Wroth's narrator occasionally scolds Amphilanthus for his behaviour, but he remains glamorous, gifted, and wildly successful as a ruler and warrior—eventually king of Naples, Rome, and the Holy Roman emperor, 'master of the greater part of the Western world' (1.568) not by conquest or inheritance but by universal consent of the governed. Some critics have suggested that Amphilanthus' effortless unification of Europe constitutes a fantasy alternative to the situation in the fractured real world of the 1620s, in which James's daughter and son-in-law had been violently ejected from their thrones, and in which England's half-hearted and incompetent efforts at intervention failed disastrously.[61]

Because both circumstances and affections are prone to waver and change in the world of *Urania*, marriage, so often a romance plot *terminus ad quem*, tends to seem a mere way-station. The emphasis on a one-way trajectory of the female characters from maid to wife, from untouched virgin to honourably monogamous matron, so central to many romances by male authors, is here almost entirely absent. Characters, including both the hero and the heroine, marry people they respect but do not adore, even while sustaining their emotional connection to their original beloveds. Especially in the second part of *Urania*, though it features even more shipwrecks, lost children, giants, and other fantastic elements than the first part, many standard plot tropes seem to be critiqued or undermined. As Clare Kinney puts it, 'the continuation, while apparently offering a more conventional romance narrative, also betrays a growing impatience with that mode'.[62] A new generation, the children of the main characters in the first part, are growing up and pursuing their own varied objectives. Meanwhile, Amphilanthus, wanting to become 'sure possessor of what I most desire', marries Pamphilia before witnesses 'but not as absolute marriage, though as perfect as that, being only an outward ceremony of the church, this as absolute before God

---

[60] Mary Wroth, *The First Part of the Countess of Montgomery's Urania*, ed. Josephine Roberts, pp. 468–470.

[61] Ibid., Roberts, Introduction, pp. xxxix–xliv.

[62] Clare R. Kinney, '"Beleeve this butt a fiction": Female Authorship, Narrative Undoing, and the Limits of Romance in *The Second Part of the Countess of Montgomery's Urania*', *Spenser Studies* 17, pp. 239–250.

and as fast a tying' (2.45). Nonetheless, after a complicated series of misunderstandings, Amphilanthus goes on to marry the Princess of Slavonia, and Pamphilia marries Rodomandro, King of Tartaria. Yet Amphilanthus and Rodomandro remain friends and military allies, circumstances unthinkable in the emotionally unqualified worlds of Fletcherian tragicomedy.

Both parts of Wroth's romance end in mid-sentence, possibly in imitation of her uncle's unfinished *Arcadia*, but also suggesting the impossibility of imposing an ending on a narrative that undermines the satisfactory nature of what conventionally counts as a conclusion. It is understandable that the possibility of a romance happy ending would have seemed delusional to Wroth by the late 1620s, when she finally abandoned work on the second part. Pembroke had deserted her once again for a new love, and—although he had no legitimate children, and although her children were acknowledged by the family to be his and took his last name—apparently made no financial arrangements for their education or their futures. 'By the time Wroth laid aside *Urania*, she knew that her affair with Pembroke would bring her neither happiness nor security', writes her biographer; 'She had been widowed for at least a decade, and perhaps had come to realize that, given Pembroke's betrayal, her greatest loss was her husband.'[63] Although Wroth had vastly more social and material resources than her contemporary Aemelia Lanyer, both women found themselves constrained in middle age by the lack of options available for gifted females to make their own way outside of a marital framework.

In many prose romances, it is routine to include poems—in Sidney's *Arcadia*, not only are there many interpolated poems but each book concludes with an extended poetic interlude. *Argenis*, too, showcases a variety of Latin verse forms, although they are not a major focus. In the *Urania*, however, the reading and writing of poetry, especially poetry by women, is foregrounded. Both Pamphilia and Urania write love poems, and when the volatile Antissia, a sometime rival for Amphilanthus' love, goes mad, her malady manifests as vile poetry and ludicrously high-flown language. Pamphilia is an especially skilled poet, celebrated as such by the people around her. Wroth's sonnet sequence *Pamphilia to Amphilanthus*—which I discuss at greater length in Chapter 6—was appended to the printed edition of the first part of the

---

[63] Margaret P. Hannay, *Mary Sidney, Lady Wroth*, pp. 267, 272. Mary Ellen Lamb similarly comments on the 'increasingly painful inadequacy of romance to shadow the events occurring in the lives around [Wroth]': 'Topicality and the Interrogation of Wonder in *The Second Part of the Countess of Montgomery's Urania*', *Renaissance Historicisms: Essays in Honor of Arthur Kinney*, ed. James Dutcher and Anne Lake Prescott, p. 256.

romance, adapting to this more public context many of the poems Wroth had originally written to Pembroke.[64] Wroth not only makes a strong case for female poetic merit, but she uses her own experience rather like Robert Burton: representing her own suffering as an impetus to her own and her avatar's creativity, and her writing as a therapy.

Kenelm Digby's *Loose Fantasies*, like Wroth's *Urania* which conceivably inspired it, draws upon his own life, so much so that it is sometimes considered under the rubric of autobiography: its first printed edition, in 1827, retitled it *Private Memoirs*. The first reference to the existence of *Loose Fantasies* occurs in 1669, four years after Digby's death, and is quite explicit about the autobiographical component, describing the manuscript as 'some notes . . . of the *amores* between him and Mistress Venetia Stanley, he going therein by the name of Theagenius and she by the name of Stelliana . . . and others in disguised names'.[65] By the time the manuscript next surfaces in 1808, a key to those names has been provided in another handwriting.

Unlike Barclay or Wroth, Digby seems to have written his romance entirely for himself and perhaps his wife, and made no attempt to publish or circulate it. Indeed, in an afterword, he asks his literary executors to destroy it after his death, for, he writes, it

> was at the first begun only for my own recreation, and then continued and since preserved only for my own private content . . . I may not be thought to have grown unto such a height of immodesty, as to desire that my follies may after me remain upon record.[66]

Digby was a Catholic Jacobean courtier and intellectual, a loyal subject of James, and later Charles, despite what he calls 'a foul stain on his blood'[67] — his father, Everard Digby, had been executed for treason in 1606, for his part in the Gunpowder Plot. In the mid-1620s Kenelm Digby married Venetia Stanley, a court beauty and fellow Catholic, and they had four children together before her death in 1633. During the 1620s Digby made several privateering expeditions in the Mediterranean and Aegean Sea, and probably wrote the first draft of 'Loose Fantasies' in 1628, while awaiting the repair

---

[64] For the differing manuscript and print versions of *Pamphilia to Amphilanthus*, see Gavin Alexander, 'Constant Works: A Framework for Reading Mary Wroth', *Sidney Journal* 14 (1996–97): 5–32.
[65] Quoted in Vittori Gabrieli, introduction, *Loose Fantasies*, xi.
[66] Kenelm Digby, *Loose Fantasies*, ed. Vittorio Gabrieli, p. 173.
[67] Ibid., p. 20.

of his ship on the Greek island of Milo. There are signs, however, that he revised his work at a later date, perhaps after the death of Venetia.

Digby frames his romance as an argument for marriage based on companionate love. While some, he notes, believe that women are incapable of noble friendship, he argues that emotional and spiritual compatibility, combined with physical attraction, 'make the blessing of friendship full on every side by an entire and general communication'. The marriage of true lovers is

> the height of that happiness which this life can afford, and which representeth notably the infinite blessed state wherein the almighty God reigneth, by uniting two persons, two souls, two wills, in one; which by breathing together produce a divine love; and then their bodies may justly strive to perpetuate that essence by succession, whose durance in themselves is limited: and thus they become types of that trinity and unity living in eternity, which infused the spirit of life into him of whom all men derive themselves, and enjoy in security within themselves the perfection of blessedness and content.[68]

Loose Fantasies holds up a fictionalized version of his own courtship and marriage as evidence of this claim.

Digby's close focus on the experiences of his two main characters make *Loose Fantasies* much more straightforward and less digressive than the *Urania* (or, for that matter, *Argenis* or *Arcadia*). And yet it is not clear how closely episodes of the romance track with events in Digby's life. Some of his peregrinations—his sojourn in France and Italy, his presence in Prince Charles's entourage during Charles's visit to Madrid to court the Spanish Infanta, and his eventual marriage to 'Stelliana'—are externally verifiable. Other episodes, such as the kidnapping of Stelliana by an ardent nobleman and her daring escape from his clutches, and the infatuation of the 'Athenian' (French) queen with Theagenes, may have some basis in fact but rehearse common romance plot devices. Still other elements, such as the long, stylized dialogues on love and honour, on the nature of God and spirits, on the active and contemplative life, and so on, are pretty clearly fabrications. So, doubtless, is Theagenes' encounter during his travels with a 'Brahmin priest' who magically shows him an image of Stelliana back at home, mourning his supposed death.

---

[68] Ibid., p. 6.

The most interesting aspect of *Loose Fantasies*, in fact, is how Digby, like Wroth, struggles to capture his experience in a romance form that does not quite fit. Before her marriage to Digby, Stanley was apparently the concubine of the Earl of Dorset, and was rumoured to have borne an illegitimate daughter in this relationship. In *Loose Fantasies*, Theagenes argues that a husband ought not to concern himself too closely with his wife's premarital behaviour:

> I will go further in controlling the fond imaginations of the world concerning women's honour; for they are deceived that place it only in chastity, since they are capable of worse corruptions, and that there are innumerable vices incident to them, as well as to men, that are far more to be condemned than the breach of this frozen virtue.[69]

Yet Digby cannot incorporate this sensible, but heterodox view into his plot. Instead, he predictably insists upon Stelliana's undying fidelity to Theagenes and her steadfast chastity in the face of outrageous tribulations, attributing any blemish on her reputation to slanders.

The Prose of Everyday Life

While the intellectual writers profiled earlier in this chapter use their writing to delineate markedly distinctive, frequently sceptical points of view, and often self-consciously hope to be writing for the ages, there were a number of other writers less interested in advancing the sum of human knowledge or in engaging an international readership than in describing the world around them for a local audience. The impulse is similar to that which produces satiric city comedy and, perhaps not surprisingly, Thomas Dekker excelled in both modes. Dekker was a professional writer, with an urban, probably artisanal family background similar to that of his sometime theatrical collaborator, Ben Jonson. Yet his sympathies and his acquaintance were with the denizens of London City proper rather than with the court circles to which Jonson eventually gravitated. In the 'War of the Theatres' at the end of Elizabeth's reign, Jonson had lampooned Dekker as a hopelessly derivative hack in his satiric Roman comedy, *Poetaster*, and Dekker had replied with *Satiro-Mastix* ['Whipping the Satirist'] (1601), ridiculing

---
[69] Ibid., pp. 144–145.

Jonson's highfalutin classical airs and his pretensions to genius. Lacking the patronage of the wealthy, Dekker occupied an even more precarious economic niche than did Jonson; he was briefly imprisoned for debt in 1599, and then imprisoned again in 1612, a confinement which lasted seven years. Throughout his career he wrote prolifically in varied modes, apparently turning out whatever he could sell, but his most memorable work features lively descriptions of London life.

Dekker's career as a writer of colourful occasional pamphlets begins with *The Wonderful Year* (1603). The treatise opens with the history-making changes at the beginning of 1603, when Elizabeth died and James acceded to the English throne. These are described from the point of view of an ordinary Londoner who watches Elizabeth's impressive funeral procession but doesn't take part in it, and voices some rather anodyne patriotic sentiments. But the majority of the pamphlet focuses on an outbreak of plague later in the year, which killed thousands of city residents and completely upended the normal routines of urban life. Dekker paints a vivid picture of the stricken city and of the villages roundabout, horrified by Londoners who have attempted to flee the infection but bring contagion with them to highways, inns, and taverns.

Though conditions in plague-ridden London were undoubtedly dire, some of the blackly ironic anecdotes in *The Wonderful Year* seem likely to have been urban legends. A man orders a coffin for his plague-stricken companion but ends up occupying it himself, 'called into the company of his grave neighbours', puns Dekker, 'an hour before his infected friend'.[70] A bride, on her wedding day, collapses at the moment during her vows when the priest intones the words 'in sickness and in health':

> The maiden-blush into which her cheeks were lately dyed now began to lose colour: her voice like a coward would have shrunk away but that her lover, reaching her a hand, which he brought thither to give her, (for he was not yet made a full husband) did with that touch somewhat revive her. On went they again so far till they met with 'for better, for worse.' There was she worse than before, and had not the holy officer made haste, the ground on which she stood to be married might easily have been broken up for her burial.[71]

---

[70] Thomas Dekker, *The Wonderful Year, The Gull's Hornbook, Penny-Wise, Pound-Foolish, English Villainies Discovered by Lantern and Candlelight, and Selected Writings*, ed. E. D. Pendry, p. 51.

[71] Ibid., p. 55.

A married woman, near death, confesses her infidelities to her husband and others clustered around her bed, but then she unexpectedly recovers and finds she must cope with the enraged wives of her adulterous partners. Out in the country, a carefree tinker takes money from an innkeeper for burying a plague victim that has fled from London, and compounds his profits by stealing the clothes and pocket money from the Londoner before tipping him into the grave.

Dekker's other prose tracts feature the same mixing of literary and fictional elements with lifelike observation of what purports to be truth. *The Gull's Hornbook* (1609), modelled ironically on popular conduct books such as *The Complete Gentleman* and *The Courtier*, purports to instruct an ignorant 'ninnyhammer' on how, exactly, to excel as a pretentious dandy in the distinctive environs of Jacobean London. Each chapter deals with an episode in the fop's day: when to rise in the morning, how to behave when perambulating in St Paul's, how to eat at an 'ordinary', how to draw attention to oneself by behaving obnoxiously at the theatre, how to drink and dice at a tavern in the evening. Like satiric city comedies, *The Gull's Hornbook* trades in the notion of London as presenting a distinct set of pitfalls and opportunities. Dekker's fop understands the fact that in a crowded urban environment, people do not know one another well and thus must base their social judgements on superficial impressions, a situation that encourages pushy but fake-casual self-promotion. The advice-giver of *The Gull's Hornbook*, of course, not only recognizes these apparently unstudied manoeuvres as calculated strategies, but recognizes too that the awkward sprezzatura of the fake gentleman most likely conceals poverty and hardship.

Dekker's interest in social tactics is even more obvious in *The Bellman of London* (1608), a treatise on crime and fraud that advertises itself on the title page as 'profitable for gentlemen, lawyers, merchants, citizens, farmers, masters of households, and all sorts of servants'. But the format of the book is hardly straightforwardly instructional. Although much of its content is indebted to Robert Greene's amusing coney-catching pamphlets of the 1590s, which similarly expose common scams, Dekker's style of presentation is quite different. The narrator begins with a fairy-tale like excursion through a beautiful sylvan landscape. Soon he discovers a mysteriously uninhabited grove in which a house has been readied for a large gathering. It turns out that a rogues' get-together is about to begin. The narrator, spying on the festivities, discovers that the vagabonds, beggars, and petty criminals of England, though they seem ragged, miserable, and disorganized, meet here at regular 'quarter dinners' just as if they were prosperous burghers or masters of a guild. After the rogues depart, the narrator learns more about their different varieties from the woman who keeps the house. She explains how the criminal world duplicates the 'straight' world, with its own division of labour, caste hierarchies, customs, and culture, and, most importantly, with its own language: 'canting'. Disillusioned by the corruption of what had seemed so idyllic a place, the narrator returns to the city, where a new informant, a 'bellman' or night watchman, provides him with further information about the criminal underworld, this time organized not as a typology of criminals but of varieties of fraudulence and petty crime. As in *The Gull's Hornbook*, the ironic tone recalls satiric city comedy; in fact, Dekker reprises much of his 'knowledge' of the underworld in his collaboration with Thomas Middleton in *The Roaring Girl*.

Another genre with strong ties to the theatre and to early modern theatrical technique was the character sketch. The genre was a very old one, apparently originating with Theophrastus, one of Aristotle's students, whose sketches delineated moral types as a method of ethical instruction.[72] In the first decade of the seventeenth century, this ancient mode was revived by Joseph Hall. Hall had begun his literary career as a young man in the 1590s, as an edgy 'railing satirist' in the vein of Juvenal. But verse satire was proscribed by the Bishop's Ban in 1599; moreover, after Hall took holy orders and began a rapid rise in the Church of England establishment (he was chaplain to Prince Henry and eventually became a bishop), he may well have found the ferociously contemptuous tone of Juvenalian satire inconsistent with his clerical role. In 1608 he published *Characters of Virtues and Vices in Two Books*, modelled closely on Theophrastus' example.[73] The first book details virtues, sketching 'the wise man', 'the humble man', 'the valiant man', 'the good magistrate', and so on. The second book is devoted to the vices: 'the hypocrite', 'the busybody', 'the unthrift', 'the malcontent'. The features of each 'character' are listed in a way that accumulates apparently discrete bits of information rather than developing a cause-and-effect argument. Here, for instance is the opening of the portrait of 'The Honest Man':

> He looks not to what he might do, but what he should. Justice is his first guide: the second law of his actions is expedience. He had rather complain than offend: and hates sin more for the indignity of it than the danger. His

[72] J. W. Smeed, *The Theophrastan 'Character': The History of a Literary Genre*.
[73] For Hall's career, see Richard A. McCabe, *Joseph Hall, A Study in Satire and Meditation*.

simple uprightness works in him that confidence which ofttimes wrongs him, and gives advantage to the subtle, when he rather pities their faithlessness than repents of his credulity. He hath but one heart, and that lies open to sight; and, were it not for discretion, he never thinks aught whereof he would avoid a witness. His word is his parchment, and his yea his oath; which he will not violate for fear or for loss.

The interest here lies in Hall's memorably punchy sentences, which aim not to describe a human being—the honest *man*—but to describe the nature, or 'character' of honesty—the *honest* man. In Hall's words, he aims to '[draw] out the true lineaments of every virtue and vice'—hence the segregation of the virtues and the vices into different books: the first set of sketches designed to inspire emulation, the second set to arouse disgust.

The year 1614 saw the publication of another series of character sketches, these attributed to the courtier Thomas Overbury, but most of them probably the work of other hands.[74] Posthumously printed with Overbury's poem 'The Wife', these *Characters* were very widely read, partly because of the scandalous circumstances of Overbury's death (he had been poisoned in prison at the instigation of the Countess of Somerset, the wife of King James's favourite, Robert Carr.) Their popularity helped to enshrine the genre of the character sketch for later essayists, such as Richard Steele and Joseph Addison in the early eighteenth century. Overbury's 'characters', like Hall's, are descriptions that tend to accrue by presenting a series of discontinuous observations, sentence to sentence. Here is the opening of 'The Puny Clerk'—that is, a young employee in a law office:

He is ta'en from grammar school half coddled, and can hardly shake off his dreams of breeching in a twelvemonth. He is a farmer's son, and his father's utmost ambition is to make him an attorney. He doth itch towards a poet, and greases his breeches extremely with feeding without a napkin. He studies false dice to cheat costermongers, and is most chargeable to the butler of some Inn of Chancery, for pissing in their green-pots. He eats gingerbread at a playhouse; and is so saucy, that he ventures fairly for a broken pate at the Banqueting House, and hath it.[75]

---

[74] For the actual authorship of the character sketches collected in Overbury's *Characters*, see Donald Beecher, ed., *Characters: A Jacobean Miscellany*, pp. 116–128.
[75] *The Overburian Characters*, ed. W. J. Paylor, p. 52.

Yet, as even this short excerpt demonstrates, these sketches differ from Hall's in their fundamental conception. Although they often pass ethical judgement, they represent themselves not primarily as depicting virtues and vices, but as 'witty descriptions of the properties of sundry persons'[76]—a footman, country gentleman, a military commander, a milkmaid—as Henry Newman puts it, 'estranging and trademarking forms of humanity'.[77] Hence, the characteristics noted tend to be tightly bound to social status and contexts; the unstated implication is that one's behaviour is conditioned upon one's situation in life, rather than founded upon considered moral principles. A puny clerk yearns for advancement, a milkmaid radiates health and innocence, a Dutch buttonmaker is a hypocritical Puritan because they are puny clerks or milkmaids or Dutch buttonmakers, not because they have chosen to conduct themselves according to an articulated code of conduct. And since their circumstances make them what they are, gritty details like the butler's pisspot or the playhouse gingerbread become determinative rather than exiguous. Like Dekker's coney-catching tracts, Overbury's character sketches draw on techniques of description commonly used onstage to introduce characters to the audience. They resemble Antonio's asides in the first scene of Webster's *The Duchess of Malfi*, describing Ferdinand, Bosola, the Cardinal, and the Duchess to his friend Delio, or Vindice's similar explication in *The Revenger's Tragedy* as his enemies parade past. Indeed, Webster and other playwrights have been proposed as the authors of the character sketches added to later editions of the volume.

Memoir and Biography

In Ben Jonson's *Volpone*, the idiotic Sir Politic Would-be, an English visitor in Venice, attempts to impress his fellow tourist, Peregine, with his sophisticated habits:

> SIR POLITIC This is my diary,
> Wherein I note my actions of the day.
> PEREGRINE Pray you let's see, sir What is here?
> *Notandum*,
> A rat had gnawn my spur-leathers; notwithstanding,

[76] Ibid., p. 3.
[77] Harry Newman, 'Character ™: Character-Writing, Drama, and the Shape of Literary History', *Journal for Early Modern Cultural Studies* 21 (2021): 143.

> I put on new and did go forth; but first
> I threw three beans over the threshold. Item,
> I went, and bought two toothpicks, whereof one
> I burst immediately in a discourse
> With a Dutch merchant bout *ragion' del stato*.
> From him I went and paid a *moccenigo*
> For piecing my silk stockings; by the way
> I cheapened sprats; and at St. Mark's I urined.
> ...
> SIR POLITIC Sir, I do slip
> No action of my life, thus, but I quote it.
>
> (4.1.133–14)

Jonson mocks not only Sir Politic's pretentiousness but his hopeless narcissism, treating every moment of his life, no matter how crushingly mundane, as if it were of momentous importance. And, as usual, he is seizing on and parodying a new fashion. As we have already seen, there is a notable increase of interest in this period in the unique experience of individuals, and in the ways in which one person's apprehension of reality may differ from another's. The seventeenth century saw a steep rise in diary-keeping: some apparently intended for purely private use, and some freely shared among groups of supportive friends.[78] As John Beadle wrote in *The Diary of a Thankful Christian* (1656),

> Of all histories of lives ... the history of a man's own life (even out of common principles of self-love) must needs be most acceptable. To be able to read our lives even from the womb to this present moment; from the cradle, within some few days of the grave, would surely be a study as profitable as delightful.
>
> (p. 104)

Diaries could provide not only a memorial record of one's activities, but fodder for spiritual reflection.

As Alan Stewart remarks, clear distinctions between diary and memoir can only be anachronistically applied to this period:

---

[78] Paul Delany, *British Autobiography in the Seventeenth Century*; Alan Stewart, *The Oxford History of Life Writing*, volume 2, *Early Modern*.

Processes of revision and rewriting reveal connections between diary, autobiography, and biography: lists of expenses in almanacs get rewritten as diary entries, diary entries are re-read and re-meditated on in the writing of spiritual autobiography, diaries are quoted in biographies, autobiographies are absorbed into personal memoirs and biographies, which act in turn as models for future life-writers.[79]

I will focus primarily on the more extended memoirs and journals because they constitute deliberate literary acts of retrospection and composition, generally attempting to find instructive patterns in what might otherwise seem to be a series of haphazard experiences.

One class of memoir was written by well-born ladies and gentleman, intensely conscious of family, who write for their own posterity. 'Certainly it will be found much better', writes Edward, Lord Herbert of Cherbury, 'for men to guide themselves by such observations as their father, grandfather, and great-grandfather might have delivered to them, than by those vulgar rules and examples, which cannot in all points so exactly agree unto them'.[80] Edward Herbert, George Herbert's older brother, was, as the firstborn, the heir to the bulk of the family estate—a fortune he improved by marrying his first cousin, Mary Herbert, the heiress of his uncle Sir William Herbert. Although locally significant in their home territory of Montgomeryshire, Wales, the wealth and power of this branch of the family paled before that of their relations, the brothers William and Philip Herbert, who became Earls of Pembroke in turn. Edward, intelligent and ambitious, sought advancement in the courts of James and Charles. His memoir, probably written in the early 1640s when he was about sixty, begins with a detailed account of his male ancestors on his father's and mother's side, and then relates his life from his birth in 1583 to 1624, when he published his book, *De Veritate* ['On Truth']. In these decades he studied and travelled extensively, and found employment as a soldier in the Low Countries and as an ambassador to France.

Like Browne and Digby, Herbert evidently developed cosmopolitan, personally tolerant religious views in the course of his European travels; *De Veritate*, which argues that all religions share a few crucial precepts, later earned him the title of 'the father of deism'. But Herbert's memoir is little

---

[79] Alan Stewart, *Life Writing*, p. 8.
[80] *The Autobiography of Edward, Lord Herbert of Cherbury*, ed. Sidney L. Lee, p. 1.

concerned with philosophical or religious issues, instead detailing his illnesses, his physical oddities (he claims to have grown taller in middle age, and notes that he has a pulse at the crown of his head), and his chequered experience as a Jacobean courtier. In 1603 King James creates him Knight of the Bath, a ceremonial honour which in his mind obliges him to gallantry, especially because, according to him, ladies find him irresistible. When he first comes to court the elderly Queen Elizabeth kisses his hand and laments that he was married so young; soon after he is made a Knight of the Bath, an unnamed 'principal lady of the court, and certainly in most men's opinion the handsomest', fastens his knight's tassel on her sleeve.[81] In France, he sends a challenge to a duel to a man who had rudely stolen a young woman's hair ribbon; back in England, a jealous husband, wrongly believing that Herbert had debauched his wife because she treasures his miniature portrait in her bosom, tries to have him assassinated. Herbert's blow-by-blow accounts of his various conflicts—in which he invariably triumphs—recalled decades after the fact, sometimes seem heavily embroidered by nostalgia, and his touchy sense of honour nearly quixotic: as Paul Delany comments, 'it is a curious paradox that this man, who in his philosophical ideas was a century ahead of his time, should in his life have guided himself by the antiquated notions of a chivalry that he attempted vainly to revive'.[82] Unfortunately, Herbert's memoir ends just as he is recalled from a second term as ambassador in France. In the ensuing years, he did not receive the recognition or advancement that he might have reasonably expected; whether he could not find a way to accommodate his later life to a tale of triumph and derring-do, or whether the cessation was simply coincidental, is impossible to tell. Yet the combination of memoir with a romance paradigm is not all that different from what we encounter in Wroth and Digby; like them, Herbert seems to struggle to re-imagine his life in terms of a literary pattern that is not entirely suitable.

Anne Clifford's memoirs make an interesting female counterpart to Herbert's. Throughout her long life she produced several kinds of autobiographical writing. Her surviving diaries, which record the events of her life from 1603 to 1619, intersperse comments on political and court affairs with terse remarks upon her marriage, friendships, children, and Bible study. She was married twice: first to Richard Sackville, Earl of Dorset, then, after his death, to Philip Herbert, Earl of Pembroke and Montgomery (Herbert's first

---

[81] Ibid., p. 85.
[82] Delany, *British Autobiography*, p. 141

wife had been the dedicatee of Mary Wroth's *Urania*). Both marriages were apparently tumultuous, and Clifford seems to have drawn more sustenance from her relationships to her mother, daughters, and circle of female friends than from the men in her life. Yet her most passionate lifelong attachment was to what she saw as her natural inheritance: the vast Clifford family landholdings spreading across three counties in the north of England. When her father, George Clifford, Earl of Cumberland, died, she was his only surviving child, and the terms of the 'entail' that governed the succession of his landed estate seemed to designate her as heir. Yet George Clifford had made a will conferring the estate upon his brother and his brother's children, reserving a substantial dowry for Anne but only if she declined to contest the will. Clifford's estranged widow, Anne's mother, fought this arrangement on Anne's behalf in court, and Anne continued the litigation after her mother's death, stoutly withstanding severe pressure by her first husband, the Earl of Dorset, by King James, and by other powerful males in her life to accept a financial settlement. In 1617, the court decided against her claim and the lands were assigned to her uncle, though she still refused to sign a document acceding to the judgement. Clifford's diaries from this period detail the grief and disorientation into which she was plunged by this loss. Decades later, however, she had the last laugh when her cousin died without male heirs and she finally came in to what she had always seen as her due. In 1643 she rode north into what was now her dominion, never to leave, and embarked upon an ambitious building programme: reconstructing castles and churches, erecting funeral monuments for her parents and herself, and, in 1646, placing a marker at the site at which she had last taken leave of her mother forty years earlier. In 1651, she wrote 'The Life of Me', reprising her life as wife and widow of first Richard Sackville and then of Philip Herbert. Later in life—she lived until 1676, well into the reign of Charles II—Clifford produced annual summaries of her activities and living arrangements in the 'Great Books of Record', in which she recounts the story of the entire Clifford dynasty to which she belongs.

Like Edward Herbert, Clifford does not lack self-esteem. In her sixties when she writes her autobiography, she remarks upon the 'exquisite shape of body' she possessed in her youth, 'and though I say it, the perfections of my mind were much above those of my body'.[83] Her retrospective of her life understandably casts her as triumphant victrix over adverse circumstances: she calls her cousin's failure to produce an heir and her subsequent

---

[83] *Anne Clifford's Autobiographical Writing, 1590–1676*, ed. Jessica L. Malay, p. 97.

regaining of her inheritance 'deliverances so great, as would not befall to any who were not visibly sustained by a divine favour from above'.[84] And, like Herbert, Clifford was intensely proud of her lineage—one of the oldest and most distinguished in England—and apparently wrote her memoirs with the idea that they would be valuable to her heirs. The Great Books of Record, in particular, are meant not merely to chronicle her activities but to cement her posterity's title to her extensive landholdings. Anne Myers has argued that for Clifford, her 'autobiographical writing and her architectural work . . . were not parallel pursuits but interdependent ones', ways of asserting spatial and temporal control over her world.[85] Her writings survived in manuscript, eventually edited and printed in the early twentieth century by her descendant, Vita Sackville-West.

The theme of family prestige that looms so large for Herbert and Clifford, and which seems to have underwritten their robust sense of self-importance, is much less visible in the other class of memoir in the period: the religious autobiography. This is partly due to the fact that the writers of such works came from humbler walks of life, but it is also true that the genre, like devotional poetry, naturally downplays the worldly forms of display in which Clifford and Herbert take such pleasure. The most famous examples of religious autobiography postdate the chronological limits of this volume—the Baptist John Bunyan's *Grace Abounding to the Chief of Sinners* was published in 1688 and the autobiography of George Fox, founder of Quakerism, in 1694. Yet the habits of scrupulous life-review that these documents manifest are not new: they were encouraged among Catholics by the obligation to confess their sins to a priest, and among Protestants by clergy who exhorted their flock to practices of constant critical self-assessment. And both faith traditions find a prestigious precedent in Augustine's *Confessions*, with its autobiographical tale of a youthful sinner who undergoes a profound experience of conversion and spiritual awakening.

John Beadle, in *The Journal or Diary of a Thankful Christian* (1656), argues that a written record provides the Christian with a guard against the sin of forgetfulness. The practice of journal-keeping encourages the writer to remark upon God's manifestations in one's own life and in the world around one, in matters both great and trivial: 'the name of God, that is, the wisdom of God, the power and faithfulness of God, is written upon every spear

---

[84] Ibid., p. 124.
[85] Anne M. Myers, 'Construction Sites: The Architecture of Anne Clifford's Diaries', *ELH* 73 (2006): 582.

of grass, upon every drop of rain, in such great letters, that he who cons may read'. (67). Beadle recommends that the diarist record summaries of major political events and 'the more remarkable judgments that God in our time has inflicted upon notorious offenders', but his emphasis is firmly upon recognizing the presence of God in one's own life, blessing and chastening. Yet Beadle's expansive view of the spiritual diary or memoir was not always realized in practice: the Puritan practice of written self-examination most likely was disseminated by preaching and local example. 'Virtually all the surviving early Puritan self-examination diaries can be tracked to a narrow circle of godly men in Cambridge', writes Alan Stewart in his recent survey of early modern life-writing.[86] One of these, Samuel Rogers, the son and grandson of important Puritan clergymen, kept a diary between 1634 and 1638, when he was a student at Cambridge and a young minister serving as a family chaplain. It is dreary reading—expressions of spiritual desolation and self-loathing familiar in early seventeenth-century devotional verse, but unmitigated by the self-irony or verbal facility of a Donne or a Herbert. Rogers' fraught relationship with his forbidding clergyman father seems to have reproduced itself in his yearning for a distant God he is never able to satisfy:

> June 27. I am ashamed to consider this week past, I am wholly undeserving, dead, dull, unsavory; I have yet prayed, and will wait to see whether the Lord will be gracious in the Sabbath to me, Lord, stir up thine angels to stir the waters, that I may dip and be healed, and quickened to a better serving of thee.
>
> June 30. I am faint, to go out of my study anxious, alas how fruitless am I; I am ashamed, Lord pardon, pardon, if thou regardest the sins of one day I am undone.
>
> July 1. Little worth the writing, still I give myself occasion to bewail my unfruitfulness, and careless walking with God.

Roger's self-absorbed sense of his own inadequacies is matched by his disgust with his acquaintances, particularly his employers, who annoy him by their requests for more succinct prayers at family worship. It is not entirely

---

[86] Stewart, *The Oxford History of Life-Writing*, pp. 142–143.

surprising that when the manuscript was discovered and printed in the eighteenth century, its editor gave it the title 'Diary of a Fanatic'.

Tobie Matthew's *True Historical Relation of the Conversion of Tobie Matthew to the Holy Catholic Faith*—not printed until 1904—is a very different sort of document. The manuscript is dated September 1640 but, as Alan Stewart demonstrates, it actually stitches together writings produced and revised at various times during his life. Unlike Rogers, who describes his religious experience as solitary and alienated, Matthew frames the story of his conversion to Catholicism as, primarily, a series of social interactions, from his early conversations with the English Jesuit Robert Persons in Florence to his later debates, back in England, with such interlocutors as Francis Bacon, John Donne, and the Archbishop of Canterbury. Matthew was brought up in the Church of England but found himself attracted to Catholicism in his early twenties, when he spent a period of time living on the Continent. He had promised his worried parents that he would not visit Italy but as soon as he got permission to travel, he hurried to Florence and Siena, eager to perfect his language skills. Immersing himself in local life, he soon found himself impressed by the fervour of Italian religious devotion. In addition, various incidents conspired to spur his concern with providence and divine judgement: for instance, his life was, he thought, miraculously spared when his mule tripped on high bridge, plunging him into a raging waterfall below. Yet he relinquishes his worldly interests only reluctantly:

> This only accident was cause enough in itself to have made me vow myself to the service of his Divine Majesty for ever after; whereas yet I considered much more where I might find a fire to dry my clothes, than how to secure myself from the fire of Hell, wherein my soul was undoubtedly, and instantly and eternally afterward to have been tormented, if the infinite mercy of God had not enabled me, by the prolongation of my life, to become a member of the holy Catholic Church.[87]

After a number of years abroad, Matthew returned to England, living for a while with his friend Francis Bacon. But it was not easy to be a Catholic in England in the years immediately after the Gunpowder Plot. English subjects were required to take the Oath of Allegiance, which recognized the sovereignty of the monarch over the English church and disavowed the

---

[87] *A True Historical Relation of the Conversion of Sir Tobie Matthew to the Holy Catholic Faith*, ed. A. H. Matthew, p. 13.

power of the Pope. When Matthew refused to do so, he was remanded to Fleet Prison and eventually to house arrest.

During this period of confinement, Matthew was visited by many of his acquaintances, discussing not only the Papal supremacy but the doctrine of Purgatory, the intercessory powers of the Virgin and the saints, and other matters of dispute between Catholics and Protestants. The bulk of the memoir, in fact, is Matthew's summary of these conversations, in which, of course, he represents himself as invariably getting the better of his interlocutor. He considers Bacon, although 'a kind of monster both of wit and knowledge also in other things ... a poor kind of creature in all those which were questionable about religion'. But Bacon's theological ineptitude does not disqualify him as a companion. After Mattthew, by his account, trounces Bacon in a theological debate, 'We seldom met after upon such arguments, but I passed my time with him in much gust [pleasure]; for there was not such company in the whole world'.[88] A modern reader is likely to find Matthew's observations of his friends and acquaintances considerably shrewder and more entertaining than his summaries of their religious discussions. He describes Edwin Sand as

> a man of a very great wit, and of good learning, and flowing speech, yet the tediousness of his discourse, the solemnness of his understanding, the visible delight which he had to be extremely admired, and his resolution to reduce all religion to human reason, made me apt to fear him a little, and to like him less.[89]

Of one Christopher Perkins, Matthew remarks that he 'loved music very much, and had a boy whom he was yet suspected to love more; but at least he had a desire to make him profit well in that art'.[90]

Eventually Matthew was permitted to sell much of his property and go abroad. He was allowed to return to England in 1622 and (like his fellow-Catholic, Kenelm Digby) participated in Prince Charles's expedition to Madrid to court the Spanish Infanta. The Caroline period was an easier period for English Catholics than the preceding decades had been, since Charles's French Queen Henrietta Maria came attended with a large Catholic entourage. During the 1630s, Matthew became a familiar figure at court. Yet his memoir suggests that his loyalties may still have been suspect,

---

[88] Ibid., pp. 112–113
[89] Ibid., p. 87.
[90] Ibid., p. 70.

since in 1640 he is at pains to delineate not only his faithful Catholicism but also his irreproachable loyalty to King and country. With civil war underway, Matthew departed England again in 1641, shortly after signing his memoir; he would die in Ghent in 1655.

An interesting permutation of religious memoir began to develop in the 1650s with the burgeoning of the Quaker movement, although the more elaborate personal testimonies of this kind would not flourish until the years after the Restoration. The Quakers were followers of the religious radical George Fox, whose charismatic preaching attracted an enthusiastic following beginning in the 1640s. Foxe preached a reliance on the inner light of inspiration over the doctrines of an established church or even the teachings of Scripture: unlike orthodox Christians, who believed that the divine will had been perfectly revealed in the teachings of Christ and the apostles, Fox taught that revelation was ongoing and that anybody—male or female, of humble birth or noble—might become a vessel of new truths. In consequence, his followers rejected social and gender hierarchies and the distinction between clergy and laypersons. They refused to practice customs of deference, such as doffing the hat or using the formal 'you' with social superiors, they objected to paying tithes to support the ministries of the Church of England, and they refused to swear oaths.

Quaker unconventionality led to considerable persecution; Quaker women, whose public preaching violated gender norms, were particularly vulnerable to arrest and prosecution. As radical pacifists, the Quakers could not react to violent treatment with more violence, but they could record and publish their own accounts of the cruelties to which they were subjected. Their convictions about the equal value of all souls before God encouraged them to believe that the experiences of all persons, not merely the stories of the rich, powerful, and well-connected, were worth recording. They were, moreover, acutely aware of the propaganda value of victimhood. From the outset of Fox's ministry, they had attracted allies and converts from among those who were horrified by witnessing the disproportionate abuse meted out to them. By recording and printing such abuse, the Quakers effectively expanded the potential audience for it.

The first such tract, *The Lamb's Defense Against Lies*, was published in 1656. Most of the tract records the persecution of James Parnell, a young Quaker arrested in Colchester for disturbing a church service. Although acquitted by the jury, he was nonetheless assessed a forty-pound fine—an enormous sum for a person of modest means. Unable to pay, Parnell was imprisoned in Colchester Jail, where he was beaten, starved, and confined in cramped and unhealthy conditions. Eventually, after months of dreadful treatment, Parnell died either as a result of his accumulated injuries or in the aftermath of a hunger strike. The presentation of these events closely recalls the procedures of Foxe's *Acts and Monuments*, familiar to mid-seventeenth-century English readers, alternating narration with copies of official documents and signed attestations by witnesses. Even more interesting is the short first-person narration that follows Parnell's story, in which Quaker evangelist Dorothy Waugh relates the cruelty to which she was subjected after she attempted to preach at the market cross in Carlisle. She was punished as a 'shrew' or uppity woman: jailed, whipped, and forced to wear a 'scold's bridle', a tortuous metal gag that fastened around the head. Waugh's rhetorically unembellished first-person account enhances her credibility; the unmistakable implication is that she, like Parnell, follows in the footsteps of the many other Christians who have suffered heroically for their faith. Yet if these short accounts hark back to Foxe's *Acts and Monuments*, they also look forward to the memoirs that will become popular in the following decades, and remain popular today.

Developing in tandem with the impulse for recording one's own life was an interest in investigating other people's. There were important classical precedents for biographical writing—most notably Plutarch's *Lives of the Noble Grecians and Romans*, translated into English by Thomas North in 1580, and Tacitus' biography of his father-in-law, Agricola. There was, as well, a venerable Christian tradition of recording (and sometimes elaborating) upon the lives of saints and martyrs. Yet in his 1605 *Advancement of Learning*, Francis Bacon was correct to identify 'the writings of lives' as one of the 'deficiencies of knowledge' that he hoped would be supplied in the future.[91] The early seventeenth-century censorship laws, which severely punished the criticism of eminent persons in the state, made the frank discussion of powerful contemporaries a perilous matter; as Walter Ralegh remarked in his *History of the World*, he who follows the heels of truth too closely is likely to get kicked in the teeth. Still, an interest in the vicissitudes of individual lives shows up in a variety of forms. It became increasingly common for funeral services to include a sermon recounting the life of the deceased and for printed editions of collected works to be prefaced by a short biographical account of the author.

---

[91] Bacon, *Advancement of Learning*, ed. Michael Kiernan, *The Oxford Francis Bacon*, vol. 4, pp. 68–69.

INTELLECT AND EXPRESSION   441

After the Restoration, spurred on by the turmoil of the Civil War and its aftermath, the popularity of biography burgeoned dramatically. In 1662, the antiquarian Thomas Fuller published the *History of the Worthies of England*, a systematic attempt to record and memorialize the notable persons in each of the various counties of England: a human version of the locally oriented chorography that has already been discussed in Chapter 4. The Puritan Lucy Hutchinson and the royalist Margaret Cavendish wrote biographies of their own husbands, Clarendon included extended biographical sketches in his *History of the Rebellion*, and, in the last decades of the century, John Aubrey published his *Brief Lives*.[92] Yet a few pre-Restoration biographies deserve mention both for their literary interest and their closeness to memoir. They relate the lives of individuals with whom the biographer himself was personally acquainted, and as such recirculate many of the same tropes and concepts that underlie the period's friendship poetry.

Fulke Greville's *Life of Sir the Renowned Philip Sidney* was printed in 1652, decades after Greville's death in 1628, but it was most likely written around 1610. And it seems to have been designed not, in the first instance, as a 'life' but as a lengthy dedication to Sidney's memory of some of Greville's own tragedies and political treatises: Greville's modern editor therefore retitles the work 'A Dedication to Sir Philip Sidney'.[93] It falls into three unequal parts. The first, and longest, section is a memorial to Sidney, Greville's lifelong friend (they met as boys in the same grammar school class). Greville eulogizes Sidney as the ideal gentleman-courtier: brave, staunchly Protestant, patriotic, discerning, and literate. Although Greville discusses the politics of the *Arcadia* in some detail, he emphasizes that Sidney is not a mere scribbler: 'his end was not writing, even while he wrote; nor his knowledge moulded for tables, or schools; but both his wit and his understanding bent upon his heart to make himself and others, not in words or opinions, but in life and action, good and great'.[94] After recounting Sidney's short life and premature death from a battle wound, Greville briefly mentions his own distinguished political career and literary productions as inspired by Sidney's example: 'to sail by his compass was . . . one of the principal reasons I can allege which persuaded me to steal minutes of time from my daily services, and employ them in this kind of writing'.[95] The third part of the Life is devoted to the reign of Queen Elizabeth, who is by Greville's account

---

[92] For a more comprehensive discussion of the development of biography than I am able to provide here, see Alan Pritchard, *English Biography in the Seventeenth Century*.
[93] John Guows, *The Prose Works of Fulke Greville, Lord Brooke*.
[94] Ibid., p. 12.
[95] Ibid., p. 89.

the ideal ruler to Sidney's ideal courtier. Apparently Greville had originally intended to write a separate history of the Tudor monarchs, but he could not gain access to the necessary archival materials, so he appended his account of Queen Elizabeth to his life of Sidney.

Despite the rather curious organization of *The Life*, taken as a whole it makes several coherent arguments. One is that there exists a natural aristocracy of outstanding individuals who recognize and admire one another across the boundaries of nation or creed. Everyone, according to Greville, acknowledges Sidney's greatness: the Huguenot scholar and diplomat Hubert Languet; William of Nassau, Prince of Orange; the future James I, then king of Scotland; Henry of Navarre; Elizabeth's advisor and Sidney's father-in-law Francis Walsingham. Even Sidney's Spanish enemy Bernardino de Mendoza, after Sidney's death, 'acknowledged openly that howsoever he was glad King Philip his master had lost, in a private gentleman, a dangerous enemy to his state, yet he could not but lament to see Christendom deprived of so rare a light in those cloudy times'.[96] The universities admire Sidney's scholarship, soldiers his valour, 'men of affairs' his wise counsel. Consequently, Greville argues, princes ought to encourage and promote such meritorious individuals. Sidney's genius and ambition, in the service of the Tudor monarchy, contribute to the glorious reign of his Queen.

Greville's Sidney is a forthright man who does not hesitate to voice his opinions and stand up for himself. When, as a mere knight, he becomes embroiled in a quarrel with the Earl of Oxford, Queen Elizabeth calls him in to 'lay before him the difference in degree between earls and gentleman'. Unintimidated, Sidney 'with such reverence as became him ... besought her Majesty to consider that although [Oxford] were a great lord by birth, alliance, and grace, yet he was no lord over him'. In this contretemps and others, Greville claims that Sidney's 'constant tenor of truth ... protected this gentleman (though he obeyed not) from the displeasure of his sovereign', an immunity that reflects as much credit to Elizabeth as to Sidney. Both, Greville claims, recognize that while tyrants insist upon absolute power, wise monarchs allow 'a latitude for subjects to reserve native and legal freedom'.[97] It is this sense of a mutual and complementary understanding of the appropriate roles of prince and courtier that motivates Greville's yoking of Sidney's career to Elizabeth's. In order to depict the harmony between ruler and subject, Greville does not hesitate to suppress facts when they are inconvenient.

[96] Ibid., p. 21.
[97] Ibid., pp. 40–41.

He gives a detailed account of Sidney's objection to Queen Elizabeth's proposed marriage to the Duke of Anjou, but omits her angry reaction to his unsolicited advice: in the face of her fury Sidney temporarily withdrew from court, and in fact wrote the *Arcadia*, which Greville discusses in detail, while retired to his sister's estate outside Salisbury.

When Greville wrote *A Life* around 1610, his idealized portrait of ruler and subject has an unstated polemical edge. Sidney, and Greville after him, supported a strong and unified alliance of the Protestant states of Europe against what they saw as the malign power of the Pope and Catholic Spain. From that point of view James's pacific policies, and in particular his 1604 treaty with Spain, dangerously underestimated the Catholic threat. In addition, Elizabeth's supposed awareness of the advantages of tolerating loyal but refractory counsellors, and her appreciation for the freedoms of her subjects, offers an implied contrast to James's apparent reliance upon 'unworthy' male favourites and his more openly authoritarian views. In 1610, hopes for the revival of the Elizabethan programme would have lain in the court of the heir apparent, Prince Henry, whose military ambitions and strong Protestant views produced some friction with his father and also contributed to a wave of Elizabethan nostalgia among his followers. Henry's death in 1611 crushed these hopes as a practical matter, but by 1652, when the *Life* was finally published, the Thirty Years War on the Continent and the memories of civil war at home might have convinced many readers, at least those on the Parliamentary side, of the original correctness of the Greville / Sidney position.

Between 1640 and 1673, Isaak Walton wrote and published the biographies of five eminent clergymen of the Church of England: John Donne, Henry Wotton, George Herbert, Richard Hooker, and Robert Sanderson. Although in 1670 the first four of Walton's *Lives* were printed as a collection, and although Walton continued to revise them and add material over the course of decades, each biography was initially conceived as a one-off accompaniment to the published works of their subjects. The first version of Walton's life of John Donne appeared in 1640, introducing an edition of the sermons, and was reissued in 1658 as a stand-alone piece. The first version of the Wotton biography appeared in 1651, as a preface to *Reliquiae Wottonianae*, a collection of Wotton's letters, poems, aphorisms, and other writings. Walton had been one of Donne's parishioners in the 1620s, and Wotton was a personal friend of both men: in fact, Wotton was originally supposed to write the preface to Donne's sermons, but died in 1639 before he could do so, at which point Walton took over the assignment. Walton claims, in the preface to his 1670 volume, that 'having writ these two lives, I lay quiet twenty years', and he undertook the other biographies much later in life.

Like Fulke Greville, Walton envisages biography as a tribute to a valued acquaintance—in fact, he seems to take for granted a personal relationship between the biographer and his subject, exhorting the 'relations and friends' of other great men to write their biographies as well.[98] He imagines Donne watching him from his perch in Heaven: 'If the author's glorious spirit... can have the leisure to look down and see me, the poorest, the meanest of all his friends, in the midst of this officious duty, confident I am that he will not disdain this well-meant sacrifice to his memory.'[99] In its eulogizing and idealizing spirit Walton's biography of Donne, like Greville's of Sidney, celebrates an ideal community created among men of ability, who put aside their rivalries and disagreements in generous appreciation of one another's merits. Even after Donne's secret marriage to Anne More leads to his dismissal from Lord Ellesmere's service and to some years of hand-to-mouth existence, his intelligence and winning ways recommend him, Walton tells us, to 'many of the nobility and others of this nation, who used him in their counsels of great consideration, and with some rewards for his better subsistence':

> Nor did our own nobility only value and favour him, but his acquaintance and friendship was sought for by most ambassadors of foreign nations, and by many other strangers, whose learning or business occasioned their stay in this Nation.[100]

Because Walton intended to introduce Donne's sermons, not the poems, and because his personal acquaintance with Donne commenced only after Donne's ordination, it is perhaps not surprising that the biography emphasizes Donne's clerical *persona*: his conscientious piety, his charity to the poor and the imprisoned, his dutiful care of his Catholic mother, and his memorable presence in the pulpit. Like Greville, Walton gives detailed attention to his subject's last illness and death, not only because he was likely an eyewitness, but because Donne's embrace of his own mortality reveals his faith in God's mercy and his own salvation.

The vividness with which Walton conveys his subject's life and his own interactions with Donne made the biography immediately popular and

---

[98] Isaak Walton, 'Epistle to the Reader', *Walton's Lives*, ed. Thomas Zouch, p. 46.
[99] Isaak Walton, *The Life of John Donne, Doctor of Divinity and Late Dean of Saint Paul's Church London*, p. 4.
[100] Ibid., p. 34.

still influences Donne's reception among modern readers and critics. Yet the impulsive, intensely sexual personality that emerges from some of the poems, the combative tone of the controversial treatises Donne wrote early in James's reign, and the baroque weirdness of some of the devotional prose and sermons all go unremarked. Walton acknowledges Donne's youthful 'infirmities' (p. 44): in fact, they make the story of his transformation into a great man of the church all the more dramatic. But Walton provides few details about them and seems to regard them as entirely superseded in a saintly later phase.

Walton undertook his biography of Henry Wotton, like the Donne biography, 'in gratitude to the memory of my dead friend',[101] and in fact harps even more strongly in this work upon the theme of friendship. Wotton studied at Oxford, where he befriended Donne and Albericus Gentilis, and then spent several years travelling in Italy and Germany, where he befriended distinguished intellectuals of a wide variety of religious persuasions. In the latter 1590s Wotton returned to England to study law at the Inns of Court, eventually becoming a trusted secretary to the Earl of Essex. In 1601, in the wake of Essex's failed insurrection, he fled to the Continent—prudently, since not only Essex but Essex's other secretary, Henry Cuffe, was executed for treason. Walton represents what must have been a traumatic episode in Wotton's life as mainly another chance for Wotton to expand his social circle, describing him back in Italy 'happily renewing his intermitted friendship and interest, and indeed his great content in a new conversation with his old acquaintance in that nation'.[102] After James's accession to the throne, Wotton served for years as ambassador to Venice and also took part in a number of other sensitive diplomatic missions. For Walton, these functions are a worthy extension of Wotton's talent for making alliances, since diplomacy enhances the rapport between nations and sovereign states, not merely between individuals. In his fifties, after a distinguished diplomatic career, Wotton accepted the position of provost of Eton College and took holy orders. Here, again, his amiability manifests itself in the care he takes of his students, and in his reputation for hospitality: 'a great lover of his neighbors, and a bountiful entertainer of them very often at his table, where his meat was good, and his discourse better'.[103] By Walton's account, Wotton 'was a

---

[101] Isaak Walton, 'The Life of Sir Henry Wotton' (introduction to Sir Henry Wotton, *Reliquiae Wottoniana*), p. 11.
[102] Ibid., p. 16.
[103] Ibid., p. 25.

great enemy to wrangling disputes of religion'. He orders a gravestone that reads, in Latin, 'The itch of disputation will prove the scab of the church'.[104]

Like *The Complete Angler*, which Walton was writing during the same years, these biographies comment on some of the burning issues of the day from a royalist perspective. Donne and Wotton of course both died well before the onset of civil war, but Walton strongly implies that they would have been appalled by the dismantling of the Church of England's ecclesiastical structure, and by the execution of Laud and Charles. The truly wise, Walton claims, conduct themselves without resort to violence, or even to incivility, even when they differ on theological matters. In the Wotton biography, he mentions an incident in which Wotton serves as intermediary between the theologian Jakob Arminius, 'a man of most rare learning, and ... of a most strict life, and of a most meek spirit', and William Perkins, also a person 'of most meek spirit and of great and sanctified learning'.[105] Although the two men disagree on the topic of predestination, they query one another politely, respectfully, and in private. The implication is that open controversy, even on issues of importance, does more harm than good by rending the body of the Universal Church. In the civil war and interregnum years, to someone of Walton's persuasion, the dangers of religious schism seemed obvious. As in *The Complete Angler*, where Walton associates primitive Christianity with openhearted fellowship rather than with particular doctrinal convictions, human solidarity seems to offer the true ground of sanctity. The process of memorializing one's friendships thus becomes a profoundly religious undertaking.

---

[104] Ibid., p. 25.
[105] Ibid., p. 26.

Bibliography

Aasand, Hardin. '"To blanch an Ethiop, and revive a corse": Queen Anne and *The Masque of Blackness*', *SEL* 32 (1992): 271–285.

Achinstein, Sharon. *Literature and Dissent in Milton's England*. Cambridge: Cambridge University Press, 2003.

Adams, Christine. 'Francis Bacon's Wedding Gift of "A Garden of a Glorious and Strange Beauty" for the Earl and Countess of Somerset', *Garden History* 36 (2008): 36–58.

Adlington, Hugh. 'Donne and Diplomacy', in *Renaissance Troplogies: The Cultural Imagination of Early Modern England*, ed. Jeanne Shami. Pittsburgh: Duquesne University Press, 2008. pp. 187–216.

Alexander, Gavin. 'Constant Works: A Framework for Reading Mary Wroth', *Sidney Journal* 14 (1996–1997): 5–32.

Allinson, Mark. 'Re-Visioning the Death Wish: Donne and Suicide', *Mosaic* 24 (1991): 31–46.

Altman, Joel. *The Tudor Play of Mind: Rhetorical Inquiry and the Development of Elizabethan Drama*. Berkeley: University of California Press, 1978.

Andrea, Bernadette. 'Black Skin, The Queen's Masques: Africanist Ambivalence and Female Authority in the Masques of "Blackness" and "Beauty"', *English Literary Renaissance* 29 (1999): 246–281.

Andreadis, Harriette. *Sappho in Early Modern England: Female Same-Sex Literary Erotics*. Chicago: University of Chicago Press, 2001.

Asp, Carolyn. *A Study of Thomas Middleton's Tragicomedies*. Salzburg: Institut fur Englische Sprache und Literatur, 1974.

Attridge, Derek. *Well Weighed Syllables: Elizabethan Verse in Classical Metres*. Cambridge: Cambridge University Press, 1974.

Bacon, Francis. *The Advancement of Learning*, ed. Michael Kiernan, *The Oxford Francis Bacon*. Oxford: Oxford University Press, 2000.

Bacon, Francis. *The Essays or Counsels, Civil and Moral*, ed. Michael Kiernan, *The Oxford Francis Bacon*. Oxford: Oxford University Press, 2000.

Bacon, Francis. *The Instauratio Magna Part II Novum Organum and Associated* Texts, ed. Graham Rees and Maria Wakeley. *The Oxford Francis Bacon*. Oxford: Oxford University Press, 2004.

Bailey, Amanda. *Flaunting: Style and the Subversive Male Body*. Toronto: University of Toronto Press, 2007.

Baldwin, T. W. *William Shakespeare's Small Latine and Lesse Greeke*. Urbana: University of Illinois Press, 1944.

Bamber, Linda. *Comic Women, Tragic Men: A Study of Gender and Genre*. Stanford: Stanford University Press, 1982.

Barbour, Richmond. *Before Orientalism: London's Theater of the East 1576–1626*. Cambridge: Cambridge University Press, 2003.

Barbour, Richmond. 'Jonson and the Motives of Print', *Criticism* 40 (1998): 499–528.

Barbour, Reid. *Sir Thomas Browne: A Life*. Oxford: Oxford University Press, 2013.

Barclay, John. *Argenis*, ed. and trans. Mark Riley and Dorothy Pritchard Huber. Tempe: Arizona Center for Medieval and Renaissance Studies, 2004.
Barroll, Leeds. *Anna of Denmark, Queen of England: A Cultural Biography*. Philadelphia: University of Pennsylvania Press, 2001.
Barton, Anne. 'Harking After Elizabeth: Ben Jonson and Caroline Nostalgia', *ELH* 48 (1980): 706–731.
Beaumont, Francis and John Fletcher. *Philaster, or Love Lies a-Bleeding*, ed. Andrew Gurr. London: Methuen, 1969.
Bednarz, James P. *Shakespeare and the Poets' War*. New York: Columbia University Press, 2001.
Beecher, Donald, ed. *Characters: A Jacobean Miscellany*. London: Dovehouse, 2003.
Bell, Ilona. 'Joy's Sports: The Unexpurgated Text of Wroth's *Pamphilia to Amphilanthus*', *Modern Philology* 111 (2013): 231–252.
Belsey, Catherine. *The Subject of Tragedy*. London: Methuen, 1985.
Benet, Diana Trevino. 'Sexual Transgression in Donne's Elegies', *Modern Philology* 92 (1994): 14–35.
Bentley, G. R. *The Profession of Dramatist in Shakespeare's Time 1590–1642*. Princeton: Princeton University Press, 1971.
Bevington, David, Katharine Eisaman Maus, Lars Engle, and Eric Rasmussen, eds. *English Renaissance Drama: A Norton Anthology*. New York: W. W. Norton, 2002.
Bliss, Lee, 'Tragicomic Romance for the King's Men, 1609-1611: Shakespeare, Beaumont, and Fletcher,' in A.R. Braunmuller and J. C. Bulman, eds., *Comedy from Shakespeare to Sheridan*. Newark: University of Delaware Press, 1986.
Blank, Paula. *Broken English: Dialects and the Politics of Language in Renaissance Writings*. New York: Routledge, 1996.
Bodley, Thomas. *Letters of Sir Thomas Bodley to Thomas James, Keeper of the Bodleian Library*, ed. G. Wheeler. Oxford: Bodleian Library, 1926.
Bowers, Fredson. *Elizabethan Revenge Tragedy 1587–1642*. Princeton: Princeton University Press, 1940.
Bradbrook, Muriel. *Themes and Conventions of Elizabethan Tragedy*. Cambridge: Cambridge University Press, 1980.
Bradbrook, Muriel and M. C. Lloyd-Thomas. *Andrew Marvell*. Cambridge: Cambridge University Press, 1940.
Braden, Gordon. *Renaissance Tragedy and the Senecan Tradition: Anger's Privilege*. New Haven: Yale University Press, 1985.
Braden, Gordon, 'Unspeakable Love: Petrarch to Herbert', in *Soliciting Interpretation: Literary Theory and Seventeenth-Century Poetry*, ed. Elizabeth Harvey and Katharine Eisaman Maus. Chicago: University of Chicago Press, 1990. pp. 253–272.
Braunmuller, A. R. and J. C. Bulman, eds., *Comedy from Shakespeare to Sheridan*. Newark: University of Delaware Press, 1986.
Bray, Alan. *The Friend*. Chicago: University of Chicago Press, 2003.
Bray, Alan. *Homosexuality in Renaissance England*. London: Gay Men's Press, 1982.
Britland, Karen. *Drama at the Courts of Queen Henrietta Maria*. Cambridge: Cambridge University Press, 2006.
Browne, Thomas. *Pseudodoxia Epidemica*, ed. Robin Robbins. Oxford: Clarendon, 1981.
Browne, Thomas. *Religio Medici, The Complete Works of Sir Thomas Browne, vol. 1*, ed. Reid Barbour and Brooke Conti. Oxford: Oxford University Press, 2023.
Bruster, Douglas. 'The Representation Market of Early Modern England', *Renaissance Drama* 41 (2013): 1–23.

Burgess, Glenn. *The Politics of the Ancient Constitution: An Introduction to English Political Thought, 1603–1642.* State College: Pennsylvania State University Press, 1993.

Burrow, Colin. *Epic Romance: Homer to Milton.* Oxford: Oxford University Press, 1993.

Burrow, Colin. 'Shakespeare's Sonnets as Event', in *The Sonnets: The State of Play*, ed. Hannah Crawforth, Elizabeth Scott-Baumann, and Clare Whitehead. London: Bloomsbury Arden Shakespeare, 2017. pp. 97–116.

Burton, Robert. *The Anatomy of Melancholy*, ed. Thomas C. Faulkner, Nicolas Kiessling, and Rhonda Blair. Oxford: Clarendon, 1989.

Bush, Douglas. *English Literature in the Early Seventeenth Century.* Oxford: Oxford University Press, 1945.

Bushnell, Rebecca. *Tragedies of Tyrants: Political Thought and Theater in the English Renaissance.* Ithaca: Cornell University Press, 1990.

Butler, Martin. '"Servant But Not Slave": Ben Jonson at the Jacobean Court', *Proceedings of the British Academy* 90 (1996): 65–93.

Butler, Martin *The Stuart Court Masque and Political Culture.* Cambridge: Cambridge University Press, 2008.

Cadman, Daniel, Andrew Dufield, and Lisa Hopkins, eds. *The Genres of Renaissance Tragedy.* Manchester: Manchester University Press, 2019.

Callaghan, Dymphna. *Women and Gender in Renaissance Tragedy: A Study of King Lear, Othello, The Duchess of Malfi, and The White Devil.* London: Harvester Wheatsheaf, 1989.

Camden, William. *Remains Concerning Britain.* ed. R. D. Dunn. Toronto: University of Toronto Press, 1984.

Campbell, Gordon and Thomas Corns. *John Milton: Life, Works, and Thought.* Oxford: Oxford University Press, 2008.

Carey, John. *John Donne: Life Mind, and Art.* London: Faber and Faber, 1981.

Carleton, Dudley. *Dudley Carleton to John Chamberlain, 1603–1624: Jacobean Letters*, ed. Maurice Lee. New Brunswick: Rutgers University Press, 1972.

Cary, Elizabeth. *The Tragedy of Mariam the Fair Queen of Jewry: With the Lady Falkland: Her Life*, ed. Barry Weller and Margaret Ferguson. Berkeley: University of California Press, 1994.

Cave, Terence. *The Cornucopian Text: Problems in Writing in the French Renaissance.* Oxford: Clarendon, 1979.

Chamberlain, John. *The Letters of John Chamberlain*, ed. Norman Egbert McClure. Philadelphia: The American Philosophical Society, 1939.

Clark, Peter and David Souden, eds. *Migration and Society in Early Modern England.* London: Hutchinson, 1987.

Clarke, Elizabeth. *Theory and Theology in George Herbert's Poetry: 'Divinitie and Poesie Met'.* Oxford: Clarendon, 1997.

Clarkson, L. A. *The Pre-Industrial Economy in England, 1500–1750.* London: B. T. Batsford, 1971.

Clifford, Anne. *Anne Clifford's Autobiographical Writing, 1590–1676*, ed. Jessica L. Malay. Manchester: Manchester University Press, 2018.

Coiro, Ann. *Robert Herrick's Hesperides and the Epigram Book Tradition.* Baltimore: Johns Hopkins University Press, 1985.

Coiro, Ann Baynes. 'Writing in Service: Sexual Politics and Class Position in the Poetry of Aemila Lanyer and Ben Jonson, *Criticism* 35 (1993): 357–376.

Coles, Kimberley Ann. *Bad Humor: Race and Religious Essentialism in Early Modern England.* Philadelphia: University of Pennsylvania Press, 2022.

Colie, Rosalie. *My Echoing Song: Andrew Marvell's Poetry of Criticism*. Princeton: Princeton University Press, 1970.
Colie, Rosalie. *The Resources of Kind: Genre-Theory in the Renaissance*. Berkeley: University of California Press, 1973.
Cook, Ann Jennalie. *The Privileged Playgoers of Shakespeare's England*. Princeton: Princeton University Press, 1981.
Cottegnies, Line. 'The Sapphic Context of Lady Mary Wroth's *Pamphilia to Amphilanthus*', in *Early Modern Women and the Poem*, ed. Susan Wiseman. Manchester: Manchester University Press, 2013. pp. 60–76.
Coward, Barry. *Oliver Cromwell*. New York: Routledge, 2000.
Cowley, Abraham. *The Collected Works of Abraham Cowley, volume 2. 1656 part 1: The Mistress*, ed. Thomas O. Calhoun, Laurence Heyworth, and J. Robert King. Newark: University of Delaware Press, 1993.
Cowley, Abraham. *Poems: Miscellanies, The Mistress, Pindarique Odes, Davideis, Verses Written on Several Occasions* ed. A. R. Waller. Cambridge: Cambridge University Press, 2014 (originally published 1905).
Crawford, Julie. *Mediatrix: Women, Politics, and Literary Production in Early Modern England*. Oxford: Oxford University Press, 2014.
Creasar, John. '"Jocund his Muse Was": Celebration and Virtuosity in Herrick', in *Lords of Wine and Oil: Community and Conviviality in the Poetry of Robert Herrick*, ed. Ruth Connolly and Tom Cain. Oxford: Oxford University Press, 2011. pp. 39–64.
Creaser, John. 'Time's Trans-shifting: Chronology and the Misshaping of Herrick', *ELR* 39. (2009): 163–196.
Cressy, David. *Literacy and the Social Order: Reading and Writing in Tudor and Stuart England*. Cambridge: Cambridge University Press, 1980.
Croll. Morris. *'Attic' and Baroque Prose Style: The Anti-Ciceronian Movement*, ed. J. Max Patrick, Robert O. Evans, and John Wallace. Princeton: Princeton University Press, 1969.
Croll, Morris. *Style Rhetoric, and Rhythm: Essays by Morris Croll*. Princeton: Princeton University Press, 1966.
Cubeta, Paul M. 'Ben Jonson's Religious Lyrics', *JEGP* 62 (1963): 96–100.
Cunningham, Karen. *Imaginary Betrayals: Subjectivity and the Discourses of Treason in Early Modern England*. Philadelphia: University of Pennsylvania Press, 2001.
Curtis, Mark. 'The Alienated Intellectuals of Early Stuart England', *Past and Present* 23 (1962): 25–43.
Curtis, Mark. *Oxford and Cambridge in Transition: 1558–1642*. Oxford: Clarendon, 1959.
Cust, Richard. *Charles I: A Political Life*. New York: Routledge, 2007.
Cust, Richard and Ann Hughes, eds. *Conflict in Early Stuart England: Studies in Religion and Politics 1603–1642*. New York: St Martin's, 1987.
Danson, Lawrence. 'The Shakespeare Remix: Romance, Tragicomedy, and Shakespeare's "distinct kind"', *Shakespeare and Genre*, ed. Anthony Guneratne. New York: Palgrave, 2012. pp. 101–119.
Davis, Natalie. *The Gift in Sixteenth-Century France*. Madison: University of Wisconsin Press, 2000.
Degenhardt, Jane Hwang. 'Catholics Prophylactics and Islam's Sexual Threat: Preventing and Undoing Sexual Defilement in *The Renegado*', *Journal for Early Modern Cultural Studies* 9 (2009): 62–92.

Dekker, Thomas. *The Wonderful Year, The Gull's Horn-Book, Penny-Wise, Pound-Foolish, English Villainies Discovered by Lantern and Candlelight, and Selected Writings*, ed. E. D. Pendry. Cambridge: Harvard University Press, 1968.
Delany, Paul. *British Autobiography in the Seventeenth Century*. New York: Columbia University Press, 1969.
DeLuna, B. N. *Jonson's Romish Plot: A Study of Catiline and Its Historical Context*. Oxford: Clarendon, 1967.
Digby, Kenelm. *Loose Fantasies*, ed. Vittorio Gabrieli. Rome: Edizione di Storia e Letteratura, 1968.
Digby, Kenelm. *Observations upon Religio Medici Occasionally Written by Sir Kenelm Digby, Knight*. London, 1643.
Dixon, Mimi Still. 'Tragicomic Recognitions: Medieval Miracles and Shakespearean Romance', in *Renaissance Tragicomedy: Explorations in Genre and Politics*, ed. Nancy Klein Maguire. New York: AMS Press, 1987. pp. 56–79.
Doerksen, Daniel. *Conforming to the Word: Herbert, Donne, and the English Church Before Laud*. Lewisburg: Bucknell University Press, 1997.
Dollimore, Jonathan. *Radical Tragedy: Religion, Ideology and Power I the Drama of Shakespeare and his Contemporaries*. London: Harvester Wheatsheaf, 1984.
Donne, John. *Devotions Upon Emergent Occasions*, ed. Anthony Raspa. Montreal: McGill-Queen's University Press, 1975.
Donne, John. *John Donne: Selected Prose*, ed. Evelyn Simpson, Helen Gardner, and T. S. Healy. Oxford: Oxford University Press, 1967.
Donne, John. *Selected Letters*, ed. P. M. Oliver. London: Taylor and Francis, 2017.
Donne, John. *The Sermons of John Donne*, ed. Evelyn Simpson and George Potter. Berkeley: University of California Press, 1954.
Dryden, John. *The Works of John Dryden*, ed. A, B. Chambers, William Frost, and Vinton Dearing, et al. Berkeley: University of California Press, 1978–2002.
Dubrow, Heather. '"And Thus Leave Off": Reevaluating Mary Wroth's Folger Manuscript, V.a.104', *Tulsa Studies in Women's Literature* 22 (2003): 273–291.
Dubrow, Heather. *Captive Victors: Shakespeare's Narrative Poems and Sonnets*. Ithaca: Cornell University Press, 1987.
Dubrow, Heather. *Genre*. London: Methuen, 1982.
Dubrow, Heather. '"Incertainties Now Crown Themselves Assur'd": The Politics of Plotting in Shakespeare's Sonnets', *Shakespeare Quarterly* 47 (1996): 291–305.
Durston, Christopher. *James I*. New York: Taylor and Francis, 2016.
Dutton, Richard. *Mastering the Revels: The Regulation and Censorship of Early Modern Drama*. Oxford: Oxford University Press, 2022.
Easterling, Heather. *Parsing the City: Jonson, Middleton, Dekker, and City Comedy's London as Language*. New York: Routledge, 2007.
Edmondson, Paul and Stanley Wells. *Shakespeare's Sonnets*. Oxford: Oxford University Press, 2004.
Eliot, Sir John. *Negotium Posterorum*, or An Apology for Socrates. ed. A. B. Grosart. London: 1881.
Elton, William R. *King Lear and the Gods*. Los Angeles: Huntington Library, 1966.
Empson, William. *Some Versions of Pastoral*. London: Chatto and Windus, 1935.
Engle, Lars, Patrick Gray, and William Hamlin, eds., *Shakespeare and Montaigne*. Edinburgh: Edinburgh University Press, 2023.
Enterline, Lynn. *The Tears of Narcissus*. Stanford: Stanford University Press, 1995.
Erickson, Amy. *Women and Property in Early Modern England*. New York: Routledge, 1993.

Erne, Lukas. *Shakespeare as a Literary Dramatist*. Cambridge: Cambridge University Press, 2003.
Fallon, Stephen. *Milton's Peculiar Grace: Self-Representation and Authority*. Ithaca: Cornell University Press, 2007.
Ferguson, Margaret. *Dido's Daughters: Literacy, Gender, and Empire in Early Modern England and France*. Chicago: University of Chicago Press, 2003.
Finkelpearl, Philip. *Court and Country Politics in the Plays of Beaumont and Fletcher*. Princeton: Princeton University Press, 1990.
Finkelpearl, Philip. *John Marston of the Middle Temple: An Elizabethan Dramatist in His Social Setting*. Cambridge: Harvard University Press, 1969.
Fish, Stanley. 'Author-Readers: Jonson's Community of the Same', *Representations* 7 (1984): 26–58.
Fish, Stanley. *How Milton Works*. Cambridge: Harvard University Press, 2001.
Fish, Stanley. 'Marvell and the Art of Disappearance', in *Revenge of the Aesthetic: The Place of Literature in Theory Today*, ed. Michael P. Clark. Berkeley: University of California Press, 2000. pp. 25–44.
Fish, Stanley, *Self-Consuming Artifacts: The Experience of Seventeenth-Century Literature*. Berkeley: University of California Press, 1972.
Fisher, F. J. *London and the English Economy, 1500–1700*, ed. P. J. Corfield and N. B. Harte London: Hambledon, 1990.
Fleming, Juliet. *Graffiti and the Writing Arts of Early Modern England*. Philadelphia: University of Pennsylvania Press, 2001.
Floyd-Wilson, Mary. *English Ethnicity and Race in Early Modern Drama*. Cambridge: Cambridge University Press, 2003.
Floyd-Wilson, Mary. 'Temperature, Temperance, and Racial Difference in Ben Jonson's "The Masque of Blackness"', *English Literary Renaissance* 28 (1998): 183–209.
Fowler, Alastair. *The Country House Poem: A Cabinet of Seventeenth-Century Estate Poems and Related Items*. Edinburgh: Edinburgh University Press, 1994.
Fowler, Alastair. 'The Formation of Genres in the Renaissance and After', *New Literary History* 34 (2003): 185–200.
Fowler, Alastair. *Kinds of Literature: An Introduction to Genres and Modes*. Oxford: Oxford University Press, 2002.
Fox, Adam. *Oral and Literate Culture in England 1500–1700*. Oxford: Clarendon, 2000.
Foxley, Rachel. *The Levellers: Radical Political Thought in the English Revolution*. Manchester: Manchester University Press, 2013.
Frank, Joseph. *The Beginnings of the English Newspaper 1620–1660*. Cambridge: Harvard University Press, 1961
Fraser, Antonia. *The Gunpowder Plot: Terror and Faith in 1605*. London: Weidenfeld and Nicholson, 1996
Fumerton, Patricia. *Unsettled: The Culture of Mobility and the Working Poor in Early Modern England*. Chicago: University of Chicago Press, 2006.
Gamboa, Brett. *Shakespeare's Double Plays: Dramatic Economy on the Early Modern Stage*. Cambridge: Cambridge University Press, 2018.
Gibbons, Brian. *Jacobean City Comedy: A Study of Satiric Plays by Jonson, Marston, and Middleton*. Cambridge: Harvard University Press, 1968
Gibbons, Daniel. *Conflicts of Devotion: Liturgical Poetics in Sixteenth- and Seventeenth-Century England*. Notre Dame: University of Notre Dame Press, 2017.
Goldberg, Jonathan. *Endlesse Worke: Spenser and the Structures of Discourse*. Baltimore: Johns Hopkins University Press, 1981.

Goldberg, Jonathan. *James I and the Politics of Literature*. Baltimore: Johns Hopkins University Press, 1983.
Goldberg, Jonathan. *Sodometries: Renaissance Texts, Modern Sexualities*. Stanford: Stanford University Press, 1992.
Goody, Jack. *Family and Inheritance: Rural Society in Western Europe 1200-1800* Cambridge: Cambridge University Press, 2008.
Gossett, Suzanne. *The Influence of the Jacobean Masque on the Plays of Beaumont and Fletcher*. New York: Garland Publishing, 1988.
Gouge, William. *Of Domestical Duties*. London, 1622.
Grantley, Daryll. *London in Early Modern English Drama: Representing the Built Environment*. New York: Palgrave Macmillan, 2008.
Greenblatt, Stephen. *Hamlet in Purgatory*. Princeton: Princeton University Press, 2002.
Greenblatt, Stephen. *Renaissance Self Fashioning*. Chicago: University of Chicago Press, 1981.
Greenblatt, Stephen. *Shakespearean Negotiations: The Circulation of Energy in Renaissance England*. Berkeley: University of California Press, 1988.
Greenblatt, Stephen. *Shakespeare's Freedom*. Chicago: Chicago University Press, 2010.
Greene, Thomas. *The Light in Troy: Imitation and Discovery in Renaissance Poetry*. New Haven: Yale University Press, 1982.
Greville, Fulke. *The Prose Works of Fulke Greville, Lord Brooke*, ed. John Guows. Oxford: Clarendon, 1986.
Griswold, Wendy. *Renaissance Revivals: City Comedy and Revenge Tragedy in the London Theatre 1576-1980*. Chicago: University of Chicago Press, 1986.
Guibbory, Aschah. *Ceremony and Community from Herbert to Milton*. Cambridge: Cambridge University Press, 1998.
Guillen, Claudio. 'Notes toward the Study of the Renaissance Letter', in *Renaissance Genres: Essays on Theory, History, Interpretation*, ed. Barbara Lewalski. Cambridge: Harvard University Press, 1986. pp. 70-110.
Gurney, John. *Brave Community: The Digger Movement in the English Revolution*. Manchester: Manchester University Press, 2007.
Gurr, Andrew. *Playgoing in Shakespeare's England*. Cambridge: Cambridge University Press, 1986.
Gurr, Andrew. 'The Shakespearean Stage', in *The Norton Shakespeare, first edition* ed. Greenblatt, Stephen, Walter Cohen, Jean Howard, and Katharine Eisaman Maus. New York: W. W. Norton, 1997.
Habermas, Jurgen. *The Structural Transformation of the Public Sphere: An Inquiry into a Category of Bourgeois Society*, trans. T. Burger. Cambridge, MA: Harvard University Press, 1989.
Hall, Kim. *Things of Darkness: Economies of Race and Gender in Early Modern England*. Ithaca: Cornell University Press, 1995.
Hamlin, William. *Tragedy and Scepticism in Shakespeare's England*. London: Palgrave, 2005.
Hammond, Paul. 'The Date of Marvell's "The Mower Against Gardens"', *Notes and Queries* 53 (2006): 178-181.
Hammond, Paul. 'Marvell's Sexuality', *The Seventeenth Century* 11 (1996): 87-123.
Hannay, Margaret. *Mary Sidney, Lady Wroth*. New York: Routledge, 2010.
Harbage, Alfred. *Shakespeare and the Rival Traditions*. New York: Macmillan, 1952.
Harding, Vanessa. 'The Population of London, 1550-1700: A Review of the Published Evidence', *London Journal* 15 (1990): 111-128.

Harington, John. *Nugae Antiquae: Being a Miscellaneous Collection of Original Papers, in Prose and Verse*. London, 1804.
Harrison, William. *The Description of England. 1587*. ed. Georges Edelen. Ithaca: Cornell University Press, 1968.
Heal, Felicity and Clive Holmes, *The Gentry in England and Wales, 1500–1700*. London: Macmillan, 1994.
Helgerson, Richard. *The Elizabethan Prodigals*. Berkeley: University of California Press, 1977.
Helgerson, Richard. *Forms of Nationhood: The Elizabethan Writing of England*. Chicago: University of Chicago Press, 1992.
Helgerson, Richard. *Self-Crowned Laureates: Spenser Jonson Milton and the Literary System*. Berkeley: University of California Press, 1983.
Hendricks, Margo and Patricia Parker, eds. *Women, 'Race', and Writing in the Early Modern Period*. New York: Routledge, 1994.
Herbert, Edward. *The Autobiography of Edward, Lord Herbert of Cherbury*, ed. Sidney L. Lee. Cambridge: Cambridge University Press, 2014.
Herrick, Marvin. *Tragicomedy: Its Origin and Development in Italy, France, and England*. Urbana: University of Illinois Press, 1955.
Herrick, Robert. *The Complete Poems of Robert Herrick*, ed. Tom Cain and Ruth Connolly. Oxford: Oxford University Press, 2013.
Hibbard, G. R. 'The Country House Poem of the Seventeenth Century', *Journal of the Warburg and Courtauld Institutes* 19 (1956): 159–174.
Hirst, Derek and Stephen Zwicker, *Andrew Marvell: Orphan of the Hurricane*. Oxford: Oxford University Press, 2012.
Hobbes, Thomas. *Leviathan*, ed. J. C. A. Gaskin. Oxford: Oxford University Press, 1998.
Hobby, Eleanor. 'Katherine Philips: Seventeenth-Century Lesbian Poet', in *What Lesbians Do in Books*, ed. Eleanor Hobby and Chris White. London: Women's Press, 1991. pp. 183–204.
Hodgkins, Christopher. *Authority, Church, and Society in George Herbert: Return to the Middle Way*. Columbia: University of Missouri Press, 1993.
Holberton, Edward. *Poetry and the Cromwellian Protectorate: Culture, Politics, and Institutions*. Oxford: Oxford University Press, 2008.
Holbrook, Peter. *English Renaissance Tragedy: Ideas of Freedom*. London: Bloomsbury, 2015.
Holland, Peter. '*Hamlet* and the Art of Acting', *Themes in Drama* 6 (1984): 39–61.
Hollander, John. *Vision and Resonance: Two Senses of Poetic Form*. New York: Oxford, 1975.
Holmes, Martin. *Proud Northern Lady: Lady Anne Clifford 1590–1676*. London: Phillimore, 1975.
Hooker, Richard. *Of the Laws of Ecclesiastical Polity*, ed. Arthur Stephen McGrade. Oxford: Oxford University Press, 2013.
Howard, Jean. *Theater of A City: The Places of London Comedy 1598–1642*. Philadelphia: University of Pennsylvania Press, 2006.
Hoxby, Blair and Anne Coiro, eds. *Milton in the Long Restoration*. Oxford: Oxford University Press, 2021.
Hoy, Cyrus. 'Massinger as Collaborator: The Plays with Fletcher and Others', in *Philip Massinger: A Critical Reassessment*, ed. Douglas Howard. Cambridge: Cambridge University Press, 1985. pp. 51–82.
Hughes, Ann. *The Causes of the English Civil War*. New York: Palgrave MacMillan, 1998.

Hughes, Charles, ed. *Shakespeare's Europe: Unpublished Chapters of Fynes Moryson's Itinerary. Being a Survey of the Condition of Europe at the End of the 16th Century.* New York: B. Blom, 1967.
Hutchinson, Lucy. *Memoirs of the Life of Colonel Hutchinson*, ed. James Sutherland. New York: Oxford University Press, 1973.
Hutson, Lorna. *The Usurer's Daughter: Male Friendship and Fictions of Women in Seventeenth-Century England.* London: Routledge, 1994.
Hutton, Ronald. *The Making of Oliver Cromwell.* New Haven: Yale University Press, 2022.
Hyman, Wendy. *Impossible Desire and the Limits of Knowledge in Renaissance Poetry.* Oxford: Oxford University Press, 2019.
IJselwiin, J. 'John Barclay and his *Argenis*: A Scottish neo-Latin Novelist', *Humanistica Lovaniensia* 32 (1983): 1–27.
Iyengar, Sujata. *Shades of Difference: Mythologies of Skin Color in Early Modern England.* Philadelphia: University of Pennsylvania Press, 2005.
Jackson, MacDonald P. 'Vocabulary and Chronology: The Case of Shakespeare's Sonnets', *Review of English Studies* 52 (2001): 59–75.
James VI and I. *King James VI and I: Political Writings*, ed. Johann Somerville. Cambridge: Cambridge University Press, 1994.
Jardine, Lisa. *Francis Bacon: Discovery and the Art of Discourse.* Cambridge: Cambridge University Press, 1974.
Jardine, Lisa. *Still Harping on Daughters: Women and Drama in the Age of Shakespeare.* Sussex: Harvester, 1983.
Johnson, Samuel. *The Lives of the Most Eminent English Poets: With Critical Observations on their Works*, ed. Roger Lonsdale. Oxford: Oxford University Press, 2006.
Jones, Ann Rosalind, and Peter Stallybrass, 'The Politics of Astrophil and Stella', *SEL* 24 (1984): 53–68.
Jones, Richard Foster. *Ancients and Moderns: A Study of the Rise of the Scientific Movement in Seventeenth-Century England.* Berkeley: University of California Press, 1965.
Jonson, Ben. *The Cambridge Edition of the Works of Ben Jonson*, ed. David Bevington, Martin Butler, Ian Donaldson, et al., Cambridge: Cambridge University Press, 2012.
Kahn, Victoria. *Machiavellian Rhetoric: From the Counter-Reformation to Milton.* Princeton: Princeton University Press, 1994.
Keble, N. H. ed. *The Cambridge Companion to Writing the English Revolution.* Cambridge: Cambridge University Press, 2001.
Kermode, Frank. 'The Date of Cowley's *Davideis*', *The Review of English Studies* 25 (1949): 154–158.
Kerrigan, John. *Archipelagic English: Literature, History, and Politics 1603–1707.* Oxford: Oxford University Press, 2008.
Kerrigan, John, *Revenge Tragedy: Aeschylus to Armageddon.* Oxford: Clarendon, 1996.
Kerrigan, John. 'Thomas Carew', in *On Shakespeare and Early Modern Literature: Essays.* Oxford: Oxford University Press, 2001. pp. 181–216.
Kinney, Clare R. '"Beleeve this butt a fiction"': Female Authorship, Narrative Undoing, and the Limits of Romance in The Second Part of the Countess of Montgomery's Urania', *Spenser Studies* 17 (2003): 239–250.
Kirsch, Arthur. *Jacobean Dramatic Perspectives.* Charlottesville: University of Virginia Press, 1972.
Kishlansky, Mark. 'The Emergence of Adversary Politics in the Long Parliament', *Journal of Modern History* 49 (1977): 617–640.

Klawitter, George. *Andrew Marvell, Sexual Orientation, and Seventeenth-Century Poetry*. Madison: Fairleigh Dickinson University Press, 2017.
Knapp, Jeffrey. *Shakespeare's Tribe: Church, Nation, and Theatre in Renaissance England*. Chicago: University of Chicago Press, 2002.
Knight, G. Wilson *The Wheel of Fire: Interpretations of Shakespearean Tragedy*. Oxford: Oxford University Press, 1930.
Lake, Peter. *The Antichrist's Lewd Hat: Protestants, Papists, and Players in Post-Reformation England*. New Haven: Yale University Press, 2002.
Lamb, Mary Ellen, 'Topicality and the Interrogation of Wonder in *The Second Part of the Countess of Montgomery's Urania*', in *Renaissance Historicisms: Essays in Honor of Arthur Kinney*, ed. James Dutcher and Anne Lake Prescott. Newark: University of Delaware Press, 2008.
Lamb, Mary Ellen and Valerie Wayne, eds., *Staging Early Modern Romance: Prose Fiction, Dramatic Romance, and Shakespeare*. New York: Routledge, 2009.
Lamb, Mary Ellen. *Gender and Authorship in the Sidney Circle*. Madison: University of Wisconsin Press, 1990.
Langford, Gerald. '*Argenis*, a Seminal Novel', *SEL* 26 (1947): 59–76.
Laslett, Peter. *The World We Have Lost*. London: Methuen, 1965.
Laslett, Peter, *The World We Have Lost: Further Explored*. New York: Routledge, 2000.
Leggatt, Alexander. *Citizen Comedy in the Age of Shakespeare*. Toronto: University of Toronto Press, 1973.
Leinwand, Theodore. *The City Staged: Jacobean Comedy 1603–1613*. Madison: University of Wisconsin Press, 1986.
Lemon, Rebecca. 'Scaffolds of Treason in *Macbeth*', *Theatre Journal* 54 (2002): 25–43.
Levy-Navarro, Elena. 'Breaking Down the Walls That Divide: Anti-Polemicism in the *Devotions Upon Emergent Occasions*', in *John Donne and the Protestant Reformation*, ed. Mary Arshagouni Papazian. Detroit: Wayne State University Press, 2003. pp. 273–292.
Lewalski, Barbara. *The Life of John Milton: A Critical Biography*. Oxford: Blackwell, 2000.
Lewalski, Barbara. *Protestant Poetics and the Seventeenth Century Religious Lyric*. Princeton: Princeton University Press, 1979.
Lewalski, Barbara ed., *Renaissance Genres: Essays on Theory, History, and Interpretation*. Cambridge: Harvard University Press, 1986.
Lewis, C. S. *Mere Christianity*. New York: Harper Collins, 1952.
Liebler, Naomi, ed., *The Female Tragic Hero in English Renaissance Drama*. New York: Palgrave Macmillan, 2002.
Liebler, Naomi Conn *Shakespeare's Festive Tragedy: The Ritual Foundations of Genre*. London: Routledge, 1995.
Llewellyn, Mark. 'Katherine Philips, Friendship Poetry, and NeoPlatonic Thought in Seventeenth-Century England, *Philological Quarterly* 81 (2002): 441–468.
Loewenstein, Joseph. *The Author's Due: Printing and the Prehistory of Copyright*. Chicago: University of Chicago Press, 2002.
Loewenstein, Joseph. *Ben Jonson and Possessive Authorship*. Cambridge: Cambridge University Press, 2002.
Loewenstein, Joseph. 'The Jonsonian Corpulence: Or the Poet as Mouthpiece', *ELH* 53 (1986): 491–518.
Loewenstein, Joseph. *Responsive Readings: Version of Echo in Pastoral, Epic, and the Jonsonian Masque*. New Haven: Yale University Press, 1984.

Loomba, Ania. '"Break her will, and bruise no bone sir": Colonial and Sexual Mastery in Fletcher's The Island Princess', *Journal of Early Modern Cultural Studies* 2 (2002): 68–108.

Love, Harold. *Scribal Publication in Seventeenth-Century England*. Oxford: Oxford University Press, 1993.

Low, Anthony. *The Georgic Revolution*. Princeton: Princeton University Press, 1985.

Low, Anthony. *The Reinvention of Love: Poetry, Politics, and Culture from Sidney to Milton*. Cambridge: Cambridge University Press, 1993.

Lyons, Tara. 'Reading a Lost Book: Ben Jonson's *Epigrammes*. c. 1612 and Disposable Authorship', *ELR* 53 (2023): 1–34.

MacFarlane, Alan. *The Origins of English Individualism: Family, Property, and Social Transition*. Oxford: Basil Blackwell, 1978.

Mack, Maynard. *Everybody's Shakespeare: Reflections Chiefly on the Tragedies*. Lincoln: University of Nebraska Press, 1993.

Manley, Lawrence. *Convention, 1500–1700*. Cambridge: Harvard University Press, 1980.

Mansky, Joseph. 'Rethinking Royalism in Herrick's *Hesperides*', *Review of English Studies* 73 (2022): 476–489.

Marcus, Leah. *The Politics of Mirth: Jonson, Herrick, Milton, Marvell, and the Defense of Old Holiday Pastimes*. Chicago: University of Chicago Press, 1986

Marcus, Leah. *Unediting the Renaissance: Shakespeare, Marlowe, and Milton*. London: Taylor and Francis, 1996.

Marotti, Arthur. *The Circulation of Poetry in Manuscript in Early Modern England*. New York: Routledge, 2021.

Marotti, Arthur. *John Donne, Coterie Poet*. Madison: University of Wisconsin Press, 1986.

Marotti, Arthur. '"Love is Not Love": Elizabethan Sonnet Sequences and the Social Order', *ELH* 49 (1982): 396–428.

Marotti, Arthur. *Manuscript, Print, and the English Renaissance Lyric*. Ithaca: Cornell University Press, 1995.

Martin, Catherine Gimelli. 'Milton and Donne's Stargazing Lovers: Sex and the New Astronomy', *Studies in English Literature* 54 (2014): 143–171.

Martin, Jessica and Alec Ryrie, eds. *Private and Domestic Devotion in Early Modern Britain*. Burlington: Ashgate, 2012.

Martz, Louis. *The Poetry of Meditation: A Study in English Religious Literature*, revised edition. New Haven: Yale University Press, 1965.

Mascetti, Yaakov. 'Here I have Prepar'd My Paschal Lambe: Reading and Seeing the Eucharistic Presence in Aemilia Lanyer's "Salve Deus Rex Judaeorum"', *Partial Answers: Journal of Literature and the History of Ideas* 9 (2011): 1–15.

Masten, Jeffrey. '"Shall I turne blabbe?": Circulation, Gender, and Subjectivity in Mary Wroth's Sonnets', in *Reading Mary Wroth: Representing Alternatives in Early Modern England*, eds. Naomi Miller and Gary Waller. Knoxville: University of Tennessee Press, 1991. pp. 67–87.

Masten, Jeffrey. *Textual Intercourse: Collaboration, Authorship, and Sexualities in Renaissance Drama*. Cambridge: Cambridge University Press, 1997.

Matthew, Tobie. *A True Historical Relation of the Conversion of Sir Tobie Matthew to the Holy Catholic Faith*, ed. A. H. Matthew. London: Burnes and Oates, 1904.

Maus, Katharine Eisaman. *Ben Jonson and the Roman Frame of Mind*. Princeton: Princeton University Press, 1984.

Maus, Katharine Eisaman. *Four Revenge Tragedies of the English Renaissance*. Oxford: Oxford University Press, 1995.

Maus, Katharine Eisaman. 'Why Read Herrick?', *Lords of Wine and Oil: Community and Conviviality in Robert Herrick and his Contemporaries*, ed. Tom Cain and Ruth Connelly. Oxford: Oxford University Press, 2011. pp. 25–38.

Mauss, Marcel. *The Gift: The Form and Reason for Exchange in Archaic Societies*, trans. W. D. Halls. London: Routledge, 1990.

McAlindon, Thomas. *English Renaissance Tragedy*. Basingstoke: Macmillan, 1986.

McCabe, Richard A. *Joseph Hall, A Study in Satire and Meditation*. Oxford: Clarendon, 1982.

McCabe, Richard A. *'Ungainefull Art': Poetry, Patronage, and Print in the Early Modern Era*. Oxford: Oxford University Press, 2016.

McCanles, Michael. *Jonsonian Discriminations: The Humanist Poet and the Praise of True Nobility*. Toronto: University of Toronto Press, 1992.

McColley, Grant. 'The Astronomy of *Paradise Lost*', *Studies in Philology* 34 (1937): 219–247.

McCullough, Peter, Hugh Adlington, and Emma Rhatigan, eds. *The Oxford Handbook of the Early Modern Sermon*. Oxford: Oxford University Press, 2011.

McDonald, Charles Osborne. *The Rhetoric of Tragedy: Form in Stuart Drama*. Amherst: University of Massachusetts Press, 1966.

McDowell, Nicholas. 'Classical Liberty and Cavalier Poetics: The Politics of Literary Community in Caroline England from Jonson to Marvell', *Yearbook of English Studies* 44 (2014): 120–136.

McDowell, Nicholas. *Poetry and Allegiance in the English Civil Wars*. Oxford: Oxford University Press, 2008.

McKeon, Michael. '*Paradise Lost*: Poem of the Restoration Period', *Eighteenth Century Life* 41 (2017): 9–27.

McLuskie, Kathleen E. and Felicity Dunsworth. 'Patronage and the Economics of Theatre', in *A New History of Early English Drama*, ed. John D. Cox and David Scott Kastan. New York: Columbia University Press, 1997. pp. 423–440.

McMullan, Gordon. *The Politics of Unease in the Plays of John Fletcher*. Amherst: University of Massachusetts, 1994.

McRae, Andrew and Philip Schwyzer. eds. *Poly-Olbion: New Perspectives*. Rochester: Boydell and Brewer, 2020.

Mears, Natalie and Alec Ryrie, eds. *Worship and the Parish Church in Early Modern Britain*. Burlington: Ashgate, 2013.

Menges, Hilary. 'Authorship, Friendship, and Forms of Publication in Katherine Philips', *SEL* 52 (2002): 517–541.

Middleton, Thomas. *Thomas Middleton: The Collected Works*, ed. Gary Taylor, John Lavagnino, et al. Oxford: Clarendon, 2007.

Miehl, Dieter, Angela Stock, and Anne-Julia Zwerlein, eds. *Plotting Early Modern London: New Essays on Jacobean City Comedy*. Aldershot: Ashgate, 2014.

Miller, Naomi. *Changing the Subject: Mary Wroth and Figurations of Gender in Early Modern England*. Lexington: University Press of Kentucky, 1996.

Miller, Perry. *The New England Mind. The Seventeenth Century*. Harvard: Harvard University Press, 1939.

Milton, John *An Apology For Smectymnuus, with The Reason of Church-Government*. London, 1641.

Milton, John. *Paradise Lost*, ed. Alastair Fowler. New York: Routledge, first edition 1968, second edition, 2007.

Montaigne, Michel de. *Essays, or Moral, Politic, and Military Discourses*, trans. John Florio. London, 1603.

Morris, David. 'Drama and Stasis in Milton's Ode on the Morning of Christ's Nativity', *Studies in Philology* 68 (1971): 207–222.

Montrose, Louis. 'The Place of a Brother in As *You Like It*: Social Process and Comic Form.' *Shakespeare Quarterly* 32 (1981): 28–54.

Moul, Victoria. 'Abraham Cowley's 1656 Poems: Form and Context', *Royalists and Royalism in 17th-Century Literature: Exploring Abraham Cowley*, ed. Philip Majors. New York: Routledge, 2019. pp. 150–179.

Muldrew, Craig. *The Economy of Obligation: The Culture of Credit and Social Relations in Early Modern England*. New York: Palgrave MacMillan, 1997.

Myers, Anne M. 'Construction Sites: The Architecture of Anne Clifford's Diaries', *ELH* 73 (2006): 581–600.

Neill, Michael. *Issues of Death: Mortality and Identity in English Renaissance Tragedy*. Oxford: Clarendon, 1997.

Newman, Harry. 'Character": Character-Writing, Drama, and the Shape of Literary History', *Journal for Early Modern Cultural Studies* 21 (2021): 142–177.

Newman, Karen. 'City Talk: Women and Commodification in Jonson's *Epicoene*', *ELH* 53. (1989): 503–518.

Newman, Karen *Fashioning Femininity and English Renaissance Drama*. Chicago: University of Chicago Press, 1991.

Norbrook, David. *Poetry and Politics in the English Renaissance: Revised Edition*. London: Routledge, 2002.

Norbrook, David. '"What Care These Roarers for the Name of King?": Language and Utopia in The Tempest', in *The Politics of Tragicomedy: Shakespeare and After*, ed. Gordon MacMullan and Jonathan Hope. New York: Routledge, 1992. pp. 21–54.

Norbrook, David. *Writing the English Republic 1627–1660*. Cambridge: Cambridge University Press, 1999.

O'Callaghan, Michelle. *The English Wits: Literature and Sociability in Early Modern England*. Cambridge: Cambridge University Press, 2009.

O'Hehir, Brendan. *Expans'd Hieroglyphics: A Critical Edition of Sir John Denham's Cooper's Hill*. Berkeley: University of California Press, 1969.

Oppenheimer, Paul. *The Birth of the Modern Mind: Self, Consciousness, and the Invention of the Sonnet*. Oxford: Oxford University Press, 1989.

Orgel, Stephen. *The Illusion of Power*. Berkeley: University of California Press, 1975.

Orgel, Stephen. *The Impersonations of Gender in Shakespeare's England*. Cambridge: Cambridge University Press, 1996.

Orgel, Stephen. *The Jonsonian Masque*. Cambridge: Harvard University Press, 1966.

Orgel, Stephen and Guy Fitch Lytle, eds. *Patronage in the Renaissance*. Princeton: Princeton University Press, 1982.

Orgel, Stephen and Roy Strong, *Inigo Jones: The Theater of the Stuart Court*. Berkeley: University of California Press, 1973.

Orlin, Lena Cowen, ed., *Material London*. Philadelphia: University of Pennsylvania Press, 2000.

Ornstein, Robert. *The Moral Vision of Jacobean Tragedy*. Madison: University of Wisconsin Press, 1960.

Overbury, Thomas, et al. *The Overburian Characters*, ed. W. J. Paylor. New York: AMS, 1977.

Parker, Patricia. *Inescapable Romance: Studies in the Poetics of a Mode*. Princeton: Princeton University Press, 1979.

Parker, Patricia. *Literary Fat Ladies: Rhetoric, Gender, Property*. New York: Routledge, 1987.
Patterson, Annabel. *Censorship and Interpretation: The Conditions of Writing and Reading in Early Modern England*. Madison: University of Wisconsin Press, 1984.
Patterson, W. B. *King James VI and I and the Reunion of Christendom*. Cambridge: Cambridge University Press, 2000.
Peck, Linda Levy. *Consuming Splendor: Society and Culture in Seventeenth-Century England*. Cambridge: Cambridge University Press, 2005.
Peck, Linda Levy. *Court Patronage and Corruption in Early Stuart England*. London: Routledge, 1990.
Perkins, William. *The Whole Treatise of the Cases of Conscience, Distinguished into Three Books*. London, 1628.
Perry, Curtis. *Literature and Favoritism in Early Modern England*. Cambridge: Cambridge University Press, 2006.
Perry, Curtis. *The Makings of Jacobean Culture: James I and the Renegotiation of Elizabethan Literary Practice*. Cambridge: Cambridge University Press, 1997.
Perry, Curtis. *Shakespeare and Senecan Tragedy*. Cambridge: Cambridge University Press, 2020.
Potter, Lois. *Secret Rites and Secret Writing: Royalist Literature 1641–1660*. Cambridge: Cambridge University Press, 1989.
Prall, Stuart. *Church and State in Tudor and Stuart England*. Arlington Heights: Davidson, 1993.
Prior, Charles W. A. *Defining the Jacobean Church: The Politics of Religious Controversy 1603–1625*. Cambridge: Cambridge University Press, 2005.
Pritchard, Allan. *English Biography in the Seventeenth Century*. Toronto: University of Toronto Press, 2005.
Pritchard, Allan. 'Marvell's "The Garden"', *SEL: Studies in English Literature* 23 (1980): 371–388.
Prynne, William. *Histrio Mastix: The Players Scourge, or Actors Tragaedie*. London, 1633.
Purkiss, Diane. *The English Civil War: A People's History*. London: HarperPress, 2006.
Puttenham, George. *The Art of English Poesy: A Critical Edition*, ed. Frank Whigham and Wayne Rebhorn. Ithaca: Cornell University Press, 2007.
Quilligan, Maureen. 'The Constant Subject: Instability and Authority in Wroth's *Urania* Poems', in *Soliciting Interpretation: Literary Theory and Seventeenth-Century English Poetry*, ed. Elizabeth Harvey and Katharine Eisaman Maus. Chicago: University of Chicago Press, 1990, pp. 307–335.
Quint, David. *Epic and Empire: Politics and Generic Form from Virgil to Milton*. Princeton: Princeton University Press, 1993.
Quint, David. 'Expectation and Prematurity in Milton's Nativity Ode', *Modern Philology* 97. 1999: 195–219.
Rambuss, Richard. *Closet Devotions*. Durham: Duke University Press, 1998.
Rappaport, Steven, *Worlds Within Worlds: Structures of Life in Sixteenth-Century London*. Cambridge: Cambridge University Press, 1989.
Raylor, Timothy. *Cavaliers, Clubs, and Literary Culture: Sir John Mennes, James Smith, and the Order of the Fancy*. Newark: University of Delaware Press, 1994.
Raymond, Joad. *The Invention of the English Newspaper: English Newsbooks 1641–49*. Oxford: Clarendon, 1996.
Ribner, Irving. *Jacobean Tragedy: The Quest for Moral Order*. New York: Barnes and Noble, 1962.

Rogers, Edward, ed., *Some Account of the Life and Opinions of a Fifth-Monarchy-Man: Chiefly Extracted from the Writings of John Rogers, Preacher.* London, 1867.
Rogers, John. *The Matter of Revolution: Science, Poetry, and Politics in the Age of Milton.* Ithaca: Cornell University Press, 1996.
Rose, Mary Beth *The Expense of Spirit: Love and Sexuality in English Renaissance Drama.* Ithaca: Cornell University Press, 1988.
Rush, Rebecca. *The Fetters of Rhyme: Liberty and Poetic Form in Early Modern England.* Princeton: Princeton University Press, 2021.
Rush, Rebecca. 'Like Alcestis: Milton's Twenty-Third Sonnet and Lyric Personhood', *Milton Studies* 64 (2022): 173–199.
Russell, Conrad. *The Causes of the English Civil War: The Ford Lectures Delivered in the University of Oxford 1987–1988.* Oxford: Clarendon, 1990.
Russell, Conrad. *King James I and his English Parliaments: The Trevelyan Lectures Delivered at the University of Cambridge 1995*, ed. Richard Cust and Andrew Thrush. New York: Oxford University Press, 2011.
Russell, Conrad. *Unrevolutionary England, 1603–1642.* London: Hambledon Press, 1990.
Ryrie, Alec. *Being Protestant in Reformation Britain.* Oxford: Oxford University Press, 2013.
Sachse, William. 'The Migration of New Englanders to England, 1640–1660', *American Historical Review* 2 (1948): 251–278.
Salzman, Paul. *Literary Culture in Jacobean England: Reading 1621.* New York: Palgrave Macmillan, 2002.
Salzman, Paul. *Reading Early Modern Women's Writing.* Oxford: Oxford University Press, 2006.
Sanchez, Melissa. *Erotic Subjects: The Sexuality of Politics in Early Modern Literature.* Oxford: Oxford University Press, 2011.
Sandberg, Julianne. 'Book, Body, and Bread: Reading Aemilia Lanyer's Eucharist', *Philological Quarterly* 96 (2017): 1–25.
Sanderson, William. *Reign and Death of King James.* London, 1656.
Sandstroem, Yvonne. 'Marvell's "Nymph Complaining" as Historical Allegory', *SEL* 30 (1990): 93–115.
Saunders, J. W. 'The Stigma of Print: A Note on the Social Bases of Tudor Poetry', *Essays in Criticism* 1 (1951): 140–165.
Schalwyck, David. *Speech and Performance in Shakespeare's Sonnets and Plays.* Cambridge: Cambridge University Press, 2002.
Schnell, Lisa. 'So Great a Difference is There in Degree: Aemilia Lanyer and the Aims of Feminist Criticism', *Modern Language Quarterly* 57 (1996): 23–35.
Schoenfeldt, Michael. 'That Ancient Heat: Sexuality and Spirituality in *The Temple*', in *Soliciting Interpretation: Literary Theory and Seventeenth-Century Poetry*, eds. Elizabeth Harvey and Katharine Eisaman Maus. Chicago: University of Chicago Press, 1990. pp. 273–306.
Schoenfeldt, Michael. *Prayer and Power: George Herbert and Renaissance Courtship.* Chicago: University of Chicago Press, 1991.
Scott Brown, Denise. 'Room at the Top? Sexism and the Star System in Architecture', in *Architecture: A Place for Women*, eds. Ellen Perry Berkeley and Matilda McQuaid. Washington: Smithsonian Institution Press, 1989.
Scott Brown, Denise. 'A Worm's Eye View of Recent Architectural History', *Architectural Record* 172 (1984): 69–81.
Shakespeare, William. *The Norton Shakespeare, Third Edition.* Ed. Stephen Greenblatt et al. New York: W. W. Norton, 2015.

Shakespeare, William. *Shakespeare's Sonnets and Poems*, ed. Colin Burrow. Oxford: Oxford University Press, 2008.

Shami, Jean. *John Donne and Conformity in Crisis in the Late Jacobean Pulpit*. Suffolk: Boydell and Brewer, 2003.

Shannon, Laurie. *Sovereign Amity: Figures of Friendship in Shakespearean Contexts*. Chicago: Chicago University Press, 2002.

Shuger, Debora. *Habits of Thought in the English Renaissance: Religion, Politics, and the Dominant Culture*. Toronto: University of Toronto Press, 1990.

Siddiqi, Yumna. 'Dark Incontinents: The Discourses of Race and Gender in Three Renaissance Masques', *Renaissance Drama new series* 23 (1992): 139–163.

Sidney, Philip. *The Defence of Poesie*. London, 1595, in *Sir Philip Sidney: The Defence of Poesie, Political Discourses, Correspondence, Translation*, [*The Prose Works of Sir Philip Sidney* vol 3], ed. Albert Feuillerat. Cambridge: Cambridge University Press, 1962.

Simkin, Stevie, ed., *Revenge Tragedy*. New York: Palgrave, 2001.

Simpson, James. *The Oxford Literary History: Volume 2: 1350–1547: Reform and Cultural Revolution*. Oxford: Oxford University Press, 2004.

Siochru, Michael O. *God's Executioner: Oliver Cromwell and the Conquest of Ireland*. New York: Faber and Faber, 2000.

Skinner, Quentin. *Liberty Before Liberalism*. Cambridge: Cambridge University Press, 1998.

Smeed, J. W. *The Theophrastan 'Character': The History of a Literary Genre*. Oxford: Clarendon, 1985.

Smith, Bruce R. *Homosexual Desire in Shakespeare's England*. Chicago: University of Chicago Press, 1991.

Smith, Emma, ed. *The Cambridge Companion to English Renaissance Tragedy*. Cambridge: Cambridge University Press, 2010.

Smith, Nigel. *Literature and Revolution in England*. New Haven: Yale University Press, 1994.

Smith, Nigel. *Perfection Proclaimed: Language and Literature in English Radical Religion 1640–1660*. Oxford: Clarendon, 1989.

Smuts, Malcolm. 'Cultural Diversity and Cultural Change at the Court of James I', *The Mental World of the Jacobean Court*, ed. Linda Levy Peck. Cambridge: Cambridge University Press, 1991. pp. 99–112.

Song, Eric. *Dominion Undeserved: Milton and the Perils of Creation*. Ithaca: Cornell University Press, 2013.

Speght, Rachel. *Mortalities Memorandum, with a Dreame Prefixed, imaginarie in manner; real in matter*. London, 1621.

Spring, Eileen. *Law, Land, and Family: Aristocratic Inheritance in England 1300–1800*. Chapel Hill: University of North Carolina Press, 2000.

Spufford, Peter. 'Population Movement in Seventeenth-Century England', *Local Population Studies* 4 (1970): 41–50.

Stallybrass, Peter. '"We Feast in Our Defense": Patrician Carnival in Early Modern England and Robert Herrick's "Hesperides"', *English Literary Renaissance* 16 (1986): 232–254.

Stallybrass, Peter and Ann Rosalind Jones. 'The Politics of Astrophel and Stella', *SEL* 24 (1984): 53–68.

Starke, Sue. '"The Eternal Now": Virgilian Echoes and Miltonic Premonitions in Cowley's Davideis', *Christianity and Literature* 55 (2006): 195–219.

Stephen, James. *Francis Bacon and the Style of Science*. Chicago: University of Chicago Press, 1975.
Stevens, Andrea. *Inventions of the Skin: The Painted Body in Early English Drama, 1400–1642*. Edinburgh: Edinburgh University Press, 2013.
Stewart, Alan. *The Cradle King: The Life of James VI and I*. New York: St Martins, 2003.
Stewart, Alan. *The Oxford History of Life Writing, volume 2, Early Modern*. Oxford: Oxford University Press, 2018.
Stewart, Alan and Lisa Jardine. *Hostage to Fortune: The Troubled Life of Francis Bacon, 1561–1626*. New York: Farrar Strauss Giroux, 1999.
Stirling, Brent. *The Shakespeare Sonnet Order: Poems and Groups*. Berkeley: University of California Press, 1968.
Stone, Lawrence. *The Causes of the English Revolution, 1529–1642*. New York: Routledge, 1986.
Stow, John *The Annals or General Chronicle of England*. London, 1615.
Straznicky, Marta. *Privacy, Playreading, and Women's Closet Drama, 1550–1700*. Cambridge: Cambridge University Press, 2004.
Strier, Richard. *Love Known: Theology and Experience in George Herbert's Poetry*. Chicago: University of Chicago Press, 1983.
Strier, Richard. 'Milton Against Humility', in *Religion and Culture in Renaissance England*, ed. Debora Shugar and Claire McEachern. Cambridge: Cambridge University Press, 1997. pp. 258–286.
Strier, Richard. *Shakespearean Issues: Agency, Skepticism, and Other Puzzles*. Philadelphia: University of Pennsylvania Press, 2023.
Strong, Roy. *Henry, Prince of Wales and England's Lost Renaissance*. London: Thames and Hudson, 1986.
Summers, Joseph. *George Herbert: His Religion and Art*. Cambridge: Harvard University Press, 1954.
Targoff, Ramie. *Common Prayer: The Language of Public Devotion in Early Modern England*. Chicago: University of Chicago Press, 2001.
Targoff, Ramie. *John Donne, Body and Soul*. Chicago: University of Chicago Press, 2008.
Teskey, Gordon. *Delirious Milton: The Fate of the Poet in Modernity*. Cambridge: Harvard University Press, 2009.
Teunissen, John J. and Evelyn Hinz. 'What is the Nymph Complaining For?', *ELH* 45 (1978): 410–428.
Thirsk, Joan. *Economic Policy and Projects: The Development of a Consumer Society in Early Modern England*. Oxford: Oxford University Press, 1978.
Thirsk, Joan. 'England's Provinces: Did They Serve or Drive Material London?', in *Material London, ca. 1600*, ed. Lena Cowen Orlin. Philadelphia: University of Pennsylvania Press, 2000. pp. 97–108.
Thirsk, Joan. *The Rural Economy of England: Collected Essays*. London: Hambledon, 1984.
Thirsk, Joan and J. P. Cooper, eds. *Seventeenth-Century Economic Documents*. Oxford: Clarendon, 1972.
Thomas, Keith. 'The Meaning of Literacy in Early Modern England', in *The Written Word: Literacy in Transition*, ed. Gerd Baumann. Oxford: Clarendon, 1986. pp. 97–131.
Tillyard, E. M. W. *The Elizabethan World Picture: A Study of the Idea of Order in the Age of Shakespeare, Donne, and Milton*. New York: Random House, 1959.
Toliver, Harold. 'Herrick's Book of Realms and Moments', *ELH* 49 (1982): 429–448.

Traub, Valerie. '"Friendship so Curst": *Amor Impossibilis*, the Homoerotic Lament, and the Nature of Lesbian Desire', in *The Noble Flame of Katherine Philips: A Poetics of Culture, Politics, and Friendship*, ed. David L. Orvis and Ryan Singh Paul. Pittsburgh: Duquesne University Press, 2015. pp. 276–325.

Traub, Valerie. *The Renaissance of Lesbianism in Early Modern England*. Cambridge: Cambridge University Press, 2002.

Trevor, Douglas. *The Poetics of Melancholy in Early Modern England*. Cambridge: Cambridge University Press, 2004.

Turner, James. *The Politics of Landscape: Rural Scenery and Society in English Poetry, 1630–1660*. Oxford: Blackwell, 1979.

Van Es, Bart. *Shakespeare in Company*. Oxford: Oxford University Press, 2013.

Vickers, Brian. *Francis Bacon and Renaissance Prose*. Cambridge: Cambridge University Press, 1968.

Vitkus, Daniel. *Turning Turk: English Theater and the Multicultural Mediterranean, 1570–1630*. New York: Palgrave Macmillan, 2003.

Waith, Eugene. *The Pattern of Tragicomedy in Beaumont and Fletcher*. New Haven: Yale University Press, 1952.

Wall, Wendy. *The Imprint of Gender: Authorship and Publication in the English Renaissance*. Ithaca: Cornell University Press, 1993.

Waller, Gary. *The Sidney Family Romance: Mary Wroth, William Herbert, and the Early Modern Construction of Gender*. Detroit: Wayne State University Press, 1993.

Walton, Isaak. *Isaak Walton: The Complete Angler, 1653–1676*, ed. Jonquil Bevan. Oxford: Oxford University Press, 1983.

Walton, Isaak. *The Life of John Donne, Doctor of Divinity and Late Dean of Saint Paul's Church London*. London, 1658.

Walton, Isaak. *The Life of Mr George Herbert*. London, 1670.

Walton, Isaak. 'The Life of Sir Henry Wotton', in Henry Wotton, *Reliquiae Wottoniana*. London, 1651.

Walton, Isaak. *Walton's Lives*, ed. Thomas Zouch. Boston: Crosby, Nichols, Lee, and Company, 1860.

Wasserman, Earl. 'Denham: Cooper's Hill', in *The Subtler Language: Critical Readings of Neoclassic and Romantic Poems*. Baltimore: Johns Hopkins University Press, 1959. pp. 45–88.

Wayne, Don. *Penshurst: The Semiotics of Place and the Poetics of History*. Madison: University of Wisconsin Press, 1984.

Webber, Joan. *The Eloquent 'I': Style and Self in Seventeenth-Century Prose*. Madison: University of Wisconsin Press, 1968.

Webster, Tom. *Godly Clergy in Early Stuart England*. Cambridge: Cambridge University Press, 1997.

Whigham, Frank. *Seizures of the Will in Early Modern English Drama*. Cambridge: Cambridge University Press, 1996.

White, Micheline. 'A Woman With Saint Peter's Keys?: Aemelia Lanyer's "Salve Deus Rex Judaeorum" 1611 and the Priestly Gifts of Women', *Criticism* 45 (2003): 323–341.

White, Paul Whitfield and Suzanne Westfall, eds. *Shakespeare and Theatrical Patronage in Early Modern England*. Cambridge: Cambridge University Press, 2002.

White, Peter. *Predestination, Policy, and Polemic: Conflict and Consensus in the English Church from the Reformation to the Civil War*. Cambridge: Cambridge University Press, 1992.

Williams, Raymond. *The Country and the City*. London: Chatto and Windus, 1973.

Williamson, George. *The Senecan Amble: A Study in Prose Form From Bacon to Collier*. Chicago: University of Chicago Press, 1951.

Wills, Gary. *Witches and Jesuits: Shakespeare's Macbeth*. Oxford: Oxford University Press, 1996.

Wilson, Arthur. *The History of Great Britain, Being the Life and Reign of King James I*. London, 1653.

Wilson, Edward. 'Did John Fletcher Read Spanish?', *Philological Quarterly* 27 (1948): 187–190.

Witmore, Michael. *Culture of Accidents: Unexpected Knowledge in Early Modern England*. Stanford: Stanford University Press, 2002.

Wood, Anthony. *Athenae Oxoniensis*, ed. Philip Bliss. London, 1817.

Woodbridge, Linda. 'Queen of Apricots: The Duchess of Malfi, Hero of Desire', in *The Female Tragic Hero in English Renaissance Drama*, ed. Naomi Conn Liebler. New York: Palgrave, 2002. pp. 161–184.

Wrightson, Keith. *Earthly Necessities: Economic Lives in Early Modern Britain*. New Haven: Yale University Press, 2002.

Wrightson, Keith. *English Society, 1580–1680*. London: Routledge, 1993.

Wrigley, E. A. and R. S. Schofield, *The Population History of England, 141–1871: A Reconstruction*. Cambridge: Cambridge University Press, 1981.

Wroth, Mary. *The First Part of the Countess of Montgomery's Urania*, ed. Josephine Roberts. Binghamton: Medieval and Renaissance Texts and Studies, 1995.

Wroth, Mary. *The Second Part of the Countess of Montgomery's Urania*, ed. Josephine Roberts, Suzanne Gossett, and Janel Mueller. Tempe: Arizona Center for Medieval and Renaissance Texts and Studies, 1999.

Wroth, Mary. *The Abridged Countess of Montgomery's Urania*, ed. Mary Ellen Lamb. Tempe: Arizona Center for Medieval and Renaissance Texts and Studies, 2011.

Wymer, Rowland. 'Jacobean Pageant or Elizabethan Fin-de-siecle? The Political Context of Early Seventeenth Century Tragedy', in *Neo-Historicism: Studies in Renaissance Literature, History, and Politics*. Ed. Robin Headlam Wells, Glenn Burgess, and Rowland Wymer. Cambridge: D.S. Brewer, 2000. pp. 138–151.

Zagorin, Perez. *The Court and the Country*. New York: Routledge, 1969.

Zucker, Adam, *The Places of Wit in Early Modern English Comedy*. Cambridge: Cambridge University Press, 2011.

Index

Aasand, Hardin 220, 447
Achinstein, Sharon 394, 447
Adams, Christine 223, 447
Addison, Joseph 429
Adlington, Hugh 292, 447
Aesop 375
Agricola 440
Alexander, Gavin 348, 423, 447
Alighieri, Dante 305, 324, 340, 405
Alleyn, Edward 359
Allinson, Mark 407, 447
Altman, Joel 447
Anacreon 375
Andrea, Bernadette 218, 447
Andreadis, Harriette 336, 379–380, 447
Andrewes, Lancelot 76, 393
Anne of Denmark, Queen consort of James I and VI 10, 24, 50, 110, 115, 116, 119–120, 121, 122, 138, 213, 216, 218–220
Anne, Queen of Great Britain (d. 1714) 35
Aquinas 336
Arden of Faversham 390
Ariosto, Ludovico 324
Aristotle 149, 273, 359, 377, 380, 428
   Organon 397
   Poetics 232, 243
Arminius, Jakob 446
Arnold, Matthew 'Dover Beach' 196
Asp, Carolyn 261, 447
Aston, William 105, 121
Attridge, Derek 388, 447
Aubrey, John 441
Aubrey, Mary 378
Augustine 336, 359, 405
   Confessions 80, 435
Austin, William 283, 295
   Devotionis Augustinianae Flamma 295

Bacon, Anthony 400
Bacon, Francis 1, 5, 72, 74, 82, 110, 223, 225, 273, 395–402, 403–404, 405, 408, 409, 412, 415, 416, 437, 438, 447
   'Of Greatness and Goodness of Nature' 401
   'Of Marriage and Single Life' 401
   'Of Suspicion' 401
   'Of Usury' 401
   The Advancement of Learning 72, 82, 397, 398, 440
   De Augmentis Scientarum 397
   Essays, or Counsels 38, 39, 72, 82, 152, 395, 400–402
   The History of Henry VII 82, 400
   Instauratio Magna, or Great Instauration 82, 397
   The New Atlantis 397
   Novum Organon (The New Organon) 54, 72, 395, 397–400, 410
Bailey, Amanda 166, 447
Baldwin, T. W. 50, 447
Bamber, Linda 253, 447
Barbour, Reid 409, 447
Barbour, Richmond 140, 279
Barclay, John, *Argenis* 54, 415–417, 418–419, 422, 424, 448
Barnes, Barnaby 340
Barroll, Leeds 51, 120, 218, 448
Barry, Lording *Ram Alley* 100, 160
Barton, Anne 128, 448
Bastwick, John 287
Beadle, John *The Diary of a Thankful Christian* 431, 435–436
Beaumont, Francis 74, 89, 93, 103, 112, 215, 261, 359, 414, 448. *see also* Fletcher, John
   A King and No King 263, 264, 265, 275
   The Knight of the Burning Pestle 47, 97, 100, 102, 160–161
   The Maid's Tragedy 212, 230, 244, 251, 252, 253, 254

Philaster 262, 263–264, 265, 266, 274, 275, 448
The Works of Beaumont and Fletcher 93, 144
Bednarz, James 56, 448
Beecher, Donald 429, 448
Bell, Ilona 348, 448
Belsey, Catherine 231, 237, 253, 448
Benet, Diana Trevino 352, 448
Bentley, G. R. 90, 448
Bevington, David 448, 455
Bible 3, 19, 54, 80–81, 189, 204, 289–291, 296, 301–303, 304, 317, 318–319, 320–321, 324, 327, 329, 331, 335, 363, 400–401, 406, 408
'King James' version 16, 119, 390
Blair, Rhonda 396, 403, 449
Blake, William 9
Blank, Paula 56, 448
Bliss, Lee 268, 448
The Bloody Banquet 230
Bloom, Harold 131
Bodley, Thomas 38, 102
Boethius 83, 377
Book of Common Prayer 204, 287, 310, 311
Book of Sports 224
Bowers, Fredson 230–231
Bradbrook, Muriel 231, 385, 448
Braden, Gordon 232, 299, 448
Brahe, Tycho 395
Brathwaite, Richard *Panthalia* 417
Bray, Alan 336, 448
Bright, Timothy *Treatise of Melancholy* 403
Britland, Karen 212, 223, 448
Brome, Richard 90, 91, 144, 154, 155
The Antipodes 174
Brooke, Christopher 358
Browne, Thomas 82, 409–412, 416, 432, 448
Religio Medici 38, 39, 82, 410–412
Pseudodoxia Epidemica 396, 410
Bruster, Douglas 90, 448
Bunyan, John *Grace Abounding to the Chief of Sinners* 435
Burbage, James 65
Burbage, Richard 65
Burgess, Glenn 21, 449
Burrow, Colin 324, 342, 345–346, 359, 449, 461
Burton, Henry 287
Burton, Robert 82, 402–405, 409, 423, 449

The Anatomy of Melancholy 82, 396, 402–405
Bush, Douglas 385, 449
Bushnell, Rebecca 231, 245, 449
Butler, Martin 122, 212, 214, 362, 449, 455

Cadman, Daniel 231, 449
Cain, Thomas 369
Caius, John, *Of English Dogs* 61, 63
Calhoun, Thomas 144–145
Callaghan, Dymphna 231, 449
Calvin, John 297
Camden, William 7, 82, 135, 195, 359, 361
Britannia 54, 193
Remains Concerning Britain 193, 194, 393, 449
Campbell, Gordon 315, 449
Campion, Thomas 74, 215, 368, 389
Carew, Richard *Survey of Cornwall* 193
Carew, Thomas 74, 112, 116, 181, 190, 194, 224, 366, 368
'To My Friend G. N. From Wrest' 153, 189–190
'A Rapture' 369
'To Saxham' 153, 188–189, 191, 192, 194
Coelum Britannicum 189
Carey, John 310, 355–356, 406, 407, 449
Carleton, Dudley 112, 220, 419, 448
Carr, Robert, Earl of Somerset 25, 109, 429
Cartwright, Thomas 286
Cartwright, William 367
Cary, Elizabeth, Viscountess Falkland 50, 231, 288, 449
The Tragedy of Mariam 39, 243, 257–258, 289
Cary, Henry, Lord Hunsdon 114
Cary, Lucius 31, 364
Cary, Patrick 283, 287–288
Castiglione, Baldassare, *The Courtier* 77, 427
Catullus 335, 344, 358
Cave, Terence 49, 129, 449
Cavendish, Margaret 29, 50, 51, 86–87, 441
The Blazing World 39
Cavendish, William 51
Caxton, William 389
Cecil, Robert 10, 23
Cecil, William 396
Cervantes, Miguel de 244, 394
Don Quixote 394, 414
Persiles and Sigismunda 394

Chamberlain, John 220, 419, 449
Chapman, George 5, 88, 89, 93, 100, 105, 109, 111, 117, 118, 120, 129, 215, 232, 241, 243, 247, 262
  'Andromeda Liberata' 109
  Bussy d'Ambois 100, 126, 230, 242, 243, 248, 249, 251
  The Conspiracy and Tragedy of Charles, Duke of Byron 230, 242, 243, 249
  Eastward Ho 12, 93, 100, 160, 169, 170, 171, 175, 178
  A Memorable Masque 216
  The Revenge of Bussy d'Ambois 100, 120, 126, 230, 234–235, 243, 248, 251
  The Tragedy of Chabot, Admiral of France 230
  The Widow's Tears 64
Charles I, King 1, 18–19, 21, 24–31, 52, 81, 82, 113, 116, 121, 122, 138, 157, 190, 197–198, 208, 210–211, 216, 221, 223–226, 246, 279, 283, 287, 289, 366, 370, 373, 382, 385, 391, 407, 417, 423, 424, 432, 438, 446
  Eikon Basilike 392
Charles II, King 1, 30, 32–33, 83, 370, 381, 434
Charles, Thomas 368
Chaucer, Geoffrey 5, 104
Chettle, Henry 94
  The Tragedy of Hoffman 251
Christian IV, King of Denmark 214
Chute, Walter 114
Cicero 8, 357, 362, 377, 392
Clark, Peter 449
Clarke, Elizabeth 310, 449
Clarkson, L. A. 11, 449
Clifford, Anne 50, 84, 110, 112, 113, 118, 133, 156, 186–187, 433–435
  'The Life of Me' 434–435
  'Great Books of Record' 434, 435
Clifford, George, Earl of Cumberland 50, 110, 115, 186, 434
Clifford, Margaret, Countess of Cumberland 108, 115, 118, 186–188, 434
Clyomon and Clamydes 258
Cocke, John 138
Coiro, Ann Baynes 321, 328, 370, 449, 454
Coke, Edward 21, 208
Coleridge, Samuel Taylor 417
Coles, Kimberly Ann 219, 449

Colie, Rosalie 149, 450
Condell, Henry 140
Congreve, William 2–4, 161
Connolly, Ruth 369
Cook, Ann Jennalie 98, 450
Cooper, J. P. 463
Copernicus 395
Corneille, Pierre 378
Corns, Thomas 315, 449
Cottignies, Line 351, 450
Cotton, Charles 376
Cotton, Robert 108
Coward, Barry 32, 450
Cowley, Abraham 143, 144, 295, 326, 328, 330, 332, 366, 369, 450
  'The Dissembler' 369
  Davideis 143, 289, 324–327, 413
  De Plantis 54
  The Mistress 144, 366, 368, 369
Cox, John 458
Crashaw, Richard 57, 144, 152, 283, 288, 289, 291
  'Luke 11: Blessed Be the Paps Which Thou Hast Sucked' 301–302
  Steps to the Temple 295
Crawford, Julie 51, 450
Creasar, John 311–312, 369, 370, 450
Cressy, David 45–48, 450
Croll, Morris 392, 403, 450
Cromwell, Richard 32
Cromwell, Thomas 116
Cromwell, Oliver 30–33, 83, 142, 190, 246, 289, 326, 382, 388, 391, 413
Cubeta, Paul 292, 450
Cuffe, Henry 445
Cunningham, Karen 74, 450
Curtis, Mark 48, 64, 249, 450
Cust, Richard 23, 25, 450, 461

D'Avenant, William 116, 143, 215, 224, 280–282, 326
  The Cruelty of the Spaniards in Peru 281–282
  Gondibert 143, 326, 413
  Salmacida Spolia 223, 230
  The Siege of Rhodes 143, 230, 280–281, 282
Daniel, Samuel 5, 50, 67, 88, 105, 110, 111, 118, 119, 122, 132, 215, 389, 390
  Delia 132, 340
  Philotas 241

The Vision of the Twelve Goddesses 213
Danson, Lawrence 266, 450
Danvers, John 113
Davies, Sir John 50, 74, 83
   Nosce Teipsum 83
Davies, John of Hereford 117
   The Scourge of Folly 137
Davis, Natalie 107, 450
De Gruys, Robert 416
De las Casas, Barthome 281
Defoe, Daniel 142
Degenhardt, Jane Hwang 279, 450
Dekker, Thomas 5, 56, 89, 90, 94, 95, 98, 102, 154, 155, 164, 393, 425–428, 430, 451
   The Bellman of London 427–428
   The Gull's Hornbook 90–91, 98, 102, 427, 428
   Northward Ho 160
   The Roaring Girl 55, 162, 164, 165, 172–173, 178, 179, 428
   Satiro-Mastix 425
   The Shoemaker's Holiday 64, 159–160, 163
   The Wonderful Year 426–427
   Westward Ho 100, 160, 162, 163
Delany, Paul 431, 433, 451
DeLuna, B. N. 16, 451
Democritus 404
Denham, John 282
   Cooper's Hill 144, 153, 196–200, 413
Denny, Edward 419
Dering, Edward 378
De Vere, Edward, Earl of Oxford 104, 118, 133
Devereux, Robert, 2nd Earl of Essex 10, 104, 105, 225, 445
Devereux, Robert, 3rd Earl of Essex 109, 218
Digby, Everard 423
Digby, Kenelm 411, 432, 433, 438, 451
   Loose Fantasies 423–425
Dixon, Mimi Still 271, 451
Doerksen, Daniel 310, 451
Dollimore, Jonathan 231, 237–238, 451
Donaldson, Ian 81, 339, 455
Donne, Henry 356
Donne, John 1, 4, 5, 38, 39, 52, 56, 69, 74, 76, 79–80, 82, 84–85, 104, 105, 108, 110–112, 114, 117, 118, 120, 125–126, 134, 135, 141, 152, 156, 245, 283, 287–288, 289, 291–294, 295, 299–301, 305, 310, 311, 313, 315, 337, 339, 356–359, 360, 362, 367, 368, 371, 374, 379, 393, 405–409, 413, 436, 437, 443, 444–445, 446, 451
   'Air and Angels' 356
   'The Calm' 358
   'The Canonization' 337, 344, 353–354
   'Community' 353
   'The Extasie' 354
   'The Flea' 74, 354–355
   'The Funeral' 356
   'Good Friday, 1613. Riding Westward' 297–298
   'The Good Morrow' 59, 353–354
   Holy Sonnet 4: 'O my black soul' 294, 303–304, 306
   Holy Sonnet 11: 'Spit in my face, you Jews' 300–301
   Holy Sonnet 14: 'Batter my heart' 79, 298
   'Holy Sonnet 17: 'Since she whom I loved' 79, 357
   Holy Sonnet 18: 'Show me, dear Christ' 79, 301
   'A Hymn to Christ, at the Author's Last Going into Germany' 292–294
   "Hymn to God My God, in My Sickness" 303
   'A Litany' 290
   'Love's Alchemy' 353
   'The Relic' 356
   'The Storm' 358
   'The Sun Rising' 337, 355, 387
   'To the Countess of Bedford' 106
   'To the Countess of Huntingdon' 105
   'To his Mistress: Going to Bed' 337, 369, 371–372
   'A Valediction: Forbidding Mourning' 354, 378–379
   Sermon preached at the funeral of Sir William Cockayne, Dec. 12 1626 291–292
   The Anniversaries 4, 108, 112, 141
   Bia-Thanatos 405–407
   Devotions upon Emergent Occasions 79–80, 303, 407–409
   Elegies 352–353
   Holy Sonnets 290, 294, 351, 357
   Ignatius His Conclave 112
   La Corona 290
   Songs and Sonnets 352, 353–357
   Pseudo Martyr 112

Dowland, John 368
Drayton, Michael 5, 7, 67, 105, 111, 114, 120, 125, 132–133
  Idea's Mirror 125, 133
  Poly-Olbion 39, 153, 193–196
Dreiser, Theodore 240
Drummond, William 58, 71–72, 81, 84, 89, 96, 283, 339, 360
Drury, Robert 108, 112, 114, 134
Dryden, John 2–4, 7, 33, 34, 36, 161, 180, 451
  'To My Dear Friend Mr. Congreve' 2, 36
  Essay of Dramatic Poesy 2
  Preface to *Troilus and Cressida* 263
  The Tempest, or the Enchanted Island 3
Du Bartas, Guillaume 324
Dubrow, Heather 149, 342, 347, 348, 451
Dudley, Robert, Earl of Leicester 104, 133
Dufield, Andrew 231, 449
Dunsworth, Felicity 138, 458
Durston, Christopher 451
Dutcher, James 422, 456
Dutton, Richard 53, 451
Dyer, John 'Grongar Hill' 196
Dymok, Tailboys 261

Easterling, Heather 160, 451
Edmondes, Clement 359
Edmondson, Paul 343, 451
Edward VI, King of England 184, 285
Egerton, John, Earl of Bridgewater 121, 123, 227
Egerton, Thomas 111, 353
Eliot, Sir John 210, 451
Elizabeth I, Queen of England 1, 9–10, 15–17, 20, 21–22, 24, 64, 104, 116, 127, 131–132, 138, 180, 193, 212–213, 225, 246, 285–286, 337, 396–397, 415, 433, 442–443
Elizabeth, Princess 18, 115, 118, 120, 138, 139, 268, 292, 421
Elton, William R. 237, 451
Enterline, Lynn 451
Empson, William 151, 179, 386, 451
Engle, Lars 394, 448, 451
Epicurus 377
Erasmus, Desiderius 87
  Praise of Folly 87, 404
Erickson, Amy 60, 451
Erne, Lukas 452
Euripides 258

Everyman 89

Fairfax, Thomas 31, 110, 190–192, 382
Fallon, Stephen 315, 452
Fane, Mildmay 71–72, 181
Farington, William 225
Farrar, Nicholas 295
Faulkner, Thomas 396, 403, 449
Featly, Daniel 80
Felton, John 26
Ferguson, Margaret 46, 50, 288, 449, 452
Ferrabosco, Alfonso 359
Finkelpearl, Philip 73, 75, 121, 274, 452
Fish, Stanley 107, 307–308, 310, 323, 331, 362, 387–88, 400, 411, 452
Fisher, F. J. 165, 452
Flecknoe, Richard 181
Fleming, Juliet 46, 452
Fletcher, Giles 78, 319, 340
  Christ's Victory and Triumph in Heaven and Earth Over and After Death 78, 319–20, 322, 323
Fletcher, John 53, 56, 74, 88, 89, 91, 93, 94, 103, 111, 112, 120, 129, 139, 143, 232, 244, 247, 264–266, 268–269, 271–273, 282, 394, 414, 420, 421
  Beggars' Bush 99
  Cardenio 266
  The Custom of the Country 260, 263, 264, 275
  The Elder Brother 60
  The Faithful Shepherdess 97, 180, 259, 261–262, 275
  Henry VIII 260, 266
  The Island Princess 266, 277–278, 279, 374
  A King and No King 263, 264, 265, 275
  The Maid's Tragedy 212, 230, 244, 247–248
  Philaster 262, 263–264, 265, 266, 274, 275
  Two Noble Kinsmen 260, 265, 343
  The Queen of Corinth 264
  A Wife for a Month 263, 274
  The Works of Beaumont and Fletcher 93, 144
Fletcher, Phineas 7, 78, 99
  The Purple Island 78, 80
Florio, John 105, 110, 377, 394, 400, 458
Floyd-Wilson, Mary 218, 452
Ford, John 74, 103, 139, 232
  The Broken Heart 231, 244, 255–256
  Perkin Warbeck 231, 242, 243, 244, 256

'Tis Pity She's a Whore 231, 240, 251, 252, 256
Fowler, Alastair 149, 180, 332, 452, 458
Fox, Adam 46, 298, 452
Fox, George 435, 439
Foxe, John *Acts and Monuments* 285, 389–390, 440
Foxley, Rachel 394, 452
Frank, Joseph 393, 452
Fraser, Antonia 16, 452
Frederick, Elector Palatine 18, 120, 139, 268, 292, 421
Fuller, Thomas *History of the Worthies of England* 441
Fumerton, Patricia 66, 452

Gabrieli, Vittori 423, 451
Galen 395
Galileo Galilei 395
Gamble, John 368
Gamboa, Brett 92, 452
Gardner, Helen 406
Garrard, George 141
Gawain-poet 5
George, David 225
Gibbons, Brian 161, 452
Gibbons, Daniel 311, 452
Goffe, Thomas (attrib.) *The Careless Shepherdess* 89
Goldberg, Jonathan 115, 231, 336, 419, 452, 453
Golding, Arthur 118
Goodere, Henry 105, 110, 133, 359
Goodman, Godfrey 25
Goody, John 60, 453
Gorges, Katherine 223
Gossett, Suzanne 268, 417, 453, 465
Gouge, William *Of Domestical Duties* 207, 453
Grantley, Daryll 453
Gray, Patrick 393, 451
Gray, Thomas 'Elegy Written in a Country Churchyard' 45, 59
Greenblatt, Stephen 60–61, 66, 115, 202, 238, 239, 453, 461
Greene, Robert 5
  Alphonsus King of Aragon 258
  History of Orlando Furioso 258
  Pandosto 390
Greene, Thomas 361, 453

Gregory (Pope) 286, 288
Greville, Fulke 71–72, 415, 441–443, 444, 453
  Life of the Renowned Sir Philip Sidney 415, 441–443
  Mustapha 231
Grierson, Herbert 300
Griswold, Wendy 160, 162, 453
Guarini, Battista
  Il pastor fido 261, 271–272
Guibbory, Achsah 314, 453
Guillen, Claudio 357, 453
Guows, John 441
Gurney, John 394, 453
Gurr, Andrew 98, 263, 448, 453

Habermas, Jurgen 393, 453
Hakluyt, Richard *Principal Navigations, Voyages, and Discoveries of the English Nation* 200
Hall, Joseph 117, 428
  Characters of Virtues and Vices in Two Books 428–429
Hall, Kim 218, 453
Hamlin, William 237, 394, 451, 453
Hammond, Paul 382, 386, 453
Hannay, James 27
Hannay, Margaret 51, 417, 419, 422, 453
Harbage, Alfred 98, 453
Harding, Vanessa 11, 453
Hardy, Thomas 240
Harington, John 74, 118, 214, 454
Harrison, William 44, 60–61, 63, 72, 454
Harvey, Elizabeth 448, 461
Harvey, William, *De Motu Cordis* 54, 395–396
Hastings, Henry, Earl of Huntingdon 120–121, 123
Hawkins, John 14
Hay, James 108
Heal, Felicity 44, 454
Healey, T. S. 406
Helgerson, Richard 64, 153, 157, 192–193, 195, 367, 454
Heminges, John 140
Hendricks, Margo 218, 454
Henrietta Maria, Queen consort of Charles I 18, 24, 198, 223–228, 262, 287, 326, 378, 390, 438
Henry VII, King of England 10

Henry VIII, King of England 33, 52, 104, 116, 198, 285, 288
Henry, Prince of Wales 16, 17–18, 109, 119–120, 122, 138, 195, 216, 220–221, 428, 443–444
Henslowe, Philip 89–90, 92
Herbert, Edward 52, 71–72, 77, 113, 117, 432–433, 434, 435, 454
  The Autobiography of Edward, Lord Herbert of Cherbury 432–433
  De Veritate 432
Herbert, George 1, 19, 52, 54, 57, 62, 69, 77–79, 82, 84, 99, 110, 113–114, 117, 152, 156, 283, 289, 290, 291, 292, 295–296, 310, 311, 313, 315, 330–331, 344, 405, 413, 432, 436, 443
  'Affliction I' 77, 113, 294
  'The Altar' 307–308, 310
  'The Bunch of Grapes' 303
  'The Church Militant' 19, 311
  'The Church-Porch' 290, 311, 312
  'The Collar' 77, 294, 303
  'Easter Wings' 307, 308
  'The Flower' 303, 344
  'The Forerunners' 77, 305
  'The Holdfast' 306–307
  'Jordan II' 308–309, 318
  'Love III' 298–299
  'The Priesthood' 77
  'The Pulley' 303
  'Redemption' 304–305
  'The Temper' 299–300
  The Country Parson 77
  The Temple 294–295, 303, 309
Herbert, Henry 52
Herbert, Magdalen 52, 105, 112, 295
Herbert, Mary Sidney, Countess of Pembroke 50, 51, 110, 111, 115, 118, 132, 156, 360, 418, 443
  The Psalms of David 51, 290
Herbert, Percy *The Princess Cloria* 417
Herbert, Philip, Earl of Pembroke and Montgomery 113, 118–119, 432, 433, 434
Herbert, Susan De Vere, Countess of Montgomery 114, 118, 120, 418, 433–434
Herbert, Thomas 52

Herbert, William, Earl of Pembroke 51, 77, 104, 105, 113, 117–119, 121, 122, 126, 127, 132, 348, 359, 418, 422–423, 432
Herrick, Marvin 259, 454
Herrick, Robert 1, 29, 76, 78–80, 83–84, 99, 144, 156, 181, 282, 283, 287, 289, 290, 291, 311–315, 316, 329, 366, 368, 369–373, 387, 413, 454
  'Another' 313
  'Art Above Nature' 373
  'Corinna's Gone A-Maying' 78, 371
  'Delight in Disorder' 373
  'Discontents in Devon' 83
  'Gather Ye Rosebuds While Ye May' 371, 383
  'Her Legs' 371
  'His Creed' 312–313
  'His Protestation to Perilla' 370
  'The Hock Cart' 58–59, 78
  'To his Savior, a Child; A Present, By a Child' 313–314
  'To the Reverend Shade of His Religious Father' 78
  'Upon Himself' 80, 368, 369, 370
  'Upon Julia's Clothes' 370, 372
  'The Vine' 80
  Hesperides 47, 78, 311, 339, 366, 369–373
  His Noble Numbers 78, 283, 295, 311–314, 369, 372
Heywood, Jasper 356
Heywood, Thomas 5, 91, 94, 160
  The English Traveller 94
  Four Prentices of London 259
  If You Know Not Me, You Know Nobody part 2 161
  A Woman Killed With Kindness 240, 244
Hibbard, G. R. 180, 454
Hinz, Evelyn 385, 463
Hirst, Derek 386, 454
Hobbes, Thomas 29, 454
  Leviathan 246, 392, 393
Hobby, Eleanor 379, 454
Hoby, Thomas 77
Hodgkins, Christopher 310, 454
Holberton, Edward 142, 454
Holbrook, Peter 231, 237, 454
Holland, Peter 244, 454
Holland, Philemon 193
Hollander, John 364–365, 454
Holinshed, Raphael, *Chronicles* 243, 390

Holmes, Clive 44, 454
Holmes, Martin 133, 454
Homer 324
'Homily on Obedience' 210
Hooker, Richard 443, 454
    The Laws of Ecclesiastical Polity 205
Hopkins, John 290
Hopkins, Lisa 231, 449
Horace 135, 335, 336, 344, 357
    The Art of Poetry 149
Howard, Frances, Countess of Somerset 25, 109, 218, 429
Howard, Henry, Earl of Surrey 73, 340
Howard, Henry, Earl of Northampton 10
Howard, Jean 160, 454
Howell, James 295
Hoxby, Blair 328, 454
Hoy, Cyrus 264, 454
Huber, Dorothy Prichard 415
Huggarde, Miles 116
Hughes, Ann 450, 454
Hughes, Charles 454
Hutchinson, John 31
Hutchinson, Lucy 24–25, 225–226, 228, 441, 455
Hutson, Lorna 361, 455
Hutton, Ronald 32, 455
Hyde, Edward, Earl of Clarendon 31, 441
Hyman, Wendy 372, 373, 455

Ibsen, Henrik 240
Ijselwiin, J. 417
Iyengar, Sujata 218–219, 455
Ireton, Henry 31

Jackson, MacDonald P. 342, 455
James I and VI, King of England and Scotland 1, 4, 6, 10, 15–25, 27, 56, 79, 109, 112, 113, 116, 118, 119, 121, 123, 126, 127, 134, 138, 157, 158, 185, 192–193, 195, 207, 208, 213, 214–215–217, 219–222, 246–247, 279–280, 286–287, 294, 337, 366, 391, 396, 397, 416, 421, 423, 432, 433, 434, 443, 445, 455
    Basilikon Doron 20, 204
    Demonology 221
    The True Law of Free Monarchies 20–21, 329–330
Jardine, Lisa 253, 396, 402, 455, 463

Jesus 290–291, 300–303, 304, 305, 319, 321–323, 325, 326, 361, 406, 412–413
John of Gaunt 104
Johnson, Samuel 4, 355, 455
Jones, Ann Rosalind 132, 337, 455, 462
Jones, Inigo 109, 117, 212, 216, 217, 224
Jones, Jenkin 380–381
Jones, Richard Foster 392–393, 455
Jonson, Ben 1, 4, 6, 38, 44–45, 49, 53, 56, 62, 65, 67, 69, 70–71, 81, 84, 88, 89, 90, 93, 94–97, 104, 105, 108, 109, 111, 114, 116, 117, 119, 121, 122, 124, 129–131, 135–137, 155, 160–169, 172–173, 178, 194, 215, 216, 224, 225, 232, 240, 243, 244–245, 247, 261, 266–267, 283, 288, 289, 292, 294, 295, 335, 344, 358–366, 367, 368, 371, 372, 374, 376, 379, 414, 416, 425–426, 455
    'A Celebration of Charis in Ten Lyric Pieces' 359
    'Come, my Celia' 358
    'Drink to me only with thine eyes' 358
    'An Epistle Answering to One that Asked to be Sealed of the Tribe of Ben' 363–364
    'An Epistle to Master Arthur Squib' 362
    'Epistle to Katherine, Lady Aubigny' 121, 360
    'Garland of the Blessed Virgin Mary' 283
    'Inviting a Friend to Supper' 361–62
    'Ode to Himself' 85, 266–267
    'On Lucy, Countess of Bedford' 126, 360
    'That Women are But Men's Shadows' 359–360
    'To Elizabeth Countess of Rutland' 361
    'To Heaven' 283
    'To the Immortal Memory of that Noble Pair, Sir Lucius Cary and Sir Henry Morison' 364–366
    'To the Memory of My Beloved, the Author William Shakespeare' 94–95, 130, 362–363
    'To Mary, Lady Wroth' 106
    'To My Lady Covell' 359
    'To My Muse' 136
    'To Old End Gatherer' 129–130
    'To Penshurst' 126, 127, 136, 153, 181–184, 187, 188, 189, 191, 192, 194, 361
    'To Sir Henry Neville' 360

Jonson, Ben (*Continued*)
　'To Sir Robert Wroth' 121, 126, 153, 185, 225, 361
　'To William, Earl of Pembroke' 106, 126, 360
　The Alchemist 7, 55, 101, 124, 160, 164, 168, 172, 173, 176–177, 178, 200, 222
　Barriers at a Marriage 218
　Bartholomew Fair 47, 97, 100–101, 160, 162–163, 164, 165, 173–174, 176–177, 209, 266
　Catiline 16, 230, 243, 245
　Chloridia 224
　Cynthia's Revels 100
　The Devil is an Ass 160, 169, 176
　Eastward Ho 12, 93, 100, 160, 169, 170, 171, 175, 178
　Epicene 55, 97, 99, 100, 126, 160, 162, 164, 165, 167–168, 171, 173, 176, 208
　Epigrams 126, 135, 358–363, 369
　Every Man in His Humour 74, 153, 160
　Every Man Out of His Humour 75, 185
　For the Honour of Wales 217–218
　The Forest 126, 135, 283, 358, 359, 362, 363, 418
　The Fortunate Isles and Their Union 221
　The Gypsies Metamorphosed 222
　The Haddington Masque 216
　Hymenaei 154, 218
　Informations to William Drummond of Hawthornden 81, 89, 275, 283, 339, 360
　The Irish Masque at Court 217–218
　The King's Entertainment at Welbeck 224
　Lovers Made Men 222
　Love's Triumph Through Callipolis 224
　Love's Welcome at Bolsover 224
　The Masque of Beauty 213, 215–216, 218
　The Masque of Blackness 213, 215, 218–220
　Masque of Queens 126–127, 216, 218, 221–222, 225
　Mercury Vindicated from the Alchemists at Court 222
　Neptune's Triumph for the Return of Albion 221
　The New Inn 153, 359, 416
　News From the New World Discovered in the Moon 88, 222, 391
　Oberon, the Fairy Prince 216, 217
　Poetaster 55, 74, 100, 135, 425
　Sejanus 230, 231, 235, 239, 240, 241, 242, 243, 246, 249, 250
　The Staple of News 88, 160, 163, 167–168, 222, 391
　A Tale of A Tub 47
　Timber, or Discoveries 70–71, 124, 361
　The Underwood 283, 358, 359, 365
　The Vision of Delight 222
　Volpone 7, 55, 124, 137, 259, 430–431
　The Works of Ben Jonson 140, 181, 358, 362
Josephus, Flavius 243, 289
Juvenal 428

Kahn, Victoria 229, 455
Kastan, David Scott 458
Keats, John 9
Keble, N. H. 455
Kepler, Johannes 395
Ker, Robert 80
Kermode, Frank 325, 455
Kerrigan, John 52, 189, 250, 455
Kiessling, Nicholas 396, 403, 449
King, Henry 283, 287
　'The Labyrinth' 295–296
King, William 368
Kinney, Clare 421, 455
Kirsch, Arthur 237, 271, 455
Kishlansky, Mark 33, 455
Klawitter, George 386, 455
Knapp, Jeffrey 237, 319, 455
Knight, G. Wilson 237, 456
Knox, John 286
Kyd, Thomas 4, 5, 57
　The Spanish Tragedy 7, 90, 151, 165, 201, 232, 250
　Ur-Hamlet 251

Lake, Peter 237, 456
Lamb, Mary Ellen 51, 414, 417, 422, 456, 465
The Lamb's Defense Against Lies 439–440
Langford, Harold 415, 456
Langland, William 5
Lanier, John 368
Lanier, Nicholas 368
Lanier, Richard 368
Lanier, William 368
Lanyer, Aemilia 1, 108, 114–115, 118, 137, 155, 181, 194, 283, 328, 422
　'The Description of Cookham' 115, 153, 186–188, 191, 192, 194

INDEX

'To the Virtuous Reader'
  Salve Deus Rex Judaeorum 39, 58, 114, 137, 283, 289, 319, 320–322
Lanyer, Alphonso 114
Laslett, Peter 12, 35, 43–44, 456
Laud, William, Archbishop of Canterbury 18, 27, 28, 81, 211, 225, 279, 287, 312, 315, 373, 446
Lawes, Henry 226, 230, 280, 368
Lawes, William 368
Lee, Maurice 220, 449
Leggatt, Alexander 160, 456
Leibniz, Gottfried 417
Leinwand, Theodore 160, 456
Lemon, Rebecca 16, 456
Levy-Navarro, Elena 311, 456
Lewalski, Barbara 149, 292, 310, 315, 323, 456
Lewis, C. S. 311, 456
Liebler, Naomi Conn 231, 253, 456
Lilburne, John 391
Lindley, David 154, 213
Llewellyn, Mark 380, 456
Lloyd-Thomas, M. C. 385
Lodge, Thomas 289, 340
Loewenstein, Joseph 69, 212, 361, 456
Long, Kingsmill 416
Loomba, Ania 277–278, 456
Love, Harold 141, 145, 391, 456
Lovelace, Richard 1, 29, 82, 144, 190, 366, 373–377, 387
  'The Grasshopper' 374–376
  'To Althea from Prison' 376–377
  'To Lucasta, From Prison: An Epode' 374
  'To Lucasta, Going to the Wars' 374
  Lucasta: Epodes, Odes Sonnets 366, 367, 368, 374, 375, 382
  Lucasta: Posthume Poems 374
Low, Anthony 180, 290, 456, 457
Lownes, Matthew 394
Lucretius 237
Luther, Martin 288, 336
Lyly, John 5, 57, 117
  Euphues 390
Lyons, Tara 358, 457

McDowell, Nicholas 366
MacFarlane, Alan 166, 457
Machiavelli, Niccolo 237
Mack, Maynard 247, 457

Majors, Philip 325
Malory, Thomas 389
Manley, Lawrence 149, 457
Mannners, Elizabeth Sidney, Countess of Rutland 51, 361
Mansky, Joseph 370, 457
Manwaring, Roger 116
Marcus, Leah 154, 185, 314, 373, 457
Marlowe, Christopher 4, 5, 7, 49, 57, 95, 231, 336, 344, 390, 413
  Doctor Faustus 89, 231, 232, 238
  Tamburlaine I and II 201, 243, 255
  Edward II 243
  Hero and Leander 163, 336
  The Massacre at Paris 243
Marotti, Arthur 75, 110, 132, 337, 338, 347, 457
Marston, John 56, 74, 76, 93, 94, 103, 117, 164
  Antonio's Revenge 151
  The Dutch Courtesan 160
  Eastward Ho 12, 93, 100, 160, 169, 170, 171, 175, 178
  The Insatiate Countess 231, 253
  The Malcontent 260–261
Martial 135, 336, 359, 360, 361
Martin, Catherine Gimelli 332, 457
Martin, Jessica 457
Martz, Louis 292, 310, 457
Marvell, Andrew 1, 68, 110, 181, 190, 194, 199–200, 283, 289, 328, 366, 382–388
  'Bermudas' 283
  'The Coronet' 283, 305–306, 309–310
  'Damon the Mower' 384
  'Daphnis and Chloe' 383–384
  'A Definition of Love' 382, 386
  'The Garden' 386–388
  'An Horatian Ode Upon Cromwell's Return from Ireland' 31–32, 143–144, 382, 388
  'The Mower Against Gardens' 384
  'The Mower's Song' 384
  'The Mower to the Glow-Worms' 384
  'A Nymph Complaining for the Death of her Fawn' 383, 384–385, 386, 388
  'A Portrait of Little T. C. in a Prospect of Flowers' 382–383
  'To His Coy Mistress' 383
  'The Unfortunate Lover' 383, 386, 388
  'Upon Appleton House' 153, 190–192

Marvell, Andrew (*Continued*)
  'Young Love' 382–383
  Miscellaneous Poems 339
Mary I, Queen of England 116, 285
Mary, Queen of Scots 10, 415
Mascetti, Yaacov 321, 457
The Masque of Flowers 223
The Masque of Indian and China Knights 213, 217
Massinger, Philip 56, 91, 94, 117, 129, 144, 264, 268, 282
  Beggars' Bush 99
  The City Madam 161, 174, 179
  The Custom of the Country 260, 263, 264, 275
  A New Way to Pay Old Debts 64, 259–260
  The Renegado 260, 264, 278–280
  The Roman Actor 231, 243
Masten, Jeffrey 93, 350, 457
Matthew, Tobie *The True Historical Relation of the Conversion of Tobie Matthew to the Holy Catholic Faith* 437–439, 457
Matthew, A. H. 457
Maus, Katharine Eisaman 250, 359, 448, 457, 461
Mauss, Marcel 107, 458
McAlindon, Thomas 231, 458
McCabe, Richard 104, 428, 458
McCanles, Michael 365, 458
McClure, Norman Egbert 419
McColley, Grant 332, 458
McDonald, Charles Osborne 232, 458
McDowell, Nicholas 143, 366, 368, 458
McEachern, Claire 315, 463
McGrade, Arthur Stephen 205, 454
McKeon, Michael 328, 458
McLuskie, Kathleen 138, 458
McMullan, Gordon 121, 261, 274, 458
McRae, Andrew 193, 458
Mears, Natalie 458
Menges, Hilary 382, 458
Middleton, Thomas 1, 6–8, 53, 57, 65, 88, 89, 92, 93, 94, 95, 117, 121–122, 123, 129, 131, 144, 154, 155, 160–164, 170–173, 174–179, 215, 223, 231, 241, 247, 458
  The Changeling 64, 92, 230, 240, 242, 243, 249, 251, 252
  A Chaste Maid in Cheapside 60, 64, 160, 169, 170, 175, 176, 177, 259
  A Game at Chess 117, 121

The Masque of Cupid 122
A Mad World, My Masters 160, 176, 178–179
Michaelmas Term 100, 160, 170–171, 172, 174, 175–176
More Dissemblers Besides Women 131, 160
The Puritan 160
The Revenger's Tragedy 7, 17, 64, 121, 212, 231, 235, 242, 248, 249, 251–253, 259, 261, 430
The Roaring Girl 6–8, 55, 160, 162, 164, 165, 172–173, 178, 179
The Second Maiden's Tragedy 121
Timon of Athens 128, 231
A Trick to Catch the Old One 100, 160, 170, 171, 172, 173, 175
Women Beware Women 121, 122, 131, 230, 243, 251, 252, 253, 254
Your Five Gallants 160
Miehl, Dieter 160, 458
Miller, Naomi 417, 458
Miller, Perry 393, 458
Milton, John 1, 8–9, 54, 62, 67, 69, 81–83, 143, 144, 152, 226–227, 283, 314–318, 319, 324, 328, 351–352, 366, 388, 391, 393, 405, 458
  'On the Morning of Christ's Nativity' 322–323, 331
  Sonnet 7 "How soon hath Time' 317
  Sonnet 12 'I did but prompt the age' 86
  Sonnet 19 'When I consider how my light is spent' 317–318
  Sonnet 23 'Methought I saw my late espoused saint' 351
  An Apology for Smectymnus 315
  Areopagitica 317
  Lycidas 81, 315, 318, 319, 367, 372
  A Masque Presented at Ludlow Castle (Comus) 226–230, 262, 316, 319, 334
  Paradise Lost 9, 82, 83, 226, 283, 289, 297, 316–318, 319, 323, 327–334, 374
  Paradise Regained 83, 289
  Poems of Mr. John Milton 283, 295, 315, 328, 366
  Samson Agonistes 83, 226, 289
Montagu, Walter 215
Montaigne, Michel de 377, 394, 400, 410, 458
  "Of Friendship" 377
  Essays 276, 394
Montalvo, Garci, *Amadis de Gaule* 414

Montrose, Louis 64, 458
More, Anne 353–354, 357, 444
More, Thomas 87
Morison, Henry 364
Morris, David 323, 458
Moryson, Fynes 88–89
Moseley, Humphrey 131, 144
Moul, Victoria 325, 459
Mucedorus 258
Meres, Francis 339
Mueller, Janel 417, 465
Muldrew, Craig 73, 108, 166, 459
Myers, Ann M. 435, 459

Nashe, Thomas 5, 390
Neill, Michael 239, 459
Newman, Henry 430, 459
Newman, Karen 174, 253, 459
Norbrook, David 115, 195, 274, 328, 367, 393–394, 459
North, Thomas 394, 440
Norton, Thomas 290

O'Callaghan, Michelle 368, 459
O'Hehir, Brendan 197, 459
O'Neill, Phelim 28
Oppenheimer, Paul 340, 459
Orgel, Stephen 110, 212, 336, 459
Orlin, Lena Cowen 13, 165, 459, 463
Ornstein, Richard 230, 237, 459
Overbury, Thomas 25, 393, 429–430, 459
 Characters 152, 429–430
 'The Wife' 429
Ovid 83, 118, 335, 86
Owen, Ann 378

Painter, William, *The Palace of Pleasure* 243, 394
Papazian, Mary Arshagouni 311, 456
Parker, Patricia 218, 419, 454, 459
Parnell, James 439–440
The Passionate Pilgrim 339
Patterson, Annabel 115, 459
Patterson, W. B. 17, 459
Paul (apostle) 320
Paul, Ryan Singh 379, 463
Peacham, Henry, *The Complete Gentleman* 77, 427
Peck, Linda Levy 104, 116, 165, 460
Pendry, E.D. 426, 451

Penry, John 286, 390
Perkins, Christopher 438
Perkins, William 39, 76, 79, 446, 460
Perry, Curtis 26, 128, 157, 180, 232, 249, 261, 460
Persons, Robert 437
Petrarch and Petrarchism 131–136, 305, 340, 348, 352, 405
Philip, King of Spain 288
Philips, James 378, 379
Philips, Katherine 1, 84, 143, 377–382
 'Content: To Lucasia' 379
 'A Friend' 377–378
 'Friendship in Emblem, or the Seal' 378–379
 'On the Double Murder of King Charles' 381
 'A Retired Friendship: To Ardelia' 380
 'To Antenor, on a Paper of Mine' 381
 'To His Grace Gilbert, Lord Archbishop of Canterbury' 381
 'To Mrs. Mary Aubrey' 380
 'To My Dearest Antenor, on his Parting' 379
 Poems by the Most Deservedly Admired Katherine Philips, the Matchless Orinda 339
 Pompey (trans. Corneille) 378
Philostratus 358
Plato 335–336
 Symposium 361
 Phaedrus 375
Plautus 258
Pliny the Younger 357
Plutarch *Lives of the Noble Grecians and Romans* 394, 440
Pocohantas 200
Pope, Alexander 4, 180, 367
 'Windsor Forest' 196
 First Epistle of the Second Book of Horace Imitated 366
Porter, Endymion 370
Pory, John 88
Potter, George 451
Potter, Lois 143, 275, 394, 417, 460
Powell, Mary 451
Powhatan 200
Prall, Stuart 296, 460
Prescott, Ann Lake 422, 456
Pride, Thomas 29

Prior, Charles W. A. 296, 460
Pritchard, Allan 382, 441, 460
Prynne, William 19, 28, 75, 117, 226, 287, 390–391, 460
  Histriomastix 19, 75, 117, 390–391
Purcell, Henry 368
Purkiss, Diane 28, 460
Puttenham, George, *The Art of English Poesy* 54, 149, 180, 233, 389, 460

Quarles, Frances 80, 283
'Oh Wither Shall I Fly' 298
Quilligan, Maureen 350, 460
Quint, David 323, 324, 328, 460

Ralegh, Walter 5, 17, 82, 111, 117, 120, 132, 141, 440
Rambuss, Richard 292, 460
Rappaport, Steven 159, 460
Raylor, Timothy 56, 368, 460
Raymond, Joad 391, 393, 460
Rees, Graham 398, 447
Reggio, Petro 368
Ribner, Irving 231, 237, 460
Rich, Penelope 120, 133
Richelieu, Cardinal 417
Riley, Mark 415
Roberts, Josephine 417, 421, 465
Roe, John 359
Roe, Thomas 14, 120, 135, 158
Rogers, John (preacher) 15, 460
Rogers, John (critic) 332, 460
Rogers, Samuel 436–437
Rolfe, Thomas 200
Rose, Mary Beth 253, 460
Rossingham, Edward 88
Rowley, William, *The Changeling* 93, 230, 240, 242
Rush, Rebecca 340–341, 351, 389, 461
Russell, Conrad 23, 34–35, 461
Russell, Lucy, Countess of Bedford 51, 104, 105, 110, 112, 114, 115, 118, 120, 125–126, 134, 359
Ryrie, Alec 291, 296, 390, 393, 457, 458, 461

Sachse, William 17, 461
Sackville-West, Vita 84, 435
Sackville, Richard, Earl of Dorset 127, 425, 433, 434, 435
Sales, William *Theophania* 417

Salzman, Paul 391, 415, 417, 461
Sanchez, Melissa 337, 461
Sand, Edwin 438
Sandberg, Julianne 321, 461
Sanderson, Robert 443, 461
Sanderson, William 33
Sandstrom, Yvonne 385, 461
Saunders, J. W. 144, 461
Savile, Henry 359
Scaliger, Julius Caesar 149
Schaffer, Peter 131
Schalwyck, David 342, 342, 461
Schnell, Lisa 321, 461
Schoenfeldt, Michael 113, 306, 461
Schofield, R.S. 11, 465
Schwyzer, Philip 193, 458
Scott Brown, Denise 94, 461
Scott, William 389
Second Shepherd's Play 258
Selden, John 332, 359, 393, 396
Seneca 135, 232, 357, 362, 377, 392
Shakespeare, William 1, 3–4, 5–6, 8–9, 38, 43–45, 49, 53, 56, 57, 65–66, 67, 69, 88, 91, 94, 95, 104, 105, 129, 132, 135, 231, 243, 245, 266–275, 280, 335, 352, 353, 358, 362, 371, 374, 379–380, 390, 394, 414, 461
  All's Well That Ends Well 266
  Antony and Cleopatra 4, 8, 230, 242, 256–257, 343, 394
  As You Like It 60, 99, 179–180, 259
  Cardenio 266
  Coriolanus 4, 101, 230, 242, 245, 256, 394
  Cymbeline 4, 61, 266, 268, 269, 272, 274
  Hamlet 4, 7, 151, 165, 209, 230, 232, 235, 241, 242, 247, 251, 259, 262, 406
  Henry IV parts 1 and 2 8, 55, 163, 177–178, 243, 258–259, 343, 346
  Henry V 55, 66, 97, 259
  Henry VI parts 1–3 243
  Henry VIII 260, 266
  Julius Caesar 4, 8, 230, 232, 245, 394
  King Lear 4, 17, 20, 43, 127, 139, 172, 205, 230, 237, 241–242, 243, 247, 249, 250, 251, 259, 330
  Macbeth 4, 16, 93, 139, 230, 231, 236, 238–239, 242, 247, 256, 259
  Measure for Measure 4, 93, 139, 176, 259, 261, 266, 346

The Merchant of Venice 8, 66, 201, 259, 278, 343
The Merry Wives of Windsor 47, 153–154, 209
A Midsummer Night's Dream 47, 97
Much Ado About Nothing 259, 335
Othello 4, 66, 165, 172, 230, 243, 249, 250, 252, 254, 255, 262
Pericles 259, 266, 267, 269, 274
The Rape of Lucrece 105, 129, 320, 406
Richard II 8, 105, 200, 232, 243
Richard III 232, 243, 247
Romeo and Juliet 4, 231, 232
Sonnets 55, 132, 151, 339, 341–348
Tempest 3, 4, 43, 61, 105, 139, 205, 266, 267, 268, 269–272, 273–274, 275–277, 346
Timon of Athens 128, 231, 266, 394
Titus Andronicus 7, 232
Troilus and Cressida 202–204, 205, 259, 266
Twelfth Night 61, 75, 343, 344
Two Gentlemen of Verona 343
Two Noble Kinsmen 260, 265, 343
Venus and Adonis 105, 129, 320
The Winter's Tale 4, 47, 61, 205, 266–268, 270–271, 272–273, 274, 275, 384
Mr. William Shakespeare's Comedies, Histories, and Tragedies (the 'First Folio') 117, 140, 266, 418
Shami, Jean 296, 461
Shannon, Laurie 249, 336, 461
Shelton, Thomas 394, 414
Shirley, James 74, 94, 103, 144, 215, 230
  The Cardinal 231, 244, 251
  The Triumph of Peace 225
Shuger, Debora 295, 315, 461, 463
Siddiqi, Yumna 218, 461
Sidney, Philip 4, 5, 64, 69, 73, 77, 83, 132, 133, 244, 371, 441–443, 444, 461
  Arcadia 51, 83, 151, 179, 180, 243, 258, 418, 390, 414, 415, 418, 422, 424, 443
  Astrophil and Stella 133, 151, 308, 340, 419
  Defense of Poesy 38, 80–81, 149–150, 258, 389
  The Psalms of David 51, 83, 290
Sidney, Robert, Earl of Leicester 50, 51, 108, 118, 127, 181–184, 341, 418
Simkin, Stevie 250, 462
Simpson, Evelyn 292, 406

Simpson, James 55, 462
Siochru, Michael 32, 462
Skelton, John 104
Skinner, Quentin 394, 462
Smeed, J. W. 428, 462
Smith, Adam 206
Smith, Bruce R. 336, 462
Smith, Emma 231, 462
Smith, Nigel 394, 462
Smuts, Malcolm 115–116, 462
Socrates 83
Solomon and the Queen of Sheba 214–215
Song, Eric 333, 462
Souden, David 449
Southwell, Richard 283
Speed, John *Theatre of the Empire of Great Britain* 193
Speght, Rachel, 'The Dream' 85–86, 462
Spenser, Edmund 4, 5, 6, 49, 69, 73, 117, 118, 371, 390
  Amoretti 337, 340
  The Faerie Queene 5, 180, 320, 324, 414, 415, 418
  The Shepherd's Calendar 179
Sprat, Thomas 325
Spring, Eileen 60, 462
Spufford, Peter 155, 462
Stafford, Anthony 133
Stallybrass, Peter 132, 314, 337, 455, 462
Stanley, Thomas 143, 368, 375
Stanley, Venetia 423–425
Starke, Sue 326, 462
Steele, Richard 429
Stephen, James 396, 462
Sternhold, Thomas 290
Stevens, Andrea 220, 362
Stewart, Alan 10, 25, 396, 402, 431–432, 436, 437, 462, 463
Stirling, Brent 342, 463
Stock, Angela 160
Stone, Lawrence 34, 463
Stow, John, *The Annals of England* 56–57, 463
Straznicky, Marta 289, 463
Strier, Richard 276, 310, 315, 463
Strong, Roy 122, 212, 463
Stuart, Esme 108
Stuart, Lady Arbella 115
Stubbes, John 390

Suckling, John 74, 144, 366
   'A Session of the Poets' 130
   Fragmenta Aurea 366
Suetonius 243
Summers, Joseph 310, 463
Sutherland, James 25
Sylvester, Joshua 324, 359

Tacitus 8, 392, 440
Targoff, Ramie 77, 290, 310, 357, 407, 463
Tasso, Torquato 324
Taylor, Gary 458
Taylor, John 58
Tertullian 336
Teskey, Gordon 334, 463
Teunissen, John J. 385, 463
Theophrastus 428*t*
Thirsk, Joan 11, 13, 60, 463
Thirty-Nine Articles 210
Thomas, Keith 46, 463
Thrush, Andrew 23, 461
Tillyard, E. M. W. 202, 463
Toliver, Harold 371, 463
Tourneur, Cyril 231
   The Atheist's Tragedy 236, 259–260
Townsend, Francis 108
Townshend, Aurelian 215, 224
   Tempe Restored 216, 223, 224–225, 227–228
Traub, Valerie 336, 379, 463
Trevor, Douglas 403, 463
Turner, James 180, 464

Van Es, Bart 91, 464
Vaughan, Henry 57, 144, 152, 283, 289, 291, 291
   'The World' 301
   Silex Scintillans 294, 295
Vaughan, Thomas 287
Vere, Horace 359
Vickers, Brian 396, 464
Villiers, George, Duke of Buckingham 25–26, 222, 395
Virgil 324, 325, 326, 327, 330, 335
Vitkus, Daniel 279, 464

Waith, Eugene 260, 264, 464
Wakeley, Maria 398, 447
Wall, Wendy 321, 464
Waller, A. R. 369, 450

Waller, Edmund 29, 366
   'At Penshurst' 153
Waller, Gary 51, 350, 464
Walton, Isaak 282, 294, 412–413, 443–446, 464
   The Complete Angler 412–413, 446
   Lives 443–446
Wasserman, Earl 199, 464
Waugh, Dorothy 440
Wayne, Don 180, 183, 464
Wayne, Valerie 414, 456
Webb, John 280
Webbe, William 389
Webber, Joan 396, 464
Webster, John 53, 57, 74, 94, 231, 241
   The Duchess of Malfi 17, 64, 230, 233–235, 236, 237, 242, 243, 248–249, 251, 252, 255, 256, 430
   Northward Ho 160
   Westward Ho 100, 160, 162, 163
   The White Devil 230, 243, 251, 252, 253
Webster, Tom 296, 456
Weller, Barry 50, 288, 449
Wells, Stanley 343, 451
Wentworth, Thomas, Earl of Strafford 27–28, 199
Westfall, Suzanne 138, 464
Whigham, Frank 54, 149, 180, 231, 233, 460, 464
White, Chris 379, 454
White, Micheline 321
White, Peter 296, 464
Wilkins, George
   The Miseries of Enforced Marriage 260
   Pericles 259, 267, 269, 274
Williams, Raymond 183, 464
Williams, Roger 391
Williamson, George 392, 464
Wills, Gary 16, 464
Wilson, Arthur 33, 464
Wilson, Edward 394, 465
Wilson, John 368
Winstanley, Gerrard 391
Wither, George 74, 137, 283, 290
Witmore, Michael 273, 465
Wood, Anthony 374, 465
Woodbridge, Linda 255, 465
Woodcock, Katherine 351
Wordsworth, William
   'Tintern Abbey' 196

Wotton, Henry 358, 443, 445–446
  Reliquiae Wottonianae 443, 445
Wright, Thomas *Passions of the Mind* 403
Wrightson, Keith 11, 35, 43–44, 49, 465
Wrigley, E. A. 11, 465
Wriothesley, Henry, Earl of Southampton 104, 105, 119, 129, 132
Wroth, Mary Sidney 7, 50, 51, 118, 120, 341, 352, 368, 374, 393, 414, 433, 465
  Urania 39, 51, 118, 151, 180, 418, 341, 348, 393, 415, 417–422, 424
  Pamphilia to Amphilanthus 51, 118, 133, 341, 348–351
Wroth, Robert 121, 185
Wyatt, Thomas 73, 340
Wycherley, William 161
Wymer, Rowland 232, 465

Zagorin, Perez 157, 465
Zucker, Adam 154, 465
Zwerlein, Ann-Julia 160
Zwicker, Stephen 386, 454